**With the new Longman Comparative Politics Web site, students can "visit" countries throughout the world with a click of the mouse.**

## www.ablongman.com/comparativepolitics

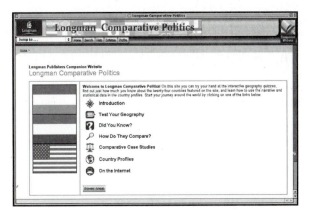

This one-of-a kind Web site lets you explore over 20 countries, check your knowledge of geography and key issues in comparative politics, learn how to interpret the data with case studies, and more!

**Longman Comparative Politics Web site features—**

- *COUNTRY PROFILES* offer both narrative summaries and statistical data regarding the geography, people, religion, government, military, and the economy of over 20 countries – plus the national flags, anthems, and maps.

- *TEST YOUR GEOGRAPHY* contains several interactive map quizzes.

- *DID YOU KNOW?* multiple-choice and true/false quizzes help you find out the most important aspects of each nation's politics and government.

- *HOW DO THEY COMPARE QUIZZES* let you check your knowledge of how the countries compare to one another.

- *COMPARATIVE CASE STUDIES* offer an opportunity to explore the data provided in the various country profiles to draw conclusions.

- *ON THE INTERNET* provides Web links to official sites like the United Nations, embassies and consulates, IGOs, NGOs, etc.

# Western European Government and Politics

## SECOND EDITION

**Michael Curtis, General Editor**
*Rutgers University*

**Giuseppe Ammendola**
*City University of New York*

**Jean Blondel**
*European University Institute*

**Ken Gladdish**
*University of Reading*

**Donald Kommers**
*University of Notre Dame*

**Thomas D. Lancaster**
*Emory University*

**A. James McAdams**
*University of Notre Dame*

New York  San Francisco  Boston
London  Toronto  Sydney  Tokyo  Singapore  Madrid
Mexico City  Munich  Paris  Cape Town  Hong Kong  Montreal

Vice President/Publisher: Priscilla McGeehon
Executive Editor: Eric Stano
Executive Marketing Manager: Megan Galvin-Fak
Supplements Editor: Kristi Olson
Production Manager: Ellen MacElree
Project Coordination, Text Design, and Electronic Page Makeup: Electronic Publishing
    Services Inc., NYC
Cover Designer/Manager: John Callahan
Cover Photo: PhotoDisc
Photo Researcher: Photosearch, Inc.
Manufacturing Manager: Dennis J. Para
Printer and Binder: Hamilton Printing Company
Cover Printer: Phoenix Color Corps.

**Library of Congress Cataloging-in-Publication Data**

Western European Government and Politics/Michael Curtis, general editor; Giuseppe
Ammendola . . . [et al.].—2nd ed.
       p. cm.
    Includes bibliographical references and index.
    ISBN 0-321-10477-3
    1. Europe, Western—Politics and government. 2. Comparative government. I. Curtis,
Michael, 1923– II. Ammendola, Giuseppe, 1957–

    JN94.A58 W57 2002
    320.3'094—dc21

                                                        2002073177

Please visit our website at http://www.ablongman.com

ISBN 0-321-10477-3

1 2 3 4 5 6 7 8 9 10—HT—05 04 03 02

*To*
*Harold and Diana,*
*Ruth and Sam,*
*Gina and Sam*

# Brief Contents

*Detailed Contents*   ix
*Preface*   xxv

CHAPTER **1**   THE NATURE OF WESTERN EUROPEAN POLITICS
*Michael Curtis*   1

CHAPTER **2**   THE GOVERNMENT OF GREAT BRITAIN   *Michael Curtis*   33

CHAPTER **3**   THE GOVERNMENT OF FRANCE   *Jean Blondel*   115

CHAPTER **4**   THE GOVERNMENT OF GERMANY   *Donald Kommers and A. James McAdams*   177

CHAPTER **5**   THE GOVERNMENT OF ITALY   *Giuseppe Ammendola*   253

CHAPTER **6**   THE GOVERNMENT OF SPAIN   *Thomas D. Lancaster*   327

CHAPTER **7**   THE GOVERNMENT OF THE NETHERLANDS   *Ken Gladdish*   397

CHAPTER **8**   THE EUROPEAN UNION   *Michael Curtis*   451

*Credits*   482
*Index*   483

# Detailed Contents

*Preface*   *xxv*

**CHAPTER 1**   THE NATURE OF WESTERN EUROPEAN POLITICS   *Michael Curtis*   **1**

Introduction   1
**A CLOSER LOOK 1.1** THE BALKANS   3
**A CLOSER LOOK 1.2** BALTIC STATES   3
**A CLOSER LOOK 1.3** BENELUX   4
**A CLOSER LOOK 1.4** NORDIC COUNTRIES   5
Political Development   5
**A CLOSER LOOK 1.5** COMMONWEALTH OF INDEPENDENT STATES   5
**REVIEW 1.1** MONARCHIES IN WESTERN EUROPE   6
    *Affluent Societies*   *8*
    *Economic and Social Modernization*   *8*
    *Postindustrial Societies*   *8*
**REVIEW 1.2** THE COLD WAR FROM BEGINNING TO END   9
    *Class and Politics*   *9*
    *Women in Western European Societies and Politics*   *10*
    *Aging Societies*   *13*
    *Religious or Secular Societies*   *13*
    *Multiethnic and Multiracial Societies*   *15*
**REVIEW 1.3** REGIONAL AND CULTURAL DIVERSITY   16
    *Liberal Democracies*   *16*
    *Electoral Systems and Party Systems*   *17*
**REVIEW 1.4** ELECTORAL SYSTEMS   18
    *Political Parties*   *20*
    *Cabinet and Presidential Government Systems*   *24*
**REVIEW 1.5** REGIONAL PARTIES IN RECENT YEARS   24
    *Political Consensus*   *25*
    *Unitary and Federal Systems*   *25*
**REVIEW 1.6** UNITARY AND FEDERAL STATES   26
    *The Growth of Government*   *26*
    *The Welfare System*   *27*
Western European Integration   28
**A CLOSER LOOK 1.6** NORTH ATLANTIC TREATY ORGANIZATION NAID   28
**REVIEW 1.7** KEY EVENTS IN THE HISTORY OF NATO   29
**REVIEW 1.8** EUROPEAN DEFENSE ORGANIZATIONS   30
Further Readings   31

CHAPTER **2**    **THE GOVERNMENT OF GREAT BRITAIN**   *Michael Curtis*   **33**

**A.** POLITICAL DEVELOPMENT   36

Historical Background   36

**A CLOSER LOOK 2.1** Magna Carta   36

Evolution of the Political System   38

Britain as a Model in Politics   40

The Importance of Consensus and Its Limits   41

Political Stability   42

> *Political Culture   42*
> *Deference of the People   42*
> *Pattern of Authority   42*
> *Relative Deprivation   43*
> *Effect of Geography   43*

The Unified System   43

A New Pluralistic System?   44

**A CLOSER LOOK 2.2** The Good Friday Agreement   44

**REVIEW 2.1** The Irish Problem   46

**A CLOSER LOOK 2.3** The West Lothian Question   47

Political Problems   48

**REVIEW 2.2** A Summary of Recent Constitutional Change   49

**A CLOSER LOOK 2.4** British Sovereignty   49

The Nature of British Society   50

> *A Postindustrial Society   50*
> *A Class Society   51*
> *A Pluralistic Religious Society   51*
> *A Multicultural Society   53*
> *A Welfare State   53*
> *A Mixed Economy   53*

The Socialization Process   54

> *Education and Class   54*

A Changing Britain   55

**THINKING CRITICALLY**   56

Key Terms   57

Further Readings   57


**B.** POLITICAL PROCESSES AND INSTITUTIONS   58

Voting   58

Is the Electoral System Working?   61

Elections   62

**A CLOSER LOOK 2.5** The June 2001 General Election   63

> *Who Are the Candidates?   64*

**A CLOSER LOOK 2.6** Some Record Postwar Elections   64

> *The Nature of Voting   65*

**A CLOSER LOOK 2.7** PARTY IDENTIFICATION AND CLASS   67

Political Parties   68

Party Organizations   69
   *Local and Regional   69*
   *National Organization   70*

The Parties in Parliament   72

Party Leadership   72

Power within the Parties   73

Interest Groups   74
   *Business   74*
   *Trade Unions   75*

The Executive   76

The Monarchy   76

**REVIEW 2.3** LONG LIVE THE QUEEN: A EUROPEAN TIME LINE   77

The Government   77

The Cabinet   79

**REVIEW 2.4** SOME KEY TERMS IN BRITISH POLITICS   80
   *Cabinet Membership   81*
   *Procedure in the Cabinet   81*

**A CLOSER LOOK 2.8** THE CABINET, 2002   81

The Prime Minister   82
   *Functions   83*

**A CLOSER LOOK 2.9** TONY BLAIR: LABOUR LEADER AND PRIME MINISTER   83
   *Is the Prime Minister a Quasi President?   84*

**REVIEW 2.5** THE CENTER OF BRITISH GOVERNMENT   85

The Civil Service   86

**REVIEW 2.6** QUANGOS (QUASI AUTONOMOUS NONGOVERNMENTAL ORGANIZATIONS)
   OR NONDEPARTMENTAL PUBLIC BODIES   87
   *The Role of the Civil Service   87*

**A CLOSER LOOK 2.10** CIVIL SERVANTS AND POLICY ADVICE   88

The Legislature   88
   *Composition of Parliament   89*
   *House of Lords   89*
   *House of Commons   90*

**A CLOSER LOOK 2.11** THE HOUSE OF LORDS: INTERIM REFORM   90
   *Who Becomes an MP?   91*

**A CLOSER LOOK 2.12** DID I HEAR A WORD?   91
   *MPs and Political Parties   92*
   *The Opposition   93*
   *How Important Is the MP?   94*
   *An Assenting Assembly   94*

Judges and Politics   95

**THINKING CRITICALLY   96**

Key Terms   96

Further Readings   97

**C.** PUBLIC POLICY   98

The Mixed Economy   98

The Decline of Nationalized Industries   99

Economic Planning   100

**REVIEW 2.7** THATCHER AND BLAIR ECONOMICS   101

The Welfare State   101
   *Social Security*   *101*

**REVIEW 2.8** ECONOMIC AND SOCIAL POLICIES OF THE BLAIR GOVERNMENT,
   1997–2002   102
   *The National Health Service*   *103*

Foreign Affairs   104
   *From Special Relationship to Ally*   *104*
   *From Empire to Commonwealth*   *105*

**A CLOSER LOOK 2.13** SPLITTING THE ROCK   108
   *Britain and the European Union*   *108*

Conclusion   110

**THINKING CRITICALLY**   **111**

Key Terms   111

Abbreviations   111

Further Readings   112

Web Sites   112

CHAPTER **3**    **THE GOVERNMENT OF FRANCE**  *Jean Blondel*  **115**

**A.** POLITICAL DEVELOPMENT   118

History and Society: Traditions and Contradictions in French Politics   118
   *The Instability of French Politics through the 1960s*   *118*
   *Social and Economic Development*   *118*
   *The Clash between Liberalism and Authoritarianism*   *118*
   *Nationalism and Internationalism*   *119*
   *Centralization and Decentralization*   *120*

**A CLOSER LOOK 3.1** FRENCH CULTURE AND THE FRENCH LANGUAGE   120

The Historical Perspective of French Politics   121
   *The Revolution of 1789*   *121*
   *Traditionalists and Liberals in the Nineteenth Century*   *121*
   *The Napoleonic Tradition*   *122*
   *Republicanism and Its Elements*   *123*
   *The Second World War and Its Consequences: The Vichy Regime,
      the Resistance, and the Fourth Republic*   *123*
   *The Fall of the Fourth Republic*   *123*

The Background of the Social Order   124
   *Peasant Origins*   *124*
   *Regional Sectionalism and the Influence of Paris*   *125*
   *Social Class*   *126*

Church and State   127

The Administrative and Cultural Centralization of Modern France   128
**THINKING CRITICALLY**   129
Key Terms   129
Further Readings   129


**B.** POLITICAL PROCESSES AND INSTITUTIONS   130

Interest Groups   130
    *Trade Unions   130*
    *Business Organizations   132*
    *Farmers' Organizations   134*
    *Other Groups   134*
**A CLOSER LOOK 3.2** THE WEAKNESS OF PROTEST GROUPS IN FRANCE   135
    *Groups and the Political System   136*
The Party System   137
    *Streamlining the Parties: Gaullists and Socialists   137*
    *The Effect of the Electoral System   138*
    *The Right and Center   138*
    *The Resilience of the Center   140*
    *The Extreme Right   141*
    *The Left   142*
The Spirit of the Constitution of 1958   146
    *De Gaulle and the Constitution of 1958   146*
    *A Hybrid System of Executive Power   148*
**A CLOSER LOOK 3.3** DE GAULLE AND MITTERRAND   147
President and Government   148
    *The Formal Powers of the President   148*
    *The Presidential Power of Dissolution   148*
    *Constitutional Amendments and Referendums   148*
    *Emergency Powers   150*
    *Popular Election of the President   150*
**A CLOSER LOOK 3.4** THE POPULAR ELECTION OF THE PRESIDENT MAY WEAKEN
    POLITICAL PARTIES   150
The Government   151
    *The Role of the Prime Minister   151*
    *The Structure and Composition of the Government   152*
President, Prime Minister, and Government in the Fifth Republic   153
    *The Extent of Presidential Intervention   153*
    *The Semipresidential Character of the Fifth Republic   154*
    *Cohabitation   154*
The Legislature   155
    *The Traditional Role of the French Parliament   155*
    *Parliamentary Organization in the Fifth Republic   156*
    *Scope of Legislation   157*
    *The Legislative Struggle   157*
    *Parliamentary Committees   158*
    *The Power of the Government to Curb Debate   158*
    *The Vote of Censure   159*

The Constitutional Council   160
The New Equilibrium of Powers   160
**A CLOSER LOOK 3.5** The Judiciary and Politicians   161
**THINKING CRITICALLY   162**
Key Terms   162
Further Readings   162

**C.** PUBLIC POLICY   163
The Organization of the State   163
  *The Civil Service   163*
  *The Idea of the State   163*
The Civil Service and Its Characteristics   164
  *The Grands Corps   164*
  *The Grandes Ecoles   164*
  *The Role of the* Grands Corps *in the Nation   165*
**A CLOSER LOOK 3.6** Education: Still Strongly Elitist   165
  *Civil Service Control   166*
Local Government   166
  *Département and Commune   167*
  *Regionalism   167*
**A CLOSER LOOK 3.7** The French Media   168
Economic Intervention and Public Enterprise   168
  *The Plan   168*
  *The Size of the Public Sector   169*
  *The Move toward Privatization   170*
Foreign Policy   170
  *De Gaulle's Worldwide Policy   170*
  *Pompidou's Greater Realism   170*
  *France's Role in World Affairs   171*
  *France and the European Union   171*
Conclusion   172
**THINKING CRITICALLY   174**
Key Terms   174
Further Readings   175
Web Sites   175

CHAPTER **4**   **THE GOVERNMENT OF GERMANY**   *Donald Kommers and
A. James McAdams*   **177**
  **A.** POLITICAL DEVELOPMENT   180
  Historical Background: Molding the German Nation   180
    *The First Reich (800–1806)   180*
    *Napoleon to Bismarck (1806–1871)   181*
    *The Second Reich (1871–1918)   181*
    *The Weimar Republic (1919–1933)   182*

*The Third Reich (1933–1945)   183*
Toward a New Framework of Government   183
*The Occupation (1945–1949)   183*
*Reunification   184*
**A CLOSER LOOK 4.1** INCOMPATIBLE SOCIAL REALITIES?   185
Society and Economy   185
*Economic Background   185*
**A CLOSER LOOK 4.2** THE SOCIAL MARKET ECONOMY   187
*Territory and Population   187*
*From Bonn to Berlin and In Between   189*
*Economic and Social Stratification   190*
*Security and Equality   191*
*Women, Law, and Society   193*
*Ethnic Minorities   196*
**A CLOSER LOOK 4.3** NOT QUITE A MELTING POT   197
Culture: Social and Civic   197
*Education and the Media   197*
*Religion and the Churches   198*
*Political Attitudes and Participation   199*
*Politics and Literature: A Footnote   201*

Conclusion   202
**THINKING CRITICALLY   202**
Key Terms   202
Further Readings   203


**B.** POLITICAL PROCESSES AND INSTITUTIONS   204

Political Parties   204
*Christian Democrats   204*
*Social Democrats   205*
*Free Democrats   206*
*Splinter Parties   207*
*Greens   207*
*Party of Democratic Socialism   208*
**A CLOSER LOOK 4.4** THE PDS TAKES ROOT   208
*Party Organization   209*
*Party Finance   209*
Interest Groups   211
*Citizen Initiatives* (Bürgerinitiativen)   *212*
*Major Interest Aggregations   212*
Electoral Politics   214
*The Electoral System   214*
*Split-Ticket Voting   216*
*Candidate Selection   216*
*Campaign Styles and Techniques   216*
German Politics in Transition   217
*The Postwar Years to Reunification   217*
*A Change of Government   219*

Policy-Making Institutions   221
    *The Federal President   221*
    *The Federal Government   223*
**REVIEW 4.1** THE BASIC LAW: SELECTED BASIC RIGHTS   223
    *The Bundestag: Legislative Branch   226*
    *The Law-Making Process   228*
    *Federalism and Bureaucracy   228*
    *The Bundesrat   229*
    *An Emerging Instrument of Opposition   230*
    *The Legal System and the Judiciary   231*
**THINKING CRITICALLY   233**
Key Terms   233
Further Readings   234

**C.** PUBLIC POLICY   235
Civil Liberties: An Ordering of Constitutional Values   235
**A CLOSER LOOK 4.5** ARTICLE 65 OF THE BASIC LAW—THE CHANCELLOR   235
Asylum and Citizenship   236
Public Administration: Decentralized Federalism   238
Social and Economic Policy   238
    *Fiscal Policy   238*
    *General Economic Policy   239*
**A CLOSER LOOK 4.6** GERMANY'S SOCIAL CODE   241
    *Social Welfare Policy   241*
    *Summary   242*
Foreign Policy, National Unity, and the Road to Normalcy   242
    *Resolving the "German Problem"   242*
    *Gorbachev and Glasnost   243*
    *The Progress and Politics of German Unity   244*
**A CLOSER LOOK 4.7** AN INDIVISIBLE NATION   244
**REVIEW 4.2** THE PATH TO GERMAN UNITY   246
    *Post-Unification Foreign Policy   248*
**A CLOSER LOOK 4.8** FOREIGN POLICY: A SPECIAL RESPONSIBILITY TO HISTORY   249
Conclusion   250
**THINKING CRITICALLY   250**
Key Terms   250
Further Readings   250
Web Sites   251

CHAPTER **5**    **THE GOVERNMENT OF ITALY**   *Giuseppe Ammendola*   **253**
    **A.** POLITICAL DEVELOPMENT   256
The Land   256
**A CLOSER LOOK 5.1** THE COMMUNE (*IL COMUNE*)   257
Historical Development   257

**REVIEW 5.1** THE MAKING OF ITALY    258

The New Century    259

The Rise of Fascism    260
 *Mussolini in Power    260*
 *Aggressive Foreign Policy    261*

World War II    261

After the War    261

The Relevance of History    262
 *Language    262*
 *The Church, Secularism, and Socialism    262*
 *Fascism and Centralization    263*
 *Trasformismo    263*

The Regions    264
 *The Southern Question    264*
 *Crime and Punishment    265*

**REVIEW 5.2** PROFILE OF ITALY    266
 *The Third Italy    267*

Social Classes    267
 *Standards of Living and Status    268*

The Family    268
 *The Family since the 1980s    269*

**REVIEW 5.3** THE FAMILY: POLITICS AND PUBLIC POLICY    270
 *Closeness in the Family    270*

**REVIEW 5.4** FACTS ABOUT THE ITALIAN FAMILY    271

Gender Issues    271

**THINKING CRITICALLY    272**

Key Terms    273

Further Readings    273


**B.** POLITICAL PROCESSES AND INSTITUTIONS    274

Elections    274

Political Parties    275
 *The Individual Parties    276*

Christian Democrats and Post–World War II Politics    279
 *The Elections of 1948    279*
 *Less Stable Majorities    280*
 *The 1960s: The Socialists out of Quarantine    280*
 *The Center-Left Governments    281*
 *Politics as Usual    281*
 *Historic Compromise: Enter the Communists    281*
 *The End of DC-PCI Cooperation    282*
 *The 1980s: The Rise of the Socialists    282*
 *The 1990s: Referendums, Judges, and the Northern League    283*

The End of the Traditional Political System    *283*

The Elections of 1994    284

A New Party System?    285

The Elections of 1996    286
The Elections of 2001    287
Interest Groups    288
 *The Unions*    288
 *Unions' Waning Power*    289
 *Interest Groups since the 1990s*    289
The Parliament    290
 *Lawmaking*    291
 *Other Powers*    291
 *A Changing Parliament*    292
The Government: The Prime Minister and the Council of Ministers    292
 *Government's Legislative Powers*    295
The President    295
 *Presidents Scalfaro and Ciampi*    296
**REVIEW 5.5** PRESIDENTS OF THE REPUBLIC    296
The Public Administration    297
 *A Large State Presence*    298
 *The Auxiliary Organs*    298
 *Regions, Provinces, and Communes*    298
 *Demand for Efficiency*    299
The Constitutional Court    299
The Judicial System    300
 *Operation Clean Hands*    301
**THINKING CRITICALLY**    301
Key Terms    301
Further Readings    302

**C.** PUBLIC POLICY    303

The Post–World War II Years: Between Market and State    303
 *The Free-Market Choice*    303
 *The Western Choice*    304
 *Economic Intervention in the South*    304
 *The Economic Miracle*    304
 *Trade and Europe*    305
 *Investments in the South*    305
The 1960s and Economic Planning    305
 *The End of the Miracle*    306
 *European Integration*    306
 *Stronger Unions*    306
The Inflationary 1970s    307
 *Entrepreneurial Choices*    308
 *A Postindustrial Society*    308
The 1980s    308
 *Changing Labor Relations*    308
 *Less Participation*    309
 *A Second Economic Miracle?*    309
**REVIEW 5.6** HIGHLIGHTS OF ITALIAN FINANCE    310

Policy Courses since World War II   311
    *The Center-Left   311*
    *Consociational Politics   311*
    *The Fight against Inflation   312*
    *The Public Deficits   312*
    *Out of the ERM   312*
    *Into the EMU   313*
    *The Former Communist in Power   313*
    *Amato Is Back   313*
    *The Economic Policies of the Olive Tree   314*
    *Enter Berlusconi   315*
The Road Ahead   315
    *European Economic Integration   315*
    *Privatization and Capital Markets   316*
    *Deregulation and Antitrust Legislation   317*
    *Unemployment   317*
    *The South   317*
    *Public Administration   318*
    *Decentralization   318*
    *The Justice System   319*
    *Institutional and Electoral Reforms   321*
Foreign Policy   321
Conclusion   323
**THINKING CRITICALLY   324**
Key Terms   324
Further Readings   324
Web Sites   325
Note   325

CHAPTER **6**   **THE GOVERNMENT OF SPAIN**   *Thomas D. Lancaster*   **327**
    **A.** POLITICAL DEVELOPMENT   330
Historical Background   330
    *Modern Political History   331*
**REVIEW 6.1** KEY EVENTS IN SPANISH HISTORY   332
    *The Transition to Democracy   336*
**REVIEW 6.2** KEY EVENTS IN DEMOCRATIC SPAIN   338
Society and the Economy   339
    *Physical Characteristics   339*
    *The Regions   340*
    *The Societies: Nationalism and Language   340*
    *The Population   341*
    *The Economy   341*
    *Francoist Economic Policy   341*
    *The Moncloa Pacts   342*
Culture: Social and Civil   343
    *Education   343*

*Religion and the Church  345*
*The Press  345*
**THINKING CRITICALLY  347**
Key Terms  347
Further Readings  347

**B.** POLITICAL PROCESSES AND INSTITUTIONS  349

The Spanish Party System  349
*Social and Political Cleavages  349*
*The Central Parties  350*
*The Nationalist Parties  356*
The Electoral System  357
*Frequency of Elections  358*
*Electoral Performances  358*
Interest Groups  359
*Economic Organizations  359*
*The Church  361*
*The Military  363*
Major State Institutions  365
*The Monarchy  365*
*The Government  368*
*The Parliament  370*
*The Legislative Process  372*
*The Regional System of Government  374*
*The Judicial System  377*
**THINKING CRITICALLY  379**
Key Terms  380
Further Readings  380

**C.** PUBLIC POLICY  381

Regional Politics  381
*Fiscal Policy  382*
*Institutionalization of Regionalism  382*
*Political Terrorism  383*
The Politics of European Integration  384
*The European Union  384*
*NATO  385*
Economic Policy  387
*Macroeconomic Policy Making  387*
*Monetary Policy: From the Bank of Spain to the Euro  388*
*Fiscal Policy  389*
*Budget Deficits  390*
*Unemployment: The Persistent Problem  391*
Corruption and Scandals  392
Conclusion  393

**THINKING CRITICALLY**  393

Key Terms  394

Further Readings  394

Web Sites  394

CHAPTER **7**  **THE GOVERNMENT OF THE NETHERLANDS**  *Ken Gladdish*  **397**

**A.** POLITICAL DEVELOPMENT  399

The Setting  399

Historical Background  399

> *Origins of the State  399*
> *Religion  401*
> *Republican Virtues  401*
> *The New Kingdom  401*

Parliamentary Government  402

> *The Liberal Era  403*
> *Development of Modern Politics  404*

**REVIEW 7.1** Chief Features of the 1917 Pacification  405

The Pacification and Its Sequel  405

The Pillars of Society  406

Consociational Democracy  407

War and Reconstruction  408

The Corporatist Package  408

The Crumbling of the Pillars  409

Post-Pillarization Politics  410

Quality of Life  412

Women's Political Participation  413

**THINKING CRITICALLY**  413

Key Terms  413

Further Readings  414

**B.** POLITICAL PROCESSES AND INSTITUTIONS  415

Proportional Representation  415

> *Elections before PR  415*
> *Meticulous Proportionality  416*

**A CLOSER LOOK 7.1** The 2002 Election  418

> *Parties and PR  418*

The Party Universe  419

> *Major Parties  421*
> *Minor Parties  423*
> *Party Programs  423*
> *Party Membership and Resources  425*
> *Party Organization  426*

*Party Support*  427
Interest Groups  428
The Constitution  429
The Monarchy  429
The Political Executive  430
  *Cabinet Formation  431*
  *Coalition Negotiations  432*
  *The Cost of Delay?  432*
  *Executive and Legislative Relations  433*
The Professional Executive  434
The Parliament  434
  *Parliament's Functions  435*
  *Parliamentary Group and Members of Parliament  436*
Subnational Government  437
Supranational Politics  438
**THINKING CRITICALLY**  438
Key Terms  438
Further Readings  439

**C.** PUBLIC POLICY  440
Policy Generation  440
Economic Policy  441
The State in the Marketplace  442
Social Security  444
Foreign Policy  445
  *Defense and Domestic Politics  446*
  *European Integration  447*
  *Aid and International Visibility  448*
**THINKING CRITICALLY**  448
Key Terms  448
Further Readings  448
Web Sites  449

CHAPTER **8**     **THE EUROPEAN UNION**  *Michael Curtis*  **451**
Historical Background  453
  *A United States of Europe?  454*
  *European Coal and Steel Community  455*
**REVIEW 8.1** KEY TERMS IN EUROPEAN INTEGRATION  456
  *The European Economic Community  457*

**A CLOSER LOOK 8.1** THE COUNCIL OF EUROPE   457

**REVIEW 8.2** THE SINGLE ECONOMIC ACT (SEA)   458

    *The Maastricht Treaty   458*

**A CLOSER LOOK 8.2** THE EUROPEAN ECONOMIC AREA (EEA)   458

**REVIEW 8.3** MAJOR FEATURES OF MAASTRICHT   459

The Basic Structure of the European Union   459

**REVIEW 8.4** KEY EVENTS IN EUROPEAN INTEGRATION   461

**A CLOSER LOOK 8.3** THE EUROPEAN COMMUNITIES AND THE EU   462

EU Financial Structure   463

The Institutions of the EU   465

    *The European Commission   465*

**A CLOSER LOOK 8.4** ROMANO PRODI—PRESIDENT OF THE EUROPEAN COMMISSION   465

    *The Council of Ministers   468*

    *Other Executive Bodies   469*

The European Parliament   469

**A CLOSER LOOK 8.5** WHO MAKES EU POLICY?   470

The Court of Justice   471

Other Agencies   472

The Single or Common Market   472

EU Policy Issues   472

    *A Common Currency   472*

**REVIEW 8.5** A TALE OF SEVEN CITIES   474

    *Security and Defense   474*

**A CLOSER LOOK 8.6** NO MORE FRANC, NO MORE LIRA—NOW THE EURO   475

    *Justice and Home Affairs   475*

    *Common Agricultural Policy   476*

**REVIEW 8.6** MAJOR FEATURES OF THE EUROPEAN UNION   476

Foreign Affairs   477

    *Trade   477*

    *Diplomatic Relations and Development Programs   477*

**A CLOSER LOOK 8.7** CENTRAL AND EASTERN EUROPE   477

The EU's Future   478

**THINKING CRITICALLY   480**

Key Terms   480

Further Readings   481

Web Sites   481

*Credits   482*

*Index   483*

# Preface

## OUR APPROACH

This book introduces students to the subject of Western European governments and politics through both an analytical and institutional approach. The authors believe it is desirable, even essential, to use this double approach to provide a valid and meaningful understanding of the subject. Our approach allows unusual flexibility for purposes of instruction, since students can benefit from exposure to alternative ways of comparing political systems.

This book, like its companion volume, *Introduction to Comparative Government*, is not based on any narrow or rigid theoretical approach. It does not force the material into categories that do not provide understanding or that make learning difficult for beginning students. This book instead allows each instructor and student to choose the comparative approach that he or she thinks is most helpful for understanding the whole or parts of political systems.

To help that understanding, the authors have written with clarity and have throughout tried to avoid unnecessary jargon, unfamiliar terminology, and unduly complex classifications. What is important about this book is that the authors have used a more descriptive, accessible style than other texts available at the present time so that all can learn about the realities and performances of the countries we cover.

Each chapter is divided into three discrete sections. The first is the history and socio-economic development of the country and the bases on which the regimes rest, the norms and rules of each society. The second section is devoted to political processes and institutions, a subject that so many other texts have neglected or relegated to minor significance. The third section looks at various aspects of public policies, including economic, social, and foreign affairs. By this method, we can obtain comparisons among the chapters as well as within them, a method that again provides instructors and students with flexibility.

## OUR FEATURES

This edition introduces a number of new features, helpful for understanding factual material and theoretical approaches.

### Country Profile

The chapters begin with a profile of the country, constructed in a consistent way across the chapters, thus providing uniformity for the whole book. We recognize that the statistics in these profiles, taken from official sources, may not always correspond exactly to those provided by international organizations that may appear elsewhere within a chapter, but the small differences do not detract from their essential validity.

### Thinking Critically

The authors have provided a number of questions for instructors to use and students to ponder at the end of each of the three sections of each chapter. Students will therefore be encouraged to think about the reading and be prepared for the next section.

### Web Sites

Each chapter provides a list of Web sites that students can use for up-to-date, detailed information on the individual system or parts of it.

### Boxes

This edition also introduces two new features, "A Closer Look" and "Review" boxes, both of which provide succinct information on a particular aspect of each system.

## Visuals

All tables and statistics have been brought up-to-date, including electoral results up to the point of publication. The photos in each chapter illustrate significant people and institutions. The maps have been drawn for easy comprehension.

This text is now accompanied by Longman's new Web site for comparative politics, found at www.ablongman/comparative politics. On the site, students can try their luck at interactive geography quizzes, find out how much they know about the 24 countries featured on the site, and utilize a wealth of narrative and statistical data in the site's "Country Profiles."

## ACKNOWLEDGMENTS

Both individually and collectively, the seven authors of the book owe intellectual debts to many colleagues who have given valuable advice, and also to our students at different institutions.

We also want to thank the various readers of drafts of the manuscript, for this and previous editions, whose comments and suggestions improved the end result.

Nancy Bermeo, Princeton University

Manoutchehr Eskandari-Qajar, Santa Barbara City College

Michael W. Foley, Catholic University of America

Michael Levy, Southeast Missouri University

George Moyser, University of Vermont

Thomas Nichols, Westminster College

Sofia Perez, Boston University

Richard Piper, University of Tampa

George Romoser, University of New Hampshire

Kaare Strom, University of California–San Diego

Christopher Van Houten

Robert E. Williams, Pepperdine University

Dwayne Woods, Purdue University

*Michael Curtis*

# Western European Government and Politics

CHAPTER

1

# THE NATURE OF
# Western European Politics

*Michael Curtis*

## INTRODUCTION

This book is an introduction to contemporary Western European political systems, to the major features and institutions of those systems, and to the challenges they now face at the beginning of the twenty-first century. It does this first by denoting the major characteristics of Western European societies in this chapter, and then by providing an in-depth analysis of six of the more important and significant of those societies and of the European Union in following chapters.

Other great civilizations in the world, especially those of China, India, and the Middle East, have been important in world history. Yet, with its diversity of peoples, its great and complex 2,000-year history, its widely varying social, economic, and political traditions, and its rich cultural, artistic, philosophic, and scientific contributions, Western Europe was for a long time seen by many as the central feature of world history, at least until World War II, and as the area which had the most influential impact on other parts of the world.

In the aftermath of World War II, Western Europe seemed overshadowed by the emergence of the two superpowers, which dominated world politics. With the dissolution of one of those superpowers, the Soviet Union, the role of Western Europe is again becoming significant with its remarkable economic growth and prosperity, its intellectual vitality, its strategic importance, its political stability, and the influence of its institutions. Study of the Western European systems is not simply a matter of intellectual curiosity, but is also vital for analysis of a renewed political and military power, one which has a population about 50 percent larger than that of the United States and a larger gross domestic product.

The six countries examined in this book have been chosen to illustrate the main ways of political life in Western Europe. They are examples of modern political systems and the various forms taken to become democratic. Included here are the four countries with the largest populations, which are also notable as some of the world's leading industrial democracies (see Table 1.1).

**TABLE 1.1**

**SIX COUNTRIES OF WESTERN EUROPE**

| | Population (millions) | Area (thousands of sq km) | Employment (%) | | |
| --- | --- | --- | --- | --- | --- |
| | | | Agriculture | Industry | Service |
| Great Britain | 58 | 245 | 1 | 19 | 80 |
| France | 59 | 552 | 4 | 25 | 71 |
| Germany | 82 | 357 | 2.8 | 33.4 | 63.8 |
| Italy | 57 | 301 | 5.5 | 32.6 | 61.9 |
| Netherlands | 15 | 37 | 4 | 23 | 73 |
| Spain | 39 | 505 | 8 | 28 | 64 |

Britain has been crucially important as the model, sometimes referred to as "the Westminster model," of a parliamentary-cabinet system and a flourishing two-party system. France gave the world the model of revolutionary change, the idea of grandeur in international politics, the image of political nationalism, and a heritage of ideological politics mixed with practical reality. Recently reunited, Germany illustrates the successful transition after a turbulent history to a stable political order and economic prosperity. Italy, with its acute internal divisions and social problems and its multiparty system, illustrates the political characteristics of coalition making in a democratic society. Spain has shown how an authoritarian system can be transformed into a democracy. The Netherlands is an important example of a particular kind of pluralistic politics and of political arrangements sometimes referred to as "consociational." These six countries, with other Western countries, are now engaged in the construction of some new, as yet undefined, form of European identity.

The term "Western Europe" has been defined in different ways—geographically, economically, and politically—and has usually been seen as a cultural entity with a distinctive character, the source of ideas and artistic expressions throughout history. Geographically, Western Europe consists of 18 major states, 11 on the mainland continent, 5 Nordic nations, and the 2 island states of Great Britain and Ireland. Currently, its population is 380 million, with a density about four times greater than that of the United States. Four of the states—Britain, France, Germany, and Italy—have populations over 50 million. In all countries of Western Europe, women constitute a majority of the population. Territorially, Western Europe is defined on three sides by the sea; only on the eastern side have the boundaries between Western and Central Europe been disputed. For most of the post–World War II period, until the fall of the Communist Central and Eastern European states and the end of the Soviet Union, those boundaries were in reality defined by the Iron Curtain, which divided Europe.

Since that curtain fell in 1989 with the end of Communist domination in the Soviet Union and the Warsaw Pact countries, no neat boundaries can be drawn dividing Western, Eastern, and Central Europe. The three Baltic countries—Estonia, Latvia, and Lithuania—can now be considered part of Western Europe from certain points of view. The placing of others such as Slovakia, Poland, Romania, Hungary, and Bulgaria, is less clear as some of these countries are being considered for membership in the European Union.

European countries can usefully be studied as parts of certain groups: the Balkans, the Baltic states, Benelux, the Nordic countries, NATO, and the EU. For over 40 years following World War II, Europe was divided into two blocs: a Democratic West, becoming more prosperous, and a Com-

## A CLOSER LOOK 1.1

### THE BALKANS

The Balkans, the area of southeast Europe, south of the Danube River, between the Adriatic Sea, the Black Sea, and the Mediterranean, contains a diversity of ethnic groups speaking eight major languages and belonging to three major religions and cultures. Because of the rivalries and conflicts among them, the term "Balkanization" is used to convey political fragmentation. After the fall of the Ottoman Empire which dominated the area until the end of World War I, a number of new states came into existence. Almost all of them were under Communist domination after World War II until 1989–1991, when the Balkan Communist regimes were overthrown. Yugoslavia disintegrated when Croatia, Bosnia-Herzegovina, and Slovenia declared independence in 1991. The present Balkan states, still embroiled in conflicts, are Yugoslavia (Serbia and Montenegro), Bosnia-Herzegovina, Croatia, Macedonia, Albania, and Slovenia.

munist East, relatively poor with political systems modeled on that of the Soviet Union. The latter nations were ruled by a Communist Party (the only legal party), a large secret police, a Marxist ideology, central planning and direction of the economy, strict censorship, control of information, and restrictions on travel. They were also dominated by the Soviet Union itself and were members of Comecon and the Warsaw Pact.

At the end of the 1980s the changes in Central and Eastern European systems were rapid and dramatic and have transformed the European continent. Much of this was due not only to their own economic, social, and political problems, but also to the people of the Soviet Union and their differences over the proposals of Soviet leader Mikhail Gorbachev for *perestroika,* or restructur-

ing. The Central and Eastern Europeans were aware of the decline of Communism as a force, of the lack of support for Communist Party leadership, and of the fact that the Soviet Union under Gorbachev would no longer intervene in their internal affairs or use force to prevent change.

Eastern Europe also appreciated that the Communist decline and the policy of *perestroika,* calling for economic and political reforms, was leading to moderation of the Cold War between the Soviet Union and the United States. The tension in the postwar period between the two countries was partly an ideological struggle between a liberal democracy with a market economy and a Communist system with a centrally planned economy, and partly a conflict over influence and competing interests in a world

## A CLOSER LOOK 1.2

### BALTIC STATES

The Baltic states are Estonia, Latvia, and Lithuania, which border the Baltic Sea. The three countries became independent after World War I, then became "union-republics" of the Soviet Union in 1940, and again independent in 1991–1992 after the fall of the Soviet Union. The Baltic Council, originally set up in 1990, with a consequent new agreement in June 1994, aims at cooperation between the three countries in many areas. This takes place in different forums: parliamentary, govenmental, and among heads of state. The three Baltic countries have applied for membership of in both NATO and the EU.

## A CLOSER LOOK 1.3

### BENELUX

Benelux comprises Belgium, the Netherlands, and Luxembourg. Originally a customs union signed in 1944 and operative in 1948 to remove customs barriers among the three countries and to set up a common external tariff, it became a full economic union in 1960, and a single customs area. The three countries were founding members of the European Community (now the European Union).

dominated by two superpowers. The tension was lessened in the 1980s with a growing mood of political cooperation with the West.

Internal dissension within the Central and Eastern European system came to a head in 1989. Movements for an end to Communist rule and for change to a more prosperous and productive economy began in Poland and Hungary and rapidly spread to Czechoslovakia, East Germany, Bulgaria, and to a lesser extent, Romania (see Table 1.2). This revolution, almost entirely peaceful, was most dramatic in East Germany, the German Democratic Republic. On November 9, 1989, the Berlin Wall, a symbol of the Cold War dividing East and West, came down; in December 1989 and March 1990, two Communist governments collapsed; and in October 1990 the GDR was united with the Federal Republic of Germany.

The former Communist systems are in different phases of transition to some other form of political system. So is the former Soviet Union and the republics within it, most of which are in the Commonwealth of Independent States, led by Russia.

After renouncing their Communist systems and after the collapse of the Warsaw Pact and the Comecon trading bloc, the Central and Eastern European countries formed new political parties and wrote new or adapted their existing constitutions. The countries all have parliaments, reflecting free elections and a multiparty system, free markets, mixed economies that are part state-owned and part privatized, and a civil society not controlled by the state.

The Eastern European states have been taking varied roads, and at different speeds, in search of pluralistic democratic systems, protection of political and human rights, and economies more oriented to the market and private ownership than to management by state-owned enter-

### TABLE 1.2

#### PROFILE OF CENTRAL AND EASTERN EUROPE

|  | Area (thousands of sq km) | Population (millions) | $ GDP Per Capita, 2000 | GDP ($ billion), 2000 |
|---|---|---|---|---|
| Poland | 312 | 38.5 | 8,500 | 325 |
| Czech Republic | 79 | 10.3 | 12,900 | 132 |
| Slovakia | 49 | 5.4 | 10,200 | 55 |
| Hungary | 93 | 10.0 | 11,200 | 114 |
| Slovenia | 20 | 2.0 | 12,000 | 23 |
| Bulgaria | 111 | 7.7 | 6,200 | 48 |
| Romania | 238 | 22.7 | 5,900 | 132 |

## NORDIC COUNTRIES

The Nordic countries are Denmark, Norway, Sweden, Finland, and Iceland. The Faroe Islands and Greenland, part of Denmark, enjoy a degree of self-government. The Nordic Council, a cooperative structure of parliaments and governments, was set up in 1952 to make proposals for action on most issues except defense and foreign policy, but it does not have final authority over decisions. Denmark and Norway are members of NATO, and Denmark, Finland, and Sweden are in the EU.

prises, price controls, and central planning. In this period of transition these states have experienced problems of economic hardship, inflation, high taxes, and unemployment. Many of the states also face complex internal problems because of the presence of ethnic minorities in their territories, territorial disputes with their neighbors, and mutually hostile national movements.

## POLITICAL DEVELOPMENT

Western Europe has been the arena for a long and influential historical process and varied paths to political development which reflect the diversity of its changing society, culture, and politics, from the civilizations of Greece and Rome from about 800 B.C.E. until the fall of the Roman Empire in 476 C.E., to the present.

The Greeks created the political form of the city-state, or *polis,* from which our word "politics" comes. The city-states had different kinds of political institutions, including monarchy, tyranny,

democracy (rule by the people), and assemblies controlled by the aristocracy (rule of the best). From Rome, with its complex political history and institutions, came strong codes of law and an elaborate set of legal principles. In an effort to unify the Roman Empire, in 313 the Emperor Constantine adopted Christianity as the official religion.

In the medieval period, between the eighth and fifteenth centuries, economic relations and political institutions were connected. Economically, feudalism was based on agricultural estates or manors in a hierarchy of landlords, vassals, and serfs. Politically, the feudal monarch was limited in his exercise of power. Personal rights were based on the social category into which an individual was born and lived. Simple parliamentary assemblies represented some of those ranks such as the nobles and the Church and advised the monarch on taxation and other policy issues.

Significant intellectual, economic, and political changes shaped Western Europe after the fifteenth century: the Renaissance, which brought a new learning and style in literature, art, and

## COMMONWEALTH OF INDEPENDENT STATES

The Commwealth of Independent States (CIS), an association of 12 of the 15 republics of the former Soviet Union, was formed in 1991 to establish cooperation in a number of policy areas. The three Baltic states did not join. The CIS is supposed to coordinate economic and foreign policies of its members, working through councils of heads of state, heads of governments, and ministers, and a parliamentary assembly. But the members have been divided by territorial disputes, economic difficulties, and complaints about domination by Russia.

life; the Protestant Reformation in the sixteenth century and the Catholic Counter-Reformation; the rise of science in the late seventeenth century and the Enlightenment in the eighteenth; the change from feudalism and serfdom to an industrial system based on wage labor and increased commercial activity; the emergence of the political state and national monarchies in the sixteenth century; the exploration and colonization of a considerable part of the world from the Americas to East Asia; the Industrial Revolution in the nineteenth century, which transformed the essentially agricultural countries of the West into manufacturing countries.

Three of our countries—England, France, and Spain—in the sixteenth century embodied the essential characteristics of the state; political institutions that exercised power and had a monopoly on the use of legitimate force, territory with recognized boundaries, and a population in that territory. In these three countries, power was centralized under the monarchs as different territorial areas were united to form the state boundaries.

In our other three countries, the state was created at a later time; the Netherlands in 1648, Italy in 1861, and Germany in 1871. The Netherlands fought for its independence from Spain for 80 years (1568–1648) and can trace its monarchical system back to 1813. The states of Italy and Germany were created as a result of successful wars and on the basis of the common nationality of a people.

In the main, our six states have been politically unstable. Only Great Britain—with its clear, recognized boundaries, its strong central government, its acknowledged civil liberties, and absence of invasion for a thousand years—has had a long, stable continuity. Since its Revolution in 1789, France has had 12 constitutions, 5 republics, 2 empires, and 2 monarchies; the present Fifth Republic began in 1958. Since 1861, Italy has had a constitutional monarchy, a totalitarian Fascist dictatorship, and a republic which began in 1946. Since 1871, Germany has had an empire, two republics, the totalitarian Nazi dictatorship and occupation by Allied forces following World War II. In 1949, the country was divided into East and West Germany but was reunified in 1990 as a federal republic. Spain over the last century has had two republics, two dictatorships, and two monarchies; the present regime dates from 1975.

Political development in our countries took different forms from the authoritarian and autocratic regimes of the past to the present liberal, democratic systems. The varied ways in which the feudal system was modified or ended conditioned whether European countries would become liberal democracies, unstable republics, or authoritarian systems.

Most of Europe during the seventeenth and eighteenth centuries was ruled by absolute monarchies—typified by Louis XIV of France, (1643–1715)—which controlled political decision making, the royal court, the military, and some

---

**REVIEW**

**1.1**

## MONARCHIES IN WESTERN EUROPE

Today monarchies exist in ten Western European countries:

| Country | Head of State | Country | Head of State |
|---|---|---|---|
| Belgium | King Albert II | Monaco | Prince Rainier III |
| Britain | Queen Elizabeth II | Netherlands | Queen Beatrix |
| Denmark | Queen Margrethe II | Norway | King Harald V |
| Liechtenstein | Prince Hans-Adam II | Spain | King Juan Carlos |
| Luxembourg | Grand Duke Henri | Sweden | King Carl XVI Gustaf |

economic activities. The monarchs appointed the bureaucracies of regular administrators and ruled without any real parliamentary assembly. However, in some countries, primarily Great Britain and the Netherlands, the royal power was limited by an assembly. Moreover, at the same time as the power of central government grew, restraints on that power were proposed by political theories calling for limits on executive power, separation of powers, and protection of individual rights.

Relations between the aristocracy and the rising middle class in the eighteenth and nineteenth centuries largely shaped the direction taken by the chief European political systems. The entrance of the middle class in Great Britain into the political system, hitherto largely dominated by the aristocracy, provided a social base for constitutional government. Britain moved in gradual and generally nonviolent fashion from a traditional system controlled by a small elite to a more open and democratic system. The middle class acquired political power but the aristocracy continued to participate in political affairs, and British society continued to incorporate the aristocratic values of birth, family, and deference. In the Netherlands by 1813, the governing class had virtually merged with the old landed aristocracy.

In France the aristocracy was enfeebled by the strong monarchs who forced members of the royal family and of the aristocracy to reside at court, thus preventing them from productive activity. The resistance by the monarchy, aristocracy, and the Church to modernization contributed to a considerable degree to the violence following the Revolution in 1789, which ended the traditional monarchy. The aristocracy rejected, and remained hostile to, the rising middle class and its values and refused to accept the republic that replaced the monarchy. The legitimacy of the new regime was thus not fully upheld by the whole French society.

The German aristocratic group, the Junkers, who were the large landowners in the East, remained on their land, giving the tone to culture, and conserving their power. In the nineteenth century in Germany, political power did not coincide with economic power. The economy was dominated by businessmen, industrialists, and rich financiers, while the state and military were largely the aristocratic domain. The middle-class attempt in 1848 to create a constitutional democratic political system failed. As a result, the authoritarian nature of German politics was reinforced.

Throughout the nineteenth century in Western Europe, the new liberal forces and ideas competed with traditional, conservative elements. Revolutionary uprisings occurred in most of the six countries examined here. The main exception was Great Britain, which already had a functioning parliamentary system, the franchise for which was extended in 1832, 1867, and 1884.

Political power in the West gradually moved from the weakened, though still important, aristocracy to other social groups. Constitutions were adopted, assuring individual and group rights and equality under the law; parliamentary power was expanded and the voting suffrage was extended to larger numbers of people and social classes; though women were excluded until the twentieth century.

Political development was uneven in the different countries in spite of some similar trends. The power of the monarchy in most countries was reduced or ended. Political parties were established, reflecting to some degree the variety of political ideas: liberalism, conservatism, socialism, and nationalism. Workers began to organize in trade unions. At the end of the nineteenth century, a feminist movement began, demanding female suffrage and equal rights for women.

During the nineteenth and early twentieth centuries, a number of the Western European countries became imperialistic powers by acquiring large amounts of territory throughout the world. This control over colonies and their markets added to the West's dominance of the world economic market as well as affecting the traditional economic, social, and cultural life of much of the world.

After World War I, political development was checked in a number of Western countries. They suffered from high inflation, a major economic depression that began in 1929, a substantial rise in unemployment, fluctuating levels of production, and domestic political unrest. One consequence of these problems was the rise to power in 1922 of Fascism in Italy and in 1933 of Nazism in Germany under Adolf Hitler. In both countries, totalitarian regimes were established with similar characteristics: a dominant single dictator; a one-party system; an ideology imposed on the nation; monopoly control over the media and censorship of speech and meeting; a powerful secret police; the use of terror; concentration camps, and, in the case of Nazi Germany, extermination camps in which millions were killed and the Holocaust perpetrated.

During World War II, the political systems of Western Europe were for the most part destroyed by the Nazi conquest of the continent. Over 30 million people were killed in battle or in acts of atrocity against civilians. Europe became, in the words of Winston Churchill, the British prime minister, "a charnel house, a rubble heap." The economies suffered immense losses; a considerable part of the national wealth of the countries was destroyed or liquidated. Industrial production fell, livestock was lost, arable land laid waste, communications of all kinds slowed or paralyzed, millions of houses were destroyed, and most large cities suffered considerable damage. At least 60 million Europeans were driven from their homes, and a substantial shift of population occurred.

By the end of the twentienth century, Western Europe had recovered economically with a high level of prosperity, an unparalleled standard of living, and almost constant growth, and politically with generally stable systems with some uncertainties. The large colonial empires of the West ended as the nations of Africa and Asia gained independence. The internal challenge to political systems from Communist parties, especially in France and Italy, and the external threat from the Soviet Union were overcome. The Cold War, which divided the European continent into two parts, began in 1947 and ended in 1989–1990 with the collapse of the Soviet Union and the changes in Central and Eastern Europe. The Western European nations have not only lived together in peaceful coexistence, especially in the case of France and Germany, since the end of World War II, but have also established the set of security, economic, and political organizations that have bound the countries together. Almost all the boundary disputes between the countries have been settled, though some remain, such as the area of Alto Adige or South Tyrol, which is claimed by both Italy and Austria.

## Affluent Societies

At the start of the twenty-first century, Western Europe is at its most prosperous level ever, marred only by persistent unemployment in some countries. Every statistical index indicates the high standard of living: gross domestic product (GDP) as a whole; GDP per capita; length of education and numbers in higher education; universal literacy for the whole population; better health and increased longevity of life; material possessions, such as cars, phones, television sets, and washing machines; patterns of consumption; and leisure activities. The average income of citizens in the 15 countries in the European Union in 2002 is about $20,000 annually, one of the highest in the world.

## Economic and Social Modernization

All six states examined here have moved from economic feudalism to systems based on private ownership of property and resources or on different mixes of private and public ownership or control. The Western European countries are among the principal examples in the world of those processes of economic, social, and cultural change generally referred to as modernization, which originated in technological change and then affected the rest of human affairs. They illustrate the move to modernity, with their societies based on rationality, science and technology, control over the environment, high urbanization, high or universal literacy, geographical, social, and occupational mobility, greater separation of individuals from family and kinship relations, and a more secular outlook.

## Postindustrial Societies

Economic modernization has transformed Western Europe into what can be termed "postindustrial societies." The largest part of the occupied population works in services, not in industrial or agricultural activity; by the 1970s over half of all workers in Western Europe were already

## THE COLD WAR FROM BEGINNING TO END

| | |
|---|---|
| 1947 | Marshall Plan—U.S. aid to Europe. |
| 1947–1948 | Pro-Communist governments take power in Poland, Hungary, Bulgaria, Romania, Czechoslovakia |
| 1949 | NATO established; Germany divided into two states: the Federal Republic and the German Democratic Republic; Soviet Union creates Council for Mutual Economic Assistance (Comecon). |
| 1950–1953 | Korean War—Korea divided. |
| 1955 | Warsaw Pact of Communist countries established. |
| 1956 | Hungarian uprising suppressed by Soviet Union. |
| 1957 | European Economic Community set up. |
| 1961 | East Germany builds Berlin wall—city divided. |
| 1963 | Soviet Union and United States sign Nuclear Test Ban Treaty. |
| 1968 | Uprising in Prague suppressed by Soviet Union. |
| 1972 | Strategic Arms Limitation Treaty between Soviet Union and United States. |
| 1989 | Fall of Communist systems; Berlin wall opened. |
| 1991 | Soviet Union dissolved. |

employed in services. The proportion of people working in agriculture has long been steadily declining; in some countries it is only about 2 percent. Partly because of the feminist movement and the liberation of women, a larger number of women are in the workforce, either in a full- or part-time capacity, primarily in the service sector.

One result of the relative decline of manufacturing and of jobs in that sector has been the decrease in the membership of Western Europe trade unions, except those in the public or governmental sector. As a consequence, during the last decade the unions have been less influential than in the early postwar period in shaping government policy.

## Class and Politics

The decline in trade unions reflects the changing nature and significance of social class in Western societies, whether class is defined in the Marxist sense of the relation of groups to the process of production or in terms of different lifestyles and life chances as a result of economic position. The changes in social class result from the reduction of the industrial working population, the increase

of the service sector, and the general rise in the standard of living.

Class, in both an objective and a subjective sense, has been important in Western European relationships and politics since the Industrial Revolution. Consciousness of class differences or cleavages has long been demonstrated in voting preferences. Broadly speaking, support of the working class has gone to socialist, and later Communist, parties, while the middle class and upper class voted for liberal and conservative parties.

The postwar Western European countries have been open societies that are socially mobile, and where classes do exist they are not rigid. With greater affluence and changes in lifestyles, especially in what was the traditional working class, class identification is more unclear than in the past, and class consciousness is less apparent.

Though the data are not altogether clear-cut on the subject, voting on the basis of class is more fluid now than in the immediate postwar years, though the working class and the less affluent still tend to support political parties of the Left. Moreover, parties have tried to appeal to different classes. The Christian Democratic parties of Germany and Italy have sometimes been termed "catch-all parties," because of their broad and nonideological appeal.

## Women in Western European Societies and Politics

Though the lives of men and women are still considerably different, women in contemporary Western Europe participate to a greater degree than ever before in economic, social, and political life and organizations. Women's issues have also become more central to European political dialogue.

Women are better educated now than they were in the past; more young women than men who complete their compulsory schooling now go on to higher education. They are healthier and have a life expectancy of over 80 years in all our six countries; for some not very clear reasons, they outlive men by several years, up to eight years in France and Spain (see Table 1.3).

Women are marrying later or not at all, and have fewer children. In Western Europe the birthrate is below two, the reproduction level (see Table 1.4). Divorce is more common, more in northern than in southern Europe, and cohabitation has risen, and with it the number of children born out of wedlock. In Scandinavia, the proportion of children born to unmarried mothers has risen to over 40 percent. The size of households therefore has fallen, and single-person or single-

### TABLE 1.3

#### GENDER COMPARISONS

| | Life Expectancy | | Women as percentage of the Workforce |
|---|---|---|---|
| | w | m | |
| Great Britain | 80 | 75 | 44 |
| France | 82 | 74 | 45 |
| Germany | 80 | 74 | 43 |
| Italy | 81 | 75 | 38 |
| Netherlands | 81 | 75 | 42 |
| Spain | 82 | 75 | 39 |

Source: *World Development Report,* 2000.

### TABLE 1.4

#### HOUSEHOLDS AND FAMILIES

| | Average Household Size | Fertility Rate | Abortion Allowed |
|---|---|---|---|
| Great Britain | 2.5 | 1.7 | Yes |
| France | 2.6 | 1.7 | Yes |
| Germany | 2.3 | 1.3 | No |
| Italy | 2.9 | 1.2 | Yes |
| Netherlands | 2.5 | 1.5 | Yes |
| Spain | 3.5 | 1.2 | No |

Source: *The World's Women,* 2000.

parent families are more common. The population of all the six countries is not only aging but is becoming increasingly female (see Table 1.5).

Legislation for equal opportunities as well as economic necessity has meant more women working outside the home. Women play a large part in the economies of the six countries, constituting about half the workforce. They continue to earn less than men, though the gap has been reduced since the 1970s. Also, while men lost almost 3 million jobs in Western Europe in the 1980s, women gained almost that number. They constituted over 40 percent of the labor force in the European Union countries in 2002.

Women tend to work in different kinds of jobs than men, in clerical, sales, and service employment rather than in production and transport: about three-quarters of women in the labor force work in the service sector (see Table 1.6). They also tend to occupy positions that are less well paid and less prestigious and have lower status than those of men. Some combine part-time or temporary jobs with child care. These jobs are often unskilled and offer little training or possibility of advancement. Women are also often in occupations that are losing status, while new occupations of higher status, such as the computer industry, are dominated by men.

In their jobs women do not have comparable advantages to men regarding pay, pensions, sickness benefits, type of work, hours of employ-

**TABLE 1.5**

**POPULATION: AGE AND SEX STRUCTURE, 2000**

| | Women per 100 Men | % under 15, Both Sexes | % over 60 | | Population Distribution | |
|---|---|---|---|---|---|---|
| | | | w | m | urban | rural |
| Great Britain | 104 | 19 | 23 | 19 | 90 | 10 |
| France | 105 | 19 | 23 | 18 | 76 | 24 |
| Germany | 104 | 16 | 27 | 20 | 88 | 12 |
| Italy | 106 | 14 | 27 | 21 | 67 | 23 |
| Netherlands | 102 | 18 | 21 | 16 | 89 | 11 |
| Spain | 105 | 15 | 24 | 19 | 78 | 22 |

*Source: The World's Women, 2000.*

ment, and opportunities for promotion. In addition, women work more hours than men in Western Europe; in particular they do between two-thirds and three-quarters of the unpaid work in the home. The working time of women fluctuates more widely than that of men because of their different responsibilities.

The postwar period in Western Europe, as in the United States, saw the rise of a feminist movement concerned with sexual equality, the liberation of women, and the implementation of women's economic, political, and social rights, including pay, equal rights at work and in social relations, abortion, and divorce. The impact of feminism reflects a number of factors: the larger number of highly educated women; the reality of the greater number of women, divorced or separated, living alone or as a single parent; the decline in the birthrate and thus smaller families; the substantial increase in the number of women with full-time, part-time, or temporary employment outside the home.

Though European women are better educated than ever before, this has not automatically ensured economic or political advancement, particularly in positions of senior executives, managers, editors, or producers. Women, for example, constitute about a third of doctors in Great Britain,

**TABLE 1.6**

**WOMEN IN THE WORKFORCE**

| | Women per 100 Men in Occupational Groups, 1990 | | | | | | |
|---|---|---|---|---|---|---|---|
| | Professional, Technical | Administrative, Managerial | Clerical | Sales | Service | Agricultural | Production, Transport |
| Great Britain | 78 | 49 | 318 | 181 | 195 | 109 | 18 |
| France | 71 | 10 | 180 | 94 | 219 | 48 | 18 |
| Germany | — | — | — | — | — | — | — |
| Italy | 86 | 60 | — | 86 | — | 57 | 24 |
| Netherlands | 74 | 16 | 138 | 75 | 238 | 31 | 10 |
| Spain | 89 | 10 | 97 | 83 | 141 | 39 | 15 |

*Source: The World's Women, 1995.*

but only 10 percent of senior corporate managers, and less than 1 percent of executive directors. Though some improvement has occurred in recent years, women remain very underrepresented in political positions, whether in the governmental, administrative, or legislative areas, or in the leadership of political parties. They have, however, been more prominent in Western European nongovernmental organizations (NGOs) at the grassroots, national, and international levels.

The record of women in Western European legislatures is mixed. Their membership is highest in the Nordic countries; in Finland and Norway 39 percent of the lower chamber were women. Of the six countries studied in this book, the highest proportions in the lower chamber were in the Netherlands (36 percent) and Germany (31 percent) (see Table 1.7). In all the countries, issues of particular concern to women—such as equal rights and nondiscrimination in employment and promotion—and social matters—such as divorce and abortion—have been discussed to a greater degree in the national parliaments and in local councils.

The number of women candidates for the legislatures has been increasing; in France in 1993 it rose to 20 percent of the candidates for the first round of elections of the National Assembly. Political parties have responded to the pressure for more women candidates, especially now that women have organized political groups of their own and pressed for women's sections in parties, trade unions—which they have joined in larger numbers—and professional bodies. Among our six countries, the British Labour Party decided in the 1980s that at least one woman should be on the short list of candidates for each parliamentary seat. Similarly, in Spain two of the three main parties set quotas for women candidates. Quotas for a larger number of women candidates were also introduced in the French Socialist Party. However, the number of women candidates is still small; in France it has not been over 6 percent. In the Scandinavian countries women have had some appreciable success, gaining between 32 and 38 percent of the seats.

Women are also underrepresented in ministerial positions. In only two of our countries have women become prime ministers: Margaret Thatcher in Great Britain (1979–1990) and Edith Cresson in France (1991–1992). Among other Western systems, Norway had its first woman prime minister in 1981. The number of women governmental ministers has been low; in 1998 it was highest in the Netherlands (28 percent), followed by Spain (18 percent), and Germany (16 percent) (see Table 1.8). Women ministers are most likely to be found in departments of law and justice, and, above all, social affairs.

Not until the twentieth century did women get the vote in Western Europe; in Switzerland it was as recent as 1971. In our six countries, women's suffrage was obtained in Great Britain in 1918 and 1928, France in 1944, Germany in 1919, Italy in 1945, the Netherlands in 1919, and Spain in 1931.

## TABLE 1.7

### WOMEN IN PARLIAMENT, 2002

| | Unicameral or Lower House | | | Upper House | | |
|---|---|---|---|---|---|---|
| | Total Seats | Women | % | Total Seats | Women | % |
| Great Britain | 659 | 118 | 18 | 713 | 117 | 16 |
| France | 577 | 63 | 11 | 321 | 35 | 11 |
| Germany | 666 | 207 | 31 | 69 | 17 | 24 |
| Italy | 630 | 62 | 10 | 321 | 25 | 8 |
| Netherlands | 150 | 54 | 36 | 75 | 20 | 26 |
| Spain | 350 | 99 | 28 | 259 | 63 | 24 |

**TABLE 1.8**

**WOMEN IN PUBLIC LIFE**

| | Government Ministerial Positions, 1998 | | Subministerial Positions, 1998 | | Professional and Technical Workers |
|---|---|---|---|---|---|
| | Number of Women | Women as % | Number of Women | Women as % | Women as Percentage, 1995–1997 |
| Great Britain | 23 | 8.7 | 56 | 7.1 | 33 |
| France | 29 | 6.9 | 113 | 11.5 | 10 |
| Germany | 25 | 16.0 | 153 | 5.2 | 19 |
| Italy | 25 | 13.0 | 45 | 9 | 54 |
| Netherlands | 16 | 28.0 | 39 | 8 | 17 |
| Spain | 21 | 18.0 | 28 | 4 | 12 |

*Source: The World's Women, 2000.*

Women have generally voted in higher proportion than men for the political Right, partly because they have tended to be more religious than men. This began to change in the 1970s when, for a number of reasons, including the feminist movement and the greater economic and social independence of women, they began to vote more heavily for the political Left. At present no strong generalization can be made about the direction of voting by women.

## Aging Societies

A noticeable feature of the changing postwar Western European social and cultural picture is the steady decline in the birthrate after the baby boomer period from the late 1940s to the early 1960s. At the same time life expectancy has increased to an average of 75 years. Since the total population has been relatively stable in recent years, it is aging with an increasing proportion of older people in the six countries. In Germany, for example, one in seven persons is now under age 15, and one in six is over age 65. The aging societies now encounter serious economic and political problems, including the decline in baby-based industries and probably in housing

construction in the future, and above all the increasing burden and costs of medical care, social security, and pensions.

The reality that the number of native-born residents working in the future will be a declining proportion of the population raises new questions. Should the age of retirement be raised? Should taxes to cover social security and health be increased? Should more immigrants be allowed into the countries in order to fill manual jobs?

More is being spent on health sevices not only as the population ages but also as patients come to expect better treatment with up-to-date, expensive technical equipment (see Table 1.9).

## Religious or Secular Societies

Since the sixteenth century, Western Europe has not had a common religion. Eight countries— including France, Italy, Portugal, and Spain—are nominally Catholic; seven—including Great Britain and the northern European states—are Protestant; and three—Germany, the Netherlands, and Switzerland—are mixtures of Catholics, Lutherans, Calvinists, and Presbyterians (see Table 1.10). Jews are a small part of the total population; the largest number in any country is the

**TABLE 1.9**

**HEALTH SPENDING, 1998 (% OF GDP)**

|  | Public | Private | Total |
|---|---|---|---|
| Great Britain | 5.7 | 1.1 | 6.8 |
| France | 7.3 | 2.1 | 9.4 |
| Germany | 7.8 | 2.5 | 10.3 |
| Italy | 5.5 | 2.7 | 8.2 |
| Netherlands | 6.0 | 2.7 | 8.7 |
| Spain | 5.4 | 1.7 | 7.0 |
| EU average | 6.4 | 2.1 | 8.5 |

700,000 in France. The major change in postwar Europe has been the large-scale immigration of Muslims, thus presenting problems of accommodation to different practices and codes.

Religious attendance has declined, even if nominal adherence to a religion remains. Over three-quarters of the French population describes itself as Catholic, but less than 10 percent go regularly to services. With some exceptions, such as Northern Ireland and new issues arising from the Muslim immigration, religion has not recently been the divisive political factor it was in the past. However, problems stemming from differences over discrimination or privileges regarding religion remain. They take the form of religious teaching or prayers in the school system, public funds for private Catholic schools—in France

**TABLE 1.10**

**CATHOLIC POPULATION AS A PERCENTAGE OF TOTAL**

| | |
|---|---|
| Great Britain | 8.5 |
| France | 76.4 |
| Germany | 38.0 |
| Italy | 83.2 |
| Netherlands | 36.1 |
| Spain | 99.0 |

about one-fifth of school pupils attend Catholic schools—or crucifixes in public places as in Italy.

A noticeable feature of postwar European politics has been, contrary to the role of the Catholic Church in the nineteenth and early twentieth centuries, the moderate position of political parties based to some extent on Catholic principles and of many individual Catholics on social and political issues. These individuals do not abide by church doctrine on issues such as contraception, abortion, and divorce.

Those political parties that are based, at least theoretically, on the moral principles of the different religions—as in the case of the Christian Democratic parties of Germany, Italy, and France, or six such parties in the Netherlands—are not officially connected with their churches. However, in some of the Catholic countries, the Catholic Church has maintained a network of institutions, including economic institutions, social clubs, and trade unions, which have an impact on political affairs.

In general, the areas in the different countries that are most religiously observant are likely to vote for right-wing parties. Conversely, those areas considered to be anticlerical, opposed to the privileged role of the church, tend to vote for parties of the Left.

The increasing presence of Muslims is a new and potentially challenging feature in Western Europe society and politics (see Table 1.11). About 12 million Muslims now live in Western Europe and their experience has varied in the different countries.

The largest number live in France, to which they have come from the Maghreb, the countries of Algeria, Morocco, and Tunisia. They have worked in factories and agriculture and many have adapted to the French way of life. Germany made little effort to integrate its immigrants until 2000, when citizenship was granted to children born in Germany to foreign parents. About two-thirds of Germany's immigrant population are Turks who were admitted as temporary "guest workers" (*Gastarbeiter*) but stayed and brought their families. Half of these Turks are under 30.

Muslims in Britain have come from a number of countries, mostly from Pakistan and

**TABLE 1.11**

**MUSLIMS IN WESTERN EUROPE, 2002**

|  | Number (millions) | % of Population |
|---|---|---|
| Great Britain | 2 | 3.3 |
| France | 4–5 | 7.5 |
| Germany | 3.25 | 3.9 |
| Italy | 0.5 | 1.2 |
| Netherlands | 0.5 | 4.4 |
| Spain | 0.5 | 1.8 |

*Source: Europa.*

Bangladesh, and these have, among other occupations, been employed in textile mills of northern England, which have become economically depressed. People from these two countries have experienced higher than average unemployment and have tended to remain segregated rather than becoming integrated into British society. One result of this alienation was riots in the summer of 2001 in northern cities.

Spain, which was dominated by the Arabs—the "Moors"—from 711 to 1492, when they were expelled by King Ferdinand and Queen Isabella, has about half a million legal Muslim residents and many illegal ones. They are likely to remain in the country rather than return to the Maghreb.

## Multiethnic and Multiracial Societies

Western European societies have sometimes appeared to be homogeneous with citizens coming from only one cultural group and background and speaking a single common language. In fact, almost all those societies, because of historical factors, have what is sometimes called a center-periphery cleavage. The center, and its political institutions, seeks to impose a common rule and culture in the state; the periphery consists of areas within the state that were independent or autonomous before the state, including the areas, was created.

About 9 percent of the total population of the European Union, living in over 30 regions, speak minority languages. In our six countries, some of the major indigenous ethnic groups speaking their own languages are the following:

| | |
|---|---|
| Great Britain | Gaelic, Celtic |
| France | Corse, Breton, Basque |
| Italy | German (Alto-Adige or South Tyrol) |
| Spain | Catalan, Basque |

Western societies are also now multiracial because of the large influx of immigrants, migrant workers, and political refugees who have come from non-Western cultural and ethnic backgrounds since the 1960s. The migrant workers, brought in as temporary laborers or "guest workers," have not returned home as expected, but instead have sent for their families to live in the host country. In addition to the economic migrants, Western Europe has been handling about 700,000 requests for asylum a year.

Of the 369 million population in the 15 countries of the European Union, about 12 million are immigrants or descendants of immigrants (see Table 1.12). France has about 4.5 million, Great Britain 2.5 million, the Netherlands about 500,000, and Italy about 800,000 legal immigrants and about 500,000 illegal immigrants working in the hidden economy. In Germany the 6.8 million foreign residents formed their own political party, the Democratic Party of Germany, in 1995.

For Western Europe, the problem is a continuing one because of the discrepancy in birthrates between the countries in the European

**TABLE 1.12**

**MAJOR IMMIGRANT GROUPS**

| | |
|---|---|
| Great Britain | West Indians, Indians, Pakistanis, Bangladeshis |
| France | Algerians, Moroccans, Portuguese, West Africans |
| Germany | Turks, Yugoslavs, Greeks, Italians |
| Italy | West Africans, North Africans |
| Netherlands | Indonesians, South Moluccans, Surinamese |
| Spain | Moroccans, Algerians, Ecuadorians |

## REGIONAL AND CULTURAL DIVERSITY

| | |
|---|---|
| Great Britain | Wales, united with England in 1536; 600,000 speak Celtic. |
| | Scotland, united with England and Wales in 1707 to form Great Britain; 75,000 speak Gaelic. |
| | Northern Ireland, united 1921 with Great Britain to create United Kingdom. |
| France | Brittany, absorbed by France in fifteenth century; speak form of Celtic. |
| | Languedoc, incorporated into France in thirteenth century; speak Provencal Corsica. |
| Germany | German states create Germany in 1871; country divided after World War II and reunited 1990. |
| Italy | Alto Adige (South Tyrol), considerable Germanic culture. |
| | Sardinia, some autonomy. |
| Netherlands | Friesland, lost separate identity in 1748; Frisian language spoken by 300,000. |
| Spain | Euzkadi, Basques who want separation. |
| | Catalonia, long history of struggle against central government; got some autonomy in 1932 but not independent. |

Union, where the rate is now about 1.5, and the developing countries from where the immigrants mainly come, where it is considerably higher. France has a particularly difficult problem because its immigrants come from the three countries of the Maghreb (Algeria, Morocco, and Tunisia) where the population is expected to expand to over 125 million by 2025.

In general, the immigrants, many nonwhite and Muslim by religion, live in urban ghettos; are segregated in cities, schools, and housing; are differentiated from natives by their religion, food, and clothes; and have their own associations, schools, and religious houses of worship. Their presence has occasioned considerable tension, racial animosity, and at times riots and violence in most of our six countries. The political response to the immigration has been of two kinds: stricter control over immigration, and laws and regulations to limit or eliminate racial discrimination. Hostility against immigration has contributed to the growth of extreme nationalist groups and political parties in recent years.

## Liberal Democracies

With the defeat of Nazi Germany and Fascist Italy in the World War II, new political systems were established in Western Europe. The totalitarian regimes were replaced by democratic political institutions in Italy and West Germany, and in 1989 in East Germany. France, which had been partly under German occupation and partly under the Vichy French State, restored its parliamentary system with the Fourth Republic in 1946 and the Fifth in 1958; its democratic institutions have survived in spite of threats in 1958 and 1961. The Netherlands, which had also been under German occupation, restored its constitutional monarchy. A new constitutional monarchy replaced the authoritarian political system in Spain after the death of General Francisco Franco, who had ruled from 1939 to 1975.

Danger from the extreme Right, neo-Fascist and Nazi groups, was virtually eliminated in the early postwar years though it has become more manifest since the 1980s in some countries. Threat from the extreme Left, the Communist parties, remained strong in France and Italy, though it began declining as moderate socialist and democratic parties became more popular, and as the appeal of the Soviet Union waned.

Two interesting features were included in a number of the new constitutions: judicial review or oversight of constitutional issues, and declarations of human rights. The judiciary in France,

Germany, Italy, and Spain can either oversee the constitution or reject those parliamentary laws it holds to be in violation of the constitution. The human rights protected by the different constitutions, and by the European Convention for the Protection of Human Rights to which the countries belong, include not only individual freedoms but also collective rights, such as those of trade unions, economic public ownership, and social welfare of health and employment.

Since Portugal and Greece in 1974 and Spain in 1975 ended their authoritarian systems, all Western European systems can be said to be liberal or constitutional democracies. They constitute a majority of the countries in the world that have had free, competitive elections in the whole postwar period since 1945.

Besides having free elections, the liberal, constitutional democracies have many similar features:

1. Competing political parties in different forms of electoral systems.

2. Freedom of speech, assembly, and association.

3. Rights of private property within certain limits.

4. Acceptance of peaceful change and of the electoral result by the losers.

5. Agreement that an opposition is free and able to criticize the existing government.

6. Limits on the exercise of power, whether imposed by a constitution or understood by convention.

7. Open, voluntary organizations to which citizens can belong.

8. Civilian control of the military and of decision making in general.

9. The rule of law.

The countries have different versions of the rule of law, which imposes restraints on individual and group behavior that does not comply with accepted legal principles. In Great Britain it is the common law, in France the *Etat de Droit*, in Germany the *Rechtsstaat*. In four of the countries—Germany, Italy, the Netherlands, and Spain—human and social rights are part of the

constitution. The German Basic Law of 1949 begins with an elaboration of basic rights. The Italian Constitution of 1947 contains 41 articles on the rights and duties of citizens. About a third of the Spanish Constitution of 1978 deals with rights. The Netherlands Constitution was amended in 1983 to add social rights to the individual rights already present. In France, rights rest on the 1789 Declaration of the Rights of Man and Citizen. Only in Great Britain, without a written document, are rights uncodified.

In most Western European countries, the political parties have alternated in the capture of political power, though sometimes one party has dominated for a considerable length of time, as the Christian Democrats have done in Germany and Italy, and the Socialists have done in Scandinavia. In all the countries a two-party or multiparty system exists, based on a variety of different factors: class, religion, language, nationality, and ideology.

## Electoral Systems and Party Systems

Western European countries use different forms of representative democracy for the lower legislative chamber, based either on single-member constituencies (SMC) and mostly on plurality decision, or on proportional representation (PR), or mixtures of the two kinds.

Historically, SMC, which registers major but not minor shifts in opinion, has led to or reinforced a two-party system, handicapping and being unfair to small or new parties. PR, which reflects the diversity of opinions in a country in a more or less accurate way, results in a multiparty system, usually with no one party getting an overall majority of votes or of legislative seats. Instead, small parties have an undue influence, extremist parties are able to gain some seats in the legislature, and government coalitions are fragile. The SMC system is more likely to lead to stable, durable government, which can control a majority in parliament, than is the PR system.

The classic case of SMC is Great Britain, with a well-entrenched system in which the bulk of the seats and most, if a declining proportion, of the total electoral votes are won by the major

**TABLE 1.13**

**CONSERVATIVE AND LABOUR PARTIES IN SELECTED BRITISH ELECTIONS**

| Year | % of Total Vote | % of Total Seats |
| --- | --- | --- |
| 1945 | 88.1 | 94.7 |
| 1951 | 96.8 | 98.6 |
| 1964 | 87.5 | 98.6 |
| 1974 | 74.9 | 94.2 |
| 1983 | 70.0 | 93.2 |
| 1992 | 76.3 | 93.2 |
| 1997 | 75.8 | 88.6 |
| 2001 | 72.4 | 87.7 |

parties, with other parties obtaining only a small number of seats (see Table 1.13). Only regional parties, such as the Scottish National Party, with a limited territorial base have done reasonably well on some occasions.

At the opposite extreme is the equally classic PR in the German Weimar Republic (1920–1933), which allocated legislative seats to a party in exact proportion to the votes cast for it. A number of European systems today follow this pattern with some qualifications and variations; they include the Netherlands and Spain (see Table 1.14). Italy had this pattern until 1994 when it changed to a new system in which 75 percent of the seats came from SMC, and 25 percent from PR.

The new Italian system is imitative of what had been a unique German system, which entails a double vote, one for a single-member constituency and one for a PR party list. Half of the German legislature is elected by each method. One important qualification is that a party can only receive a list seat if it gets over 5 percent of the list votes, or wins three constituency seats. The German system combines SMC and PR with half of the seats in each category. Every voter has two ballots, one for a SMC candidate and one for a party list. The vote for the party list determines the number of seats obtained (see Figure 1.1).

France, which has had five different electoral procedures since 1945, has settled on a SMC system with two rounds of voting; if no majority is obtained in a constituency, a second round is held a week later. This voting system tends to favor the dominant parties. In the first round of the 1993 election for the National Assembly, the Gaullist Party (RPR) with 20.39 percent of the vote won 42 seats, and the Union pour la Démocratie Française (UDF) with 19.08 percent of the vote got 36; the extreme right-wing National Front with 12.41 percent got no seat.

**REVIEW**

**1.4**

## ELECTORAL SYSTEMS

| | |
| --- | --- |
| Great Britain | SMC, plurality; 659 constituencies; candidate with the most votes wins. |
| France | SMC, two rounds of voting: 555 constituencies in metropolitan France, 577 in all of France; a candidate needs an absolute majority to win in the first round. A second round is held a week later, and the candidate with the most votes wins. |
| Germany | 603 seats, half by SMC and half by party list in PR. Each voter casts a vote in each part. No seats are allocated by PR unless a party obtains 5 percent of the list vote or three constituency seats. For the 1998 election there were 669 seats. |
| Italy | Had PR with country divided into 32 regions until 1994; new system allocates 75 percent of seats by SMC and 25 percent by PR. Total seats 630. |
| Netherlands | Party list and PR using whole county as a constituency for the 150 seats. |
| Spain | Party list and PR with country divided into 52 constituencies, each returning seven deputies. Total seats 350. |

**TABLE 1.14**

**ELECTIONS IN THE NETHERLANDS UNDER PROPORTIONAL REPRESENTATION SYSTEM**

|  | % of Votes | | Seats | |
| --- | --- | --- | --- | --- |
| Party | 1994 | 1998 | 1994 | 1998 |
| Communist | — | — | — | — |
| Green | 4.8 | 7.3 | 7 | 11 |
| Labor | 24.9 | 29.0 | 37 | 45 |
| Democrats' 66 | 15.5 | 9.0 | 24 | 14 |
| Liberal | 19.9 | 24.7 | 31 | 38 |
| Center | 2.5 | — | 3 | 1 |
| Christian Democrat | 22.2 | 18.4 | 34 | 29 |
| Reformed Political League | — | 1.3 | — | 2 |
| Political Reformed | 3.5 | 1.8 | 5 | 3 |
| Reformed Political Federation | — | 2.0 | — | 3 |
| Others | — | 2.5 | 3 | — |

The voice of the people in Western Europe can be registered not only in parliamentary elections, but also by direct vote, a referendum, on a specific issue. Switzerland uses this method far more frequently than any other country in the world (58 times between 1978 and 1986). Some of the Western constitutions provide for the device; Italy consequently voted on divorce in 1974 and on abortion in 1981, while France voted on a number of issues, including the amendment of the constitution itself in 1962. Germany and the Netherlands have not used the referendum, but Great Britain in the 1970s did on two occasions, on the issue of adherence to the European Community in 1975 and on the devolution of power to Scotland and Wales in 1979.

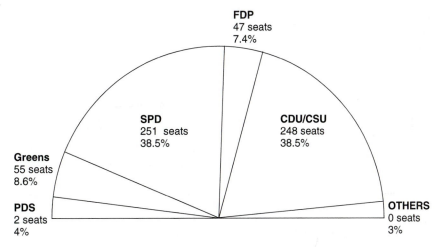

**Figure 1.1 THE GERMAN ELECTION 2002**

## Political Parties

Since the downfall of the remaining authoritarian or one-party systems, all the Western European countries now have two-party or multiparty systems. Whether two main parties obtain most of the votes and legislative seats, or whether a number of parties share the votes and seats depends on a number of factors: historical development of the country; the process of economic modernization; the strength of divisions or cleavages in society, such as class, ethnic, racial, religious, national, regional, linguistic, or ideological policy divisions; the political powers of the executive and legislature and the relations between them; and the character of the electoral system. In some countries, one factor has dominated the origin and nature of parties, as in Great Britain, where economic and social class has been crucial. In other countries, a diversity of factors has affected the creation of parties.

The parties, now over 120, reflect the wide differences and the great variety of political opinion in Western Europe (see Table 1.15). In a broad spectrum, they can be characterized as Christian Democracy, Social Democracy, Communist, Liberal, Conservative, Extreme Right, Greens, and Regional.

***Christian Democracy***   Christian Democracy (CD) emerged as an important political movement after 1945. It has been significant in many of the continental countries, and particularly successful in Italy, where the party got almost 35 percent of the vote until 1987, as well as in Germany, Austria, Luxembourg, and for a time France (see Table 1.16).

Theoretically, CD parties are based on ideas such as concern for all parts of society; end of class conflict; some form of welfare state; decentralization; Christian values in education; criticism of individualism, capitalism, and collectivism; support for a European community; and reconciling Catholic principles with democracy.

Though the main support of CD parties has come from Catholics individually and organizationally, and though the parties favor religious education in schools and more generous funding for the Church, they also combine policies of social welfare with those of the free market and try to appeal to non-Catholics and to all social groups.

***Social Democracy***   The European socialist and social democratic movement is some 150 years old, stemming from the criticism of nineteenth-century capitalism and industrialism,

## TABLE 1.15

### PAST AND PRESENT WESTERN EUROPEAN POLITICAL PARTIES

| Type | Main Theme | Example |
| --- | --- | --- |
| Agrarian | Supports farmers | France in the Third Republic |
| Christian Democracy | Traditional morality, family values, welfare | Germany: CDU |
| Communist | Common ownership of production and distribution | Italy: Communist Refoundation |
| Conservative | Order, traditional institutions, strong military | Britain: Conservative Party |
| Ethnic, National | Autonomy or self-determination for particular groups | Spain: Catalan Nationalist, Basque Nationalist |
| Extreme Right | Anti-immigrant, highly nationalist, militant | France: National Front |
| Green | Environmental concerns | All 6 countries |
| Liberal | Freedom from controls; limited government | Britain: Liberal Democrats |
| Socialist | Government controls of certain parts of economy, welfare | Netherlands: Labor |

**TABLE 1.16**

**CHRISTIAN DEMOCRAT VOTE, SELECTED ELECTIONS (PERCENTAGES)**

| | |
|---|---|
| Austria | 28.1 (1995), 26.9 (1999) |
| Belgium | 24.5 (1991), 19.9 (1999) |
| Germany | 35.1 (1998), 38.5 (2002) |
| Italy | 11.1 (1994), 4.1 (2001) |
| Netherlands | 22.2 (1994), 18.4 (1998) |
| Spain | 34.8 (1993), 45.2 (2000) |

and calling for the end of perceived social and economic inequalities by state intervention in the economy, redistribution of wealth, and public ownership of major industrial and commercial concerns. Though major support for socialist parties has always come from the working class and from trade unions, the parties have also been supported by people in other social classes who believe that the existing social and political order should be changed.

After the Russian Revolution of 1917 and the consequent establishment of Communist parties, which absorbed the more revolutionary socialists, the Western European socialist parties were mainly moderate groups. They did not collaborate with Communist parties except for a short time in the mid-1930s. After World War II, no Socialist-Communist collaboration was possible because of the Cold War. Social Democratic parties call for gradual improvement of social and economic conditions through the procedure of parliamentary democracy. They have followed this path while in power, as in Great Britain, France, Germany, Spain, and the Scandinavian countries.

In the postwar period, Social Democratic parties renounced any Marxist or revolutionary philosophy; the West German party did this at Bad Godesberg in 1959, the Italian party in 1964 when it entered into a center-left coalition government, the Spanish party in 1979 when it adopted a moderate policy position, the British in the mid-1980s when its leadership tamed the more extreme elements, and the French party

when it was reformed and renamed as the PS (Socialist Party) in 1969.

The problem for Social Democratic parties since the 1970s has been the increasing affluence of Western societies and the occupational changes to the service sector, which have meant that more of the population was in reality or psychologically part of the middle class, not the working class. The customary base for parties of the political Left has therefore been shrinking. In addition, socialist policies and programs, including public control of enterprises, have been criticized as being inefficient, or wasteful, and necessitating too high a burden of taxation.

***Communist Parties***   In postwar Europe, Communist parties have been relatively small and unsuccessful, except in Italy, France, Finland, and Portugal (see Table 1.17). This is largely due to three factors: the increased affluence of Western societies; the diminished attractiveness of the Soviet Union, the world's major Communist country; and the fear of revolution and of dictatorship, even if it were a theoretical one of the proletariat.

Communist parties became less attractive after the revelations of the brutal dictatorship of Stalin by the Communist leader Nikita Khrushchev, the Soviet invasion of Hungary in 1956 and of Prague in 1968, and finally by the collapse of the Soviet and Central and Eastern European Communist regimes in the late 1980s. In the 1970s, Western Communist parties, to increase their electoral support, introduced a more moderate concept of "Eurocommunism," which was pledged to abide by parliamentary government, and attempts were made at political compromises, with the Socialist Party in France in a common program in 1972 and with the Christian Democrats in a "historic compromise" in Italy in 1973. These attempts to win more parliamentary seats failed, except in Italy. Even there the party has renounced not only any revolutionary character but also its name, when in 1990 it became the Democratic Party of the Left (PDS).

***Liberal Parties***   Liberal political parties were prominent movements in the nineteenth century

**TABLE 1.17**

**COMMUNIST PARTY VOTE (PERCENTAGE)**

|               | 1940s  | 1950s  | 1960s  | 1970s  | 1980s  | 1990s–2001 |
|---------------|--------|--------|--------|--------|--------|------------|
| Great Britain | (1945) | (1955) | (1966) | (1979) | (1987) | (2001)     |
|               | 0.4    | 0.1    | 0.2    | 0.1    | 0.02   | —          |
| France        | (1946) | (1956) | (1967) | (1978) | (1986) | (1997)     |
|               | 28.0   | 26.0   | 22.5   | 20.6   | 9.7    | 9.9        |
| Germany (FDR) | (1949) | (1957) | (1969) | (1976) | (1987) | (2002)     |
|               | 5.7    | —      | 0.6    | 0.4    | —      | 4.0        |
| Italy         | (1948) | (1958) | (1968) | (1976) | (1987) | (2001)     |
|               | 31.0   | 22.7   | 26.9   | 34.4   | 26.6   | 5.0        |
| Netherlands   | —      | —      | —      | —      | (1986) | (1998)     |
|               | —      | —      | —      | —      | 0.6    | —          |
| Spain         | —      | —      | —      | (1979) | (1986) | (2000)     |
|               | —      | —      | —      | 10.8   | 4.6    | 5.5        |

and until World War I. Believing in limited government, gradual reform, individual liberty, a free market, free trade, private property, and national self-determination, and opposed to church controls or privileges in politics and education, liberal parties appealed to political moderates and to the middle class, which supported constitutional, democratic systems.

In the twentieth century, and particularly in the postwar period since 1945, liberal parties, often divided on policy issues and organizationally less disciplined than rival parties, have had less electoral appeal, though they have favored the principles of a free market and also a welfare state. On average, liberal parties get about 11 percent of the vote in Western Europe as a whole, but it varies substantially in the different countries. In the 1980s in the Netherlands and Great Britain, liberal parties got over 20 percent of the electoral vote, but in France, Germany, Italy, and Spain, they received less than 10 percent.

In some countries the liberals have participated in coalition governments. In West Germany and now in united Germany, the liberal Free Democrat Party (FDP) with a relatively small number of seats in the Bundestag, the German lower house, was part of the government coalitions for 40 years during the 1946–1996 period. Liberals have also been in coalition governments in the Netherlands and in Italy.

*Conservative Parties*   Like the liberal parties, Western European conservatives from the nineteenth century on have supported the free market and private property and a moderate welfare system, and have rejected radical change. But they have also upheld the place of traditional authorities in social, religious, and political issues; believed in a tranquil, stable order; emphasized nationalism and national appeals to overcome social and political cleavages; called for limits on government spending; and laid stress on government efficiency.

In the postwar period, these principles have for the most part been observed in a moderate, opportunistic fashion, sometimes making conservative parties barely distinguishable from Christian Democrats or the Gaullist parties in France. In Western Europe as a whole, voting from the 1940s until the present for conservative parties has averaged about 17 to 18 percent. They have been most successful in Ireland, in

**TABLE 1.18**

**CONSERVATIVE VOTE IN GREAT BRITAIN**

| Election | % | Seats |
|---|---|---|
| Feb. 1974 | 37.8 | 297 |
| Oct. 1974 | 35.8 | 277 |
| 1979 | 43.9 | 339 |
| 1983 | 42.4 | 397 |
| 1987 | 42.2 | 375 |
| 1992 | 41.9 | 336 |
| 1997 | 31.4 | 165 |
| 2001 | 31.7 | 166 |

France (if we include the Gaullist parties), and in Great Britain, where they have held power for 34 of the 51 years since 1945 (see Table 1.18).

In the late 1970s and 1980s, conservative parties, particularly in Great Britain, tended to adopt more hard-line positions on issues, emphasizing the market system to a greater degree, stressing the reduction of government expenditure and of taxation, and eliminating nationalized enterprises in favor of privatization by selling them to the public. Yet, if the role of the state was to be reduced in economic matters, it was to remain pronounced on social and cultural issues.

***Extreme Right Parties***    More extreme than the conservative parties are the postwar movements of the far Right, small except in France and Italy, which often resort to violence. They proclaim themselves as both antidemocratic and anti-Communist, and derive from or are influenced by the Fascist and Nazi parties of the years between the two world wars.

Essentially the extreme Right parties appeal to negative emotions, blaming enemies or scapegoats for existing problems, and fostering hostility to Jews, foreigners, and immigrants in their countries. They call for a strong disciplined state with authority to limit immigration and to control large-scale commercial enterprises and banks, which will emphasize national strength (see Table 1.19). Among the more prominent of these parties is the National Front in France, whose leader, Jean-Marie Le Pen, got up to 30 percent in southern France, which has a large number of immigrants, in the presidential election in 1988. The Italian right-wing National Alliance got 13.5 percent of the vote and won 109 seats in the Chamber of Deputies in 1994 and was given four cabinet positions. In recent years, Germany has had two such parties, the Republicans, led by a former Waffen SS officer, and the German People's Union. In Great Britain, the Netherlands, and Spain, right-wing, anti-immigrant parties have done less well and gotten little support at elections.

***The Greens***    In the 1970s, environmental or ecological groups soon became concerned with the issues of nuclear weapons, the search for alternative energy supplies after the 1973 oil crisis, and the military in general. The groups, composed mainly of young, middle-class, well-educated people, at first organized demonstrations and called for referendums on environmental issues. In the late 1970s and in the 1980s, they formed political parties, the Greens, which were loosely organized

**TABLE 1.19**

**EXTREME RIGHT VOTE, SELECTED ELECTIONS**

| | Party | Year | % |
|---|---|---|---|
| France | National Front | 2002 | 11.10 |
| Germany | National Democratic Republicans | 1998 | 1.80 |
| | German People's Union | 1998 | 1.20 |
| Italy | National Alliance | 2001 | 12.00 |

and disciplined. The Greens attracted support from those concerned about pollution of air and water, and from those opposed to the 1979 NATO decision to upgrade its nuclear defensive system and to the U.S. policy to station medium-range nuclear missiles on the European continent.

By the late 1980s, the Greens had gained representation in a number of legislative bodies. In Western Europe as a whole, the Greens got only about 2 percent of the vote in the 1980s, and in most of our six countries they have had little success. But they have had an impact on the policies of other political parties, as well as being more prominent in Germany, where in 2002 the Greens got 8.6 percent of the national vote and won 55 seats in the Bundestag. The Greens have become part of the governing process in some countries; in recent years they have supported governments in France and Germany. In the European Parliament in 2002, they had 47 seats.

***Regional Parties***  Most Western European systems, while existing as nation-states, also contain within their territories regional or local minority groups based on national, ethnic, or linguistic solidarity. A surprising feature of recent politics in Western Europe has been the emergence of many parties based on these factors and making claims for devolution of power or regional autonomy as a minimum or to a call for independence from the rest of the nation-state as a maximum.

Such parties have been important in Belgium, with both Flemish- and Walloon-speaking regional parties, and in Finland, with its Swedish People's Party. In our six countries, they are prominent in Great Britain, Italy, Spain, and France.

## Cabinet and Presidential Government Systems

In democratic systems the two main types of government, and relations between the executive and the legislative branches, are the cabinet and presidential systems. In the latter type, the president is separately elected by the people and is not responsible to the legislature. In the former type, the government is not elected independently but results from the party or parties controlling a majority in the legislature, to which it is responsible.

Most of Western Europe has varying forms of cabinet government, many influenced by Great Britain, the model for this type of political system. Of our six countries, five are of this type. The French Fifth Republic is a hybrid with some characteristics of both types.

Great Britain throughout the postwar period has had single-party governments. The other four cabinet-type systems, with the partial exception of Spain, have had coalition governments because a single party has rarely been able to control a majority of the seats in the legislature (see Table 1.20). The Netherlands differs from the others in some respects because it has illustrated what is sometimes termed "consociational decision making" or "pillarization." Dutch governments not only contain representatives of some of the subcultures—Catholics, Calvinists, and secular—but also allow powerful political and social groups a

---

**REVIEW**

**1.5**

### REGIONAL PARTIES IN RECENT YEARS

| | |
|---|---|
| Great Britain | Sinn Fein; Ulster Unionists; Plaid Cymru (Welsh Nationalists); Scottish National Party; Social Democratic and Labour Party. |
| France | Breton Democratic Union; Liberation Front of Brittany; Union of the Corsican People. |
| Italy | South Tyrol People's Party; Sardinian Action Party; Lombard League; Northern League. |
| Spain | Basque separatists. |

**TABLE 1.20**

**ONE-PARTY GOVERNMENT OR COALITIONS**

|  | % Votes Won by Two Largest Parties | Likelihood of Coalitions, 2002 |
|---|---|---|
| Great Britain | 72.4 (2001) | None |
| France | 39.2 (1997) | Very likely |
| Germany | 69.3 (1998) | Always |
| Italy | 46.0 (2001) | Always |
| Netherlands | 53.7 (1998) | Always |
| Spain | 78.7 (2000) | Always |

role in formulating policies and sometimes helping administer churches, economic organizations, hospitals, and leisure associations.

France has a mixed system. Its president is directly elected and is the leading political figure who participates in the making of government decisions. But it also has a prime minister and a government that also make those decisions and must have the confidence of Parliament. Therefore, built into the system is both a potential conflict between the two executive leaders and a certain ambiguity about who is to wield power in the different areas of public policy.

## Political Consensus

With the generally pragmatic and less ideological politics, apart from Communist groups in France and Italy, in the immediate postwar years, a consensus on major economic and political objectives was accepted by all the mainstream political spectrum. Economically, the main objectives were full employment, prosperity and a rising standard of living, low inflation, and a mixed economy with varying amounts of public and private ownership. Politically, the consensus entailed a stable state; a role for the state in decisions on social issues and on the economy; the maintenance of a liberal democracy with freedoms of speech, press, assembly, and religion; a governmental decision-making process in which interest groups participated; and a welfare

system paid for by individual contributions in part but mostly by the state.

As new problems arose in the 1970s, this postwar consensus was more difficult to sustain and policy making was altered. The energy crisis, caused by the dramatic increase in the price of oil in 1973, burdened the European economies with higher inflation and more unemployment. The mounting costs of the welfare system—in health, social security and pensions, and education—necessitated increased taxation. Separatist movements, or those wanting greater autonomy, troubled the coherence and stability of even the most well-established systems. Militant terrorism, caused by both internal and external factors, became of concern in the late 1970s and again in the mid-1980s, particularly in Italy and Germany, which experienced bombings and murders of judges, officials, and politicians, including Aldo Moro, former Italian prime minister, and which necessitated counteraction by police and security agencies. As a consequence of these factors and electoral victories by conservative parties, the postwar consensus became more difficult to sustain.

## Unitary and Federal Systems

Except for Germany, all our states are unitary with centralized political and administrative structures in which political power and sovereignty resides in the central institutions. By contrast, because of its historical origin, Germany has been, except in the Nazi years (1933–1945), a federal system with powers shared between the central authorities and the *Länder*, or states.

However, in spite of the centralized power in unitary systems, the Western European systems have been obliged to take account of regional sentiments and to make provision in their constitutions or to provide economic and political concessions to these sentiments. The 1948 Italian Constitution calls for the creation of 15 partly autonomous regions to which some power would be given. In addition four special regions with particular ethnic identities were created after the constitution. Regional government was introduced in 1970, with powers to legislate on a

## UNITARY AND FEDERAL STATES

*Unitary*—Britain, Finland, France, Greece, Ireland, Netherlands, Norway, Portugal, Sweden

*Federal*—Austria, Belgium, Germany, Switzerland

*Mixed (some regional)*—Italy, Spain

Spain has 17 regions with wide powers to use at their discretion. Some (Basques and Navarra) collect their own taxes and pay the central government for services. Regional governments control over 30 percent of all public spending, though the funds for all except Basques and Navarra come from central government.

number of issues: town planning, urban and rural police, health and hospital assistance, and education and culture.

Britain, France, and Spain have made concessions to regional demands on issues such as economic development, industrial policy, taxation, and autonomy on local languages and ways of life. Starting in the 1950s, demands for regional autonomy in France led to the re-creation of regions that would coordinate the departments into which France is administratively divided. The first elections for regional councils took place in 1986.

The Spanish system, established in 1975 as a unitary state, has also decentralized power by creating 17 regions or "autonomous communities," each with its own parliament and executive, and acting in legislative and administrative matters. The Basques, the most determined regional group, have been given special powers in the areas of police, taxation, education, and television.

Great Britain in the 1970s confronted the Scottish and Welsh nationalist movements, which were making claims for autonomy or independence. The central government proposed devolution, or transfer of certain powers from the center to parliaments and governments in the two nations, but the proposals were rejected in referendums in Scotland and in Wales in 1979. However, devolution was introduced in 1998.

Germany is the only federal state of our six countries. By its Basic Law, power is shared between the central institutions and the *Länder*, now 16 in number in the united Germany. The *Länder* share concurrent legislative authority with the central government in some areas, have their own authority in other defined areas, have the function of administering federal law as well as that of their own land, and send representatives to the Bundesrat, the second house of the German Parliament.

## The Growth of Government

In postwar Europe, central government has tended to become more powerful because of its increased participation in economic, monetary, and fiscal policy, including planning, and because of the welfare system, which absorbs a great part of the budget and the GDP (see Table 1.21). In addition, partly because of the concentration of

**TABLE 1.21**

**GOVERNMENT SPENDING AS PERCENTAGE OF GDP, 2001**

| | |
|---|---|
| Great Britain | 39.5 |
| France | 50.5 |
| Germany | 46.2 |
| Italy | 46.8 |
| Netherlands | 42.9 |
| Spain | 37.6 |

the media, more attention has been focused on national politics.

Government has grown in terms of functions, in the amount of spending, and in the numbers and proportion of the workforce employed in the public sector. Spending on the public sector increased from about 25 percent of the GDP in Western Europe at the end of World War II to about 45 percent today. In Italy and the Netherlands, it reached 53 percent in 1993. Social policy, including welfare, has taken an increasing share of GDP in the West as well as a larger proportion of the total employed population.

The cost of government spending is also shown by the increase in budget deficits as a proportion of GDP. This proportion in 1995 reached 2.3 percent in Germany, 4.2 percent in Britain, 5 percent in France, and 7.8 percent in Italy. Since large deficits lead to high interest rates and divert investment from productive uses, Western governments have eagerly sought ways to cut the deficits by reducing expenditures.

The functions of government expanded beyond law and order and defense to include economic planning, more state ownership, assistance to economic enterprises, and a comprehensive welfare system. This system usually covers a universal health program, unemployment and sickness benefits, pensions, family support, housing subsidies, and education. Welfare now accounts for up to one-third of GDP in Western Europe. In similar fashion, governments there pay over two-thirds of health care costs.

This increased intervention by Western European states led in the last two decades to a certain amount of criticism. The state has been viewed by some as exerting too great an influence over the allocation of resources through taxation and spending policies. The high level of social spending and costs is viewed as a great disadvantage in international competition. Western governments have faced the dilemma that voters are reluctant to pay and to be taxed for higher levels of public spending, but at the same time people want more of those goods, such as health care and education, that are provided by the state, and thus it is difficult to cut spending.

## The Welfare System

The postwar welfare systems in Western Europe have been a major success in providing social services and transfer payments to all those in society who need them, thus trying to ensure a decent standard of living for all. However, the systems have imposed great financial strains for a number of reasons. Unemployment has persisted, up to 21 percent in Spain, thus necessitating both more unemployment benefits and general family support for low-income families.

The larger number of older people has meant two things. One is the increase in pension benefits, due to automatic increases to match increasing earnings, and in pension coverage, now provided for about a quarter of the Western populations. Pensions account for about one-quarter of the increase in public expenditure since 1960. The other fact is the increase in health costs, partly due to the use of more expensive equipment, new drugs, and more generous treatment, but also resulting from the larger number of older people who require more care. In Great Britain, for example, more than 3 million people are over 75, and their health care costs are some six to seven times that for people of working age.

As a consequence of the rising costs of welfare, since the 1980s European governments have been faced with budget deficits and debt financing problems, as well as resentment of high taxes. Economic recession worsens the problem because most European social insurance programs are paid for by payroll taxes on workers and employers. Therefore, if unemployment rises, less funding goes into social security budgets.

The countries have tried to reduce the financial burden in different ways. Great Britain has proposed abolition of earnings-related unemployment benefits, France increased social security contributions, the Netherlands froze benefits. Germany delayed an increase in pensions by stopping the automatic linking of pensions to earnings, and Italy suggested raising the pension age. A number of countries even tightened requirements for unemployment benefits.

The welfare problem, especially in health care, remains serious for the West. The increase in life expectancy means more spent on pensions and geriatric care, with a decreasing proportion of younger workers to carry the cost. Social changes, such as the decline of the extended family, and the rapid increase of single-parent families which rely more heavily on welfare than do two-parent families, mean greater demands on governments.

Governments, however, are reluctant to increase taxes to pay for higher costs or to increase borrowing, since government debt is already so high. Businesses resist higher contributions for welfare funding, which they fear would mean increased prices for their products, causing their goods to become less competitive internationally. In Germany in 1994, social security contributions were 40 percent of gross pay, while social spending accounted for about one-third of GDP.

## WESTERN EUROPEAN INTEGRATION

In the postwar period, the concept took shape and institutional form of a Western European entity culturally and politically distinct from the United States and the Soviet Union and its Central and Eastern European allies, an entity with its own values and attitudes. At the same time, interrelated with that concept was the idea of an Atlantic community in which the United States would participate in the defense of the West and of Western political and economic values.

These two concepts have given rise to the set of military, economic, and political institutions created in the postwar period and discussed in Chapter 8. These institutions have been responsible for the remarkable political development in Western Europe; the general political stability, occasionally interrupted, in most of the countries; the harmony between former enemies, especially France and Germany; and the set of links with the United States. Two organizations have been particularly important: NATO and the European Union.

**NATO**    The North Atlantic Treaty Organization (NATO), established in 1949 as a mutual defense organization in the Cold War helped define the boundaries of Western Europe. It can be regarded as highly successful in that it contained any contemplated Soviet expansion westward. The Soviet threat did not materialize and ended in 1991 with the disintegration of the Soviet Union.

The problem for NATO today is that it is a defensive alliance without any particular enemies. What is its function in the absence of perceived enemies, acknowledging that the external threat held the countries together? It must decide whether to enlarge its membership to include Central and Eastern European countries, thus

**A CLOSER LOOK**

**1.6**

### NORTH ATLANTIC TREATY ORGANIZATION (NATO)

NATO for over 50 years has been the primary shield in defense of common U.S. and European interests. NATO, with headquarters in Brussels, at its core is still a military alliance but it has also undertaken some political functions. The North Atlantic Treaty of 1949, in Article 5, states that an attack on one or more NATO members will be considered an attack on all, in defense of which all other members will collectively take appropriate action including the use of force. Article 5 was invoked after the terrorist attacks on the United States on September 11, 2001. There are now 19 member countries: Belgium, Canada, Czech Republic, Denmark, France, Germany, Greece, Hungary, Iceland, Italy, Luxembourg, Netherlands, Norway, Poland, Portugal, Spain, Turkey, the United Kingdom, and the United States.

blurring the distinction between Eastern and Western Europe and extending its territorial guarantee. It also has to decide whether to expand its functions to act in non-NATO areas, and whether to participate in peacekeeping or peace support operations.

The Western European countries in NATO have been considering greater emphasis on their own European security identity and defense organization rather than continuing to rely on NATO and the United States, whose commitment to Western Europe has been a fundamental basis for its peace and prosperity. This emphasis would mean the revival of the Western European Union through closer military and security cooperation, starting with France and Germany.

***The European Union***   The original intention of the European Community, now the European Union, was to create, by establishing an economic organization, the basis for a broader and deeper community among peoples long divided by bloody conflicts. The institutions of the organization have gradually been created, obtaining closer cooperation among the Western countries, extending European law to the member nations, setting up an elected parliamentary assembly, and establishing executive and judicial bodies.

### TABLE 1.22

### NATO DEFENSE EXPENDITURES AS PERCENTAGE OF GDP

| | |
|---|---|
| Belgium | 1.4% |
| Canada | 1.2 |
| Czech Republic | 2.3 |
| Denmark | 1.5 |
| France | 2.7 |
| Germany | 1.5 |
| Greece | 4.9 |
| Hungary | 1.7 |
| Iceland* | — |
| Italy | 1.9 |
| Luxembourg | 0.7 |
| Netherlands | 1.6 |
| Norway | 1.9 |
| Poland | 2.0 |
| Portugal | 2.2 |
| Spain | 1.3 |
| Turkey | 6.0 |
| United Kingdom | 2.4 |
| United States | 3.0 |

*Iceland has no armed forces

**REVIEW**

**1.7**

### KEY EVENTS IN THE HISTORY OF NATO

| | |
|---|---|
| 1949 | NATO formed. |
| 1955 | West Germany joins NATO. |
| 1961 | NATO condemns building of Berlin wall. |
| 1979 | Soviet Union invades Afghanistan. |
| 1987 | NATO secretary general negotiates Turkish-Greek dispute. |
| 1989 | Berlin wall falls. |
| 1990 | Germany reunited; remains NATO member. |
| 1994 | NATO begins airstrikes in Bosnia. |
| 1995 | Bosnia peace accord; NATO deploys troops. |
| 1999 | NATO launches airstrikes in Kosovo; Yugoslavia withdraws troops. |
| 1999 | Czech Republic, Hungary, and Poland join NATO. |
| 2001 | NATO dispatches troops to Macedonia; supports United States in war against terrorism. |

## REVIEW 1.8    EUROPEAN DEFENSE ORGANIZATIONS

| Organization | Members | Purpose |
| --- | --- | --- |
| Western European Union (WEU) | Great Britain, Belgium, France, Germany, Greece, Italy, Luxembourg, Netherlands, Portugal, and Spain are full members; 18 other countries are associates or observers. Headquarters in Brussels. | Created in 1954 as the successor of the Brussels Treaty Organization of 1948 to provide for collective self-defense. It is an intergovernmental organization for security. It is now seen as the probable future defense component and peacekeeping military organization of the European Union. |
| North Atlantic Treaty Organization (NATO) | 16 European countries, plus Canada, Turkey, and the United States. Headquarters in Brussels. | Created in 1949 for collective security against the Communist Warsaw Pact led by the Soviet Union, Now discussing its role since the end of the Cold War. It has acted as a regional peacekeeping authority under U.N. auspices. |
| Organization for Security and Cooperation in Europe (OSCE) | 55 nations including all European states, the United States, and Central Asian States. Headquarters in Vienna. | Created in 1975 at Helsinki to provide a forum for NATO, Warsaw Pact, and non-aligned countries to cooperate on security issues, including arms control and economic and environmental factors that affect security. The largest regional security organization in the world. |

The European Community officially became the European Union on November 1, 1993, and is preparing for full monetary union, a single currency, and a common defense and foreign policy. The countries can move towards these objectives at different speeds and can decide whether to participate in joint economic or security organizations. Though the process has begun by which individual states are giving up some of their traditional independence, tension remains between the nation-states and the European institutions.

How will that tension be resolved? The individual states remain independent but have pooled their resources to a certain degree. They have also given up some of their sovereign power to the European Union, the institutions of which are able, on some issues, to make decisions or rules for all the member states.

The question remains open whether Western Europe can forge a greater measure of political unity and become a superpower comparable to the United States. The Western European countries have collaborated in arrangements of international cooperation and collective security. It is not yet clear whether they can also form an ever more perfect union.

# FURTHER READINGS

Blondel, Jean, and Ferdinand Müller-Rommel, eds. *Cabinets in Western Europe,* 2nd ed. (New York: St. Martin's, 1997).

Blondel, Jean, and Ferdinand Müller-Rommel, eds. *Governing Together* (New York: St. Martin's, 1993).

Bowler, Shaun, et al., eds. *Party Discipline and Parliamentary Government* (Columbus: Ohio State University Press, 1999).

Budge, Ian, et al. *Mapping Policy Preferences* (New York: Oxford University Press, 2001).

Budge, Ian, and Hans Keman. *Parties and Democracy: Coalition Formation and Government Functioning in Twenty States* (New York: Oxford University Press, 1990).

Budge, Ian, et al. *The Politics of the New Europe* (New York: Longman, 1997).

Colomer, Josep. *Political Institutions: Democracy and Social Choice* (New York: Oxford University Press, 2001).

Cortada, James N. *Can Democracy Survive in Western Europe?* (Westport, CT: Praeger, 1996).

Farrell, David M. *Electoral Systems: Comparative Introduction* (New York: Palgrave, 2001).

Hanley, David L. *Christian Democracy in Europe: A Comparative Perspective* (New York: St. Martin's, 1994).

Hayward, Jack and Edward C. Page, eds. *Governing the New Europe* (Cambridge: Polity Press, 1995).

Keating, Michael. *The New Regionalism in Western Europe* (Northampton: Elgar, 1998).

Kitschelt, Herbert, et al. *Post-Communist Party Systems* (New York: Cambridge University Press, 1999).

Lane, Jan-Erik, and Svante Ersson. *European Politics: An Introduction* (Thousand Oaks, CA: Sage, 1996).

Lijphart, Arend. *Patterns of Democracy: Government Forms and Performance in Thirty-Six Countries* (New Haven, CT: Yale University Press 1999).

Linz, Juan. *Totalitarian and Authoritarian Regimes* (London: Rienner, 2000).

Maor, Moshe. *Parties, Conflicts, and Coalitions in Western Europe* (New York: Routledge, 1998).

Menon, Anand, and Vincent Wright, eds. *From the Nation State to Europe?* (New York: Oxford University Press, 2001).

Redmond, John, and Glenda Rosenthal, eds. *Expanding European Union: Past, Present, Future* (Boulder, CO: Rienner, 1998).

Siaroff, Alan. *Comparative European Party Systems* (New York: Garland, 2000).

Siedentop, Larry. *Democracy in Europe* (London: Lane, 2000).

Steiner, Jürg. *European Democracies,* 4th ed. (New York: Longman, 1998).

Wilson, Frank L., ed. *The European Center-Right at the End of the Twentieth Century* (New York: St. Martin's, 1998).

# THE GOVERNMENT OF
# Great Britain

*Michael Curtis*

## INTRODUCTION

**Background:** Great Britain, the dominant industrial and maritime power of the 19th century, played a leading role in developing parliamentary democracy and in advancing literature and science. At its zenith, the British Empire stretched over one-fourth of the earth's surface. The first half of the 20th century saw the UK's strength seriously depleted in two World Wars. The second half witnessed the dismantling of the Empire and the UK rebuilding itself into a modern and prosperous European nation. As one of five permanent members of the UN Security Council, a founding member of NATO, and of the Commonwealth, the UK pursues a global approach to foreign policy; it currently is weighing the degree of its integration with continental Europe. A member of the EU, it chose to remain outside of the European Monetary Union for the time being. Constitutional reform is also a significant issue in the UK. Regional assemblies with varying degrees of power opened in Scotland, Wales, and Northern Ireland in 1999.

### GEOGRAPHY

**Location:** Western Europe, islands including the northern one-sixth of the island of Ireland between the North Atlantic Ocean and the North Sea, northwest of France

**Area:** 244,820 sq km

**Area—comparative:** slightly smaller than Oregon

**Land boundaries:** 360 km

  *border countries:* Ireland 360 km

**Climate:** temperate; moderated by prevailing southwest winds over the North Atlantic Current; more than one-half of the days are overcast

**Terrain:** mostly rugged hills and low mountains; level to rolling plains in east and southeast

**Elevation extremes:** *lowest point:* Fenland –4 m
*highest point:* Ben Nevis 1,343 m

**Geography note:** lies near vital North Atlantic sea lanes; only 35 km from France and now linked by tunnel under the English Channel; because of heavily indented coastline, no location is more than 125 km from tidal waters

## PEOPLE

**Population:** 59,647,790

**Age structure:** *0–14 years:* 18.89% (male 5,778,415; female 5,486,114)
*15–64 years:* 65.41% (male 19,712,932; female 19,304,771)
*65 years and over:* 15.7% (male 3,895,921; female 5,469,637)

**Population growth rate:** 0.23%

**Birthrate:** 11.54 births/1,000 population

**Sex ratio:** 0.97 males/female

**Life expectancy at birth:** 77.82 years
*male:* 75.13 years
*female:* 80.66 years

**Nationality:** *noun:* Briton, Britons, British (collective plural)
*adjective:* British

**Ethnic groups:** English 81.5%, Scottish 9.6%, Irish 2.4%, Welsh 1.9%, Ulster 1.8%, West Indian, Indian, Pakistani, and other 2.8%

**Religions:** Anglican 27 million, Roman Catholic 9 million, Muslim 1 million, Presbyterian 800,000, Methodist 760,000, Sikh 400,000, Hindu 350,000, Jewish 300,000

**Languages:** English, Welsh (about 26% of the population of Wales), Scottish form of Gaelic (about 60,000 in Scotland)

**Literacy:** *definition:* age 15 and over has completed five or more years of schooling
*total population:* 99%

## GOVERNMENT

**Country name:** *conventional long form:* United Kingdom of Great Britain and Northern Ireland
*conventional short form:* United Kingdom, Great Britain
*abbreviation:* UK, GB

**Government type:** constitutional monarchy

**Capital:** London

**Dependent areas:** Anguilla, Bermuda, British Indian Ocean Territory, British Virgin Islands, Cayman Islands, Falkland Islands, Gibraltar, Guernsey, Jersey, Isle of Man, Montserrat, Pitcairn Islands, Saint Helena, South Georgia and the South Sandwich Islands, Turks and Caicos Islands

**Independence:** England has existed as a unified entity since the 10th century; the union between England and Wales was enacted under the Statute of Rhuddlan in 1284; in the Act of Union of 1707, England and Scotland agreed to permanent union as Great Britain; the legislative union of Great Britain and Ireland was implemented in 1801, with the adoption of the name the United Kingdom of Great Britain and Ireland; the Anglo-Irish treaty of 1921 formalized a partition of Ireland; six northern Irish counties remained part of the United Kingdom as Northern Ireland and the current name of the country, the United Kingdom of Great Britain and Northern Ireland, was adopted in 1927

**Constitution:** unwritten; partly statutes, partly common law and practice

**Legal system:** common law tradition with early Roman and modern continental influences; no judicial review of Acts of Parliament; accepts compulsory International Court of Justice jurisdiction, with reservations; British courts and legislation are increasingly subject to review by European Union courts

**Suffrage:** 18 years of age; universal

**Executive branch:** *chief of state:* Queen Elizabeth II (since 6 February 1952); Heir Apparent Prince Charles (son of the queen, born 14 November 1948)
*head of government:* Prime Minister Anthony (Tony) Blair (since 2 May 1997)

*cabinet:* Cabinet of Ministers appointed by the prime minister

*elections:* none; the monarch is hereditary; the prime minister is the leader of the majority party in the House of Commons (assuming there is no majority party, a prime minister would have a majority coalition or at least a coalition that was not rejected by the majority)

**Legislative branch:** bicameral Parliament comprised of House of Lords (consists of approximately 500 life peers, 92 hereditary peers and 26 clergy) and House of Commons (659 seats; members are elected by popular vote to serve five-year terms unless the House is dissolved earlier)

**Judicial branch:** House of Lords (highest court of appeal; several Lords of Appeal in Ordinary are appointed by the monarch for life); Supreme Courts of England, Wales, and Northern Ireland (comprising the Courts of Appeal, the High Courts of Justice, and the Crown Courts); Scotland's Court of Session and Court of the Justiciary

## ECONOMY

**Overview:** The UK, a leading trading power and financial center, deploys an essentially capitalistic economy, one of the quartet of trillion dollar economies of Western Europe. Over the past two decades the government has greatly reduced public ownership and contained the growth of social welfare programs. Agriculture is intensive, highly mechanized, and efficient by European standards, producing about 60% of food needs with only 1% of the labor force. The UK has large coal, natural gas, and oil reserves; primary energy production accounts for 10% of GDP, one of the highest shares of any industrial nation. Services, particularly banking, insurance, and business services, account by far for the largest proportion of GDP while industry continues to decline in importance. The economy has grown steadily, at just above or below 3%, for the last several years.

**GDP:** purchasing power parity—$1.36 trillion

**GDP—real growth rate:** 3%

**GDP—per capita:** purchasing power parity—$22,800

**GDP—composition by sector:** *agriculture:* 1.7%
   *industry:* 24.9%
   *services:* 73.4%

**Population below poverty line:** 17%

**Labor force:** 29.2 million

**Labor force—by occupation:** agriculture 1%, industry 19%, services 80%

**Unemployment rate:** 5.5%

**Currency:** British pound (GBP)

# A. POLITICAL DEVELOPMENT

## HISTORICAL BACKGROUND

Why study the British political system? There are a number of answers to this understandable question. Britain has the oldest operating political system in the world; some of its governmental institutions have been in continuous existence for nearly a thousand years. Symbolically this is illustrated by the memorials to many notable figures in public and cultural life in Westminster Abbey, the building of which was begun in the eleventh century. No one needs to be reminded of the intellectual and literary influence of Britain's writers, such as Chaucer, Shakespeare, Milton, Austen, Dickens, Shaw, Woolf, and Auden, and its philosophers, such as Hobbes, Locke, Hume, Mill, Bentham, and Russell. Its political influence, both directly and indirectly, has been equally important.

Through its former control of about one-quarter of the world's population on every continent, Britain has directly influenced many countries, including the United States. From Britain, the United States has absorbed a similar idea of the rule of law and a concern for personal freedoms. There are similar political institutions, such as a single-member-constituency electoral system for the lower house, a two-chamber legislature, a two-major-party system, a cabinet, and a civil service based on merit. Oscar Wilde once said that Britain and the United States were two countries separated by a common language. Certainly there are great differences in the way that political power is exercised and institutions function in the two countries. Nevertheless, it was appropriate that the British memorial to President John F. Kennedy be placed at Runnymede, where King John was tamed by the feudal barons into signing the Magna Carta in 1215.

Today the British Empire, on which the sun never set, no longer exists. But most of the countries once ruled by Britain belong to the 54-member Commonwealth with its population of over 1.7 billion. Though not a political power in itself, the Commonwealth is a unique multiracial association.

Indirectly, Britain has influenced other countries by its political ideals and values and by some of its political practices, such as a meaningful parliament which could control the excesses of executive power, an officially recognized loyal opposition, political moderation and tolerance, and a process of change by gradual and peaceful means.

The British system is also instructive for those interested in modernization and political development. Britain was the world's first industrialized country, a process which began at the end of the eighteenth century. For Karl Marx, Britain was the model of the capitalist system in the middle of the nineteenth century. The proportion of the working population employed in factories and manufacturing rose while that in agriculture declined. With the repeal of the Corn Laws in 1846, allowing the entry of cheap food, and the adoption of free-trade principles, Britain lived by exporting its manufactured goods and by importing food and raw materials. As a result, the country has been very concerned with problems of foreign trade and international exchange. London became the financial center of the world in banking, insurance, and shipping: the British

**A CLOSER LOOK**

**2.1**

### MAGNA CARTA

No freeman shall be taken, imprisoned ... or in any other way destroyed ... except by the lawful judgment of his peers, or by the law of the land. To no one will we sell, to none will we deny or delay, right or justice.

currency, the pound sterling, became the medium for much of the world's trade.

A century ago Britain was the workshop of the world, producing two-thirds of the world's coal, half of its iron, over half of its steel, half of its cotton goods, and almost all of its machine tools. Britain's exports of capital goods—machines and technology—led to industrialization in other major countries, which soon became competitors and began to supplant Britain technologically and industrially. Yet with the industrial exports had also gone other exports such as ideas, institutions, and ways of life. Britain was the foremost example of the process of modernization and industrialization without a revolution from either above or below.

But Britain has also paid a heavy price for having the first mature industrial system and for being dependent on international trade. Its cap-ital equipment became outmoded, and its relative economic position in the world weakened as other countries advanced industrially. Its dependence on imports of food and raw materials made it vulnerable to outside forces.

In the modern age, Britain has become a postindustrial society with a mixed economy and a significant social welfare system, in which private enterprise coexists with a public sector and public expenditure now amounts to about 40 percent of the gross national product. In the 1980s Britain was acutely troubled by problems such as inflation, less-than-full employment, and comparatively slow economic growth, which have plagued other advanced nations to differing degrees. Yet productivity grew by over 3 percent a year between 1980 and 2001. The British economy is still the sixth largest in the world, and Britain is still the fifth largest trading nation.

No. 10 Downing Street, the residence and office of the prime minister, is located in a small street off Whitehall about half a mile from Parliament. The only other houses in the street are occupied by the chancellor of the Exchequer and by the office of the government chief whip.

The High Court, which hears most important cases of common law, equity, divorce, and custody, and hears appeals from lower courts in certain instances in civil and criminal cases.

# EVOLUTION OF THE POLITICAL SYSTEM

The British political system illustrates the gradual evolution from internal chaos and divisions, which resulted in the Wars of the Roses between rival contenders for the throne in the fifteenth century and the Civil War between the king and parliament and the peaceful "Glorious Revolution" in the seventeenth century, to a stable unitary system with a long process of development of political structures, institutions, and behavior (see Figure 2.1). The country changed from a mainly rural, isolated, religious nation to a democratic, largely urban, industrial society, essentially secular in practice, and the center of an empire.

Britain exemplifies political change from a strong monarchy with an important aristocratic

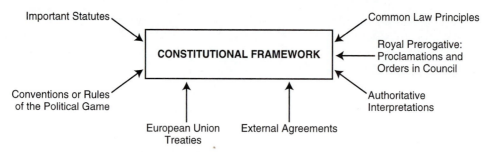

**Figure 2.1** THE CONSTITUTIONAL FRAMEWORK OF BRITISH GOVERNMENT

class to a political democracy. A constitutional monarch reigns over a country in which the parliamentary cabinet system and political parties are the dominant political organizations representing the different political expressions of the power of the people. With the gradual expansion of rights and privileges and the removal of civil and religious disabilities, all can legally participate in politics without discrimination (see Table 2.1).

All political systems retain certain traditional practices and institutions that seem to run counter to the logic of political development. In Britain these would include anomalies such as the presence until 1999 of over 700 hereditary peers in the House of Lords; the rebuilding of the destroyed House of Commons after World War II so that it physically resembles the old chamber and can seat only half of its members; and the uses until recently of eighteenth-century wigs by the Speaker of the House of Commons and by the judges and barristers in the High Courts of Law. Indeed, it is ironic that the leading political figure, the prime minister, was long paid for holding an office, First Lord of the Treasury, which no longer has a function, but was not paid for being prime minister, the functions of which are nowhere legally or precisely defined.

In recent years the British system has been responding to social and cultural changes as well as to economic difficulties and political problems. Innovations such as the referendum on the European Community in 1975, the devolution of power to Scotland and Wales in 1998, and the restoration of direct rule in Northern Ireland in 1972 and then the creation of a Northern Ireland Assembly in 1998, the direct election of a mayor of London and the establishment of a Greater London Authority, and setting up of Regional Development Agencies have been just some of the responses. New parties of the political center such as the Social Democrats and later the Liberal Democrats came on the scene. The nationalist parties in Wales and particularly in Scotland obtained greater support from the electorates in the two countries, though the support has fluctuated. The Greens, a group and party reflecting the growing concern about environmental issues, emerged in the 1980s.

## TABLE 2.1

### REMOVAL OF POLITICAL AND CIVIL DISABILITIES

| | |
|---|---|
| 1656 | Jews allowed back into the country |
| 1689 | Toleration Act—members of all religious orders except Catholics and Unitarians permitted freedom of worship |
| 1774 | Residency qualifications for members of Parliament declared unnecessary |
| 1778 | Some restrictions against Roman Catholic worship removed |
| 1779 | Dissenters relieved from subscribing to some of the 39 Articles |
| 1807 | Slave trade abolished |
| 1828 | Dissenters allowed to become members of Parliament |
| 1829 | Catholics permitted to become members of both houses of Parliament |
| 1858 | Jews permitted to become members of both houses of Parliament |
| | Property qualification for members of Parliament ended |
| 1871 | University religious tests abolished |
| 1872 | Secret ballot instituted |
| 1888 | Atheists allowed to become members of Parliament |
| 1918 | Women over 30 obtain the vote |
| 1928 | Women over 21 obtain the vote |

# BRITAIN AS A MODEL IN POLITICS

For the student of politics, Britain has long been useful as an example in the comparison of different systems. Britain with its constitutional and civilian government, essentially two-party system, and representative democracy has been instructive for this purpose. The British system has sometimes been called the "Westminster model" after the area of London in which Parliament is located.

Britain has adhered for three centuries to the subordination of the military to political power, and the military has been loyal to governments of all political complexions. Not since Oliver Cromwell's government (1653–1658) has Britain had a military dictator or been seriously threatened by fear of a military coup. Britain had also been an example of an essentially two-party system as distinct from regimes with one dominant party, a number of parties, or none at all. In Britain, as in the United States, only two parties have, in effect, been strong enough to share the bulk of the electoral vote and exert political control while alternating in the exercise of executive power. However, a third party is still an important presence.

Britain is a constitutional democracy as well as a constitutional monarchy. All citizens, individually and through organizations, can participate and attempt to influence political decisions. For the most part this is done indirectly through the electoral system, by which the representatives of the people are sent to the House of Commons, the powerful chamber of Parliament, the supreme legal power in the country. The representative system based on the majority principle, by which a plurality is sufficient to win, is also based on the permitted existence of political minorities, which have the right to try to become the majority in their turn, and on basic freedoms of speech, meeting, and the press which allow political commentary of all kinds.

Britain is one of few countries which do not have a single formal document regarded as a constitution to define the political system and state the rights and duties of citizens. Unlike most other systems, all changes of a constitutional nature take place without any special legal provision for them; nor is there a supreme or constitutional court to decide on the constitutionality of legislation passed by Parliament. But Britain is the classical example of a system that is "constitutional" in the sense of adherence to rules and to accepted ways of political behavior as contrasted with countries that are nonconstitutional, or arbitrary, in their political practices.

The British constitutional framework results from the following different components (see Figure 2.1).

1. A number of legislative statutes and documents of outstanding importance have provided the foundations of a considerable number of political institutions. These include the Magna Carta, 1215; the Petition of Right, 1628; the Bill of Rights, 1689; the Habeas Corpus Act, 1679; the Act of Settlement, 1701; the Acts of Union with Scotland in 1707 and with Ireland in 1801; the Franchise Acts of 1832, 1867, 1884, 1918, 1928, 1948, 1958, 1963, and 1969; the Parliament Acts, 1911 and 1949; the Crown Proceedings Act, 1947; the Ministers of the Crown Act, 1937; the Nationalization Acts between 1947 and 1950; the European Communities Act, 1972; the British Nationality Act, 1981; the European Communities (Amendment) Act, 1986; the House of Lords Act, 1999. They differ from other statutes, not in a technical sense, but only in their political importance.

2. Certain principles have been established by common law, which comprises the decisions of judges and the courts in individual cases. Personal liberties of speech, press, and assembly are to a considerable degree the result of judicial decisions over the last two centuries.

The most important principle is the rule of law, which implies the certainty of legal rules rather than arbitrary judgments in determining the rights of individuals and in examining the behavior of authorities. There is no punishment unless a breach of the law has been established in a court of law. False imprisonment is prevented by a writ of habeas corpus, by which an individual obtains an explanation of the reason for detainment. The rule of law also implies that everyone is subject to the law, including officials. No one can plead the orders of a superior official in defense of illegal actions or can claim the right to be tried in a special court under a different code for official actions.

The demand for a more formal bill of rights has grown, largely as a result of two of Britain's external agreements. Britain ratified the European Convention of Human Rights in 1951 and has thus been subject to grievances taken before the European Commission on Human Rights. Furthermore, British membership in the European Union, the laws of which may take precedence over British law, has allowed judges to decide on conflicts between the two sets of law.

Though the British judiciary since the 1970s occasionally ruled against the interpretation by ministers of the extent of their powers, it still cannot rule on the validity of statutes passed by Parliament. Britain does not have a court like the United States Supreme Court that can declare legislation unconstitutional. However, the British courts in recent years have reviewed some actions of government ministers and administrative officials to see if they have exceeded the powers allowed them by parliamentary statute and encroached on rights of individuals. The courts have sometimes declared such actions *ultra vires* (beyond legal power) and even exercised some judicial review.

3. Certain books written by constitutional experts are regarded as so authoritative that some of their views on constitutional issues are commonly accepted. They include such works as Walter Bagehot's *The English Constitution,* A. V. Dicey's *Introduction to the Study of the Law of the Constitution,* and Erskine May's *Parliamentary Practice.*

4. Numerous political rules and practices, known collectively as conventions, are observed by all participating in the system. Though they have never been passed in any formal or legal manner, they are usually observed as completely as any laws. Occasionally, however, there may be differences about the exact meaning of a convention. Among the most important of these conventions are the following:

a. The real heads of the government are the prime minister and the cabinet.

b. The government is formed from the party that can control a majority in the House of Commons.

c. Cabinet ministers will normally be chosen from the two houses of Parliament, and the prime minister will come from the House of Commons.

d. The cabinet will operate on the basis of collective responsibility to ensure political unity.

e. The government will resign or ask for a dissolution of Parliament if defeated in the House of Commons on a motion of no confidence.

f. The monarch will ultimately accept the wishes of his or her government.

g. Only the government can propose votes on grants of money in the House of Commons.

h. Those affected by a proposed action will normally be consulted by the government before a final decision is made.

Without these conventions, regular and orderly government in its present form could not function. They create harmony between the executive and legislative branches of the government through various understandings about the workings of the parliamentary cabinet system. The conventions ensure that government is ultimately responsible to the will of the people because an election decides which party is to form the government and thus who is to be prime minister. In a society such as the British, in which traditional institutions have survived changing political circumstances, as the monarchy has done in a political democracy, conventions allow institutions to adjust to political reality.

Conventions are observed not because it is illegal to disregard them, but because they enable the political system to work in accordance with the agreed fundamental principles on which consensus exists.

## THE IMPORTANCE OF CONSENSUS AND ITS LIMITS

Britain until very recently has been a model of political stability and consensus on the nature of the regime and on the method of change. British politics has depended on all participants abiding by "the rules of the political game" or understandings. These rules include the pragmatic working and adaptation by gradual change of political institutions and organizations; tolerance of different political positions; the belief that government should govern and have adequate powers; agreement on procedural matters, the validity of political dissent and of trade union organization, through which the working class has a stake in the system; the view that the people should be consulted about political action, through their representatives and groups to which they belong; and moderation in political behavior.

The essence of the British political system is a stable democracy which provides for the exercise of strong power by the government, but which also allows substantial personal freedoms and rights. There has been an alternation of political power between the parties in a system characterized by a limited constitutional monarchy, a bicameral parliament, the supremacy of parliament, the linking of the executive and the legislature through the members of the government sitting in parliament, the responsibility of the government to parliament and indirectly to the people, and on an independent nuclear deterrent.

There has also been acceptance of the welfare state, the need for full employment and adequate incomes, free collective bargaining, a mixed economy with both private and state enterprises, and a foreign policy based on membership in the Western alliance.

## POLITICAL STABILITY

The last revolution was in 1688 when the struggle between the king and the parliament led to the overthrow of the monarch. The principle was established that Parliament, not the king, had supreme power. The monarch could not suspend laws, levy taxes without parliamentary consent or maintain a standing army in peace-time. How is this remarkable political stability to be explained? There are various explanations of why the British people accepted the political institutions and those classes which controlled

them. Some of them are analyzed in the following paragraphs.

## Political Culture

The acceptance by the population of political authority, on the one hand, and the existence of individual rights, on the other, has resulted in political moderation. The balance among the British people between limited political activity and general acquiescence in what government does has led to an attachment to the political system and to agreement on the rules of political behavior. Britain has been regarded as the model of a democratic political culture in which there is regular competition for the control of government (the existence of which is dependent on the electoral will of the people). Training in this civic culture takes place in many social institutions—for example, the family, peer group, school, and workplace—as well as in the political system itself.

## Deference of the People

Since Bagehot introduced the idea in the nineteenth century, some have stressed the deference until quite recently of the population, including a significant part of the working class, to the social elite or members of the upper social classes, the well-born or the wealthy, who because of their social position are regarded as the natural or uniquely qualified political leaders by a people that accepts traditional values and authority. In practice, the Conservative Party came to be regarded by many as the embodiment of the natural ruling class or as particularly gifted to govern. But whatever the significance of the deference of people in the past, the fact that the Conservative Party, though it governed from 1979 to 1997, did not win 6 of the 11 elections since 1964 has suggested that deference is less important today and not the sole explanation of the political stability.

## Pattern of Authority

Some analysts suggest that there is a correlation between the pattern of authority in government and administration, and that in parties, interest groups, and nonofficial organizations and institutions. In Britain the pattern is strong leadership, which is efficient and can make itself obeyed but which is limited by substantive and procedural restraints. There is minimal direct participation by the vast majority of the population. Voters choose between alternatives presented by party leaders. The parties themselves are not only disciplined but also dominated by the leadership.

Traditional values uphold leadership and authority in politics and society. They permeate the elite institutions such as the monarchy, the established Church, the "public" schools, Oxford and Cambridge, the military and administrative hierarchy, and the senior civil service. The Conservative Party has controlled the government for the majority of years since 1895.

### Relative Deprivation

One hypothesis suggests that the feeling of people that they are deprived economically or socially—and their consequent political behavior—depends on which other people or group they compare themselves with rather than on real social conditions. The British working class has usually not taken the nonmanual privileged classes as a comparative reference group. Therefore, the working class's feeling of deprivation has not been as strong as objective inequalities might have led them to believe. This, in turn, has produced a less disruptive and less revolutionary political attitude than in other major countries.

### Effect of Geography

Perhaps the most important single factor explaining British stability and the continuity of social and political life is that Britain is an island. Since 1066 the existing political institutions have not been disrupted by military invasion. This happy fact permitted the creation of stable borders, a luxury not enjoyed by other European countries that were forced into wars to create or maintain national unity. Moreover, this island power developed both a navy (until 1939 the largest in the world) for its protection, as well as a shipping fleet that became the basis for its commercial expansion, capital accumulation, and the conquest of an empire, which at its height consisted of over 15 million square miles of territory on every continent of the world.

## THE UNIFIED SYSTEM

The process of unification of the country took more than five centuries. The United Kingdom is now composed of four national units on two main islands and surrounding small islands. England constitutes 52 percent, Wales 9 percent, Scotland 33 percent, and Northern Ireland 6 percent of the total area. Northern Ireland, or Ulster, constitutes 16 percent of the area of the second island, the rest of which is occupied by the Republic of Ireland (see Table 2.2).

The British population is a heterogeneous multiracial society of Celts, Romans, Scots, Picts, Angles, Jutes, Danes, Norsemen, Normans, East Europeans, West Indians, Asians, and other groups. But the prospect of much greater immigration from the Caribbean and Asian Commonwealth countries such as India, Pakistan, and Bangladesh led to limitations on that immigration by statutes in 1962, 1968, and 1971, which were passed after a certain amount of opposition, and by political policies.

Though English is the standard language (the form spoken in the southeast is the most prestigious norm), other languages are also spoken. About 20 percent of the Welsh population

| TABLE 2.2 | | |
|---|---|---|
| **THE UNITED KINGDOM** | | |
| | **Area (square miles)** | **Population (millions)** |
| England | 50.3 | 49.5 |
| Scotland | 30.4 | 5.1 |
| Wales | 8.0 | 2.9 |
| Northern Ireland | 5.4 | 1.7 |
| Total | 94.1 | 59.2 |

speaks Welsh, a form of British Celtic which is of equal validity with English in the administration of justice and the conduct of government business in Wales. Some 2 percent of the population of Scotland, mainly in the Highlands and western coastal regions, speak Gaelic, and about 2 percent in Northern Ireland speak the Irish form of Gaelic. The newer Asian communities speak a variety of languages.

## A NEW PLURALISTIC SYSTEM?

Although Britain is a pluralistic society in ethnic origin, language, religion, and race, the differences have rarely caused political problems affecting the unity and centralization of the system. But in recent years the issues of race, ethnicity, and religion and the emergence of nationalist sentiment have upset the stability of the political order.

After World War II the presence of the new nonwhite communities, with their different languages, religions, lifestyles, and tendency to remain in certain inner-city areas, has caused friction and riots and led to statutes such as the 1976 Race Relations Act, which makes discrimination unlawful on grounds of color, race, or ethnic and national origins in employment, housing, education, and provision of goods and services (see Table 2.3). Some extreme members of the Islamic community called for the recognition by the state of Islamic laws on marriage, divorce, and inheritance.

The areas of Scotland, Wales, and Northern Ireland until the late 1990s were ruled by departments of the central government in London. The centralized, unitary political system has been troubled in the last decades by the rise of nationalist sentiment in Scotland and Wales, and the constitutional framework has been disturbed by political problems in Northern Ireland.

In Northern Ireland the minority Catholic population, numbering about 600,000, has long objected to discrimination against it in political rights, employment, and housing by the Protestant majority of about 1 million. The Catholic civil rights campaign in 1969 resulted in greater tension between the two separate communities and an increasing level of violence, which led the British government to send army units to maintain order. Though some concessions were made on civil rights, no agreement could be reached on the larger Catholic political demands. As a result of the continuing violence and the terrorist activity by the Irish Republican Army (IRA), the powers of the Northern Irish government and Parliament were suspended, and direct rule by the British government began in March 1972. Britain in 1978 shifted the responsibility for security back to the local police and a part-time civilian corps, almost exclusively Protestant.

An assembly elected in Northern Ireland in 1982 charged with making proposals for devolu-

---

**A CLOSER LOOK**

**2.2**

### THE GOOD FRIDAY AGREEMENT

Multiparty negotiations in 1998, aided by former U.S. senator George Mitchell, led to the Good Friday Agreement in Belfast. Under the agreement, the fate of Northern Ireland was to be decided by vote. The Catholic minority would be part of the new power-sharing executive. A council would link Northern Ireland and the Republic of Ireland; another council would link Ireland and Great Britain. In addition, weapons of paramilitary organizations were to be "decommissioned." A Northern Ireland Assembly would be elected, to include 108 members in 18 six-member constituencies. After the Good Friday Agreement was approved by the people through referendum, the Northern Ireland Assembly was elected, with legislative and executive authority for Northern Ireland in those matters devolved by Great Britain. The Assembly is led by a First Minister and Deputy First Minister, chosen by the members.

---

**TABLE 2.3**

**IMMIGRATION AND CIVIL RIGHTS IN BRITAIN**

---

*Immigration and Nationality*

From the early seventeenth century, Britons were British subjects by birth within the realm of the monarch; this was extended to British colonies. By the 1940s, over 800 million people were British subjects and had rights in the United Kingdom.

| | |
|---|---|
| 1948 | British Nationality Act: 2 classes of citizenship: (1) UK and colonies—full rights of citizens; (2) independent Commonwealth citizens could enter Britain. Citizens of the Republic of Ireland given special status to enter. Over half a million nonwhite British subjects immigrated to Britain in the 1950s and 1960s. |
| 1962 | Commonwealth Immigration Act: restricted entry for overseas British subjects. By 1971, over 1.5 million had immigrated. |
| 1971 | Immigration Act: entry for those with at least one British grandparent, or who were naturalized, or who had lived in Britain for five years. |
| 1981 | Nationality Act: British citizenship limited to those already legally in Britain, or who had one British parent and were registered abroad, or long-standing family connections with UK (patriality). |
| 1990 | Citizenship granted to 50,000 Hong Kong "heads of household"; about 135,000 Hong Kong nationals acquire citizenship. |
| 1996 | Distinction between "economic" and "political" refugees. Asylum seekers denied social benefits. |
| 1998 | Citizens of all dependent territories receive UK citizenship. |

*Civil Rights*

| | |
|---|---|
| 1965 | Racial discrimination in housing and jobs outlawed. |
| 1968 | Racial discrimination in provision of goods and services outlawed. |
| 1970 | Women to get same pay as men for similar work. |
| 1975 | Discrimination on grounds of sex forbidden; Equal Opportunities Commission set up. |
| 1976 | Criminal offense to incite racial hatred; Race Relations Board to assist conciliation among races; Commission for Racial Equality set up to investigate complaints of racial discrimination. |
| 1976 | Discrimination unlawful on grounds of color, race, nationality, or ethnic or national origin. |
| 1986 | Amended 1975 Act prohibiting sexual discrimination in housing, training, provision of goods and services, and employment. |
| 1996 | Women given right of paid maternity leave. |
| 1998 | New offenses of racial harassment and racially motivated violence created. Race Relations Forum established to advise on issues affecting ethnic minority communities. |

---

tion failed and was dissolved. By a 1985 agreement with Britain, the Republic of Ireland was given a consultative role about the future of Ulster. Attempts in 1991 to foster talks among Britain, the main constitutional parties in Northern Ireland, and the Irish government on home rule for Ulster failed. In December 1993 the British and Irish prime ministers agreed on the Downing Street Declaration for general principles for peace talks on Northern Ireland. These include agreement of the people in both the north and the south (Ireland). Since then the leaders of

## REVIEW 2.1

### THE IRISH PROBLEM

| | |
|---|---|
| 1690 | Battle of the Boyne—Catholic King James II beaten by Protestant King William III of Orange. Siege of Derry. |
| 1795 | Battle of the Diamond—the two religions clash over land ownership in Armagh. Orange Society formed. |
| 1886 | Gladstone introduces Home Rule bill, which fails. |
| 1893 | Second Home Rule bill leads to violence. |
| 1912 | Protestants sign Ulster Covenant to resist home rule. |
| 1916 | Easter rebellion in Dublin against Britain. |
| 1920 | Ireland becomes independent, but six northern counties form Northern Ireland or Ulster. |
| 1937 | Ireland becomes Eire. |
| 1968 | Riots in Londonderry over Catholic civil rights. |
| 1969 | Police ban most marches. British troops in streets of Northern Ireland. |
| 1972 | Britain suspends Northern Ireland Parliament and assumes direct rule. |
| 1985 | Anglo-Irish agreement on search for a peaceful solution. |
| 1993 | British and Irish prime ministers agree on the Downing Street Declaration for general principles for peace talks on Northern Ireland, which include agreement of the people in both the north and the south (Ireland). |
| 1995–97 | Peace talks break down and then resume with cease-fire. |
| 1997 | Parades Commission to deal with contentious parades. |
| 1998 | Multiparty negotiations lead to Good Friday Agreement. Assembly to be elected. General de Chastelain appointed to supervise decommissioning of paramilitary arms. |
| 1999 | Police Service of Northern Ireland to replace Royal Ulster Constabulary, to get a balance between Protestants and Catholics. |
| 2000 | Power-sharing executive in Northern Ireland forms coalition, then suspends, then resumes. |
| 2001 | IRA declares it will decommission its weapons; process begins to place them permanently and verifiably beyond use. |
| 2002 | Four years of power sharing government between Protestant and Catholic communities in Northern Ireland ended, and direct rule from London imposed. |

the different parties in Ulster have met with the British government to discuss the peace process. The Good Friday Agreement reached in Belfast in 1998 led to the establishment of the Northern Ireland Assembly and elections to it.

In Scotland after the Act of Union of 1707, the continuation of separate educational, legal, and religious institutions and a local government system provided the country with a distinctive historical and cultural identity. But not until recently has there been a revival of the political nationalism that was strong in the eighteenth century. Economically, industrial production and commerce in Scotland has been tied to the rest of the British economy, with which it trades two-thirds of its imports and exports.

Politically, Scotland sends 72 members to the House of Commons, which is 11 percent of the total members even though Scotland represents only 9.5 percent of Britain's electorate. The British system responded to Scottish concerns by the establishment in London of the position of Secretary of State for Scotland, a cabinet minister who had responsibility for the formulation and execution of a wide range of policies.

The argument that Scotland's problems, especially those of ailing heavy industry and shipbuilding, were due to neglect or exploitation by London, the increased emphasis on national pride, and the discovery of large oil reserves in the North Sea off the Scottish coast stimulated the Scottish National Party (SNP) to become the proponent of self-government in the 1960s.

In the sixteenth century, Wales was united with England and became part of the English system of administration. Nationalist expression had been more literary and cultural than political. But for some years demands were made for administrative arrangements similar to those of Scotland. In 1964 a Welsh Office was set up in Cardiff, the Welsh capital, and a Secretary of State for Wales with a seat in the British cabinet was appointed. In Parliament, to which Wales sends 40 MPs, there was a Welsh Grand Committee to discuss Welsh affairs in general, as well as all legislation pertaining to Wales.

In 1969 a Royal Commission on the Constitution—the Kilbrandon Commission—was appointed to examine the problem of Scotland and Wales. Reporting in 1973, the commission rejected both the division of the United Kingdom into independent states (separatism) and the creation of states sharing sovereignty with Parlia-ment (federalism). It recommended the devolution of political and administrative powers from London for both countries. The British Parliament in 1978 passed two statutes that would establish elected assemblies with responsibility for a wide range of internal affairs in Scotland and Wales.

Both statutes were submitted to referendums in March 1979 with the stipulation that they would only take effect if at least 40 percent of the electorate, as well as a simple majority, approved. The voters in Wales rejected the statute by nearly 4 to 1. Scottish voters approved their statute by 51.6 percent of the voters but only 32.5 percent of the total electorate. Both statutes were therefore repealed in June 1979.

Twenty years later, in 1998, in major constitutional changes, devolution was introduced for both Scotland and Wales with the creation of a Scottish Parliament, the first since 1707, and a Welsh Assembly, the first since 1495, with local executives to follow with responsibilities formerly performed by government departments in London. The Scottish Parliament in Edinburgh, with 129 members, has lawmaking and some tax powers, while the Welsh Assembly in Cardiff, with 60 members, has powers only of secondary legislation and is wholly dependent for its budget on an annual grant from London.

## A CLOSER LOOK 2.3

## THE WEST LOTHIAN QUESTION

Devolution now exists for Scotland and Wales, but what about England? Raised by a Scottish Labour MP during the devolution debates in the 1970s, the West Lothian question concerned the anomaly of Scottish MPs being able to vote on legislation relating purely to England and Wales when English and Welsh MPs could not vote on purely Scottish issues. Scotland and Wales still send members, in disproportionate numbers, to the House of Commons and therefore deal with issues pertinent to England, but English MPs cannot deal with Scottish or Welsh issues. The question now is whether an English Parliament should be established for the 80 percent of British citizens who live in England.

The government has acknowledged the problem in a number of ways. Among these attempts were the introduction of Regional Development Agencies for England, appointed by ministers, supposedly to coordinate regional economic development; some unelected Regional Chambers; a standing committee on regional affairs in the House of Commons; select committees in the House of MPs from English constituencies; and a joint ministerial committee on devolution. Little visible result was evident by 2002 on this complicated constitutional issue.

## TABLE 2.4

### THE SCOTTISH PARLIAMENT AND THE WELSH ASSEMBLY, 1999 ELECTIONS

*Election to Scottish Parliament: 129 members*

| Party | First Vote (%) | Second Vote (%) | Constituency | PR | Total |
|---|---|---|---|---|---|
| | | | **Seats** | | |
| Labour | 38.8 | 33.8 | 53 | 3 | 56 |
| SNP | 28.7 | 27.0 | 7 | 28 | 35 |
| Conservative | 15.6 | 15.4 | 0 | 18 | 18 |
| Liberal Democrat | 14.2 | 12.5 | 12 | 5 | 17 |
| Others | 2.7 | 11.4 | 1 | 2 | 3 |
| Turnout: 59 percent | | | 73 | 56 | 129 |

*Election to Welsh Assembly: 60 members*

| Party | First Vote (%) | Second Vote (%) | Constituency | PR | Total |
|---|---|---|---|---|---|
| | | | **Seats** | | |
| Labour | 37.6 | 35.4 | 27 | 1 | 28 |
| Plaid Cymru | 28.4 | 30.5 | 9 | 8 | 17 |
| Conservative | 15.9 | 16.5 | 1 | 8 | 9 |
| Liberal Democrat | 13.4 | 12.6 | 3 | 3 | 6 |
| Others | 4.7 | 5.1 | 0 | 0 | 0 |
| Turnout: 46 percent | | | 40 | 20 | 60 |

*Source:* Inter-Parliamentary Union.

Elections took place in both countries in 1999 by a form of proportional representation; each elector cast two votes, (1) in the familiar constituency method of victory by plurality (first past the post), and (2) by regional party lists and proportional share of seats (see Table 2.4).

## POLITICAL PROBLEMS

Britain confronts a number of complex political problems. The relationship of the four countries within the United Kingdom is changing. The impact of membership in the European Union on British sovereignty and on the rights and duties of citizens is uncertain. The growing numbers of nonwhite immigrants have led to greater racial tension. There are now six parliamentary constituencies in which nonwhites are a majority, and ten others in which they are prominent.

The British system has been troubled by difficult economic, social, and constitutional issues.

The weakness of the currency was shown when Britain withdrew from the Exchange Rate Mechanism of the European Union in 1992. The downturns in the economic cycle helped increase ethnic tensions which led to urban riots, mostly of blacks, in 1981 and 1985. The monarchy has come under sharp criticism with questioning of the finances and cost of the Queen and her household and concern about the drama of the failure of the marriage of the heir to the throne, Prince Charles, and Princess Diana. The question arises of whether a divorced Charles could become King, and therefore head of the Church of England.

Among the various problems facing Britain today some are high on the political agenda. One is a certain dissatisfaction with some aspects of the political system and of the unwritten constitution. Proposals have been made for modernization of procedures of the House of Commons, change of the electoral system, further reform or abolition of the House of Lords, regional auton-

## REVIEW 2.2

### A SUMMARY OF RECENT CONSTITUTIONAL CHANGE

| | |
|---|---|
| 1998 | Devolution to Scotland and Wales, and new Assembly in Northern Ireland. |
| 1999 | Regional Development Agencies, and 8 Regional Chambers, voluntary bodies, to scrutinize the RDAs, which are nondepartmental public bodies accountable through ministers to Parliament. |
| 1999 | Direct election of mayor of London, with considerable authority but limited financial powers. Creation of a Greater London Authority. |
| 1999 | Reform of House of Lords—interim arrangement with elimination of hereditary peers except 92. |
| 1998 | Human Rights Act incorporates the 1950 European Convention on Human Rights into British law; British courts will enforce the provisions of the Convention. |
| 1998 | Accepted Social Chapter of Maastricht Treaty of European Union; Britain bound to European Union rules on working life, equal treatment of the sexes, and protection of workers. |
| 1999 | European Parliament Elections Act adopts proportional representation system and party lists for voting in European Parliament elections. |

omy for England, and peace in Northern Ireland. Above all, some call for a bill of rights, on U.S. lines, to provide better protection for basic British freedoms.

A second problem is the increased attempt to decentralize government after the reduction of powers of local authorities, and the more central intervention in decisions about universities, police authorities, and health service regions in postwar policies.

A third issue is the strong difference of opinion in political parties and in the country about the development and powers of the European Union and the extent to which its laws and regulations may limit the sovereignty of Britain.

A continuing economic and political problem is the disparity between an ailing industrial northern England and the more prosperous service economy in southern England. The gap is growing in income, average disposable household income, number of unemployed, and migration patterns. The population of London has grown considerably in the 1990s, while that in the northeast has declined.

## A CLOSER LOOK 2.4

### BRITISH SOVEREIGNTY

Traditional British sovereignty, the final legal and political authority to make decisions, is affected in a number of ways. International economic globalization, especially freedom of capital movements, has influenced and placed limits on domestic monetary policies and meant more difficulty in controlling exchange and interest rates. Britain is not independent from the continent of Europe politically, nor from the world economically.

Politically, the UK is bound by the European Union treaties and decisions, and by the European Convention on Human Rights (ECHR) and the European Court of Human Rights, which has found the UK guilty in some cases of violation of rights. The 1998 Human Rights Act requires that all British legislation be implemented in a way compatible with the ECHR. British courts have also accepted the ruling of the EU's Court of Justice of the primacy of EU law over national law; a UK statute will not be given effect by the courts if it is incompatible with EU law.

# THE NATURE OF BRITISH SOCIETY

Political systems inevitably reflect economic, social, and cultural forces in the country, though there is no inevitable or automatic link among them. The British system has reflected, among other forces, a prosperous industrialized economy; sharp differences between social classes; the aristocratic values such as obedience, fair play, and sportsmanship that lasted into the present era; the ideal. of the gentleman; a working-class subculture; and religious differences.

Certain significant characteristics of and changes in contemporary British society will be discussed in the following sections.

## A Postindustrial Society

Britain is now a postindustrial society in which there has been a shift from the production of goods to a service economy, with a very prominent professional and technical class and with a sophisticated technology. Services now account for 80 percent of the workforce of the country, industry for 19 percent, and agriculture for 1 percent. There has been a dramatic increase in the service sector in the last two decades. Services now account for about 67 percent of the gross domestic product, manufacturing for about 25 percent, construction for 6 percent, and agriculture, fishing, and mining for about 1.7 percent.

The public sector grew at a faster rate than the private sector until the late 1970s, after which private employment increased relative to public jobs. Of the 29 million in the current workforce, 23.9 million (82.4 percent) are employed in the private sector, and 5.1 million in the public sector. About 3.5 million of the latter work for the government. The number of self-employed rose from 1.9 million in 1979 to 3.4 million in 2000.

About 7.1 million belong to the 221 trade unions; of these, 6.8 million in 74 unions are affiliated with the Trades Union Congress (TUC). Union membership has declined 40 percent since 1979, especially among manual workers and particularly in southeast England. This decline can be attributed to the replacement of old industries, a base for strong unionization, by high-technology firms; the increase of the self-employed to 3.4 million; and the privatization which reduced the numbers working in the public sector, a union stronghold. By 2002, only 30 percent of British workers were unionists. The largest union is Unison, public employees, with 1.2 million members. The highest density of union members are those working in public authorities, and the lowest in agriculture and in services.

Women, over 40 percent of the labor force, are now almost as equally unionized as men. With their consciousness raised by the women's liberation movement, women have been more eager to obtain a job than remain in the home. Women in Britain now tend to marry younger, have children later, bear fewer children, and stay in a job at least until their first child is born. Increasingly they return to full- or part-time work after having children. The higher divorce rate has reinforced the trend for women to work.

Women have been protected by law in a number of ways. The 1970 Equal Pay Act states that women are entitled to the same pay as men when performing similar work. The 1975 Sex Discrimination Act makes sexual discrimination unlawful in employment, education, occupational training, and provisions of housing, goods, facilities, and services. With regard to both statutes, the Equal Opportunities Commission exists to promote equal opportunities for women. Through legislation in 1996 and 2000, women have the right of paid time off before and after pregnancy. Yet women are still underrepresented in senior managerial positions and overrepresented in lower paid, part-time work.

There has been a steady rise in the general standard of living and in the consumption of goods, especially of housing, cars, better-quality food and drink, and recreation, and more credit borrowing. At the beginning of the twentieth century only 1 in 10 families owned their own home; in 1952 the proportion was less than 1 in 3; by 2001, 68 percent of the 21 million homes in Britain were owner-occupied. In spite of occupational changes, Britain is still a highly urban as well as densely populated country. About 60 percent of the population lives in cities of over 50,000 people, though only 28 percent of the population of Wales does so. Only one-fifth of the total population lives in rural communities. In recent years there has been an increase in the population of the suburbs and a decline in those in the inner-city areas.

## A Class Society

Britain has remained a divided, though changing, society in which people of different occupations, income levels, and education have different lifestyles, modes of dress, speech patterns and accents, favorite games, social habits, ways of leisure, and mortality rates due to different standards of health. It has been dominated by an elite, albeit an open elite into which the successful could enter, that has occupied the key positions in the financial world, the professions, government administration, and the Conservative Party. The principles of the elite have been moderation, fair play, loyalty, and its ideal of the gentleman and the cultivated amateur.

A class theory of politics would argue that class is the major factor influencing voting behavior and that the political parties are representative of the different social classes. In Britain this would mean that the working class would vote for the Labour Party, and the middle and upper classes for the Conservative Party. But this broad generalization is only partly true. About one-third of the working class does not vote Labour, while one-fifth of the middle class does. Nor are the leaders and members of the parties recruited from one class. The programs of the parties do not reflect the interest of one class, as all of them have tried to broaden their appeal.

Britain is still a country with great inequality in the distribution of wealth. About 25 percent of total personal wealth is owned by 1 percent of the adult population and about 61 percent by 10 percent. In 1914 the bottom 90 percent of the population owned 8 percent of all personal wealth; by 1974 they owned 37 percent. The top tenth got 30 percent of pretax income in 1987, compared with the 22 percent obtained by the bottom 50

percent. Britain remains a society in which class differences, due to these inequalities in wealth and income, are strongly felt, and where barriers to social and economic mobility still exist. Yet dramatic changes in the last few years have reduced the old class consciousness, with the shrinkage of the manual working class and with the striking increase in shareholders to 11 million in 1991, compared with 3 million in 1979. This has resulted from three factors: the sale of public enterprises (privatization), employee share schemes, and personal equity plans making it more attractive for small savers to invest.

## A Pluralistic Religious Society

Britain is a pluralistic society in its religious diversity after centuries of discrimination (see Table 2.5). There is now no religious disqualification for public office. (The only exception is the monarch, who must be a member of the established Church of England.) About 40 percent of the population regards itself as secular, unattached to any religion.

***Protestant***    Though few people go to any church on a regular basis, Protestantism is still the dominant religion, with the Anglican Church nominally accounting for 40 percent of the English and 45 percent of the Welsh population. The free or nonconformist churches account for 20 percent of the population in England and 45 percent in Wales.

The Church of England is the established church (the concept of "establishment" derives from this fact) and the monarch is its Supreme Head. The chief dignitaries of the Church—the two archbishops of Canterbury and York, the 43 bishops, and the deans—are formally appointed by the monarch, who accepts the recommendation of the prime minister, who is advised by ecclesiastical representatives. Politically, 26 of the higher clergy sit as members of the House of Lords, but no clergy of the Church of England can sit in the House of Commons. The Church is a large landowner and has considerable possessions in industrial shares and property; however, though many of the senior figures in the Church

**TABLE 2.5**

**ACTIVE FAITH MEMBERSHIP IN THE UNITED KINGDOM**

| Group | Adult Members (in thousands) | | | |
|---|---|---|---|---|
| | 1970 | 1980 | 1990 | 1998 |
| Christian: Trinitarian | 9,272 | 7,529 | 6,624 | 6,012 |
| Anglican | 2,987 | 2,180 | 1,728 | 1,650 |
| Roman Catholic | 2,746 | 2,455 | 2,198 | 1,833 |
| Free Churches | 3,539 | 2,894 | 2,698 | 2,529 |
| Christian: Non-Trinitarian | 276 | 349 | 455 | 537 |
| Hindu | 80 | 120 | 140 | 161 |
| Jewish | 120 | 111 | 101 | 94 |
| Muslim | 130 | 306 | 495 | 637 |
| Sikh | 100 | 150 | 250 | 380 |
| Others | 26 | 52 | 86 | 107 |
| Total membership | 10,004 | 8,617 | 8,151 | 7,928 |

*Source:* Christian Research.

have come from elite backgrounds, the Church does not speak with a monolithic voice in political, social, and economic affairs. The present Archbishop of Canterbury, George Carey, comes from a working-class background. The monarch is also head of the Presbyterian Church of Scotland, which has been the established Church since 1707.

The free or nonconformist Protestant churches, strong in the west of England and in Wales, have historically been critical of or opposed to the establishment. In general, there has been a correlation between areas of religious nonconformity and those of political dissent, associated first with the Liberal Party and later with the Labour Party. The largest of the free churches are the Methodist Church and the Baptist Church.

***Catholicism*** There are some 9 million adherents to Roman Catholicism. The religion is strongest in Northern Ireland, where it accounts for about 40 percent of the population, and in northwest England. Though some old aristocratic families are Catholic, as are some prominent converts and members of the upper class, most Catholics are members of the working class and the majority stem from Irish immigrants. Catholicism has not been the politically divisive issue that it has been in many other political systems, but the Labour Party has sometimes nominated Catholic candidates in heavily Catholic constituencies.

***Other Religions*** The Jewish community dates from 1656, after being expelled from Britain in 1290. In the twentieth century it was increased by immigration from Eastern Europe after pogroms and anti-Semitic outbreaks and from Germany during the Nazi regime in the 1930s. It now consists of about 300,000 people. As a result of the recent immigration of Asians, there is now a considerable number of non-Christian adherents, primarily Muslims, Buddhists, Hindus, and Sikhs. Most live in large urban areas.

Since World War I, religion has not been a divisive political issue, except in Northern Ireland. In general, the correspondence between a particular religion and a particular party has remained—the Anglican Church with Conservatives, the Catholics with Labour and the nonconformists with the Liberals and Labour—but the ties are much less strong, especially among Anglicans, than in previous generations. In the late 1980s, a small Islamic fundamentalist movement emerged, demanding separate status and insisting on Islamic law.

## A Multicultural Society

The population of Britain is not ethnically homogeneous but contains ethnic, religious, and cultural diversities, bringing changes in social structure, geographical mobility, and educational patterns (see Table 2.6). Minority groups can be defined in two ways: Afro-Caribbean (from West Indies and Africa) now about 1 million, and Asian (from India, Pakistan, Bangladesh, Sri Lanka) now about 2 million. The first group tends to be less segregated than the Asian. In East London, public notices are printed in Bengali as well as English. Riots occurred in summer 2001 in northern industrial cities with pockets of poverty and unemployment, where some Asian groups live in self-segregated communities with Islamic schools that receive state funding, halal butchers, and mosques. In Birmingham, where Asian Muslims constitute 12 percent of the total 1 million population, the party based on Pakistani

immigrants has won a number of seats in the local council. The three major political parties ran 57 nonwhite candidates in the 2001 election, of whom 12 were elected.

Nonwhites are younger on average than whites and are more concentrated in the fertile age groups. They are located in the more populous areas of England. About three-fifths of people from black ethnic groups live in London. Indians and Pakistanis are in the midlands and northern England. About 2 million Muslims live in the United Kingdom. There are over 600 mosques and numerous Muslin community centers.

## A Welfare State

The British welfare system developed to deal with problems of poverty and unemployment; to provide for the aged, the sick, and the infirm; and to maintain minimum living standards. The main elements of the current welfare system are the national health service, personal social services, and social security, which now account for about 40 percent of total public expenditure.

The national health service provides almost free treatment for all who want to use it and allows free choice of medical practitioners and hospitals. Personal social services include services for the elderly, the physically disabled and mentally ill, home care, social clubs, and day care for children under age 5. Social security exists to provide a basic standard of living for people in need through nonemployment benefits, retirement pensions, sickness benefit and invalidity pensions, child benefits, benefits to widows, and death grants.

### TABLE 2.6

### ETHNIC GROUPS IN THE UNITED KINGDOM, 2002

| Group | % |
| --- | --- |
| White | 93.2 |
| Nonwhite | 6.7 |
| Caribbean | 0.9 |
| African | 0.7 |
| Other black | 0.5 |
| Indian | 1.7 |
| Pakistani | 1.2 |
| Bangladeshi | 0.5 |
| Chinese | 0.2 |
| Others | 1.1 |

*Source:* U.K. Government, Sationery Office.

## A Mixed Economy

Britain was the first capitalist country in the world when, in the eighteenth and nineteenth centuries, the ownership and control of industry was in private hands. Today it is more appropriate to regard the economy as a mixture of private enterprise and various public controls.

Most manufacturing enterprises are privately owned except for the steel, aeroengine, and (since 1977) most of the aircraft and ship-building industries. Few, since 1945, argued a laissez-faire position and a minimal role for public control over the economy. Although only the left wing of the Labour Party believes in the state ownership of the means of production, distribution, and exchange, most people in the different political parties accepted a substantial role for the state, the largest employer in the country. Since 1979 public policy under the Thatcher and Major governments emphasized the reduction of the state sector, the sale of public enterprises to private ownership, and a freer market economy. This has been continued by the Blair government since 1997.

## THE SOCIALIZATION PROCESS

### Education and Class

Class distinctions have long been a prominent feature of British society. Though classes have been defined in different ways—the easiest way is to talk of the upper class, the upper middle, the lower middle, and the lower class—they differ in accent and language used, dress, style of life, nature of schooling, and occupations.

The educational system has reflected and helped to perpetuate the class structure. In 1944 the system was reorganized and students were streamed into separate modern secondary, technical, and grammar schools. Most students ended their education between 14 and 16 years of age to become manual workers. The occupational pattern and the working-class status of these youngsters who had left school was in most cases set for life. Those who left school at age 18 entered white-collar or minor managerial jobs and became part of the lower middle, sometimes middle, class. Only those who had further education beyond 18 years of age were likely to enter the professions or become managers and executives, the middle-class occupations.

In the 1970s comprehensive schools, which like high schools in the United States provide a wide range of education and educate students of different backgrounds and abilities together, replaced many of the selective secondary and grammar schools to help end the class stratification of educational streaming based on passing of examinations at an early age. During the 1980s, Conservative governments removed many of these comprehensive schools from local government control to enable them to become more selective again. Whether schools are comprehensive, as in the United States, and local government controlled, or selective and self-governing, varies on whether the Labour or Conservative Party, respectively, is in power.

Outside the state system are parochial schools, independent grammar schools stressing academic achievement (many have impressive reputations), and the 260 "public" schools, which are expensive and socially significant. The most prominent of the public schools—such as Eton. Harrow, Winchester, and Rugby—are prestigious institutions, consciously training young people for leadership positions in politics and society by discipline, building of character, and inculcation of traditional values. They have been a unique means of recruiting members of elite groups, constituting an "old boy" network in prominent positions. Though they represent only 4 percent of the British student population, graduates of the public schools, like those of the older universities, have occupied a highly disproportionate number of positions in the cabinet, the House of Commons, the senior civil service, the upper ranks of the armed forces, the High Courts, and the Church of England, as well as in major banking and financial institutions. Perhaps more surprisingly, public school graduates also accounted for 42 percent of the Labour Cabinet in 1966–1970 and 18 percent of Labour MPs in 1978. About 75 percent of Conservative MPs in the House of Commons elected in 1987 attended a public school. Between 1900 and 1985 old Etonians alone accounted for almost one-fourth of government ministers and top ambassadors. It is interesting in light of this that none of the last five prime ministers before Blair, including three conservatives, attended a public school.

Traditionally, higher education has been dominated by Oxford and Cambridge, which have provided the political and social elite. Eight of the last ten prime ministers attended Oxford, as did three-quarters of the present senior judges, two-thirds of the top civil servants, and many of the prominent media personalities.

In the last two decades, there has been a considerable expansion of higher education for both social and educational reasons. The full-time student body has increased to over 844,000, about 20 percent of the 18-year-old population. There are now 47 universities attended by about 270,000 students. Another 250,000 take courses on a wide range of topics at the 35 former poly-technics in England and Wales or attend other colleges providing further education in Britain. The most prestigious of the universities remain Oxford, with its 39 individual colleges, and Cambridge, with 29. Graduates of "Oxbridge" still constitute a high proportion of the elite groups in the country, including the Cabinet and the House of Commons. Nevertheless, the Conservative government in 1991 called for abolishing the distinction between universities and polytechnics, which have increased in importance in recent years, thus removing barriers between academic and vocational education.

Class barriers still exist, linked to educational achievement, in spite of more social mobility and emphasis on meritocracy and equal opportunity. Labour and Conservative prime ministers alike have been critical of the class system. Labour leaders have regarded it as responsible for lack of innovation. Margaret Thatcher attacked the upper-class amateurs in her Conservative Party and in the BBC and Foreign Office; John Major spoke of the need for a classless society.

## A CHANGING BRITAIN

Britain has long been a free and—despite unnecessary secrecy in government—open society. It has also generally been a peaceful society in which the police went unarmed. A sign of increased social problems has been the considerable rise in crime. The increasing violence and the terrorist acts, perpetrated mostly by the IRA

in British cities, have meant that some of the police now carry weapons, though the majority still go unarmed.

Britain is still a significant industrial and economic power. It is the fifth largest trading nation, exporting nearly 9 percent of total exports of manufactured goods by the industrial countries of the world. These exports constitute about one-half of all British exports. Britain still accounts for nearly one-third of all international banking business. About 10 percent of "invisible" trade in the world (banking, insurance, shipping, tourism, and income from overseas investment) is handled by Britain.

As Britain became industrialized, it also became a larger importer of foods and raw materials; today its imports also include a growing proportion of semimanufactured and manufactured goods. For almost 200 years the value of British imports of goods was usually larger than the value of exports. The deficit on this balance of "visible" trade was overcome in the total balance of payments by a surplus on invisible trade, the receipts from which are about one-third of total receipts. But as the deficit in visible trade has increased, partly due to the rise in raw materials prices, the dramatic rise in oil prices, the large contribution to the budget of the European Union, the lower exchange rate of sterling, foreign competition, and the loss of many Commonwealth markets to other industrialized countries, the earnings on invisible trade were often not enough to overcome the deficit.

Britain has suffered the disadvantages, as well as having gotten the rewards, of being the first mature industrial nation in the world and of now having old capital equipment. Its older industries—coal, textiles, and shipbuilding—have contracted, and productivity per worker remained low compared with that of other advanced nations. It suffered from having exported capital abroad rather than using it internally and for being dependent on the international economy, which has made Britain vulnerable to external factors. The persistent balance of payments problem discouraged sustained investment and limited the rate of growth.

The postwar British performance in production, trade, and growth disappointed its political leaders. In the 1950s Britain was one of the ten richest countries in the world. From the mid-1960s to the mid-1970s, the economy grew by only 2.7 percent per year. By 1976 Britain ranked twenty-fourth in per capita gross national product, which was about half that of the United States.

There have been differing explanations for the low level of productivity per worker and the relatively slow economic growth. Some criticize the overmanning of jobs and the restrictive practices and obstructions of the powerful trade unions, which they see as more interested in job security than in increases in production, as well as the immobility of the labor force. Other critics stress inadequate management that is slow to introduce innovations, insufficient research and development, low levels of replacement of capital goods, reluctance to adapt production to new needs, and poor sales drive. The ethos of the social system and the ideal of the cultivated amateur and gentleman have been blamed for the failure to attract well-educated people as industrial managers and for the view of industrial activity as distasteful. Britain's desire to remain an important world power has meant large expenditure on overseas bases, large military forces, and considerable expenditure on nuclear research and development and on expensive delivery vehicles in the attempt to become a nuclear power.

Government policies have been criticized for many reasons: the disincentive of high tax rates, the lack of effective economic planning, the slowness in retraining unemployed workers, the concentration on prestigious and wasteful items such as supersonic aircraft rather than on more profitable industries likely to grow, and the inability to control inflation. Though there is validity in all of these criticisms, much of the British economic problem has been caused by external factors: the inevitable growth of other countries, many of which are industrializing rapidly and some of which are technologically mature; the rising cost of imports of food and raw materials; the loss of protected markets for exports to the former colonies; the sacrifices made by Britain in the two world wars, which seriously depleted British capital and led to the sale of overseas investments; and large external debts.

All British governments tried to solve the economic problem by increasing productivity, growth, and exports; by reducing the rate of inflation; and by maintaining confidence in the British pound. In the decade after 1979 the Thatcher government tried to encourage growth by cutting taxes, controlling the money supply for a time, approving only those wage settlements connected with increases in productivity, and stressing the value of competition. The economy has grown faster, inflation fell, and strikes declined, while trade unionism was weakened. But the share of manufacturing in the economy has declined, and deficits have occurred in some years.

In addition to economic problems and the issue of sovereignty, a new troubling issue is that of international terrorism. This has led to the Terrorism Act 2000, which allows the Home Secretary to ban organizations engaged in violence, in Britain or abroad, to advance a political religious or ideological cause, or to create a serious risk to public health or safety.

## Thinking Critically

1. Can Britain still be considered a unitary state? Do you think that devolution of Scotland and Wales has been helpful from a political and administrative point of view?
2. Do you think that Britain ought to have a written constitution?
3. Is it still valid to talk of British parliamentary sovereignty?
4. From a comparative point of view, would you regard Britain as a class society?
5. Is Britain a country of equal opportunity and affirmative action?

6. Do you believe that Britain should limit immigration?

7. Have economic changes and the increasing concentration of ownership and control of the media in Britain been harmful to free speech and political democracy?

# KEY TERMS

Anglican church *(51)*
Bill of Rights *(40)*
class *(51)*
consensus *(41–42)*
constitutional democracy *(40)*
conventions *(40–41)*
deference *(42)*
devolution *(47)*
Magna Carta *(36)*
majority principle *(40)*
mixed economy *(53–54)*
Northern Ireland (Ulster) *(44)*
Oxbridge *(55)*
pluralistic society *(44)*
postindustrial society *(37, 50)*
privatization *(54)*
public school *(54)*
referendum *(47)*
Reform Acts *(40)*
representative system *(39)*
rule of law *(40)*
sovereignty *(49)*
United Kingdom *(43)*
welfare state *(53)*

# FURTHER READINGS

Bagehot, Walter. *The English Constitution* (Ithaca, NY: Cornell University Press, 1966).

Barker, Rodney. *Political Legitimacy and the State* (Oxford: Clarendon Press,1990).

Beetham, David. *The Legitimation of Power* (London: Macmillan, 1991).

Blackburn, Robert, and Raymond Plant, eds. *Constitutional Reform: The Labour Government's Constitutional Reform Agenda* (New York: Longman, 1999).

Crick, Bernard, ed. *National Identities* (Oxford: Blackwell, 1991).

Dunleavy, Patrick, et al. eds. *Developments in British Politics 6* (London: Macmillan 2000).

Ewing, Keith, and C. A. Gearty. *Freedom under Thatcher: Civil Liberties in Modern Britain* (New York: Oxford University Press, 1990).

Foley, Michael. *The Politics of the British Constitution* (New York: Manchester University Press, 1999).

Gamble, Allen. *The Free Economy and the Strong State: The Politics of Thatcherism* (London: Macmillan, 1988).

Jones, Nicholas. *Sultans of Spin: The Media and the New Labour Government* (London: Orion, 2000).

Jowell, Jeffery, and Dawn Oliver. *The Changing Constitution,* 4th ed. (London: Oxford University Press, 2000).

Kavanagh, Dennis. *British Politics: Continuities and Change,* 4th ed. (London: Oxford University Press, 2000).

Kearney, Hugh. *The British Isles: A History of Four Nations* (New York: Cambridge University Press, 1989).

# B. POLITICAL PROCESSES AND INSTITUTIONS

## VOTING

The electoral system for the House of Commons is a simple one, comprising single-member constituencies, plurality decision or top-of-the-poll winner, and the principle of one person, one vote. Since the first Reform Act of 1832, which began the process of standardizing the qualifications for voting, the suffrage has gradually been extended to the whole citizenry over the age of 18. During the same period, factors such as the necessary ownership of property, double or triple voting based on ownership of a business or possession of an MA degree, residential qualification, feminine gender, and deliberately unequally sized constituencies have been eliminated (see Table 2.7).

Registration of voters is the responsibility of the local authorities, not of the individual, and an annual register of those eligible to vote in each constituency is issued every February. Since 1948, a postal vote has been possible for those who are incapable of voting in person, have moved from the constituency, or will be away on business. Middle-class voters are more likely to register for a postal vote than working-class voters, and the Conservative organization is better able to mobilize postal voters than other parties.

There are now 659 constituencies with boundaries that are a compromise between population and geographical size. In 1944, four boundary commissions—one each for England, Wales, Scotland, and Northern Ireland—were set up to ensure an equitable relationship between

| TABLE 2.7 | | |
|---|---|---|
| **EXTENSION OF THE FRANCHISE** | | |
| **Year** | **Main Group Enfranchised** | **Other Features** |
| 1832 | Industrial middle class | Redistribution of seats from small boroughs to the counties and towns |
| | | Registration of voters necessary |
| | | Increased suffrage by 217,000 |
| 1867 | Urban workers | Increased suffrage by 1 million |
| 1872 | | Secret ballot |
| 1883 | | Bribery and corrupt electoral practices become criminal offenses |
| 1884 | Agricultural workers | Increased suffrage by 2 million |
| 1885 | | Equal-sized constituencies |
| 1918 | Women over age 30 | Increased suffrage by 12.5 million |
| | | Redistribution of seats |
| | | Limit to two votes (places of residence and business or university) |
| 1928 | Women over age 21 | Increased suffrage by 7 million |
| | | Universal suffrage over age 21 |
| 1948 | | One person, one vote |
| | | Abolition of university vote and seats |
| | | Abolition of business vote |
| | | Redistribution of seats |
| 1969 | Persons over age 18 | Increased suffrage by 3 million |

representation and population and to recommend, every five to seven years, alteration of constituency boundaries as population shifts. Wales and Scotland are deliberately overrepresented as a concession to nationalist sentiment. An Electoral Commission, an independent body, now oversees controls on donations to and campaign spending by political parties and others, and reviews electoral law and practice.

Election by plurality has helped to sustain the system of two major parties. The Conservative and Labour parties have shared the bulk of the electoral vote and seats in the House of Commons. These two parties alternated in political power for almost the same number of years between 1945 and 1979—the Conservatives remained in power from 1979 to 1997—while until 1983 the third party, the Liberal, had not obtained more than 14 seats (see Figure 2.2).

The plurality system has produced serious inequities and distortions of the will of the people at both the level of the individual single-member constituency and the national level. At the individual constituency level, seats may be won by a minority vote where there are more than two parties and the successful candidate polls fewer votes than those of all the other candidates. In February 1974 there were 408 seats (64.3 percent of the total) won by less than a majority. Between 1945 and 1979, 30 percent of all seats were won by a minority vote. At the national level the opinion of the people may be distorted and political parties may not be truly represented in proportion to the votes they receive in the country, as is shown in Table 2.8.

There is no exact correlation between the votes obtained by a party in the country as a whole and the number of seats it wins in the House of Commons. Indeed, it may even happen, as in 1951 and February 1974, that the party with the smaller percentage of votes in the country may win more seats than the party with a larger percentage of votes. Labour in 2001 won 62 percent of seats with only 40 percent of the vote.

A second problem is that a relatively small change in electoral opinion may produce a much larger proportional change in the distribution of seats between the parties. This disproportionate result is produced by changes in voting in the "marginal seats," those that are normally won by small numbers of votes.

The main inequity in the system is that the Liberals, in spite of considerable support all over the country, have not won more than a few seats in the postwar period until 1997. Unlike a regional party such as the Scottish National Party (SNP) or the Plaid Cymru, whose votes are concentrated in a small number of constituencies, the Liberal and, in 1983 and 1987, the Social Democratic vote was spread throughout the country. The Liberal Democrats only got 20 seats in 1992 with 17.8 percent of the vote. Minority parties are underrepresented in the House of Commons.

The present system is unfortunate for the Liberal Democrats and other minor parties in two other respects. The first is that candidates lose their deposit—the registration fee paid in order to run for election—if they get less than 5 percent of the constituency vote; in 1992, 897 candidates lost deposits of £500 each. The second is that Liberal Democrat electoral support is very fluid. Persons who might vote Liberal are reluctant to do so if they believe the candidate is likely to lose and the party as a whole will do badly. They might prefer to influence the outcome of the election by voting for a candidate of one of the two major parties. Not surprisingly, the Liberal Party and the former Social Democratic Party (SDP) advocated a change in the electoral system. But the two major parties are still unwilling to approve a change because they benefit from the present system. This method has helped perpetuate the two-party system in the postwar period by normally producing a majority of seats for one of the two major parties, which is then able to form a government. Not since 1935 has one party obtained 50 percent of the total poll, but parties have had comfortable majorities in 12 of the 16 postwar elections. A different electoral system would result in a fairer distribution of seats in relation to the votes cast for the parties; but it would also lead to an increase in the number of parties represented in the House of Commons, make it difficult to obtain a majority, and therefore change the formation and functioning of government.

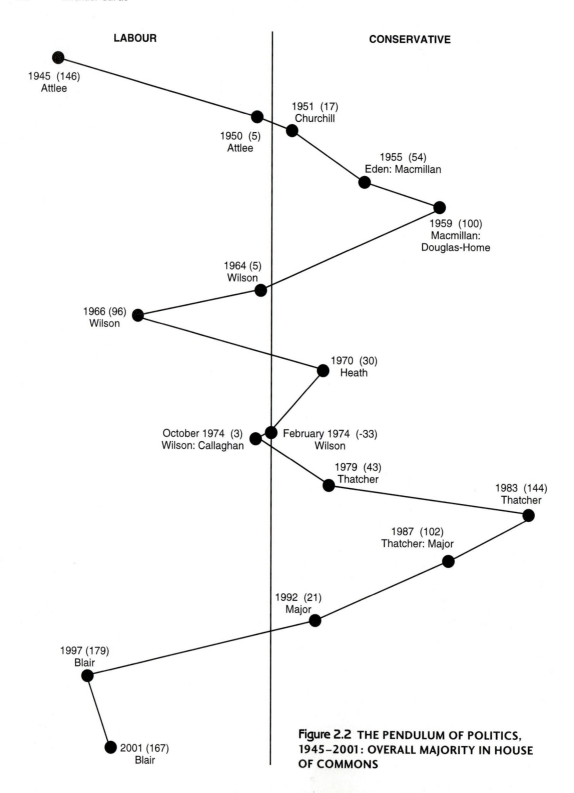

LABOUR                                                CONSERVATIVE

1945 (146)
Attlee

1951 (17)
Churchill

1950 (5)
Attlee

1955 (54)
Eden: Macmillan

1959 (100)
Macmillan:
Douglas-Home

1964 (5)
Wilson

1966 (96)
Wilson

1970 (30)
Heath

October 1974 (3)          February 1974 (-33)
Wilson: Callaghan          Wilson

1979 (43)
Thatcher

1983 (144)
Thatcher

1987 (102)
Thatcher: Major

1992 (21)
Major

1997 (179)
Blair

2001 (167)
Blair

**Figure 2.2 THE PENDULUM OF POLITICS,
1945–2001: OVERALL MAJORITY IN HOUSE
OF COMMONS**

**TABLE 2.8**

**GENERAL ELECTIONS, 1974–2001**

| Year | % of Votes Cast | | | | Number of Seats Won | | | | Total number of seats | Turnout % of electorate |
|------|------|------|----------|--------|------|------|----------|--------|------|------|
| | Con. | Lab. | Lib.Dem. | Others | Con. | Lab. | Lib.Dem. | Others | | |
| 1974 (Feb) | 38.2 | 37.2 | 19.3 | 5.7 | 297 | 301 | 14 | 23 | 635 | 78.7 |
| 1974 (Oct) | 35.8 | 39.3 | 18.3 | 6.7 | 277 | 319 | 13 | 26 | 635 | 72.8 |
| 1979 | 43.9 | 36.9 | 13.8 | 5.4 | 339 | 269 | 11 | 16 | 635 | 72.0 |
| 1983 | 42.4 | 27.6 | 25.4[a] | 4.6 | 397 | 209 | 23 | 21 | 650 | 72.7 |
| 1987 | 42.3 | 30.8 | 22.6[a] | 4.3 | 376 | 229 | 22 | 23 | 650 | 75.3 |
| 1992 | 41.8 | 34.4 | 17.8[b] | 5.8 | 336 | 271 | 20 | 24 | 651 | 77.7 |
| 1997 | 31.4 | 44.4 | 17.2 | 7.0 | 165 | 418[c] | 46 | 29 | 659 | 71.3 |
| 2001 | 31.7 | 40.7 | 18.3 | 9.3 | 166 | 412[c] | 52 | 28 | 659 | 59.4 |

[a]Combined vote of the Liberal and Social Democratic parties (Alliance)
[b]Liberal Democratic Party
[c]Excludes the Speaker

## IS THE ELECTORAL SYSTEM WORKING?

The present electoral system has been defended essentially on the grounds that it provides one of the two major parties with a comfortable majority in the House of Commons. The winning party can then form a strong government which is able to formulate a coherent policy that will be approved by Parliament. This has generally been true in the postwar period when the Conservative and Labour Parties have obtained the bulk of the electoral vote and one of them has obtained a majority of seats. The peak was reached in 1951, when their combined vote was 96.8 percent of the poll and 79.9 percent of the total electorate.

But from 1951 there was a steady drop in their electoral support, as well as a decline in the proportion of those voting in general. The decline in strength of the two major parties resulted in February 1974 in a minority government, with Labour getting 33 seats less than an absolute majority, and in October 1974 in an overall majority of only 3 seats. The two major parties got only 72 percent of the poll in 2001 (see Table 2.9).

**TABLE 2.9**

**PERCENT SHARE OF THE VOTE BY THE TWO MAJOR PARTIES, SELECTED ELECTIONS**

| Election | % Total Electorate | % Actual Vote | Seats Won | | % Seats Won by 2 parties | Total Seats |
|------|------|------|------|------|------|------|
| | | | Con. | Lab. | | |
| 1945 | 64.6 | 88.1 | 213 | 393 | 94.1 | 640 |
| 1951 | 79.9 | 96.8 | 321 | 295 | 98.6 | 625 |
| 1966 | 68.1 | 89.8 | 253 | 363 | 97.8 | 630 |
| 1974 (Oct.) | 54.6 | 75.0 | 277 | 319 | 94.0 | 635 |
| 1983 | 50.9 | 70.0 | 397 | 209 | 93.2 | 650 |
| 1992 | 58.8 | 76.3 | 336 | 271 | 93.2 | 651 |
| 1997 | 53.1 | 75.8 | 165 | 419 | 88.5 | 659 |
| 2001 | 43.0 | 72.4 | 166 | 412 | 87.5 | 659 |

The decline in recent electoral support for the two major parties is attributable to two main factors: the rise in nationalist sentiment and in Liberal-Social Democratic support, and the decrease in the strength of partisanship for the Conservative and Labour Parties.

The cumulative rise in Scottish nationalist strength has been rapid in recent elections. The SNP slogan "It's Scotland's oil" appealed to those who believe that Scotland should control the North Sea oil revenues. By 1974 the SNP had become a broad-based party drawing support from all social classes, geographical regions, and age groups, and from former voters, especially younger people, from other parties. In 2001 it got the second highest proportion of votes in Scotland (see Table 2.10).

In October 1974 the Welsh Plaid Cymru won three seats, with 10.8 percent of the Welsh vote, and came in second in six constituencies, but its strength was largely confined to the rural, Welsh-speaking part of the country. Influenced by literary figures, the party has been more concerned about the extinction of the Welsh culture and language than about broader political issues. The Welsh protest vote against the major parties—unlike the Scottish, which has increasingly gone to the nationalist party—has often gone to the Liberals and more recently to Labour (see Table 2.10).

The Ulster Unionists, once automatically associated with the Conservative Party, are now more independent. Elections in Northern Ireland had little reference to the rest of the United Kingdom and were primarily concerned with political affairs in Ulster since 1974.

Many electors have a partisan self-image or psychological commitment to one of the two major parties, but there has been a drop in support for them. The Conservative vote fell in 1997, and in 2001 to 31 percent, the lowest in its history. Labour lost considerable support in the 1980s. In 1979 the party got the votes of less than half of the working-class voters. But after 1983 it recovered a considerable part of the working-class vote. Both parties have experienced a decline in membership, a weakening of party allegiance, and expressions of dissatisfaction with their leadership.

Nevertheless, despite the decline in the major party vote of the electorate as a consequence of the rise of minor parties and the decline in partisanship, there has not been a similar decrease in the number of seats gained by the major parties. The working of the present electoral system still allowed Conservatives and Labour to obtain 87 percent of the seats while getting only 72 percent of the electoral vote in 2001.

## ELECTIONS

When are general elections held? The whole House of Commons is elected for a period of five years, but only two Parliaments since 1945 have lasted the full allotted time. Most elections are called by the prime minister at a time thought best for the ruling party to win. Campaigns last less than a month, and in recent years, especially because of television coverage, they have concentrated on the major party leaders.

---

**TABLE 2.10**

**VOTING IN SCOTLAND AND WALES FOR HOUSE OF COMMONS, 2001**

| Scotland: turnout 58.2% | | | Wales: turnout 61.6% | | |
|---|---|---|---|---|---|
| Party | % Vote | Seats | Party | % Vote | Seats |
| SNP | 20.1 | 5 | Plaid Cymru | 14.3 | 4 |
| Labour | 43.9 | 56 | Labour | 48.6 | 34 |
| Conservative | 15.6 | 1 | Conservative | 21.0 | 0 |
| Liberal Democrat | 16.4 | 10 | Liberal Democrat | 13.8 | 2 |
| Others | 4.0 | 0 | Others | 2.3 | 0 |

*Source:* The Constitutional Unit: Constitutional Update.

## THE JUNE 2001 GENERAL ELECTION

Britain in June 2001 had a strong economy, low inflation, low interest rates, an independent Bank of England, a mostly unified Labour Party, a divided Conservative Party, and a new leader of the Liberal Democrats (since 1999). The Labour government had not lost any by-election between 1997 and 2001. The electoral system favored Labour, and the British press was mainly supporting Labour at the election. The Labour campaign was the most effective. Conservative organization was weak at the local level; many constituencies were without a full-time Tory agent. The Liberal Democrats seemed to be left of Labour, calling for more spending on public services and speedy entry into the euro single currency. Labour focused on health, education, transport, law and order, and information technology. The Conservatives called for tax cuts, limits on state intervention, no euro during the next parliamentary term, and no participation in a military structure independent of NATO. Conservative leader William Hague had low rating as "most capable leader." The parties concentrated on marginal seats.

The 3,318 candidates included 375 women and 63 persons of ethnic minorities (blacks and Asians). Almost all constituencies in Great Britain were contested by the three major parties. The Scottish National Party (SNP) contested all 73 seats in Scotland, and the Welsh nationalists, Plaid Cymru, all 40 seats in Wales. The UK Independence Party, an anti–European Union party, put up 420 candidates, the Greens 149, and the far-right British National Party 50, mostly in northern England where racial tensions were high in some cities.

The June 2001 election saw a dramatic drop in turnout; it was 59.4 percent, the lowest since 1918. More people abstained than voted for the winning party. About 60 percent of young people abstained. Many people took a Labour victory for granted. The result was a Labour landslide in terms of seats. Labour was reelected with 40.7 percent of the vote and 412 seats. In 1997, Labour had the biggest overall majority in the House of Commons in recent years. Yet in 2001, with almost the same majority, it got fewer votes (10.7 million) than any government since 1924. In the 1997 and 2001 elections, Labour got less than 50 percent of the vote. Labour won a considerable part of the middle-class vote, marginal seats, and owner-occupiers. The Conservative Party suffered its second consecutive defeat, getting 31.7 percent of the vote and 166 seats in 2001. In 1997 the party had received 31.4 percent of the vote and 165 seats, its worst performance since 1832. Its vote fell from 1992 to 2001 by 40 percent, to 8.3 million. The Conservatives lost the upwardly mobile, skilled working-class male in the southeast, to whom the Tories appealed in the 1980s. They won no seat in Scotland in 1997, and only one in 2001. The Conservatives won no seat in Wales in either election, though they were the second party in terms of votes (21 percent). They won no seat in any large city or town outside London. In some areas the party's candidates came in third. It lost many of its stronghold seats in southeast England, the old conservative working-class, and marginal seats. It suffered in both elections by tactical voting by Labour and Liberal Democrats in some individual constituencies to defeat the Tories though there was no formal pact to do so. William Hague resigned immediately after the 2001 election, the first Conservative leader in 80 years to have resigned without having been prime minister.

The Liberal Democrats made considerable gains in seats in 2001, with 18.3 percent of the vote and 52 seats; in 1997, they had received 17.2 percent and 46 seats. The 2001 result was the best for any third party since 1923. The Liberal Democratic Party now has representation in all regions of the country. It offered the main challenge to Labour in working-class areas, and to Conservatives in rural areas. It got more votes than the Conservatives in Scotland and was second in a number of northern constituencies. The UK Independence Party, the Greens, and the BNP got about 2 percent of the vote and no seats. The SNP got 1.8 percent and 5 seats, and Plaid Cymru 0.7 percent and 4 seats. Parties in Northern Ireland got 2.8 percent and 18 seats.

Women were elected to 118 seats in 2001, down from 120 in 1997. Ethnic minorities, who held 9 seats in 1997, were elected to 12 seats in 2001, all from Labour. The June 2001 election saw considerable class dealignment. Labour got substantial support from the salaried middle class and public sector professionals.

By-elections in an individual constituency are held on the death or resignation of a member of Parliament (MP). The number of by-elections during the life of a Parliament thus depends on the duration of the Parliament and the age of MPs.

There are two interesting features of by-elections. The first is that the vote is always considerably lower than in the same constituency at general elections. The second is that the voters usually register a more antigovernment view than they did at the previous general election, thus decreasing the strength of the government party in the House of Commons. However, Labour between 1997 and 2001 did not lose a single by-election.

There are no primaries or nominating conventions in British politics. Primaries are virtually impossible in the British context because of the unpredictable timing of elections. Almost all candidates are sponsored by a political party. It has been rare for a nonparty candidate to run or for a candidate not associated with a major party to win.

Any person over age 21 can stand as a candidate, with certain exceptions: those who are disqualified from voting; clergymen of the churches of England, Scotland, and Ireland, and of the Roman Catholic Church; and people holding certain offices, including judges, civil servants, members of the armed forces, police officers, and various public officials, except members of the government. Candidates need not reside in their constituencies.

One requirement is that each candidate must deposit £500 with the registrar, which is returned if the candidate gets over 5 percent of the total vote in a constituency.

## Who Are the Candidates?

An implicit problem in representative democracies is that the candidates and the representatives elected are not a model of their constituents. The British system bears out this generalization. The percentage of male candidates is far greater than the percentage of men in the general population, and candidates are wealthier and better educated than the average constituent (see Table 2.11).

Among Conservative candidates it is noticeable that 57 percent attended a public school, 35 percent went to Oxbridge (Oxford or Cambridge), and 33 percent to some other university. What is perhaps more surprising in a party that gets most of its support from the working class is that 14 percent of the Labour candidates went to public school, 13 percent went to Oxbridge, and 45 percent to some other university.

In 1992 the two dominant occupations among the candidates were business and the professions. Most Conservative professionals were lawyers, while most Labour professionals were teachers at some educational level. The Liberals also had a high proportion of teachers. The Conservatives have become a less aristocratic group and Labour more professional.

**A CLOSER LOOK 2.6**

### SOME RECORD POSTWAR ELECTIONS

- Labour's largest share of the vote: 48.8 percent in 1951.
- Labour's lowest share of the vote: 27.6 percent in 1983.
- Conservatives' lowest share of the vote: 31.4 percent in 1997.
- Largest overall majority: 179 by Labour in 1997; 144 by Conservatives in 1983.
- Best third-party performance: 25.4 percent by the Alliance (Liberals and Social Democrats) in 1983, though only 23 seats.
- Highest voter turnout: 84 percent in 1950.
- Lowest voter turnout: 59.4 percent in 2001.

## TABLE 2.11

### EDUCATION AND OCCUPATIONS OF CANDIDATES, 2001

| | Labour | | Conservative | | Liberal Democrat | |
|---|---|---|---|---|---|---|
| | Total | Elected | Total | Elected | Total | Elected |
| *Education* | | | | | | |
| State secondary | 461 | 342 | 360 | 60 | 507 | 34 |
| Public school | 103 | 68 | 280 | 106 | 132 | 18 |
| Oxford or Cambridge | 88 | 65 | 145 | 79 | 75 | 14 |
| All universities | 420 | 275 | 422 | 138 | 356 | 36 |
| *Main Occupations* | | | | | | |
| Barrister | 25 | 13 | 46 | 28 | 9 | 2 |
| Solicitor | 28 | 10 | 47 | 13 | 23 | 4 |
| Accountant | 5 | 2 | 25 | 3 | 31 | 1 |
| Civil service | 51 | 30 | 15 | 2 | 26 | 3 |
| Military | 2 | 1 | 20 | 11 | 8 | — |
| University and college teachers | 66 | 49 | 7 | 1 | 34 | 3 |
| School teachers | 81 | 49 | 25 | 6 | 75 | 9 |
| Business: directors and executives | 29 | 15 | 172 | 49 | 78 | 13 |
| Insurance | 10 | 2 | 52 | 6 | 33 | — |
| White collar workers | 108 | 73 | 31 | 2 | 91 | 1 |
| Politician | 60 | 44 | 47 | 18 | 43 | 4 |
| Publishers and journalists | 51 | 32 | 32 | 14 | 24 | 4 |
| Farmer | 1 | — | 17 | 5 | 5 | 1 |
| Skilled Worker | 50 | 37 | 4 | — | 17 | 1 |
| Miner | 11 | 11 | 1 | 1 | 2 | — |
| Total | 640 | 412 | 640 | 166 | 639 | 52 |

*Source:* David Butler and Dennis Kavanagh, *The British General Election of 2001* (New York: Palgrave, 2002).

In all parties there have been a limited number of women candidates, though the number has been increasing. The highest number was the 640, or 19 percent of the total, who ran in 2001 (see Table 2.12).

## The Nature of Voting

Though recent changes in voting behavior must be borne in mind, and despite the fluid political situation, certain general statements

## TABLE 2.12

### WOMEN CANDIDATES AND MPs, 2001

| Party | Candidates | MPs |
|---|---|---|
| Conservative | 95 | 14 |
| Labour | 150 | 95 |
| Liberal Democrat | 139 | 5 |
| Others | 260 | 4 |
| | 644 | 118 |

*Source:* Inter-Parliamentary Union.

about voting in the post–World War II period can be made.

***A High but Declining Poll***   Voting is not compulsory, but the vote in general elections in the postwar period has tended to be over 72 percent of the electorate, though smaller at by-elections. Turnout reached a peak of 83.9 percent in 1950, but there has been a steady, though irregular, decline. In October 1974, it dropped to 72.8 percent, increased 77 percent in 1992, and dropped to 59.4 percent in 2001.

The abstention rate is higher among younger people, new residents of a constituency, the unmarried or divorced, blacks, the unemployed, and private rather than council tenants. These groups are less involved in political parties, less interested in politics, and less exposed to political information in general. Demographic factors have reinforced an overall decline in political interest and the belief, perhaps temporary, that the outcome of elections is not important. The decline in the poll may also be explained by the greater mobility of the population and the reduction of voting in safe seats in the inner cities.

***Class***   There has been a strong correlation between class and party voting. Until the late 1990s the Conservatives normally got 90 percent of the upper-middle-class vote and between two-thirds and three-quarters of the middle-class vote. Labour gets some two-thirds of the working-class vote, while the Liberal Democrats draw from all social classes.

Yet the link between class and party voting has never been complete. About one-third of the electorate does not vote according to this premise. The most serious qualification of class-party voting has always been the working-class Conservative vote, which has amounted to about one-third of the total working-class vote. There are a number of possible explanations for this contradiction of class voting. Those among the working class who see themselves as middle class and adopt middle-class values and ways of life are more likely to vote Conservative than those who think of themselves as working class. Mem-

bers of the working class who have had more than the minimum secondary and further education are more likely to vote Conservative than those who have not. Workers in agricultural areas who have close contacts with their employers, who do not belong to unions, who are religious, who belong to local organizations and are integrated into the local community are more likely to vote Conservative than the average worker.

Another explanation has been the deference of the working class. It used to be argued that this group preferred a socially superior political leadership, which it believed to be a natural ruling group. But it is more likely that this group believes that the Conservative Party is more efficient than its rivals and that its wielding of power will ensure greater material benefits.

Whatever the explanation, the Conservatives have done particularly well in the working class among older people, women until 1979, those who own their own homes, and those who own shares. The increase in home ownership—66 percent of voters now own homes—has meant greater Conservative support. About 44 percent in 1987 and 40 percent in 1992 of the home-owning working class voted Conservative; 32 percent voted Labour in 1987 and 41 percent in 1992. By contrast, about 57 percent of working-class tenants in public housing voted Labour in the same election. In the same way, a majority of first-time shareholders voted Conservative and only 17 percent voted Labour, in 1987. However, in the 1997 and 2001 elections, Labour obtained considerable support from the middle class.

The evidence is mixed at present, but there appears to be less subjective class identification, a weakening of class alignment, especially by young voters, and less acceptance of the basic principles of a party by its supporters. In 1992, 1997, and 2001, the Conservatives did less well than in previous elections with voters of the "new" working class, those who live in the south of England, are homeowners, work in the private sector, and are non-unionists.

***Party Identification***   The best guide to voting choice for most of the electorate has been identification with a party and psychological commitment to it. This allegiance has been the basis for response to party programs, for evaluation of the competence of party leaders, and for voting and political behavior in general. Among Labour and Conservative voters in 1974, 9 out of 10 thought of themselves as Labour or Conservative. In contrast, only half of the Liberal voters felt a similar identification with the party.

Why do people identify with a party? The strongest single influence has been the party preference of parents, especially if both parents voted the same way. Identification also results from other factors, including the supposed link between the party and a class, and the image of what policies and principles the party represents. For the Conservatives, the image has included capable leadership, skill in foreign policy, patriotism, and maintenance of the free enterprise system. For Labour it has been the pursuit of a more egalitarian society and concern for the underprivileged. Part of the dilemma of the Liberals is that their image is rather diffuse, devoid of specific policy content of general appeal.

In the early 1980s the Labour Party moved to the left and alienated some traditional supporters. In the 1990s it moved to more centrist positions, renounced extreme policies that lost votes, gave up unilateral disarmament, accepted the market economy, and agreed not to revoke privatization of enterprises.

In the recent past the party identification factor has given considerable stability and pre-dictability to the voting pattern for the major parties. But in the 1970s and 1980s strength of party identification appears to have declined and the ties of voters to a particular party to have grown weaker. Voters are less prone to vote for the party of their parents. Changes in the social structure, a general criticism of the performance of governments of both parties, and the presence of new issues that cut across party lines have contributed to this decline in party identification, the rise of the Social Democrats, and perhaps also to a certain cynicism about parties. In particular, part of the decline since 1970 in the Labour and Conservative vote and in turnout has been attributed to two factors: (1) less party identification in the young and newly enfranchised part of the electorate, and (2) a decline in the number of those who define themselves as "very strong identifiers" with a party.

***Gender***   Women constitute 52 percent of the electorate. Until recently, men have been more politically active than women, with a particularly low political interest among working-class women. Women tended to vote Conservative to a greater degree than did men until 1979. In 1983, for the first time, the Conservatives got less support from women than from men. In recent elections, Labour received a majority of the votes of women.

***Race***   Nonwhite immigrants have overwhelmingly voted Labour, partly because the vast majority are

**A CLOSER LOOK**
**2.7**

### PARTY IDENTIFICATION AND CLASS

Social class has been the main form of identity, and British voters have identified in general with the party they think represents the interests of their social class. In elections between 1945 and 1970, nearly two-thirds of all voters voted for their class-party. Since 1974, the percentage has declined, though class remains the single most important factor. On one hand the increase in public sector professions, whose members are more concerned with service than with wealth, meant more middle-class support for Labour. On the other hand, social factors (home ownership, mobility from north to south and from inner cities to suburbs, decline in trade union membership) meant working-class support for non-Labour parties. Moreover, the working class has declined from 41 percent of all voters in 1979 to 30 percent in 2002. The new social cleavages have weakened, though not ended, class voting.

members of the working class. But the presence of a significant number of immigrants in a constituency and the nonwhite immigration issue have another effect on voting. In the 1970 election the Conservatives were believed to have gained about six seats as a result of their being perceived—largely owing to the speeches made by the then-prominent Conservative Enoch Powell—as the more restrictive major party on allowing immigration.

In the 1990s, all mainstream parties increased their number of ethnic minority candidates. In 2001, 12 were elected to the House of Commons.

***Religion***    In contemporary times, religion has not been a politically divisive issue, except in Northern Ireland and among parts of the Islamic community. But there is a link between class and membership in a particular religion, and thus a link between religion and voting behavior. In general, members of the Anglican Church vote more Conservative than do individuals of other religious denominations; members of the non-conformist churches are likely to support the Labour or Liberal Parties; and Catholics, largely working class, vote strongly Labour.

***Age***    Younger people tend to vote Labour in greater proportions than their elders, especially those between 50 and 64. But the youngest people also have the lowest rates of turnout. On the whole it is true that the Conservatives are supported more by older than younger voters. This has been explained by the argument that it is the conservation of those political tendencies that were established when young that increases with age, not conservatism itself. Voting habits will therefore be influenced by those tendencies that were dominant when people first entered the electorate. Older people became adults when Labour was still a minor party and therefore have less allegiance to it than younger people.

***Regional Variations***    For generations, certain areas have been strongholds of particular parties. Labour does well in south Wales, central Scotland, the industrial north of England, and in the inner cities. The Conservatives have been strong in southern and eastern England,

and in the suburbs and country areas, which have grown in population and economic prosperity. In 1987 Labour won only 3 of the 176 seats in southern England, excluding London, but did better in 1997 and 2001. The Liberal Democrats do best in the west of England, Wales, and the Scottish islands. Labour has a plurality in Wales and Scotland. The Conservatives usually have a plurality in England and, until recently, in Northern Ireland. From the 1970s, politics in Ulster have been very fluid because of complex internal problems.

***Occupation***    Those employed in nationalized industries and public service organizations are more likely to vote Labour than those working in commercial organizations and the self-employed. People in both the working and middle class who have experienced unemployment are more likely than the average to vote Labour. Trade unionists vote Labour to a greater degree than do non-unionists. The strongest working-class support for Labour comes from predominantly working-class constituencies in large towns, industrial areas, and mining villages; union members; workers in large factories and offices with over 250 employees; those with working-class parents; those living in council apartments; and those who have been unemployed for a period of time. However, the number of manual workers and of those working in large factories, and the number of council tenants all have been declining.

***Party and Leader***    Voting may depend on the images people have of the parties and their leaders and on perceptions of party positions on issues. The assumption that people are more likely to vote for a party than a leader may no longer be true in view of the prominence of the leaders on television and the time given to their speeches and personalities.

## POLITICAL PARTIES

British parties have been largely unregulated by law until very recently. The Registration of Political Parties Act 1998 forbade misleading descriptions of candidates who run under labels easily confused with those of other parties. It also provided for noncompulsory registration of parties. The Political Parties, Elections, and Referendums Act 2000 made registration compulsory and set up an independent Electoral Commission with wide executive and investigative powers over party funding, as well as administration of elections and referendums. Each political party must publish annual accounts and information on donations, gifts, subscriptions, and affiliation fees. Donations must not be anonymous nor come from a foreign source.

The British system has often been regarded as the classic example of a two-party system in which the Conservative and Labour Parties—national, large, cohesive, disciplined, ideological but generally moderate—have alternated as the government and the opposition. The Liberals did not win more than 20 seats until 1997. A considerable number of minor parties have existed and run candidates in national and local elections. But none, except the nationalists in recent years, has had much success. Extremist parties have fared poorly. On the left, the Communist Party, founded in 1920, has never gained more than two parliamentary seats and since 1950 has been unrepresented. On the right, the party opposing nonwhite immigration has not been able to win a parliamentary seat. The Green Party emerged in 1985 out of an ecological group. In 1987 it received less than 1 percent of the vote, but in the 1989 election for the European Parliament it obtained 15 percent. In the 2001 election, its candidates got between 1 and 2 percent of the vote.

A possible change to a multiparty system appeared with the formation of the Social Democratic Party (SDP) in 1981 by some prominent Labour politicians who were disturbed by militant leftism in their party and by organizational changes allowing more influence to extraparliamentary forces, extremists in some of the constituency parties, and the trade unions.

The SDP and the Liberals agreed to form an Alliance to support each other electorally. This did well at some by-elections and in local elections. But the Alliance was less successful nationally, though it won 23 seats and came second in 311 constituencies and got 25 percent of the poll in 1983, and it won 22 seats and came second in 260 constituencies and got 22 percent in 1987.

As a result of this disappointment, a majority in SDP agreed to merge with the Liberals and form a new party, the Social and Liberal Democrats (SLD), who were generally called Liberal Democrats in 1988. A minority of the old SDP remained as a small separate group, transforming itself in 1990 into the Campaign for Social Democracy. In the 1992 election the Liberal Democrats got 17.8 percent of the vote and 20 seats, which in 2001 increased to 18.3 percent and 52 seats.

## PARTY ORGANIZATIONS

### Local and Regional

All the major parties have the parliamentary constituency as the basic unit of party organization. The Conservative and Liberal constituency associations are composed of individual members who subscribe to the party and who manage the local organizations, elect their own officers, select parliamentary and local government candidates, raise funds, engage in educational work, and conduct the electoral campaign in their area. However, the constituency Labour parties are composed not only of individual members but also of affiliated organizations, such as trade unions, cooperative societies and branches of the Cooperative Party, branches of Socialist societies and some professional organizations, and trade councils.

Total membership of all parties has declined in the last two decades. The Conservative Party has declined from about 3 million in the late 1950s to about 300,000 members, the Liberals now have about 60,000 members, and the Labour Party has about 311,000 individual and 4 million affiliated members. A number of factors may explain this decline away from party membership: other political outlets such as social movements and pressure groups, the lessening of partisan alignment, the erosion of working-class communities, the increase in middle-class working women who are no longer Conservative volunteers, and the reliance on television and not personal activity for electoral campaigns.

## National Organization

Each party has a national organization that works through different committees, holds an annual conference in the autumn, has a central headquarters to control the working of the party machinery and prepare publications, and has geographical regional groups and policy committees.

The National Union of Conservative and Unionist Associations is a federation of constituency associations. It is responsible for the organization and growth of these associations and acts as a link between the leader of the party and the associations. The Union is nominally governed by the Central Council, which meets once a year and which, in the postwar period, has chosen the officers of the Union. But because the Central Council is too large a body for effective action, the group that acts on its behalf and meets more frequently is the Executive Committee; this committee is composed of the party leader, chief officials, and representatives of the regional organizations.

The Conservatives hold an annual conference to discuss the reports of the Council and of the Executive Committee. Until recently the conference was usually a platform for the main party leaders rather than a challenge to them. However, because of internal differences, especially over the EU, the conferences over the last decade have become less placid and more divisive. Since 1998 a Conservative Policy Forum oversees the policy discussions at constituency level. It is characteristic of the Conservative conference that it is usually more right-wing than the leadership.

The Conservative Central Office, the party headquarters, is concerned with the efficient organization of the party. It provides general guidance and technical assistance, helps the formulation of policy by supplying background material through its research department, and offers advice on electioneering. It is headed by a chairperson, appointed by the party leader, and officers who are responsible for the different departments concerned with specific functions.

The Central Office cannot coerce the constituency associations, which operate through local volunteer workers and obtain and spend their own funds. The local associations also, in the main, control the process of selection of parliamentary candidates, though the Central Office supplies a list of available candidates on request and may influence the final choice.

The Labour Party has the most complex organizational structure. It began as, and has remained, a federal body composed of four main groups (see Figure 2.3):

1. The more than 600 constituency associations, which now have about 300,000 members. They are responsible for their own organization and selection of parliamentary candidates. The number of activists is relatively small, and they are usually more left-wing than either the party leaders or their MPs. Most party members spend little or no time at party meetings or activities.

2. The 23 affiliated trade unions, which account for 4 million, or 95 percent, of the members. Not all unions are affiliated with the party—74 unions are now attached to the Trades Union Congress—and not all members of a union that is affiliated want to be members of the party. About one-third of the membership of the affiliated unions have "contracted out," or refused to have part of their union dues go to a political levy for the party. About three-quarters of the Labour Party's funds come from the unions.

Since all organizations are represented at the annual conference in proportion to their membership, the four largest unions constituted a majority if they all voted the same way. But the union vote has been reduced to a third of the whole conference.

A number of unions sponsor parliamentary candidates, most of whose election expenses they pay. Because their constituencies are usually safe seats, those candidates are much more likely to win than nonsponsored candidates. In 1992, of the 634 Labour candidates, the unions sponsored 173. Of these, 143 won, of whom 22 were women.

3. The cooperative organizations linked to the Labour Party. One cooperative society, the Royal Arsenal, has been affiliated since 1927 and another since 1979. There is a separate Cooperative Party, founded in 1917, but it is now in real-

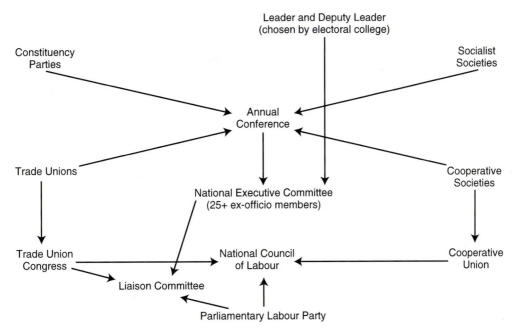

Constituency Parties

Socialist Societies

Leader and Deputy Leader (chosen by electoral college)

Annual Conference

Trade Unions

Cooperative Societies

National Executive Committee (25+ ex-officio members)

Trade Union Congress

National Council of Labour

Cooperative Union

Liaison Committee

Parliamentary Labour Party

**Figure 2.3 ORGANIZATION OF THE LABOUR PARTY**

ity an adjunct of the Labour Party. Since 1922 all Cooperative Party parliamentary candidates have been endorsed by the Labour Party and have run as Labour and Cooperative.

4. A number of Socialist societies, small in size and composed largely of professionals or intellectuals. The most well-known of these bodies is the Fabian Society, which was founded in 1884. The total membership of these societies and of the cooperative groups is about 54,000.

The nominal policy-making body in the Labour Party is the annual party conference, which debates resolutions, changes the constitution of the party, and elects the major administrative organ, the National Executive Committee (NEC). The conference is attended by representatives from the four different elements making up the party and by the chief officials of the party, MPs, and parliamentary candidates.

The NEC consists of the leader of the party, the deputy leader, the treasurer, and 28 other members who are elected at the conference. Of

these people, 12 are chosen by the trade union delegates, 7 by those from the constituency parties, 4 by representatives of the cooperative and Socialist societies, and 5 women by the whole conference. At least 11 members must be women.

The NEC is the administrative authority of the party and is the body responsible between annual conferences for deciding policy matters and enforcing the rules of the party. It controls the central organization, supervises the work of the party outside Parliament, decides disputes between members or associations, and manages the party funds. Together with the Parliamentary Labour Party (PLP), the NEC draws up the election manifesto based on conference proposals, but there is sometimes friction between them.

The NEC also plays a role in the selection of parliamentary candidates. Like the Conservative Central Office, it maintains a list of acceptable candidates that the local constituencies can request, but the final choice is made by the local parties.

The NEC can expel a member or disaffiliate an organization for activity contrary to party decisions. In recent years Labour has enforced its rules stringently. Since 1998 the NEC has vetted the voting and absentee record of Labour MPs to see if they are suitable to be reselected as parliamentary candidates. The party expelled two Labour members of the European Parliament who had repeatedly criticized the leadership of Prime Minister Blair and suspended two others for breaking party or parliamentary rules.

## THE PARTIES IN PARLIAMENT

The major Conservative organ in Parliament is the 1922 Committee, which is composed of the nongovernmental Conservative MPs and expresses their opinions to the leadership of the party. When the party is in power, its leaders, now members of the government, do not attend the committee's weekly meetings. After the discussion of policy issues or political problems, the chairperson of the committee expresses its views to the leadership.

From 1881, after the death of Disraeli, until 1963 the Conservative leader "emerged" after a series of informal "soundings" of the views of different sections of the party. Of the 11 leaders in this period, 5 were of aristocratic descent and the others came from business or professional politics. The method adopted in 1963 was that the Conservative leader would be elected by the MPs in the House of Commons and then presented for confirmation to a meeting composed of the Conservative MPs and peers, prospective candidates, and members of the Executive Committee of the National Union.

In 1998 new rules were adopted. Each Conservative MP can vote for a candidate to be leader. One or more ballots take place until only two candidates remain. The party members in the country then choose between the two in a postal ballot. The two candidates are allowed campaign managers and can spend up to £100,000. A new leader, Iain Duncan Smith, a former officer in the Scots Guards who had never been a cabinet minister and is regarded as on the right wing of his party, was elected in 2001.

The Parliamentary Labour Party (PLP) consists of Labour members in the House of Commons and those in the House of Lords. It is led,

when the party is in opposition, by the Parliamentary Committee, or "shadow cabinet," which consists of the leader and deputy leader, 15 others elected by Labour MPs, and 1 elected representative of Labour peers. The leader and deputy leader of the PLP are the same people who have been elected as the leaders of the party by the electoral college. In this electoral college, the trade unions, the constituency parties, and the PLP each have one-third of the votes.

In recent years most of the members of the shadow cabinet have become cabinet ministers if the party gains power. This custom was reinforced by a party rule, which states that 16 members of the shadow cabinet will be given cabinet positions if the party wins the next election. When the party is in power, a liaison committee links the government and other Labour MPs, who thus have the opportunity to influence the policies of the government. Groups of Labour MPs based on territory and subject matter have also been formed for that purpose.

## PARTY LEADERSHIP

In all the parties the parliamentary leader has until recently been regarded as leader of the whole party. Unlike the formal process of democratic decision making in the SLD and Labour Parties, the Conservative Party leader is responsible for deciding party policy and for the choice of the shadow cabinet, or consultative committee, when the party is in opposition. The leader controls the party headquarters and appoints the chief officials, who are responsible to him or her.

The Labour Party has been more loyal to its leaders than have the Conservatives. In the twentieth century the Conservatives have had 13 leaders, 7 of whom were overthrown by a party revolt, while an eighth was almost overthrown twice, and another two resigned after electoral defeats. During the same period Labour had eight leaders, one of whom (MacDonald) left his party, and another (Lansbury) resigned because of disagreements with party policy. All the others died in office or resigned voluntarily. The current leader, Tony Blair, who reflects a moderate liberal position, was elected in July 1994.

Until 1976 the Liberal leader was also elected by the MPs of the party. In that year the Liberals established a new procedure by which the leader was chosen by an electoral college composed of about 20,000 delegates from the constituencies. The new SLD party elects its leader by ballot of all members, using the alternative vote method. The present leader, Charles Kennedy, was elected in this way in the fourth round of balloting in August 1999.

## POWER WITHIN THE PARTIES

A complex relationship exists among the different sections of the parties, in which no one element has complete power over the others, and in which each section has some, if unequal, influence on decision making in the party. Differences over policy and personnel exist between the central party organizations and the constituency associations, especially the activists in them; between the organizations in the country and the parliamentary party; and between the leadership of the party, especially when it is in power, and the MPs of the party (see Table 2.13).

Important as the party organizations are, the real power in the formulation of policy has remained with the parliamentary elements of the parties. The Liberal and Conservative parliamentary parties, from which come the prime minister and governmental leaders, existed before the mass organizations in the country were created. The dominance of the Conservative parliamentarians over the rest of the party is understandable in view of the fact that between 1886 and 2002 the Conservatives were in power for 79 years and the party leaders were also prime ministers and cabinet ministers.

Although the Labour Party is different from the others in having begun as a mass organization, by the 1920s the Parliamentary Labour Party had become the strongest element and the body that chose the political leaders. This has been partly due to the strong support of the parliamentary leaders by the trade union leaders, who for the most part held similar political opinions.

Activists of the party, at both the national and local level, have rarely been able to challenge the parliamentary leadership successfully. The political reality is that the national electoral decision and the parliamentary representatives, not the party as a whole, determine who is to be prime minister. The party organizations have been able to influence and sometimes limit the

### TABLE 2.13

#### POWER IN THE POLITICAL PARTIES, 2002

|  | Conservatives | Labour | Liberals |
|---|---|---|---|
| Leader | Iain Duncan Smith, makes policy, controls party HQ, chooses shadow cabinet, chooses cabinet, approves election manifesto | Tony Blair, chooses cabinet | Charles Kennedy, shares policy making, controls party HQ, approves election manifesto |
| Parliamentary party | Chooses two candidates for leader | Shares in election of leader, chooses shadow cabinet | Shares policy making, approves manifesto |
| Party conference | — | Makes policy | Makes policy |
| Party HQ executive | — | Makes policy, approves manifesto, controls party organization | Makes policy, controls party organization |
| Constituency associations | The constituency associations in all the parties choose or help choose parliamentary candidates | | |
| Individual members | Elect leader | | Elect leader |

activity for the parliamentary leadership, but they rarely formulate policy.

Skillful manipulation by political and union officials controlled the agenda and the debates of the annual conference, and tended to exalt the parliamentary part of the Labour Party over the mass movement. In recent years the Labour conference has asserted itself and changed the organization of the party. In 1979, when the left wing of the party controlled a majority, resolutions were approved for all Labour MPs to be automatically subject to a reselection process by their constituency parties in order to remain as candidates for the next election and for the NEC to take, after appropriate consultation, the final decision on the contents of the general election manifesto.

A decision at the 2000 conference was that any resolution passed by a two-thirds majority at conferences would be embodied in the party platform from which the electoral manifesto is composed. The Labour Party in 2000 also created a network of policy forums at regional and constituency levels and a National Policy Forum to oversee them, on lines similar to those adopted by the Conservatives two years earlier.

The constituency parties on a number of occasions have attempted, sometimes successfully, not to renominate MPs who differ politically from the activists controlling the local organization. Selection of candidates is now in the hands of the local organizations. Though the central offices keep a list of nationally approved candidates and can veto an undesirable local choice, they cannot force the local organization to accept a candidate, and only very rarely have they exercised a veto even when it involved an individual who had rebelled against party policy or leadership.

The internal struggle for power within the parties continues. This has recently been shown in a number of ways. All the parties have made the choice of the party leader open to wider participation: the Conservatives by choice of two candidates by MPs and then election by party members; the Liberals by bringing the whole membership of the party into the process; and Labour by establishing an electoral college in which the trade unions and other affiliated organizations, the PLP, and the constituency parties would each have one-third of the vote.

# INTEREST GROUPS

Interest groups have long existed in British politics and now play a significant role. They are usually differentiated from parties in that they do not hold or seek political office, though some groups sponsor parliamentary candidates. Interest group leaders now participate in consultative or even administrative functions and serve on government committees and advisory boards. In certain matters, they may even have a veto on government decisions.

There are numerous interest groups concerned with all aspects of life. For analytical purposes, a frequently used distinction is between sectional interest and promotional groups. *Sectional interest groups* defend and promote the interests of their members, whether individuals or enterprises. They include organizations concerned with the economic interests of labor, business, and agriculture, with social affairs such as automobile organizations, or with living arrangements such as tenants' groups. *Promotional groups* are concerned with a particular general cause, principle, or policy issue. They advocate a specific conception of the public interest. Examples of such groups are the Howard League for Penal Reform, the National Society for the Prevention of Cruelty to Children, and the Royal Society for the Prevention of Accidents.

Recent years have seen the rise of a number of protest movements, of which the most vocal has been the Campaign for Nuclear Disarmament, and groups concerned with welfare and environmental issues, such as Greenpeace with nearly half a million supporters, and Friends of the Earth, which has a quarter million members.

The most significant interest groups affecting the working of the political system are the business organizations and the trade unions.

## Business

There are hundreds of business organizations concerned with a number of functions: providing common services, exchanging information, regulating trade practices, negotiating with trade unions on wages and conditions of work, and representing the business position to the government.

Most employers' groups are organized on an industry rather than product basis. Some are local or deal with a part of or the whole of an industry. There are about 150 national employers' organizations, most of which belong to the Confederation of British Industry (CBI), formed in 1965 of a number of industrial groups. The CBI is the central body representing national business and industry. It acts as an advisory and consultative body for its members and presents their views publicly. Its representatives sit on many official bodies and advisory groups. The CBI has been called the voice of British business, but this is only partly true because of the widely varied interests of industrial and commercial organizations.

The CBI has had little consistent direct influence over government policy as a whole, though it has had an impact on some industrial and business issues. On the other hand, the important financial institutions—usually referred to as the City—have been politically important.

This importance results from two factors. First, the City is still the world's most significant financial and credit center, including the Bank of England and the central offices of many British banks, the largest number of foreign banks, the stock exchange, the largest gold market and international insurance markets, and international insurance and commodity markets. Second, many public issues have been connected with regulation of money, credit, price levels, and currency relationships and balance of payments, all of which need the expertise of the City. The leading persons in the City are usually closely connected with the Conservative Party in the same way that union leaders are with the Labour Party.

## Trade Unions

Trade unions began with the Industrial Revolution, but not until the mid-nineteenth century did unions of skilled and semiskilled workers become well organized in their demands for higher wages and better working conditions. In the latter part of the century, unions of unskilled workers that pursued a more active industrial policy were formed. The attacks on the unions by court decisions led to the establishment of a political lobby, the Trades Union Congress (TUC), and later to the Labour Party.

The TUC is a loose confederation which does not direct individual unions and has little power over them, but acts on behalf of the whole union movement to achieve objectives that would be difficult for separate unions to obtain. Since World War II, the TUC has sat on countless governmental committees, advisory bodies on economic issues, agricultural marketing boards, and consumer councils, and has given its views on questions of general economic and social policy. The leaders of the TUC have become members of numerous QUANGOs (Quasi Autonomous Nongovernmental Organizations).

The unions have been linked with the Labour Party since their decision to establish a pressure group in Parliament. The unions still provide the bulk of party membership and financing. Of the 67 unions in the TUC in 1996, 27 were affiliated with the party. About 60 percent of the members of these affiliated unions have paid the political levy which automatically makes them party members, though many do not realize they are doing so. They represent about 4 million members, or over 95 percent of the total party. The large manual and industrial unions form the basis of Labour's main union strength. They supply not only most of the annual funds of the party but also the extra money needed for campaigns. The unions constitute one-third of the electoral college which chooses the leader and deputy leader of the party. The unions also sponsor parliamentary candidates.

But the alliance between the unions and the party has been an uneasy one. There was considerable cooperation between 1945 and 1951, when there was a voluntary restraint on wage demands, largely because of the close personal relations between the government and union leaders. Under the Labour government of 1964–1970, the unions generally supported the government, including its income policy, until 1969, when an attempt was made to introduce legislative controls over unions. Similarly, in the Labour government of 1974–1979, the unions abided by the social contract and restraint in wage increases, until 1978–1979, when they defied the government's income policy that sought to limit wage increases to 5 percent per year.

The significant influence of the unions on policy—especially in 1974, when a series of strikes led the Conservative government to call an election which resulted in its defeat—brought calls for limits on their power; the Conservatives after their return to power in 1979 imposed such limits. The most important of these are ending the legal case for the closed shop; allowing employers the right not to recognize unions; union contributions to political parties have to be approved by secret vote of members; forbidding political strikes; forbidding mass picketing; strikes must be approved and union leaders must be elected by secret ballot. Working days lost through strikes have been substantially reduced. So has the membership of unions, which dropped from 13.3 million in 1979 to 7.1 million in 2001. The power of unions in relation to government and to employers has greatly declined.

## THE EXECUTIVE

About 150 years ago, Bagehot in *The English Government* distinguished between the dignified and efficient parts of the political system. Some institutions, such as the monarchy, were important for symbolic reasons, while others exercised real power.

The British executive can still be viewed in the same fashion. The head of the state is the monarch, who reigns but has virtually no political power and only limited influence. The real political power is centered in the prime minister and the cabinet, with the civil service assisting and influencing the exercise and administration of that power. The British system has been based on the existence or possibility of strong, effective government. Over the last three centuries, the executive power of the king was first restrained by Parliament and then transferred to ministers.

## THE MONARCHY

The present monarch, Queen Elizabeth II, can trace her descent back to at least the ninth century. The powers formerly exercised by the monarch are now in the hands of various individuals and institutions. By a series of arrangements beginning in 1760, the monarchy turned over to the government the hereditary revenues derived from the Crown Lands and other sources and has received in return an annual grant (Civil List) to cover the salaries and expenses of the royal household.

Queen Elizabeth II greets her people during the 50th anniversary of her reign, celebrations June 2002.

## LONG LIVE THE QUEEN: A EUROPEAN TIME LINE

In June 2002, Britain's Queen Elizabeth II celebrated 50 years on the throne. During that time she witnessed, among other things:

- The end of the Soviet Union, leading to 8 new republics and 7 dictatorships.
- Two republics in France.
- The end of East Germany as a separate state.
- Over 50 governments in Italy, where these were also four political assassinations and the criminal indictment of two former prime ministers.
- Yugoslavia fragmented into 6 republics.
- Czechoslovakia partitioned into 2 states.
- Spain transformed from an authoritarian dictatorship to a parliamentary democracy, constitutional monarchy, and market economy.
- Portugal changed from an authoritarian regime to a republic.
- Greece transformed from a monarchy and 7 years of dictatorship to a republic.
- Three constitutional changes in Belgium.

The functions of government are now exercised by political ministers who are collectively and individually responsible to Parliament, but the monarch still participates in a formal way in some executive and legislative activities. The monarchy survived in Britain because the sovereign became a constitutional monarch, neither exercising the wide powers of the crown nor being responsible for their exercise. According to constitutional procedure, the sovereign always ultimately accepts the will of the government, although the monarch may make known his or her opinion and can attempt to influence the decision made.

The most important single political power of the sovereign is the choice of a prime minister. When there is a clearly recognized leader of a party that is able to control a majority in the House of Commons, the choice of the individual is obvious and immediate. But where one or both of these conditions are not present, a real choice may exist for the sovereign.

Referring to the monarchy, it used to be said that "we must not let daylight in upon magic," but in this television age, the royal family has been more exposed to the public eye. The monarch today still has a symbolic and ceremonial role to play in the system, but the monarchy has been divested of its former political power, though legally it still has the power to dissolve Parliament.

## THE GOVERNMENT

The real power is exercised by the government, composed of the political ministers and junior ministers, of whom the most politically important are the prime minister and the cabinet (see Figure 2.4).

The government consists of about 100 members, all nominated by the prime minister and appointed by the monarch. It essentially consists of holders of administrative posts of a political character and the whips of the government party. It never meets as a whole to discuss policy or to take action. There is no fixed number of departments. These are established to deal with issues

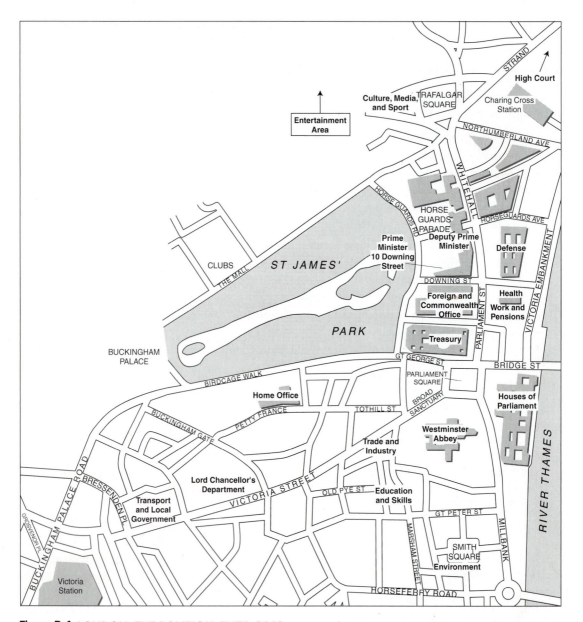

**Figure 2.4** LONDON: THE POLITICAL ELITE, 2002

or to meet changing conditions or political and social crises. In the postwar period the number of major departments has been reduced and almost all of them are now in the present cabinet, usually 20 to 25. Five of the 22 persons in the cabinet in 2002 are women, as are 17 of the 67 ministers of state and junior ministers.

Ministers are individually responsible to Parliament for the work of their departments. They introduce legislative proposals, press the concerns of their department, and argue its case and requests for money in cabinet and interdepartmental committees. They discuss departmental issues with interest groups and others affected by or interested in those issues and speak in defense of the department in Parliament. It is their task to see that decisions and policies are correctly implemented by the civil servants in the department.

## THE CABINET

The most significant members of the government constitute the cabinet, those ministers who are chosen by the prime minister to attend cabinet meetings and are made privy councillors. The cabinet has replaced the privy council as the chief source of executive power since the eighteenth century, but the latter still exists as an executive organ, largely giving formal effect to policy decisions made by the cabinet and making orders-in-council. A significant heritage from the past is the Judicial Committee of the Privy Council, which is the final court of appeal on certain legal issues arising in the colonies and in those independent countries of the Commonwealth that have decided to retain the arrangement.

The cabinet, which is not a legal body, is based on political understandings or conventions. Its members are normally the leading figures of the party controlling a majority in the House of Commons. The cabinet is the chief single body concerned with the initiation, control, and implementation of political policy and the most important decision-making body. It initiates most legislation and controls the legislative process. It is responsible for the coordination of governmental activity; all ministers must implement cabinet decisions insofar as their departments are affected.

For politicians, the cabinet is the top of the political ladder, except for the position of prime minister. It constitutes the core of the British political elite. A number of conventions underlie the existence and operation of cabinet government:

1. The cabinet is ultimately dependent on the support of the House of Commons that has come into existence as a result of the general election. A government that is defeated on a major issue or on a vote of censure or no confidence is expected to resign or to ask for a dissolution of Parliament. A government whose party has been clearly defeated at a general election will resign immediately.

2. Unlike the American cabinet, the members of which are drawn from a wide variety of sources and backgrounds, the British cabinet is drawn, with rare exceptions, from members of the two Houses of Parliament. This fusion of executive and legislative functions in the hands of the same people is a striking denial of the concept of the separation of powers. This convention also means that the members of the cabinet are selected from a relatively small pool of available people. Moreover, in recent years most of the members of both Labour and Conservative cabinets have come from the shadow cabinets of the two parties.

3. Except in wartime or in a serious political or economic crisis, the entire cabinet will be members of the same political party if that party can control a majority in the Commons. In this way, political coherence and unity can be obtained. Britain is the only country in Western Europe that has not had a coalition government in the postwar period.

4. The monarch is excluded from the discussions of the cabinet, though he or she is kept informed of its conclusions by the prime minister, who is the acknowledged head of the cabinet. The advice offered by the cabinet, even on personal issues (as in 1936 on the marital plans of King Edward VIII, who was eventually obliged to abdicate), must be accepted by the monarch or a constitutional crisis will result.

5. All members take the oath of privy councillors and are bound to secrecy by this and the Official Secrets Act. There is now a 30-year limitation on the publication of cabinet documents, and secrecy is generally preserved.

6. The members of the cabinet are collectively responsible for all decisions and actions, as well as individually responsible for the performance of the particular department or unit each may head. There is free and frank discussion of issues in the cabinet.

## REVIEW 2.4

### SOME KEY TERMS IN BRITISH POLITICS

**Backbencher**—members of the House of Commons (MPs) who are not members of the government or leaders of the opposition; they sit on the back benches of the chamber.

**Cabinet**—the most senior ministers in the government, usually about 20.

**Constituency**—the geographical area represented by an MP; there are now 659 constituencies.

**Dissolution**—the ending of the life of the House of Commons by royal proclamation on the advice of the prime minister (PM).

**Government**—the ministers, usually about 100, who form the political executive; most are in the House of Commons (HoC).

**Great Britain**—the countries of England, Scotland, and Wales.

**Hansard**—the daily official report of the proceedings in Parliament.

**Law Lords** (Lords of Appeal in Ordinary)—senior judges appointed to the House of Lords to hear appeals in civil and criminal cases.

**Money bill**—legislation on spending and taxation introduced in HoC; it becomes law within one month.

**Opposition**—second party in HoC with an officially paid leader and a "shadow cabinet."

**Prime minister (PM)**—head of the government and the cabinet.

**Public bill**—proposed legislation on public policy, which affects everyone.

**Question time**—one hour four times a week when ministers answer questions in HoC.

**Shadow cabinet**—the group of opposition party leaders in Parliament.

**Speaker**—presiding officer of the HoC.

**10 Downing Street**—home of the PM.

**United Kingdom**—the countries of Great Britain and Northern Ireland.

**Usual channels**—consultations between whips of different parties on parliamentary business.

**Whips**—MPs who provide information to and from their party members and leaders and who discipline their party in HoC.

**Whitehall**—term used for civil service and administration.

---

Members may and do disagree about the desirability of a policy, but they must support and implement policy decisions once they have been made. The British system is based on the premise that a government that is publicly divided on a given subject cannot govern.

The principle of collective responsibility means that all ministers must support and defend government policy and not speak or act against it. The principle applies now not only to cabinet ministers but also to all members of the government. If ministers continue to oppose or cannot accept a decision made on an important issue, the principle suggests that they should resign. In recent years cabinets have some-times remained divided but without resignations. In addition, the development of the system of cabinet committees and the dominant role of the prime minister has meant that cabinet members tend to feel less personally committed to every decision.

Collective responsibility also implies that an attack on a minister in regard to important policy, as distinct from criticism of the administration of that minister's department, will be taken as an attack on the whole government unless it disclaims responsibility. If the latter is the case, strong criticism of a minister may lead to resignation, but not to a vote on the government as a whole.

This concept of collective responsibility and decision making is to be distinguished from the principle of ministerial responsibility, which means that individual ministers are responsible for all the work and actions of the government departments that they head. Though it is most improbable that ministers will be familiar with all the work of the department, they must respond to parliamentary criticism of or inquiry about it.

Theoretically, if parliamentary criticism of a department or of a minister's performance or neglect of duties or competence is sufficiently great, the minister is obliged to resign. Resignation has also resulted from ministerial indiscretion, either inadvertent or more blatant, as in sexual escapades, improper behavior, or the use of indiscreet language. But there are many more examples of ministers not resigning in spite of considerable parliamentary criticism of their activity.

## Cabinet Membership

The number and members of the cabinet depend on the prime minister, whose appointments result partly from the administrative needs and governmental functions to be performed and partly from political necessity to accommodate the ambitions of colleagues, to have different ideological sections of the party and territorial parts of the country represented, and to include some individuals loyal to himself or herself. The cabinet, which realistically contains the political rivals and possible successors of the prime minister, is thus the result of administrative, political, and personal factors.

Except during the two world wars, when the size of the cabinet was reduced to 8 or 9, it has numbered between 18 and 23 ministers. Usually, the important departments will be included in the cabinet, though no one becomes a member simply because of his or her office. The minister of a department has been included in one cabinet but excluded from the next, depending on the priority given it by the different cabinets or the political weight of the minister.

Although members of the cabinet are drawn from both Houses, certain ministers, especially those with financial responsibilities, will almost always be chosen from the Commons. Only occasionally will someone outside Parliament be appointed. The average tenure of a departmental office between 1964 and 1991 was under 2½ years. Ministers are not experts and rarely have executive experience, as they have spent much of their lives in politics.

In reality, the choice of the prime minister is constrained by the existence of the shadow cabinet led by the PM when his party was in opposition. Though there is no compulsion, prime ministers in recent years have appointed most of the members of the shadow cabinet to the cabinet itself. This is now mandatory in the Labour Party.

## Procedure in the Cabinet

Cabinet meetings are called by the prime minister, usually once a week. Members ask the cabinet

**A CLOSER LOOK**

**2.8**

### THE CABINET, 2002

In recent years, the cabinet as a body appears to have become less significant for a wide range of political affairs. It now largely deals with foreign issues, some immediate important questions of the day, any item brought up by the PM, and issues that have not been resolved by cabinet committees or interministerial meetings. The normal process today is for a ministerial proposal to go to the relevant cabinet committee, which virtually decides if it should become policy; that decision is usually accepted as a cabinet decision. Ministers are reluctant to take some matters to the cabinet, and almost always try to get agreement from the Treasury.

secretariat to put items on the agenda and receive copies of it before each meeting. They are thus able to study the issues and to attend meetings with an informed opinion on them. Ministers who are not cabinet members are normally invited to attend when a subject affecting their department is on the agenda.

It has usually been assumed that the cabinet does not vote on issues, but that discussion takes place until a collective decision is reached when the prime minister sums up "the sense of the meeting." But some cabinet ministers have stated that voting did sometimes take place on substantive as well as procedural matters.

There are other qualifications of the principle of collective decision making by the cabinet. First, members do not always participate in discussion, especially as the range of subjects has increased. This is largely the result of the heavy burden of duties imposed on cabinet members, which includes the reading of official papers, attending and speaking in Parliament, supervising the work of their departments and giving directions to officials, attending official functions, maintaining contact with their parliamentary constituencies, and undertaking a round of speeches throughout the country, as well as attending cabinet meetings. Ministers tend to fight in cabinet for their departmental policies and budgets.

Second, not all issues are fully discussed by the cabinet as a whole. Various devices are used to reduce the burden on it. Decisions made by individual ministers have sometimes been accepted by the whole body. Agreement on issues has been reached by interdepartmental ministerial meetings or in private meetings between ministers, including the prime minister. Above all, cabinet committees, consisting of a small number of cabinet members, and occasionally nonmembers, have been established to relieve the burden on the cabinet as a whole and to speed up decision making now that there has been a great increase in governmental activity. Sometimes the real decisions are made by a small committee rather than by the cabinet as a whole. In crisis or wartime, a small cabinet of five or six members is usually set up to make major decisions.

# THE PRIME MINISTER

The prime minister is the acknowledged head of the executive. Unlike the U.S. presidency, the office of the prime minister is largely based on conventions. Despite the office now being over 280 years old, there are still few statutes referring to it or to the functions to be performed. The prime minister was once regarded as *primus inter pares* (first among equals) in the cabinet, but this is an inadequate description for an individual who is preeminent in it and is the dominant political personality.

Legally the prime minister is chosen by the monarch, who selects the person capable of forming a government. The choice is obvious if one political party possesses or controls an absolute majority of seats in the House of Commons and if that party has an acknowledged leader. This was the case in 1979 with the appointment of Margaret Thatcher, the first woman to become prime minister, and Tony Blair in 1997.

But there are occasions when the monarch has a real choice between individuals. If the prime minister dies or resigns, the choice of a successor is not always obvious. The monarch had to choose between rival candidates in 1957 and 1963. If no party has an absolute majority in the Commons, as in February 1974, the monarch might have a choice between the leaders of the different parties. In those situations the monarch will not act without directly or indirectly consulting a number of political leaders.

A convention of the twentieth century has limited the monarch's choice to members of the House of Commons. Since 1923, all prime ministers have been members of the lower chamber. When Lord Home was appointed in 1963, he immediately disclaimed his title, left the House of Lords, and won a seat in the Commons. This convention illustrates the predominance of the Commons over the Lords. Governments can be defeated and forced to resign by vote of the Commons but not by the Lords.

Prime ministers differ in personality, energy, political interests, and administrative abilities, but all are seasoned politicians with experience in Parliament. In the twentieth century as a whole, as in the postwar period, the prime minister's average tenure as an MP has been 28 years. Most of them have held a number of other cabinet positions. The average tenure in this century has been three different posts and eight years in the cabinet. Thatcher had only one previous post and four years in cabinet, and Major had only one year in a senior cabinet post before becoming prime minister. Blair had not served in a previous cabinet.

In the twentieth century there have been 20 prime ministers. They have differed in social background: five came from the aristocracy, eight from the middle class, six from the lower middle class, and one from the working class. All the aristocrats and six of the eight middle-class prime ministers went to a public school, five of them went to Eton and two to Harrow. Thirteen attended university at Oxford or Cambridge. It is distinctive that the last five before Blair came from the lower middle class, attended state (non-public) schools, and can be regarded as examples of the principle of meritocracy. John Major, like James Callaghan, Labour PM (1976–1979), is unusual in never having gone to a university.

## Functions

The prime minister chooses and can dismiss members of the government. But, unlike the U.S. president, the prime minister's range of choice is restricted; rarely does he or she choose someone from outside Parliament and even more rarely from outside the government party. Many choices will be obvious because the leading members of the successful party, especially many of those who have been in the shadow cabinet, will be appointed; the most important of them may even be consulted by the prime minister in choosing the others. The prime minister must keep the confidence of senior colleagues. He or she can dismiss or demand the resignation of ministers, but may not always be able to get rid of those who have some independent political strength in the party or country.

The prime minister decides the size and composition of the cabinet. He or she forms a cabinet that is satisfactory from both a political and an administrative point of view. Thus, prime ministers will usually include not only people who reflect different elements or political opinions in

**A CLOSER LOOK**

**2.9**

### TONY BLAIR: LABOUR LEADER AND PRIME MINISTER

- Born in Edinburgh, Scotland, in 1953. Educated at Scottish private school and at Oxford University.
- Lawyer specializing in employment and industrial law; married to fellow lawyer.
- Became Labour MP in 1983 for constituency in northern England, formerly a coal-mining area.
- Member of NEC of Labour Party in 1989; member of shadow cabinet.
- Elected leader of Labour Party in 1994, its youngest leader.
- Self-proclaimed modernizer and moderate, left of center.
- Spoke of "New Labour"—called for reduced influence of trade unions in party policies, removing "common ownership of the means of production, distribution, and exchange" from the party's constitution, closer ties with EU, and devolution.
- Became Prime Minister in 1997 after Labour electoral victory.
- Advocated "the Third Way," a mixture of public and private enterprise, less governmental interference with the economic market balanced with social justice.
- Continued as Prime Minister after Labour's 2001 victory; focus on "tough choices."
- Strongly supports U.S. war on terrorism.

the party but also some on whose loyalty they can rely or whose counsel they value.

The prime minister also establishes and appoints the members of cabinet committees. He or she sets up task forces, working parties, and ad hoc meetings as may seem necessary to deal with issues.

The prime minister calls cabinet meetings, takes the chair, determines the items of business, and controls the agenda, as well as also chairing some cabinet committees. In the task of summing up the sense of the meeting, the prime minister is allowed to interpret to some extent the decision reached. He or she is also the ultimate decider and spokesperson of cabinet policy, controlling the flow of information about the government.

The prime minister reports the conclusions of the cabinet and is the chief channel of political communication to the monarch. By convention, no minister can see the monarch without first informing the prime minister. Many of the prerogatives of the Crown, such as declarations of war and peace and dissolution of Parliament, are, in fact, exercised by the prime minister.

The prime minister acts as an arbiter and tries to resolve disputes between departments. The degree of interest the prime minister today has in any particular department varies, but traditionally he or she is always in close touch with the Foreign Office.

The prime minister dispenses considerable patronage and has a power of appointment that includes not only the members of the government but also the senior members of the civil service, the chief members of the judiciary, military leaders, and the archbishops of the Church of England. Twice yearly an official Honors List bestows some title or honor on individuals chosen by the prime minister for some contribution to public life.

The prime minister controls the major appointments in the civil service, especially those of the permanent secretary to the Treasury and the secretary of the cabinet, who is the prime minister's chief adviser on problems concerning the machinery of government.

The prime minister is also the leader of his or her party within Parliament and in the country. In Parliament he or she answers questions in the House of Commons and speaks on important occasions and in debates. Blair spends less time in the House than did his predecessors and answers questions only once a week.

The prime minister's task is to keep the party as united as possible, and his or her political survival depends on it. When the prime minister loses control of the party, as did Chamberlain in 1940, Eden in 1956–1957, and Thatcher in 1990, he or she is obliged to resign. But normally the prime minister can expect loyalty from his or her party, and he or she is aided in the maintenance of discipline by the whips, who since 1964 are paid and are regarded as part of the government team. Thatcher served as prime minister for 11 years, the longest consecutive term in the twentieth century. In 1995, 1997, and again in 2001, a deputy prime minister was appointed and given special duties in the cabinet. In 2002 he was given additional departmental responsibility. The title, however, does not imply a right to succeed the prime minister.

## Is the Prime Minister a Quasi President?

There is universal agreement that the prime minister is the most important political figure in Britain. This has led some to regard the office as similar in the extent and degree of its power to that of the U.S. president. Some argue that the country is governed by the prime minister, who leads, coordinates, and maintains a series of ministers who are advised and supported by the civil service. In this view, prime ministerial government has replaced cabinet government as a result of the increased role of political parties, the influence of the cabinet secretariat, which is close to the prime minister, the control of the prime minister over patronage and major civil service appointments in the departments, and the influence of the mass media and television in particular, which normally focus attention on the leader. In addition, the prime minister has more time for thinking about general policy issues or current problems than do the ministers at the head of particular departments who are responsible for a heavy administrative load.

Certainly it is true that the prime minister has sometimes taken the initiative in foreign affairs and in emergencies and has been personally responsible for political decisions, of which in recent years the Falklands war in 1982 to resist the seizure by Argentina of the Falkland Islands administered by Britain and Blair's support of the U.S. war on terrorism were the most striking. In addition, until recently, the cabinet did not discuss the annual budget and was only informed about it a day before the budget was introduced in the House of Commons.

Although the powers of the prime minister are strong, they are qualified in certain respects. The prime minister can retain power only as long as he or she retains control over the party,

## REVIEW 2.5

## THE CENTER OF BRITISH GOVERNMENT

The center of British government in 2002 comprises the Prime Minister's Office, the Cabinet and its committees, and the Cabinet Office, as well as the Treasury, the Law Officers, and the parliamentary business managers.

### THE PRIME MINISTER'S OFFICE

Located in 10 Downing Street, the Prime Minister's Office is run by a chief of staff, appointed as a temporary civil servant. It includes a number of units: the Private Office, the Political Office, the Press Office, the Strategic Communications Unit, and the Policy Unit, and also a small number of special advisers to help with specific areas of policy.

The Private Office manages the flow of business to and from Prime Minister Blair, arranging his timetable and the documents he needs to see, and briefing him before public meetings and the House of Commons. The Political Office handles Blair's relations with the Labour Party in Parliament and in the country; its members are political appointees, not civil servants. The Press Office deals with the government's relations with the media; its head, Alastair Campbell, appointed as a temporary civil servant, was a powerful and controversial figure between 1997 and 2001. The Strategic Communications Unit provides a unified presentation of government policy to reflect the government's overall program. The Policy Unit, staffed by special advisers, is concerned with the main policy issues of the government, proposing and evaluating initiatives taken by the departments.

### THE CABINET OFFICE

Created in 1916, the Cabinet Office headed by the PM is run by the Cabinet Secretary, who since 1983 has been the head of the Home Civil Service. The Cabinet Office is at the center of British government, responsible for coordinating government business and for reviewing expenditures on and managing government security and intelligence operations. It assists the PM and ministers on selection of senior civil servants. Its two main functions are to assist the Cabinet and its committees and to manage the civil service and the machinery of government. It ensures the efficient dispatch of business in those bodies, records decisions, and distributes them to relevant ministers and officials.

Connected with the Cabinet Office are innovations by Tony Blair aimed at dealing with issues that cut across a number of departmental lines. The most important of these are the Social Exclusion Unit and the Performance and Innovation Unit.

### THE TREASURY

In 2002 the Treasury is headed by Gordon Brown, a political rival of Prime Minister Blair. The Treasury is the guardian of the public purse, coordinating and supervising the spending of public departments and offices. It has considerable influence over the direction of government policy.

and over both the cabinet and Parliament. Unlike the U.S. president, he or she does not have a fixed term of office.

The range of the prime minister's choice of cabinet is very limited compared with that of the U.S. president; moreover, he or she is always aware of potential successors in the cabinet.

The prime minister still relies more than the U.S. president on collective decision making, but the relationship between the prime minister and the cabinet changes with the personality of the individuals and issues involved. Thatcher often appeared to act in an authoritarian way. By contrast, Major was a more tactful and less abrasive person. Blair has been forceful and commanding, and has tended to put less stress on decisions made at the full collective cabinet level. He has been criticized for "presidentialism."

One can conclude that the relationship between the prime minister and the cabinet is molded by the personality and preferences of the prime minister and by the political conditions and problems of the country. Other PMs besides Blair, such as Churchill and Thatcher, have also been accused of being presidential or being elected dictators exercising strong power and leadership, and ignoring both cabinet government and the House of Commons.

## THE CIVIL SERVICE

The British civil service has long been admired for its competence, political impartiality, and dedication, and only in recent years have mounting criticisms led to structural changes in its organization. In the nineteenth century, the civil service was based on patronage and was sometimes corrupt and inefficient. The modern civil service is based on the 1854 Northcote-Trevelyan report, most of whose recommendations were implemented. The civil service became a single organization instead of a series of separate departmental staffs. Entry into the service was based on open competition, not on patronage. The successful candidate entered the service, rather than a particular department, and could be transferred from one department to another.

All examinations were conducted by the Civil Service Commission, not the individual departments, and corresponded to both the level and academic content of those taken in the educational system at the same age of applicants. The exams were always general rather than specific.

The civil service is organized into departments according to subject matter. Almost all departments have their headquarters in London in or near Whitehall, and some have branch offices throughout the country. The civil service, based on the distinction between intellectual and routine work, was divided into three servicewide classes: administrative, executive, and clerical. Outside these classifications were the professional, scientific, and technical officials, as well as the manual and manipulative workers, mostly in the postal and telegraph systems.

Criticism of various aspects of civil service organization and behavior mounted in the 1960s, based largely on the elitist nature of the senior civil service, their limited experience, their lack of initiative, the lack of scientists in top administrative positions, narrowness of outlook, and poor methods of training. As a result, the Fulton Committee on the civil service was established. Reporting in 1968, the committee was critical of the civil service's stress on the gifted amateur and generalist who was expected to be able to deal with any subject matter. It was also critical of the division of the civil service into general classes, the inferior status of scientists, the relative lack of specialized experts, and the frequent movement of senior civil servants between departments.

Only some of the changes recommended were introduced. A Civil Service Department was established, taking over the management of the service from the Treasury Department. A Civil Service College was set up to give courses in management techniques to new entrants. The three-class organization was ended, and part of the service was restructured along classless, unified lines. In the currently reduced (full-time 460,000 by 2002) civil service, the largest unit is the administrative group, composed of the former three classes. An important change was a new grade, administrative trainee, made to strengthen middle management. The Civil Ser-

---

REVIEW
2.6

### *QUANGOS* (QUASI AUTONOMOUS NONGOVERNMENTAL ORGANIZATIONS) OR NONDEPARTMENTAL PUBLIC BODIES

- About 6,700 QUANGOS in 2002, spending one-third of public expenditure.
- Responsible for administration (e.g., Audit Commission, Medical Research Council, Forest Commission) or advice (e.g., Parole Board, Consumers Panel, Political Honors Scouting Committee).
- Mostly appointed by ministers; many business people appointed.
- Decentralize administration and bring in non–civil servants.
- Not directly accountable to those who use public services.

---

vice Department was abolished by Margaret Thatcher in 1981, but the prime minister remains in charge of the machinery of government. In 1988, Thatcher proposed a plan for semiautonomous agencies to manage services now administered by departments. By 2002, over 100 such agencies had been set up, employing 200,000 civil servants. The general idea behind these agencies is to introduce a more entrepreneurial and competitive spirit into administration. Besides the executive agencies a large number of QUANGOs have been set up, run by non–civil servants appointed by a minister.

A constant cause of criticism of the senior civil service—the 3,000 top positions in the home and foreign service—has been that its members come largely from the middle and upper class, with less than 5 percent coming from the working class, and that a high proportion of those in the elite group, the former administrative class, was educated at the public schools and at Oxford and Cambridge. About three-quarters of top officials come from Oxbridge and about half from the public schools. The proportions are even higher for entrants into the senior foreign civil service, of which about 10 percent were educated at Eton.

## The Role of the Civil Service

The senior civil servants advise ministers on formulating policy and decision making. Their role is based on impartiality and anonymity, though the latter has been eroded in recent years. All governments, irrespective of political persuasion, have been served loyally by the nonpolitical permanent civil servants.

The work of the civil service is anonymous because of the principle of ministerial responsibility; the minister alone is responsible to Parliament for the operation of his or her department, even though in practice the minister may not always be aware of what has been done. Civil servants are free to give unbiased and frank advice to ministers without having to defend their views.

The obverse of anonymity has been the secrecy behind the making of decisions, both in form and content. The shielding of the civil service from the glare of partisan politics has also meant that it is restricted in its political activities. No member of the senior administrative group, above the clerical staff, can participate in national political activity; a member can take part in local politics only with departmental permission.

The determination of policy is the responsibility of ministers; the task of the civil service is to carry out that policy with energy and goodwill. The minister is a politician, not an expert on the issues of his or her department, and he or she must decide policy not only on its own merits, but in light of the government program as a whole and of what is politically rather than administratively possible at a certain point.

## CIVIL SERVANTS AND POLICY ADVICE

During the 1990s, and especially during the Blair government since 1997, two new factors have been apparent. One factor is that, ministers, who have tended to appear less frequently before Parliament and who have nonofficial advisers and spin doctors, have seemed less dependent on civil servants, who have become more a vehicle for managerial responsibilities than for policy advice. The other factor is a certain tension between two different views of a proper public service ethos. One view, the traditional one, is that civil servants are concerned with protecting the public good, ensuring good government, which might entail checks on ministers. The second view is that the primary function of civil servants is to serve ministers, whose will and political interests are paramount. The traditional view seems less certain today than in the past.

But the reality of ministerial–civil service relations is often different from the theory. Departmental policy may often result from past administrative experience and the cumulative decisions made by the civil servants while dealing with individual cases. Moreover, civil servants do not merely implement policy; they also play a role in policy making, advising on options for new policies. The long experience and great knowledge of the senior administrators may often lead them to take the initiative in suggesting new policies. Ministers are not experts in the affairs of their departments and have time to pay attention to only a relatively small number of those affairs.

Ministers may often accept the advice or acquiesce in the views of their civil servants. The role of the civil service has grown with the vast increase in government business, owing to the expanded activity of government in internal affairs; the time pressures on ministers; the influence of the cabinet secretariat; the growth of interdepartmental committees, which tend to settle problems at an early stage; and the creation of high-level civil service committees to parallel and give advice to cabinet committees.

But influential as the civil service may be, ministers are not its puppets, nor are civil servants "statesmen in disguise." Senior civil servants are mostly concerned with the administration of existing policies rather than policy planning, with immediate needs rather than long-term policy.

The interaction between ministers and senior civil servants is complex, but the political ministers are still the dominant element in the policy-making process.

## THE LEGISLATURE

Parliament—or strictly speaking the Queen-in-Parliament, since the monarch must assent to all legislation—is the supreme legislative body. It has the authority to pass, change, or repeal any law without being subject to restraint or veto by the courts of law or any other body; on the contrary, Parliament can reverse the decisions of the courts. No issues are outside the control of Parliament. It can pass retrospective legislation that legalizes past illegalities and punishes actions that were lawful when performed. By the 1911 Parliament Act, the term of Parliament is fixed at five years, though it can be dissolved at any time. But Parliament is able to prolong its own life as it did during both world wars. One Parliament cannot bind its successors.

In fact, Parliament uses self-restraint in the exercise of this legal supremacy. It is conscious of the common law tradition and of political conventions that foster moderation. The effective power of Parliament is limited in real ways. Parliament rarely passes legislation which is contrary to the views of the population or deprives individuals of rights. The principle of the mandate suggests that the electorate has given general approval of changes proposed by the electoral manifesto of the successful party. Though this does not mean that the electorate has approved of all proposals in the manifesto, it implies that a major change will only rarely be introduced in Parliament if it was not included in the party manifesto, except in a time of emergency or crisis.

Parliamentary action is also affected and influenced by the major interest groups in the country, which by convention are always consulted on legislation related to them. In the 1960s and 1970s some regarded the trade unions as having a virtual veto power on proposals concerning industrial relations and incomes policy. Perhaps most important of all, Parliament is dominated by the government, which, as the majority party, generally controls the time, procedure, and actions of Parliament and is responsible for the initiation of all financial and most legislative proposals.

In the 1970s a new factor, British membership in the European Community (EC), now the European Union (EU), affected parliamentary supremacy. Britain is now pledged to adhere to EU decisions, which signifies qualification of Parliament's legal supremacy. The European Court of Justice ruled in 1990 that British courts could suspend a statute that was incompatible with law of the European Community. The Court ruled in 1991 that parts of a British law breached the law of the EC and therefore had to be changed. Parliamentary supremacy has also been limited by the 1950 European Convention on Human Rights, by which Britain accepted the obligation to recognize certain fundamental rights.

## Composition of Parliament

The two chambers of Parliament now at Westminister have existed for seven centuries. Though for some time the House of Commons has been the more significant political body, the House of Lords had an unlimited veto power over legislation until 1911. In that year the Parliament Act limited the veto of the Lords to two years over bills passed by the Commons in three successive sessions and abolished the veto over financial bills. In 1949 this delaying power of the Lords was reduced to one year.

## House of Lords

Until 1999, the House of Lords consisted of about 1,330 members. Its heterogeneous composition reflected the nature of its origin with the greater noblemen and higher clergy. The main categories were the following:

1. Some 760 hereditary peers (since 1958 including women) who inherit or have been appointed to the peerage and who pass on the titles to their heirs; since the Peerage Act of 1963 they can disclaim their titles for their lifetime.

2. About 550 life peers, men and women, created under the Life Peerage Act of 1958; their title expires at their death.

3. Twelve Lords of Appeal in Ordinary (Law Lords), who are appointed to act as judges when the House of Lords acts as a court of law; they must have been barristers for at least 15 years and have held high judicial office for at least 2 years.

4. Twenty-six senior dignitaries of the Church of England; they are the archbishops of Canterbury and York, the Bishops of London, Durham, and Winchester, and 21 other bishops in their order of seniority as bishops.

The House of Lords Act 1999 ended the right of all but 92 of hereditary peers to sit in the upper chamber. Further changes are to come. In future, members may be chosen through an electoral system and through appointment.

Although the House of Lords still has the function of considering and approving all legislation, its powers have been significantly limited by the Parliament Acts of 1911 and 1949. The Lords can propose amendments to bills and can delay them by voting against them, but they have no power of absolute veto. Since 1949, a bill passed by the Commons in two successive sessions does not need the consent of the House of

Lords. This procedure has been used five times between 1911 and 2002.

The House of Lords has no power over finances. It can still reject, however, delegated legislation, which requires the approval of both Houses. By convention, it will not vote against the principles of a government bill if the bill was featured in the governing party's electoral manifesto.

The Lords are unpaid; however, since 1957, attending members receive a daily allowance for expenses and lodging. Because of the experience in public affairs and the intellectual caliber of many of the new life peers—as well as the presence of past and present cabinet ministers, other public servants, and former MPs—debate on important topics in the House of Lords may often be on a high level.

On the whole, the House of Lords exercised its functions with discretion. The subordination of the Lords to the Commons and to the executive has been accepted in general, but proposed legislation has sometimes been delayed.

It is this power of delay and the Conservative majority in the House of Lords that have been the main reasons for criticism. In a democratic system like the British, it seems paradoxical for a nonelected body to delay the legislation passed by the elected lower chamber and to claim it is acting in the best interests of the country. Because of the automatic Conservative plurality in the House of Lords, a Labour government had more to fear in this regard than a Conservative one.

The House of Lords still performs a useful role as an organ of review in the revision of legislation, the initiation of noncontroversial legislation, the discussion of important topics, and the examination of delegated legislation—which all save the time of the Commons. It performs an important judicial function as the final Court of Appeal and Court of Criminal Appeal. By convention, only the Law Lords and the lord chancellor attend these sittings of the House as a court.

## House of Commons

There are now 659 members (MPs) of the House of Commons elected from the territorial constituencies of the country. The number and distribution of the seats can be altered according to population changes after recommendations by the four boundary commissions. Currently, 529 represent English, 40 Welsh, 72 Scottish, and 18 Northern Ireland constituencies. Members are elected at a general election or at a by-election on the death or resignation of an MP.

There are no property, religious, sex, or education disqualifications. Any person over 21 can be elected, except members of the House of Lords, aliens, clergy of the established churches and the Catholic Church, felons, and holders of most official positions other than members of the government. Since 1963, an MP who has succeeded to the peerage can disclaim his title and remain in the Commons.

**A CLOSER LOOK 2.11**

### THE HOUSE OF LORDS: INTERIM REFORM

A major constitutional change was made by the House of Lords Act 1999, which removed the automatic right of hereditary peers to sit in the upper house of Parliament, ending 700 years of tradition. By a compromise agreement, the House of Lords will retain 92 hereditary peers until the second stage of its reform. Two of these are ceremonial persons, 15 were elected by the whole house, and 75 were chosen by hereditary peers voting in political party groups. Proposals by a Royal Commission for the second stage of reform were introduced in January 2000; the essential one was that a new chamber would be chosen, part appointed and part elected, to represent the countries and regions of the nation. No immediate action was taken. In terms of declared political affiliation in 2002, the House of Lords has 736 members, consisting of 227 Conservatives, 198 Labors, 62 Liberal Democrats, 195 nonaffiliated, 26 bishops, and 28 current and former Law Lords.

MPs are paid less and have inadequate facilities compared with U.S. congressional members. Only in recent years have they obtained some secretarial assistance and office space. They now receive a salary of about £48,371 and another £51,500 for secretarial costs. Nevertheless, there is no shortage of candidates for the Commons. People are attracted to it for nonmaterial rewards, including public service, personal prestige, and the opportunity to exert influence on public affairs. However in recent years, as a result of certain improper or questionable behavior, MPs have to register their financial interests and, since 1996, cannot accept payment for lobbying.

The glory of Parliament may have dimmed somewhat in recent years, but the Commons still plays a significant role in the political system (see Table 2.14). Parliament not only possesses legislative supremacy and authorizes all expenditure and taxation; the Commons is politically important because its party composition is the basis for the formation of governments. It enables the leaders of one political party to rule and those of the opposition party to be considered as a possible alternative government. It is the major political arena in which there is continuous interaction among the parties. Ministers explain and defend their policies in it against the attacks of the opposition.

If it is not the real determinant of policy or decisions, Parliament wields influence over the executive which makes concessions to it. For its members, Parliament is a forum for the raising of complaints and grievances on behalf of their constituents, for arguing political views of their own, and for subjecting the executive to criticism. It is also the main path to political distinction and to membership in the government.

## TABLE 2.14

### THE POWERS AND LIMITS OF THE HOUSE OF COMMONS

*Powers*

Provides road to political success and to becoming a minister

Main forum for discussion of grievances of constituents

Approves legislation and policy thus giving them greater legitimacy; debates legislation and motions

Allows representation and expression of different views of citizens on policy

Asks questions of ministers

Greater independence of MPs in voting; governments defeated in some standing committees

Departmental select committees in House of Commons investigate administration and recommend policy

Some committees discuss issues of European Union

*Limits*

Power of executive

Increasing impact of interest groups outside of Parliament

Increasing burden of work

Little impact on decisions of European Union

## Who Becomes an MP?

MPs have become increasingly professional in their background and lifestyle and, therefore, less characteristic of their constituents. This is especially true in the Parliamentary Labour Party, where the proportion of manual workers has fallen and that of professionals has increased

## A CLOSER LOOK 2.12

### DID I HEAR A WORD?

MPs may not utter certain words or phrases about each other in the House of Commons. The forbidden locutions include: *black guard, cad, criminal, liar, coward, hypocrite, murderer, Pharisee, rat, traitor, guttersnipe, dog, stool-pigeon, swine, ruffian, snail, jackass, jerk, impertinent pup.*

since 1945. The average age of the PLP has fallen; recruiting younger MPs generally means less opportunity for working-class candidates, who tend to emerge later in life.

The Conservative MPs illustrate the postwar shift away from landowners, farmers, and people with an aristocratic background to businesspeople and industrial technocrats. A considerable number have been local councillors. Conservative MPs have rarely had working-class backgrounds.

The number of women MPs in the postwar period was small: about 5 percent until 1987 and 8 percent in 1992. In 1997, a record number of 120 women were elected. Women have always been underrepresented in the Commons, which has been a male-dominated "club."

There has been a trend for MPs to remain longer in Parliament and thus to be regarded as professional politicians. The House of Commons has always been attractive to people in the professions, who in many cases combine their careers as lawyers, journalists, or businesspeople with afternoon and evening attendance in the House.

## MPs and Political Parties

All MPs are members of political parties, and the arrangements in the Commons reflect the fact that its working is interrelated with the party system and the operation of government.

The only exception to the partisan nature of MPs is the Speaker (with three deputies), who is the chief officer of the House of Commons. Unlike the U.S. counterpart, the British Speaker is an impartial, nonpartisan figure who gives up party associations. The general rule is that the Speaker, who is elected at the beginning of a Parliament, will be reelected in subsequent Parliaments irrespective of which party controls a majority. For the first time a woman was elected in 1992.

The chamber in which MPs meet is small and rectangular. It is a political arena in which the opposing parties physically face each other, as shown in Figure 2.5. The Speaker sits at one end of the chamber. The benches to his or her right are used by the government party, while the official opposition party and other parties not supporting the government sit on his or her left.

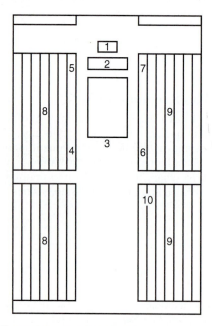

1. Speaker
2. Clerks
3. Mace
4. Prime minister
5. Cabinet
6. Leader of opposition
7. Shadow cabinet
8. Government party MPs (backbenchers)
9. Main opposition party MPs (backbenchers)
10. MPs of other opposition parties

Figure 2.5 HOUSE OF COMMONS

The members of the government and the shadow cabinet sit on the front benches, with their supporters behind them on the back benches. The physical separation reflects the political differences between the two sides.

The smallness of the chamber, which seats only 350 MPs, together with the fact that MPs speak from their places rather than from a rostrum, has led to a more intimate style of speech than is often the case in other countries. By tradition, MPs do not read speeches or speak boisterously. They refer to colleagues in a dignified and polite way.

With rare exceptions the MPs are organized in parliamentary parties. The Parliamentary Labour Party (PLP) is composed of Labour members of both Houses. The major organ of the Conservative Party in Parliament is the 1922 Committee, composed of all Conservative backbenchers.

## The Opposition

The official opposition, the largest nongovernment party in Parliament, is a vital part of the British system. Its leaders are seen inside and outside Parliament, as an alternative government. Its function is both to subject government to criticism and to seek to replace it, as well as to participate in the working of the system.

The opposition acts as a responsible group in criticism of the government. It proposes alternative policies and tries to change government policies, get concessions on government bills, and defeat the government. By convention, governments resign or request dissolution of Parliament if defeated on a major question, though since 1867 only five governments have resigned for this reason. In 1979 the opposition successfully moved a vote of no confidence for the first time since 1892. In Parliament, the opposition is continually addressing itself to the electorate as a whole with its eyes on the next election.

The opposition also cooperates with the government party in formulating the business of the Commons. It chooses the subjects for debate on a number of occasions, currently on the 16 days available to it. It is given time at the committee stage of bills to move amendments and time in

Prime Minister Tony Blair, 2002.

the House of Commons itself for both opposition leaders and backbenchers to question ministers. The government even provides the time for the opposition to move motions of censure against it.

Since 1937 there has been an official, paid leader of the opposition who is consulted by the prime minister on political arrangements; by convention, the shadow cabinet receives information from cabinet ministers relevant to the conduct of affairs. There is consultation between the two sides on some questions concerning foreign affairs and defense.

The opposition is represented on standing and select committees, now about 40, in proportion to its membership in the Commons. An accepted rule is that the chairpersons of some committees are members of the opposition.

## How Important Is the MP?

Important though MPs are, their prominence has declined for several reasons: the extension of the suffrage, the organization of constituency associations and the rise of disciplined political parties; the increase in the function and activity of government and the growth in power of the bureaucracy; and the nature of modern general elections, which are to a large degree about which party leader will become prime minister.

MPs are aware that the electorate is the ultimate political sovereign and that their reelection depends on their activity in Parliament. Attendance is not compulsory, and no financial loss is attached to nonattendance, but it is rare for MPs to neglect their parliamentary duties. MPs also frequently visit their constituencies, particularly on weekends, and hold "surgeries," at which they meet their constituents. They ask questions in the Commons and speak in debates on matters affecting their areas.

The crucial fact about MPs is that, with rare exceptions, they are members of parties that they are expected to support loyally and without which they could not have been elected. In the Commons, MPs are still subject to the persuasion, if not the discipline, of the whips and rarely engage in a conflict with the parliamentary leadership. Party cohesion exists partly because of agreement by party MPs on policy issues, partly because of ambition for promotion, especially among those of the government party, and partly because of the probable political isolation experienced by those consistently opposing party policy. The ultimate threat by a prime minister, faced by revolt within his party, is to dissolve Parliament, but this is a theoretical rather than a real menace. Nevertheless, some revolts against the leaders, when the party is in power and in opposition, have occurred.

This recent greater assertiveness and independence of MPs can be attributed to a number of factors. MPs found that they were seldom denied readoption as candidates or ministerial promotion because of their rebellious actions. Defeats of the government—65 times between 1972 and 1979, and 26 times a session during the Blair government in 2000—did not mean resignation or the dissolution of Parliament, which will occur only on a motion of no confidence. The major parties have been internally divided on significant recent issues such as the European Union, devolution, and income policy. MPs have believed, correctly in a number of cases, that fear of defeat may make a government change its mind.

For some time the dominant body in the operation of the Commons has been the government, which controls the timetable, the allocation of time, and the procedure of the Commons and is responsible for the initiation of most legislation. During the years from 1939 to 1948, backbenchers had no legislative initiative; they currently have 12 days to introduce bills as well as 10 days to move motions.

The great increase in the amount of legislation, and in its scope, variety, and technical nature, has meant both that few MPs are knowledgeable about much of the legislation and the wide range of problems with which the Commons deals and that little time is available for the discussion of government legislation. Most amendments of that legislation are minor, and they are made or agreed to by the government. Of those amendments proposed by ministers, almost all are accepted by the Commons; of those proposed by backbenchers, few are successful.

In addition, many rules are now made by ministers in the form of delegated legislation. There are several reasons for this large development of ministerial power: the technical nature of the rules, the speed with which they can be made, the flexibility available to change them, and the opportunity of discretionary choice. Although some opportunity to discuss delegated legislation is available to MPs, there is little parliamentary scrutiny of it.

## An Assenting Assembly

MPs participate in the work of the Commons in a variety of ways: through question time, participation in debates on legislation and on policy, membership on standing and select committees, and proposal of motions and initiation of some legislation.

In the parliamentary golden age of the mid-nineteenth century, the Commons regularly defeated governments without being dissolved. Since that period, few governments have been defeated and obliged to resign or have Parliament dissolved as a result of the actions of the House of Commons.

A number of criticisms can be made of the failings of contemporary parliaments. Parliamentary control over administration and finance is ineffective. Most MPs feel inadequately informed about administration. The real initiative in the legislative process and policy making is in the hands of the executive. Procedure in the Commons is still poorly organized and archaic. The majority political party is the real strength underlying the operation of the political system. Nevertheless, recent experience has shown that MPs can exercise some control over governments. The assertiveness and dissent among MPs led to a surprising number of government defeats in the 1970s and 1980s.

## JUDGES AND POLITICS

Unlike the United States, Britain does not have a system of judicial review, and courts cannot declare legislation void. As the legal sovereign, Parliament, not the courts, decides on the nature and extent of legislative power. The function of British judges is to apply the law to the particular cases before their courts rather than to decide on the desirability or correctness of the law itself. Some judges interpret the law in a way that upholds individual liberty or in accordance with social and personal justice. But most judges interpret statutes narrowly, holding that it is Parliament, not judicial interpretation, that should change a law that is unjust.

British judges have long had the reputation of being impartial and neutral. The judges' impartiality results partly from the common law tradition and judgment based on precedent and partly from the method of their appointment. Judges are not political appointees; few of them have been MPs, and even fewer have been partisans of a political party, as they come from the ranks of barristers with long and successful careers. In the legal profession, there are now about 5,500 barristers, of whom 750 are women, and over 40,000 solicitors (see Table 2.15).

Judges are independent of the other branches of government and their salaries are not open to discussion by Parliament. Since 1701, judges have been appointed on "good behavior," meaning until retirement, which since 1959 has been at age 75. They can only be dismissed by resolutions of both Houses, an event that has not yet occurred. They are scrupulous about a fair hearing in court and impartial application of the law.

The qualities of impartiality and neutrality are always present in cases concerning disputes between private individuals. But there are also other cases in which decisions of judges may affect a wider group of people, or in which they can exercise some discretion. These cases have recently included subjects such as immigration, industrial relations, race relations, police powers, and human rights. It is on questions of this kind that the generally conservative view of judges may be felt.

Judges form one of the prominent elite groups of the country. Over 75 percent of senior judges were educated at public schools and at Oxford and Cambridge; over 80 percent come from upper-class or upper-middle-class backgrounds. A conservative position is to be expected from individuals who not only come from these social

### TABLE 2.15

### BRITISH JUDGES

| Position | Men | Women |
| --- | --- | --- |
| Lords of Appeal in Ordinary (Law Lords) | 12 | — |
| Lords Justice of Appeal | 31 | 1 |
| High Court Judges | 88 | 6 |
| Circuit Judges | 486 | 30 |
| Recorders | 853 | 53 |
| Assistant Recorders | 297 | 52 |
| District Judges | 273 | 29 |
| Deputy District Judges | 632 | 84 |

Source: *The Times*, April 10, 1995.

backgrounds but also have had a successful career and adhere to the tradition of the common law and precedent.

Judges have been reluctant to limit the scope of ministerial powers and have habitually upheld the exercise of the discretionary power of ministers (who can take action under a statute if they think it necessary). Judges have approved executive action, provided it was not out of bounds or exercised unfairly, unreasonably, or in bad faith.

But in the last three decades, some judges have tried to control ministerial administrative action and assert judicial discretion in cases on the scope of executive prerogative in war or on ministerial privilege, or if they decided that ministers had exceeded their legal powers and had encroached on individual rights.

Britain does not have a strong system of administrative or constitutional law to control the actions of the political executive or administration. Yet in recent years the judiciary has been more active in scrutinizing and challenging executive actions, largely by reference to "fundamental rights" which need to be safeguarded as well as to the will of Parliament, the traditional basis for judgement. This kind of judicial review, though still rare, results from the increase of powers claimed by an active government and from the impact of European Union laws and charters which judges interpret.

The Human Rights Act 1998 not only provides for individuals to challenge executive actions but also allows the courts wide interpretive powers regarding those actions. Since 1998 the courts have decided on a number of occasions that ministers acted beyond their powers, and decided on issues stemming from British statutes in a way that they thought compatible with the European Convention on Human Rights. In addition to this convention, a series of international agreements such as the UN Convention on Refugees and the UN's Dublin Convention give judges the power to block deportation and repatriation of individuals suspected by the government to be linked to terrorist organizations.

## Thinking Critically

1. Is it still true to speak of the British system as cabinet government?
2. Do you think the present electoral system in Britain should be changed?
3. Do you believe that the role of Parliament has been reduced in recent years?
4. Should the House of Lords be abolished?
5. What are the major differences between the British political parties?
6. Do you agree with those who say that civil servants are the real rulers in Britain?

## KEY TERMS

backbencher *(43)*
by-election *(64)*
the City *(75)*
civil service *(86–88)*
common law *(88)*
Confederation of British Industry (CBI) *(75)*
Conservative Party *(70)*
constituency *(58)*
Crown *(76–77)*
legislation *(94)*
House of Commons *(90–91)*
House of Lords *(89–90)*
Labour Party *(70–72)*
marginal seat *(59)*
National Executive Committee (NEC) *(71)*
opposition *(93)*
party identification *(66–67)*
Plaid Cymru *(62)*
prime minister *(82–86)*
QUANGO *(87)*
Scottish National Party (SNP) *(62)*
Social and Liberal Democrats (SLD or Liberal Democrats) *(59, 69)*
Trades Union Congress (TUC) *(70, 75)*
Treasury *(85)*
Westminster *(89)*
whip *(94)*
Whitehall *(86)*

# FURTHER READINGS

Blackburn, Robert. *The Electoral System in Britain* (London: Macmillan, 1995).

Butler, David, and Martin Westlake. *British Politics and European Elections 1999* (New York: St. Martin's 2000).

Butler, David, and Dennis Kavanagh. *The British General Election of 1997* (New York: St. Martin's, 1997).

Conley, Frank. *General Elections Today,* 2nd ed. (New York: Manchester University Press, 1992).

Crewe, Ivor, et al. *The British Electorate 1963–87* (New York: Cambridge University Press, 1991).

Hart, Jenifer. *Proportional Representation; Critics of the British Electoral System, 1820–1945* (New York: Oxford University Press, 1992).

Kavanagh, Dennis, ed. *Electoral Politics* (New York: Oxford University Press, 1992).

Miller, William, et al. *How Voters Change* (New York: Oxford University Press, 1990).

Norris, Pippa. *Electoral Change since 1945* (Oxford: Blackwell, 1997).

Richardson, Jeremy, ed. *Pressure Groups* (New York: Oxford University Press, 1993).

Seyd, Patrick. *The Rise and Fall of the Labour Left* (New York: St. Martin's, 1987).

## *The Executive and Judiciary*

Barber, James P. *The Prime Minister since 1945* (Cambridge: Blackwell, 1991).

Bogdanor, Vernon. *The Monarchy and the Constitution* (London: Oxford University Press, 1995).

Foley, Michael. *The British Presidency: Tony Blair and the Politics of Public Leadership* (Manchester: Manchester University Press, 2000).

Griffith, J.A.G. *The Politics of the Judiciary,* 5th ed. (London: Fontana, 1997).

Hennessy, Peter. *The Prime Minister: The Office and Its Holders since 1945* (London: Penguin, 2000).

Hennessy, Peter. *Whitehall* (London: Secker and Warburg, 1989).

James, Simon. *British Cabinet Government,* 2nd ed. (New York: Routledge, 1999).

Laver, Michael, and Kenneth Shepsie, eds. *Cabinet Ministers and Parliamentary Government* (New York: Cambridge University Press, 1994).

Pilkington, Colin. *The Civil Service in Britain Today* (Manchester: Manchester University Press, 1999).

Shell, Donald, and Richard Hodder-Williams. *Churchill to Major: The British Prime Ministership since 1945* (Armonk: Sharpe, 1995).

## *The Legislature*

Adonis, Andrew. *Parliament Today,* 2nd ed. (New York: Manchester University Press, 1993).

Bluth, Christopher, et al. *The Future of European Security* (Brookfield: Dartmouth, 1995).

Franklin, Mark, and Philip Norton, eds. *Parliamentary Questions* (Oxford: Clarendon Press, 1993).

Griffith, J.A.G., and Michael Ryle. *Parliament: Functions, Practice and Procedure* (London: Sweet and Maxwell, 1989).

Jogerst, Michael. *Reform in the House of Commons* (Lexington: University of Kentucky, 1993).

Norris, Pippa, and Joni Lovenduski. *Political Recruitment: Gender, Race and Class in the British Parliament* (New York: Cambridge University Press, 1995).

Norton, Philip. *Does Parliament Matter?* (New York: Harvester Wheatsheaf, 1993).

Norton, Philip, and David Wood. *Back from Westminster: British MPs and Their Constituents* (Lexington: University Press of Kentucky, 1993).

Rush, Michael, ed. *Parliament and Pressure Politics* (New York: Oxford University Press, 1990).

Shell, Donald. *The House of Lords,* 2nd ed. (New York: Harvester Wheatsheaf, 1992).

Silk, Paul, and Rhodri Walters. *How Parliament Works,* 4th ed. (New York: Longman, 1998).

Weir, Stuart, and David Beetham. *Political Power and Democratic Control in Britain* (London: Routledge, 1999).

# C. PUBLIC POLICY

## THE MIXED ECONOMY

Like other Western countries, Britain has a mixed economy. Part of it is owned and administered by public authorities; this public sector employs 5.1 million workers, including central and local government and public corporations. However, most of the economy is under private ownership and control. The private sector has increased since 1979 as the Conservative government cut the public sector and denationalized or "privatized" many enterprises.

Both Labour and Conservative governments intervened in economic affairs in the postwar period in differing degrees. This intervention stemmed partly from the desire to implement social principles such as the public ownership of resources, the welfare of citizens, and the reduction of unemployment, but also from the effort to solve economic problems by increasing production and trade. Governments therefore not only nationalized industries, but also promoted industrial development, supplied money and credits to both public and private enterprises, increased the level of investment, helped firms in trouble, proposed "targets" and planning agreements for industry and the restructuring of industry, and attempted to restrain wage increases.

The public sector today comprises three parts: central government, local government, and public–private partnerships, which have largely replaced the former nationalized industries and aim to deliver public services through private sector management.

Central government is responsible for all spending on social security benefits, health, defense, trade, industry, overseas payments and foreign aid, and central administration (see Table 2.16 and Figure 2.6). It also partly finances housing, education, transport, and law and order programs. The largest spending programs are on social security, health, the environment, education, transport, and defense. Most of the expenditure is paid for by taxation and social security

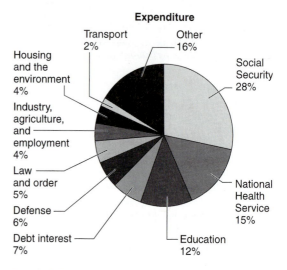

**Expenditure**

**Figure 2.6** UK GOVERNMENT EXPENDITURE FORECAST 2000–2001

contributions, which in the late 1990s amounted to about 35–37 percent of GNP.

Local government now accounts for about one-quarter of total public spending. The largest item is education, followed by housing, transport, law and order, and social services. This expenditure is paid for by property taxes and by grants from the central government.

The nationalized industries in 1979 accounted for 10 percent of gross domestic product (GDP), employed almost 2 million (8 percent of the workforce), and took 14 percent of fixed investment. The industries dominated areas such as coal, electricity, gas, broadcasting, public transport, communications, and iron and steel. Because they were producers of basic goods and services, as well as large consumers of raw materials, they significantly affected investment, employment, prices, and cost of living in the whole economy. By 1988, denationalization had reduced them to 6 percent of GDP, 750,000 workers, and 9 percent of investment.

## TABLE 2.16

### GOVERNMENT SPENDING LIMITS, 1998–2001

The Economic and Fiscal Strategy Report in June 1998 introduced changes to the public expenditure control regime. Three-year departmental expenditure limits (DELs) now apply to most government departments. Spending which cannot easily be subject to three-year planning is reviewed annually in the Budget as annually managed expenditure (AME). Current and capital expenditure are treated separately.

| Departmental Expenditure Limits | £ billion | | |
| Current Budget | Outturn 1998–1999 | Estimate 1999–2000 | Plans 2000–2001 |
| --- | --- | --- | --- |
| Education and Employment | 13.6 | 14.8 | 16.6 |
| Health | 37.5 | 40.5 | 44.2 |
| of which NHS | 36.8 | 39.9 | 43.5 |
| DETR—main programs | 4.0 | 4.6 | 4.7 |
| DETR—local government and regional policy | 32.4 | 33.9 | 35.3 |
| Home Office | 6.5 | 7.3 | 7.6 |
| Legal departments | 2.6 | 2.7 | 2.8 |
| Defense | 20.8 | 21.6 | 21.3 |
| Foreign and Commonwealth Office | 1.0 | 1.1 | 1.0 |
| International Development | 2.1 | 2.2 | 2.5 |
| Trade and Industry | 2.6 | 3.0 | 3.2 |
| Agriculture, Fisheries and Food | 1.2 | 1.2 | 1.1 |
| Culture, Media and Sport | 0.8 | 0.9 | 0.9 |
| Social Security (administration) | 3.3 | 3.3 | 3.2 |
| Scotland | 11.6 | 12.3 | 13.0 |
| Wales | 5.9 | 6.4 | 6.9 |
| Northern Ireland | 5.1 | 5.5 | 5.5 |
| Chancellor of the Exchequer's departments | 3.1 | 3.5 | 3.6 |
| Cabinet Office | 1.0 | 1.1 | 1.1 |
| Welfare to Work | 0.3 | 0.5 | 0.8 |
| Invest to save budget | 0 | 0 | 0 |
| Reserve | 0 | 0 | 2.0 |
| Allowance for shortfall | 0 | −1.4 | 0 |
| Total Current Budget | 155.3 | 165.1 | 177.3 |

*Source:* Stationery Office: Budget 2000.

## THE DECLINE OF NATIONALIZED INDUSTRIES

The motives to nationalize industries were varied. They included public control over significant parts of the economic system; efficient organization and development of the economy; influencing the level of investment to achieve full employment; better industrial relations; preventing possible abuse of a monopoly situation; continuation of enterprises, even if unprofitable, to provide a social service or minimize unemployment; or assistance to failing firms. Added to these economic and social reasons was the ideology of the Labour Party, whose constitution (Clause IV) called for "public ownership of the means of production, distribution, and exchange."

A major change took place with the privatization policy of the Thatcher government that consisted of selling off the assets and shares of nationalized industries to private owners. This policy also allowed some services previously administered by public authorities to be performed by private firms. Prime Minister Thatcher argued that privatization brought certain benefits: the industries would be more efficient and profitable in a more competitive market, away from interference of officials; their objectives would not be overridden by irrelevant political, social, and economic factors, thereby increasing business confidence; the government would raise large amounts by sales; Britain would become a property-owning democracy (now 11 million shareholders). By 1991 about 60 percent of state industry had been privatized. The government claimed that output, profits, investment, and industrial relations in those enterprises had all improved.

The Conservative government also sought to promote competition by ending the monopoly of a number of enterprises, such as long distance buses and express delivery services, and of certain professional activity, such as some legal work.

## ECONOMIC PLANNING

All postwar British governments accepted the need for planning, which resulted from increased government activity and expenditure. They saw the need for creating nationalized industries and increasing productivity, economic growth, and exports. Governmental intervention took a variety of forms: financial aid and incentives to stimulate industrial investment; taxation changes and loans to strengthen development areas and transfer workers from services to manufacturing; physical controls to induce firms to move to less

developed areas; subsidies to aid failing enterprises and controls on wages, prices, and foreign exchange. Bodies such as the National Economic Development Council (NEDC) and the National Enterprise Board were set up to assist the economy and to foster greater efficiency.

These governments sought, mainly through the annual budget, to maintain a high level of economic activity, and strove for full employment, economic growth, and a rising standard of living. They stressed expansion of demand rather than anti-inflationary measures, and relatively little attention was paid to restraint of money supply.

The Thatcher government broke with this approach. It sought, at first, to reduce inflation by restricting the money supply, hoping to increase output and employment. It tried to revitalize the private sector by lowering taxes and interest rates that would result from cuts in public expenditure and borrowing. It emphasized free market forces by reducing the public sector, taming the trade unions, ending controls on prices and wages, and trying to curb the spending of local authorities.

The government from 1979 on was particularly interested in limiting or controlling the power of the trade unions. Unions must now hold secret ballots for the election of union leaders, before a strike is called, and on their political funds. Limits have been set on picketing, secondary strike action, and closed shops. Union funds are now liable for damages in civil actions. Union membership declined substantially during the 1980s.

In the late 1980s, a policy at first called New Steps was introduced to separate executive functions of officials from policy making. The civil service would be reduced to a small core responsible for policy making, while many activities would be transferred to agencies which would deliver services and which would have a good deal of operational and budgetary autonomy, thus replacing civil service departments. By 2002 about 150 such agencies have been set up, employing three-quarters of all civil servants. Regulatory agencies have been set up to get public utility

---

**REVIEW**

**2.7**

### THATCHER AND BLAIR ECONOMICS

THATCHER

- Monetarism; minimal government intervention in economic affairs except for control of money supply.
- Chief concern to control inflation, which was linked to supply of money circulating in the economy.

BLAIR

- Continued policy of keeping inflation low.
- Financed expenditure with taxation, usually low indirect tax.
- Accepted that free market, not the state, should be the main provider of goods and services.

---

companies to provide good service for consumers and to protect the environment.

In 2002 the private sector is employing three-quarters of civilian workers, of whom 19 percent belong to trade unions; by contrast, about 60 percent of public sector employees are union members. Public spending as a proportion of GDP between 1997 and 2000 fell from 41.2 to 37.7 percent. Both Major and Blair have wanted to extend private sector management in some major public services, especially in medical care and transport and education; outside contractors provide a range of services.

## THE WELFARE STATE

The term *welfare state* implies the provision by the state of benefits and services, elements of social and economic security, including health care, subsidies for housing, sick and unemployment benefits, pensions, disability help, and family allowances. Britain has long concerned itself with the poor. Before 1914, national insurance, old-age pensions, and unemployment insurance were adopted. But it was not until after World War II that the plans for a welfare state and for social improvement were implemented. The Beveridge Report in 1942 had proposed the extension of the process of insurance to provide adequate subsistence for all. Two years later Beveridge called for a system of full employment.

The Labour government of 1945–1950 introduced the basic elements of a welfare system which has been modified and extended during the ensuing years. Three elements of this system have been particularly important: social security, the national health service, and personal social services. The last is the responsibility of local authorities and voluntary organizations, though central government is responsible for setting national policies; the first two are the direct responsibility of central government.

Personal services help the elderly, the disabled, children, and young people. Older people represent the fastest growing part of the population, with consequent greater demands for services including advice by social workers, domestic help, provision of meals in homes, day centers, and recreational facilities.

### Social Security

The social security system is a complex one with over 30 different benefits. It is the largest single area of government spending. The major postwar reform in this area has been the extension of national insurance to cover unemployment, sickness, maternity, retirement, industrial injuries, and death. A National Insurance Fund was established,

REVIEW

### 2.8    ECONOMIC AND SOCIAL POLICIES OF THE BLAIR GOVERNMENT, 1997–2002

#### ECONOMIC

- Bank of England given independent control of interest rates; Monetary Policy Committee of Bank of England officials and other economists to decide on those rates.
- Rise in tax burden (37.7 percent of GDP in 2000) though cut in basic rate of income tax.
- Abolished dividend tax credit for pension schemes.
- Abolished mortgage interest tax relief and married couple's allowance; increased child benefits.
- Less government intervention in industrial disputes and wage bargaining; less close collaboration with trade unions.
- Limited stress on redistribution of income.
- Labour Party gives up Clause IV; stress on public–private partnerships: privatization of some state-owned assets, including National Air Traffic Services, Horserace Totalisator Board, Royal Mint.

#### SOCIAL

- Increased number of university students, now 35 percent of age group.
- Maintained Conservative policies of national school tests and inspections.
- Abolished system of maintenance grants by which students qualified for help with living expenses.
- Recourse to private sector by National Health Service and some state schools.
- Benefits for employed parents, and maternity leave increased to three months; protection for workers if dismissed.
- New official categories of social class; now seven classes reflecting a person's position in the labor market and the nature of the employment contract.
- Minimum income guarantee for pensioners; free TV licenses for those over 75.

---

to which insured persons and their employers contribute and from which they are paid when necessary. The contributions cover about 90 percent of the benefits paid, with the state paying the rest. The system is universal, applying to everyone, but individuals can have their own private insurance in addition to the national system.

Unemployment benefit is payable for one year in each case of unemployment. Sickness benefits of various kinds cover loss of earnings during absence from work. Maternity pay, normally for 18 weeks, is now usually paid by employers. A variety of different grants, depending on the individuals and relationships, are paid on death. The most significant of these grants go to widows who receive allowances for the first 26 weeks of widowhood, as well as other possible allowances.

Since 1946 pensions have been paid to men at age 65 and women at age 60; individuals may defer retirement for five years and qualify for a higher pension, however. Since 1959, the basic pension has been supplemented by an additional amount in return for larger contributions, an earning-related scheme. Pensions are also paid to disabled veterans. An injured worker receives benefits for a period depending on the disablement.

Family allowances have been given since 1945 to mothers who receive a sum for all children who are below the minimum school-leaving age or in full-time education (now up to the age of 19). In 1977, child benefits replaced family allowances and the income tax allowances, which have been phased out. Children also receive other benefits: medical examinations, free milk (which since 1971 has been limited to those under 7 years of age), and school meals. Benefits introduced in 1988 included income support for families whose income is under a certain level, a family credit for low-income working families with children, and aid for rent and local rates.

The cost of these services has been high. Social security accounts for about 9 percent and retirement pensions alone for 6 percent of GNP. If health and education are included, the social services account for over 23 percent of GNP and 47 percent of total public expenditure. But in spite of the cost, for political reasons Conservative governments did not reduce the services and benefits. Indeed, expenditure increased under Thatcher and Major, partly because of the larger numbers of elderly and unemployed people and single-parent families.

## The National Health Service

Introduced in 1946, the National Health Service (NHS) was one of the towering achievements of the Labour government. It was a centrally planned, government-funded institution, providing a full range of medical services available to all residents, regardless of income. It is financed through general taxation, national insurance contributions, and charges for prescribed drugs.

When the NHS was established, the state acquired all hospitals except teaching hospitals. Doctors could no longer sell their practices or set up practice in an area that already had too many doctors. But concessions included the right of doctors to private practice, maintenance of private paying beds in hospitals, the right of the patients to choose their doctor, and local rather than central administration of hospitals. Medical and dental services were free to all who used the service. Doctors in the service receive a basic salary plus a certain fee for each patient. Hospitals have been run by regional boards and committees. Over 90 percent of doctors decided to enter the service.

Residents in Britain can choose to join the system, as over 90 percent have done. They have free choice of an NHS doctor, dentist, optician, and pharmacist and have access to specialists and hospital treatment through their doctor. About 11 percent of the population in 2002 is covered by various forms of private health insurance. Spending on publicly funded patients treated privately currently accounts for about 5 percent of total expenditure on the NHS.

The creation of the NHS and the provision of free medicine resulted initially in higher costs than had been anticipated. Charges, covering only a small part of the cost, were therefore imposed for drug prescriptions, dental treatment, dentures, and spectacles. But over 80 percent of the cost is financed from the regular tax. The most costly item has been the hospitals, which now account for about three-fifths of the total cost; the teaching hospitals are particularly expensive. The NHS, employing 1 million people, including 30,000 doctors, now accounts for 10 percent of public expenditure and 6 percent of GDP, and about $70 billion a year.

Considerable variation exists in the performance of NHS trusts, hospitals, and doctors' surgeries throughout the country. There are now fewer doctors per 1,000 patients than in most Western European countries, and about half the comparable number in the United States. The NHS has faced some difficulties in recent years because of the demands on it. Problems have arisen over pay for medical personnel, industrial disputes, low morale, waiting lists in hospitals and for operations, a shortage of specialists, demands caused by the increasing proportion of older people, and the high cost of medical care and high-technology equipment. The cost of the NHS, which treats 30 million patients a year, rose 50 percent in real terms between 1979 and 1990.

The government has therefore recently tried to shift emphasis from the treatment of illness to the promotion of health and the prevention of disease, and to decentralize the system by allowing some hospitals to administer their own budgets and to become self-governing trusts with their own boards of directors. In 2000 the government agreed that health authorities could arrange for citizens to travel to continental Europe for operations, largely paid for by the NHS.

# FOREIGN AFFAIRS

At the end of World War II, Britain was still one of the three major powers; its empire and Commonwealth contained one-quarter of the world's population. It remained the major European economic and military power until the mid-1950s. By 1952 Britain had manufactured atomic bombs, and in 1957 it exploded a thermonuclear bomb. It was the dominant power in the Middle East and the second most important power in the Far East, and had a "special relationship" with the United States.

But in the postwar period, Britain has become an important but middle-sized power. It declined economically, in both production and trade, as other nations developed industrially. British economic growth was lower than that of other major Western European countries. Britain increased its imports not only of raw materials but also of manufactured chemical and semi-manufactured products. Britain never fully recaptured its export markets, over half of which had been lost as a result of World War II. Although Britain has been technologically inventive—for example, television, radar, the jet engine, and the swing-line plane—it has been deficient in exploiting inventions.

The British Empire has been almost completely transformed into independent nations, most of them now members of the Commonwealth. Unable to produce missiles to launch its bombs, Britain became dependent on the United States, which supplied it with the Polaris missile. Britain could not sustain the burden of supporting other countries, such as Greece and Turkey, or of protecting Palestine, from which it withdrew in 1948. It began withdrawing its forces from other areas: the Suez Canal zone in 1956, Jordan in 1957, Iraq in 1958, the Persian Gulf in 1969, Singapore in 1971, and Hong Kong in 1997.

Britain's relative economic decline, as well as the demand for independence of its former colonies, affected its foreign policy. Both major parties agreed that Britain should be a nuclear power and for a time sought to maintain its bases east of Suez. Both Labour and Conservatives intervened to help keep the peace, to safeguard oil, tin, and rubber supply lines, and to protect other countries, such as Malaya from 1948 on, Kenya between 1952 and 1960, and Kenya and Tanganyika in 1964, as well as the Middle East. About 10 percent of the central government's expenditure was for defense.

Britain had to adjust its foreign policy to three developments: the decline in its special relationship with the United States, the end of the empire and the increase in the Commonwealth, and the creation of the European Community (now the European Union).

## From Special Relationship to Ally

The close British-American relationship during World War II was transformed by postwar events, the first of which was the quick termination of the U.S. lend-lease program in 1945; this forced Britain to borrow heavily in the immediate postwar period. The strategic strength and economic might of the United States and its emergence as the dominant world power meant that Britain was an ally, not an equal partner. The relationship is now one of consultation and exchange of information, intelligence, and opinions on issues of common interest. Britain has been a staunch U.S. ally in recent conflicts: the Gulf War of 1991, the war in the Balkans and Kosovo, sanctions against Iraq, and the fight against terrorism following extremist attacks on the United States in 2001.

Britain is one of the few countries in the world with a military nuclear capacity, and it intends to maintain that capacity. The core of its defense effort is now based on its membership in the North Atlantic Treaty Organization (NATO). Britain is committed to the deterrent strategy of NATO and to consultations of the Nuclear Planning Group within it. It contributes forces to all three elements of NATO's strategy: strategic nuclear, theater nuclear, and conventional armaments.

Britain has a Trident submarine force, but has reduced its reliance on nuclear weapons. The Royal Navy, the strongest European navy in NATO, contributes its wide variety of ships—the third largest number of surface combat ships in the world—including aircraft carriers, antisubmarine helicopters, nuclear-powered attack submarines, frigates, and guided missile destroyers to the alliance. In addition to its NATO assignments in the Atlantic and the North Sea, the navy sends task forces into the Indian Ocean, party to help safeguard oil supplies.

Britain has 55,000 regular army troops assigned to NATO's force. It has two divisions in Germany and one in Britain. It is supported by a tactical unit of the Royal Air Force (RAF). The RAF as a whole has some 500 combat aircraft at its disposal, including units in Britain that provide part of NATO's mobile force, a contribution to NATO's Intermediate and Rapid Reaction Forces.

Out of the NATO area, Britain still stations troops or plays a role in a number of areas such as Cyprus, Gibraltar, the Falklands, and in the major oceans. Britain played a significant role in the Gulf War of 1991. With the end of the Warsaw Pact in 1991, Britain made substantial cuts in all its armed forces. In 2002 there were 110,000 in the army, 54,000 in the RAF, and 42,000 in the navy. For Britain, NATO, rather than an EU force, should be Europe's major security unit.

## From Empire to Commonwealth

Before World War II the British Commonwealth, as it was then called, consisted of Britain and six dominions, which (except for South Africa) were largely populated by individuals of British extraction, economically modernized and politically developed, with democratic systems and values (again except for South Africa) similar to the British. Preferential trading arrangements, adopted in Ottawa in 1932, were extended to all the dominions.

The rest of Britain's possessions throughout the world were colonies ruled by Britain. They began demanding independence soon after the end of the war, beginning in Asia and then throughout Africa and the rest of the world. Most nations on gaining independence have chosen to be members of the Commonwealth, which in 2002 numbers 54 countries with a population of 1.7 billion. Britain, however, is still responsible for 16 dependent territories around the world.

The Commonwealth, now consisting of diverse races, religions, and cultures, is a voluntary association with members all being equal in status. Some are republics which acknowledge the monarch as head of the Commonwealth, some 16 are constitutional monarchies owing allegiance to the monarch, and four have their own monarchs. Some are political democracies in the British sense, but others have one-party systems or are under military control. Some are based on private ownership, while others regard themselves as socialists. A few are wealthy, but most are poor countries with a low per capita income.

The Commonwealth accounts for 23 percent of world trade and about 20 percent of global investment. It is a loose association of independent nations, all once ruled by Britain, which have in no way chosen each other but are linked by accident. British law no longer extends to the Commonwealth. It does not reach collective decisions or take united political action. It is neither a trade bloc—although some economic privileges do exist—nor a military alliance, though its weapons, uniforms, and military training are similar to Britain's and there are combined exercises and joint research organizations. In the Commonwealth the Queen is the symbol of free association, but this is not a position of executive power. It has no center of sovereignty, no central law-making body or parliament, and no organ to speak for it; in 1965, a secretariat was established, but it does not make decisions that are binding on Commonwealth members. However, a Commonwealth Ministerial Action Group was set up in 1995 which addresses violations of democratic principles in the countries.

The Commonwealth does not have a written constitution but it does have a number of statements outlining its objectives. The most important of these are the Declaration of Commonwealth Principles agreed in Singapore in 1971 and the Harare Declaration in 1991, which committed the Commonwealth to promote democracy, human

The Commonwealth Member Countries
(with date of membership and populations)

| 1 Antigua and Barbuda (1981) 67,000 | 11 Cyprus (1961) 760,000 | 22 Lesotho (1966) 2,105,000 |
|---|---|---|
| 2 Australia (1901) 18,967,000 | 12 Dominica (1978) 73,000 | 23 Malawi (1964) 10,788,000 |
| 3 The Bahamas (1973) 298,000 | 13 Fiji Islands (1970) 801,000 | 24 Malaysia (1957) 22,710,000 |
| 4 Bangladesh (1973) 127,669,000 | 14 The Gambia (1965) 1,251,000 | 25 Maldives (1982) 269,000 |
| 5 Barbados (1966) 267,000 | 15 Ghana (1957) 18,785,000 | 26 Malta (1964) 379,000 |
| 6 Belize (1981) 247,000 | 16 Grenada (1974) 97,000 | 27 Mauritius (1968) 1,174,000 |
| 7 Botswana (1966) 1,588,000 | 17 Guyana (1966) 856,000 | 28 Mozambique (1995) 17,299,000 |
| 8 Brunei Darussalam (1984) 322,000 | 18 India (1947) 997,515,000 | 29 Namibia (1990) 1,701,000 |
| 9 Cameroon (1995) 14,691,000 | 19 Jamaica (1962) 2,598,000 | 30 Nauru (1968) 11,000 |
| 10 Canada (1867) 30,491,000 | 20 Kenya (1963) 29,410,000 | 31 New Zealand (1907) 3,811,000 |
| | 21 Kiribati (1979) 88,000 | 32 Nigeria (1960) 123,897,000 |

## THE COMMONWEALTH

*Source:* Commonwealth Secretariat Publications.

rights, gender equality, economic and social development, eradication of poverty, and opposition to racial discrimination.

Tangible and intangible bonds have linked the Commonwealth. The latter result from the use of English by the professional classes, similar educational experiences, and common backgrounds in some cases. More tangible have been the regular meetings of heads of governments, political leaders, and profes-

33  Pakistan (1947) 134,790,000
34  Papua New Guinea (1975) 4,705,000
35  St. Kitts and Nevis (1983) 41,000
36  St. Lucia (1979) 154,000
37  St. Vincent and the Grenadines (1979) 114,000
38  Samoa (1970) 169,000
39  Seychelles (1976) 80,000
40  Sierra Leone (1961) 4,949,000
41  Singapore (1965) 3,952,000
42  Solomon Islands (1978) 429,000
43  South Africa (1931) 42,106,000

44  Sri Lanka (1948) 18,985,000
45  Swaziland (1968) 1,019,000
46  Tonga (1970) 100,000
47  Trinidad and Tobago (1962) 1,293,000
48  Tuvalu (1978) 11,000
49  Uganda (1963) 21,479,000
50  United Kingdom 59,501,000
51  United Republic of Tanzania (1961) 32,923,000
52  Vanuatu (1980) 193,000
53  Zambia (1964) 9,881,000
54  Zimbabwe (1980) 11,904,000

sional people; collaborative functions in areas such as health, especially the fight against HIV/AIDS, education, law, technical cooperation, teacher training, youth groups, sports, arts festivals, and agriculture; and representa-tion of the members by High Commissioners in London. Some preferential trade arrangements still exist. Most of Britain's bilateral and much of its multilateral foreign aid has gone to the Commonwealth.

**A CLOSER LOOK**
**2.13**

## SPLITTING THE ROCK

Britain still has 15 overseas territories; one of them, Gibraltar, has been British since 1713. A few square miles of rock with a population of 30,000, Gibraltar voted in 1967 to remain British, but Britain in 2002 was discussing with Spain the possibility of sharing sovereignty over it in return for the lifting of Spanish restrictions on border crossing, air traffic, and telecommunications.

---

But Britain's ties with the Commonwealth have weakened. The very diversity of its members means that no common ethnic or cultural bonds exist. Controls have been imposed on non-white immigration into Britain. Britain can no longer offer military protection to the members. Few of them retain the Judicial Committee of the Privy Council in London as the final court of appeal from their own courts.

The Commonwealth is a useful bridge among races, areas of the world, and richer and poorer nations. But it has declined in economic value and political importance for Britain. This is especially true in the changing pattern of trade as Britain has turned to Europe, and the Commonwealth countries have begun manufacturing their own products. British exports to the Commonwealth decreased from 37.3 percent of the total in 1958 to 8.5 percent in 1987. In the same period, exports to the European Community increased from 13.9 to 42 percent, and imports from it rose from 9 to 52 percent. British trade has shifted from the Commonwealth to other industrial countries, especially those of Western Europe.

## Britain and the European Union

In the immediate postwar period, Britain was not interested in joining in the proposals for greater European unity. Its status as one of the "Big Three" powers, its worldwide role, its Commonwealth, its special relationship with the United States, its higher standard of living and trade pattern, and its insular political tradition and

fear of European entanglement—all led Britain to refuse to participate in the Economic Coal and Steel Community in 1951, the proposed European Defense Community in the 1950s, and in the formation of the European Economic Community (EEC) and European Atomic Energy Community (Euratom) in 1957.

Britain preferred to maintain a much looser free-trade area and organized the European Free Trade Association in 1959 as an alternative. But the speedy success of the EEC, popularly known as the Common Market, the rapid recovery of Western Europe after the war—at first assisted by U.S. economic aid—the realization of the importance of a large single market, and weakening relations with the United States and the Commonwealth led Britain to apply for membership in the European Community (EC), which is now the European Union (EU). After being vetoed twice by France, in 1963 and 1967, Britain was accepted and joined the Community in January 1973.

When the Labour Party, split on the issue of the EC, formed the government in 1974, it decided to renegotiate the terms of Britain's membership and then put the issue to a vote by the people. A number of changes were made, including the system of financing the EC budget, the reduction in the cost of the common agricultural program, and better access for certain Commonwealth produce. As a result, the government, though still divided, recommended that Britain remain in the EC. The referendum, the first in British history, was approved by 67 percent of the vote in 1975.

British Eurostar train at Victoria Station in London.

Britain accepted the EC's agricultural policy, which means higher prices for food and the gradual reduction of Commonwealth trade preferences. In return, it hoped that the larger market and progressive removal of European tariff barriers would induce a faster rate of economic growth, a restructuring of the British economy, and greater economies of scale in production.

Membership in the EC did not immediately revive British industry, but trade with it increased. Trade with the EU now accounts for over half of Britain's imports and exports.

Britain was also concerned about the size of its net contribution to the EC budget, as it contributed considerably more than it received in return. The EC raised revenue from customs duties, farm levies, and value-added taxation (VAT), which was costly to Britain, which imports most of its food; most EC expenditure was to farmers, thus benefiting countries with a larger farming population than Britain's. As a result of vigorous protest by Prime Minister Thatcher, Britain's contribution was reduced in the 1980s.

Britain is now subject to the laws of the European Union; it accepts and gives the force of law to the rules, principles, and procedures of the EU. It is bound by all EU treaties. The Court of Justice of the European Union has ultimate authority to rule on interpretation of the law. In the institutions of the EU, now composed of 15 states. Britain has 2 of the members of the European Commission, the executive of the EU, and 87 of the 626 members of the enlarged European Parliament, which was directly elected for the first time in 1979.

For Britain some new political problems exist. The historic concept of the supremacy of Parliament is now qualified by the right of EU institutions to make rules applying to Britain without parliamentary consent and by the ability of the EU Court of Justice to rule on whether British law is compatible with European Union law. Though there has not been any serious constitutional clash between Britain and the EU institutions, problems remain now that there is a level of government above that of Britain and now that Britain is for the first time bound to some extent by the written constitution of the European Union. Britain welcomed the EU objective of a free internal market by 1992, and approved of a greater European role in world affairs, but it has been reluctant to become a member of the European Monetary System or to accept the idea of a European bank, let alone a United States of Europe.

It did, however, join the exchange rate mechanism of the European Monetary System in October 1990, though it remained opposed to rapid moves to an economic and monetary union, and to a single European currency (the euro). It also still insists that any such union must be based on free markets and price stability. Equally, the Conservative governments under Thatcher and Major rejected the idea of a federal Europe, and have been concerned about any reduction of British sovereignty. The Conservatives agreed that some common European policies, such as a single market and a negotiating position on world trade, are necessary and that Europe should have a more coordinated foreign policy and a stronger voice in world affairs; they did not accept the view that all European cooperation must take place through the institutions of the European Union. However, the Blair government in 1997 accepted, after the previous Conservative government had refused to do so, the Social Chapter of the Maastricht Treaty, and minimum wage regulations.

Britain has been troubled by the diminution of its sovereignty, as in late 1991 when the Community threatened to take legal action to stop British Rail construction projects for environmental reasons. Parliamentary sovereignty is even more challenged by the European integration process and the move to common European employment, budgetary, taxation, and defense policies, and by the 1999 Amsterdam Treaty.

# CONCLUSION

Whether examined from an international, social, economic, or political point of view, the British system has changed in the postwar world. Internationally, Britain cannot be seen as a superpower, though it is still a significant world power with a capacity for independent action as was displayed in the 1982 Falklands war. It has drawn closer to Western Europe and its membership in the European Union now accounts for over half of British trade. Britain maintains a variety of important foreign ties, especially with the United States, with which it shares common political and democratic values as well as military and intelligence-gathering connections.

It is a leading member of NATO and the European Union, a permanent member of the Security Council of the United Nations, and one of the Group of Seven Economic Summit countries. British troops are deployed or stationed in over 40 countries.

Britain is the world's sixth largest economy, though its share of world trade has fallen from 11.5 percent in the early postwar years to 5.5 percent in 2002. It is the world's second biggest foreign investor and the biggest foreign investor in the United States. Promoting trade is as important as diplomatic activity; about a quarter of GDP comes from the overseas market. Over 85 percent of that trade is with OECD countries.

Socially, Britain is a country with a mixture of peoples of different races and background, a less rigid class system, and, for most individuals, a more affluent lifestyle. Economically, Britain has experienced mixed success. Long-term economic growth has averaged about 2.25 percent a year in recent years. Fastest growth has been in the services sector, especially in transport, storage, and communications. Inflation has been kept to a low level. Trade unions, with a declining membership, have in general been less militant. Under both Conservative and Labour governments, the proportion of total GDP spent by government did not diminish significantly.

Britain in the mid-1990s witnessed an increasing centralization of public administration as the Conservative government under John Major reduced the autonomy of local councils, universities, police authorities, health regions, armed forces, and nationalized industry boards. The Blair government reversed this trend by the policy of devolution, thus qualifying the unitary nature of Britain and decreasing centralized authority.

The Thatcher government stressed individual responsibility, encouraged economic initiative, sold off many nationalized industries, and dismantled state controls over the economy. To a considerable degree the Blair government has accepted this and the new consensus on the free market, maximizing individual choice, more concern for costs, no return to nationalization of enterprises, and limits on powers of government in normal times. This has merged with the previous consensus of full employment, a welfare state, and free collective bargaining.

Difficult issues, such as the Irish question, environmental problems, the role of Britain externally (particularly in the EU, which is a very divisive issue), class and ethnic differences, the question of equal opportunity for women, and protective laws for ethnic minorities, remain to be adequately resolved. It is clear that there will be no shortage of difficult problems on the British political agenda.

The need for constitutional and political changes including reform of the House of Lords has been raised. Britain is the only country in Western Europe which does not have a bill of rights providing constitutional protection for individual and group rights. It set up a considerable number of independent government agencies and QUANGOs whose political responsibility is unclear. This has led some to argue that Britain should have a formal bill of rights, a fairer electoral system, and more parliamentary scrutiny of the executive. This has yet to be done.

On the other hand, Britain remains a stable democracy in no danger of military defeat, revolution, or political collapse. In a country where tradition and conventions have played such a large role, peaceful political and constitutional change is taking place.

## Thinking Critically

1. Why was Britain reluctant to join the European Community? Why is Britain still unwilling to adopt the euro?
2. How would you explain Britain's changing policies on nationalization and privatization?
3. Does Britain have, and did it ever have, a special relationship with the United States?
4. Has the welfare state changed during the postwar period? Is it working satisfactorily?
5. Is British government expenditure excessive?
6. Should the Commonwealth be ended?

## KEY TERMS

Commonwealth *(106–107)*
devolution *(111)*
economic planning *(100)*
European Community (EC) *(108)*
European Monetary System *(110)*
European Union (EU) *(109)*
family allowances *(103)*
mixed economy *(98)*
National Health Service (NHS) *(103)*
nationalized industries *(98)*
North Atlantic Treaty Organization (NATO) *(104)*
privatization *(100)*
public–private partnerships *(100)*
social security *(102)*
special relationship *(104)*
welfare state *(101)*

## ABBREVIATIONS

| | |
|---|---|
| BBC | British Broadcasting Corporation |
| CAP | Common Agricultural Policy |
| CBI | Confederation of British Industry |
| EC | European Community |
| ECHR | European Convention on Human Rights |
| EMS | European Monetary System |
| EMU | European Monetary Union |
| EP | European Parliament |
| EU | European Union |

| GB | Great Britain |
|---|---|
| GDP | Gross Domestic Product |
| GNP | Gross National Product |
| HoC | House of Commons |
| HoL | House of Lords |
| Lib Dem | Liberal Democrat |
| MP | Member of Parliament |
| NATO | North Atlantic Treaty Organization |
| NHS | National Health Service |
| PM | Prime Minister |
| PR | Proportional Representation |
| SNP | Scottish National Party |
| TUC | Trades Union Congress |
| UK | United Kingdom |

# FURTHER READINGS

Atkinson, A. B. *Incomes and the Welfare State* (Cambridge: Cambridge University Press, 1996).

Bagilhole, Barbara. *Equal Opportunities and Social Policy* (New York: Longman, 1997).

Bartlett, Christopher J. *British Foreign Policy in the Twentieth Century* (Basingstoke: Macmillan, 1989).

Bulmer, Simon, et al., eds. *The United Kingdom and European Community Evaluated* (London: Pinter, 1992).

Curwen, Peter, ed. *Understanding the United Kingdom Economy* (London: Macmillan, 1997).

Deakin, Nicholas, and Richard Parry. *The Treasury and Social Policy* (New York: St. Martin's, 2000).

George, Stephen, ed. *Britain and the European Community: The Politics of Semi-Detachment* (New York: Oxford University Press, 1992).

Giddens, Anthony. *The Third Way and Its Critics* (Cambridge: Polity Press, 2000).

Grant, Wyn. *Pressure Groups, Politics and Democracy in Britain* (New York: Allan, 1989).

Grant, Wyn. *Business and Politics in Britain,* 2nd ed. (London: Macmillan, 1993).

Grant, Wyn. *The Politics of Economic Policy* (New York: Harvester Wheatsheaf, 1993).

Hampton, William. *Local Government and Urban Politics* (New York: Longman, 1991).

Hills, John, ed. *The State of Welfare: The Welfare State in Britain Since 1974* (New York: Oxford University Press, 1990).

Jenkins, Simon. *Accountable to None: The Tory Nationalization of Britain* (London: Hamish Hamilton, 1995).

Kavanagh, Dennis. *The Reordering of British Politics: Politics after Thatcher* (New York: Oxford University Press, 1997).

Kellas, James. *The Politics of Nationalism and Ethnicity* (Basingstoke: Macmillan, 1991).

Kellas, James. *The Scottish Political System,* 4th ed. (New York: Cambridge University Press, 1989).

Lister, Ruth. *Citizenship: Feminist Perspectives* (London: Macmillan, 1998).

Louis, Wm. Roger, and Hedley Bull, eds. *The Special Relationship: Anglo-American Relations Since 1945* (New York: Oxford University Press, 1986).

Marsh, David. *The New Politics of British Trade Unionism: Union Power and the Thatcher Legacy* (Ithaca, NY: ILR Press, 1992).

Pierson, Christopher. *Beyond the Welfare State? The New Political Economy of Welfare* (Cambridge: Polity Press, 1991).

Robins, Lynton, and Bill Jones, eds. *Half a Century of British Politics* (Manchester: Manchester University Press, 1997).

Sanders, David. *Losing an Empire, Finding a Role: British Foreign Policy since 1945* (Basingstoke: Macmillan, 1990).

Savage, Stephen P., and R. Atkinson, eds. *Public Policy under Blair* (New York: Palgrave, 2001).

Smith, Michael, et al., eds. *British Foreign Policy: Tradition, Change and Transformation* (Boston: Allen and Unwin, 1988).

Timmins, Nicholas. *The Five Giants: A Biography of the Welfare State* (New York: Harper Collins, 1995).

# WEB SITES

**www.ukpol.co.uk**
information on many subjects
**www.pm.gov.uk**
information on prime minister
**www.parliament.uk**
information on Parliament
**www.cabinet-office.gov.uk**
information on the cabinet
**www.parliament.uk/commons**
information on House of Commons

www.publications.parliament.uk/pa/ld/ldhome.htm
information on House of Lords and its committees

www.civil-service.gov.uk
information on the civil service

www.hm-treasury.gov.uk
information on Treasury

www.fco.gov.uk
information on Foreign and Commonwealth Office

www.thecommonwealth.org
information on the Commonwealth

www.tuc.org.uk
information on Trades Union Congress

www.humanrights.gov.uk
information on Britain and Human Rights treaties

www.scotland.gov.uk
information on Executive of the Scottish Parliament

www.scottish.parliament.uk
information on Scottish Parliament

www.alba.org.uk
information on Scottish politics

www.wales.gov.uk/assembly.dbs
information on Welsh Assembly

www.nio.gov.uk
information on Northern Ireland Office

www.ni-executive.gov.uk
information on Executive in Northern Ireland

www.niassembly.gov.uk
information on Northern Ireland Assembly

**CHAPTER 3**

THE GOVERNMENT OF
# France

*Jean Blondel*

## INTRODUCTION

**Background:** Although ultimately a victor in World Wars I and II, France suffered extensive losses in its empire, wealth, manpower, and rank as a dominant nation-state. Nevertheless, France today is one of the most modern countries in the world and is a leader among European nations. Since 1958, it has constructed a presidential democracy resistant to the instabilities experienced in earlier parliamentary democracies. In recent years, its reconciliation and cooperation with Germany have proved central to the economic integration of Europe, including the advent of the euro in January 1999. Presently, France is at the forefront of European states seeking to exploit the momentum of monetary union to advance the creation of a more unified and capable European defense and security apparatus.

### GEOGRAPHY
**Location:** Western Europe, bordering the Bay of Biscay and English Channel between Belgium and Spain, southeast of the UK; bordering the Mediterranean Sea between Italy and Spain

**Area:** 547,030 sq km

**Area—comparative:** slightly less than twice the size of Colorado

**Land boundaries:** 2,889 km

> *border countries:* Andorra 56.6 km, Belgium 620 km, Germany 451 km, Italy 488 km, Luxembourg 73 km, Monaco 4.4 km, Spain 623 km, Switzerland 573 km

**Climate:** generally cool winters and mild summers, but mild winters and hot summers along the Mediterranean; occasional strong, cold, dry, north-to-northwesterly wind known as mistral

**Terrain:** mostly flat plains or gently rolling hills in north and west; remainder is mountainous, especially Pyrenees in south, Alps in east

**Elevation extremes:** *lowest point:* Rhone River delta –2 m

*highest point:* Mont Blanc 4,807 m

**Geography note:** largest West European nation

## PEOPLE

**Population:** 59,551,227

**Age structure:** *0–14 years:* 18.68% (male 5,698,604; female 5,426,838)

*15–64 years:* 65.19% (male 19,424,018; female 19,399,588)

*65 years and over:* 16.13% (male 3,900,579; female 5,701,600)

**Population growth rate:** 0.37%

**Birthrate:** 12.1 births/1,000 population

**Sex ratio:** 0.95 males/female

**Life expectancy at birth:** 78.9 years

*male:* 75.01 years

*female:* 83.01 years

**Nationality:** *noun:* Frenchman (men), French-woman (women)

*adjective:* French

**Ethnic groups:** Celtic and Latin with Teutonic, Slavic, North African, Indochinese, Basque minorities

**Religions:** Roman Catholic 90%, Protestant 2%, Jewish 1%, Muslim 3%, unaffiliated 4%

**Languages:** French, rapidly declining regional dialects and languages (Provençal, Breton, Alsatian, Corsican, Catalan, Basque, Flemish)

**Literacy:** *definition:* age 15 and over can read and write

*total population:* 99%

## GOVERNMENT

**Country name:** *conventional long form:* French Republic

*conventional short form:* France

**Government type:** republic

**Capital:** Paris

**Administrative divisions:** 22 regions: Alsace, Aquitaine, Auvergne, Basse-Normandie, Bour-gogne, Bretagne, Centre, Champagne-Ardenne, Corse, Franche-Comté, Haute-Normandie, Ile-de-France, Languedoc-Roussillon, Limousin, Lorraine, Midi-Pyrénées, Nord-Pas-de-Calais, Pays de la Loire, Picardie, Poitou-Charentes, Provence-Alpes-Côte d'Azur, Rhône-Alpes

**Dependent areas:** Bassas da India, Clipperton Island, Europa Island, French Polynesia, French Southern and Antarctic Lands, Glorioso Islands, Juan de Nova Island, New Caledonia, Tromelin Island, Wallis and Futuna

*note:* the US does not recognize claims to Antarctica

**Independence:** 486 (unified by Clovis)

**National holiday:** Bastille Day, 14 July (1789)

**Constitution:** 28 September 1958, amended concerning election of president in 1962, amended to comply with provisions of EC Maastricht Treaty in 1992, amended to tighten immigration laws 1993

**Legal system:** civil law system with indigenous concepts; review of administrative but not leg-islative acts

**Suffrage:** 18 years of age; universal

**Executive branch:** *chief of state:* President Jacques Chirac (since 17 May 1995)

*head of government:* Prime Minister J.-P. Raffarin (since June 2002)

*cabinet:* Council of Ministers appointed by the president on the suggestion of the prime minister

*elections:* president elected by popular vote for a five-year term; at election June 2002 prime minister nominated by the National Assembly majority and appointed by the president

**Legislative branch:** bicameral parliament con-sists of the Senate or Senat (321 seats; mem-bers are indirectly elected by an electoral college to serve nine-year terms; elected by thirds every three years) and the National Assembly (577 seats; members are elected by popular vote under a single-member majoritar-ian system to serve five-year terms)

**Judicial branch:** Supreme Court of Appeals (judges are appointed by the president from nominations of the High Council of the Judiciary); Constitutional Council (three members appointed by the president, three appointed by the president of the National Assembly, and three appointed by the president of the Senate); Council of State

## ECONOMY

**Overview:** France is in the midst of transition, from an economy that featured extensive government ownership and intervention to one that relies more on market mechanisms. The government remains dominant in some sectors, particularly power, public transport, and defense industries, but it has been relaxing its control since the mid-1980s. The Socialist-led government has sold off part of its holdings in France Telecom, Air France, Thales, Thomson Multimedia, and the European Aerospace and Defense Company (EADS). The telecommunications sector is gradually being opened to competition. France's leaders remain committed to a capitalism in which they maintain social equity by means of laws, tax policies, and social spending that reduce income disparity and the impact of free markets on public health and welfare. The government has done little to cut generous unemployment and retirement benefits which impose a heavy tax burden and discourage hiring. It has also shied from measures that would dramatically increase the use of stock options and retirement investment plans; such measures would boost the stock market and fast-growing IT firms as well as ease the burden on the pension system, but would disproportionately benefit the rich. In addition to the tax burden, the reduction of the work week to 35-hours has drawn criticism for lowering the competitiveness of French companies.

**GDP:** purchasing power parity $1.448 trillion

**GDP—real growth rate:** 3.1%

**GDP—per capita:** purchasing power parity $24,400

**GDP—composition by sector:** *agriculture:* 3.3%
   *industry:* 26.1%
   *services:* 70.6%

**Labor force:** 25 million

**Labor force by occupation:** services 71%, industry 25%, agriculture 4%

**Unemployment rate:** 9.7%

**Currency:** euro (EUR)

   *note:* on 1 January 1999, the EU introduced the euro as a common currency to be used by financial institutions; the euro has replaced the franc for all transactions in 2002

# A. POLITICAL DEVELOPMENT

## HISTORY AND SOCIETY: TRADITIONS AND CONTRADICTIONS IN FRENCH POLITICS

### The Instability of French Politics through the 1960s

France refuses, almost doggedly, to fit the framework of the rest of Western Europe and of the Atlantic world. The Fifth Republic, set up by Charles de Gaulle in 1958, has been a stable regime, but as recently as 1958 the country seemed on the verge of political catastrophe, with generals in Algiers threatening a military invasion. The previous regime, the Fourth Republic, had ended after 12 years marked by great political instability. During the 150 years before that, France had had about 20 constitutions, of which only one—that of the Third Republic, inaugurated in 1870—lasted more than 20 years. The First Republic was installed at the end of the eighteenth century and lasted 7 years (1792–1799); the Second was established in 1848 and lasted 3 years to 1851; the Fourth Republic was set up after World War II and lasted 12 years (1946–1958).

Indeed, both the Third and Fourth Republics were characterized by instability greater even than that of contemporary Italy. During that period, governments rarely lasted more than half a year and almost never had any real authority. It may be that France has at last acquired real political stability in the Fifth Republic, but at a price. France's political system is somewhat different from those of other Western countries and poses as yet unresolved problems about the respective position of president and government.

### Social and Economic Development

Explanations for France's political instability are not easy to find. Economic performance does not provide the answer. France is one of the richest countries in the world. Its per capita GDP of $21,900 in 2000 is the same as that of Denmark (also $21,900), somewhat lower than that of Germany ($22,800), and appreciably lower than that of the Netherlands ($23,200) and Britain ($23,800), though the differences are much smaller if one takes into account the purchasing power parity of the various currencies. If, as political scientists believe, on the basis of considerable evidence, wealth and political stability are closely associated, France should be as stable as the other Western European countries.

The distribution of wealth and the class structure do not provide clues either. Incomes and wealth are somewhat more unevenly distributed in France than in northern Europe, but the large majority of the population has sizeable incomes, and a very substantial proportion are small property owners. Indeed, France has traditionally been a nation of small businesspeople—shopkeepers, artisans, and above all farmers. While in Latin America and the countries of southern Europe political unrest can be attributed to conflict over land reform, in France the land is owned by large numbers of smallholders, making agricultural workers and sharecroppers a tiny minority.

The sources of French contemporary difficulties are therefore not the direct consequence of social and economic characteristics common to Latin or other countries that experience instability. Political unrest is more deeply embedded in the culture of the country, in its history, and in many of its structures, especially the administrative structures. Conflicts appear to arise in large part from a number of contradictions which the French do not seem able to surmount. The result has been that, for a long period at least, the legitimacy of the regime has been relatively low; only recently has the political system been fully accepted by almost all the French citizens.

### The Clash between Liberalism and Authoritarianism

Since the eighteenth century, perhaps the most obvious contradiction has been between traditional authoritarianism and liberal democracy. It has left its scars. The Revolution of 1789 stressed the values of republicanism, liberalism, and egalitarianism, but these values had to be imposed on a substantial segment of the French population which did not readily accept them and at times combatted them by force. France was the first continental country to adopt constitutionalism and liberalism; it was also the first country to experience modern authoritarian rule, under the two Napoleons at the beginning and in the middle of the nineteenth century. It escaped with difficulty twentieth-century totalitarianism in peacetime, but did succumb to it, with the so-called Vichy regime, under the impact of the German occupation between 1940 and 1944. Liberal democracy became fully legitimate in the last decades of the twentieth century only.

## Nationalism and Internationalism

France sees itself as having an international mission, but this results in another contradiction, between nationalism and internationalism. France's international mission has tended to be to propagate its national values. Thus the Revolution of 1789 was the only time when the contradiction was resolved, since the imperialism of the French was then associated with the desire to spread an idealistic gospel. The armies of the Republic invaded Europe to defeat the "tyrants" and liberate the "people." This same idea existed a hundred years later, as France made "assimilation" its colonial policy. By contrast, British colonial policy was based on the principle of noninterference with local traditions. Opposition to French colonial rule was often held to be wholly misguided as

Arrival of the TGV in Marsalles on the Mediteranean Coast.

it did not recognize the blessings of France's "civilizing mission."

France's view of the outside world reveals a third contradiction: a belief in the greatness of the country that does not correspond to reality. When political power was based on the strength of armies and on cultural prestige, France did rather well. It was the most populous of European countries and it had spread its language and civilization all over Europe; European aristocrats worshipped French culture, while French armies periodically fought and imposed their will. But the Industrial Revolution gradually changed the basis of power, and suddenly a small country like England could control the world by its exports of manufactured goods. France was caught unprepared. Although it had a rich tradition of public works (on roads and urban planning), it entirely lacked one of industrial enterprise. To this day, objects of French national pride are more likely to be grand projects of dubious commercial value, such as the Concorde, rather than successful ventures in light engineering or consumer goods. Hence a bitter resentment and jealousy has extended to this day to the "Anglo-Saxon" countries.

Cultural pride helps to explain the peculiar relationship France had with the former Soviet Union. In the late 1940s, the French Communist Party had over 25 percent of the votes; only very slowly did it fall to under 10 percent four decades later. The French Communist Party was also probably the most Stalinist of Western Communist parties, following quite faithfully the policy dictated by the Soviet Union in the pre-Gorbachev era. Communist Russia exercised some attraction in part because France always wanted to be independent of the United States and wanted the Western nations that form part of the Atlantic alliance to be more independent. In reality, France's geographical position as well as its culture and history make it a part of the West. Thus, it can scarcely be independent. In spite of this, its leaders periodically by various means endeavor to affirm, typically rather symbolically, France's independence.

## Centralization and Decentralization

***The Role of the Bureaucracy***   The final fundamental contradiction in French government is the role of the bureaucracy. Historically it has been a major instrument of change and a major hindrance to decentralization and development. Authorities had viewed the centralization of the French state as a necessity dictated by the fact that civil servants and technocrats had been the originators of industrial strength who

**A CLOSER LOOK 3.1**

### FRENCH CULTURE AND THE FRENCH LANGUAGE

In some ways, France remains outside the major social and cultural changes that took place in the second half of the twentieth century. The determined resistance to Americanization accounts in large part for the awkwardness with which French governments, but also the French people, react to world developments. Many of the country's elites believe that French culture must be defended against all kinds of encroachments, particularly against the invasion of Anglicisms into the French language. The enduring belief that the French language is a flagship that helps to propagate French culture has prompted French governments to continually extol the "francophonie" (the supposed cultural realm defined by French-speaking peoples throughout the world). In the mid-1990s a law was passed to attempt to protect the language. Such a policy helps to keep some weakening ties from dissolving completely, particularly in Africa, but it isolates France from the rest of the world. Foreign language skills are not seen as essential, and French citizens are often officially told that they must use the French language while abroad.

often saw themselves as agents in the midst of a population that was passive and often markedly antagonistic to their innovations. Further justifications were added. Government centralization meant a uniform structure. Who would want education to be less developed in some parts of the country than in others? Moreover, if the civil service did not intervene, so the argument went, localism would prevail and there would be much patronage and graft. A centralized bureaucracy was thus morally justified. Nevertheless, some decentralization has occurred with the movement away from central control to move decision making by local groups such as municipalities, *départements*, and regions. This decentralization has been recognized in the constitution as "free administration of local collectivities."

These contradictions remain, although they are less acute than in the past. The cultural prestige of France has dwindled and many know it. Many also know that industrial strength is the key to prosperity and world influence, as the growth of West Germany and Japan has shown. Yet, while there is awareness of these realities in some circles, old views about French greatness still linger on, as the utterances of many leaders, even at the beginning of the twenty-first century, clearly demonstrate.

# THE HISTORICAL PERSPECTIVE OF FRENCH POLITICS

France's political history has been highly complex. To unravel this jumble, one must begin with the great rent in French history—the Revolution of 1789. With great drama, with a missionary and military zeal that threatened *anciens régimes* in much of the rest of Europe, the French routed the monarchy, the aristocracy, and the privileged Roman Catholic Church in the name of liberty, equality, and the republican form of government. Yet the old order, though defeated, was not destroyed. Its defenders were able to revive the monarchy in the nineteenth century and delay for decades any final regulation of the Church's powers. Meanwhile, the antirepublican tradition resisted through time; after

attempting to undermine all the republics from the First (1792) to the Fifth (1958), its supporters took until the last decades of the twentieth century to reconcile themselves to the processes of popular sovereignty.

## The Revolution of 1789

The defenders of the Revolution and Republic were not long in becoming divided over whether they should give priority to equality or liberty. In the early revolutionary period, great effort was made to destroy the political privileges of the titled and aristocratic classes. The Declaration of the Rights of Man and the Citizen, adopted tumultuously in the revolutionary Assembly of 1789, detailed the expectations of French citizens to be given basic freedoms and to be granted justice on the basis of the law. The Declaration represented the momentary ascendancy of libertarians over egalitarians.

However, strong undercurrents in the Revolution were bent on leveling all economic and social distinctions. The dictatorship of the progressive party of the time, known as the Jacobins (1793–1794), was a move toward the use of the state as an instrument of vigorous social change. The efforts of the Jacobins failed, and Napoleon installed a much more conservative (and stabilizing) regime after taking power in 1799. However, the Jacobins added to the matrix of French political development a powerful political strain.

## Traditionalists and Liberals in the Nineteenth Century

For most of the nineteenth century the libertarians had only a shaky hold on France, and the antirevolutionaries came back in 1814–1815. As the returning monarch, Louis XVIII agreed to a considerable dose of liberalism, which did not sit well with his brother and successor, Charles X. Charles's reactionary attempts ended in revolution in 1830, when the French put Louis Philippe d'Orléans on the throne. The new Orleanist monarchy started as a parliamentary regime but ended once more in revolution, after having made too many efforts to manipulate parliament instead of concentrating on the new political aspirations of the French. The Revolution of 1848 (which swept over continental Europe as well) put an end to the liberal monarchy, and to the monarchy altogether.

## The Napoleonic Tradition

The most curious intermixture of political strands flowing from the French Revolution was the imperial tradition, into which Napoleon Bonaparte (1799–1814) stumbled, which his nephew Louis Napoleon perfected in the Second Empire (1852–1870), and which some contemporary commentators felt was reincarnated in the Fifth Republic of General de Gaulle (see Table 3.1). Claiming that they were embodying the general will of the nation as expressed in the plebiscites that chose them, the Bonapartes could thus pretend that they were descendants of the revolutionary assemblies.

The imperial tradition, despite some trappings borrowed from the Revolution, was both politically antiliberal and socially conservative. It was aimed essentially at maintaining the rights of the newly enfranchised bourgeoisie. Napoleon I's primary achievement was to develop the bureaucracy inherited from the monarchy. Through him, France was given a well-functioning civil service, codes of law, and a theory of the administrative process that were envied by many countries for several generations. Much of the Napoleonic bureaucracy is still in existence. Political battles have been fought largely over governments and their policies, not over the administrative instruments of government.

The Second Empire went further than the First by placing great emphasis on industrial and commercial development, often with substantial state help. This was the time when some of the great banks were set up, for instance. It was under the Second Empire that France began moving decisively away from being a predominantly agricultural economy.

| TABLE 3.1 | |
|---|---|
| **CHRONOLOGY OF POLITICAL DEVELOPMENT IN FRANCE** | |
| To 1789 | *Ancien régime* (dates of reign): Louis XIV, 1643–1715. Louis XV, 1715–1774. Louis XVI, 1774–1792. |
| 1789–1792 | Constitutional Monarchy. Constituent Assembly. Constitution of 1791. First legislative Assembly. |
| 1792–1799 | First Republic. Convention Constitution of 1793 (not applied). Directory Constitution of 1795. |
| 1799–1804 | Consulate. Napoleon, first consul. Constitutions of 1799 and 1802. |
| 1804–1814 and 1815 | First Empire. Napoleon I, emperor. Constitutions of 1804, 1814 (not applied), and 1815. |
| 1814–1815 and 1815–1830 | Restoration. Louis XVIII, 1814–1824. Charter of 1814 Charles X, 1824–1830. |
| 1830–1848 | Orleans monarchy. Louis-Philippe I, 1830–1848. Charter of 1830. |
| 1848–1851 | Second Republic. Napoleon Bonaparte (nephew of Napoleon I), president. Constitution of 1848. |
| 1852–1870 | Second Empire. Napoleon III, emperor. Constitutions of 1852 and 1870. |
| 1870–1940 | Third Republic. Constitution of 1875. |
| 1940–1944 | Vichy regime. Pétain "head of state." |
| 1945–1958 | Fourth Republic. Constitution of 1946. |
| From 1958 | Fifth Republic. Constitution of 1958. Presidents: Charles de Gaulle, 1958–1969; Georges Pompidou, 1969–1974; Valéry Giscard d'Estaing, 1974–1981; François Mitterrand, 1981–1988, reelected, 1988–1995; Jacques Chirac, 1995–2002, reelected 2002. |

## Republicanism and Its Elements

Nineteenth-century French republicanism originally comprised only a few simple elements: the expression of the public will through a sovereign and directly elected assembly, a society free from the institutionalized influence of the Church, and distrust of executive authority as a threat to freedom, against which the people had an obligation to rise when and if tyranny appeared imminent. Several times the people did take to the barricades. From when the monarchy was returned in 1815 to the Commune of 1870, the people, particularly the people of Paris, took periodically to the streets. On at least two occasions, in 1830 and 1848, civic violence led to the collapse of a regime. A rising of this kind occurred in 1944 when the German occupation forces were leaving Paris; students rose also in the university district of Paris, the Latin Quarter, in 1968.

The egalitarian strand of French republicanism never succeeded for long. The 1793–1794 Reign of Terror eventually led to Napoleon; the 1848 revolution led to the Second Empire. When this regime fell after being defeated by Prussia in 1870, the Paris Commune seized power in the capital, but it was smashed, ending in one of the bloodiest episodes of repression in French history.

Moderate republicanism became truly established after the Paris Commune. A national assembly composed mainly of monarchists drafted constitutional laws, hoping that a monarchical restoration could take place. The republic triumphed by default, and almost by accident, in 1875. The constitution then grudgingly adopted lasted until 1940. It was destroyed by German arms after a series of attacks coming from both Right and Left and by the weakness and internal divisions of its supporters.

## The Second World War and Its Consequences: The Vichy Regime, the Resistance, and the Fourth Republic

Modern French history spans the Third, Fourth (1946–1958), and Fifth Republics (since 1958); it was interrupted between 1940 and 1944 by the "corporate state" of Pétain, whose authority derived from the German victory over France and not, despite the appearances of a legal transfer, from the will of the French people. In many ways, the Vichy regime (so called because the seat of government was transferred to Vichy, in central France, while northern France was occupied) symbolized what was antirepublican in French life.

Meanwhile, a Resistance movement against German occupation began organizing. It contained elements from all shades of French republicanism, from conservative nationalists to Communists. Although General de Gaulle had created a government in exile long before, first in London and later in Algiers, at the time of liberation in 1944 the Resistance remained the main political force in the country. The new constitution, adopted in 1946, established the Fourth Republic on the basis of traditional republican principles, but with left-wing overtones inherited from the Resistance. The Left was not strong enough to retain power, however, and the Fourth Republic resembled the Third. It was characterised by a powerful popular assembly, a weak executive, and an administrative apparatus floating in an ambiguous limbo below the government.

## The Fall of the Fourth Republic

Being weak and transient, the governments of the Fourth Republic were unable to solve the major political problem of the time: decolonization. Defeat in Indochina in 1954 severely undermined the political system. A strong prime minister, Mendès-France, produced a settlement that effectively disengaged France from its Indochinese colonies, but he remained in power for only six months afterwards. By then, the war had begun in the French possession of Algeria between supporters of the status quo (mostly comprising the million French settlers in Algeria) and those who demanded Algerian independence. Successive governments proved too weak to make any move in the direction of reform. Despite the presence of a million French conscripts on the other side of the Mediterranean, France lost the war. By May 1958, pushed by civilian extremists, commanders in Algiers ceased to recognize the authority of the Paris government and even landed a small military force in Corsica. Rumors of an impending army coup spread throughout France; these created a climate of tension, plots, and counterplots. De Gaulle was recalled to office by a large majority of the Assembly on June 1, 1958, some hoping he could keep Algeria French, others thinking that he alone had the power to solve the problem. The Fifth Republic was born.

# THE BACKGROUND OF THE SOCIAL ORDER

In the 1950s and 1960s, France leapt forward both socially and economically. Many consider the tragedy of modern France to be the inability to keep pace with socioeconomic change. At the same time aspects of the traditional background of French society remain visible in many parts of the country. Four characteristics of this traditional social order have special prominence. First, the French population—long static at 40 million and now about 60 million—has peasant origins. Second, France is geographically and even linguistically divided. Third, the class system and particularly the division between bourgeois and worker (*ouvrier*) has long affected lifestyles. Fourth, France is traditionally Roman Catholic, but it also was fiercely anticlerical in the nineteenth and early twentieth centuries. It was on such a social landscape that the kings first and Napoleon later built a centralized administrative machine and that the Republic imposed a centralized political culture.

## Peasant Origins

France was long a peasant nation—indeed perhaps the only peasant nation with a substantial proportion of its population who worked as smallholders instead of farm laborers. By the outbreak of World War II, as many as one-third of the population worked on plots inherited from their parents and to which they were strongly attached (see Table 3.2). Though owners of the land, these farmers had a difficult life. Plots were small and often fragmented because the civil code of Napoleon required that estates be divided equally among all the children. This led to low productivity even in rich areas and to low incomes—a state of affairs that fostered pessimism among large numbers of farmers. This also led to a low birthrate—lower, before 1945, than in all other developed nations.

Migrations from village to city were characteristic of Western Europe, yet in France they had less influence on the new city-dweller than

**TABLE 3.2**

**OCCUPATIONS OF THE FRENCH POPULATION**

|  | Percentage of the Active Population | | | |
|---|---|---|---|---|
|  | 1954 | 1962 | 1975 | 1990 |
| Farmers and farm laborers | 26.5 | 24.0 | 9.4 | 4.5 |
| Owners of businesses | 12.0 | 10.0 | 7.8 | 7.9 |
| Higher management and professions | 3.0 | 4.0 | 6.7 | 11.7 |
| Middle management | 6.0 | 7.5 | 12.7 | 20.0 |
| White-collar workers | 16.0 | 17.0 | 22.3 | 26.5 |
| Manual workers | 33.5 | 35.0 | 37.6 | 29.4 |
| Other (army, police, etc.) | 3.0 | 2.5 | 3.5 | — |
|  | 100.0 | 100.0 | 100.0 | 100.0 |
| Total (millions) | 19.3 | 20.1 | 21.7 | 22.3 |

*Source:* Europa World Yearbook, various years (origin ILO Yearbooks of Social Statistics.)

in other countries. Peasant origins remained very important, and residents of cities often took on attitudes more characteristic of rural than of urban communities. Preconceptions, fears, worries, and a rather negative and anarchistic individualism came to dominate much of the middle and lower-middle levels of French society—shopkeepers, artisans, mechanics, and workers in commerce and even in industry, as well as the many civil servants.

The peasant complex, as this orientation might be called, has been a strong element in that much discussed French characteristic: individualism. It has manifested itself in the negative way in which the French have traditionally reacted to voluntary groupings. They did not believe in them and supported them with great hesitation, thus demonstrating, in a self-fulfilling prophecy, that most groupings conferred few benefits. The respect for negative criticism, the fear of appearing naive, and the suspicion of all men and institutions had considerable drawbacks for the French economy. This individualism rendered experimentation an object of ridicule and it became the very cause of the outside imposition of rules that the peasant community could not and would not establish.

Since World War II the characteristics of the farming community have altered markedly. The flight from the land took such proportions in the late 1950s and the 1960s that the weight of the peasantry in society diminished notably: from 1954 to 1975 the farming population was more than halved, from 5.2 million to under 2 million; there was a further decline to a little over 1 million by 1990. Farmers who remained on the land acquired larger plots and mechanization, and the commercialization of farm products gave farmers a different outlook on their role in society. With less than one person in 20 engaged in agriculture and with farms becoming businesses, modern France no longer has a large body of citizens who alone can tilt the scales in elections and generally flavor the political culture. But attitudes die hard and memories are long. The past political order on the land still plays a substantial part in the political life of the present, as can periodically be seen in the way the government defends French farming in the European Union and other international settings.

## Regional Sectionalism and the Influence of Paris

The second characteristic of the traditional French social structure is its sectionalism. This was maintained partly by the size of the peasantry, but general historical and geographical characteristics are also at play. Mountains and plateaus separate the country into natural regions and isolate certain areas from the main communication axes. Brittany in the west, the Southwest (sometimes known as Aquitaine), the Alpine area, and Provence (of which the southeastern tip on the Mediterranean has a very hilly interior and is known to tourists as the Côte d'Azur) all constitute sharply differentiated regions. These regions are somewhat isolated from the more accessible northern and northeastern parts of the country, whose wide plains give them an easier agriculture, more industry, and more natural lines of communication. History has in large part been molded by these geographical constraints, and local particularism has been widespread.

French sectionalism manifests itself in many ways. As everywhere, there are differences in accent, in turn often the product of the survival of local dialects, some of which, as in the south, have a Latin origin and are related to Italian (Provençal) or Spanish (Catalan), while others (Alsatian and Flemish) have Germanic roots and yet others (Breton and Basque) have little or nothing in common with the main European languages. But different forms of living are often also the consequences of different climates, which vary sharply as one moves from humid but temperate Brittany to the cold Massif Central or Alsace and to the pleasant, almost Californian Mediterranean coast. Architectural styles make towns and villages in Alsace, Provence, or the Paris area so distinct that they seem to belong to different countries. But these variations are the symbols of other, more profound variations in modes of living; the outdoor life in the clement south and southeast contrasts with the indoor life of the tougher north and east.

These differences naturally led the French to be attached to their *petite patrie*—to their traditional districts—while strangers who come to an area find real human relationships slow to develop. Important consequences follow; for instance, for a long time, political candidates had little chance of being elected if they ran for office in areas where they had no local roots.

The peculiar position of Paris has to be considered in this context. The political, social, economic, and cultural preeminence of the capital is beyond doubt, but it is resented. Paris is much larger than any other French city or metropolitan area. Eight million people live in the Paris area (the city proper has a population of only about 2 million). The next three largest metropolitan areas—Marseilles, Lyons, and Lille— barely reach a million, while the fifth largest town, Toulouse, has about half a million. Provincial capitals are therefore not in a position to challenge the metropolis. Those who have "arrived" have to be in Paris; those who are not in Paris often feel they have not "arrived," although there are exceptions. The weight of Paris, however, is felt even by those who do not wish to move to the capital.

Factors such as the car and television are minimizing sectionalism and bringing Paris nearer to the provinces. The wider economic context of the European Union decreases the preeminence of Paris, but the capital remains a pole of attraction, as well as a drain on the better resources of the provinces, to a much greater extent than in other European countries.

## Social Class

Class consciousness, the third main influence on French society, is a function of the cleavages that have torn the fabric of modern society and an outgrowth of the Industrial Revolution, which acquired full momentum in France only at the end of the nineteenth century. Social distinctions run sharp and deep, particularly in the large cities, although these have decreased since the 1950s. The size of the Communist vote was clearly a consequence of the bitterness that these conflicts caused.

Social mobility does occur, of course, indeed at about the same rate as in other developed societies. Moreover, this development is not new. Through education in particular, large numbers of sons and daughters of peasants, of lower-middle-class employees, and of manual workers have entered the middle class. Some educational channels have long made social promotion possible, in particular through prestigious graduate schools, such as the Ecole Polytechnique and the Ecole Normale Supérieure, as well as numerous other schools or examinations leading to the middle ranks of the civil service or the armed forces. Thrifty working-class young people often set up small businesses that they hope slowly to expand.

In France, social class is based to a large extent on occupation, education, and income. Though there is in France a tradition of respect for the crafts (the skills of artisans are often extolled), the esteem for industrial manual work is low. Class tension has decreased somewhat, however, partly as a result of the "embourgeoisement" of many workers who have adopted a middle-class lifestyle, from cars to holidays abroad.

Class tension may also have decreased because large-scale immigration enabled the French to avoid working in the building trades and sections of the automobile and other engineering industries, where they have been replaced by workers from Poland, Italy, Spain, and, since the 1950s, Portugal and, even more, North Africa. This situation may have helped the French avoid less pleasant forms of work, but it is at the root of the major ethnic tensions that have characterized contemporary France. Tension between the native French and North Africans has erupted in violence in many vast suburban high-rise estates where immigrants often are in the majority. While government policy is officially against all forms of discrimination, repressive measures, including forced repatriation, have occasionally been taken against immigrants. Terrorist incidents have from time to time provided authorities with grounds for surveillance and repression of the immigrant population. These measures have been taken in part to compete with and hopefully stop (so far unsuccessfully) the development of a strong extreme-right movement, the National Front, which emerged in the 1980s.

There has also been an increase in the proportion of women in higher-status positions, particularly in the civil service and the professions and more recently in business, but still less so in politics, especially at the parliamentary level. Improvement has taken place despite the fact that there has been markedly less pressure from women's organizations than in Anglo-American countries. Nonetheless, France has not, any more than most industrial countries, ceased to be mainly male dominated.

## CHURCH AND STATE

France is nominally a Catholic nation. One million Protestants (Calvinists in the south, Lutherans in Alsace) and fewer than half a million Jews are the only other sizeable indigenous religious groups. While these groups are static or in decline, Muslims have gained appreciably in the course of the last decades. Numbering more than a million, they are drawn from among immigrants, mainly from North Africa. The many Muslims born in France may feel religiously but also culturally least at ease in an environment that is often hostile and at best uncomprehending. A number of highly symbolic difficulties have occurred in schools with respect to the right of girls to wear the veil or not to participate fully in physical education classes. However, despite tensions that are often close to the surface, French and non-French Muslims have become somewhat uneasily integrated in the life of the nation.

While France is in theory overwhelmingly a Catholic nation, it also is profoundly anticlerical, in parts wholly dechristianized, and still somewhat affected by the great political battles that led to the separation of church and state in 1905. For the majority of French people, Roman Catholic practice relates only to social rites such as baptisms, marriages, and funerals. Weekly attendance at mass and general observance of religious prescriptions is limited to a rather small minority that is not uniformly spread throughout the nation. Brittany and Alsace are Catholic areas; the western part of the Massif Central and the southeast are antireligious or at best areligious. The historical origins of these variations are complex and are often due less to the priests than to the behavior of the local gentry before or during the Revolution of 1789.

As in most predominantly Roman Catholic countries of Western Europe, church and social order are associated in France. Since the Catholic Church was close to the Right in the nineteenth century, the Left, both moderate and extremist, has always attacked it. The attempt to restore the monarchy in the 1870s was viewed partly as an effort of the Church. Anticlericalism therefore spread among supporters of the Republic. The climax was reached in the 1890s with the Dreyfus case, in which a Jewish military officer was unjustly accused and convicted of treason. In spite of numerous signs that a judicial error had been committed, the case was reopened only after a long and bitter struggle between his defenders and his accusers (the Church, the military, and the conservatives). In 1905, partly in response to the Dreyfus Affair, Parliament passed a law separating church and state. Priests, Protestant ministers, and Jewish rabbis lost their status as civil servants, and various religious orders were disbanded or had to leave the country (among them the Jesuits, who were tolerated again after 1918 and not formally allowed in the country before World War II).

Many Roman Catholics became embittered against the Republic, but others began to realize that a change of attitude had to take place. The pronouncements of Pope Leo XIII helped in this respect, though his successor, Pius X, returned to more traditional ways and condemned a progressive Catholic movement, *Le Sillon,* created in 1894. Development of a strong Christian Democratic party therefore was difficult and was to occur only in the 1940s, too late to enable the party to have a permanent social base, as the country was by then rather dechristianized. On the other hand, progressive Catholics played a large part in the development of some trade unions and other organizations.

The climate has changed since the 1950s, although some antipathy against the Catholic Church still exists. However, the status of Catholics and of the Church has increased and there are no longer the big battles of the early part of the century. Major skirmishes have centered on church schools, to which state subsidies were granted in the 1950s. After the 1981 Socialist victory, when the government attempted to establish greater control over the schools, vast demonstrations occurred—so large that the proposals had to be abandoned. There is still sensitivity with respect to the Catholic Church, but the issue has ceased to be truly central.

## THE ADMINISTRATIVE AND CULTURAL CENTRALIZATION OF MODERN FRANCE

Divisions run deep in France. Not all are due to the Revolution, as we have seen; many date back to an earlier period. They cut across each other and lead to a fragmentation of the basic social attitudes, which accounts for much of the ideological and political sectionalism of the country.

The very number and complexity of the social divisions account for state centralization, both administrative and cultural. It is often thought that, had not the French kings and later the Empire set up a strong administrative system, the country would not have survived. It is also often thought that, had not the Republic introduced a uniform political culture cutting across geographical and social barriers, the Republic would not have survived. Administrative centralization was thus practiced by all regimes in order to defend themselves; not surprisingly, the strength of the impressive network of state agencies existing throughout the country has proved difficult to reduce.

The Republic did introduce a new political culture, mostly since the 1880s. This was spread by means of a centralized educational system, which was to be liberal, lay, and egalitarian. It

was not totalitarian, as it aimed at developing critical faculties, but it was uniform. It was largely based on the frame of mind of the writers of the eighteenth-century French Enlightenment, particularly Voltaire, who for about half a century had waged a war against the power of the Church and the state, which were viewed as opposed to rational thinking in order to reduce criticisms of the social order.

This critical ideology clearly undermined the authority on which all states, even republican ones, have to be based; only the centralized administration was therefore able to maintain the state. This, of course, made France more difficult to govern, although one can understand why republican politicians thought it necessary to spread their somewhat negative ideology. By emphasizing the right to criticize, they created problems for their successors. The political system has been bedeviled by the very success of the republicans of the 1880s and 1890s, who bequeathed their political culture to millions of their fellow citizens. But had the republicans not been so successful, France might not have been a republic for long.

Such is the background with which modern French governments have had to contend; not surprisingly, the various traditions reduced the ability of ministers and governments to maneuver. The centralizing tendencies are of course the most visible—and the most overwhelmingly strong—of these traditions. But the weight of tradition can be seen also in the very large part played by the public sector, in its various facets, on the French economy, at least up to the last decade of the twentieth century and even to an extent since then. Centralization brought about a spirit of enlightened despotism and *dirigisme*, the strong role of the state in administering the economy, which has prevailed in the political, administrative, and economic life of the country. France underwent major changes in the second half of the twentieth century, but the impact of the past lies close to the surface. It would be as foolish for observers to forget these traditions as it would be fatal for politicians to disregard them.

## *Thinking Critically*

1. Would you agree with those who say, "All roads in France lead to Paris"?
2. How would you define "anticlericalism" in France?
3. What was the impact of Napoleon on French history and politics?
4. Would you regard France as an example of political instability?
5. What are the major social and political divisions in France?

## KEY TERMS

administative centralization *(128)*
church and state *(127)*
class consciousness *(126)*
The Declaration of the Rights of Man and the Citizen *(121)*
The Dreyfus Affair *(127)*
Jacobins *(121)*
Napoleon Bonaparte *(122)*
regional sectionalism *(125)*
republicanism *(123)*
Revolution of 1848 *(122)*
Revolution of 1789/Revolutionary Assembly *(121)*

## FURTHER READINGS

Ardagh, J. *The New France* (Baltimore: Penguin Books, 1973).

Bodley, J. E. *France* (London: Macmillan, 1898).

Brogan, D. W. *The Development of Modern France* (London: Hamish Hamilton, 1940).

Cerny, P., ed. *Social Movements and Protest in France* (London: Pinter, 1982).

Howarth, J., and P. Cerny, eds. *Elites in France* (London: Pinter, 1981).

Ehrman, H. *Politics in France,* 3d ed. (Boston: Little, Brown, 1974).

Frears, J. R. *France in the Giscard Presidency* (London: Allen and Unwin, 1981).

de Gaulle, C. *Memoirs* (New York: Simon and Schuster, 1968–1972).

Hall, P. A., J. Hayward, and H. Machin, *Developments in French Politics* (London: Macmillan, 1990).

Hoffmann, S., G. Ross, and S. Malzacher, eds. *The Mitterrand Experiment,* (Oxford: Polity Press, 1987).

Stevens, A. *The Government and Politics of France* (London: Macmillan, 1992).

Todd, E. *The Making of Modern France* (Oxford: Blackwell, 1991).

Williams, P. M. *Crisis and Compromise* (New York: McKay, 1964).

Williams, P. M., and M. Harrison. *Politics and Society in de Gaulle's Republic* (New York: Doubleday, 1973).

Wylie, L. *Village in the Vaucluse* (Cambridge: Harvard University Press, 1964).

# B. POLITICAL PROCESSES AND INSTITUTIONS

The advent of the Fifth Republic in 1958 marked the emergence of truly modern politics in France, although as we already noted, elements of the past are still prominent. The constitution was changed, transforming the roles of president, government, and parliament. At the same time, the strength and characteristics of groups and of parties were markedly affected, although these remain weaker and less well-organized than elsewhere in Western Europe.

## INTEREST GROUPS

Interest groups have long been frowned upon in France. To this day, they have remained rather weak, at least by comparison with other Western countries. In the 1830s, Tocqueville went to America and saw the part that associations played in bringing about democracy. Nearly 200 years later, France has still not become a truly associational society, and this has important consequences for the democratic character of the society.

The Revolution of 1789 fought the corporate state of the *ancien régime,* in which each trade was organized in closed craft networks that were entered only after long periods of apprenticeship, but which provided their members with monopoly privileges. In the name of liberty the Revolution abolished these guilds and forbade individuals to coalesce to limit production or regulate the entry of others into a profession (with several important exceptions). Trade unions came to be tolerated 75 years after the Revolution, but they had to wait another 25 years to be fully recognized.

Political parties were undermined by the conception that politicians should have direct contacts with electors and remain free from the bureaucratic influence of headquarters and leaders. In the 1950s a major change of attitude occurred, paradoxically as de Gaulle continued to attack groups and parties, but he needed a party to maintain his hold on the country.

While more pluralistic than at any time since 1789, present-day France still has fewer associations than other Western countries. The target of group attacks is often the state, and the typical approach is still to ask the state to meet the demands or to force (for instance, by law) private employers to make concessions. The idea of partnership between economic actors is only slowly gaining ground, and not in a regular manner.

## Trade Unions

***Workers' Unions*** The French trade union movement is very divided, largely for political reasons. Its membership is small, proportionately the smallest in Western Europe, indeed smaller than in the United States, though participation is high in works councils mandated by law in firms of a certain size. The relatively late development of the union movement and political divisions account for these weaknesses.

The early history was difficult. Full recognition was achieved only in 1884. Very quickly, trade unions came to be controlled by militants who believed in direct action. By the turn of the twentieth century, they displaced the more reformist or even Marxist elements from the leadership. These "syndicalists" were against employers and against all politicians. The *Confédération Générale du Travail* (CGT), created in 1895 as a federation of all major trade unions, did not look for piecemeal victories through parliament. Rather, it sought one major push through the general strike. The union was never powerful enough to launch any such action and, when war broke out in 1914, even trade unionists rushed to defend the "bourgeois" state.

After World War I, the majority of labor leaders adopted a more reformist stance, but the emergence of Communism brought about a split and introduced party politics into the trade union movement. The CGT followed more closely the Socialist Party, while the more militant elements set up a Communist-led trade union, which was disbanded in 1936 in a "popular front" alliance.

This move enabled Communists to acquire influence gradually in the newly reunited body and to dominate it in 1945. In 1947, when the CGT was openly used for political reasons in a wave of strikes launched by the Communists, the Socialists broke away and set up a new union, the CGT-*Force Ouvrière* (the name of the newspaper of those who held these views).

Meanwhile, a Catholic union, the *Confédération Française des Travailleurs Chrétiens* (CFTC), created in 1918, quickly acquired substantial support among white-collar employees and in strongly Christian parts of the country (Alsace in particular); it then slowly gathered followers in the whole of the country. Having grown to be the second largest trade union, it changed its name in 1964 to widen its appeal and became the *Confédération Française Démocratique du Travail* (CFDT), although a small segment continued under the old name.

There are thus three main trade union organizations catering to manual and white-collar workers. Yet the membership is small, perhaps 2 to 2.5 million for all three organizations. Under 10 percent of the workforce is thus unionized, although there are substantial variations among occupational groups.

***Consequences of the Divisions among Workers' Unions***   The division of the workers' unions has been detrimental to workers' interests. Employers and governments have been able to play one union against the other. This also has led unions to make demagogic proposals in order not to be overtaken and convinced many French workers that unionization was not necessary. There are exceptions to these divisions, admittedly. In printing, for instance, all the members belong to the CGT. In many firms and offices, one or at most two unions predominate. The CGT is strong mostly on the docks and in mechanical engineering (particularly around Paris). The CFDT's strength tends to be in light industry and among white-collar workers. *Force Ouvrière* leads among textile workers in the north and among civil servants everywhere, though it is not, as is sometimes claimed, the main trade union among civil servants. Competition between two unions

is common. At the national level, all three major unions take stands and are involved in consultations among themselves, with the government, and with employers.

The combination of this traditional weakness of unions and of legislative efforts to integrate the working-class representatives into the rest of society led to a mixture of compulsory cooperation at the top and of semi-anarchistic and often ineffective outbursts at the bottom. Formally, unions are often involved, as in the social security system, which is largely administered by them; there are also factory committees (*comités d'entreprise*) in charge of large sums devoted to leisure and cultural activities; boards of nationalized industries have union representatives. Many advisory committees of the government in the planning field, for instance, include trade union members. Yet unions are often unable to press seriously their claims at the level of the firm, as they often do not agree on a common stand and cannot promise financial help in case of strikes. Many workers thus often continue to work when a strike is called. This occurs despite the fact that the CFDT has regularly campaigned for a new approach to the relationship between workers and society; instead of emphasizing the need for workers' organizations to prepare for an onslaught on the state, as the CGT traditionally tended to do, the CFDT aimed at developing cooperation. It thus played a large part in developing collective bargaining, which came about in France only in the 1950s, although it was legalized in 1936. It was also the first union to place emphasis on the need to improve job conditions, in particular to reduce boredom and repetitiveness.

Yet these moves have not altered patterns of behavior fundamentally. Unions are weak; workers are generally passive. Occasionally, however, there are somewhat anomic massive protest movements which start from the grass roots and extend to a large proportion of the workforce. This was the case in 1968, the catalyst being provided by the student movement. From time to time, especially among students, revolts seemed about to occur, but strikes have become rarer, in part perhaps because of the reforms of the

Socialist government of the first half of the 1980s. The influence of the CGT has markedly declined, as was shown at elections for the social security boards, since the 1980s in particular. The entrenched class antagonism of the past seems to be giving way to more realism and greater moderation.

However, in December 1995, a large movement took place against a proposed governmental reform of pensions and social security. Strikes, in particular in the railways, urban public transport, and to an extent the post office, were on a scale which resembled the 1968 outburst, although the unrest occurred only in the public sector. The movement thus seemed to indicate that some of the old forms of discontent continued to exist, especially as the (conservative) government had tried to impose changes without consultation.

***Other Unions***    The three major trade union organizations cover, in theory at least, all types of employees. But many white-collar workers, most lower and middle management (*cadres* is the French expression), the professions, and students have typically been organized in different unions (though a minority belong to the three major organizations). There has even been a substantial spread of "autonomous" trade unions among some categories of skilled workers, such as train drivers. Sectional unions have long existed among professionals—doctors, dentists, and lawyers, for instance, who are typically self-employed. Special unions also exist among some other groups, such as school and university teachers. For a while, in the 1950s and early 1960s, students succeeded in creating one of the best and most active French trade unions, the *Union Nationale des Etudiants de France,* but the Algerian war and the events of 1968 led to a radicalization of the leadership, which proved unacceptable to the mass of the students and led to union splits. Finally, much of the employed middle class—the various levels of management in commerce and industry—are organized in a general union, the *Confédération Générale des Cadres* (CGC), which aims at maintaining the pay differentials which *cadres* have acquired in the

growing French economy. Together with the three major workers unions it participates in general government-union discussions, but clashes with workers' unions are frequent in view of status and ideological differences.

## Business Organizations

Business organizations are somewhat divided because of the traditional influence of small business and because of the economic changes that have benefited large firms. Before 1945, industrial pressure—mainly from industrialists—on government was frequent, but it tended to occur in secret and outside the framework of organizations. Change began to take place with the first ever French Socialist government, elected in 1936, which initiated general negotiations between government, unions, and business. This led to an overall agreement, the Matignon Accord, which indirectly strengthened the role of business organizations as well as that of trade unions. After World War II the reconstituted *Conseil National du Patronat Français* (CNPF) first started to operate in an unfriendly environment of strong antibusiness ideology. Employers seemed divided among themselves. Though the CNPF was a federation covering all types of firms, small and medium-sized enterprises were organized into a semi-independent confederation, the *Confédération Générale des Petites et Moyennes Entreprises* (CGPME), which because of the larger number and smaller incomes of its members and the prevailing cult of the "petit" in France was often more militant. Meanwhile, a section of the *patronat,* organized into a *Centre des Jeunes Patrons,* now the *Centre des Jeunes Dirigeants d'Entreprise,* displayed a more progressive attitude and criticized their colleagues for their conservatism.

The division between the CGPME and the CNPF—reorganized and renamed *Mouvement des Entreprises de France* (MEDEF) in 1998—has remained a feature of the contemporary French business scene. On the whole, the CNPF used to cooperate with government, but this has been markedly less the case in its new MEDEF incarnation. The earlier cooperation arose in

French public sector workers on strike.

part because governments have usually been of the Right or Center, in part because of many personal ties between leaders of large businesses and civil servants. Business leaders and top civil servants tend to go through the same elite schools or be members of the *grands corps,* as we shall see later. Big business has also been broadly sympathetic with the policy of growth and industrialization promoted by French governments since the 1950s, which still prevailed, albeit in a somewhat bruised manner, in the conditions of economic depression of the late 1970s and early 1980s. Relations had been relatively good even with Socialist governments of the 1980s, despite the large-scale nationalization program. They deteriorated to a substantial extent in the late 1990s, the leaders of the MEDEF taking an appreciably more radical,

"free enterprise" line than the leaders of the CNPF had previously adopted.

***Defensive Attitudes of Small Business***    From the mid-1950s, small businesses, in particular proprietors of small shops and small repair stores, had come increasingly to view with major suspicion both civil servants anxious to rationalize the economy and big businesses that seemed to benefit from the changing economy, in particular supermarkets and discount stores. This led to the development of a number of strong protest movements, the earliest of which, that of Pierre Poujade, the *Union de Défense des Commerçants et Artisans,* became so famous for its populist ideology that it acquired the status of a political symbol. The expression "poujadism" was used widely, in France and abroad, to refer to bodies based on and aiming to represent "small men" fighting against the "tentacles" of the state and of big business. The protest was not just on the economic plane; it was also political (the poujadists obtained 12 percent of the votes at the 1956 parliamentary election). It was often violent, direct action against tax offices being one of the methods used by the movement. The return of de Gaulle to power in 1958 abruptly ended the success of poujadism, but another movement with similar aims and similar tactics was founded in the late 1960s, though that body never had the political success of the prior organization and it quickly faded out. Meanwhile, the CGPME continued throughout the period to voice, in a more responsible manner, the basic grievances of shopkeepers and small businesspeople. Results were indeed occasionally obtained, for instance in the form of restrictions placed on the development of large discount stores.

Outbursts of the underdogs of French business thus did occur in the Fifth Republic, especially in the 1960s, but more sporadically than before 1958, though, under the Socialist governments, truck drivers in particular have more than once adopted direct action and blocked roads and superhighways. On the whole, however, the party system of the Fifth Republic has been better able to contain the activities of these groups. Yet the contrast between the "civilized" forms of pressure exercised by large businesses and the somewhat anomic and occasionally violent actions of small businesspeople shows that traditionalism has not ceased to play a part in the panorama of French social and political life.

## Farmers' Organizations

The evolution of agriculture has been rapid, though outbursts of discontent are not unknown among farmers. The flight from the land and the development of mechanization have altered farming conditions everywhere in the country; those who stayed gained more elbow room and some scope for expansion, though they also confronted acute problems of capital and investment. Small farms are the norm except in the north and the Paris area, where wheat and beetroot growers have long constituted an aristocracy, with larger plots, widespread mechanization, and rather high incomes. Elsewhere, the prevailing culture emphasizes, and is adamant to protect, the tradition of the small farm. This culture prevails, not just among the members of the agricultural community, but widely across many segments of the population and in the political world.

The main pressure group of farmers is the *Fédération Nationale des Syndicats d'Exploitants Agricoles* (FNSEA), created in 1945 and originally led by the northern farmers. This body was challenged as agriculture rapidly changed in structure and its relation to the rest of the community. The first anomic protests resembled those of shopkeepers; roadblocks and the dumping of unsold vegetables were fairly common means of demonstrating anger. Gradually, however, a change began to occur when a number of associations, mainly of Catholic origin, started to stress the long-term benefits of the modernization of agriculture, cooperation among farmers being presented as the best way of solving the problems posed by the need to undertake large investments, especially in machinery. The agricultural policy of the European Community, as the European Union was then known, also suggested that huge opportunities were becoming open to French farmers. The *Jeunesse Agricole Chrétienne* and the *Centre National des Jeunes Agriculteurs* (CNJA) thus succeeded in converting large sections of the farming community to their views, to the extent that these eventually came to be adopted by the FNSEA as CNJA leaders took over that organization.

Yet recurring complaints continue to be voiced by farmers. Many of them feared the effect on their incomes of the expansion of the European Community and of the liberalization of farm products on a worldwide basis. On the whole, farmers' unions have succeeded in forcing French governments to support their cause on the international scene, indeed to an extent that seems out of proportion with the size of the farming population.

## Other Groups

Since the mid-1960s, interest groups have played a large part in the panorama of French political life, although their development has remained patchy. Until the late 1950s, promotional groups had not been influential. For instance, while the nuclear disarmament campaign was reaching a climax in Britain, there was almost no equivalent in France, though the subject could have become controversial when de Gaulle embarked on a worldwide nuclear strategy.

The Algerian war was instrumental in the development of protest organizations, as political parties seemed impotent and none of them, not even the Communist Party, was able or willing to take a firm line against the war. The end of the Algerian war in 1962 made these protest organizations obsolete, but gradually new groups emerged. Consumer associations started to inquire into the quality of products, forms of marketing, and relative costs. Environmental societies have campaigned against the pollution of the seaside and the development of private beaches, attacked the takeover of vast areas of land for army camps, and opposed plans for highways and, more recently, for new lines for "very rapid" trains. Some groups are purely local and exclusively concerned with one issue; others are national and foster general aims. From the mid-1970s, antinuclear groups have become vocal and often violent, while women's groups have begun to make themselves felt, but both types have remained relatively low-key.

In the late 1960s and early 1970s, there was an upsurge in the activity of regionalist groups. Long limited to the Bretons and (though less so) the Basques, regionalist ideas extended for a while to large parts of the country, particularly the southern half, where the *Mouvement Occitan* stated that the "colonization" of the country by the north and by Paris had to be ended. The strength of most of these movements declined, however, in part probably because the Socialist government of 1981–1986 introduced regionalist and decentralization measures. Only to an extent in French Overseas Territories (in New Caledonia, in the Caribbean) and above all in Corsica did radicalization occur. Yet even in Corsica, the terrorist activities of autonomist movements has remained rather patchy, in part because of the division among these movements. These terrorist activities are beginning to have an effect on politicians' attitudes, however, the Socialist Party being, on the whole, the only party which is truly prepared to grant substantial autonomy to the island. In continental France, the one set of serious terrorist activities which the country has known since World War II occurred during the Algerian war in the early 1960s. In the late 1980s and mid-1990s, however, there were sporadic outbursts of bombing connected with Muslim, and

## A CLOSER LOOK 3.2

## THE WEAKNESS OF PROTEST GROUPS IN FRANCE

Groups are unquestionably much weaker in France than in other Western democracies. What was true in the nineteenth century continues to be true, despite some changes, at the beginning of the twenty-first. It is not just that trade unions are less strong and more divided than elsewhere; it is that the groups which flourish in other countries do not emerge, or scarcely emerge, in the French context. The huge antinuclear protests in Britain had no counterparts in France, despite the fact that France has nuclear weapons. The limited reactions within France to the bombs exploded in the Pacific in the mid-1990s are a case in point. Moreover, there have also been on balance relatively few demonstrations against nuclear power stations despite the fact that France has more nuclear power stations than other countries. Even feminist groups have been weak, and not because women have made more advances in France than elsewhere, though they have not made fewer advances than elsewhere either. The low level of associationalism in France was mentioned by Tocqueville in his *Democracy in America* in the 1830s and, remarkably, the same trend still prevails. This characteristic is unquestionably among the most important aspects of French political culture.

in particular Algerian, opposition to French government policies.

## Groups and the Political System

### *The Role of Consultation*

The Fifth Republic began in 1958 with an anti–interest-group bias. Yet de Gaulle was soon confronted with large waves of protest on the part of veterans and of opponents of church schools. The government took little notice of the huge demonstrations and won. De Gaulle seemed to have proved his point—that when the state is strong, it can withstand the pressure of groups. However, his policy of benign neglect led to an accumulation of grievances which finally exploded in May and June 1968. Since then, leaders of the Fifth Republic have been more cautious and have developed consultation as a means of addressing grievances.

The origin of consultation can be traced to the *ancien régime* and the Napoleonic system. Although it was initially limited to narrow sectors of the population, representation gradually increased. After World War I, it was institutionalized through an economic council that was given constitutional status in 1946. The Economic and Social Council is composed of representatives of all sectors of the population, including consumers and intellectuals. In addition to advising on bills and the more important government regulations, it debates economic and social plans. Together with the many representative bodies on which trade unionists are present (boards of nationalized industries, social security boards, and others) and with the associations of farmers (*Chambres d'Agriculture*) or of business leaders (*Chambres de Commerce*), the council provides a broad formal basis to the consultative process.

Yet what had been lacking until recently was not so much a formal machinery, but a will to discuss or a climate of consultation. Previously partnership existed only in one privileged sector, big business, where personal ties between leaders of industry and higher civil servants made informal discussions possible and indeed frequent. For small business, agriculture, employ-

ees, and consumers, no similar relations existed. Admittedly, the uncooperative and unrealistic attitudes of many trade unions and of many other groups can be blamed, but these uncooperative attitudes were also in part the product of an earlier lack of partnership.

Some change began to occur in the 1970s with Presidents Pompidou and Giscard d'Estaing. Pompidou's first prime minister, Chaban-Delmas, undertook to bring about a partnership between the various "live forces" *(forces vives)* of the nation. Then, in the 1980s, having accused the Gaullists and their associates of not giving enough scope for consultation, the Socialists who

General Charles de Gaulle (1890–1970) was the leader of the Free French movement in London during World War II, the head of government in 1944–1946, the last prime minister of the Fourth Republic in 1958, and president of France 1959–1969.

came to power in 1981 attempted to increase consultation; however, the program of reforms which they undertook was so large in the fields of local and regional government, public enterprise, and workers' participation that the government was primarily anxious to act quickly. The return of the Right to power, first in the late 1980s and subsequently in 1993, did not lead to much change, if any, in the direction of greater consultation. Under the Socialist government of the late 1990s, consultation suffered a setback when the leaders of the new business organization, the MEDEF, declared that they would no longer participate in the management of the social security bodies if major changes in structure were not introduced; no way out of the impasse had been found by the time the Socialists left power in 2002.

The role of interest groups has increased: the civil service can no longer implement its big projects without engaging in discussions with vocal groups. Yet much has still to be done to reconcile the French with the basic need for and the real value of association. As few workers belong to unions, these are weak and their leaders often feel impotent. Much has still also to be done, despite recent changes, to bring government and civil service nearer to the nation. A centralizing spirit and centralized structures are major handicaps to a real partnership between groups and the state. Therein lies perhaps the major problem of French society, a problem which the 1981–1986 Socialist government began to tackle, but to which high priority has not been given since then, although lip service is periodically paid to the need to find a solution.

# THE PARTY SYSTEM

## Streamlining the Parties: Gaullists and Socialists

Before 1958, French parties were weak, poorly organized, and undisciplined. This was largely due to the traditions that we examined earlier and in particular to the high degree of localism. With the advent of the Fifth Republic, the situation changed somewhat, but neither regularly nor indeed continuously. In a first period, roughly during the 1960s, the Gaullist party established itself as the dominant party. It won an unprecedented victory in 1968, when it gained a large majority of seats (though only 45 percent of the votes), but this was followed by a decline in the 1970s. The Gaullist party has scarcely polled above 20 percent since the 1980s, most of the votes lost going to groups of the Center, which are only loosely held together.

The election of 1981 changed the party configuration, in more ways than one. The French Socialist Party, for the first time in the history of the country, won an absolute majority of seats; it gained only 38 percent of the votes, admittedly, but never had it obtained before the support of more than a quarter of the electorate. For the first time since 1958, there was a change in the party in power. The victory of the Socialists in 1981 was also remarkable in that it signalled the end of the Communist Party as a major force in French politics. That party declined first to 16 percent and subsequently to under 10 percent.

The 1986 parliamentary election brought about the return of the Right with a small majority, but when reelected in 1988, the Socialist president, Mitterrand, immediately dissolved parliament. The Socialist Party did win, though this time short of an absolute majority. It was to suffer a crushing defeat at the parliamentary election of 1993, in part as a result of a number of financial scandals. The Right confirmed its victory at the 1995 presidential election, which was won by the Gaullist Chirac with a relatively small majority. However, in view of the squabbles within the right-wing coalition in power, Chirac dissolved parliament a year early, in 1997; this led, somewhat unexpectedly, to a victory of the Socialist Party at the head of a coalition including Communists and Greens. Lionel Jospin's tenure as prime minister was to last five years, up to the 2002 election, the longest that any Socialist prime minister in France ever enjoyed. The 1997 election also led to the longest period during which a president of one party (the Gaullists) was to "cohabit" with a government of the other main party (the Socialists).

In the first ballot vote for the May 2002 presidential election, Socialist candidate Jospin came in third, behind extreme-Right candidate Le Pen. Chirac won an easy victory over Le Pen in the run-off, and in June 2002 the Socialists were roundly defeated. As a result, the Right held both the presidency and the government.

In the Fifth Republic, the French party system is somewhat more streamlined than under the two previous Republics. It still has a multiparty character, but these parties come under the umbrella of two main blocs, Center-right, in which Gaullists and Center parties now share power equally, and Center-left, in which the Socialist Party dominates. Thus even when, as in the 1970s and typically in the 1990s, complex coalitions have controlled the government, these have remained more disciplined and cohesive than at almost any time since the beginning of the twentieth century.

## The Effect of the Electoral System

The streamlining of the party system was helped by the electoral system that (with the exception of the 1986 parliamentary election) has been in force since 1958. The system is known as the *scrutin d'arrondissement à deux tours,* a two-ballot system within single-member districts taking place on two successive Sundays. This type of electoral system had been in use during most of the Third Republic, but it was replaced in 1945 by proportional representation, traditionally advocated by the Left as being fairer. Proportional representation was reintroduced by the Socialist majority in 1985, but the conservative coalition that won in 1986 returned to the majority system. At the first ballot, only candidates receiving 50 percent or more of the votes cast in a district are elected. At the second round, the candidate who gets the most votes is elected, but only candidates who obtained more than 12.5 percent of the votes at the first round may run. Between the first and second round, deals take place and candidates withdraw voluntarily, sometimes in favor of other candidates better placed in the race.

The effect of this two-ballot system on the French party system has varied somewhat over time and is not entirely straightforward. In some cases, it has the same apparent consequences as the British first-past-the-post system. It has made it possible for one party to be temporarily dominant, as in the case of the Gaullists between 1962 and 1973 and of the Socialists during most of the last two decades of the twentieth century. At other times, the effect has been to create two blocs—on the Right and on the Left—within which agreements are made between component parties. This type of agreement has become truly imperative to governments of the Right. After the decline of the Gaullist party in the mid-1970s, the scene has also been occupied by the *Union pour la Démocratie Française* (UDF), a coalition of loosely organized medium-sized and small parties closely connected at the time with President Giscard d'Estaing. This coalition consistently obtained between a fifth and a quarter of the votes at parliamentary elections. On the Left, the Socialist Party has dominated but has tended to associate with some Center-left groupings, some Communists, and increasingly some members of the Green Party.

The French system thus remains multiparty, with only some tendencies toward having dominant parties (see Table 3.3). The effect of the electoral system consists perhaps more in bringing parties within two broad blocs than in forcing the merger let alone the disappearance of parties.

## The Right and Center

Unlike Britain, France never had a Conservative party. Yet on at least two occasions, it seemed that the Gaullist party would be able to unite the large majority of the electors of the Right. The first time was in the late 1940s, when de Gaulle created the *Rassemblement du Peuple Français* (RPF), which was pointedly called a "rally" because its founder wanted to indicate that his organization was different from all other political movements. The RPF was for a time very successful. At the municipal elections of 1947, it swept most large towns, obtained nearly 40 percent of the votes cast, and seemed a major challenge to the government of the Fourth Republic. Traditional parties of the Center, however, proved to be resilient and gradually eroded

## TABLE 3.3

### ELECTIONS TO THE FRENCH NATIONAL ASSEMBLY (SELECTED DATES)

| | | Party Votes (%) | | | | | | |
|---|---|---|---|---|---|---|---|---|
| | Total (millions) | Communist and Other Left Parties | Socialists | Center-left and Greens | Center | Gaullists | National Front | Other |
| 1962 | 18.3 | 22.0 | 15.0 | 8.0 | 29.0 | 32.0 | | |
| 1981 | 25.0 | 16.2 | 37.6 | 1.3 | 19.1 | 20.9 | | 4.9 |
| 1988 | 24.0 | 11.1 | 37.7 | 0.3 | 40.3* | | 9.9 | 0.6 |
| 1993 | 25.2 | 11.0 | 17.6 | 10.1 | 19.2 | 20.4 | 12.5 | 9.1 |
| 1997 | 25.3 | 12.1 | 25.5 | 6.7 | 14.7 | 16.8 | 15.1 | 9.1 |
| 2002 | 26.3 | 7.6 | 25.2 | 4.4/3.1 | 4.2 | 34.2 | 11.1 | 4.6 |

| | Total | Seats per Party | | | | | | |
|---|---|---|---|---|---|---|---|---|
| 1962 | 480 | 41 | 67 | 45 | 89 | 234 | — | 4 |
| 1981 | 491 | 45 | 289 | — | 73 | 84 | — | — |
| 1988 | 577 | 27 | 277 | 12 | — | 130 | 128 | 1 |
| 1993 | 577 | 25 | 67 | — | 206 | 242 | 1 | 36 |
| 1997 | 577 | 37 | 245 | 37 | 109 | 140 | 1 | 8 |
| 2002 | 577 | 21 | 154 | 3 | 22 | 369 | — | 8 |

*Combination of Center and Gaullists for 1988 election only. Before and after 1988 they were separate.

Gaullist strength. At the 1951 general election, the Gaullists obtained little more than one-fifth of the votes; a year later they split, and by 1956 Gaullism as a movement had all but disappeared.

The resurgence of Gaullism was the direct consequence of de Gaulle's return to power in 1958 as a result of the inability of the Fourth Republic's political leaders to deal with the Algerian problem. But this time the return of Gaullism seemed likely to be more than a passing phenomenon. The *Union pour la Nouvelle République* (UNR), as the Gaullist party then came to be named, obtained a quarter of the votes in 1958 and 40 percent in 1962. These successes were repeated at the elections of 1967 and 1968, and by then, the Gaullist party seemed fully established. It was the closest to a mass party on the Right that France ever had, although it did not have a very large membership (unlike the old RPF of the late 1940s)—50,000 members in the early 1960s and about three times this figure in the

early 1970s. Membership drives occurred from time to time, but they were neither pushed hard nor really successful.

The policies of the first Gaullist party—that of the 1940s—were on the whole those of the authoritarian right. De Gaulle ostensibly favored ideas of collaboration between capital and labor and announced a profit-sharing scheme, but its details were not worked out in practice. What was more apparent was a nationalistic tone and a strong anticommunist stance; the policies on colonial issues were somewhat ambiguous. The first Gaullist party also allowed its militants to behave with some brutality against opponents. Fighting often broke out, and local Communist Party headquarters were occasionally burnt. The second Gaullist party, which emerged after 1958, acted more responsibly and its policies were more moderate.

In its heyday in the late 1960s, the Gaullist party seemed able to attract the support of a large proportion of the electorate without having to build a massive organization. It provided de Gaulle and his government with a solid majority, although it ceased to be as monolithic as it was once accused of being. No longer authoritarian as the first Gaullist party had been, the UNR seemed to be based on a discipline that was naturally accepted; whips were not imposed in a ruthless fashion. In parliamentary debates, criticism may not have been voiced on major matters, but it was often expressed on less important questions. This was in part because there was a "community of feeling," or common approach, between de Gaulle and his supporters in parliament and elsewhere. Some may have disagreed on tactics, but most Gaullists agreed on basic aims.

**The Decline of the Gaullist Party and Its Recovery in 2002**    In part because of the large parliamentary majority which de Gaulle bequeathed to his successor, Pompidou, the dominance of the Gaullist party in French politics survived for a time after the departure and death of the founder of the Fifth Republic. But the beginnings of the decline can be traced to one of the first decisions of Pompidou, which was to appoint to the government a number of members of small fringe parties who had hitherto remained on the sidelines. Unlike Adenauer in West Germany in the 1950s, Pompidou did not attempt to force non-Gaullist parliamentarians of the Right and Center to choose between joining the Gaullist party or abandoning effective political life. He undermined his own party by relying increasingly on non-Gaullist politicians—and in particular on Giscard d'Estaing—to counterbalance the strength of the Gaullists.

The real blow to Gaullist supremacy was administered in 1974 by one of the younger leaders of the Gaullist party at the time, Chirac, who led a substantial group of Gaullist members of parliament to support the candidacy of Giscard d'Estaing for the presidency against the official Gaullist candidate, Chaban-Delmas. Giscard d'Estaing won, and he rewarded Chirac for a while by appointing him prime minister, but the Gaullist party lost its dominant position. It lost the prime ministership in 1976, and the subse-

quent efforts of Chirac, who became Gaullist party leader, to strengthen the organization and to oppose, at times bitterly, the president whom he had so significantly helped to elect proved unsuccessful and even futile. The Gaullist party, which had by then been renamed *Rassemblement pour la République* (RPR), had ceased to embody the Fifth Republic. The electorate of the Right began to desert the party. By 1978, the Gaullist party obtained only a quarter of the votes cast, a proportion that did not change markedly during the 1980s and 1990s, despite the efforts of its leader, Chirac. In 2002, in the wake of his presidential victory, he created a new movement, the *Union pour la Majorité Présidentielle* (UMP), which went a long way, but not all the way, toward incorporating all the (non-extreme) Right.

## The Resilience of the Center

France has been characterized traditionally by an undisciplined and loosely organized Center and Right—which curiously seem nevertheless to succeed in staying in power for very long periods. The constant inability of the Right to be organized was accompanied by periodic efforts to streamline the many organizations that belonged to it, the efforts of the Gaullists being in a line of earlier endeavors. Thus, in the late 1930s, a new party, the *Parti Social Français*, seemed for a while poised to make considerable gains, but because of the Second World War, the 1940 election which would have provided the test never took place.

In 1945, when prewar conservative groups had been badly shaken by the fact that many of their members had collaborated with the Vichy regime of 1940–1944, a Christian party, the *Mouvement Républicain Populaire* (MRP), obtained a quarter of the votes. Its policies were not moderate enough to satisfy the conservative electorate, however, and its alliance with the Communists made it somewhat suspect. The emergence of de Gaulle's RPF caused the vote for the MRP to drop to about 10 percent. Yet the strength of the RPF in turn quickly eroded. By 1956, the shopkeepers' party of Poujade seemed on the verge of constituting a new catalyst, but its policies were too crude to attract the bulk of the Right; it gained only 12 percent of the votes and was soon swept away by the second Gaullist tide.

Neither organization nor ideology can provide the real explanation for the resilience or recurrence of groupings on the Center and Right; the explanation can be found only by considering the social base. Before World War II, and to a large extent in the 1950s as well, conservative and center groups were composed of prominent local politicians who had first established their influence at the municipal and county levels and had enough following to be elected to parliament. These developments flourished in a context in which political behavior was highly sectional; they accounted for the fact that parties remained both organizationally weak and undisciplined in parliament. The village and small-town basis of politics thus mirrored the rather static character of the society.

The socioeconomic changes that followed World War II seemed likely to end the dominance of these traditional politicians, especially as the war record of many of them had been poor or downright inadmissible. The old Radical party, which had long ceased to be radical except in name, was thus discredited for having led France during the years that preceded the collapse of 1940. Yet in the late 1940s and early 1950s, the same Radical party as well as other traditional groupings on the Center and Right made a surprisingly rapid comeback. Their leaders showed considerable skill and strength in opposing the first Gaullist party of the late 1940s; they became partners in government with Christian Democrats and Socialists, since those two parties alone could not command a parliamentary majority. The Radical leaders eventually provided most of the prime ministers of the last years of the Fourth Republic, only to show once more, in 1958, their inability to lead the country decisively in times of crisis.

The gradual return of small Center and Right parties to the fore in the 1970s after over a decade of Gaullist dominance is in the French political tradition in spite of major economic and social changes. In order to compete with the Gaullists, these parties have had to be better organized than in the past. From the 1978 general election, they federated under the label *Union pour la Démocratie Française* (UDF). But the various segments of the UDF have kept their identity, the two strongest elements being the Republican party founded by Giscard d'Estaing but renamed subsequently *Démocratie libérale* under a new leader, and the *Centre démocratique et social* (CDS), which is the heir to the Christian party of the 1940s and 1950s. Overall, the UDF remains an uneasy coalition of somewhat autonomous chieftains joining forces to repulse a common enemy. It is not a true federation, let alone a single party.

From the 1978 general election and throughout the 1980s and 1990s, the Right and Center have been divided into two major forces of about equal strength—the Gaullists and the non-Gaullists. Moreover, since the early 1980s, a challenge to the Gaullists and non-Gaullists has come from the extreme right, with the National Front led by Le Pen, who had been a poujadist deputy of 1956.

## The Extreme Right

The National Front has somewhat fascist undertones; its main plank—and source of success—has been an attack against immigrants, mainly those from North Africa. It gained substantial successes in particular in a number of suburban areas. The 10 percent of the votes it obtained at the 1986 election grew to 14 percent at the 1988 presidential election. Support for the Front remained static at the parliamentary elections of 1988, 1993, and 1997 as well as at the presidential election of 1995. The party then split, one of the key lieutenants of Le Pen having decided that Le Pen had become too old and perhaps too soft on some issues. The result was a temporary decline of each of the two parties (and of the votes of both parties jointly) at the 1999 European parliament election and at the 2001 local elections.

But Le Pen recovered, somewhat unexpectedly, at the 2002 presidential election. He recovered so well that he succeeded in beating Jospin, the Socialist candidate, for second place at the first ballot, thus qualifying for the run-off; Le Pen was only three points behind Chirac, scoring 17 percent against Chirac's 20 percent. This result did not mean, however, that the extreme-Right had significantly gained ground in the electorate, although the fact that Le Pen was Chirac's challenger had a great symbolic significance. One result was that it mobilized practically all the rest of the electors (82 percent) behind Chirac at the run-off. Indeed, the National Front suffered a substantial defeat at the June parliamentary election, where it obtained only 11 percent of the votes.

## The Left

While the Right and Center were traditionally based on loose, personalized groupings, the Left has long been organized around structured political parties, but always around more than one. Before World War I, the Socialists competed with the Radicals. After World War I, the Communist Party quickly gained votes, reaching 12 percent in 1932 and 15 percent in 1936, and peaking at 28 percent in 1946. Though the Communist Party lost votes when de Gaulle returned to power in 1958, it hovered around 20 percent for about two decades and was a force to be reckoned with, especially because the decline of the Socialist Party was even more pronounced in the 1950s and 1960s. Only in 1981 did the Communist Party's strength substantially diminish again, first to 16 percent, and later to under 10 percent. The party has been marginalized as a result and the Socialist Party has become the dominant party of the Left, although it suffered a major defeat in 1993 when it obtained under 20 percent of the votes. It recovered in 1997 but lost substantial support at the 2002 presidential election, where Jospin obtained only 16 percent of the votes. At the subsequent parliamentary election, it obtained a more normal 25 percent.

***The Socialist Party***    The victories won by the Socialist Party since 1981 seem almost miraculous, given what the party had been in the 1960s. Born in 1905, and for over half a century called the French Section of the (Second)

Working-Class International (SFIO), the Socialist Party originated from two groups created in the 1890s, one humanitarian and liberal, the other Marxist. Until 1914, the party practiced "noncollaboration" with bourgeois governments and seemed to be moving gradually toward a commanding position. At the 1914 general election, the party had about 100 deputies, or one-sixth of the chamber. Jaurès, the great humanitarian leader of the party, tried with all his strength to rally the antiwar forces, but he was assassinated just before hostilities started, and French Socialists, as their German colleagues, were made to accept the *Union Sacrée*. Some of their members joined the cabinet.

***Early Setbacks of the Socialist Party***    As in other European countries, a wing of the Socialist Party split in 1920 to form the Communist Party. This had little immediate effect on the Socialist organization but did hamper its electoral appeal; the party stagnated at the polls during the 1920s and 1930s, gaining votes on its right but losing about the same number on its left. At the 1936 general election, the party emerged apparently as the great winner, having led to victory the Popular Front coalition, which included the Radicals on its right and the Communists on its left, as well as various socialist splinter groups. For the first time a Socialist, Blum, was called to head the government, and for a few tense spring days the dream of the Socialist Party seemed to have become reality. But the victory was in fact small (the Socialist Party obtained only one-quarter of the votes) and hollow.

The expectations of manual workers had been raised so high by the 1936 election result that sit-down strikes soon became the norm in large factories. The Communists pushed for takeovers while the liberals were already backing out. Blum, a follower of Jaurès, a *grand bourgeois* who strongly believed in equality and liberty, made a number of important reforms (the 40-hour week, paid holidays, and collective bargaining), but he did not succeed in retaining the confidence of the workers nor, of course, in acquiring that of the employers. Financial difficulties grew and the government, in difficulty with the upper house of parliament, the Senate, resigned after a year in office.

The Socialist Party then entered a long period of decline. It was divided over the Vichy regime in 1940, and while it took an important part in the Resistance, it was far behind the Communists. It was central to many coalitions of the Fourth Republic after World War II, but perhaps as a result, its support dwindled, falling from 25 percent of the votes in 1945 to 15 percent in 1958. It entered the era of the Fifth Republic as a losing and demoralized party.

***Reorganization of the Socialist Party***   From the mid-1960s, efforts were made to broaden the base of the Socialist Party and change its image. Hopes were entertained around the creation of a federal organization that was expected to be substantially larger than the Communist Party. The Radicals and the Christian Democrats, as well as representatives of some political clubs, were to belong to the new grouping, sometimes viewed as a potentially large umbrella for the Left, but minor Socialist groups opposed the move, and the Christian Democrats, unsure of their conservative voters, rejected the proposal, while the old anti-Catholic reflex grew in the Socialist Party itself. A smaller and looser grouping comprising Socialists, Radicals, and some tiny organizations was to be a more modest but influential alternative. Its presidential candidate, Mitterrand, polled 45 percent of the votes at the presidential election of 1965, and it returned 121 members of parliament at the 1967 general election, but the old Socialist Party did not survive a crushing electoral defeat in 1968 in the wake of the Gaullist wave following the end of the 1968 "revolt."

Mitterrand was to prove stubborn in his aim to unite and lead the Left, however. Helped by the disarray caused by a further defeat of the Left at the polls at the presidential election of 1969, which followed de Gaulle's resignation, Mitterrand campaigned for the reconstruction of the Socialist Party—now known simply as the *Parti Socialiste*. Having become leader of the new party, he entered a series of negotiations with the Communist Party designed to expand the collaboration between the two organizations. A "Common Program of the Left" was adopted in 1972. It was markedly Socialist but more moderate than the Communists wanted. The result was the first upsurge in Socialist votes in 30 years at the 1973 general election.

The Socialist Party continued to increase its strength. At the 1974 presidential election, Mitterrand was once more defeated, but by a small margin. Hopes were increasingly entertained that economic difficulties and the natural unpopularity of a majority coalition in power for 20 years would result in a victory for the opposition. Divisions between Socialists and Communists appeared to have been buried, with the Socialist Party being the clear leader of the opposition. The "Common Program of the Left" was generally viewed as the natural alternative. The result of an agreement between Socialists and Communists at a time when the Communists were still the stronger partner, it had a radical flavor and included in particular large-scale nationalization proposals. At the municipal elections of 1977 the two opposition parties did particularly well—the Socialist candidates being especially successful.

In late 1977, however, the Communist Party decided to make strong demands for a redrafting of the "Common Program"; it made suggestions for major changes to sharpen the radical character of the program. Negotiations broke down. The Communist Party then endeavored to undermine the Socialist Party at the grass roots but failed. It did, however, undermine the credibility of the Left in general and therefore bore responsibility for its defeat at the 1978 general election. The 1978 result was nevertheless the best result achieved by the Socialist Party since 1945, and for the first time since World War II it was the largest party in the country.

***The Socialist Victory of 1981***   The breakdown of the "Common Program" led to a short period of stagnation, and divisions within the Socialist Party seemed to point to the reelection of Giscard d'Estaing as president in 1981. Yet, during the winter of 1980–1981, the tables were turned rapidly. Mitterrand declared himself a candidate and rallied the whole Socialist Party behind him. The Communist Party fielded their secretary general, Marchais, whose popularity was low and personal record unappealing. The scandals and arrogance associated with Giscard d'Estaing, coupled with the ever deepening economic recession, meant an upsurge in the fortunes of the Socialist Party, whose slogan (*Une force tranquille*) and whose symbol (the rose) turned out to be clear winners.

At the first round of the presidential election of April–May 1981, Mitterrand was still 2 percent behind Giscard d'Estaing, but the Communists had lost 5 percent of the votes. On the second ballot, two weeks later, when only the top two candidates could stand, Mitterrand edged out as the winner with 52 percent of the votes. A large bandwagon effect then occurred. The National Assembly was dissolved and, in June, for the first time in French history, the Socialist Party won an absolute majority of seats in parliament. The Communist representation had been halved; the Communist Party could be given four seats in the government between 1981 and 1984 without any danger.

Five years of stable government of the Left then followed—for the first time in French history. At first reforms took place rapidly and on a large scale; nationalizations, industrial reforms, and administrative decentralization were among the main changes. By 1983, however, economic difficulties led to a major rethinking, as France could not push for growth in a world in which retrenchment and "monetarism" were dominant. The Socialist government became moderate; this led the Communists to leave the government in 1984.

***Ups and Downs of the Socialist Party*** The Socialist Party lost votes at the 1986 general election but remained the largest party, with 32 percent of the votes. It had gained a reputation for moderation and statesmanship; it had shown greater unity than the conservatives who, while pledged to rule together as they did between 1986 and 1988, displayed a high level of dissension. This may explain in part the second victory of Mitterrand at the 1988 presidential election and of the Socialist Party at the subsequent general election, although the party

this time remained a few seats short of an absolute majority.

The prime minister appointed by the president in 1988, Rocard, practiced a policy of "openness" (*ouverture*) to the elements of the center parties and stressed sound management rather than ideological pronouncements. The head of the government was popular in the country, but not among the party activists throughout his three years in office. He was perhaps for this reason suddenly replaced by Mme Cresson, the first woman French prime minister. Although this was regarded as a rather skillful move by Mitterrand, largely because the new incumbent was a woman, the result proved to be a failure. Cresson was replaced a year later by a faithful supporter of Mitterrand, hitherto minister of finance, Beregovoy. By then, however, the party had become embroiled in a number of financial scandals that seemed to concern both the organization and a number of prominent personalities at national and local levels (but similar scandals also affected the parties of the Right and Center). Defeat at the 1993 parliamentary election was crushing. The Socialist Party received fewer votes than at any time since 1962; yet the result was even worse at the European parliamentary elections one year later.

The party quickly bounced back, benefiting largely from the internal dissensions within the Right and Center coalition in power between 1993 and 1997. At the 1995 presidential election, the candidate of the Socialist Party, Jospin, an ex-minister of education who had become secretary general of the party, obtained 47 percent of the votes. Under Jospin's leadership, the party was then to win decisively the 1997 parliamentary election, admittedly in combination with the Radicals, Communists, and Greens. The policies of Jospin's government were to be moderate, though not to the same extent as those of Blair and Schröder, an example being provided by the introduction of the 35-hour week. Although the prime minister was continuously popular during his five-year term of office, this was not enough to ensure a Socialist victory in 2002. At the presidential election, Jospin was in the third place and decided immediately to quit politics. At the parliamentary election, under the provisional leadership of its secretary, François Hollande, the party suffered a substantial loss of seats (because of the greater unity of the Right and the decline of the other components of the Left) despite the fact that its percentage of votes was about the same as in 1997.

### The Greens and the Communist Party

By the turn of the twenty-first century, the French Left included, alongside and indeed under the Socialist Party, a number of groupings, the two most important of which have been the Greens and the Communists. The Greens grew in strength in the 1990s, but in an uneven manner as a result of their weak organization and the serious personality conflicts that characterize them. The Communist Party, however, has a long history and was for three decades the leading party of the Left before its catastrophic decline in the 1980s and 1990s.

The hold of the French Communist Party (PCF) on French politics has much puzzled observers, as France has been one of the few European countries (with Italy, Finland, and Portugal) in which Communist strength has been large for over a generation after World War II. Simple economic explanations are obviously not sufficient: the standard of living is as high in France as in other Western European countries, indeed higher than in some. Moreover, development in France was just as fast, at least until the mid-1970s. Those who in the late 1940s had hoped that an improvement of living conditions would be accompanied by a substantial decrease in Communist Party membership have been disappointed. The Communist vote was to be reduced, but not at that time and not for economic reasons.

The resilience of the Communist Party is found in its history—a history marked in large part by the discredit of the Socialist Party and by that party's subsequent decline. The Communist Party was born of the discontent felt by many Socialists after World War I, as their party had firmly supported the war. The Resistance provided a second boost during World War II. Up to 1941, when the war was labeled bourgeois and imperialist by the Soviet Union, French Communists refused to participate in the defense of their country (their members of the parliament were dismissed in 1940) and even supported the German occupying forces in the early period. But after the Nazi invasion of the Soviet Union, the Communist Party took a leading part in the Resistance. It gained considerable prestige as a result (nicknaming itself the *parti des fusillés,* the party of the shot), successfully infiltrated the underground trade union organizations, and made inroads in parts of the countryside (particularly in those regions which the Resistance had freed from the German occupying troops long before liberation). The party went into the government in 1944, probably hoping to remain in it for long periods, but in May 1947 the Communist ministers were dismissed. With the intensification of the Cold War, the Communist Party used trade union strength to harass the government (the strikes of November 1947 were among the most difficult episodes of postwar French politics). But the government won, and the Communist challenge became less effective. By the end of the Fourth Republic in 1958, the Communist Party was a nuisance, not a menace; it could help any party to overthrow governments, but it could do little to achieve its own aims.

The Communist Party thus occupied, from the 1950s at least, the comfortable position of being the only real defender of the workers against capitalism; yet it was at the same time (its supporters would say that this was precisely for that reason) a rigid, indeed monolithic organization. Its detractors criticized it for its complacency and total lack of intellectual life as much as for its internal dictatorial methods. Purges had taken place from time to time, enabling the secretary general to remain at the helm of a large machine (potential successors were shown to be wrong or traitors to the party), but vitality was absent, in contrast with what was occurring in the Italian Communist Party.

In the 1960s, some signs of liberalization did emerge. In August 1968, for the first time in its history, the party dared to voice a criticism of the Soviet Union and (though in a somewhat lukewarm manner) attacked the occupation of

Czechoslovakia. After the 1978 defeat at the polls, however, the French Communist Party retreated once more into its characteristic position of faithful and loyal supporter of the "Socialist Motherland."

For a few more years, the tightly knit character of the party organization accounted for its maintained strength, the Communist Party being the only French party that ever created a "society," and a very disciplined and hierarchical one at that. Membership figures have been unreliable, but the party seems to have had about 300,000 to 400,000 paid-up members (about 8 to 10 percent of its voters) in the 1960s and 1970s—more than other parties had. For long periods, these members were tied closely to the party. Thus party decisions, in theory based on "democratic centralism," could be in practice imposed by the secretariat and the executive committee. Resolutions were virtually always adopted unanimously at congresses, and opponents were quickly singled out and in most cases dismissed from the party.

Dissent began to emerge with the decline of the party. This culminated with the fielding of an unofficial Communist candidate alongside the official one at the presidential election of 1988. This type of division did not occur again at the 1995 and 2002 elections and, by and large, the top leadership has been able to remain in control. While the secretary general elected in the 1990s is ostensibly more prepared to accept discussion, real behavior within the party has little changed. Yet this tight organization did not stop the electoral decline. The party's presidential candidate (and general secretary) obtained only 3 percent of the votes in May 2002, in part because of the presence of several extreme-Left candidates. With under 5 percent of the votes at the June parliamentary election of that year, the maintenance of the Communist Party as a significant political force has come into question.

Meanwhile the Greens have not succeeded in making a real breakthrough. Perhaps because of their internal divisions, especially over the leadership, they did not overtake the Communist Party, as they had hoped (they obtained just over 4 percent in June 2002). They never were as influential as their German counterparts, although they had played a significant part in the Jospin 1997–2002 government. The defeat of the Left in 2002 clearly reduced their influence, but they seem likely to see that influence rise again if and when the resurgence of the Left occurs later in the decade.

## THE SPIRIT OF THE CONSTITUTION OF 1958

### De Gaulle and the Constitution of 1958

The Constitution of 1958 was introduced primarily to strengthen the executive. From 1870 to 1958, French governments had been weak and unstable, except for about a decade at the beginning of the twentieth century, when the campaign against the Catholic Church gave cohesion to the majority and some real strength to the leader of the government. De Gaulle was convinced that chronic instability was one of the major causes of the decline of France; he believed that only by a change in the institutions could the man at the top be able to take a long-term view of the interests of the country. He thus based his cure on constitutional remedies, but the medicine was somewhat unorthodox.

### A Hybrid System of Executive Power

De Gaulle did not adhere to any of the constitutional models devised in the eighteenth and nineteenth centuries and broadly adopted in the major democracies. He wanted to ensure governmental stability and executive authority; he was not anxious—to say the least—to give representatives of the people effective means of supervising the executive, nor did he wish to devise an equilibrium between executive and legislature. Thus he proposed neither a revamped cabinet system nor a presidential system, but plumped for a hybrid system giving marked preponderance to the executive. Yet, as the cabinet system and the presidential system are the only two forms of constitutional arrangements (together with a streamlined party system) that seemed effective elsewhere in sustaining liberal democracy, the new French institutions were attacked from the start as being both authoritarian and impractical. Few expected that they would last beyond de Gaulle; indeed, though they were kept alive under the subsequent presidents, there are still doubts about the long-term future of the constitution, in that the hybrid character of the system appears to make it rather vulnerable.

This hybrid system divides executive authority into two sharply distinct segments. The president has the somewhat lofty and almost undefinable task of looking after the long-term interests of the nation; the government, headed by the prime minister, is in charge of the country's affairs. This raises two main problems. First, there is a large gray area of divided responsibility. Because the constitution does not define sectors for the president and the prime minister, clashes between the two are likely. Second, while the president appoints the prime minister, the prime minister needs the support of the legislature. There is, therefore, potential for conflict when the parliament and the presidency are controlled by different parties. This did not occur between 1958 and 1986, but it did between 1986 and 1988 and between 1993 and 1995

## A CLOSER LOOK 3.3

### DE GAULLE AND MITTERRAND

By far the two most important presidents of the Fifth Republic have been Charles de Gaulle, who founded the regime in 1958, and François Mitterrand, who reorganized the Left and gave it a new strength. Charles de Gaulle, born in 1890, had a military career during which he unsuccessfully attempted to give the French army a more modern outlook. Shocked by the defeat of June 1940, he rallied London and created the Free French Movement, which was to become the embryo of the government of liberated France in 1944. Having led this government until January 1946, he resigned in disgust at what he considered to be party domination of the regime. He founded a movement called the Rally of the French People in 1947 but remained in the wilderness of the opposition until 1958, when the events of Algeria gave him an opportunity to implement his ideas of a president-led as well as a more nationalistic form of government. Ten years later, in 1968, confronted by massive popular demonstrations, he sought to retake the initiative by proposing to the people in 1969 a reform of the constitution. He was defeated in a referendum, immediately resigned, and retired to his home in eastern France, where he died one year later, in 1970.

François Mitterrand can be regarded as having done for the Left what de Gaulle did for the nation. Born in 1916, he started as a young parliamentarian and minister in the 1940s. At the time, he belonged to a small party of the Center. He opposed de Gaulle from 1958 and moved gradually to the Left, being a strong challenger to the founder of the Fifth Republic at the election of 1965, when he obtained 45 percent of the votes. He was instrumental in giving the Socialist Party a new life in 1971 and boldly agreed to an alliance with the Communist Party in 1972, being determined to overtake that party. The policy succeeded triumphantly at the presidential and parliamentary elections of 1981, when, for the first time, the French Socialist Party gained an absolute majority of seats in the National Assembly. He agreed to appoint a conservative government in 1986, after the Socialist Party had lost its majority, but was reelected president in 1988 for a further seven years. By the early 1990s, however, as de Gaulle's earlier, his popularity began to wane; his political flair, in both internal and foreign policies, seemed to desert him. In 1993, the Socialist Party suffered a crushing defeat: Mitterrand had to appoint, once more, a conservative government with which he "cohabited" during the last two years of his term, which ended in 1995. He died in January 1996 after a long struggle with cancer, which he bore with great courage. His death was viewed as the passing of an era.

under Mitterrand and between 1997 and 2002 but only up to 2002, under his successor, Chirac. Cohabitation was relatively painless in each case, but the role of the president was clearly diminished in the process.

# PRESIDENT AND GOVERNMENT

## The Formal Powers of the President

Formally at least, the powers of the president are relatively limited. In 1958, de Gaulle had to agree to compromises with the politicians of the time who feared full-scale presidentialism. Whether de Gaulle wanted a presidency on American lines was never clarified; he had in any case to settle for much less in the constitution.

The president of the Republic was elected for seven years, but a constitutional amendment passed in 2000 reduced the term to five years. Presidents can be reelected only once. The president of the Fifth Republic has eight powers which French presidents have traditionally held:

1. Appointment of the prime minister and of the ministers on the proposal of the prime minister (without any formal power of dismissal of the prime minister).

2. Promulgation of laws voted by parliament. The president may ask parliament to reconsider a law within two weeks of its having been voted, but he has no power of veto.

3. Signature of regulations (decrees), but these must have been approved by the council of ministers.

4. Chairmanship of the council of ministers.

5. Chairmanship of the high councils of the armed forces.

6. The right to send messages to the National Assembly.

7. Ratification of treaties, after parliamentary approval.

8. The power of pardon.

As in other Western European countries, the fact that the head of state signs regulations and ratifies treaties merely means that the seal of authority of the state is given to these decisions; however, these decisions must be countersigned by the prime minister and, when appropriate, by some of the ministers. The rule of the countersignature is basic to the operation of the parliamentary system, as the government, not the head of state, is held to be politically responsible. No particular significance must therefore be attributed to the fact that the president of the Fifth Republic signs decrees or ratifies treaties.

Alongside the eight traditional powers, four others are new in the Fifth Republic and constitute the extent of the formal innovation in the regime. These powers affect the dissolution of the parliament, constitutional amendments, referendums, and emergencies. These new powers are the prerogative of the president alone. No countersignature is required, but they can be exercised at rare intervals or in emergencies only. Of these four powers, only one, the right of dissolution, has been really effective and has markedly helped to modify the conditions of political life.

## The Presidential Power of Dissolution

Before 1958, the dissolution of the parliament had been used rarely (in fact not at all between 1877 and 1955, when parliament dominated the scene). Because of the ill-organized nature of the party system, the dissolution of 1955 had no effect on political life. On the other hand, since 1958, dissolutions have been used to great effect in 1962, 1968, 1981, 1988, and 1997, in the context of a more streamlined party system. Moreover, the threat of dissolution plays a major part in helping to render governments more stable.

## Constitutional Amendments and Referendums

The other three new powers of the president have been used relatively rarely. One gives the president the power to decide that a constitutional amendment proposed by the government need not be approved by referendum after it has been adopted by parliament. In this case, the proposal has to be approved by a joint meeting of the two chambers separately. This provision was used by de Gaulle in 1960 to loosen the links between France and its African ex-colonies, by Giscard d'Estaing in 1976 with respect to the duration of parliamentary sessions, and by Chirac in 1995 to extend the duration of parliamentary sessions and the scope of legislative referendums.

Article 11 of the constitution gives the president the right to refer certain government bills to the electorate. Up to 1995, this concerned exclusively bills dealing with the organization of public authorities, those carrying approval of a (French)

François Mitterand (1916–1996), president of France in 1981–1995. He had been a government minister on many occasions in the Fourth Republic, became leader of the Socialist Party in 1971, and ran unsuccessfully for the presidency of the Fifth Republic in 1965 and 1974.

community agreement, or proposals to ratify treaties that, without being contrary to the constitution, would affect the functioning of the institutions. A 1995 constitutional amendment extended this right to bills dealing with social and economic matters, a right which has not so far been used.

De Gaulle liked referendums, as these enabled him to go directly to the people without having to bother about parties. He used the technique in a highly dubious manner from a constitutional point of view. First, he introduced the practice of bypassing parliament altogether, as if the referendum was an alternative and not merely a complement to the parliamentary approval of bills. The constitution was silent on this point, but the president's interpretation was, to say the least, highly innovative.

Yet de Gaulle went further. According to the constitution, constitutional amendments must be passed in identical terms by both chambers of parliament; a referendum then takes place, though the president has the power to avoid this referendum, as we just noted, by sending the amendment to a joint meeting of the two chambers, in which case the amendment must be approved by a majority of at least three-fifths of the votes cast. It is therefore clearly unconstitutional for an amendment to be approved without a positive vote of parliament. In 1962, however, de Gaulle proposed directly to the people an amendment stipulating that the election of the president would be by direct universal suffrage. This successful but unconstitutional move created considerable stir (including the fall of the government and the dissolution of the National Assembly). It was the last time that the referendum led to an important reform. In 1969, de Gaulle used it again on regionalism, but he lost and left power. His successor, Pompidou, used it only once; Giscard d'Estaing did not use it at all. Mitterrand proposed to use it in 1984, but the constitutional change he sought was blocked by the upper chamber. It was used in 1988 to change the status of the Pacific island of New Caledonia (when only 33 percent voted) and in 1993 to ratify the Maastricht Treaty of the European Union (when the majority in favor turned out to be wafer thin). It was used by Chirac in 2000 to approve the reduction of the duration of the presidential term to five years: there was a large majority in favor (73 percent), but only 30 percent of the electors voted, a record level of abstention.

## Emergency Powers

The fourth new power of the president is given by Article 16 of the constitution and concerns emergencies. It was used only once, in 1961, following an attempted coup by four generals in Algiers. A heated conflict had arisen at the time of the drafting of the constitution, because the clause allowed the president to assume full powers in some situations. De Gaulle wanted the power to enable the head of state to take appropriate measures in cases of national catastrophes such as the defeat of 1940. Opponents, however, saw it as a means of installing a legal dictatorship. The experience was mixed, to say the least. Such a clause does not by itself give authority to a president who does not already have it; moreover, parliament is required to meet, a somewhat ludicrous provision in the case of a national catastrophe.

The procedure proved cumbersome when it was put in use, in part because the scope of parliamentary action in the context of Article 16 was not defined. It was in fact a great relief for the government (more than for parliament) when, at the end of the of the summer of 1961, Article 16 ceased to be operative, as those who had benefited most from the emergency powers were the farmers, whose lobby was able to make itself felt in the chamber.

## Popular Election of the President

The four new powers point to de Gaulle's main preoccupation, namely that the president should be able to steer the ship of state. For this, authority was necessary. This is why de Gaulle forced a change with respect to the election of the president. He had had to accept in 1958 the setting up of a limited electoral college composed of about 80,000 delegates, mainly representatives of local authorities in which rural areas were overrepresented. By 1962, he had acquired the political strength to launch a referendum introducing the direct popular election of the president (with a two-ballot or run-off system, the second ballot taking place two weeks after the first between the top two candidates only). Opposition to the proposal was fierce, largely due to the fear of Bonapartism. The only popularly elected presi-

**A CLOSER LOOK**

**3.4**

## THE POPULAR ELECTION OF THE PRESIDENT MAY WEAKEN POLITICAL PARTIES

The election of the French president by universal suffrage contributed to an extent to the streamlining of French politics but may also have led to new divisions between and even within parties. One of the main reasons the Right of the political spectrum is not united is that both the Gaullists and the Centrists (the UDF) have their presidential hopefuls. The Socialist Party avoided major problems in the 1970s and 1980s because of the towering position of President Mitterrand. Difficulties began to arise in the party in the 1990s, however, as there were a number of presidential hopefuls. As a matter of fact, mechanisms of selection of candidates are still unclear. The idea of primaries was to an extent applied in the Socialist Party. In both 1995 and 2002, the mechanism led to the nomination of Jospin, not surprisingly in 2002, since Jospin had been prime minister for five years and was unquestionably the foremost politician of the party. Primaries took place to an extent in other parties, among the Greens in particular. The idea had been rejected by the Gaullist party in 1995, with the result that there were then two candidates of the party at the first ballot, Balladur and Chirac. The problem did not arise in 2002 as the candidate of the Gaullist party could not be other than Chirac, the outgoing president. Overall, the French Fifth Republic has still to devise a nominating mechanism that will make it possible to select presidential candidates smoothly and truly authoritatively.

dent, Louis-Napoleon, made himself emperor after a coup d'etat in 1851.

The fear proved misplaced and outdated. The popular election of the president, however unconstitutional, was approved by the people in 1962 by a majority of over 3 to 2 (62 percent voted yes). Three years later, in December 1965, the first popular election of the president led to a very active campaign. The direct election of the president has remained popular ever since, and the measure clearly enhanced the position of the president in relation to parliament and government, as de Gaulle had hoped.

Presidential elections have become the central event of French politics. It was indeed the presidential election that rendered alternance possible in 1981 when Mitterrand, the Socialist candidate, won. Thus contests have been heated; margins of victory have tended to be small; turnout has been higher than at other contests. Clearly, the Fifth Republic has succeeded in one respect; it has introduced a procedure that is very popular. The Left, which originally opposed it, abandoned its attacks and was a marked beneficiary in 1981 and 1988. The president (of whatever party) has acquired an authority he did not have in the past. The result of the second ballot of the 2002 election proved it once more, as Chirac, who had only obtained 20 percent of the votes at the first ballot, garnered 82 percent against Le Pen two weeks later, on a larger turnout. The point was clearly made by the voters that they rejected the policies and general stand of the extreme-Right. Thus the president is in a position to be a key actor, if not always the main actor, in French political life.

## THE GOVERNMENT

### The Role of the Prime Minister

The influence of the president on the government stems from his authority alone, as the constitution clearly states that the government, headed by the prime minister, is in charge of the policy; this was rediscovered after the 1986 and 1993 elections, when President Mitterrand had to appoint a government composed of Gaullists and of members of the Center parties, and after the

1997 election, when President Chirac had to appoint a government primarily composed of Socialists.

According to Article 20, "[t]he Government shall determine and direct the policy of the nation. It shall have at its disposal the administration and the armed forces." Article 21 continues: "The Premier shall direct the operation of the Government. He shall be responsible for national defense. He shall ensure the execution of the laws." There is no ambiguity; though the president of the Republic, according to customs dating back to the Third Republic, chairs the council of ministers, the government as a whole, headed by the prime minister, is responsible for national policy.

As in many other countries, the position of the prime minister grew gradually during the course of the twentieth century. The Constitution of 1875 did not formally recognize the premier, but in practice all governments had a head, then known as "president of the council of ministers" (rather illogically, since the president of the Republic chaired the meetings of ministers). However, since French governments were often uneasy coalitions, premiers tended to be compromisers rather than leaders. The Constitution of 1946 sought to increase the authority of the premier by giving him specific powers. He alone was designated by the chamber; he alone appointed the rest of the cabinet. These provisions had no effect; there was little difference between a premier of the 1930s and of the 1950s. In the Constitution of 1958, the premier—now named prime minister for the first time—retained some of these powers. He or she leads the government, has the power to implement the laws (*pouvoir réglementaire*), is responsible for national defense, and makes a number of important appointments. The constitution stresses the leadership role of the premier as much as is compatible with the position of the president of the Republic and with the collective character of the government.

The government remains legally a collective organ. Important measures of the government are taken in the council of ministers (as we noted, decrees are signed by the president after they have been approved by the council). The government as a whole is empowered to "determine and direct the policy of the nation." Collective decision making is also associated with collective responsibility through the mechanism of the vote of censure, which automatically results, if adopted, in the resignation of all the ministers. The conflict between prime ministerial leadership and collective decision making is as difficult to solve in France as elsewhere, but the matter is further complicated by the role of the president.

## The Structure and Composition of the Government

Formal arrangements have not markedly modified the internal structure of French governments. Names of ministries change from time to time, but the structure has followed a gradual evolution since the Third Republic. Typically, a government has about 20 ministers (slightly fewer than in the last years of the Fourth Republic); it includes about as many "secretaries of state" of lower status. A number of changes have markedly affected the decision-making processes and even the nature of the cabinet, however. Three of these changes in particular must be mentioned.

First, prime ministerial instability has sharply decreased. From 1958 to 2002, France has had 16 prime ministers: Debré, Pompidou, and Couve de Murville under de Gaulle; Chaban-Delmas and Messmer under Pompidou; Chirac and Barre under Giscard d'Estaing; Mauroy, Fabius, and Chirac under Mitterrand I; Rocard, Cresson, Bergegovoy, and Balladur under Mitterrand II; Juppé and Jospin under Chirac (see Table 3.4). Only two prime ministers of the Fourth Republic lasted over a year, and no prime minister since 1875 lasted continuously in office as long as Pompidou, Barre, or Jospin. Ministers, on the other hand, change fairly frequently—though rather less than under the Fourth Republic.

---

**TABLE 3.4**

**PRESIDENTS AND PRIME MINISTERS IN THE FIFTH REPUBLIC**

| Presidents | | Prime Ministers | |
|---|---|---|---|
| C. de Gaulle | 1958–1969 | M. Debré | 1959–1962 |
| (reelected 1965 for 7 years; | | G. Pompidou | 1962–1968 |
| resigned 1969) | | M. Couve de Murville | 1968–1969 |
| G. Pompidou | 1969–1974 | J. Chaban-Delmas | 1969–1972 |
| (died in office) | | P. Messmer | 1972–1974 |
| V. Giscard d'Estaing | 1974–1981 | J. Chirac | 1974–1976 |
| | | R. Barre | 1976–1981 |
| F. Mitterrand | 1981–1995 | P. Mauroy | 1981–1984 |
| (reelected 1988 for 7 years) | | L. Fabius | 1984–1986 |
| | | J. Chirac | 1986–1988 |
| | | M. Rocard | 1988–1991 |
| | | E. Cresson | 1991–1992 |
| | | P. Beregovoy | 1992–1993 |
| | | E. Balladur | 1993–1995 |
| J. Chirac | 1995–2002 | A. Juppé | 1995–1997 |
| (reelected 2002 for 5 years) | 2002– | L. Jospin | 1997–2002 |
| | | J.-P. Raffarin | 2002– |

Second, there has been a marked influx of technicians in the government. De Gaulle first brought civil servants into the cabinet in 1958, in part on the grounds that the government should in some sense (like himself?) be above the daily turmoil of political life; the government should run the state, and de Gaulle conceived of politics as an activity divorced from state policy making, a view that probably stems from the part played by the civil service in the running of modern France. Thus, Couve de Murville, successively foreign minister and prime minister, was from the career foreign service; Pompidou, a teacher and a banker, had never been in politics before 1962, except as a personal adviser to de Gaulle; Chirac was a personal adviser to Pompidou before entering politics. Since the early 1960s, civil servants have composed between one-quarter and one-third of the cabinet; many of these subsequently became members of parliament, as Pompidou or Chirac, while successive presidents continued to draw their prime ministers (Barre by Giscard d'Estaing) and ministers (Cheysson or Dumas by Mitterrand) from outside politics.

Third, in order to give the executive more independence, Article 23 of the constitution, introduced at de Gaulle's specific request, stipulates that there shall be *incompatibility* between the function of minister and that of member of parliament. This incompatibility rule also exists in some parliamentary democracies (the Netherlands, Norway, and, since the 1990s, Belgium), but it contravenes the general principle that the executive stems from the majority of the National Assembly and aims at leading it. What de Gaulle wanted was to detach ministers from the legislature, as ministerial crises often occurred in the past to help the personal careers of ambitious men. Though they can come and speak (but not vote) in parliament, ministers no longer belong to the legislature and thus can be expected to take a loftier view of daily politics. Yet the provision has been partly by-passed, as ex-ministers often seek to be reelected. This results in a cascade of by-elections at many ministerial reshuffles, as when Chirac became president in 1995. Yet the rule reduces somewhat the desire of parliamentarians to become ministers.

# PRESIDENT, PRIME MINISTER, AND GOVERNMENT IN THE FIFTH REPUBLIC

Institutional changes have brought about a new framework and introduced hurdles that have helped the Fifth Republic give France a stable political system. These institutional changes alone do not explain the whole story, however. In theory, the government is collective; in practice, it is in part hierarchical. From the very start, de Gaulle intervened in governmental life, and Pompidou, Giscard d'Estaing, Mitterrand, and Chirac followed his lead, at least outside periods of cohabitation, although even then, the president's position was never seriously challenged. Let us examine developments somewhat more closely.

## The Extent of Presidential Intervention

Until 1986, presidential intervention had gradually increased. In the early period, de Gaulle's involvement was seemingly due to the special problem of the Algerian war and was held to be confined to some fields only. The presidential sector seemed to include foreign affairs, defense, Algeria, overseas France, and key institutional problems. The prime ministerial and governmental sector seemed to comprise the rest, particularly economic and social matters. But these sectors never were recognized by de Gaulle as marking the limits of his area of intervention. De Gaulle intervened in other aspects of internal policy making, possibly because these might have had an impact on the political system. He had said in 1964: "Clearly, it is the president alone who holds and delegates the authority of the State. But the very nature, extent, and duration of his task imply that he be not absorbed without remission or limit by political, parliamentary, economic, and administrative contingencies." This meant a hierarchical distinction rather than a division between sectors. The prime minister was left to deal with those contingencies which are "his lot, as complex and meritorious as it is essential."

Subsequent presidents came to view their role as one of steering important matters affecting the well-being of the nation, directly or by implication. Hence the many instances of direct action by the president in financial matters. De Gaulle decided in 1968 not to devalue the franc; less than a year later Pompidou reversed the decision. Many aspects of regional or cultural policy, economic development, or social security reform can be ascribed to the president's steering.

## The Semipresidential Character of the Fifth Republic

The French political system under the Fifth Republic is only half-presidential in that, on many issues, the president remains an arbiter rather than an actor. On various important economic and social problems, especially under de Gaulle and Pompidou, prime ministers and individual ministers initiated policies with the president of the Republic being seemingly neutral. Giscard d'Estaing was also somewhat aloof, although his commitment to the policies of his second prime minister, Barre, was clearer than that of the two previous presidents had been to the policies of their prime ministers. In this respect, the role of the third president was greater, partly also because Giscard d'Estaing had more knowledge of and interest in economics, and economic difficulties made solutions more pressing.

Mitterrand embarked on the same path, keeping some distance from the daily turmoil and letting the prime minister deal with the major economic and social problems resulting from the government's efforts to counter economic depression. But Mitterrand was also closely associated with government policy, and he decided on a major change of economic policy in 1983 from expansion to orthodoxy. His involvement in governmental policy was less apparent but nonetheless deep between 1988 and 1993.

Intervention on such a scale implied the development of a presidential staff. Indeed, in the early period, de Gaulle seemed to want to dismantle the Council of Ministers and replace it with a number of committees chaired by the president. This was not to occur, but the president maintained a large personal staff of *chargés*

*de mission* and *conseillers techniques* who constitute a parallel organization to that of the prime minister. They cover most important fields of government action and are the sign of the president's interest in a given problem, though they are far less numerous than the members of the American presidential staff.

## Cohabitation

The 1986 general election brought about for the first time a parliamentary majority different from that of the president's party. Since the mid-1970s at least, the possibility of such an occurrence had been canvassed; what presidents would then do had remained the object of major speculation. Giscard d'Estaing had promised in 1978 that he would abide by the decision of the people if the Left were to win in parliament. This did not happen and, in 1981, the newly elected president, Mitterrand, could dissolve the chamber and obtain a socialist majority. But in 1986, with Gaullists and Centrists together having a small overall majority, Mitterrand was faced with the decision to abide—or not—by the results of the polls. He had to do so again in 1993, with the difference that the parliamentary victory of the Right and Center was then overwhelming. The same situation obtained in 1997 when Chirac dissolved the chamber and a majority of the Left was returned. As a result, between 1986 and 2002, cohabitation (president and government being from opposite political blocs) occurred during 9 years out of 16—in the years 1986–1988, 1993–1995, and 1997–2002.

Mitterrand's reaction was quick in 1986 and 1993. He appointed the prime minister from among the new parliamentary majority, choosing Chirac, the leader of the Gaullist party, in 1986, and, on the advice of Chirac, Balladur in 1993. In such circumstances, the president's role became limited: a *modus vivendi*—the "cohabitation" idea—was adopted by prime minister and president. The president would accept what the new majority would propose, provided it was within the limits of what could be regarded as fair and honest government. Thus denationalization proposals or changes in the electoral system (in fact the return to the two-ballot system) would be accepted by the president on condition that parliamentary debates not be curtailed and the rights of citizens maintained.

The cohabitation arrangement functioned well, two elements playing a major part. First, the president retained the right of dissolution in case there were conflicts with the prime minister—a threat that was real, as the popularity of the new conservative government tended quickly to decline. Second, as Chirac wished to be a presidential candidate in both 1988 and 1995 (he was to be defeated by Mitterrand in the first case and to win against Jospin in the second), neither the prime minister nor conservative politicians in general wanted to reduce the role and status of the presidency.

Cohabitation became more embedded as a result of the 1997 election, as it was to last for the whole of the five years of the life of a parliament. The system did function well, whatever has been said in the press, especially toward the end of the legislature. There was a division of labor, in that Jospin had a more limited interest in foreign affairs—even in European affairs— while being a very able, if not charismatic, leader who continuously sensed where the nation wished to go (e.g., the 35-hour working week, the need to have only some privatizations, and the desire to obtain more effective security measures). In such a context, Chirac had to concentrate on foreign affairs, including European affairs, though this was probably also his main interest. Moreover, Chirac's room for action was somewhat reduced as a result of a number of alleged scandals linked to his previous position as mayor of Paris. Yet Jospin unquestionably achieved more of what he wanted than Chirac, in part because one should not exaggerate the differences between the two leaders on foreign affairs. They both agreed broadly on the main tenets of foreign policy, whether in relation to world developments, in particular in the context of the world economy, or in relation to European integration. Both were adamant to defend French interests even in matters on which France found almost no allies. Moreover, the French people not only liked cohabitation; they also liked the two leaders who ran the country between 1997 and 2002, as opinion polls continuously showed.

The long-term consequence of the five years of the Chirac–Jospin tandem is probably a reduction of the role of the presidency. The decline of this role led, at the end of the period, to increasing attacks, especially from the Right, against the idea of cohabitation and its end, temporarily perhaps, as a result of the 2002 election. It is nonetheless probably the case that the role of the president will no longer be what it was under De Gaulle or, between 1981 and 1986 and between 1988 and 1993, under Mitterrand.

## THE LEGISLATURE

### The Traditional Role of the French Parliament

Before the installation of the Fifth Republic in 1958, much of French political life swirled around the lobbies of the Palais Bourbon, the seat of the lower house of parliament, known as the Chamber of Deputies during the Third Republic and renamed the National Assembly in 1946. The Chamber of Deputies came to symbolize the Republic and all its works; it finally became the focus of all criticism aimed at the shortcomings of French politics.

Perhaps because it was the arena where the rights of man were first enunciated and defended, the National Assembly became the repository of republican legitimacy. Inevitably, however, confusion over rights and privileges developed; members became more and more parochial and tended to regard their function as the defense of advantages that had accrued to their district by circumstance, natural good fortune, or government action. From being protectors of civil liberties, the members of the National Assembly slowly became champions of vested and purely local interests, a not uncommon development in legislatures, particularly in the U.S. Congress, whose mores resemble in many ways those of the French parliament before 1958.

In these circumstances, the mark of a promising premier was his ability to deflect or postpone the demands for the extension of special privileges which poured in on the government. Yet to survive, a premier had to nurse along the majority coalition, pleading with his own ministers not to lead an attack against him, while compromising the integrity of his legislative program to maintain the cohesion of his cabinet. To compound difficulties, the premier had to submit the plans of his legislative action to the often hostile committees of the house, whose chairmen were usually more anxious to further their own careers (perhaps by replacing the relevant minister) with brilliant critiques of the legislation under discussion than to contribute to the progress of public business. Here, too, parallels can be drawn with the committees of the U.S. Congress, though the French parliament never resorted to public grilling through hearings. This behavior was based on a supporting philosophy according to which, since the Revolution, there were crucial enemies of republicanism, namely the Church, the bureaucracy, and the armed forces. A kind of rampant anarchism (*le citoyen contre les pouvoirs,* the citizen against the powers) justified the harassment of the government, this harassment being regarded as a republican virtue.

Yet the system, despite its faults, gave France a long period of liberal government, interrupted only by the collapse of the French army in 1940 and by major colonial wars in the 1950s. Admittedly, the Napoleonic bureaucracy did help and, if the regime showed resilience, it never reformed itself. The personal stakes were too high; the life of parliamentarians was too often punctuated by the ritual of government crisis. Reform had to come from outside, as occurred in 1958, and only because of de Gaulle did a substantial curtailment of the rights of parliament take place.

## Parliamentary Organization in the Fifth Republic

The framers of the Constitution of 1958 introduced a number of devices designed to enhance the position of the government and to give parliament the power to supervise, but not block, executive action. These devices come under five headings. First, some provisions aim at reducing harassment and diminishing opportunities for conflict. Second, the scope of legislation is reduced and governmental prerogatives correspondingly increased. Third, opportunities for guerrilla warfare in parliament are limited. Fourth, the operation of censure motions is severely restricted. Fifth, parliamentary activity is controlled by the Constitutional Council. To these devices must be added the power of dissolution given to the president of the Republic.

Parliament is composed of two chambers, the National Assembly and the Senate, the upper house having regained the title but not all the powers it had under the Third Republic, while the lower house kept the name given to it by the Constitution of 1946. The National Assembly is elected for five years (if not dissolved before) by direct universal suffrage. The Senate, sometimes nicknamed the "Grand Council of French Communes," is elected for nine years (one-third of its members retiring every three years) by a complex electoral college, composed of representatives of local authorities, which favors rural areas and the Center-Right parties. Senators are elected within *département* (county) districts, in part by a two-ballot majority system, in part on a proportional representation basis.

Since the constitutional reform of 1995, parliament meets during nine months of the year (instead of during two sessions of three months each, in the autumn and the spring). The government can also call for special sessions, a procedure that was originally interpreted very restrictively but came to be used more often and led to the 1995 reform extending sittings to nine months.

The speaker of the National Assembly is elected for the duration of the legislature (instead of once a year, as was the case before 1958); thus avoiding the repeated conflicts of the past. The speaker of the Senate is elected after each partial reelection of the Senate every three years. Both speakers are assisted by a *bureau* composed of vice presidents and secretaries drawn from the various parties. The speakers of the houses, who are sometimes but not always drawn from among top politicians, are consulted by the president of the Republic, according to the constitution, in various circumstances (such as dissolution or the use of Article 16). They conceive of their role more as do speakers of the U.S. House of Representatives than as do speakers of the British House of Commons; they attempt to influence the conduct of business by informally talking to members. Indeed, before 1958, these offices were stepping stones toward the presidency of the Republic as in Italy and were strongly contested.

Since 1958, the government plays a major part in the organization of parliamentary business. Previously the order of business was decided by a "Conference of Presidents," a body that is similar to the Rules Committee of the U.S. House of Representatives and which includes chairs of committees and of the parliamentary groups (the parties in the chamber). Before 1958 the government was only represented and had no vote. In the Fifth Republic, the government's power is based on Article 43 of the constitution, which states that "Government and Private Members' Bills shall, at the request of the Government or of the Assembly concerned, be sent for study to committees especially designated for this purpose." Article 48 then stipulates that "the discussion of the bills filed or agreed to by the Government shall have priority on the agenda of the Assemblies in the order set by the Government." Government bills are thus sent automatically to a committee and are then extracted from the committee and presented on the floor of the Assembly by the government.

## Scope of Legislation

Traditionally, as in other parliamentary systems, the French parliament could legislate on any matter. Constitutions merely regulated the principles of organization of the public powers; there was no Supreme Court. Statutes (*lois*) were defined merely as texts adopted by parliament, by contrast with decrees (regulations adopted by the whole government) and *arrêtés* (adopted by a minister or a local authority). These documents derived their legal power from each other; the government could not make decrees, and ministers or local authorities could not make *arrêtés* unless a *loi* had given them the authority to do so. Parliament could invade any field and correspondingly decrease the influence of the government, although parliament often had little time to devote to major issues; it therefore often dele-

gated its statutory power to the government by means of *décrets-loi*.

Article 34 of the Constitution of 1958 attempted to provide a solution to the problem. Having stated that "all *lois* (statutes) shall be passed by Parliament," the article defines what the *lois* are by saying that "laws determine the rules" (*règles*) with respect to a list of matters as well as the "fundamental principles" with respect to others. The article then adds that its provisions "may be elaborated and completed by an organic law." Yet there are difficulties over the arrangements. While the list includes all the important matters with which one would expect a parliament to be concerned, the concept of *règle* is not precise in French law; nor is it clear what a "principle" is. Conflicts have arisen, the arbiter being the Constitutional Council. Finally, what "elaboration and completion by an organic law" means is also rather vague.

The drafters of the constitution tried to buttress the system by introducing two new distinctions among the statutes, those of "organic laws" and "ordinances." Organic laws are passed by parliament by a somewhat more stringent procedure and must be deemed to be constitutional by the Constitutional Council before being promulgated. On the other hand, when parliament delegates its legislative powers to the government, the government's texts are known as ordinances, which have to be ratified by parliament at the end of the delegation period. The procedure proved to be of value for governments anxious to pass controversial legislation rapidly, especially in 1986–1988, when the conservative majority was small. Mitterrand then used his presidential authority to ensure that the government did not overstep its rights.

This complex machinery has functioned surprisingly smoothly, although there have been occasional complaints by the opposition, both of the Left, before 1981, and of the Right, since 1981, and for the same reasons.

## The Legislative Struggle

In a parliamentary system, the two main activities of a parliament consist in voting laws and in controlling the government, but the two are intertwined. Before 1958 it was through the legislative struggle that the patience, wits, and skills of ministers were tested, as governments needed laws to implement their program. Thus, in 1958, the power of the executive over the legislative process had to be enhanced if the government was to be stronger.

A bill debated in the French parliament goes through the following sequence (not very different from that which bills go through in the U.S. Congress). After having been laid on the table of either chamber by a member of that chamber or by the government (with the exception of finance bills, which must be presented first to the National Assembly), the bill is sent to a committee which then reports to the house (a *rapporteur* from the committee is in charge of presenting this report). The house discusses the bill first in general, then clause by clause, and votes on each clause. A final vote is then taken, at which point the bill goes to the other house, which follows the same procedure. If both houses agree on the same text, the bill is sent to the president for promulgation (he can ask for a second deliberation, but has no veto). If the houses disagree, the bill goes again to each house. If there is still disagreement, a joint committee comprising an equal number of members of each house is set up with a view to drafting a common text. Only if the government intervenes, as we shall see, is there a possibility of breaking the deadlock between the two chambers.

## Parliamentary Committees

Before 1958, parliamentary committees were very powerful. Organized, as in the United States, on the basis of specialized subjects (finance, foreign affairs, etc.), the 20 or so committees of the pre-1958 parliaments had great opportunities to make trouble for the government. Their members (elected on the basis of proportional representation of the parliamentary groups) were specialists or more often had electoral reasons to be interested. Their chairs, elected every year (the seniority system never took root in France, though some office holders did remain in office for long periods), were highly influential; they were natural leaders of any opposition in their field and were the real shadow ministers.

Committees made life difficult for governments because the procedure of the chambers gave them full responsibility in relation to bills. These, whether from the government or from private members, became in effect the committee's bills; their substance could be so altered that they became unrecognizable. The government had therefore to ensure that proposed changes were overturned after the bills came on the floor of the house, a process whose outcome was always uncertain.

These practices have become impossible since 1958. The number of permanent committees in each house has been reduced to six; it was hoped these would become so large that they would include more than experts, but despite various rulings from the Constitutional Council, the government could not avoid the setting up of informal subcommittees. More importantly, committees can no longer substitute their bills for those of the government; Article 42 of the constitution states that the discussion on the floor has to take place on the government's text.

## The Power of the Government to Curb Debate

Harassment on the floor of the Assembly used to be continuous. For instance, amendments could be withheld to embarrass the government and its supporters at the last moment; this is now forbidden. There used to be no closure and no guillotine; now Article 44 allows the government to request the chamber to vote by a single vote (*vote bloqué*) on the text under discussion. The procedure is harsh, but it is designed to stop the practice of presenting hundreds of amendments that could not be reasonably dealt with but were aimed at halting the progress of bills. As a result, government bills now clearly take precedence over others (see Table 3.5).

The government has two further sets of powers with respect to legislation. First, finance bills used to be much delayed before 1958; parliament has now 70 days to discuss and decide on the budget. If the finance bill is not voted on by then, the government can promulgate it by ordinance, a stringent weapon that has not had to be used.

Second, the government, and the government alone, can end a deadlock between the two

## TABLE 3.5

### ACTIVITIES OF THE NATIONAL ASSEMBLY

| | Hours of Sitting (yearly) | Number of Bills Passed | | |
| --- | --- | --- | --- | --- |
| | | Government Bills | Private Members' Bills | Total |
| 1968 | 425 | 53 | 11 | 64 |
| 1971 | 632 | 92 | 26 | 118 |
| 1974 | 543 | 64 | 14 | 78 |
| 1977 | 609 | 144 | 35 | 179 |
| 1980 | 709 | 74 | 20 | 94 |
| 1981 | 789 | 54 | 3 | 57 |
| 1985 | 793 | 122 | 3 | 125 |
| 1989 | 835 | 85 | 17 | 102 |
| 1994 | 996 | 121 | 36 | 157 |
| 1999 | 1129 | 114 | 14 | 128 |

*Source:* Rapports Assemblee Nationale. Statistiques, various years.

chambers by asking for yet another reading by each chamber of the text adopted by the National Assembly. If there is still disagreement between the two chambers, the National Assembly then votes once more, and this decision is final. Thus the Senate is not in a position to block *governmental* legislation. This provision was used frequently between 1981 and 1986, as much of the legislative program of the Socialist government—in particular, but not only, its nationalization program—was strongly opposed by the Senate.

The balance has clearly been tilted. According to some, it has been tilted too much in favor of the government, a view which is arguable in light of the past behavior of parliament. The executive had to be strengthened. Since a variety of clever tricks were used by parliament against the government, tough rules had to be introduced to prevent the recurrence of previous tactics.

## The Vote of Censure

Only comparatively recently has the procedure of the vote of censure, in France and elsewhere, appeared to constitute a major problem. Traditionally, as is still the case in Britain, parliaments could censure governments at will. However, in France and some other countries where party discipline was weak and parties numerous, the result

was governmental instability. Yet the problem is complex because censure and legislation are often linked. If the right to censure the government is curtailed but parliament can nonetheless easily reject bills proposed by the government, and in particular reject or delay financial bills, governments will simply resign without having been censured. This was the case in the Third and Fourth Republics. Vote of censure and votes on legislation have therefore to be linked.

The 1958 Constitution does so in a curious provision which stipulates that an absolute majority is needed to defeat the government, but that only those voting for the censure motion (that is, against the government) will record their votes, while government supporters simply do not vote at all. Abstainers are thus counted on the government side. Furthermore, if the government wants to see a bill through but encounters difficulties, it can "pledge its responsibility on the vote of [the] text." In this case, the bill passes without a vote unless a motion of censure is tabled. If the censure is not adopted (the procedure is the one just described), the government is safe and the bill is adopted as well.

Thus the government has the upper hand; governments cannot be suddenly overthrown. Deputies have only two means of curbing the executive. They have the question, which was introduced in the Constitution of 1958, allegedly on the British model, but which has taken the form of short debates, not of a grilling, although its scope has been extended; there is no vote at the end of these debates. The other curb is the motion of censure. These are the Assembly's only means of supervision and control of the government; the rest of its activities are legislative and budgetary. The constitution may have gone too far. The governmental instability of the past suggested that a stringent medicine was needed, but the restrictions may be too strong. Indeed, gradually, some loosening has taken place, from the Giscard d'Estaing presidency of the second half of the 1970s onwards. With more compact majorities, the government can be more ready to make concessions, while parliament recognizes the need for self-discipline.

## THE CONSTITUTIONAL COUNCIL

An important new development of the Fifth Republic is the part played by the Constitutional Council in controlling legislation. The Constitutional Council includes nine members appointed in equal numbers by the president of the Republic and the speakers of the two chambers. It also includes the ex-presidents of the Republic. The council was set up in 1958 principally as a means of ensuring that parliament did not overstep its powers; it thus has to approve the standing orders of both houses (a matter which led to conflicts in the late 1950s). It has jurisdiction over referendums and national elections, both presidential and parliamentary, which it must officially declare and settle in cases of dispute.

Yet the main power of the council turned out to be different. Because it was entitled to assess whether laws were in conformity with the constitution, it became gradually a supreme court. Admittedly, it differs from the U.S. Supreme Court in that it can consider the validity of legislation only if the government or one of the houses asks for a ruling and does so in the period immediately following the approval of the bill by parliament, but the impact has been strong.

At first, the Constitutional Council tended to side with the Gaullist government. Gradually, it became more independent and started to rule that bills or parts of bills were not "in conformity with the constitution." In 1982, for instance, it declared that, subject to a few minor amendments (which were subsequently introduced), the nationalization program of the government was in conformity with the constitution. In 1986, it also adjudicated over the privatization legislation of the conservative coalition. In 1991, it stated that a law could not refer to a "Corsican people" as this would undermine the unity of the nation, but it added that special rules could be introduced for different areas, a major innovation in the context of centralized France. The same line was taken again in January 2002 when it quashed the first clause of the law on Corsica adopted by the parliament a few weeks earlier on the grounds that it was not in conformity with the constitution for a law to allow any body other than parliament (in this case the Corsican regional assembly) to adapt national legislation, even if only on an experimental basis. In 1993, it quashed parts of a law of the conservative government that attempted to make the French language obligatory in many fields, on the grounds that this went against the freedom of expression. It intervened in what was perhaps a more substantial manner in the laws passed under Jospin's Socialist government, in particular in relation to segments of social, economic, and budgetary policies of that government, though not the whole of these policies.

## THE NEW EQUILIBRIUM OF POWERS

The Constitution of 1958 profoundly changed the character of French political life. Parliament's power has been reduced (too much, according to some); governmental instability is a thing of the past. For the best part of three decades, the system has been dominated by the president, whose authority was enhanced by the legacy of de Gaulle and by the mechanism of the popular election. This domination has been seriously put in question by cohabitation situations, but the authority of the president has remained high throughout, even if the effective power of the head of state has

**A CLOSER LOOK**

**3.5**

## THE JUDICIARY AND POLITICIANS

In France as in a number of Western European countries, particularly Italy, the judiciary—and not merely the Constitutional Council—appear prepared to play a large part in relation to politics and politicians. Intervention of this kind has originated primarily, indeed almost exclusively, from examining magistrates (*juges d'instruction*) who, in France (as indeed in Italy), belong technically to the judiciary. A kind of war has resulted, with many examining magistrates apparently convinced of the guilt of many politicians in various scandals, involving in particular the financing of political campaigns. As a matter of fact, these magistrates have often not been followed by the judges themselves, a development that has led some of these magistrates to resign in anger. Perhaps the main example of a case which led to nothing, but after two years of investigation, was that of the first minister of finance of the Jospin government, Strauss-Kahn, who was in effect forced to resign his post as a result of (seemingly very small) accusations made against him but was subsequently acquitted of all charges. This problem has been complicated by the introduction of a law designed to clarify the complex relationship between state prosecutors (*procureurs*) and the minister of justice, a problem which appears as difficult to solve as that of squaring the circle.

diminished. Because of the popular election, the president continues to have authority; even in cohabitation he can both ensure continuity in foreign policy and exercise some supervision over the working of the executive.

Parliament also changed in character. Its social composition has been somewhat altered, although women remain markedly underrepresented and manual and white-collar workers are very few, while lawyers, members of the liberal professions, and teachers are numerous. But there are civil servants, managers, and even farmers in substantial numbers, agriculture and business being particularly represented in Center and right-wing parties. This ensures that at least parts of the active strata of the nation are in the legislature (see Table 3.6). In terms of powers, the pendulum swung originally too far against the assembly, though not quite as far as critics and parliamentarians claimed. Gradually, the right of the legislature to discuss, supervise, and suggest has been recognized, but in exchange, the government's right to lead has been fully accepted by parliamentarians.

Indeed, the constitutional reform of 1995, which increased somewhat the role of parliament by extending its sessions, is evidence that parliament is regarded as having abandoned some of the irresponsible forms of behavior in

which it engaged under previous regimes. Thus, by and through its institutions and the effects these institutions have had on the party system and on the behavior of the actors, and despite the fact that the role of the president is likely to be more limited than it was originally, the Fifth Republic has brought about a real and lasting transformation of French political life.

**TABLE 3.6**

**OCCUPATIONAL BACKGROUND OF FRENCH DEPUTIES, 1997 PARLIAMENT (PERCENTAGES)**

| | |
|---|---|
| Business proprietors | 9 |
| Professionals | 18 |
| Teachers | 26 |
| Civil servants | 16 |
| Managers (private sector) | 15 |
| Journalists | 3 |
| White-collar workers | 2 |
| Manual workers | 1 |
| Other | 10 |
| Women | 10 |
| Total (numbers) | 577 |

*Source:* Rapports Assemblee Nationale. Statistiques, 1999.

## Thinking Critically

1. Would you describe the present French system as a presidential one?
2. How would you define "Gaullism"?
3. What have been the effects of centralized bureaucracy?
4. Has the use of referendums in France been successful?
5. How would you explain the vote of between 10 and 15 percent for Jean-Marie Le Pen and his party?

## KEY TERMS

Algerian war *(135)*
*arrêtés (157)*
Chambres d'Agriculture/Chambres de Commerce *(136)*
Jacques Chirac *(140)*
Communist Party *(145)*
*Confédération Française Démocratique du Travail* (CFDT) *(131)*
*Confédération Française des Travailleurs Chrétiens* (CFTC) *(131)*
*Confédération Générale des Cadres* (CGC) *(132)*
*Confédération Générale des Petites et Moyennes Entreprises* (CGPME) *(132)*
*Confédération Générale du Travail* (CGT) *(130)*
*Conseil National du Patronat Français* (CNPF) *(132)*
Constitution of 1958 *(146)*
Constitutional Council *(160)*
Council of Ministers *(151)*
decrees *(157)*
Valéry Giscard d'Estaing *(154)*
European Union (EU), formerly European Economic Community (EEC) *(149)*
*Fédération Nationale des Syndicats d'Exploitants Agricoles* (FNSEA) *(134)*
Gaullist party (RPF, then UNR, then RPR) *(138)*
interest groups *(130)*
Lionel Jospin *(144)*
François Mitterrand *(143)*

National Assembly/Senate *(156)*
parliament *(156)*
Georges Pompidou *(140)*
Socialist Party *(142)*
*Union pour la Démocratie Française* (UDF) *(141)*
vote of censure *(159)*

## FURTHER READINGS

### Groups

Ehrman, H. *Organized Business in France* (Princeton University Press, 1957).

Kesselman, M., ed. *The French Workers' Movement* (London: Allen and Unwin, 1984).

### Parties

Anderson, M. *Conservative Politics in France* (London: Allen and Unwin, 1973).

Bell, D. S., and B. Criddle. *The French Socialist Party*, 2nd ed. (Oxford: Oxford University Press, 1988).

Charlot, J. *The Gaullist Phenomenon* (London: Allen and Unwin, 1971).

Converse, P., and R. Pierce. *Political Representation in France* (Cambridge, MA: Harvard University Press, 1986).

de Tarr, F. *The French Radical Party from Herriot to Mendès-France* (New York: Oxford University Press, 1961).

Frears, J. R. *Parties and Voters in France* (London: Hurst, 1991).

Irving, R. E. M. *Christian Democracy in France* (London: Allen and Unwin, 1973).

Kriegel, A. *The French Communists* (Chicago: University of Chicago Press, 1972).

Penniman, H. R., ed. *France at the Polls* (Washington, DC: American Enterprise, 1975).

### Institutions

Hayward, J., ed. *De Gaulle to Mitterrand: Presidential Power in France* (London: Hurst, 1993).

Keeller, J. T., and M. Schain, eds. *Chirac's Challenge* (New York: St. Martin's, 1996).

Leites, N. *On the Game of Politics in France* (Stanford University Press, 1959).

Williams, P. M. *The French Parliament* (London: Allen and Unwin, 1967).

# C. PUBLIC POLICY

## THE ORGANIZATION OF THE STATE

### The Civil Service

It is commonplace to contrast the traditional weakness of the French political institutions with the strength of the French bureaucracy. It is also commonplace to stress the virtues of this bureaucracy. There is indeed much evidence to support this praise. The French civil service helped the monarchs build the unity of the nation, actively implemented laws, and intervened in the life of the provinces. It ensured the continuity of the state—indeed embodied the state—throughout the various regimes.

There is, however, another side to the picture. The strength of the bureaucracy has the effect of stifling initiative, breeding irresponsibility, and slowing down moves toward participation and democracy. The bureaucracy's aim is to unify and develop, often against the wishes of the population. This enlightened despotism may have brought about change, but it led to paternalism. Local political and social elites were not encouraged to be entrepreneurial. This is being redressed in part, but many psychological barriers remain, two of which are particularly important: the belief in the need for uniformity, and the overwhelming importance of rules and regulations. As a result, while citizens feel impotent and aggrieved, they also accept bureaucratic canons. The role of the bureaucracy thus is far from being wholly positive.

### The Idea of the State

The pervasive nature of the bureaucracy stems from the nature and role of the French state. As in many continental European countries, the state in France is much more than a set of bodies designed to initiate and implement public policies; it is the legal embodiment of the nation. *It thus encompasses all the public organizations and corporations,* both central and local. In the United States and in Britain many public bodies began, and some still are viewed, as groupings of like-minded persons wanting to run a service. Such an associational conception of public bodies has never prevailed in France, where public services are run in the context of a general organization of the state, which can coerce or compel, but also protect citizens, as local authorities and other public corporations are deemed to be better controlled in this way. In the French legal jargon, these are merely "decentralized" entities of the state. For the French, state and law go together because the organization of the state is the embodiment of the principles of the law, and no public authority, large or small, can operate outside this framework.

Moreover, the French state is not only a legal entity; it is a legal entity with a purpose: the well-being of the citizens. From the seventeenth century, and even more so from the early nineteenth century, the tradition of the French state has been one of social engineering. Born from the strong mark that the kings and later Napoleon wanted to make on the nation, an approach that can be described as *dirigisme* (strong management), French social engineering was given its intellectual stamp of acceptability by various writers, philosophers, and sociologists, and in particular by Saint-Simon and Auguste Comte, in the early years of the nineteenth century. Society has to be molded; it is a machine, which can be perfected by appropriate means. In this the *Ecole Polytechnique* is a key element, and characteristically, Saint-Simon and Comte were associated with teaching at that school. Although Saint-Simonism faded out as a doctrine, its influence on attitudes was profound, indeed determining, during most of the nineteenth century (Napoleon III was a Saint-Simonian), particularly in those periods when economic development took place at a rapid rate.

Among the consequences of this tradition, perhaps the most important is state centralization, which includes as its corollary the spreading of public agencies across the whole nation. Another consequence, perhaps not sufficiently stressed, is the greater concern for economic than for social well-being, as the happiness of men is viewed as dependent on the better organization of society for the production of goods and services. Ideas are changing as the potential dangers of economic growth to the health of citizens and the protection of the environment become more widespread, but old ideas die hard.

## THE CIVIL SERVICE AND ITS CHARACTERISTICS

The French civil service has high prestige and considerable competence and is widely dispersed throughout the nation, although some of the differences between France and other Western countries have decreased in this respect. The strength of the civil service comes in part from its size: over 2 million men and women are employed by the central government (see Table 3.7). It comes also from the organization and the traditions of the service. The bureaucracy extends widely in the provinces in a pyramidal manner. Ministries are divided into a number of *Directions générales* and *Directions,* which have a large staff in Paris, but most of these ministries also have offices (external services) in regions, *départements* (counties), and sometimes even small towns. These offices are supervised by a prefect on behalf of the government as well as by their hierarchical superiors in Paris.

### The *Grands Corps*

Another element in the civil service tradition results from the existence of the *grands corps.*

### TABLE 3.7

#### CIVIL SERVICE OFFICIALS, 1992 (PERCENTAGES)

| | |
|---|---|
| Education | 62.1 |
| Economy and finance | 11.3 |
| Interior | 9.1 |
| Equipment | 6.0 |
| Justice | 3.2 |
| All other | 9.3 |

*Source:* Annuaire statistique de la France, 1994 (p.129).

Indeed, until 1945, the service was not united: the *fonctionnaires* (public servants) had some common rights (pensions for instance), but real unity was achieved only in 1946 by the general code for the civil service (*Statut de la fonction publique*). Before 1945, civil servants were appointed by the various ministries to fill specific jobs, and for the more technical or specialized jobs (not necessarily senior, but at least skilled) they were recruited into groups called "corps." These corps have been the basic cells of the service, with a spirit of their own (*esprit de corps*) marking them differently from other branches and divisions and with a desire to excel.

As these differences were prejudicial to the unity of the service and fostered inequality, post-1945 reforms tried to abolish the corps and replace them by general grades, but the most prestigious of the corps, the *grand corps,* were not abolished. In the economic field (Inspectorate of Finance), the administrative judiciary (Council of State), the home and local government sector (Prefectoral Corps), and various technical branches (Corps of Mines, Corps of Roads and Bridges), these bodies have for generations attracted bright, aspiring civil servants. There was an attempt to link members of these corps to the rest of the service, but it failed. Thus the French civil service continues to be run, in most of the ministries, by members of the *grands corps.* Although they may each have barely a few hundred members, they dominate the civil service and give it its tone.

### The *Grandes Ecoles*

The domination of the *grands corps* occurs through the special training given in a few elite schools, the *grandes écoles,* whose members are recruited on the basis of tough competitive examinations and in which high-quality training is given. Some are old (School of Mines, for instance), while others are recent (School of Taxes). Two are particularly important: the *Ecole Polytechnique* and the *Ecole Nationale d'Administration* (ENA). The *Ecole Polytechnique* was set up in 1795 to provide officers for the artillery and engineering branches of the army; it now gives the nation its best technical administrators. The ENA was set up in 1945 as part of the effort to unify the civil service and prepare candidates for higher management jobs in all government departments (including the foreign service). Meanwhile, a school of similar status, the *Ecole Normale Supérieure,* trains the most brilliant of the future secondary school and university teachers. Competition for entry into these schools is fierce.

The ENA is a postgraduate school. Students have first a year of field training (usually in the provinces); this is followed by a year of study in the school itself, and a further training period (usually in a large firm) before the new civil servant chooses where to go. In fact, only top candidates can truly choose; the others are left with less prestigious positions. The final examination, which leads to the posting, decides in particular whether students are to become members of a *grand corps.* Typically, about the first 20 of each class can do so, while the other 100 become *administrateurs civils* and are unlikely to reach the very top posts of the civil service.

## The Role of the *Grands Corps* in the Nation

Except for the diplomatic corps, which remains somewhat separate and whose members typically stay in the foreign service all their lives (the service still retains some of its older aristocratic flavor), members of the *grands corps* do not

work in the same department for more than a few years. They tend to be "detached" (the official expression) to be posted over a wide range of public bodies (including nationalized corporations). Thus inspectors of finance do not merely serve in the Inspectorate but are in charge of practically the whole of the Treasury and of numerous other divisions and branches in which financial or economic expertise is required. Thus graduates of the *Ecole Polytechnique* who have achieved particular excellence enter one of the two technical *grands corps,* the Corps of Mines and the Corps of Roads and Bridges, and are later detached to run not merely the relevant divisions of ministries, but other government departments and various nationalized industries. This may mean technical excellence, but there is a cost. The rigid distinction created between the very successful elements of the higher civil service and the others can lead to disillusionment and constitutes a waste of early training efforts.

The role of top civil servants does not stop at the civil service itself. The best students of the prestigious schools also provide large numbers of managers to the private sector. The situation is the converse of that which occurs in the United States, where private sector managers often join the federal service for a period. In France, the prestige of the training schools is such that their graduates transfer to business (an operation known as *pantouflage*). This gives the civil service, indirectly, a

**A CLOSER LOOK**

**3.6**

### EDUCATION: STILL STRONGLY ELITIST

The one element of social policy that is given high priority in France is education, in part because it is traditionally regarded as a ladder for upward mobility and in part because of the massive student protests that take place periodically. The best-known are those of 1968, but these have been followed by further waves of protests, for instance in the second half of the 1980s. The French education system, and in particular the French higher education system, has traditionally been elitist. The *grandes écoles* are regarded as providing their alumni with great careers, hence the tough competitive examinations set up to enter them. The rest of the higher education system tends to be a Cinderella. Despite some changes, universities remain badly provided for, and there is little contact between staff and students (of whom there are about 2 million). Centralization makes matters worse and in particular induces professors to want to reside in Paris (even if they have a post in the provinces). No real reform has as yet taken place to render universities more autonomous and more responsible.

substantial influence on the whole of the economic life of the nation.

## Civil Service Control

The quality of the *grands corps* accounts for much of the excellence of the service, but it also leads to conflicts among the various branches, each of which is primarily concerned with its own sector. Supervision and coordination can therefore be difficult, and not surprisingly, control plays a crucial and often frustrating part in the French public sector.

Control takes many forms. Some of these are internal to the civil service and date back to Napoleon. First, there are inspectorates, which are often weak, to an extent because the inspectors general stayed in the service while most of their colleagues of the same age group found a more active and more lucrative life in private business. The main role of inspectors general is now not so much to inspect but to inquire. They are often asked to examine long-term problems, and thus act in a way similar to royal commissions in Britain or presidential commissions in the United States. A second type of control is provided by the administrative courts, headed by the Council of State. These courts started as internal organs of supervision on the model of inspectorates and, as inspectors do, still conduct some inquiries and have advisory functions (on bills and decrees, the Council of State advises the government about legality, opportunity, and effectiveness), but they have become real courts and are at some distance from the active administrators.

***Ministerial Staffs (Cabinets)***   Because the civil service's internal controls seemed insufficient, there developed around each minister a staff known as the "ministerial *cabinet.*" Members of the *cabinet* (to be sharply distinguished from the "cabinet" or government) are appointed by the minister. They help him or her remain in touch with constituents and with parliament. They prepare drafts of bills and other reforms; they follow the implementation of policies; they inform their minister about what goes on in the department. They are thus both a protection against undue civil service independence and a brain trust for innovations.

The character of ministerial *cabinets* has changed somewhat in recent decades. These *cabinets* have come to include specialists drawn from the civil service itself, as ministers increasingly need technical advice. The staff of a minister of transport will thus include among others an engineer of roads and bridges, an inspector of finance (to examine costs), and a member of the Council of State (to help draft legal documents). These are civil servants, usually young and loyal to their minister (their future career depends in part on the help they give), but they are civil servants and part of their loyalty is to the civil service, and especially to the corps to which they belong. As other civil servants, they are anxious to foster development, rather than control other civil servants on behalf of constituents or politicians. *Cabinets* thus now provide only a limited check on the bureaucracy.

## LOCAL GOVERNMENT

While the civil service and central government agencies were strong, local government was traditionally weak. It was shaped by Napoleon, who, rejecting the early decentralizing schemes of the Revolution, imposed an authoritarian plan. Local authorities were not only supervised but indeed run by agents of the central government. Liberalization slowly took place in the nineteenth century, in the 1830s and 1880s in particular, but there never was a decisive break with the origins. A large amount of central government control was maintained in part for political reasons. Even liberals felt that full devolution of power to local authorities was dangerous, since much of the opposition to the government was opposition to the regime as well. Local government has thus been caught in a vicious circle, as yet not entirely broken, despite some changes in structure and a modification in attitudes, especially since the 1950s when an entrepreneurial spirit began to prevail.

## *Département* and *Commune*

The current structure of French local government dates from the Revolution of 1789, as modified by Napoleon. The French territory is divided into *départements,* of which there are now 96. This entirely artificial creation was designed to break the hold of the old provinces (such as Brittany or Provence); new counties were set up with names drawn from mountains or rivers (Jura, Var, and the like). The *départements* are in turn divided into communes—usually corresponding to the old parishes—of which there are about 37,000. This structure helped centralization and prevented real local autonomy from developing, despite the democratization of the appointment processes, as the average commune is too small to be effective and has to rely on the services of central government agents. No significant reduction in the number of communes has ever taken place, in part because of local resistance, but in part because the strength of the civil service is better maintained by the present structure. Since the 1960s there have been only a few joint authorities (urban districts), linking towns to the suburban communes, and a Paris district, which has a similar purpose for the Paris area.

Communes maintain strong sentiments of local patriotism. Their representatives play a large part in French local life. Elected every six years by universal suffrage, municipal councilors in turn elect a mayor and a number of assistants (*adjoints*). Mayors have some of the authority of the state, while running the local authority. As the basic law of municipal government of 1884 states: "The mayor is in charge of the affairs of the commune." Mayors pass by-laws relating to police or health matters, register citizens, and supervise the maintenance of roads, street lighting, street cleaning, and the like. Aspects of education and housing come directly or indirectly under their jurisdiction. Particularly in large cities, the mayor is a focal point, especially because mayors tend to stay in office for long periods—two or three terms of six years are common. The stability of communal government has always contrasted with the instability of national politics. Communal government is exec-utive centered; the municipal government is typically dominated by the mayor.

***Decentralization Efforts***    Traditionally, mayors and municipal councils were tightly supervised by central government agents, especially those at the level of the county (*département*). This is in part because counties had, up to the 1980s, a peculiar organization, based on an osmosis between central government agents and locally elected councilors. Until 1982, the executive of the *département* was indeed the prefect, who served both Paris and the elected county council. This helped to perpetuate the dependence of local authorities on the central government and has in particular prevented *départements* from being true local authorities. A major step was therefore taken by the Socialist government of the 1980s: while prefects were retained as agents of the central government, *départements* came to be run by an elected representative, the president of the "general council," the official title of the *département* council. Meanwhile, communes were given greater autonomy; they no longer need prior approval to undertake most activities.

## Regionalism

One reform to the system of local government and the problems of centralization took place through regionalism. First, regional councils composed of representatives of *départements,* communes, and economic and social groups were set up. This occurred for the Paris area in 1959, where a government-appointed post of "delegate general" was created. Regional economic development councils were introduced elsewhere in France in 1964. Participation having been one of the main themes of the 1968 revolutionary outburst, a scheme for regionalization was presented to the French people in 1969. It was limited in scope. Being coupled with a reform of the Senate, it was rejected in the referendum, and de Gaulle resigned as a result. In 1972, a regional reform was presented to parliament for approval and passed. Members of the regional councils continued to be drawn from local authorities, while regional prefects were appointed alongside the

### THE FRENCH MEDIA

France has not been well-served by its media. For a long period after World War II, state radio and television were closely controlled by the government. A number of private radio stations located at the periphery of the country provided much needed fresh air to information. Improvements took place since the de Gaulle period, the three main channels having become independent networks. Under President Mitterrand's Socialist governments, private television began to flourish. There is now more choice and genuine independence from the government, though the quality of the programs leaves much to be desired.

Most of the press is regional and of indifferent quality. Not surprisingly, the best newspapers are Parisian, *Le Monde* being the outstanding example, though some of the competitors that were set up in the 1970s and 1980s have also endeavored to develop a modern form of journalism. Weeklies have moved in the direction of investigative stories and have uncovered problems and scandals. By and large, the media suffer from the classic French characteristics of nationalistic elitism. Culture is given great emphasis—with such ministers of culture as Malraux under de Gaulle and Lang under Mitterrand—but culture is regarded as being true if it is essentially French. As a result, the Americanization of the media is (officially at least, if not necessarily in reality) markedly frowned upon: it was a strong bone of contention in the discussions leading to the 1995 GATT agreement as well as to problems arising between France and its partners in the successor body of GATT, the World Trade Organization (WTO).

regional presidents and councils; these administered a small portion of the matters hitherto handled centrally by the civil service. Finally, the Socialist government of the 1980s instituted regional elections; the councils in turn elect their executive. Independent political bodies thus exist in each region, though their powers and influence are still limited. Although these moves have been relatively slow and half-hearted, France is at last engaged in a process that may gradually dispose of many of the old habits of centralization.

## ECONOMIC INTERVENTION AND PUBLIC ENTERPRISE

The weakness of French local government stems in large part from the widespread belief that France needs a strong civil service if it is to be a modern industrial and commercial nation and the inertia of the provinces is to be shaken. A parallel view has traditionally been adopted with respect to business (see Table 3.8). Hence the large development of public and semipublic

undertakings, often taking the form of mixed companies (*sociétés d'économie mixte*), while large-scale nationalizations took place in 1945–1946 after World War II and in 1982 after the Socialist victory. An attempt was also made to supervise business generally by means of economic plans. The tide then turned. A privatization program was launched by the 1986–1988 conservative government and an effort was undertaken to reduce the traditional role of the civil service in the economy. The Socialist government of 1997–2002 followed suit, though somewhat reluctantly.

### The Plan

French economic development from the 1940s to the 1980s has often been associated with the activities of the *Commissariat général au Plan*, although its role is now almost nominal. It started under the leadership of Jean Monnet, a strong-willed ex–civil servant and ex-businessman who was to be crucial to the psychological success of the idea and was later, much in the

## TABLE 3.8

### DISTRIBUTION OF BUDGETARY EXPENDITURE, 1998 (PERCENTAGES)

| | |
|---|---|
| Economy and finance | 21.4 |
| Education (including universities) | 23.6 |
| Labor, health | 14.4 |
| Defense | 15.0 |
| Equipment and transport | 7.9 |
| Interior | 4.9 |
| Agriculture | 2.2 |
| Foreign affairs | 0.9 |
| Industry and commerce | 1.0 |
| Justice | 1.6 |
| Culture, tourism | 0.9 |
| Total budgetary expenditure | 1,585,300 francs |

*Source:* Europa World Yearbook, 2002 (p. 1593) (origin statistics of Ministere du Budget).

same vein, to foster European unity. The Plan was to be flexible; it was to be run by a team, not by a hierarchical and bureaucratic organization. Its strength came from the intellectual authority of the experts belonging to it.

The character of the Plan changed over the years. It was first concerned with reconstruction and the development of basic industries. It then extended its purview to the whole economy, to regional development (it helped decentralization to an extent), and even to social policies. Originally the Plan was prepared exclusively by officials with little discussion, even in parliament, but large segments of the community later became involved through numerous committees. Employers, leaders of nationalized industries, and trade unionists were associated with the preparation of the Plan. There were also increasingly discussions in the Economic and Social Council, in the regional economic committees, and among the public at large. However, the idea could only suffer in a climate of greater liberalization and free enterprise. With the advent of the Socialist government of 1981, its importance was revived somewhat, but because of the imperative of economic retrench-

ment, it never had again the importance it once had. By the 1990s, it had effectively disappeared in all but name.

## The Size of the Public Sector

The downgrading of the Plan coincided with the first real attempt made by post–World War II French governments to reduce the size of the public sector, which up to 1986 was among the largest in Western Europe and had already been so before the large-scale nationalization measures of the 1981 government. From a base that included, before World War II, the post office, the railways, some shipping lines, and undertakings such as potash mines in Alsace, electricity production in the Rhone Valley, and luxury china in Sèvres, the public sector expanded in 1945–1946 to include the coal mines, the major banks, insurance companies, gas, electricity, and much of aircraft manufacturing. Renault, the largest car manufacturer, was nationalized, as the owner had collaborated with Nazi Germany during the Second World War. Much of air and shipping transport also came under direct governmental control. There was a de facto monopoly of radio and television within France, and the state acquired majority capital in several of the private radio stations that operated at the periphery of the country. A public news agency, *Agence France-Presse,* replaced the private prewar *Agence Havas.* As demand for oil increased (France has very little within its territory), the state created companies, typically as a major shareholder, which engaged in research, production, and distribution of oil and natural gas on a worldwide basis.

This was the situation before 1981. The Socialist government, following to the letter the party's pledge at the election, then carried through parliament the nationalization of practically all the banks (including old, established private ones such as Rothschild) and of five major industrial groups in the chemical and electronic fields, while the major steel companies, already heavily subsidized by the state, were taken over.

These developments took a variety of legal forms that had been perfected since World War I. Originally state control was direct, as in the case of the post office. Later came the model of the *établissements publics,* whose funds are public and where control is tight, but where a board makes decisions and contracts with third parties on behalf of the agency. The formula has often been adopted by local authorities as well. To increase flexibility, companies and corporations were set up with the same structure, the same rights, and the same obligations as private firms. In the case of the large undertakings nationalized in 1945–1946 and in 1982, special legislative arrangements gave the corporations a somewhat different organization, with boards including representatives of the state, the users, and the employees, for instance. But in many other cases there was simply no difference between private and public firms, thus making it possible for state corporations to combine with private bodies to set up subsidiaries.

## The Move toward Privatization

The development of the public sector reached a peak in the mid-1980s. In 1986, for the first time, a government came to power committed both to privatization and to the abandonment of the traditional practice of linking private and public bodies. For the first time, too, the Left no longer wished to modify the new equilibrium by increasing again the public sector when it returned to power in 1988; no new nationalization was even suggested. The French governments of the 1990s thus came to follow the same direction as other European governments. In line with European Union policy, they made moves toward more classical forms of private enterprise at the expense of both wholly public and mixed economy companies, although the latter had been regarded as the way of the future for at least a generation.

Privatization spread in the 1990s and came to include, both before and under the Jospin government of 1997–2002, Air France, Renault, most banks, and television stations. However, a marked reluctance of the Socialists to move too quickly was noticeable. Some utilities, such as gas and electricity, did remain, perhaps for a while only, in the public sector. This was not merely because of the Socialists' visceral reluctance to go too far along the privatization road, however, but also because of the French tradition according to which the public sector, under the civil service, is expected to play a key part in the life of the nation.

# FOREIGN POLICY

## De Gaulle's Worldwide Policy

Foreign policy was the main interest of de Gaulle. Even the reform of the institutions was in some sense provoked by the bias of the founder of the Fifth Republic for foreign affairs, as he felt that the instability and impotence of previous regimes had been the cause both of defeat in 1940 and of the generally limited influence of the country in the world ever since. Yet although there were indeed external effects of French internal political uncertainties, de Gaulle markedly underestimated the extent to which the country could any longer be a prime mover in the contemporary world. Thus his efforts at pushing for a strong and independent foreign policy ended in failure. Indeed, he himself may have realized that he could not go much beyond symbolic gestures, such as the effort to build closer links with the Soviet Union or to defend the rights of some countries or groups against Anglo-Saxon imperialism (as he tried to do in Quebec or Latin America). In practice, he kept France within NATO (despite some changes) and within the European Community, despite a continuous emphasis on the fact that Europe should be a "Europe of nations" and despite the fact that he unquestionably retarded the development of European unity.

## Pompidou's Greater Realism

De Gaulle's departure from the scene meant a slow, indeed very slow, return to the recognition of France's international position, that of a medium-sized power, with some influence stemming from her cultural and economic ties with parts of Africa and, to a more limited extent, with Latin America. But France cannot have a direct effect on the course of events outside Western Europe. Within the European sphere, the nation has a significant part to play, albeit as a partner and not as a leader. Thus Pompidou, de Gaulle's successor and heir, began to make some moves away from grand world involvement and toward the acceptance of the country's limited European role. His acceptance of British entry into the European Community was partly motivated by the hope that Britain, as France, would reduce the spread of "supranationalism." In this he was proved right, though the entry of Britain into the European Community (now Union) also meant that the community was gradually including all Western European nations.

## France's Role in World Affairs

The third President of the Fifth Republic, Giscard d'Estaing, established a close working relationship with the German chancellor of the time, Helmut Schmidt, that continued the rapprochement of de Gaulle with Adenauer a decade or more earlier, but with a different purpose. De Gaulle used Adenauer to assert his leadership over Europe. Giscard d'Estaing was more modest; he recognized the economic superiority of Germany and was primarily concerned with economic association. A step was thus taken toward real collaboration and the abandonment of the (wholly unrealistic) idea that France could do more than partly influence the course of events in Western Europe, let alone in the rest of the world.

With Mitterrand's accession to the presidency in 1981, France's foreign policy ceased to be truly worldwide, although some interest for what had been French Africa and for the "francophonie" lingered on. Not being associated, directly or indirectly, with de Gaulle and Gaullism, Mitterrand was able to assert that France's position was in Europe and, in effect, in Europe only. His successor, Jacques Chirac, seemed torn between traditional Gaullism in words and realism in deeds. He clearly took a Gaullist line over nuclear weapons, at least in a first phase. He insisted that France should have a truly independent nuclear deterrent. He doggedly proceeded with a series of tests in the South Pacific that

antagonized almost every country, not just in the Pacific but in Europe as well. Yet Chirac then stated that the tests conducted up to January 1996 would be the last and that he would from then on act strongly in order to reduce the nuclear threat—not a line that de Gaulle would have readily adopted. As Mitterrand, he came to adopt a more realistic line in favor of Europe. However, there still is more than a lingering desire to play a large part—an unrealistically large part—in worldwide developments, whether in the Middle East, Africa, or Latin America.

## France and the European Union

Mitterrand was markedly more realistic than his predecessors about the need for France to concentrate on European affairs. This realism stemmed in part from the economic difficulties (and the consequential social problems of unemployment) of the country. These made it impossible for the president to expect to move at a different pace from his European partners. But his European conviction was also part of a general recognition that if France's commitment to Europe was wholehearted, she could play a key part in the European Community. Perhaps as a result, Mitterrand was able to appoint his ex-minister of finance, Jacques Delors, to the presidency of the European Commission in 1985, a post he was to occupy for ten years in the most able and forward-looking manner. Delors, for instance, was the architect of the single market policy and, indirectly, of the Economic and Monetary Union, which led to the adoption of the single European currency. Mitterrand could thus exercise indirect influence on Union affairs. He was not fully a federalist, but he clearly was a realist. So was Chirac, who, unlike many other members of his party, had previously supported the Maastricht Treaty of the European Union. Once in office, he began to pursue, out of sheer necessity, a European orientation.

French commitment to Europe remains somewhat ambiguous. While Joschka Fischer, the Green German foreign minister under Schröder, stressed the need to move toward a federal system, Jospin, the Socialist French prime minister, repeated that the Union had to be a Union of nations. He was indeed attacked in some quarters for being too lukewarm toward Europe and for being primarily concerned with home affairs—a point that was in some ways correct, as he did leave to Chirac many opportunities to take the lead in European matters. Yet it was under Jospin that the euro became a reality, and the support that his government showed for the move was in no way less active than that of other European governments of the "Eurozone."

Nonetheless, French governments have often been concerned, not just under de Gaulle but consistently afterwards, to use the European Union to defend their economic interests to the hilt, as over the GATT negotiations of 1993–1994, while being rather slow at applying in practice the principles that they claim to support in theory. Such a mode of behavior is perhaps inevitable in a period of transition. However, France, as the other Western European powers, has to recognize that its role in the world must diminish, and that only through a common European policy can the voice of the whole area be of real moment. The dilemma between going it alone and further integration has affected almost daily the actions of French governments over the last decades. It is likely to continue to affect them for a substantial period.

## CONCLUSION

In the 1950s and 1960s, the French economy was profoundly transformed; the colonial problems that destroyed one French regime and brought another at times near the precipice were solved and forgotten; the international status of the country was high. Yet social tensions, which seemed to diminish for a while in the 1960s, reemerged dramatically in 1968. This reinforced the feeling of many among the French that the Fifth Republic remained provisional. Yet the departure of de Gaulle one year later, in 1969, did not shake the institutions, and the transition from de Gaulle to Pompidou was smooth. Nor was the regime shaken by the transition from Giscard d'Estaing to Mitterrand in 1981, despite the many predictions made earlier that "alternance" from

Right to Left would be difficult, if not impossible. Nor was the regime at all shaken by cohabitation—twice between a president of the Left and a government of the Right and Center and once between a president of the Right and a government of the Left—despite gloomy predictions made earlier that conflicts would be intense.

In 1981, a Socialist government embarked on a major reform program. This was possible only because of institutions that had been tailor-made for de Gaulle. In 1986, a conservative government undid many of these reforms, but the regime, then too, was flexible enough to make these movements possible and to remain stable through repeated swings of the pendulum, toward the Left in 1988 and 1997, toward the Right in 1993 and 2002. The institutional ambiguity of the 1958 Constitution turned out to be a major asset of the Fifth Republic.

Cynics had claimed that de Gaulle wanted to have it both ways—to be able to run the executive and yet have considerable control over the legislature, to have the elbow room of a U.S. president but the hold over the chamber of a British premier, and, in practical terms, to be immovable for what was then seven years but be able to dissolve parliament and appeal to the people. Others had claimed that de Gaulle was unable to appreciate the importance of constitutional structures, a view which has some truth, though the attitudes of the first president of the Fifth Republic on this matter were complex. He seemed to consider that constitutional arrangements were matters for lawyers who can always find solutions if they are firmly led, and yet he had a simple, naive, almost religious belief in the virtues of constitutional reform to redress the imperfections of a political system. His approach to political analysis was more institutional than behavioral, to adopt the widely used expression of modern political scientists. Yet he made a change that, however ambiguous (or perhaps because it was ambiguous), allowed for a transition to occur and turned out to be adapted to French patterns of political behavior.

De Gaulle was often criticized because he preferred to introduce constitutional change instead of establishing a streamlined and responsible party system as Adenauer had succeeded in

Jacques Chirac was elected president in 1995, the third time he ran for the position. Chirac has been mayor of Paris since 1977, is leader of the Gaullist Rally for the Republic (RPR), and was twice prime minister.

achieving in West Germany. De Gaulle was indeed old-fashioned in this respect. He did not like parties, which he often referred to as "factions"; he saw them as divisive and as the cause of the ineffectiveness of French political life in the past. Yet, in practice, while concentrating on institutional change and endeavoring to reduce the role of parties, he streamlined the party system. He built a party on the Right, which his successors, Pompidou and Giscard d'Estaing, undermined. Indirectly, too, he enabled Mitterrand to build his popular support and to restart the Socialist Party.

The election of 1981 constituted an historic event in more than one way. In the broadest political sense, more than Pompidou and Giscard d'Estaing, Mitterrand was the heir and the continuer of de Gaulle's approach. Mitterrand, as de Gaulle, defeated the Communist Party on coming to power; he, as de Gaulle, established a strong majority party, since the election of 1981 had the same political effect of streamlining and strength-

ening the party system as the election of 1962; Mitterrand, as de Gaulle, came to power with a mission, albeit a different one. De Gaulle's mission was to solve the Algerian crisis and, beyond this crisis, to bring France back to political and psychological sanity. Mitterrand's mission was to reconcile the French among themselves, to make them no longer fear to take on their own destiny at the grass roots, whether in the regions and the communes or in the firms.

Here the comparison stops. To achieve this tall order, Mitterrand needed to exorcize the twin specters of unemployment and inflation. He reduced the latter, but unemployment probably contributed to the first setback of his party in 1986 and unquestionably led to the major Socialist defeat of 1993. As a matter of fact, Mitterrand could not hope to succeed in his mission without the collaboration of other Western European countries, the United States, and Japan. These nations practiced economic orthodoxy. Mitterrand had to accept the need for retrenchment and, with it, the clipping of many of his ideals. Yet, while the French turned away from the Left in 1993 in view of its relative failures, Mitterrand and the Socialist Party in general gained a central position in French political life of respect and of acceptability which the party had not had before, as the good performance of Jospin at the 1995 presidential election showed. That performance foreshadowed the parliamentary victory of the Socialist Party two years later in 1997. As a result, France has become a country in which pluralism and alternance are firmly established, as the 2002 election result was once more to show.

Observers around the world have tended to admire the British form of government but have been fascinated by the French political system. For a while, under the Fifth Republic, it was fashionable to say that a new French political system, streamlined and dull, had emerged. This was scarcely true at the time of the Algerian war, when virulence added unpleasantness to the political fights of the French; this has not become true with the end of the colonial wars. Since the 1970s, there has been a difficult search for a better equilibrium between the various forces in society, between Paris and the provinces, between employers and workers, as well as between the majority of the French and the many minority groups—immigrants, the young, and others. No doubt the Socialist experiment of 1981 disappointed some and repelled others, but France also changed in the process. The central bureaucracy and the elite groups are no longer able to maintain a hold on society to the extent that they once did.

By 1981 the Gaullist (and Giscardian) phase of the Fifth Republic seemed to have outlived its usefulness. By 1995, the Socialist Party, too, seemed to have proved unable to give France the brave new world that many wanted, while some among its political elite appeared to have succumbed to the lust for money as well as for power. To the lasting credit of de Gaulle, he made it possible for French citizens to bring about responsible changes in policies and changes in personnel, developments which had not been possible for many generations. It is to the credit

of the French that they seized this opportunity, though many motivations, from unemployment to scandals, have played a substantial part. Thus France may gradually overcome its social problems while also overcoming the institutional difficulties from which it suffered for almost two centuries. Yet the path is narrow and tortuous. Ingenuity and imagination will no more suffice than a competent bureaucracy. Patience and determination—not the qualities for which the French are best known—will have to be shown if the motto "Liberty, Equality, Fraternity" is to be brought, in full, closer to reality.

## Thinking Critically

1. What impact does the educational elite have on the life of France?
2. Has the role of the state been greater in France than in the United States?
3. Is it true to say that France cannot be France without "grandeur"?
4. How would you characterize France's attitude to the European Union?
5. How would you assess the impact of socialist governments on the French economy?

## KEY TERMS

adjoints (167)
bureaucracy (163)
ministerial cabinets (166)
civil service (164)
commune (167)
départements (167)
Directions générales/Directions (164)
dirigisme (163)
Ecole Nationale d'Administration (ENA) (164)
Ecole Normale Supérieure (165)
Ecole Polytechnique (164)
Grands Corps (164)
Grandes Ecoles (164)
mayors (167)
prefects (167)
regions (167)
social engineering (163)

# FURTHER READINGS

Bauchet, P. *Economic Planning: The French Experience* (London: Heinemann, 1963).

Cerny, P., and M. Schain, eds. *French Politics and Public Policy* (New York: Methuen, 1980).

Chapman, B. *Introduction to French Local Government* (London: Allen and Unwin, 1953).

Crozier, M. *The Stalled Society* (New York: Viking, 1973).

Gregoire, R. *The French Civil Service* (Brussels: Institute of Administrative Science, 1964).

Guyomarch, A., H. Machin, and E. Ritchie. *France in the European Union* (Basingstoke: Macmillan, 1998).

Machin, H., and V. Wright, eds. *Economic Policy and Policy-Making under the Mitterrand Presidency, 1981–1984.* (London: F. Pinter, 1985)

Ridley, F., and J. Blondel. *Public Administration in France,* 2nd ed. (London: Routledge and Kegan Paul, 1968).

Suleiman, E. *Politics, Power, and Bureaucracy in France* (Princeton, NJ: Princeton University Press, 1974).

Suleiman, E. *Elites in French Society* (Princeton, NJ: Princeton University Press, 1978).

# WEB SITES

**www.elysee.fr**
Information on the French president
**www.premier-minstre.gouv.fr**
Information on the prime minister
**www.archives.premier-ministre.gouv.fr**
Information on the prime minister
**www.assemblee-nationale.fr**
Information on the National Assembly
**www.senat.fr**
Information on the Senate
**www.fonction-publique.gouv.fr**
Information on the ministry for the civil service
**www.ena.fr**
Information on the National School
for Administration
**www.conseil-etat.fr**
Information on the Council of State
**www.archivesnationales.culture.gouv.fr**
National Archives
**www.conseil-constitutionnel.fr**
Constitutional Council
**www.parlement.fr**
French parliament
**www.interieur.gouv.fr**
Ministry of the Interior
**www.francetresor.gouv.fr**
Ministry for Economic Affairs
**www.diplomatie.gouv.fr**
Ministry for Foreign Affairs
**www.lemonde.fr**
France's most respected newspaper, *Le Monde*
**www.monde-diplomatique.fr**
*Le Monde Diplomatique*
**www.lefigaro.fr**
*Le Figaro*
**www.permanent.nouvelobs.com**
*Le Nouvel Observateur*
**www.rpr.org**
RPR
**www.parti-socialiste.fr**
Socialist Party

CHAPTER

4

THE GOVERNMENT OF
# Germany

*Donald Kommers and A. James McAdams*

## INTRODUCTION

**Background:** As Western Europe's richest and most populous nation, Germany remains a key member of the continent's economic, political, and defense organizations. European power struggles immersed the country in two devastating World Wars in the first half of the twentieth century and left the country occupied by the victorious Allied powers of the United States, United Kingdom, France, and the Soviet Union in 1945. With the advent of the Cold War, two German states were formed in 1949: the western Federal Republic of Germany (FRG) and the eastern German Democratic Republic (GDR). The democratic FRG embedded itself in key Western economic and security organizations, the European Community and NATO, while the communist GDR was on the front line of the Soviet-led Warsaw Pact. The decline of the USSR and the end of the Cold War allowed for German unification in 1990. Since then Germany has expended considerable funds to bring eastern productivity and wages up to western standards.

### GEOGRAPHY

**Location:** Central Europe, bordering the Baltic Sea and the North Sea, between the Netherlands and Poland, south of Denmark

**Area:** 357,021 sq km

**Area—comparative:** slightly smaller than Montana

**Land boundaries:** 3,618 km

> *border countries:* Austria 784 km, Belgium 167 km, Czech Republic 646 km, Denmark 68 km, France 451 km, Luxembourg 135 km, Netherlands 577 km, Poland 456 km, Switzerland 334 km

**Climate:** temperate and marine; cool, cloudy, wet winters and summers; occasional warm foehn wind

**Terrain:** lowlands in north, uplands in center, Bavarian Alps in south

**Elevation extremes:** *lowest point:* Freepsum lake –2 m

*highest point:* Zugspitze 2,963 m

**Geography note:** strategic location on North European Plain and along the entrance to the Baltic Sea

## PEOPLE

**Population:** 83,029,536

**Age structure:** *0–14 years:* 15.57% (male 6,635,328; female 6,289,994)

*15–64 years:* 67.82% (male 28,619,237; female 27,691,698)

*65 years and over:* 16.61% (male 5,336,664; female 8,456,615)

**Population growth rate:** 0.27%

**Birthrate:** 9.16 births/1,000 population

**Sex ratio:** 0.96 male/female

**Life expectancy at birth:** 77.61 years

*male:* 74.47 years

*female:* 80.92 years

**Nationality:** *noun:* German, Germans

*adjective:* German

**Ethnic groups:** German 91.5%, Turkish 2.4%, other 6.1% (made up largely of Serbo-Croatian, Italian, Russian, Greek, Polish, Spanish)

**Religions:** Protestant 38%, Roman Catholic 34%, Muslim 1.7%, unaffiliated or other 26.3%

**Languages:** German

**Literacy:** *definition:* age 15 and over can read and write

*total population:* 99%

## GOVERNMENT

**Country name:** *conventional long form:* Federal Republic of Germany

*conventional short form:* Germany

**Government type:** federal republic

**Capital:** Berlin

**Administrative divisions:** 16 states (Länder, singular—Land); Baden-Württemberg, Bayern, Berlin, Brandenburg, Bremen, Hamburg, Hessen, Mecklenburg-Vorpommern, Niedersachsen, Nordrhein-Westfalen, Rheinland-Pfalz, Saarland, Sachsen, Sachsen-Anhalt, Schleswig-Holstein, Thüringen

**Independence:** 18 January 1871 (German Empire unification); divided into four zones of occupation (UK, US, USSR, and later, France) in 1945 following World War II; Federal Republic of Germany (FRG or West Germany) proclaimed 23 May 1949 and included the former UK, US, and French zones; German Democratic Republic (GDR or East Germany) proclaimed 7 October 1949 and included the former USSR zone; unification of West Germany and East Germany took place 3 October 1990; all four powers formally relinquished rights 15 March 1991

**Constitution:** 23 May 1949, known as Basic Law; became constitution of the united German people 3 October 1990

**Legal system:** civil law system with indigenous concepts; judicial review of legislative acts in the Federal Constitutional Court; has not accepted compulsory ICJ jurisdiction

**Suffrage:** 18 years of age; universal

**Executive branch:** *chief of state:* President Johannes Rau (since 1 July 1999)

*head of government:* Chancellor Gerhard Schröder (since 27 October 1998)

*cabinet:* Cabinet or Bundesminister (Federal Ministers) appointed by the president on the recommendation of the chancellor

*elections:* president elected for a five-year term by a Federal Convention including all members of the Federal Assembly and an equal number of delegates elected by the state parliaments; chancellor elected by an absolute majority of the Federal Assembly for a four-year term

**Legislative branch:** bicameral Parliament or Parlament consists of the Federal Assembly or Bundestag (656 seats; elected by popular vote under a system combining direct and proportional representation; a party must win 5% of the national vote or three direct mandates to gain representation; members serve four-year terms) and the Federal Council or Bundesrat (69 votes; state governments are directly represented by votes; each has 3 to 6 votes depending on population and are required to vote as a block)

**Judicial branch:** Federal Constitutional Court or Bundesverfassungsgericht (half the judges are elected by the Bundestag and half by the Bundesrat)

### ECONOMY

**Overview:** Germany possesses the world's third most technologically powerful economy after the United States and Japan, but structural market rigidities—including the substantial nonwage costs of hiring new workers—have made unemployment a long-term, not just a cyclical, problem. Germany's aging population, combined with high unemployment, has pushed social security outlays to a level exceeding contributions from workers. The modernization and integration of the eastern German economy remains a costly long-term problem, with annual transfers from western Germany amounting to roughly $70 billion. Corporate restructuring and growing capital markets are transforming the German economy to meet the challenges of European economic integration and globalization in general.

**GDP:** purchasing power parity—$1.936 trillion

**GDP—real growth rate:** 3%

**GDP—per capita:** purchasing power parity—$23,400

**GDP—composition by sector:** *agriculture:* 1.2%
  *industry:* 30.4%
  *services:* 68.4%

**Inflation rate (consumer prices):** 2%

**Labor force:** 40.5 million

**Labor force—by occupation:** industry 33.4%, agriculture 2.8%, services 63.8%

**Unemployment rate:** 9.9%

**Currency:** deutsche mark (DEM); euro (EUR)
  *note:* in 2002, the euro replaced the local currency for all transactions.

# A. POLITICAL DEVELOPMENT

On October 3, 1990, after 45 years of painful division, Germany was once again a united nation. After midnight on that day, East Germany ceased to exist. The territory formerly governed by the German Democratic Republic (GDR) and its hard-line Communist leaders was now an integral part of the Federal Republic of Germany (FRG). For those involved, the magical term was *accession*. According to Article 23 of West Germany's constitution, "other parts of Germany" outside the territory governed by the FRG could join or "accede to" the Federal Republic. Accession meant that these "other parts" of Germany joining the FRG would henceforth be subject to its constitution, better known as the Basic Law or *Grundgesetz*. In this instance, accession took place under the terms of the German Unity Treaty signed by the FRG and the GDR. In signing the treaty the GDR agreed to dissolve itself, to embrace the Basic Law, and to bring its entire social, political, and economic system into conformity with the legal order of the FRG.

Unification did not restore to Germany all the territory lost as a result of World War II. In 1945 the Soviet Union had annexed northern East Prussia, including Königsberg, while all German territory east of the Oder and Neisse Rivers (East Prussia, Silesia, and parts of Pomerania and Brandenburg) was placed under Polish administration. The Allies divided the rest of Germany and Berlin into four zones of occupation: a Soviet zone in the east and three zones in the west occupied by France, Britain, and the United States, respectively. The western zones, united in 1949 to form the Federal Republic of Germany, constituted only 60 percent of the territory of the German nation that existed between 1871 and 1937. The Saarland, annexed by France after World War II, was returned to the FRG in 1957 after its residents voted in favor of reunion. With the GDR's accession in 1990, Germany recovered three-fourths of the territory contained within its 1937 borders.

The division of Germany after World War II recalls the tragic course of German history through the centuries. This history has been marred not only by territorial dismemberment but also by political discontinuity, which has manifested itself in recurrent patterns of revolution and reaction. It has left the German nation with a diverse and fragmented political legacy, punctuated by authoritarian, and even totalitarian rule. But importantly, since the Second World War, the German people have shown that, given the right conditions, democracy can win out.

## HISTORICAL BACKGROUND: MOLDING THE GERMAN NATION

### The First Reich (800–1806)

Centuries after Britain and France had been unified under strong national monarchs, Germany was still a dizzying patchwork of sovereign powers. In the territory where the German nation-state would eventually arise, there were over 300 feudal states and some 1,300 smaller estates, each with its own political institutions, laws, and customs. No imperial institution was prestigious enough to unify these entities, and no emperor was strong enough to merge them into a single national state. The shape of the Holy Roman Empire of the German Nation (the predominantly German parts of the Empire founded by Charlemagne and restored by Otto I—and quite rightly described as "neither holy, nor Roman, nor an empire") changed repeatedly over its thousand-year history. It stretched in and out like an accordion, depending on the fortunes of war or the outcome of princely rivalries.

Religious and political division matched the severity of Germany's territorial fragmentation. The Reformation (1517–1555) polarized Germans religiously, creating a legacy of intolerance and hatred that lasted well into the nineteenth century. The Thirty Years' War (1618–1648) was equally devastating in long-range political impact. Reputed to be the most destructive war in the first millennium of German history, it decimated the population, wrecked agriculture and industry, and destroyed an emergent middle class that might have formed the nucleus of a nationalizing and moderating force in German politics. Instead, it restored power to the princes, reinvigorated feudalism, and set the stage for the nineteenth-century struggle between feudal and modernizing forces. Moreover, Protestant religious teaching and princely absolutism combined to emphasize the duty of obedience to the State, thus inhibiting popular participation in politics.[1]

## Napoleon to Bismarck (1806–1871)

Ironically, the path to German unity was laid not by internal design but by a foreign invader. As part of his plan for European conquest, Napoleon Bonaparte occupied Germany in 1806 and forced hundreds of principalities into a confederation of some 30 states governed by a unified code of civil law. Like so much else in German history, this experience led to contradictory results that certainly Napoleon could never have foreseen, nor desired. On the one hand, French rule stimulated the development of a liberal movement focused mainly in southwestern Germany and rooted in the eighteenth-century revival of classical humanism. On the other hand, it triggered an outburst of German nationalism built almost exclusively on antipathy toward the liberal reforms of the French Revolution—a reaction paralleled in the cultural domain by a literary backlash that glorified tradition over reason, heroism over compassion, and a romantic conception of one's local community over cosmopolitanism.

France's defeat in 1815 led to the Congress of Vienna and the establishment of a new confederacy of 41 states that largely retained Napoleon's extensive remodeling of Germany. In its effort to strengthen Germany vis-à-vis France, the Congress ceded large possessions in the Rhineland and Westphalia to Prussia, a German state that by then had grown into a formidable power in central Europe. The Prussian-led conservative Hohenzollern monarchy and militaristic Junker caste were destined to finish, through "blood and iron," the work of national unification started by Napoleon. Economically, the Prussian-sponsored customs union (*Zollverein*), which removed most trade barriers among the German states, was an important tool of national integration.

A watershed year in this period was 1848, when revolutions against monarchical regimes broke out all over Europe. German liberals had gathered enough strength to persuade several princes to go along with the election of a national assembly, which convened in Frankfurt am Main. Known as the Frankfurt Parliament, it called for the creation of a united Germany to be ruled under a new federal constitution containing an impressive bill of rights, an independent judiciary, and parliamentary institutions. By the following spring, however, this attempted revolution had been put down and Germany reverted to its traditional pattern of authoritarian governance, increasingly under Prussian domination. In 1866, under the leadership of Otto von Bismarck, Prussia defeated Austria, its closest rival for hegemony in Germany. Austria's defeat led to the creation of the North German Confederation in 1867, also under Prussian domination. Four years later, after conquering France, Prussia successfully established a truly national state in the form of a constitutional monarchy.

## The Second Reich (1871–1918)

The constitutional order installed by Bismarck in 1871 was a semi-authoritarian system designed to contain and control all of the contradictory forces unleashed over the previous century. Among its diverse features, it (1) limited the franchise to the wealthier classes; (2) subordinated the popularly elected house of parliament (*Reichstag*) to the executive; (3) established a Prussian-dominated upper parliamentary chamber (*Bundesrat*) composed largely of landed proprietors and members

---

[1]This and the following historical subsections rely heavily on Geoffrey Barraclough, *The Origins of Modern Germany* (New York: Capricorn Books, 1963); Koppel S. Pinson, *Modern Germany,* 2nd ed. (New York: Macmillan, 1966); and H. W. Koch, *A Constitutional History of Germany in the Nineteenth and Twentieth Centuries* (London and New York: Longmann, 1984).

of reigning families; (4) divided executive authority between a chancellor and the emperor (*Kaiser*), with effective political power lodged in the latter; and (5) empowered the emperor (preeminently the king of Prussia) to appoint and dismiss the chancellor, dissolve the Reichstag, declare martial law, and serve as supreme commander of the armed forces.

In the socioeconomic sphere, the imperial era was marked by a similarly precarious balance of forces: (1) an economic revolution that transformed a backward and predominantly agrarian society into a powerful urban, industrialized nation; (2) the establishment of a tenuous alliance between agrarian and industrial interests in foreign policy; (3) the colonization of overseas territories and the launching of an arms race with Britain and France, reflecting many Germans' dreams of a larger and even more powerful global order under German hegemony; and (4) importantly for the later development of the nation's distinctive social and economic values, the adoption of a comprehensive program of state-supported social legislation designed to purchase the loyalty and passivity of the working masses.

The social theorist Ralf Dahrendorf has characterized imperial Germany as an "industrial feudal society,"[2] meaning that, unlike in Britain and France, industrialism in Germany failed to produce a fully modern society. Whereas modernization had brought about liberal traditions of civic equality and political participation in Britain and France, Germany retained many of the features of a preindustrial class society based on rank and status. The state bureaucracy, professional army, landed aristocracy, and patriarchal family remained the central pillars of the social structure. Human rights or other fundamental guarantees of human dignity were conspicuously absent in the imperial constitution. Conflicting social groups were either brutally repressed, or they were simply bought off through state paternalism. These devices reinforced the political compliance of the German people. It induced many to seek the satisfactions

of life by turning inward toward themselves and by cultivating private values, such as those to be gained through friends and families, rather than by turning outward toward the cultivation of public and egalitarian virtues.

## The Weimar Republic (1919–1933)

Germany's defeat in World War I gave liberals some grounds for hope. The abdication of the monarch led to the establishment at Weimar of the nation's first constitutional democracy since the short-lived National Assembly of 1848. The Constitution of 1919 confirmed the tradition of German federalism, guaranteed numerous social and political rights, and adopted a parliamentary system capped by the popular election of the president. However, it also contained structural features that contributed to the instability of the new polity. The president could dismiss the chancellor, dissolve the Reichstag (the new and increasingly vocal lower chamber), control the armed forces, suspend constitutional rights, and exercise broad emergency powers. The system of proportional representation splintered the electorate, leading to a succession of weak governments. Also, basic liberties were judicially unenforceable, and the ease with which the constitution could be amended or suspended tended to trivialize it.

It is doubtful whether any constitution, however artfully drawn, could have contained the social and political chaos of this postwar period. The disgrace of military defeat and the harsh terms of the Versailles Treaty—for example, the enforced reparations at a time of economic distress and the Allied occupation of the Rhineland—gave birth to yet another round of frenzied nationalism. Against the backdrop of an unchanged social structure, a large segment of Germany's elite failed to be persuaded about the legitimacy of Weimar's republican institutions. At length, these institutions were easily manipulated for antidemocratic purposes as social turmoil grew and the economy collapsed. Violence erupted in the streets as right-wing extremists, often fighting left-wing extremists, gathered strength and influence. This unrest led to Adolf

---

[2]Ralf Dahrendorf, *Society and Democracy in Germany* (Garden City, NY: Doubleday, 1967), p. 62.

Hitler's installation as chancellor on January 30, 1933. Nazi success in the elections of March 5, 1933, following the February burning of the Reichstag, anchored his hold on power. The passage of the Enabling Act shortly thereafter, which granted the government dictatorial powers, ended the life of the Weimar Republic.

## The Third Reich (1933–1945)

With Hitler's rise to power, constitutional government succumbed to National Socialist totalitarianism. The popular assemblies of the various states were abolished, political parties banned, autonomous groups and associations suppressed, dissent crushed, anti-Nazi political figures imprisoned, tortured, or murdered, and ordinary citizens deprived of liberty and property without due process of law. Having consolidated his power and in violation of the Versailles Treaty, Hitler took steps to remilitarize the Rhineland and build a war machine that by 1941 would sweep across Europe, threatening the security of the entire world.

Among the many atrocities committed between 1933 and 1945, Hitler engineered what Lucy S. Dawidowicz has called "the war against the Jews."[3] The dictatorship's assault began with campaigns of anti-Semitic propaganda; it continued with decrees to boycott Jewish businesses, remove Jews from the civil service and the professions, divest them of their citizenship, seize their property, and forbid them from marrying non-Jews; it culminated in the "night of the broken glass" (*Kristallnacht*), when gangs of storm troopers all over Germany assaulted Jews on the streets, invaded their homes, destroyed their shops, and set fire to their synagogues. The Holocaust followed as millions of Jews in Germany and in conquered territories throughout Europe, including women and children, were rounded up, herded into cattle cars, and sent to concen-

tration camps designed for their extermination. Six million Jews died in these camps, almost completing Hitler's goal of ridding Europe of its Jewish population.

Although the German dictatorship met with the courageous resistance of a handful of religious and political groups during this time—including even attempts on Hitler's life—it took Germany's total destruction from the outside to topple the Nazis from power. Once again, military defeat resulted in the nation's enforced dismemberment and its occupation by foreign powers. Yet provocatively, for those Germans who yearned for democracy, the situation at war's end was not completely bad. In their 12-year orgy of repression and violence, the Nazis inadvertently succeeded in destroying the old order, including many traditional institutions and values. Thus Hitler's "social revolution," combined with Germany's physical destruction, cleared the way, at least potentially, for the building of a new political order, one that would hopefully be both united and democratic.

# TOWARD A NEW FRAMEWORK OF GOVERNMENT

## The Occupation (1945–1949)

In 1945 Germany lay smoldering in ruins. Its once powerful military machine was shattered, its industrial establishment heavily damaged, its urban centers demolished, its transportation and communication networks disrupted, its government at all levels in a state of collapse, and its people demoralized and starving. Politically, Germany's future seemed bleak. At the Yalta and Potsdam conferences, the victorious powers had agreed to a number of measures to eliminate the German war threat in Europe, including the nation's total disarmament, the punishment of leaders responsible for war crimes, and the payment of reparations to nations hurt by German aggression.

In each of their zones of occupation, the Allies embarked upon programs of *denazification* and *democratization* as the first steps toward the reconstruction of a new political

---

[3]See Lucy S. Dawidowicz, *The War Against the Jews* (New York: Holt, Rinehart and Winston, 1975). See also David S. Wyman, *The Abandonment of the Jews* (New York: Pantheon Books, 1984).

order. By 1947–1948, however, cooperation among the Allies had ceased. For France, Britain, and the United States, democratization meant parliamentary institutions, competitive elections, civil liberties, and a free enterprise economy. But for the Soviet Union, it meant Communist Party dictatorship and state ownership of the means of production. Furthermore, the Soviet Union had embarked upon a policy of conquest and one-party rule in Eastern Europe, creating satellite states organized in accordance with Marxist-Leninist principles out of the countries it had liberated from the Nazis.

The Cold War was a gathering force with a vengeance, and Germany was its flash point. Unable to reach an agreement with the Soviet Union over the future of Germany, the three Western powers decided to combine their zones of occupation into a single economic unit. The Soviet Union responded by attempting to blockade the city of Berlin, but the famous airlift of 1948–1949 foiled the Soviet attempt to drive the Western powers out of Berlin.

Economic union in the western half of Germany was soon followed by political union. With the establishment of state and local governments and the licensing of political parties committed to democratic constitutionalism, the Allied military governors laid the groundwork for a new West German political system. A constituent assembly dominated by Christian and Social Democrats, elected in turn by the state legislatures, convened with Allied approval to write a new constitution. They called it the Basic Law (*Grundgesetz*), rather than the Constitution (*Verfassung*), to underscore the provisional character of the new polity pending national unification. That would take place, they argued, on the day the German people could make the choice to live together again "in free self-determination." This Basic Law, which created the Federal Republic of Germany, entered into force on May 23, 1949, after its ratification by the legislatures of more than two-thirds of the participating states (*Länder*).

The Soviet Union responded by founding the German Democratic Republic, whose constitution entered into force on October 7, 1949. From that date until 1990, Germany remained a divided nation, and for most of these 40-plus

years the FRG and GDR viewed each other with mistrust and hostility. The Berlin Wall, which cut an ugly path through the center of Berlin, stood out as the chief symbol of their mutual antagonism. Although some relaxation in relations between the two German states gradually took place by the late 1960s and throughout the 1970s, as a consequence of the West German government's efforts to ease relations with all of Eastern Europe (*Ostpolitik*),[4] tensions remained. They seemed bound to persist so long as Europe itself remained divided militarily and politically between East and West.

## Reunification

Forty-five years after the postwar division of Germany, the "impossible dream" happened. Owing to the rise of the Soviet Union's reformist General Secretary Mikhail Gorbachev, seismic changes in the geopolitics of Eastern Europe, and the subsequent end to the Cold War, the former Allied powers set the stage for Germany's reunification (see Section C for a description of these developments). Today, Germany's political and intellectual leaders often speak as though they clearly saw this event coming. But the truth is that most Germans were fully unprepared for the restoration of national unity in 1990. In earlier years, some like then-chancellor Helmut Kohl and his predecessor had repeatedly remarked that the event, however desirable, would not happen in their lifetimes. This was because they could never imagine the Soviets giving up their prized conquest in East Germany. In contrast, others, like the prominent German novelist Günter Grass, openly expressed reservations about reunification. They feared the creation of a "super-Federal Republic." Nevertheless, on Octo-

---

[4]*Ostpolitik*, which means "Eastern policy," is the term used to describe the efforts of West Germany, especially its Chancellor Willy Brandt, to normalize relations with the Communist countries of Eastern Europe. For the FRG, the high point of these efforts, which took place between 1970 and 1973, was the Basic Treaty between the Federal Republic of Germany and the German Democratic Republic.

## A CLOSER LOOK 4.1

### INCOMPATIBLE SOCIAL REALITIES?

"There can be no unification of the GDR and the Federal Republic on West German terms; there can be no uni-fication of the GDR and the Federal Republic on East German terms. What blocks such a unification—such a concentration of power—is not only the objections of our neighbors in Eastern and Western Europe, but also the fact that these two social systems are mutually exclusive…. [We] have to recognize not only the territorial and political division, but also the incompatibility of two existing German social realities."

*Source: Günter Grass, Two States—One Nation? Trans. Krishna Winston and A. S. Wensinger (New York: Harcourt Brace, 1990), pp. 54–55.*

ber 3, 1990, the entity came into being—a uni-fied *and* democratic Germany—that had been such a constant subject of debate since the mid-dle of the nineteenth century.

Helmut Kohl, the chancellor of German unity and a champion of European unification.

## SOCIETY AND ECONOMY

An understanding of contemporary German politics requires some attention to the profound social and economic changes that occurred, first in the FRG after 1945 and then in the "new states" (*Länder*) that acceded to the FRG upon the dissolution of the GDR. These five reconsti-tuted *Länder* came with a vastly different polit-ical and socioeconomic formation from that of the western *Länder*. Yet it is intriguing to note the determination with which both societies committed themselves to raising the standards of living and of production in the eastern area to parity with those enjoyed in the western area. From the beginning, Germany's more affluent leaders in the West indicated their desire to erase all vestiges of the former GDR's command economy and to replace it with the mixed economy of the advanced social welfare state. In fact, the ideal of a social welfare state has been pursued by nearly all of Germany's governments, with varying degrees of intensity, since the days when Bismarck sought to buy off his working-class and revolutionary critics with state-sponsored welfare programs.

### Economic Background

The material foundations to support the policies of a welfare state were surprisingly quick to return to Germany in the postwar period. Within a single decade, West Germany emerged from the wreckage and devastation of World War II to become one of the top industrial giants of the world. Marshall Plan aid in the amount of $4.5 billion; a preexisting industrial base available for the production of capital goods; a burgeoning export trade generated by the Korean crisis; a plentiful supply of foreign workers; and the discipline, skills, and sacrifices of the German people—all contributed to the West German economic revival.

The most important factors setting the FRG on its way to economic recovery were the currency reform of 1948 and the founding of a central bank that in time would become the main pillar of budgetary discipline and monetary stability. These were the initial building blocks of the FRG's celebrated "social market economy" (SME). Other features of the SME are competition and individual entrepreneurship, intervention by the state to ensure the realization of both, and social responsibility. Unlike in the United States, governmental regulation in Germany is not seen as a barrier to the flourishing of the market economy. Rather, the state is seen as both a guarantor of fair competition and a necessary agent in fostering social solidarity among diverse interests.

The FRG's economy percolated at an astoundingly rapid rate without any significant leveling off until the late 1960s. Motor vehicles, precision engineering, brewing, chemicals, pharmaceuticals, and heavy metal products were among Germany's strongest industries. Growth rates in the national economy in each of the four decades since 1950 were 7.96, 4.45, 2.74, and 2.21 percent, respectively,[5] placing the FRG fourth among the world's top industrial nations while transforming the country into a prosperous and mass-consumption society.

During these years, East Germany seemed to experience an economic miracle of its own, if only when compared with the struggling economies of other socialist states in the Soviet bloc. By 1970, concentrating on heavy industry, chemicals, and mechanical engineering, the GDR ranked second, after the Soviet Union, in industrial production within the bloc, outstripping all

other Socialist countries in per capita national income. In the 1970s, its leaders turned their attention to improving the everyday lives of ordinary citizens, offering a greater variety of consumer goods and improved housing. However, the good times were not to last. By the 1980s, as its totally state-owned economy proved unable to innovate and adapt to changing conditions, the GDR's increasingly outmoded industries could no longer compete in the new, postindustrial, global market. The state was on the verge of bankruptcy, workers were becoming restless, and consumer goods were scarce and markedly inferior to West German products.

Accordingly, when reunification came in the early 1990s, the FRG faced an economic challenge more formidable than the effort to revive West Germany after the war. East Germany's instantaneous integration into the FRG exposed serious weaknesses in the GDR's centrally planned economy. Its factories were unproductive and overstaffed, its technological base inferior, and its infrastructure in need of rebuilding from the ground up. The cost of reconstructing the eastern economy would require enormous financial transfers, which in turn resulted in higher taxes for West Germans and increased deficit spending. Only five years into unification, these transfers were amounting to around 640 billion in deutsche marks (DM), and billions more would be required to close the still-large gap in productivity and living standards.

Naturally, all of these changes brought heavy social costs in their wake. The rapidity of the old GDR's transformation resulted in scores of factory shutdowns. Predictably, many areas of the economy collapsed under the pressure of enormous competition from western Germany and as a result of the loss of traditional markets in the former eastern bloc. The result was massive unemployment as the region's industrial output fell by some 40 percent between 1990 and 1993. Although by 1995 over 14,000 East German industries and businesses had been privatized, productivity remained much lower than in the west. Still, for those who were willing to look down the road a bit, the future was far from bleak. Corporate-sector investment in plant and

---

[5]Eric Owen Smith, *The German Economy* (London: Routledge, 1994), p. 9.

## A CLOSER LOOK
### 4.2

### THE SOCIAL MARKET ECONOMY

An outgrowth of German neoliberal and Catholic social thought, the social market economy is predicated on the belief that a free market is compatible with a socially conscious state. It seeks to combine the principles of personal freedom and social responsibility in a unified political economy. The production of goods and services is to be left to free choice in an open market, but the marketplace is to function within a social framework created by law. This framework includes general public policies designed to enhance competition, ensure honest trade practices, and protect consumers. It is also government's duty in neoliberal economic theory to stabilize the economy as a whole and to care for the needs of persons not served by the market.

equipment over this period was far stronger in the eastern *Länder* than in the west. Also, as would be expected in the underdeveloped east, the construction industry played a dominant role in the growth of an East German economy whose gross domestic product (GDP) expanded from 5.8 percent in 1993 to 8.5 percent in 1994. By contrast, the growth rates in West Germany for these years were –1.7 and 2.4 percent, respectively. Although East Germany's economy slowed to a growth rate of 5.6 percent in 1995, it was way ahead of the 1.6 percent increase in the west.

During these years, the growth rate in the FRG as a whole bordered on 2 percent. Yet Germany remained an economic powerhouse. By 1994, the country's GDP had reached a record $1,911 billion, ranking it third in the world, just behind the United States and Japan. By 1999, as Table 4.1 shows, Germany had retained this ranking (despite having to weather an economic slowdown) as it stood on the verge of a new century.

### Territory and Population

In territorial size, reunited Germany is the fifth largest nation in Europe. Bordered by nine countries ranging from Denmark in the north to Austria in the south and flanked by Poland and the Czech Republic in the east and France and the Benelux countries in the west—a 2,350 mile border—Germany takes up 137,787 square miles in the center of Europe. Geographically, Germany is the third largest nation in the European Union,

behind France and Spain. But even if the Germany of today had the desire or the ability to return to its 1937 borders, it would nonetheless remain a medium-sized state on the global scale, even though as an industrial power, the FRG ranks third in the world.

The more revealing figures for contemporary Germany, both for its place in Europe and in the world, are those concerning its population. Before reunification, the FRG was the most populous state in Western Europe and second on the continent only to the USSR. The acquisition of

**TABLE 4.1**

**GERMANY'S GDP RANKING AMONG SELECTED NATIONS, 1999**

| Nation | GDP (billions) | GDP per Capita ($) |
|---|---|---|
| United States | $9,230 | $33,900 |
| Japan | 2,950 | 23,400 |
| Germany | 1,864 | 22,700 |
| France | 1,373 | 23,300 |
| United Kingdom | 1,290 | 21,800 |
| Italy | 1,220 | 21,400 |
| Canada | 722 | 23,300 |
| Spain | 678 | 17,300 |

*Source: CIA World Factbook, 2000. www.intellect.org/resources/cia_worldfactbook_00.*

some 16 million East Germans did not dramatically change this ranking, although everyone could see that it would eventually make an important contribution to Germany's economic future. Along with expanding its borders and its population, the FRG has gained a new neighbor, Poland, and a new set of demographics. The overall population of nearly 82 million is now somewhat more East European in origin, and proportionately more Protestant.

The population figures in Table 4.2 represent a fascinating tale of human migration and dislocation. Between 1950 and 1989 the old FRG's population increased by 13 million, while the ex-GDR lost over 2 million of its inhabitants, nearly all of whom migrated or fled to West Germany. The indigenous birthrate had little to do with these statistics. The rapid increase in population recorded over these years resulted mainly from two factors: the influx of 13 million German refugees and migrants from Poland, the Soviet Union, East Germany, and other eastern countries and the arrival of 2.5 million foreign workers who entered under the FRG's labor recruitment program in the 1950s and 1960s. The *German* "immigrants"—not technically foreigners—consisted of Polish and Sudeten Germans expelled from their homes and property (*Vertriebene*), ethnic Germans from Eastern Europe resettling in the FRG (*Aussiedler*), and East Germans who abandoned their homes and careers in the GDR to resettle in the FRG (*Übersiedler*).

Since 1970, an additional 1.9 million *Aussiedler* entered Germany from Poland, Romania, and the former Soviet Union. (Some 1.8 million East Germans moved to the western *Länder* after the collapse of the Berlin Wall.) Finally, some 900,000 asylum seekers arrived in Germany from 1988 through 1991; the figure leaped to 430,191 in 1992 alone.[6]

By 1995, there were 6.88 million foreign residents in reunited Germany, nearly 50 percent of whom had lived there for ten years or more. The FRG's foreign nationalities, which today make up more than 8 percent of the population, include 2 million Turks and 1.3 million persons from the former Yugoslavia. Italians, Greeks, Poles, Austrians, Romanians, Spaniards, Iranians, and Portuguese residents account for another 2 million residents, not to mention several hundred thousand British, American, and EU nationals and roughly equal numbers of persons of non-European origin. What is striking about these figures is that they represent a rate of entry relative to the national population that is not only twice the rate of mass immigration to America in the 1920s but, apart from Israel, several times more than that of any other EU country today.

As we shall see, the response of some Germans to these foreign entrants, particularly those from the southern and eastern parts of Europe, was sometimes far from welcoming. Sporadic incidences of violence against foreigners were registered throughout the 1990s. Further, it would prove difficult if not impossible for most of these non-Germans, even those who had lived in the FRG all their lives, to acquire actual German citizenship.

Yet despite the difficulties many foreigners encountered in living and working in the Federal Republic, one interesting fact about the native German population demonstrates just how much the FRG's economy depends on the continued presence of immigrants. Beginning in 1998, the FRG's native German population has shown marked signs of decline. According to current

## TABLE 4.2

### POPULATION OF GERMANY (MILLIONS)

| Year | Old FRG | Ex-GDR | Germany |
|------|---------|--------|---------|
| 1950 | 49.9 | 18.4 | 68.3 |
| 1960 | 55.4 | 17.2 | 72.6 |
| 1970 | 60.1 | 17.1 | 77.2 |
| 1980 | 61.5 | 16.7 | 78.2 |
| 1993 | 65.5 | 15.6 | 81.1 |
| 1999 | 65.0 | 17.2 | 82.2 |

*Source: Statistisches Jahrbuch für die Bundesrepublik Deutschland 1995, p. 46; Statistisches Jahrbuch, 2001.*

[6]"Political Asylum Seekers," *Week in Germany,* January 15, 1993, p. 2.

projections, it is conceivable that these numbers will fall from the current level of 82 million Germans to around 70 million in the year 2050, and perhaps even lower. Generally, the FRG's increasing affluence and typical postindustrial values have combined to foster this problem. Germans (and particularly western Germans) are having far fewer children than they did in the past. Additionally, they (again, particularly western Germans) are getting married at a slower rate than before. At the same time, the major factor holding the total population relatively constant is that, thanks to improved health care and living conditions, the mean age of the country's population has risen correspondingly. Now that average Germans are living longer, there are actually more persons above the age of 65 in the FRG than there are below the age of 15. This fact means that the German social welfare system is increasingly challenged to meet the costly needs of an older and presumably more demanding citizenry which is in the position to exercise considerable political clout.

One effect of this demographic shift has been to increase the demand for skilled labor. Accordingly, the German government has begun to follow the example of Canada and the United States in offering special work permits and other incentives (akin to the American "Green Card") to foreign professionals who are willing to share their talents with the FRG's high-tech industries for extended periods. Not surprisingly, critics of this initiative have been quick to point out that the German government has been much less generous when it comes to opening the country's doors to less skilled immigrants from poorer states outside Europe. As antipathy to these foreigners has risen, the Berlin government has taken strong steps to curtail the number of would-be entrants.

Still, as the native German population as a whole continues to drop in the coming years, one wonders whether the current restrictions on immigration and citizenship can be maintained. It will be interesting to see whether one of two possible outcomes is dominant. One possibility is that the necessity of recruiting labor of all kinds to keep the German economy running at full steam will have the effect of forcing the FRG's leaders to open their borders even wider. The other, more disturbing eventuality is that a greater influx of foreigners will lead to greater resentment and hostility on the part of native Germans.

## From Bonn to Berlin and In Between

Berlin is the new capital of united Germany. At last, Germany has a hub like London, Paris, or Rome and one around which the economic, cultural, and political life of the country is likely to swirl. With a population of 3.5 million, it is Germany's largest city. A sprawling urban landscape scarred by 40 years of division—half the city lay in the West and half in the old Soviet zone—Berlin experienced an unprecedented building boom in the 1990s as it prepared for the presence of the national government, parliament, and numerous federal ministries. All of these institutions were moved from Bonn to the city in 1999, marking a striking contrast between those times of national division when Germany's capital had been located in a sleepy village-like setting along the Rhine River. With its major universities, research institutes, cultural institutions, technical industries, and ongoing improvements in transportation, including its incorporation into Germany's high-speed intercity railroad network, Berlin is poised to become the gateway between East and West if not "the de facto metropolis of the new free Central Europe."[7]

Apart from Berlin, the economic and political life of the country is centered in a number of conurbations: in the Rhine-Ruhr (Essen, Dortmund, Cologne, and Düsseldorf), Rhine-Main (Frankfurt) and Rhine-Neckar (Mannheim) regions; in the business-industrial concentrations around the cities of Stuttgart, Hamburg, Hanover, and Munich; and now in the east around Dresden, Leipzig, and Chemnitz. Fourteen cities boast a population of more than 500,000. Although they are catching up, the new eastern German *Länder* remain somewhat less urbanized than those in the west. Of 19 cities

---

[7]John Ardagh, *Germany and the Germans* (London: Penguin Books, 1991), p. 63.

with more than 300,000 inhabitants, not counting Berlin, three (Leipzig, Dresden, and Halle) are in the ex-GDR. Thirty-five percent of the former FRG's population lives in cities with more than 100,000 inhabitants, but only slightly more than 10 percent of former GDR residents live in such areas. In Germany as a whole, 10 percent of the population lives in predominately rural areas—with fewer than 150 inhabitants per square kilometer—although these areas constitute over 60 percent of the national territory. Twenty-eight and 62 percent of the population live in intermediate and concentrated areas, respectively.

## Economic and Social Stratification

Germany's occupational structure shows a nation gradually transforming itself from an industrial into a postindustrial society. As is characteristic of postindustrial societies, both the service and trade sectors of the economy have grown the fastest in both western and eastern Germany, clearly overtaking traditional industries and productive enterprises. Most jobs created in West Germany over the past couple of decades have been connected with banking, insurance, education, the health professions, and the civil service. This social transformation has given way to a rising middle class composed of salaried employees associated with the worlds of finance, commerce, and increasingly the high-tech sectors of the economy. These salaried employees, along with 2.5 million public servants and 3.2 million self-employed persons constitute nearly two-thirds of the German workforce. No longer is the holding of property the decisive factor in class distinction, but rather the nature of a person's job and the prestige and income that go with it are what determine status.

The traditional crafts are another declining sector of an increasingly technological society. As in other western European states, tailors, shoemakers, painters, typesetters, and carpenters have seen their numbers dwindle in the face of a far greater demand for the services of building cleaners, automobile mechanics, TV technicians, plumbers, electricians, and hairdressers—underscoring the widespread availability of discretionary income among most occupational groups, including even common laborers. The craft trades still remain an important part of the German economy. In 1994, there were 668,000 craft firms headed by a master craftsman. The crafts employed 15 percent of the workforce, trained 37 percent of apprentices, and accounted for 9 percent of the FRG's economic output.

Of course, one cannot expect that the sort of modernization of the professions witnessed by western Germany would be equally matched in the east. The residue of socialist mismanagement will long remain in the region. The dominance of manufacturing industries in the eastern *Länder,* combined with the pathologies of central planning and the lack of competition, continues to inhibit the emergence of a modern diversified economy as well as the development of new technologies. In 1988, 94.7 percent of all persons employed in the GDR worked for state-owned enterprises. The figure was 99.9 percent in industry, 92.3 percent in construction, and 98.5 percent in agriculture and forestry. Only the traditional crafts (excluding construction) remained under some form of private ownership.

Since unification, however, progress has been made. All crafts, trades, and professions were privatized. More important, they would see their numbers increase dramatically. For example, craft firms in the ex-GDR had doubled by the end of the 1990s. In the professions, only a half-decade after the fall of the Wall, there were four times as many doctors and dentists than before unity. The number of private lawyers has more than doubled, perhaps representing an iron law of modernization, and tax advisors have shot up from only 350 into the thousands. Other professions experienced similar increases. Their number, together with the proliferation of the service trades, promises to accelerate the arrival of the postindustrial age in the eastern *Länder.*

Another major sign of postindustrialism is the increasing replacement of industrial employment by automation and the substitution of moving machines with electronic and communications technology. After years of delay, perhaps betraying an extant cultural conservatism, Germans have finally embraced the Internet revolution and the World Wide Web. These developments have coincided with the emergence of a large technocratic and managerial elite. Jobs in highly skilled professional and technical areas are increasing at a much faster rate than unskilled or semiskilled jobs. In the 1970s the number of engineers, computer technicians, economists, teachers, accountants, lawyers, and social workers in the FRG almost doubled, while university admissions in the natural and social sciences nearly tripled. By 1995 the professional-technical-managerial class contained 6.2 million persons, representing 23.4 percent of the total workforce.

The socioeconomic changes described here have affected the nature of political cleavages in Germany, largely by making them less and less important and class boundaries more permeable. While the society may reveal residues of a traditional class structure, German politics in recent decades has not been determined by the heated class conflicts of the first half of the twentieth century. The ascendancy of a new professional, technical, and managerial class supported by a vast army of white-collar employees performing highly specified roles in the social economy has blunted the class feeling of earlier generations. Additionally, as a result of Communist rule, the old class structure in the eastern *Länder* has entirely disappeared, and thus the political pressure from this part of Germany is likely to be in the direction of greater egalitarianism.

## Security and Equality

The portrait of German society sketched up to now is one of general affluence and economic opportunity, particularly in western Germany. If industrial wages, home ownership, and possession of consumer goods are considered, then income and property are widely distributed in the western *Länder*. However, as much as the *social* market economy tries to provide minimum levels of decency for all, the social *market* economy tolerates large disparities in income and economic power. As a result, as Figure 4.1 indicates, western and eastern Germany presented two rather different images of social justice and equality in the early years of unification. In the

western areas that had formed the preunification FRG, a significant gap separated the lowest and highest paid persons in the mid-1990s. In contrast, the bell-shaped curve of the ex-GDR in Figure 4.1 shows much less disparity among income levels than in the west. The figure also underscores the different levels of prosperity in the east and west. Noticeable, too, is the much larger income gap between the sexes in the west. The higher the income category, the greater the inequality, whereas in the east the inequality is far less at all income levels.

What Figure 4.1 fails to show are unemployment levels. Unemployment in the FRG reached a postwar preunification high of 10.2 percent of the workforce in 1983, tarnishing the image of the FRG's well-run social market economy. Even in 1990, with the economy running at full capacity, unemployment persisted at around 6 percent of the workforce, indicating serious structural problems in Germany's export-intensive industries. The unification-induced slump in employment drove this figure up to 9.2 percent in the early 1990s, representing 8.7 percent of unemployment in the old *Länder* and as much as 25 percent in the new. By 1996, unemployment in Germany as a whole was on the verge of reaching a postwar high of 4 million, or 10 percent of the total workforce. This figure was still lower than the rate of unemployment in France (11.5 percent) and Italy (10.5 percent), but it was significantly higher than in the United States (5.7 percent) and Japan (3.1 percent).[8]

Although the unemployment picture would begin to show significant signs of improvement in the 1998–2000 period, this was largely confined to western Germany. In the east, however, the picture remained especially painful, in part because of different attitudes in the region. Emphasizing equality over liberty, the GDR's former leaders had constructed a socialist state where the right to work was guaranteed and where there was little disparity in income among persons employed in various sectors of the economy. Finally, the state's attention to social welfare was universal in the old

---

[8]*The OECD Observer* (August–September, 1995), p. 49.

In Recent political climate of Effects of

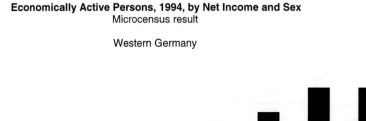

**Economically Active Persons, 1994, by Net Income and Sex**
Microcensus result

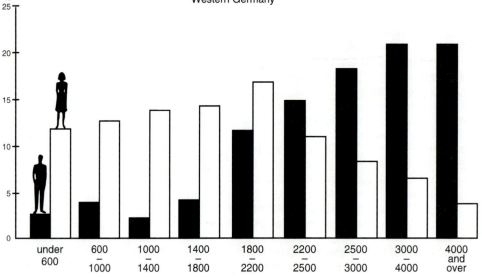

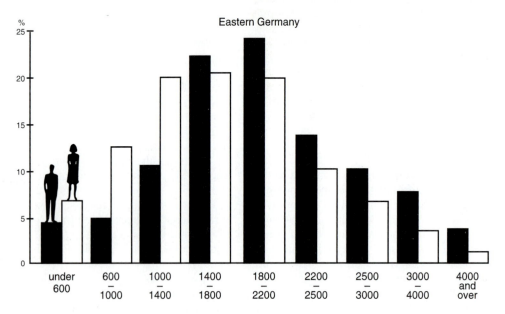

Figure 4.1 WESTERN AND EASTERN INCOME DISTRIBUTIONS IN REUNIFIED GERMANY

GDR, although the system lacked the efficiency and quality of social welfare planning in the FRG. In 1988, the year before the GDR's collapse, pensions and medical care accounted for more than 90 percent of the system's social expenditures. The average old-age pension in the GDR covered about 45 percent of net wages as opposed to about 50 percent in the FRG,[9] but again the latter was of far greater value. The child-care system and leave policy for child-bearing women, however, were more generous in the east (in large part because the Communist government wanted to stimulate population growth).

Despite its weakness, unified Germany's social security system remains one of the most comprehensive in the world. The national pension system alone covers nearly all private sector employees; for example in 1991, just after unification, it accounted for 30 percent of the social budget. Still, based as it is on an income strategy tied to lifetime earnings, its redistributive effect is limited. Elderly persons, especially widows on pensions, are the hardest hit, in part because of a discriminatory policy which allows such persons only 60 percent of the pension to which a living husband would have been entitled. Pensioners are the least well off. In the mid–1970s, approximately 35 percent of pensioners over 65 lived on or below the poverty line and in grossly inadequate housing.[10] Although Germany may not have as large an underclass of destitute persons as some other Western nations, and especially the United States, the pockets of poverty that do exist are a continuing challenge to the nation's social conscience (see Section C for additional details on German social policy).

---

[9]Günter Thumann, "The System of Public Finance in the German Democratic Republic," in Leslie Lipschitz and Donough McDonald, *German Unification: Economic Issues* (Washington, DC: International Monetary Fund, December 1990), p. 159.

[10]For a discussion of the West German social welfare system, see Wolfgang Zapf, "Development, Structure, and Prospects of the German Social State," in Richard Rose and Rei Shiratori, *The Welfare State* (New York: Oxford University Press, 1986), pp. 126–155.

## Women, Law, and Society

The West German constitution guarantees equal rights to men and women. In reality, women have not shared equally in the opportunities offered by the social economy. Even more than in many European states, Germany's legacy of male supremacy has been extremely difficult to overcome (even in the reputedly more egalitarian eastern *Länder*). This is especially true in the domain of family affairs, where tradition and law have for generations confined women to hearth, children, and the guardianship of their husbands. Although the tradition persists, the legal structure of gender discrimination has been gradually torn down, thanks in part to the Federal Constitutional Court. Laws favoring the patriarchal family have been invalidated, the last remnant of which fell in 1992 when the court struck down a provision requiring married persons to adopt a single family surname and, in the event of spousal disagreement, the surname of the husband. Already in 1977 a new family code had provided for no-fault divorce, spousal support arrangements keyed to economic status rather than gender, and an equal division of property.

Opportunities for women outside the home can be measured by comparing their participation rates in the workforce, their earnings, and the kinds of jobs they perform to those of men. In 1989 women in the FRG constituted a little more than one-third of the full-time workforce, whereas in the GDR it was about one-half. (Ninety percent of East German adult women were employed in some fashion in 1989.) Yet this was hardly a result of enlightened attitudes. In the GDR's system of state-mandated liberation, women were expected to lead a dual life of both homemaker and working person. The country's labor-intensive economy and low productivity helped to drive women into the working world. But as in the west, women were responsible for most of the household work as well.

Social policy in the GDR was designed to make a dual career possible for women. For example, child-care facilities were everywhere and free of charge, maternity leave with pay (at 75 to 90 percent of wages) was available for up to 26 weeks, and working parents could count on at least 40 days per year of paid time to care for their sick children. Yet significantly, these generous benefits were quickly abandoned in the east after reunification, at precisely the time many eastern Germans were losing their other forms of employment. As businesses remodeled and factories modernized, huge numbers of women were forced to withdraw from the labor market. By 1993, they would constitute nearly 65 percent of the unemployed in eastern Germany. Deprived of child-care facilities and other social benefits for working parents, single women with children were among the hardest hit, while women over 50 who lost their jobs had little hope of reemployment.[11] Many became depressed and bitter, feeling cheated out of their previous lives and deceived by promises of coming well-being in united Germany.

Interestingly, in terms of earning power, women lagged substantially behind men even in the affluent western *Länder,* owing both to wage-rate discrimination and to the lack of promotional opportunities associated with less stable and skilled jobs. Moreover, the disparity showed little improvement between 1983 and 1993, and in some categories of employment the gap actually widened. For example, the average gross monthly salary of female versus male white-collar employees in these years was DM 2541 and DM 3670

respectively, as opposed to more favorable male salaries of DM 4153 and DM 5987. Available household income revealed a similar gap. In 1993, the average income of a female-headed household was 63 percent of that available to a male-headed household.[12] These differences in earnings and disposable income can be attributed in part to the limited number of hours women were able to work because of their child-care and household duties.

Finally, even though the situation would gradually improve over the 1990s as women could be found in every occupation in Germany, gender-based job segregation would continue. The overall representation of women is extremely high in low to mid-level occupational categories. Textiles, retail sales, social services, and health care are almost wholly feminized. Still, the old GDR had a better record of female participation in several distinctive professional categories than West Germany. In fact, by 1985 more women than men were being admitted as students of medicine, mathematics, and economics. With unification, however, the overall figures, except for public school teachers, continue to show significant disparities. Segregation in the job market is often ascribed to employee recruitment mechanisms that, although not always overtly discriminatory, tend to channel women into traditional female roles.

As early as 1980, the West German Parliament sought to remedy these inequalities by imposing certain duties on private employers. The European Community Adaptation Act incorporated EC nondiscriminatory directives into domestic law. The act requires equal pay for equal work; bars gender discrimination in hiring, promotion, and dismissal; eliminates job descriptions based on sex; shifts the burden of proving nondiscrimination to the employer; and requires the latter to display prominently copies of equal rights legislation in the workplace. (These provi-

---

[11]On the other hand, precisely because the right and duty to work in the GDR was state-decreed, "many [East German women] appear[ed] to link self-realization to a life in which homemaking is a preferred option, and employment limited or not necessary at all." See Sabine Hübner, "Women at the Turning Point: The Socio-Economic Situation and Prospects of Women in the Former German Democratic Republic," *Politics and Society in Germany, Austria, and Switzerland,* vol. 3 (1991), p. 26. For other sources on East German women after reunification, see Marilyn Rueschemeyer, et al. (eds.), *Women in the Politics of Postcommunist Eastern Europe* (Armonk, NY: M. E. Sharpe, 1994), pp. 87–116; and Friederike Maier, "The Labor Market for Women and Employment Perspectives in the Aftermath of German Unification," *Cambridge Journal of Economics* 17 (1993), pp. 267–280.

[12]"Zur Einkommenslage der westdeutschen Arbeitnehmerinnen," *Wochenbericht* 61 (Berlin: Deutscher Institut für Wirtschaftsordnung, 21 September 1994), pp. 655 and 659.

sions were extended to public employers in 1994.) Nonetheless, the Adaptation Act has not been vigorously enforced, owing in part to the lack of enforcement agencies. Thus, the success rate of individual victims who have initiated actions against their employers under these provisions has been low.[13]

Perhaps the most important victory for women on the employment front was the *Nocturnal Employment* case of 1992. In this landmark decision, the Federal Constitutional Court invalidated as unconstitutional a federal statute that barred women from working at night. Invoking Article 3 (2) of the Basic Law, which declares that "men and women shall have equal rights," the court flatly rejected the gender stereotyping that produced the night-shift ban. *Nocturnal Employment* was decided against the backdrop of a national debate over affirmative action. By now, women were organizing in defense of their interests and the political parties were beginning to pay attention. Efforts were being made to demand more than antidiscriminatory legislation and the dismantling of legal classifications based on sex. In 1994, after years of lobbying for such an amendment, the needed two-thirds parliamentary majority added this sentence to Article 3 (2) of the Basic Law: "The state shall seek to ensure equal treatment of men and women by removing existing disadvantages [between them]."

Whatever progress has been made on behalf of women must be attributed in part to the rise of the Greens in the 1980s and the party's efforts to give greater publicity to the cause of affirmative action. By highlighting feminist issues and by requiring that 50 percent of all their party posts and parliamentary seats be held by women, the Greens effectively became a "woman's party." The Greens drew their electoral support disproportionately from women under 40 years of age. Other parties soon got the message. They grew more sensitive to women's issues, made an effort to expand their female membership, and placed increasing numbers of women on their ballots. In 1994, 176 women were elected to the Bundestag, representing 26 percent of its membership, the most ever. Four years later, in 1998, the Bundestag elections resulted in even more telling figures, as 207 women entered parliament, an increase of nearly 5 percent in the forum's total membership. In the two major parties, the SPD and the CDU/CSU, women accounted for 35.2 percent and 18.4 percent of their respective representatives (a slight decrease from the preceding election). In contrast, the Greens and the PDS were responsible for the most impressive figures, as women made up 57.4 and 58.3 percent, respectively, of their total Bundestag representation (see Table 4.3).

Significantly, in 2000, the moderate-conservative Christian Democratic Union, generally no partisan of progressive causes, elected Angela Merkel as its first female party chairperson. Merkel's ascendancy was notable both because she was a woman and because she was one of only a handful of prominent politicians to emerge from eastern Germany. Moreover, she enjoyed the

---

[13]For a discussion of the effects of the European Community Adaptation Act, see Josephine Shaw, "Recent Developments in the Field of Labor Market Equality: Sex Discrimination Law in the Federal Republic of Germany," *Comparative Labor Law Journal* 13 (1991), pp. 27–41.

**TABLE 4.3**

**WOMEN IN THE GERMAN PARLIAMENT, 1998 ELECTION**

| Party | Women | Total (Women + Men) | Women (%) |
|---|---|---|---|
| SPD | 105 | 298 | 35.2 |
| CDU/CSU | 45 | 245 | 18.4 |
| Alliance 90/ Greens | 27 | 47 | 57.4 |
| FDP | 9 | 43 | 20.9 |
| PDS | 21 | 36 | 58.3 |
| Total | 207 | 669 | 30.9 |

*Source:* Gabriela Metzler, "Women in Politics in Canada and Germany," in *Zeitschrift für Kanada-Studien—online*, v. 19, n. 2, 1999, p. 124, *http://www.kanada studien.org/ZKS/2141-992.html*

distinction of replacing Helmut Kohl, the so-called Chancellor of German unity, who had heretofore seemed a permanent fixture in the CDU because of his remarkable political longevity.

Finally, whereas women remained underrepresented in the judiciary as a whole, they would occupy no fewer than 5 of 16 seats on the Federal Constitutional Court by the mid-1990s, also a new high. In fact, with her election in 1994, Jutta Limbach became the first woman president or "chief justice" of the Federal Constitutional Court, Germany's highest tribunal. Evelyn Haas was chosen as an associate justice in the same year. Her appointment was significant because she was the first woman nominated to the high court by Christian Democrats. Still another woman was among the candidates for election to the high court in 1996. Only the future will tell whether these advances in the nation's highest judicial and legislative arenas will carry over into other areas of law and society.

## Ethnic Minorities

While grievances based on sex have been the object of the law's special solicitude, those based on ethnicity have arguably been allowed to fester. Large-scale immigration in the postwar era has transformed the FRG's racially homogeneous society into a nation of ethnic minorities. Most of the older immigrants—notably, the postwar expellees who were mainly ethnic Germans—have been almost wholly integrated into the dominant culture. Yet the story has been much different for those persons who have been unable to claim German ancestry. The new immigrants consist mainly of foreign workers recruited by industry on a massive scale during the 1950s and 1960s, who should properly be credited with playing a large role in sustaining Germany's "economic miracle." By the 1990s, there were over 5,000,000 of these workers and their families—mainly Turks, Yugoslavs, Greeks, and Italians—making up 6.4 percent of reunited Germany's total population, or nearly 8 percent of the population of the western *Länder*. Despite governmental incentives that encouraged nearly a million of these "guestworkers" (*Gastarbeiter*) to return to their homelands during the mid-1970s

recession, higher wages and the promise of a better life prompted most of them to remain in the FRG.

Many of these guestworkers and their families consider the FRG their home, but it has been anything but a "melting pot." Their experience is not unlike that of black or Hispanic Americans in the United States, or the experience of ethnic minorities in other European states like England and France. Occupying low-status jobs that Germans do not want, they live in culturally isolated urban ghettos marked by substandard housing.[14] Even though millions of guestworkers speak German fluently, send their German-born children to German schools, pay taxes, and have no plans to leave Germany, they are denied the right to vote. For them, regardless of their contribution to the FRG's well-being, citizenship is extremely difficult to secure in a nation that still defines itself largely in ethnocultural terms.

Recent waves of *Aussiedler* have also experienced difficulties in adjusting to German life and society. Although their ethnic German roots were often celebrated by the FRG during the Cold War, many have encountered a cooler reception in the period after the Soviet Union's demise. As in the past, these ethnic Germans are economically disadvantaged, come from culturally diverse backgrounds, and often have little or no knowledge of the German language. The pressures of economic reconstruction have left native Germans somewhat less accommodating.

Additionally, as noted in the section on population, hundreds of thousands of persons seeking asylum in West Germany have been added to this multicultural mix. Their presence has triggered not only acts of violence and terrorism against these "foreign elements" but also an explosive national debate over what to do about the increasing numbers of persons seeking freedom and opportunity in Germany. One recent solution has been intergovernmental agreements providing for the deportation of asylum seekers to their country of origin or other deals encour-

---

[14]See Ray C. Rist, "Migration and Marginality: Guestworkers in Germany and France," *Daedalus* 108 (spring 1979), pp. 95–108.

## A CLOSER LOOK 4.3

### NOT QUITE A MELTING POT

"Sustained and lasting progress in integration is only possible if the number of foreigners living in Germany does not increase in a way which threatens to exhaust the resources of the Federal Republic of Germany. For this reason, the immigration of foreigners from non-EU states is restricted…. [In view of the] poor employment chances of less qualified workers, which look set to remain this way, this policy is very much in the occupational interests of the foreign workers and especially to the young foreigners starting their working lives."

*Source:* German Ministry of the Interior, 2001, at *www.eng.bmi.bund.de/frameset/index.jsp.*

---

aging their return. By 1992, after extreme right-wing parties entered two state parliaments on their antiforeigner platforms, pressure was building to limit the right of asylum and to adopt an American-style system of quotas on immigration to Germany. (For a discussion of immigration and citizenship policy, see Section C.)

## CULTURE: SOCIAL AND CIVIC

### Education and the Media

Reunited Germany boasts high levels of literacy, cultural and educational diversity, and opportunities for personal development and leisure. As in Berlin, parks, sport clubs, museums, public libraries, theaters, choral societies, art galleries, opera houses, and multimillion-member book clubs abound in the country at large. There is also a high consumption rate of media output; book and magazine readership is one of the highest worldwide. In the 1990s, in terms of titles alone, Germany was second only to the United States in book publishing. By 2000, Germany had begun to catch up with the United States in terms of the percentage of Internet users among its population. German news broadcasts were also readily available on the World Wide Web.

In contrast to the United States, however, popular culture has been much more heavily funded since, in line with German state-centered traditions, most theatrical groups, orchestras, and opera houses are government-subsidized. In united Germany, for example, there are more than 100 subsidized opera houses. Hence, one could easily predict in this nation of opera lovers a swift end to any government or to the political career of any politician who would have the temerity to advocate an end to these government subsidies.

The wealth of cultural opportunities in the western *Länder* builds on their efficient and diverse educational system. A common four-year primary system splits at the secondary level into three tracks, almost seeming to mimic the country's historical class structure. These tracks are the five-year continuation of primary school (*Hauptschule*), the six-year intermediate school (*Realschule*), and the nine-year senior grammar school (*Gymnasium*); the former two emphasize preparation for vocational and technical jobs, respectively, while the latter offers the prized opportunity to the relative few, university preparation. Originally based in the classics, the *Gymnasium* offers a tough modern curriculum of arts, languages, mathematics, and science, leading to the famous school-leaving certificate, the *Abitur*. This tripartite system of secondary education has been sharply criticized for its tendency to perpetuate social and class differences. Yet its advocates note that the system has produced the most highly trained and credentialed population in Europe. Almost all nonfarm youth outside the universities are in vocational or technical schools of one kind or another. Fifty-nine percent of all German youth are in school until the age of 18, as opposed to 24 percent in England and 41 percent in France, while 44 percent are licensed to practice a trade or craft as opposed to 20 percent in England, 10 percent in Italy, and 6 percent in Spain.[15]

With the accession of the eastern *Länder* into the Federal Republic, Communist ideological control has predictably ended in the schools and universities of the former GDR, as have the jobs of Communist ideologues in law, the humanities, and social sciences. Following their western counterparts, the *Länder* themselves have taken charge. Religious instruction has been reintroduced, western language education expanded, and the humanities and social sciences reconstituted. Independent schools have reopened and the *Abitur* restored to its pride of place. True, national unification, if steered in a somewhat different direction, could have provided the opportunity to reorganize the entire system of German education on a more egalitarian basis. This strategy might have served to break down remaining class distinctions. However, to the dismay of most eastern German educators and many western critics, this opportunity was lost in the rush to reconstruct the old GDR system on the basis of the West German model alone.

## Religion and the Churches

National unity has affected Germany's religious make-up. With the accession of the five new *Länder,* the relatively equal numbers of Catholics and Protestants of the earlier FRG have been tilted in favor of the Evangelical Lutheran Church. Thus, on the eve of reunification, the FRG counted official religious affiliation among its permanent residents (German and foreign) as roughly 26 million Roman Catholics, 25.75 million Protestants (both Evangelical Lutheran and "Free Church"), 50,000 Jews, 1.5 million Muslims, 1 million members of other religions, and 4 million with no religious affiliation. Figures from the ex-GDR are more difficult to present. For years, the Communist regime was reluctant to admit any significant religious aspiration in a would-be atheist state, and citizens were reluctant to declare a religious identity that would

have reduced them to second-class status at work and in school and barred them from the upper reaches of all professions. Nonetheless, it is clear that what religious activity there was between 1945 and 1989 remained overwhelmingly Protestant. Catholic figures, which remained free of direct government intervention, showed the six bishoprics within the five eastern *Länder* as ministering to only 5 percent of the local population, approximately 800,000 out of 16,000,000 people.

Still, the denominational strife that once buffeted Bismarck's Germany has virtually disappeared, in no small part because new forms of political and social cooperation evolved out of the common struggle of the major churches against the Nazi regime. Even in the purely religious sphere, the major denominations have made great effort to reconcile their differences. An ecumenical high point was the November 1980 meeting of Pope John Paul II with German Protestant leaders in Osnabrück, the site of the signing of the Treaty of Westphalia in 1648, which confirmed the sectarian division of the German lands.

It is difficult to assess the role of religion in contemporary Germany. Figures in the preunification FRG showed a long-term decline in official affiliation. Thus, between 1950 and 1989, the proportion of Catholics decreased slightly from 44.3 to 42.9 percent, while that of Protestants dropped from 51.5 to 42.2 percent. An Allensbach Opinion Research Institute poll conducted in West Germany on the eve of the breaching of the Berlin Wall suggested that this secularization affected not only practice but basic belief. Yet even though formal religious observance in Germany is down, the biennial Catholic and Protestant national "church day" conferences remain well attended and the influence of each denomination within its own worldwide communion remains strong.

The rates of basic religious identification remain high, both in paying the church tax and in choosing a marital partner. The 1989 figures for marrying within one's faith in the preunification FRG showed 68.7 percent for Catholics, 63.0 percent for Protestants, and 32.5 percent for Jews. The social impact of the churches likewise

---

[15]*European Marketing Data and Statistics 1995* (London: Euromonitor International, 1995), p. 411.

remains high. They operate and maintain hospitals, facilities for the handicapped, nursing homes, schools, and large charitable organizations such as the Protestant Diaconal Works and the Catholic Caritas Association.

One distinct fact helps to explain their continued success at such activities. Organized as corporate bodies under public law—a constitutional status carried over from the Weimar period—Germany's organized churches are entitled to state financial support. All wage earners on the official rolls of the main denominations are subject to a church tax equal to about 8 percent of their net tax. A wage earner can escape the tax by formally resigning his or her church membership; by the mid-1990s, around one-half million Protestants and Catholics were doing so every year. Yet many Germans have remained faithful to their obligations. Collected by state revenue officers, these taxes amount to several billion dollars a year and are distributed to the major denominations in amounts proportionate to their total membership. The funds help to pay for ecclesiastical salaries, construction and maintenance, the churches' far-flung social welfare functions, and their immense overseas charitable programs.

This *modus vivendi* between church and state does have critics, both secular and religious. The most radical secular critics fear excessive church influence on politics and would divorce religion altogether from the nation's public life. By contrast, the most radical religious critics see the contemporary church as the captive of the liberal state, having compromised its spiritual mission by adopting middle-class values and copying the latter's bureaucratic forms of organization. They would have the church call society to account for its injustices and hypocrisies, and in the name of faith ally itself with the poor of Germany and the world. Most Germans who have thought about these matters situate themselves between these extremes.

## Political Attitudes and Participation

West Germans were often characterized in the first 20 years of the Federal Republic as voting in high numbers but having little feeling for their new polity. Opinion polls showed that older age groups retained some sympathy for monarchy or dictatorship and that most voters were prouder of their economic system than of its political corollary. Yet by the 1980s these attitudes had changed dramatically. The FRG was a proven success and an increasing percentage of the electorate had grown up in it and come to identify with its procedures and institutions. Nonetheless, there was still something missing. Because of the two world wars and the experience with Nazism, national pride remained well below the average for European Community member states. Reunification in 1990 thus posed two issues: Would the East Germans follow the pattern of quick adaptation to democratic practices and slow internalization of democratic feelings? In the meantime, if unforeseen economic difficulties arose, would West German civic culture now prove to be well enough rooted to weather the storm?

One measure of political democracy is the level of participation in elections. The turn-out rate for federal elections in the FRG began at 78.5 percent in 1949, exceeded a spectacular 90 percent by the 1970s, and then fell to a record low of 77.8 percent in the first all-German election of December 2, 1990. It rose again to 79.0 percent in 1994, and in 1998 it reached an impressive 82.2 percent of eligible voters.

This is a respectable rate of participation for any industrial democracy—and consistently higher than that for U.S. presidential elections. As Section B shows, the results of these elections have given the FRG a highly competitive and relatively stable party system. However, the measure of the health of a civic culture extends beyond formal electoral and institutional arrangements. Since the late 1960s, the FRG has witnessed massive demonstrations against a number of issues—the war in Vietnam, the development of nuclear power, restrictions on university admissions, NATO missiles stationed on German soil, assaults on foreign residents, and airport construction plans that threaten deforestation. These protests and *Bürgerinitiativen* (citizens' initiatives)—rivaled perhaps only by the French—have also championed other forms of democracy, such as referendums and greater popular participation. At times, commentators have asked whether this species of "politics of protest" bespeaks a widening gap between formal democratic institutions and actual grassroots democratic sentiments. For the most part, although very few Germans would support the more violent manifestations of these protests, the consensus seems to be that German democracy is holding together fairly well. Some observers have noted that these demonstrations represent a vital outlet for minority sentiments in their country, an outlet that is perfectly compatible with the functioning of any democracy. Others have contended that they represent an internalization and therefore a triumph of democratic values, while still others have acknowledged that both the Christian Democratic Union (CDU) and the Social Democratic Party (SPD) have successfully remodeled their local party electoral activities along the lines of these same *Bürgerinitiativen*.

In part, the increasingly participatory character of the FRG's civic culture seems related to changes that have taken place in family, school, and society under the impact of advanced industrialization and its accompanying patterns of social stratification—changes likely to be enhanced by the incorporation of the ex-GDR's socialist egalitarian values into the FRG. The entrance of housewives into the labor market, the separation of family and workplace, increased social mobility and income, and the enormous expansion of communications have loosened up old authoritarian structures such as the male-dominated family and the traditional school curriculum. Additionally, important instruments of socialization, such as the family and the schools, appear increasingly to promote values that are more consistent than in the past with the regime's formal values of human dignity, mutual respect and cooperation, and the pragmatic adjustment of social conflict. Generational change has also been an important source of political socialization. By the 1980 federal election, western Germany's postwar generation constituted 48.8 percent of the population and 25.5 percent of adult voters. For them, the liberal-

Supporters of the former Communist Party, the Party of Democratic Socialism (PDS) at the German election in October 1994. The PDS received 4.4 percent of the vote, thus falling below the 5 percent threshold. But it obtained 30 seats in the Bundestag because it won four directly elected seats in East Berlin.

democratic FRG was the only political and social order they had ever known. As a consequence of all these factors, while German citizens might be expected, from time to time, to challenge the political practices of one or another government, it is now reasonable to claim that the FRG's democratic system should be in the position to survive any serious threats to its authority.

## Politics and Literature: A Footnote

When unified in 1871, Germany had a humanist tradition characterized by the genius of Goethe and Schiller, renaissance men of letters and civic leadership. Yet the predominant cultural expression of the Wilhelmine and Weimar years was one of flight from political affairs as many representatives of the rising bourgeois classes retreated into an "inner freedom" or strictly private and apathetic culture. Without a strong middle class to provide an alternative political vision, persons already in authority were left to conduct public affairs as they saw fit, to define the aims and limits of state power, and to suggest, albeit broadly, the proper form and content of culture.

The works of Hermann Hesse (1877–1962), such as the novel *Siddhartha* (1922), still a favorite at many American colleges, continued the age-old inquiry into the Germanic conflict between Nature and Spirit. But they also did so in the relatively new form of stressing the need for personal, rather than communal or authoritarian, responsibility in selecting values. With Thomas Mann (1875–1955), this need was cast against the backdrop of the violent currents sweeping Germanic society: the degeneration of the great nineteenth-century mercantile order in *Buddenbrooks* (1901), the quest for regeneration and personal understanding through flight from society and its conventions in *The Magic Mountain* (1924), and the descent of artistic creativity into the demonic in *Doctor Faustus* (1947). More than anyone else, Mann gave expression to the struggle between the power and the subtle pessimism of *Germanism.*

During the life of the Federal Republic, the works of Günter Grass, such as *The Tin Drum* (1963), were especially noteworthy for their inquiry into how German culture had fallen into National Socialism and also what should be retrieved and replanted from the ashes it left in 1945. As we saw earlier, Grass opposed German reunification until the very end, claiming that Germany lacked a sense of responsibility before history and might have served as a beacon for spiritual renewal and the deflation of purely national aspirations.[16] The work of Heinrich Böll (1917–1985) was also popular. His novel *The Clown* (1963) portrayed a sense of the intrinsic worth and redemptive possibilities of life. More recently, a postunification literature has begun to appear as authors such as Martin Walser (*Die Verteidigung der Kindheit,* 1991) and Helga Königsdorf (*Im Schatten des Regenbogen,* 1993) seek to describe and to reflect on the painful changes and disorientation many East Germans have experienced since the collapse of the Berlin Wall. On the western side of the old German divide, Bernhard Schlink, a noted legal scholar, showed that his generation continues to be preoccupied with the memory of the Holocaust by publishing an allegorical novel about the subject. In *The Reader* (*Der Leser,* 1996), which received widespread attention not only in Germany but also in the United States, a young boy is swept into a love affair with an older woman (possibly Germany?) with a secret past. When it is revealed in the book that the woman was once a guard at a concentration camp, the boy is thrown into all the personal turmoil and anguish of anyone who must balance his love for an individual with his recognition of that person's guilt. Yet provocatively in view of its message for Germany, the book leaves open the possibility of reconciliation between the two persons.

In this way, where humanism temporarily failed Germany in the nineteen-century, history—and perhaps now the healing powers of national unification—may have begun to show the German people a path to normalcy. In the wake of two world wars and two major dictatorships, Germans have at least abandoned the turn to "inner freedom" and its concomitant neglect of public

---

[16]Günter Grass, *Two States—One Nation?* Trans. Krishna Winston and A. S. Wensinger (New York: Harcourt Brace, 1990), pp. 12–14.

cultural and civic responsibilities that led to such disastrous consequences. They have acknowledged Hesse's point that responsibility is personal and that, with time, it may have a redemptive effect on the whole human community. Arguably more self-consciously than any other Europeans, the Germans continue to question their values. Some observers will say this is because only the Germans have such a tortuous past to overcome. But this inclination may also have a positive side. By preventing them from taking anything for granted, it can help to extend the breadth and depth of their pluralist democracy.

## CONCLUSION

This section has traced Germany's development from a class-based feudal society into a modernized postindustrial order now completed by the accession of the nation's eastern *Länder* into the FRG. The FRG's economy, even before the incorporation of the ex-GDR, was among the richest in the world. Notwithstanding pockets of poverty, measurable discrimination against ethnic minorities, and most daunting, the massive reconstruction and clean-up of the east, the country's social system is marked by extremely high levels of economic security and welfare benefits. Finally, the political system created under the 1949 Basic Law, together with its liberal values, has been a congenial framework for the development of a social market economy. Both the system's durability in the west and its growing acceptance in the east augur well for the future.

Likewise, religious divisions are no longer readily apparent in either part of the reunited country. Also, traditional class and economic divisions have given way to the rise in the west of a new middle class of white-collar employees and professionals generated by ever-expanding service industries and technological enterprises. Western business managers, industrial trainers, and university professors hope to replicate their success in the east. Although some young people and intellectuals continue to reproach their leaders for allowing their society to sink into materialism, most Germans are no different from other Europeans, especially those recently liberated

from Communism. They are by no means willing to forego the manifest advantages of their social and economic system. On the contrary, the more likely challenge for the coming decade will be to redistribute wealth and well-being so as to convince their compatriots in the east that both parts of the nation will share equally in the benefits of unification. Germany has put its political and religious divisions behind it. As it enters the twenty-first century, it must resolve to complete the same process socially and economically.

## *Thinking Critically*

1. What political, social, and economic factors made Germany's adoption of democratic institutions and values in the twentieth century so difficult?
2. How did Hitler's "social revolution" and Germany's physical destruction after World War II ironically contribute to the country's remarkable transformation over the second half of the twentieth century?
3. How will German society change in coming years as a result of its shifting immigration and demographic patterns?
4. What are the characteristics of postindustrialism in Germany? What impact will this socioeconomic trend have on future politics in the FRG?
5. How successful was German reunification in the 1990s? Will the challenge of integrating eastern and western Germany into one united whole continue to be a problem?
6. How successful has Germany been in providing equal social and economic opportunities for all people who live within its geographic boundaries?

## KEY TERMS

*Abitur (197)*
accession *(180)*
Basic Law *(180, 184)*
*Bürgerinitiativen (199, 200)*
church tax *(199)*
deutsche mark *(186)*

Federal Republic of Germany (FRG) *(180)*
German Democratic Republic (GDR) *(180)*
guestworkers *(196)*
inner freedom *(201, 202)*
*Länder (184–185)*
North German Confederation *(181)*
reunification *(184)*
social market economy *(186–187)*
Treaty of Versailles *(182)*
Weimar Republic *(182)*

# FURTHER READINGS

## *History and People*

Barraclough, Geoffrey. *The Origins of Modern Germany* (New York: Capricorn Books, 1963).

Craig, Gordon. *The Germans* (New York: Putnam, 1982).

Elias, Norbert. *The Germans,* trans. Eric Dunning and Stephen Mennell (New York: Columbia University Press, 1997).

Koch, H. W. *A Constitutional History of Germany in the Nineteenth and Twentieth Centuries* (London: Longman, 1984).

Pachter, Henry M. *Modern Germany: A Social, Cultural, and Political History* (Boulder, CO: Westview Press, 1978).

Peukert, Detlev K. *The Weimar Republic.* (New York: Hill and Wang, 1987).

Pinson, Koppel S. *Modern Germany,* 2nd ed. (New York: Macmillan, 1966).

Schulze, Hagen. *Germany: A New History* (Cambridge, MA: Harvard University Press, 1998).

Stern, Fritz. *The Politics of Cultural Despair* (Berkeley: University of California Press, 1961).

## *Third Reich*

Bracher, Karl Dietrich. *The German Dictatorship* (New York: Praeger, 1970).

Dawidowicz, Lucy S. *The War against the Jews* (New York: Holt, Rinehart and Winston, 1975).

Gallagher, Hugh G. *By Trust Betrayed* (New York: Henry Holt, 1990).

Müller, Ingo. *Hitler's Justice* (Cambridge, MA: Harvard University Press, 1991).

Snyder, Louis L., ed. *Hitler's Third Reich: A Documentary History* (Chicago: Nelson-Hall, 1981).

## *Federal Republic*

Bork, Dennis L., and David R. Gress. *A History of West Germany,* Vols. 1 and 2 (Oxford: Basil Blackwell, 1989).

Conradt, David P. *The German Polity,* 7th ed. (New York: Longman, 2001).

Jones, Larry E. *German Liberalism and the Dissolution of the Weimar Party System, 1918–1933* (Chapel Hill: University of North Carolina Press, 1988).

Junker, Detlev, et al., eds. *Cornerstone of Democracy: The West German Grundgesetz, 1949–1989* (Washington, DC: German Historical Institute, Occasional Paper No. 13, 1995).

Merritt, Richard L. *Democracy Imposed: U.S. Occupation Policy and the German Public, 1945–1949* (New Haven, CT: Yale University Press, 1995).

Roskamp, Karl W. *Capital Formation in West Germany* (Detroit: Wayne State University Press, 1965).

Smith, Eric Owen. *The German Economy* (London: Routledge, 1994).

Spotts, Frederic. *The Churches and Politics in Germany* (Middletown, CT: Wesleyan University Press, 1973).

## *German Reunification*

Garton Ash, Timothy. *In Europe's Name* (New York: Vintage Books, 1993).

Grass, Günter. *Two States—One Nation?* trans. Krishna Winston and A. S. Wensinger (New York: Harcourt Brace, 1990).

Hancock, Donald M., and Helga A. Welsh, eds. *German Unification: Process and Outcomes* (Boulder, CO: Westview Press, 1994).

James, Harold, and Marla Stone, eds. *When the Wall Came Down* (New York: Routledge, 1992).

Maier, Charles S. *Dissolution* (Princeton, NJ: Princeton University Press, 1997).

McAdams, A. James. *Germany Divided: From the Wall to Reunification* (Princeton, NJ: Princeton University Press, 1994).

Quint, Peter. *The Constitutional Law of German Unification* (Princeton, NJ: Princeton University Press, 1996).

Wallach, Peter H. G., and Ronald A. Francisco. *United Germany* (Westport, CT: Praeger, 1992).

# B. POLITICAL PROCESSES AND INSTITUTIONS

## POLITICAL PARTIES

The Federal Republic of Germany has long been described as a two and one-half party system. For at least the first 30 years of West Germany's existence, social and political circumstances combined to facilitate a remarkable degree of continuity in the parties representing the German population. In the first national election, held in 1949, the three most popular parties—the Christian Democratic Union (CDU) and its Bavarian affiliate, the Christian Social Union (CSU); the Social Democratic Party (SPD); and the Free Democratic Party (FDP)—captured 72.1 percent of the total votes. By the 1970s, these same parties commanded the support of virtually the entire West German electorate.

In 1987, only two years before unification, the three parties still managed to win 90.4 percent of the vote (a drop from their total of 98.0 percent in 1980). But there were already signs that the party landscape was being shaken up. In 1983, a fourth party, the radical-environmentalist Greens, entered parliament for the first time since 1949. Even more surprising, the postunification elections of 1990 and 1994 resulted in the entry of a fifth party—the ex-GDR's old Socialist Unity Party (SED) now recast as the Party of Democratic Socialism (PDS)—into the national parliament. In this sense, national unification had altered German politics, at least for the time being. The established parties would have to devise strategies to recapture the allegiance of voters attracted by the upstarts. Then too, the presence of new parties in the national legislature would complicate the creation and maintenance of stable governing coalitions. But as we shall see, German democracy would prove capable of surviving these tests.

By the federal elections of 1994, observers wondered whether the Greens would replace the FDP as the balance wheel and "kingmaker" in the Bundestag. Yet the three traditional parties still managed to receive 84.8 percent of all votes cast, one sign of the remarkable continuity of German politics. This continuity—and stability—has often been traced to the Federal Election Act's 5 percent clause. Enacted early on to avoid fragmenting the electorate, the act grants parliamentary representation only to those parties securing 5 percent or more of the votes cast in a national election or at least three single-member district seats. The 5 percent rule has kept numerous splinter parties out of parliament over the years, thus avoiding the coalition instability that might otherwise have arisen. This bit of institutional engineering shows that given the right set of circumstances, election rules can effectively channel political activity in predetermined directions.

### Christian Democrats

The first party to rise to prominence in postwar German politics was the CDU. The CDU (*Christlich Demokratische Union*) was founded in 1945 as a result of the collaboration of old Center Party Catholics with liberal and conservative Protestants who had been members of other pre-1933 political parties. These groups were broadly inspired by Christian principles and the desire to present a strong united front against Leftism. But most indicative of the party's innovative style was that its founders deliberately steered away from the sectarian and dogmatic policies that had led to the ruin of the Weimar Republic. Under the canny direction of the FRG's first chancellor, Konrad Adenauer (ex-mayor of Cologne and Germany's wiliest politician since Bismarck), the CDU was cast as a modern catch-all party, espousing pragmatic values and seeking to gain the support of a majority of the German electorate. So successful was this appeal during the FRG's first two decades that the CDU would represent nearly every major occupational and class grouping in the country and completely dominate West German politics (see Table 4.4).

The party's leadership after Adenauer, however, was not nearly as capable, contributing to declining membership and its first loss of national power in 1969. As part of its recovery program, the CDU launched a major membership drive in the 1970s, leading once again to a larger—and

**TABLE 4.4**

**BUNDESTAG SEATS OCCUPIED BY THE CDU/CSU AND SPD, FEDERAL ELECTIONS, 1949–1998**

| Year | CDU/CSU (%) | Seats | SPD (%) | Seats | Total Seats |
|------|-------------|-------|---------|-------|-------------|
| 1949 | 31.0 | 139 | 29.2 | 131 | 402 |
| 1953 | 45.2 | 243 | 28.8 | 151 | 487 |
| 1957 | 50.2 | 270 | 31.8 | 169 | 497 |
| 1961 | 45.3 | 242 | 36.2 | 190 | 499 |
| 1965 | 47.6 | 245 | 39.8 | 202 | 496 |
| 1969 | 46.1 | 242 | 42.7 | 224 | 496 |
| 1972 | 44.9 | 225 | 45.8 | 230 | 496 |
| 1976 | 48.6 | 243 | 42.6 | 214 | 496 |
| 1980 | 44.5 | 226 | 42.9 | 218 | 497 |
| 1983 | 48.8 | 244 | 38.2 | 193 | 498 |
| 1987 | 44.3 | 223 | 37.0 | 186 | 497 |
| 1990 | 43.8 | 313 | 33.5 | 239 | 662 |
| 1994 | 41.5 | 294 | 36.4 | 252 | 672 |
| 1998 | 35.2 | 245 | 40.9 | 298 | 669 |

*Sources:* Peter Schindler, *Datenbuch zur Geschichte der Deutschen Bundestages 1949 bis 1982,* 4th ed. (Baden-Baden: Nomos Verlag, 1984), pp. 34–48; *Statistisches Jahrbuch 1991 für das Vereinte Deutschland,* p. 101; and *Statistisches Jahrbuch für die Bundesrepublik Deutschland 1995; Federal Election Results, 1998,* American Institute for Contemporary German Studies.

much more diverse—membership. Not coincidentally, the 1980s saw the party's return to power under the leadership of Helmut Kohl, a man whom few people were likely to credit with great charisma yet who somehow rallied his party to stunning victories from 1983 onward. Kohl loved to say about his own management instincts that he made his career on being underestimated. His leadership talents were never more evident than in his skillful role in spearheading the drive for German unification—a feat that led to his reelection in 1990 as the first freely chosen chancellor of *all* the German people since 1932.

The CDU's adaptability since the FRG's founding has partly been due to its different constituent groups. Christian social pressures within the party, particularly in its early years, long supported progressive policies such as government-sponsored savings programs and subsidized housing. Yet over time, the party's increasingly prominent business, industrial, and middle-class constituencies have led it to support policies favoring free-market economics. In recent years, the party has favored tax and spending cuts as well as government deregulation as a means of boosting an economy overburdened by the cost of unification. Outside the economic realm, the party has emphasized traditional moral values with a heavy accent on law and order. Internally, the CDU has often defended the FRG's federal structure against the centralizing influences of the national government. In foreign policy, it has been an ardent supporter of both the Atlantic Alliance and diverse efforts at European unification. In particular, the German-French axis has long been regarded as a key to European political and economic integration.

## Social Democrats

The SPD (*Sozialdemokratische Partei Deutschlands*), one of the largest mass-membership parties in Europe, can trace its roots back to the General Workingman's Association founded in

1863 by the brilliant young radical Ferdinand Lassalle. The first party to organize the working masses on a large scale, the SPD of Imperial Germany won the votes of the emerging industrial proletariat and moved on from that popular base to share power in 7 of the Weimar Republic's 21 governing coalitions.

Unlike the CDU, the Social Democrats were slower to recognize the virtues of identifying themselves with the nonideological orientation of a modern catch-all party. When the party reorganized after World War II, it failed to expand its influence much beyond the industrial working class. For almost a decade, it remained a staunchly left-wing party, openly embracing socialism and calling into question much of the Adenauer government's unabashedly pro-Atlantic and pro-European policies. This stance may have satisfied the dogmatic purists within the SPD, but to the evident satisfaction of its Christian Democratic opponents, it did not win the party any more votes. As a result, when more pragmatic elements gained the upper hand in the party leadership, like Herbert Wehner and the young Willy Brandt, its policies changed accordingly. At an historic meeting in 1959, with the passage of the famed *Godesberg Platform,* the Social Democrats finally embraced the social market economy and the basic outlines of Adenauer's foreign policy. Overnight, the SPD shed the more rigid aspects of its Marxist heritage and transformed itself from a narrow ideological party into a broadly based and pragmatic popular party.

The strategy worked. The party was able to diversify its membership by attracting more white-collar, middle-class members, and by 1966 had wide enough support to become part of a governing coalition with the CDU/CSU. After this achievement, beginning in 1969, the SPD went on, with the help of the Free Democratic Party, to elect the chancellor in four consecutive national elections. For a short period, during the 1980s, the SPD lurched abruptly back to the Left, largely as a result of internal disputes over foreign affairs and growing dissatisfaction with Western (especially American) defense policy. Perceived by voters as faction-ridden, impractical, and unfit to govern, it languished at the polls. In 1989 and 1990, in particular, the SPD blundered by seeming to oppose the immediate reunification of Germany. This costly mistake allowed Chancellor Kohl to seize the initiative and ride to yet another victory in 1990 on the CDU's speeding "unity now" train.

During the early 1990s, as the party struggled to find its way back to power, the SPD went through another series of leadership changes. The Left-leaning, minister-president of Saarland, Oscar Lafontaine, was induced to step down from his post as party chairman after the SPD's election defeat in 1990. The party then turned to Björn Engholm, the pipe-smoking and laid-back centrist minister-president of Schleswig-Holstein, who took on the challenge of ushering the Social Democrats back to the political mainstream until his sudden demise in 1993, following his admission of having given false testimony in a *Land* election scandal. Rudolf Scharping, minister-president of Rhineland-Palatinate, succeeded Engholm as party chairman. Young, intelligent, and tastefully bearded, he projected a professorial image and, given the state of public opinion polls, looked like a sure bet to emerge as chancellor in 1994. However, once again, public opinion experts underestimated Helmut Kohl's skills as a political manager. His reputation as an effective leader appeared to play a significant role in CDU/CSU–FDP victory, albeit by a single vote in the German parliament. Finally, in need of more dynamic and aggressive leadership in the face of rising unemployment and other economic problems arising out of reunification, the SPD desperately turned again, in 1995, to Lafontaine, expecting him to unify the party and produce the magic that would lead to victory in 1998. Yet surprisingly, as we shall elaborate momentarily, it was not Lafontaine but a younger and ostensibly new type of Social Democrat, Gerhard Schröder, who proved to have the mettle and the political instincts to succeed at this task.

## Free Democrats

The FDP (*Freie Demokratische Partei*), founded in 1945, is the modern counterpart of the older German liberal parties. Although considerably smaller than the CDU or SPD, the FDP is the third party to have played a consistently influential role in postwar German politics. It is the only minor party to have survived the 5 percent clause in all federal elections (although just barely in 1998), and it has determined the governing coalition in 10 out of 14 such elections. The FDP's success has in large part been a reflection of its leaders' tactical flexibility. Until 1966, it was allied with the CDU, then from 1969 to 1982 with the SPD, and from 1983 through 1994 with the CDU again. Drawing its support primarily from business people, professionals, and the secular middle classes, the FDP has profited by profiling itself as a traditional liberal party, one that stands for free enterprise and individual self-determination in all areas of social life. Thus, it has quarreled with the CDU over foreign policy and with the SPD over spending and social programs, and it has taken strong, independent stands on issues such as education reform, abortion, and church taxes. Because it has so often controlled the fate of governing coalitions, the FDP's impact on German politics has consistently far outweighed its smaller numbers, and it has used its leverage to gain important government positions—on two occasions even capturing the federal presidency.

## Splinter Parties

In addition to the three long-established parties, Germany has for years witnessed the rise and fall of numerous splinter parties. In the FRG's first few decades, the most successful of these parties seemed to predominate on the far right of the political spectrum, such as the chauvinistic National Democratic Party and, later, the *Republikaner*. Both of these parties were identified most conspicuously with their campaigns to rid Germany of its large foreign population. By exploiting the fears of the most vulnerable sectors of the electorate, especially in times of economic downturn, these parties have occasionally managed to surmount the minimum electoral hurdle (5 percent) required to gain entry into various *Land* parliaments. On the whole, however, these successes have been short-lived. Right-wing splinter parties have turned out to be localized movements with programmatically untenable platforms, and they have rarely won more than 1 percent of the national vote. The story is rather different for splinter parties on the left.

## Greens

It should not be surprising that experts were initially inclined to regard Germany's Left-leaning Greens, which began their ascent to prominence in the late 1970s, as having no better prospects than a typical splinter party. Representing a loose alliance of ecological, antinuclear, and peace groups and disgruntled Social Democrats, the Greens gradually emerged on the German scene in the wake of the student protests of the 1960s and the failed terror campaigns of the 1970s. They were something entirely new for German politics, a Left libertarian party committed to nonviolent methods of protest, which rejected politics as usual and envisioned nothing less than the total transformation of society. Popular with young voters, feminists, and middle-class environmentalists, the Greens accomplished a feat that had long eluded the traditional splinter parties of the Right. In 1983, they shocked the political establishment by attaining 5.6 percent of the national vote and hence earning 34 seats in the Bundestag. Blustery and often disdainful of formal rules of procedure, the Greens prided themselves on being the "anti-party" party. They declared war on the "bourgeois-democratic state," and sought to revitalize grassroots democracy by insisting that their representatives rotate in office and abide by the orders of their local constituencies. They also prided themselves on creating symbolically charged public spectacles, bringing live trees into debates in the Bundestag and, to the consternation of conservative parliamentarians, refusing to wear suits and ties!

After the 1987 election, when they bettered their previous success by winning 8.3 percent of the vote, the Greens began to run into the problems facing any typical protest party. Some of the party's members, the so-called *Fundis* (fundamentalists) insisted that they should brook no compromises in adhering to their original values, even if this rigidity should cost them votes at election time. In contrast, another wing of the party, the *Realos* (realists) questioned this dogmatism, wondering how the party was to survive, let alone bring its policies to fruition, if it failed to find enough loyal voters to return it to office. Slowly, the party's *Realo* wing gained the upper hand in these debates (although never decisively), and the Greens transformed themselves into a more pragmatic party willing to cooperate with other parties in achieving their aims. Having failed to clear the 5 percent hurdle in 1990, in part as a consequence of their internal squabbles, the Greens merged with Alliance 90 (*Bundnis 90*), an East German party consisting largely of citizens-rights groups that helped to topple the old GDR's Communist government. Winning 7.3 percent of the votes in 1994, Alliance 90/Greens, as the party now called itself, entered parliament with 49 seats, but interestingly, nearly all of its popular votes came from the western *Länder*. The party's postindustrial emphasis on environmental and lifestyle issues had little appeal for eastern Germans worried about unemployment and other material concerns. But this time around, undoubtedly because of the party's willingness to portray itself as a modern party of the middle, western voters proved more supportive of its programs. The prize for this conciliatory attitude, as we shall see shortly, was the Greens' inclusion in the governing coalition in 1998.

## Party of Democratic Socialism (PDS)

According to most experts in 1990, it was inconceivable that the Party of Democratic Socialism (PDS), the successor to East Germany's old Socialist Unity Party (SED), would long survive the fall of Communism. With the implosion of the GDR, the party's membership dropped from 800,000 to 320,000 in 1990 alone, and to 130,000 in 1994. Yet to the astonishment of most observers, this renamed party was able to define a distinctive role for itself in reunified Germany by campaigning for a reformed version of socialism with a human face. In 1994, although the party failed to win the necessary 5 percent of the national vote, it was still awarded 30 seats in the Bundestag by virtue of winning four single-member districts in East Berlin. Then, in 1998, it just exceeded the 5 percent hurdle and received 36 (later, 37) parliamentary seats.

In retrospect, it is clear why the PDS was able to carve out a semblance of political credibility with certain segments of the electorate. Although many of its early leaders and members were old SED comrades, the party was quickly able to attract voters from a much wider and younger segment of the electorate. While the ex-GDR's old managerial and professional elite were unification's losers and therefore had nowhere else to turn, the PDS's leaders proved skilled in gaining the support of thousands of ordinary easterners who, for one reason or another, were displeased with the course of unification. Many were angered by the seemingly arrogant behavior of their western "colonizers" and by the rapidity with which they were supposedly destroying values, such as solidarity and egalitarianism, romantically associated with the tradition of democratic socialism. Others were simply alienated as a result of the debilitating consequences

**A CLOSER LOOK**

**4.4**

### THE PDS TAKES ROOT

"In their hearts [many older persons] clung to [socialist] values that in their heads they thought to be superannuated. It is precisely this gap between heart and head upon which the PDS has been able to build its nest. That is, the party appeals neither purely to easterners' nostalgia for the past nor to their rational self-interest in the redistribution conflicts of unification. Instead, it reflects their ambivalence about the past and present.... The PDS has succeeded in positioning itself as the defender of this eastern desire to maintain biographical continuity without threatening to disrupt seriously the ongoing integration process."

*Source:* Lawrence H. McFalls, "Political Culture: Partisan Strategies, and the PDS: Prospects for an East German Party," *German Politics and Society* 13 (1995), p. 55.

of economic reconstruction in the East, mass unemployment, and general insecurity.

The PDS was able to take advantage of all of these currents of displeasure and uncertainty to elude the fate of most small parties in the past. In 1998, it achieved its first major success above the municipal level when it was invited by the SPD to form a coalition government in the eastern *Land* of Mecklenburg–West Pomerania. Of even greater proportions, however, was the successful conclusion of coalition negotiations between the PDS and the SPD in December 2001 about governing the *Land* of Berlin, after the SPD's attempts to create a "traffic light" coalition with the FDP and the Greens had broken down. Thanks to the PDS's strong appeal to voters in Berlin's eastern half, it seemed that even the reform Communists had found a measure of legitimacy in the German political system.

## Party Organization

One reason for the historical continuity and stability in Germany's parties, as well as for subtle differences among them, is their success in capturing and channeling popular opinion. The major parties are formally organized at the federal, *Land,* and precinct levels. The CDU bears the imprint of the FRG's federalized structure, with organizational power residing in the party's 13 *Land* associations. Like the American Republican and Democratic Parties, the CDU is a loosely structured party held together by a coalition of interests with a common goal of winning elections. The SPD, on the other hand, is a mass-organized party under a centralized leadership that is served by a large and disciplined core of full-time professionals who are in charge of various district parties (*Bezirksparteien*). The relative power and autonomy of the district associations have permitted the development of strong regional leaders whose views the national leadership cannot ignore with impunity.

The highest formal authority in each party is the national party convention held every two years—although the FDP meets annually—consisting of delegates elected mainly by *Land,* district, and county associations. The convention sets the general outlines of policy, votes on organizational

matters, and elects a national executive committee consisting of the party chairperson, several deputy chairpersons, secretary general, treasurer, and other elected members. At the national level, the SPD's organizational chart also includes a large party council, consisting of *Land* and local party leaders, and a nine-member presidium to supervise the work of the party executive committee.

Parties are such an important part of policy making in the FRG that the Basic Law (Article 21) actually recognizes a privileged role for them in the inculcation and articulation of democratic values. This role has been reaffirmed by the Political Parties Act of 1967. Apart from provisions on the disclosure of finances, the act largely codifies existing party practices and procedures, many of them prescribed in decisions of the Federal Constitutional Court. This act provides for a host of measures to safeguard internal party democracy: (1) the right of all members to vote for party convention delegates; (2) the right of such delegates to vote on party guidelines and programs; (3) a secret ballot for the election of party officers, who must be elected every two years; (4) a reasonable balance of *ex officio* and elected members on the party executive committee; and (5) a written arbitration procedure for the resolution of intraparty disputes.

## Party Finance

Unlike the United States, where parties have traditionally been weak organizations, Germany's parties have, at least since Bismarck's time, consistently been able to count upon strong support from their members and the state itself. One key source of support has been in funding. The parties receive their funds from a wide variety of sources, including public subsidies, private donations, receipts from party events and publications, and contributions from individual members and members of parliament. As Table 4.5 shows, some funding comes from their respective constituencies. As a mass-organized party, the SPD relies mainly on membership dues, whereas the CSU and the FDP have relied heavily on donations from corporations and other private groups. These emphases have shifted over time. Private contributions filled the CDU's coffers during the

**TABLE 4.5**

**PARTY FINANCES, 1999 (DM MILLIONS)**

| Party | Public Subsidies | Donations | Membership | Total Income |
|-------|-----------------|-----------|------------|--------------|
| SPD | 93.9 | 33.7 | 157.5 | 285.1 |
| CDU | 76.6 | 65.3 | 105.3 | 247.2 |
| CSU | 18.9 | 15.3 | 19.8 | 54.0 |
| FDP | 13.4 | 19.3 | 10.8 | 43.5 |
| Greens | 17.0 | 10.1 | 20.9 | 48.0 |
| PDS | 14.5 | 7.5 | 17.5 | 39.5 |

*Source:* Figures based upon *Deutscher Bundestag: Parteifinanzierung,* at *www.bundestag.de/datbk/finanz/pf_einnahmen.htm.*

Adenauer years, but as a result of the party's membership drive in the 1970s, when it first experienced financial difficulties, it began to catch up with the SPD in dues-paying members.

An even greater source of funding over time has been the German state. The state began to reimburse the parties for their election campaign costs in 1959. By 1990, their election campaign costs exceeded DM 400 million, representing approximately 5 DM ($3.13) for each second-ballot vote cast, an amount divided among the parties proportionate to each party's total vote. In a series of decisions, the Federal Constitutional Court has handed down rulings to ensure that the funding provisions treat all parties fairly. In 1968, the court ruled that any party receiving as little as 0.5 percent of the vote is constitutionally entitled to state support at the rate, per voter, established by federal law. The original purpose behind state funding was to help the parties compete on a more equal basis and to liberate them from the excessive influence of interest groups. Yet in the late 1970s, as the cost of campaigning skyrocketed, numerous illegal campaign finance practices dominated the news. In 1983, the Bundestag enacted a legislative reform package to put a stop to practices that deliberately circumvent the law (*Umwegfinanzierung*).[17]

---

[17]This section on party financing relies heavily on Arthur B. Gunlicks, "Campaigns and Party Finance in the West German 'Party State,'" *Review of Politics* 50 (Winter 1988), pp. 30–48.

Unable any longer to distinguish adequately between legitimate campaign costs and other party expenditures, a Constitutional Court judgment of April 9, 1992, declared major parts of the existing party finance law unconstitutional and ordered the German parliament to enact a new law. Initiated by the Greens, the case was decided against the backdrop of declining party membership and the increasing public perception that the parties were more interested in shoring up their power than in caring for the public interest. To encourage the parties to revitalize their ossified structures, increase their membership, and raise more funds on a voluntary basis, the court ruled that state subsidies and reimbursements may not exceed the amount of funds the parties raise by themselves. Then, on January 1, 1994, a new law was put into effect by the Bundestag. This statute regularized the distribution of public funds according to a revised standard, the extent to which a given party was institutionalized within society. By measuring institutionalization in terms of two factors—party performance in a variety of recent elections and the combination of membership dues and donations—parliamentarians hoped they had a fair and just means for allocating scarce public resources. Yet even with new legislation, some party leaders could not resist the temptation to cut corners. In 1999, Helmut Kohl was caught up in a well-publicized party finance scandal when he and other prominent CDU representatives were accused of maintaining secret bank accounts in Switzerland in order to fund party activities; they were also implicated in kickback schemes involving military sales and the restructuring of East German industry.

## INTEREST GROUPS

German constitutional theory regards political parties as the chief agencies of political representation, providing the vital link between state and society that facilitates effective majority rule. In reality, public policy results from the complex interplay of political parties and private interests who seek special favors from the government. This factor too is an important source of political stability in the FRG. Hundreds of national associations, ranging from recreational and fraternal to economic and professional groups, maintain offices and highly skilled professional staffs in the capital on a year-round basis. For decades, Bonn was the site of most lobbying activity because of the central importance of federal executive agencies in making public policy, and now this function has been assumed by Germany's new capital, Berlin.

Contact between interest-group representatives and public officials in the FRG is much more direct and formal than in many other other advanced democracies. This is largely a vestige of the German corporatist tradition that goes back to Bismarck's efforts to preserve political calm during Germany's initial unification in the 1870s. Under corporatist arrangements, the support of major social and economic interests, like trade unions and business associations, is guaranteed by giving them a direct stake in all decisions of consequence to the country's political welfare and its economy. These groups are represented on forums as diverse as ministerial advisory councils, agency consultative committees, regional planning councils, public broadcasting stations, and the parliamentary study groups of the political parties. Additionally, federal ministerial officials meet on a regular basis behind closed doors with the top representatives of industry, banking, agriculture, and labor for the purpose of coordinating national economic policy. Also, the quasi-official compulsory-membership trade and professional associations are still other examples of direct interest-group influence on public policy.

The link between organized interests and Germany's political parties is equally firm. Far more than in the United States, these interests are actually represented by their functionaries in the national and parliamentary parties (*Fraktionen*). Representatives of business, religious, agricultural, and refugee organizations have been conspicuous among CDU/CSU members of parliament, while not surprisingly, trade union officials are to be found in SPD leadership positions at all levels of party organization. Members of parliament associated with trade unions, business associations, and other organized interests actually dominate the membership of parliamentary committees such as labor, social policy, food, agriculture, and forestry.

This complex web of public and private interlocking directorates has prompted political scientist Peter Katzenstein to characterize the FRG as a "semisovereign state."[18] In Katzenstein's view, the FRG is semisovereign because, unlike a country like the United States which has more clearly set lines of demarcation between public and private authority, the central state in Germany shares its sovereignty with private centers of power and influence. In this conception, popular elections do not empower the victors to change policy in strict accordance with an electoral mandate. Rather, politics by consensus is the norm in Germany, a norm promoted by the regular practice of formalized cooperation between a decentralized government and highly centralized private interest associations. Thus "incrementalism rather than large-scale policy change typifies West German politics,"[19] a reality that helps to explain the stability of the FRG's political system as well as the frustration felt by those citizens who believe the system is insulated and biased against change.

---

[18]See Peter J. Katzenstein, *Policy and Politics in West Germany* (Philadelphia: Temple University Press, 1987), p. 10.
[19]Ibid., p. 362.

## Citizen Initiatives (*Bürgerinitiativen*)

The sudden appearance on the political scene of urban and rural protest groups in the 1970s and 1980s was one sign that some Germans were not happy with the inherently conservative tendencies of the political structure. Tens of thousands of German citizens staged protest rallies involving quality of life issues such as nuclear power plant construction, urban renewal, air and water pollution, new highway construction, and the cost of inner-city transportation. Their grassroots activism—protest marches, letter-writing campaigns, petition gathering, sit-ins, and other forms of spontaneous action—expressed the disenchantment felt by many citizens with the lack of responsiveness of mainstream political parties, private corporations, and official bureaucracies. These efforts were most effective at the local level, resulting in the rollback of some public transportation prices, delays in the building of nuclear power plants, and the postponement of official decisions to cut new highways through certain residential and open areas.

This culture of autonomous protest precipitated the formation and eventual electoral successes of an alternative party like the Greens. However, as a sign of the robustness of the German political system, the more mainstream parties soon recognized that they could not afford to ignore these extra-systemic protests for long. Notably, the CDU and the SPD took action on citizens' disenchantment by making the *Bürgerinitiativen* models for their local party interelection activities. Both parties were also quick to see the electoral advantage of adopting many of the alternative groups' policies (e.g., on environmental protection and gender equality) as their own.

## Major Interest Aggregations

*Business*    The three largest business associations in the FRG are the German Federation of Industry (BDI), the Federation of German Employers (BDA), and the German Chamber of Trade and Commerce (DIHT). Approximately 90 percent of employers belong to such associations,

a far higher percentage than that of employees in trade unions. For example, the German Federation of Industry, which is dominated by a few large firms, embraces 35 major industrial associations. Its financial resources, expertise, high-powered staff, and close links to the federal ministries make it one of the most effective lobbies. The Federation of German Employers, whose economic experts engage in collective-bargaining negotiations on behalf of nearly 90 percent of all private firms in the FRG, consists of 54 trade associations and 14 *Länder* organizations representing more than 1,000 regional associations. The DIHT, speaking for 82 chambers of commerce, is concerned with the legal and promotional interests of organized business. Collectively, these groups have been heavy contributors to the CDU/CSU, though the BDI's leaders have also donated funds to the FDP, a strategy calculated to secure access to the ruling circles within SPD-FDP coalition governments.

*Labor*    West German workers are organized into four major unions: the German Salaried Employees Union (DAG), the German Federation of Civil Servants (DBB), the Christian Trade Union Federation of Germany (CGB), and the German Trade Union Federation (DGB). These four unions represent a little more than one-third of the FRG's organized labor force. They are not strictly blue-collar organizations. The DGB, the largest of the unions, consists of 17 affiliated unions with a total membership of 9 million persons, only about two-thirds of whom are blue-collar workers. Higher civil servants, middle-level white-collar employees, and many Catholic workers are represented in the DBB, DAG, and CGB, respectively.

The unions serve their members with an extensive infrastructure of educational, social, and political activity, and keep them and the general public informed through a communication network that includes scores of periodicals, newsletters, and a significant presence on the World Wide Web. The unions are also heavily represented in parliament. In the ninth Bundestag (1980), for example, 69.4 percent of SPD and 30.6 percent of CDU/CSU delegates had formal interest-group ties to trade unions or other employee organizations.[20] Still, membership levels have always fluctuated. For instance, between 1982 and 1990 the CGB grew from 297,000 members to 309,000 members, while between 1980 and 1990 the DBB dropped from 821,000 to 799,000. More important, the fortunes of the trade unions have recently been similar to those of other postindustrial democracies, including the United States. In the first half of the 1990s alone, as a result of the decline of traditional industries, they lost nearly 2 million dues-paying members.

Unlike their European neighbors, German unions have also had to contend with the complicated problem of unification. The entry of East Germany's workforce into the western unions has not been smooth. As eastern workers demanded wage settlements on a par with western levels, western employers became more disinclined to invest in the less productive and all too often antiquated eastern plants. As a result, the largely western leadership of the trade unions often found themselves in the awkward position of having to support lesser wage increases in the hopes of keeping eastern industry alive. Likewise, while western unions have traditionally exercised "a sense of proportion in the national interest" by taking modest raises (e.g., the 6 percent settlement accepted by civil service union leaders in the spring of 1991), their grassroots membership has complained that it is being made to pay for the problems in the east. Calls for western union members to make direct contributions to their eastern fellow members have been particularly poorly received. Hence, the goal of achieving equality in eastern and western living standards not only has proven unsusceptible to quick or easy attainment, but has also come at the cost of union credibility.

**Churches**    The Basic Law forbids the establishment of a state church. In the consensual spirit that governs other social relations, however, it reminds the German people of "their responsibility before God." In addition, the Basic Law defines religious communities as "corporate bodies under public law," in which capacity they are entitled to levy taxes and enter into agreements with the state. While the state is constitutionally bound to remain neutral in religious matters, the neutrality that governs church-state relations in Germany is one that leans toward accommodation rather than strict separation. The prevailing view of this relationship acknowledges the important role of religion in the nation's public life. The relationship is governed by *Länder* concordats and church covenants, and they cover matters such as religious instruction in the public schools, observance of religious holidays, establishment of confessional schools, and appointment of chairs in theology at state universities.

The Evangelical Church in Germany (EKD) is an alliance of 24 largely independent Lutheran, Reformed, and United Churches. Their 29 million members include some 5 million eastern Germans. Its top legislative organ, the Synod, takes positions on various social, cultural, and educational issues, in which respect it often cooperates with the Roman Catholic Church. The Catholic Church consists of 27 dioceses, seven of which are archdioceses. Its 26 million members include 800,000 eastern Germans. The Conference of Catholic Bishops is the church's top policy-making organ. It functions independently of the Central Committee of German Catholics, an influential lay organization consisting of more than 100 Catholic associations. Other religious organizations include the Protestant Methodist Church, the Old Catholic Church, the Central Council of Jews, and even Islam. These congregations are relatively small. The Jewish community, for example, consists of around 50,000 members, a far cry from the 530,000 Jews who lived and worked in Germany prior to the Holocaust. However, some cities, like Berlin, have recently experienced an increase in the size of their Jewish communities, in part because of immigration from the former Soviet Union. At the same time, immigration from Turkey and the Middle East has led to a growing Muslim population in the FRG, which has further tested German understandings of religious tolerance.

---

[20]Russell J. Dalton, *Politics: West Germany* (Boston: Scott Foresman, 1989), p. 236.

The two major confessions—Evangelical and Catholic—continue to be influential in selected areas of public policy. Both religious establishments are represented on the governing boards of many public agencies, including those of the major public broadcasting stations. The churches are also critical players on the field of social welfare. They spend billions of dollars operating hundreds of kindergartens, hospitals, old-age homes, and homes for the handicapped, all activities that enjoy broad public support. In addition, the churches have a history of involvement in hotly contested political issues such as nuclear missile deployment, compulsory military service, and abortion. The Evangelical Church can even be credited with spearheading the West German peace movement as well as East Germany's peaceful revolution. What the churches seem unable to do today—certainly far less than in the earlier years of the Federal Republic—is to deliver votes in national election campaigns. Unlike in the late nineteenth and early twentieth centuries, German citizens have become modernized and no longer regard their religious and their political identities as inextricably intertwined.

## ELECTORAL POLITICS

### The Electoral System

In an ingenious but sometimes complicated way, the German electoral system combines single-member districts with proportional representation. This fact, which can be understood in terms of Germany's response to the chaotic conditions of the Weimar Republic, allows the electoral system to include interests across the spectrum without at the same time giving rise to political instability. Each voter receives two ballots. The first is cast for a specific candidate running in a district, the second for a party list. The second ballot includes the names of those candidates nominated by their respective parties, and they are chosen in the order in which they appear on the list. The number of parliamentary seats allocated to a party is determined by second-ballot votes, that is, by its total share of the nationwide vote. Under this system, which the *Länder* also use, party list candidates would be added to the single-member district winners until the total number of seats equals the percentage of its nationwide, second-ballot vote.

The functioning of the system can be illustrated by the election results of 1983. In winning 48.8 percent of second-ballot votes, the CDU/CSU also captured 180 districts; the figures for the SPD were 38.2 percent and 68 districts; for the FDP and the Greens they were 7.0 and 5.6 percent, respectively, and no districts. These results meant that Christian Democrats were entitled to 244 Bundestag seats. Thus, under the formula, the CDU/CSU was awarded 64 list seats which, when added to its district seats, totaled 244 or 48.8 percent of all second-ballot votes. The SPD, having won 68 district seats, was awarded an additional 125 list seats, totaling 193, whereas the FDP received 34 and the Greens 27 list seats, representing their respective shares of the national (second-ballot) vote. It is possible, however, for a party to win more district seats than it would normally be entitled to by its second-ballot vote. When this happens, such "overhang" seats are retained, thus increasing the total number of parliamentary seats by that much.

The voting system can be skewed by the 5 percent clause, which often results in "wasted" votes but also fosters stability by holding down the number of small parties in parliament. In 1990, for example, the western Greens won 4.6 percent of the votes in the old FRG, just missing the 5 percent requirement. Under "pure" proportional representation, the Greens would have been entitled to 23 seats in the Bundestag but, having failed to win 5 percent of the vote, they received none. The CDU/CSU's ten-seat majority after the 1994 election was due entirely to its overhang seats. The SPD had four such seats.

The 5 percent clause was not regarded as equitable, however, for the first all-German election of December 1990. The Federal Constitutional Court ruled that political parties in the eastern *Länder* would be severely handicapped if the rule were to apply nationwide. For this particular election, therefore, as Table 4.6 indicates, the 5 percent rule was manipulated to apply separately to Germany's eastern and western regions. If seats in the Bundestag had been allocated on a nationwide basis, as is usually the case, neither the Greens (eastern or western) nor the Party of Democratic Socialism (the old SED) would have achieved parliamentary representation. The two-constituency tabulation presented in Table 4.6 was a one-time exception to the 5 percent nationwide rule.

Finally, if a political party fails to get 5 percent of the national vote, it may still obtain proportional representation in the national parliament by winning at least three single-member districts. This happened in 1994. The PDS won 4.4 percent of the national vote, although only 0.9 percent of these votes came from the western *Länder.* However, because it won 4 constituency seats in East Berlin, the party was entitled to 30 seats in the thirteenth Bundestag (see Table 4.7).

## TABLE 4.6

### FEDERAL ELECTION RESULTS, 1990

| Party | Nationwide (%) | Old FRG (%) | Ex-GDR (%) | Seats |
|---|---|---|---|---|
| CDU | 36.7 | 35.0 | 43.4 | 262 |
| SPD | 33.5 | 35.9 | 23.6 | 239 |
| FDP | 11.0 | 10.6 | 13.4 | 79 |
| CSU | 7.1 | 9.1 | — | 51 |
| Greens (West) | 3.9 | 4.7 | — | — |
| PDS | 2.4 | 0.3 | 9.9 | 17 |
| DSU | 0.2 | — | 1.0 | — |
| Greens (East) | 1.2 | — | 5.9 | 8 |
| Republicans | 2.1 | 2.3 | 1.3 | — |

Sources: *Statistisches Jahrbuch 1991 für das Vereinte Deutschland*, p. 101; and *The Week in Germany* (New York: German Information Center, December 7, 1990).
Note: The percentages do not include the election results in Berlin. The DSU (German Social Union) ran as the "sister" party of Bavaria's CSU. The Greens (East) were allied with Alliance 90.

## TABLE 4.7

### FEDERAL ELECTION RESULTS, 1994

| Party | West (%) | East (%) | Total (%) | Seats |
|---|---|---|---|---|
| CDU/CSU | 42.2 | 38.5 | 41.5 | 294 |
| SPD | 37.6 | 31.9 | 36.4 | 252 |
| FDP | 7.7 | 4.0 | 6.9 | 47 |
| Alliance 90/Greens | 7.8 | 5.7 | 7.3 | 49 |
| PDS | 0.9 | 17.7 | 4.4 | 30 |
| Republicans | 2.0 | 1.4 | 1.9 | — |
| Other parties | 1.9 | 1.3 | 1.7 | — |
| Total | 100 | 100 | 100 | 672 |

## Split-Ticket Voting

The German system gives voters the unusual opportunity to split their tickets, a method by which coalition partners can help each other. In 1972, for example, the SPD openly encouraged its voters to cast their second ballot in favor of the FDP, while 60 percent of second-ballot FDP voters supported CDU and SPD candidates with their first ballot. Split-ticket voting was also prevalent in the 1987 election when many SPD voters, troubled by their party's military and ecological policies, cast their second ballot for the Greens, whereas many CDU voters cast their second ballot for the FDP. The FDP, in turn, appeared to convince voters that the best way to keep the CDU/CSU on the right course was to ensure its presence in the new government.

As Table 4.8 indicates, large numbers of German voters appear to be leery of one-party government. No fewer than 40.1 percent of CDU/CSU voters and 41.7 percent of SPD voters thought it would "not be good" for their respective parties to win an absolute majority of seats in the Bundestag. The corresponding percentages for the 1983 election were 27.1 and 29.5. These figures point to an increasing tendency on the part of German voters to split their ballots. This preference for governing coalitions over single-party rule contrasts sharply with the attitudes of British voters, who tend to associate responsible parliamentary government with unified party leadership backed by electoral majorities. This split-ticket voting is one indicator of the Americanization of FRG electoral behavior; another is the phenomenon of the "floating voter" who does not owe a deep and consistent attachment to any one party.

## Candidate Selection

German parties are strong in part because they monopolize the candidate selection process. Candidates seeking district seats are nominated either directly by party members or by conventions of party delegates. (There is no system of primary elections as in the United States.) In the CDU and SPD parties, executive committees select candidates for the Bundestag. Naturally the party will seek to nominate the candidate with the broadest popular appeal. But invariably he or she is a well-known party loyalist with years of faithful service to the organization. "Independent" candidates who circumvent the party organization are rarely if ever nominated. Party control over *Land* list candidates is even tighter. In principle, these lists are determined by secret ballot in party conferences, but in truth delegates vote mainly to ratify lists already put together by district and *Land* party executive committees in cooperation with national party officials. These lists are usually headed by leading party officials to ensure their election to the Bundestag.

## Campaign Styles and Techniques

West German elections have evolved into major media events and highly professionalized undertakings similar to American presidential campaigns. The CDU and the SPD continue to speak in terms of the traditional FRG mass party, the *Volkspartei* (People's Party), but both have been highly Americanized and centralized in their campaigns, especially in the use of new communication technologies and new marketing approaches. (The German courts, however, put an end to U.S.-style direct phone canvassing as an illegal infringe-

**TABLE 4.8**

**VOTERS PREFERRING ABSOLUTE MAJORITY FOR SPD OR CDU/CSU, 1987 ELECTION (PERCENT)**

| Absolute Majority | CDU/CSU | SDP | FDP | Greens | Total |
|---|---|---|---|---|---|
| Good for SPD | 0.0 | 57.7 | 1.0 | 14.3 | 22.2 |
| Good for CSU/CSU | 59.8 | 0.0 | 8.5 | 0.0 | 26.5 |
| Not good | 40.1 | 41.7 | 90.5 | 85.7 | 50.3 |

*Source: Bundestagswahl 1987: Eine Analyse der Wahl zum 11. Deutschen Bundestag am 25 January 1987* (Mannheim: Forschungsgruppe Wahlen E. V., 1987), p. 48.

ment of individual privacy.) Campaign advertisements fill newspapers and popular magazines, while election posters and richly colored lifestyle photographs of leading candidates dot the landscape. Lapel buttons, paper flags, T-shirts, and bumper stickers by the tens of thousands convey their partisan messages.

In the 1980s, the art of selling candidates reached new heights of sophistication as public relations firms assumed a central role in mapping campaign strategy. As part of this strategy, each party seeks to establish a "brand image" with matching colors and catchy slogans. For example, the CDU/CSU, in emphasizing the "take charge" quality of its leader, Helmut Kohl, sought to personalize the 1994 campaign by turning the election into a referendum on his chancellorship. One influential campaign poster showed a huge and smiling Kohl under the caption "Politics Without a Beard," referring to the bearded SPD leader at that time, Rudolf Scharping, who was thought by some to be too much of an intellectual to lead the Federal Republic. The SPD countered with its issue-oriented emphasis on "Jobs, Jobs, Jobs" in the face of rising unemployment. The FDP has cultivated itself as a "creative minority" by emphasizing its independence and portraying its leaders as persons of reason and common sense who are concerned about the lot of small businesspeople and the "besieged" middle class. The Greens have drawn upon their name as a powerful symbol of their commitment to environmental preservation.[21]

## GERMAN POLITICS IN TRANSITION

### The Postwar Years to Reunification

The year 1969 marked the turning point of West German politics in the postwar era. Prior to that year, the CDU/CSU had won five successive national elections, most of them by wide margins over the SPD. Yet the clearest observable trend, seen in Table 4.9, is the clockwork regularity of SPD gains between 1953 and 1972. The SPD's chance to enter a governing coalition occurred in 1966 when Ludwig Erhard, the CDU chancellor, resigned against a backdrop of discord within his own party and a widening rift between the CDU/CSU and its regular coalition partner, the FDP. There followed the three-year period (1966–1969) of the so-called Grand Coalition under the CDU's Kurt-Georg Kiesinger (chancellor) and the SPD's Willy Brandt (vice-chancellor). In 1969, when the Social Democrats reached a new high of 42.7 percent of the popular vote, the FDP, with 5.8 percent of the vote, decided to join hands with Brandt in producing Bonn's first SPD-led government.

The new coalition ruled with a slim voting edge of 12 votes, which by 1972 had virtually disappeared in the wake of defections from Brandt's controversial Eastern policy (*Ostpolitik*), which had sought to "regularize" the FRG's relations with the communist states of East Europe. Christian Democrats, smelling an opportunity to get back into office, moved for a vote of no confidence, the first time the parliamentary opposition had tried to topple a ruling government between federal elections. On April 27, 1972, the coalition survived the CDU/CSU challenge by a razor-thin margin of two votes. On the very next day the Bundestag rejected Brandt's budget, plunging the government into another crisis. The failure of the budget to win parliamentary approval came at a time of economic downturn and bitter wrangling in the cabinet over fiscal policy. Yet Brandt's personal popularity was at an all-time high, prompting him in late 1972, when the economic news was much brighter, to call for new elections in the hope of increasing his margin of parliamentary support. Accordingly, the chancellor invoked Article 68 and lost his vote of confidence, as planned, whereupon the federal president dissolved the Bundestag and scheduled new elections for November 19.

The 1972 federal election campaign—a bitterly fought contest—resulted in a solid victory for Brandt, marking the first time Social Democrats had exceeded the CDU/CSU in popular votes. Shortly thereafter, however, the party's fortunes

---

[21]For a study of changing campaign styles in Germany, see Susan Edith Scarrow, *Organizing for Victory: Political Party Members and Party Organizing Strategies in Great Britain and West Germany, 1945–1989* (Ph.D. dissertation, Yale University, 1991), chs. 5 and 10.

**TABLE 4.9**

**FEDERAL ELECTION RESULTS, 1949–1998 (PERCENTAGE OF VOTES CAST)**

| Year | Turnout | CDU/CSU | SPD | FDP | Greens | PDS | Others |
|------|---------|---------|------|------|--------|-----|--------|
| 1949 | 78.5 | 31.0 | 29.2 | 11.9 | — | — | 27.3 |
| 1953 | 86.0 | 45.2 | 28.8 | 9.5 | — | — | 16.5 |
| 1957 | 87.8 | 50.2 | 31.8 | 7.7 | — | — | 11.3 |
| 1961 | 87.7 | 45.3 | 36.2 | 12.8 | — | — | 6.6 |
| 1965 | 86.8 | 47.6 | 39.3 | 9.5 | — | — | 5.6 |
| 1969 | 86.7 | 46.1 | 42.7 | 5.8 | — | — | 4.9 |
| 1972 | 91.1 | 44.9 | 45.8 | 8.4 | — | — | 0.9 |
| 1976 | 90.7 | 48.6 | 42.6 | 7.9 | — | — | 0.9 |
| 1980 | 88.7 | 44.5 | 42.9 | 10.6 | — | — | 1.9 |
| 1983 | 89.1 | 48.8 | 38.2 | 7.0 | 5.6 | — | 6.0 |
| 1987 | 84.4 | 44.3 | 37.0 | 9.1 | 8.3 | — | 8.9 |
| 1990 | 77.8 | 43.8 | 33.5 | 11.0 | 5.1 | 2.4 | 4.0 |
| 1994 | 79.1 | 41.5 | 36.4 | 6.9 | 7.3 | 4.4 | 3.5 |
| 1998 | 82.2 | 35.2 | 40.9 | 6.2 | 6.7 | 5.1 | 6.0 |

declined again as the SPD suffered severe losses in several state and local elections, only to be followed by Brandt's resignation in May 1974. This set the stage, after Helmut Schmidt's takeover, for the 1976 election.[22]

In 1976 the CDU/CSU not only recovered its 1972 losses, but narrowly missed securing the majority that would have toppled the SPD-FDP coalition—a popular victory without power, as many editorial writers characterized the election. The CDU's revival was widely attributed to the expansion of its grassroots membership campaign in the early 1970s under its able general secretary, Kurt Biedenkopf, and to a highly effective national advertising campaign. Yet many spectators saw the election as an issueless campaign, decided mainly by the styles and personalities of the leading candidates.[23]

The 1980 and 1983 elections were largely a replay of 1976. However, the fortunes of Helmut Schmidt's SPD-led government declined rapidly. The popular chancellor's days were numbered in the face of increasing opposition from the FDP over his economic policy and from his own party over his strong pro-American nuclear missile policy. On October 1, 1982, after the FDP pulled out of its coalition with the SPD and switched its support to the CDU/CSU, parliament chose the CDU's leader, Helmut Kohl, as chancellor. The new chancellor pledged forthwith to call new elections in March. It turned out to be a banner year for Christian Democrats. Far ahead of the SPD in the polls, they obtained their highest percentage of the national vote since 1957 but fell just short of a majority. Again in 1987 the CDU/CSU–FDP coalition emerged victorious, this time against the challenge of Johannes Rau, the moderate SPD candidate for chancellor. Although the Greens had been gaining strength on the Left, often at the expense of the SPD, Rau promised the electorate that he would not consider a coalition with the Greens. But as the SPD organization moved steadily leftward in an attempt to draw votes from the Greens, many other voters, par-

[22]For a detailed discussion of the 1972 campaign, see Arnold J. Heidenheimer and Donald P. Kommers, *The Governments of Germany,* 4th ed. (New York: Thomas Y. Crowell, 1975), ch. 5.

[23]A treatment of the 1976 election is Karl H. Cerny, ed., *Germany at the Polls* (Washington, DC: American Enterprise Institute, 1978).

ticularly the swing vote in German politics, supported the Kohl coalition.

With the FRG's economy booming in the summer of 1989, the SPD under Oskar Lafontaine planned a 1990 campaign focusing on "a policy of ecological and social renewal of industrialized society." This postindustrial strategy, they hoped, would provide the Social Democrats with the clear sense of identity they needed to regain voter confidence. Even if this gambit would have worked, however, the Lafontaine wing of the party could not have planned on intervening events in the GDR. Massive antigovernment demonstrations in the east led to the collapse of the Communist regime and the breaching of the Berlin Wall. As East Germans prepared for their first free election in nearly 60 years and as calls for reunification became its defining feature, Chancellor Kohl seized the opportunity at his doorstep. With the active support of his FDP foreign minister, Hans-Dietrich Genscher, who had been born in the east, he obtained Allied support for negotiations with East Berlin and Moscow. By October 3, 1990, these contacts were to reunite the two German states and thereby make Kohl the first chancellor of all Germany since World War II.

Kohl's extraordinary determination and enthusiasm overcame all obstacles and all cautionary notes, including those of the president of the Bundesbank, as to the eventual costs of reunification. Wherever he went in the east, of course, Kohl was welcomed by tumultuous crowds, not least because of his willingness to predict that the integration of the GDR's economy into the FRG would produce "blooming landscapes" throughout the region. Meanwhile, Lafontaine's SPD was thrown onto the defensive by his initiatives and reduced to warning voters, in a Cassandra-like manner, that the chancellor's promises could have unpleasant side effects. Accordingly, the party's cautious support for national unity was popularly perceived in the east as far too little, and much too late. Kohl, ever the shrewd political campaigner, had both the diplomatic power and the deutsche mark to offer; Lafontaine offered voters little more than skepticism.

As a consequence, the elections to the Bundestag of 1990, the first to take place in united Germany, led to a resounding victory for Kohl's government coalition. True, the total national vote for the CDU/CSU dipped somewhat (to 43.8 percent) and was counterbalanced by a gain for Genscher's FDP (which rose to 11.0 percent). Nonetheless, the drubbing the SPD received at the polls, which fell to 33.5 percent of the national vote (its lowest level since 1957), was roundly perceived as a vindication of the chancellor's aggressive pro-unification policy.

## A Change of Government

Students of democratic politics agree that one of the most important indicators of a vibrant democracy is a "circulation of elites," an ongoing process by which even the most popular leaders are eventually subject to replacement by their opponents. By the Bundestag elections of 1994, the FRG provided a perfect test case of this proposition because Chancellor Kohl had already governed his country for 12 years. In the eyes of many citizens, it was time for a change.

Additionally, in the two decades prior to the 1994 election, the FRG's electorate had changed in significant ways. In the 1950s, voting patterns could be explained largely in terms of class and religion. By the 1970s these variables, although still important factors, were no longer sure predictors of how Germans would vote. The SPD had begun to advance beyond its labor union support into urban Catholic, white-collar Protestant constituencies, just as the CDU was beginning to broaden its appeal in urban white-collar districts previously weak in CDU affiliation. On the whole, Catholicism and ruralism correlated positively with high CDU/CSU voting, whereas the SPD's success over the long term seemed to lie less with its working-class membership than with the broadening of its base in the middle class.[24]

---

[24]For treatments of the 1969, 1972, and 1976 federal elections, see "The West German Elections of 1969," *Comparative Politics* 1 (July 1970); David P. Conradt and Dwight Lambert, "Party System, Social Structure, and Competitive Polities in West Germany: An Ecological Analysis of the 1972 Federal Election," *Comparative Politics* 7 (October 1974); and Cerny, *Germany at the Polls.*

The most dramatic shift in postwar voting patterns was due to the changing character of the German middle class. The numbers of traditional middle-class voters—property owners and farmers—had dwindled and been replaced by a new middle class of civil servants and white-collar employees connected with the FRG's mushrooming service trades. Highly urbanized, younger, and less attached to traditional values, these voters were more responsive to newer issues centering on environmental matters, educational reform, and alternative lifestyles than to older economic issues. In the 1980s, many of these voters—especially those in districts with high concentrations of students, salaried workers, and civil servants—cast their votes in favor of the Greens, seriously cutting into traditional FDP strongholds. First-time voters and younger voters (18–44) cast their ballots disproportionately for the Greens.

These factors, combined with unprecedented high levels of unemployment, both in eastern and in western Germany, and a rising national debt due to the economic costs of reunification, seemed to prime the SPD for a triumphant return to power during the so-called *Superwahljahr* (super election year) of 1994. Ten key elections would take place between March 13 and October 16, 1994: the European parliament election, eight state (*Länder*) elections, and the Bundestag election. But thanks to some clever campaigning by the CDU/CSU, which emphasized the safe virtues of continuity and stability, as well as some miscues by the SPD, which made the monumental mistake of running on a platform of large-scale income redistribution, the inevitable was postponed. In the end, Kohl inched back into the chancellorship by a single vote. Thanks to the assistance of overhang seats, the CDU/CSU–FDP coalition found a renewed lease on life with a majority of ten seats in the thirteenth Bundestag.

The Kohl government had no reason to be self-satisfied. By this point, it was clear that the German public had developed an appetite for more dynamic leadership and would not long be satisfied with Kohl's weary tributes to a now fading past. Even business leaders were unhappy with the ruling coalition's economic policies. The answer was found in a charismatic new leader of

the SPD, Gerhard Schröder, who in a stunning display of political acuity brought his party, in coalition with the Greens, back to power in the Bundestag elections of 1998. This was the first time in the FRG's history a sitting chancellor had lost his job as a result of a general election.

Looking back, there is no great mystery to Schröder's success. The new chancellor seemed to be everything for everybody, especially those in the mood for change. For Germans who had grown tired of Kohl's aging presence, Schröder seemed the epitome of youth: handsome, debonair, and excitingly fresh. More important, by cleverly modeling himself after the personal styles of other prominent left-centrist politicians on the world stage—Bill Clinton in the United States and Tony Blair in Britain—Schröder (referred to by some wits as "Clintonblair") was able to appeal to voters across the political spectrum. For unemployed workers and for easterners suffering under the burdens of unification, Schröder offered the Alliance for Jobs, a plan to create new jobs by fostering increased cooperation, in corporatist fashion, between trade unions and management. For the business community, he portrayed himself as a resurrected Ludwig Erhard (the father of Germany's "economic miracle"), someone who would be committed to the virtues of the social market economy but avoid the socialist temptations of the SPD's left wing. For the FRG's vibrant middle class, his promises of a *neue Mitte* (new middle) were expressly designed to combine postmodern values of environmental protection and equal rights with the assurance of social stability.[25]

Although the arithmetic that led to the governing coalition between the SPD and Greens was actually quite close, the major story of the 1998 election was what it signified for the electoral balance between the SPD and the CDU/CSU (see Table 4.10). The Social Democrats were the

---

[25]See Russell J. Dalton, "A Celebration of Democracy: The 1998 Bundestag Election," *German Politics and Society* 16(4) (Winter 1998), pp. 1–6; and Gerard Braunthal, "The 1998 German Election," *German Politics and Society* 17(1) (Spring 1999), pp. 32–54.

**TABLE 4.10**

**FEDERAL ELECTION RESULTS, 1994 AND 1998 (PERCENTAGES)**

| Party | 1994 | | | | 1998 | | | |
|---|---|---|---|---|---|---|---|---|
| | West | East | Total | Seats | West | East | Total | Seats |
| Christian Democrats | 42.1 | 38.5 | 41.5 | 294 | 37.1 | 27.3 | 35.2 | 245 |
| Free Democrats | 7.7 | 3.5 | 6.9 | 47 | 7.0 | 3.3 | 6.2 | 43 |
| Social Democrats | 37.5 | 31.5 | 36.4 | 252 | 42.3 | 35.1 | 40.9 | 298 |
| Greens | 7.6 | 4.3 | 7.3 | 59 | 7.3 | 4.1 | 6.7 | 47 |
| Party of Democratic Socialism | 1.0 | 19.8 | 4.4 | 30 | 1.2 | 21.6 | 5.1 | 36 |
| Other Parties | 4.1 | 2.4 | 3.6 | — | 5.1 | 8.6 | 6.0 | — |
| Total | 100% | 100% | 100% | 672 | 100% | 100% | 100% | 669 |
| Percent Voting | 80.5 | 72.6 | 79.0 | | 82.8 | 80.3 | 82.2 | |

*Source:* Forschungsgruppe Wahlen; Russell J. Dalton, *A Celebration of Democracy: The 1998 Bundestag Election*, p. 4.
*Note:* Seats include 16 overhang-mandates in 1994 and 13 overhang-mandates in 1998. West Berlin is included within the West, and East Berlin is included in the East.

big winners, able to secure 40.9 percent of the popular vote (up from 36.4 percent in 1994 and their best outcome since 1980), thanks in part to a huge shift of 1.4 million voters away from the CDU. Significantly, nearly a third of these came from the ex-GDR. In turn, the CDU/CSU fell to 35.2 percent of the vote (a loss of 6.3 percent since 1994), and for only the second time in the history of the FRG was relegated to the status of the second-largest party in parliament.

## POLICY-MAKING INSTITUTIONS

In this subsection we turn our attention to Germany's major policy-making institutions, its federal system, and its distinctive scheme of separated and divided powers. Upon their accession to the FRG in 1990, the eastern *Länder* brought their governmental systems into complete conformity with the Basic Law. Thus, unless otherwise indicated, the institutions, structures, and policy-making processes discussed here are applicable to all of Germany.

Germany's main legislative institutions are the popularly elected Bundestag (house of representatives) and the Bundesrat, the nonelected upper house of parliament, whose appointed delegates represent the *Länder* governments. The leading executive institutions are the chancellor and cabinet, collectively known as the federal government. The president, once a powerful head of state directly elected by the people, has been reduced to a figurehead akin to the British monarch. One of the most distinctive features of Germany's federal system is that the states are entrusted under the constitution with the administration of national law. This system, often dubbed *administrative federalism,* is a carryover from Germany's nineteenth-century origins. Finally, empowered to enforce the provisions of the Basic Law, the judiciary, at the top of which is the Federal Constitutional Court, serves as a check on the activities of the other branches of government.

### The Federal President

The federal president is the FRG's highest-ranking public official, but he functions mainly as a ceremonial head of state, a vestigial reminder of the once thriving presidency under the emperor. Symbolically, he remains important as a spokesman for the nation, an attribute of the office that has been acted upon to differing degrees by holders of the position. Although the presidency is perceived as a nonpartisan office, its occupant is elected for a five-year term—under Article 54 of the Basic Law he may be reelected only once—by a federal convention composed of party representatives from national and state parliaments. The president is chosen as a result of bargaining between the coalition parties forming the majority in the convention. Yet despite the complexity of the process, the office has generally been filled by respected public officials who have won recognition for their fair-mindedness and ability to communicate across party lines. Up to now, the office has served as a capstone to a successful career in politics.

In May 1999, Johannes Rau, the moderate Social Democratic and former candidate for chancellor, became the FRG's eighth president. He was preceded by Theodore Heuss (FDP, 1949–1959), Heinrich Lübke (CDU, 1959–1969), Gustav Heine-

In 1999, the well-regarded, middle-of-the-road Social Democrat Johannes Ran was elected President.

mann (SPD, 1969–1974), Walter Scheel (FDP, 1974–1979), Karl Carstens (CDU, 1979–1984), Richard von Weizsäcker (CDU, 1984–1994), and Roman Herzog (CDU, 1994–1999). Until 1979, an incumbent president who was competent and prudent in the exercise of his authority could expect, if he wished, to be reelected to a second term. Some recent elections, however, have been largely an exercise in partisan politics. In 1979, the CDU forced the resignation of Walter Scheel as presidential candidate and elected its own candidate (Karl Carstens) by a slim majority of 26 votes. In 1994, there were three serious presidential candidates: Rau (SPD), Hildegard Hamm-Brücher (FDP), and Roman Herzog (CDU)—Chancellor Kohl's personal choice for the office. Herzog won on the third ballot when the FDP switched its vote to the CDU candidate. In 1999, Rau was elected when Herzog decided not to stand for another term.

The president's powers include the appointment and dismissal of various public officials, including cabinet officials and military officers, and the pardoning of criminal offenders. His exercise of the pardoning power has occasionally caused a public uproar. This happened in 1989 when President Weizsäcker pardoned two imprisoned terrorists—female members of the terrorist Red Army Faction—after they had served 12 years of their prison terms and shown that they could reenter society as responsible citizens. The president's most common official duty, apart from receiving and visiting foreign heads of state, is to promulgate, with his signature, all federal laws.

In one respect, the president may be more than just a figurehead. Although it is disputed whether he can reject a statute on substantive constitutional grounds, presidents have done so on at least five occasions. A president's refusal to sign a properly enacted bill could conceivably bring about a constitutional crisis resulting in demands for his resignation or his impeachment. If the president resigns, dies, or is impeached—or is otherwise unable to perform his duties—the president of the Bundesrat, as the second highest official of the Federal Republic, assumes his powers. In their absence from the country, presidents have often requested the Bundesrat's president to serve as acting president.

## The Federal Government

***The Chancellor***  The Basic Law puts the chancellor in firm control of the federal government. He alone is responsible to parliament, whereas his ministers—that is, the members of his cabinet—whom he may hire and fire, are responsible only to him. Constitutionally charged under Article 65 to lay down the guidelines for national policy, he is chosen by a majority of the Bundestag and is usually the leader of the largest party in the governing coalition. Parliament is not empowered to dismiss the chancellor at will, however, as it was able to do in the Weimar Republic. Under the so-called constructive vote of no confidence, prescribed by Article 67 of the Basic Law, the Bundestag may dismiss a chancellor only when a majority of its members simultaneously elects his successor. The stabilizing effect of this provision has led many persons to label the FRG a "chancellor democracy."

The constructive vote of no confidence has succeeded only once, in 1982, when the Bundestag voted Helmut Schmidt out of office after the FDP's withdrawal from the coalition government. A new alliance between the FDP and the CDU/CSU elected Helmut Kohl as chancellor by a vote of 256 to 235, the first time in the FRG's history that a government had been replaced without an election.

Article 68 allows the chancellor to initiate a vote of confidence and to authorize him, if he loses the vote, to request the president to dissolve parliament and call for new elections. Brandt used this procedure in 1972, and Kohl used it again in 1983. Both chancellors planned to lose in the expectation that new elections would

---

**REVIEW**

**4.1**

### THE BASIC LAW: SELECTED BASIC RIGHTS

**ARTICLE 1**

1. The dignity of man shall be inviolable. To respect and protect it shall be the duty of all state authority.

2. The German people therefore acknowledge inviolable and inalienable human rights as the basis of every community, of peace, and of justice in the world.

**ARTICLE 2**

1. Everyone shall have the right to the free development of his personality insofar as he does not violate the rights of others or offend against the constitutional order or the moral code.

2. Everyone shall have the right to life and to the inviolability of his person. The liberty of the individual shall be inviolable. These rights may be encroached upon pursuant to a law.

**ARTICLE 3**

1. All persons shall be equal before the law.

2. Men and women shall have equal rights. The state shall seek to ensure equal treatment of men and women and to remove existing disadvantages.

3. No one may be prejudiced or favored because of his sex, parentage, race, language, homeland and origin, faith, or religious or political opinions. Persons may not be discriminated against because of their disability.

**ARTICLE 5**

1. Everyone shall have the right freely to express and disseminate his opinion by speech, writing, and pictures and freely to inform himself from generally accessible sources…. There shall be no censorship.

increase their parliamentary majority and thus their hold on governmental power. In both instances the strategy worked, although some constitutional lawyers argued that these were cynical political moves that circumvented the intent and spirit of the Basic Law. They held that the constitution permits the dissolution of parliament in advance of its regular expiration date only when the chancellor actually loses its confidence or is unable to govern with his current majority. To deliberately contrive a vote of no confidence for the purpose of holding new elections trivializes the Basic Law in their view by undermining the principle of regular elections.

***The Chancellor's Office***    The most powerful instrument of executive leadership in the FGR is the chancellor's office. Originally a small secretariat serving the chancellor's personal needs, it has evolved into an agency of major political importance, even overshadowing the cabinet. It contains departments corresponding to the various federal ministries as well as a planning bureau, created in 1969, to engage in long-range social and economic planning. Its staff of about 500 persons keeps the chancellor informed of domestic and foreign affairs, assists him or her in setting policy guidelines, coordinates policy making among the federal ministries, and monitors the implementation of cabinet decisions.

The chancellor's office is headed by a chief of staff, usually an experienced public official and close personal advisor. The chief of staff is a person of immense power—his influence often exceeds that of federal ministers. Other chancellery advisors have obtained national prominence in their policy-making role. Two such persons were Egon Bahr, the principal architect of Brandt's *Ostpolitik,* and Wolfgang Schäuble, a principle figure in Kohl's reunification strategy and later his political rival.

***The Cabinet***    While prescribing a chancellor-led government, the Basic Law (Article 65) also envisions a high level of cabinet responsibility. In practice, however, the cabinet has not functioned as a true collegial body. First of all, the chancellor decides how much authority is to be accorded to each minister. Adenauer and Brandt, for example, virtually served as their own foreign ministers, as

The Social Democratic leader Gerhard Schröder became chancellor in 1998 with the promise of economic and political "renewal."

did Schmidt in certain areas of foreign policy. On the other hand, certain ministers achieve enormous prominence in their own right and occasionally overshadow the chancellor. Hans-Dietrich Genscher became the dominant figure in foreign affairs under Chancellor Kohl, sometimes to the point of orchestrating his own policy.

Furthermore, cabinet members are not all equal in rank (see Table 4.11). For example, the minister of finance—probably the cabinet's most powerful official in the field of domestic policy—has a qualified veto over proposals affecting public finances. His objection to such proposals can be overridden only by the vote of the chancellor, with whom he is ordinarily closely affiliated, and a majority of the cabinet. The ministers of justice and interior also have special powers of review over cabinet proposals impinging upon their jurisdiction.

In creating the cabinet, a chancellor is constrained by the demands of coalition politics and the interests of groups allied to and rivalries within his party. Often he is required to negotiate at length over the nature and number of ministries to be awarded the minor party in his coalition government. The FDP, the perennial minor party in German coalition governments until recently, has often threatened to withhold its votes for the chancellor (i.e., the head of the major party in the coalition) until it secures agreement on certain policy issues and is assured adequate representation in the cabinet. After the 1994 election, Chancellor Kohl not only had to ensure that the FDP was satisfied with its apportionment of cabinet posts; he was also required to achieve a measure of religious and geographic balance among the CDU's cabinet members, while including members from the eastern *Länder* and granting proportionate representation to Bavaria's CSU.

***Parliamentary State Secretaries***    The office of parliamentary state secretary—to be distinguished from the permanent state secretaries of the various ministerial bureaucracies—was introduced in 1967. Parliamentary state secretaries are

**TABLE 4.11**

**FEDERAL GOVERNMENT MINISTRIES, 2001**

| Cabinet Minister | Minister's Party |
| --- | --- |
| Minister of the Chancellery | SPD |
| Foreign Minister | Alliance 90/Greens |
| Minister of the Interior | SPD |
| Minister of Justice | SPD |
| Minister of Finance | SPD |
| Minister of Economics and Technology | Independent |
| Minister of Consumer Protection, Nutrition, Agriculture, and Forestry | Alliance 90/Greens |
| Minister of Labor and Social Affairs | SPD |
| Minister of Defense | SPD |
| Minister of Family, the Elderly, Women, and Youth | SPD |
| Minister of Health | SPD |
| Minister of Transport, Building, and Housing | SPD |
| Minister of the Environment, Protection of Nature, and Nuclear Safety | Alliance 90/Greens |
| Minister of Education and Research | SPD |
| Minister of Economic Cooperation and Development | SPD |

selected from among the more junior members of the Bundestag to help the ministries run their departments, defend their records in parliament, and maintain contact with the public. A new element in the Schmidt cabinet was the high number of former parliamentary state secretaries who were elevated to cabinet posts. The office is now widely recognized as a training ground for cabinet service by all the major parties.

## The Bundestag: Legislative Branch

The Bundestag is the successor to the old imperial (1871–1918) and republican (1919–1933) Reichstag. In those regimes the legislative branch was politically, and in some respects constitutionally, subordinate to the executive establishment, just as elected representatives played second fiddle to professional civil servants. In contrast, as part of Germany's efforts to profit from the experiences of the past, the authors of the Basic Law elevated parliament to first rank among the FRG's governing institutions. Though commentators agree that parliament has fallen short of the founders' vision of a vigorously self-confident body in control of the executive, they agree that the Bundestag has evolved from the rather submissive body of the Adenauer era into an increasingly assertive agency of national policy making. Even in the event of a national emergency, which only it can declare, the Bundestag's authority remains largely intact, thereby ensuring that ultimate power will always reside in the hands of civilian leaders and the elected representatives of the people.

***Power and Functions***    While playing a role similar to that of the U.S. Congress, the Bundestag is structurally a very different institution. First of all, it is "the parliament of a parliamentary system of government" in that "it [also] determine[s] the political composition and tenure in office of the government."[26] Second, and by

the same token, the highest officials in the executive branch—that is, the chancellor and his ministers—are, at the same time, among the most important and influential members of the Bundestag. This symbiotic relationship between executive and legislative power is not at all like the U.S. notion of separation of powers. In the FRG, the idea of separation of powers is embodied largely in the role of the opposition *within* parliament. As in other parliamentary systems, such as Great Britain, the opposition's task is to call the government—and thus the executive—to account for its policies in the crucible of parliamentary inquiry and debate.

Parliament checks the executive by its power to review the national budget, to pass upon all bills introduced by the government, to hold hearings and investigations, and to confront the chancellor and his ministers in the legislative question hour, a device borrowed from British parliamentary practice. The screening of proposed legislation absorbs most of the Bundestag's time. By far, the largest number of bills are initiated by the government. For example, of the 800 bills received by the twelfth Bundestag (1990–1994), 407 were government bills, 297 originated in the Bundestag itself, and 96 were sent over by the Bundesrat. The government managed to pass 77 percent of the bills it introduced, as compared with a 16 and 7 percent success rate, respectively, for the Bundestag and Bundesrat. As these statistics show, the federal government dominates the law-making process.

***Fraktionen and Committees***    The most important groups in the Bundestag are the parliamentary parties, or *Fraktionen.* In practice, they control the Bundestag's organization and decision-making machinery. Although constitutionally regarded as "representatives of the whole people, not bound to instructions [from any group]," deputies who plan on advancing their legislative careers will not lightly oppose the policy decisions of the party hierarchy, for party unity and discipline are strongly embedded in the parliamentary party system. Party discipline, however, is exercised in only a small number of cases. Most bills—over 85 percent—are the product of group negotiation in which repre-

---

[26]Winfried Steffani, "Parties (Parliamentary Groups) and Committees in the *Bundestag,*" in Uwe Thaysen, et al., *The U.S. Congress and the German Bundestag* (Boulder, CO: Westview Press, 1990), p. 273.

The Bundestag meets in Berlin.

sentatives of the federal government, the Bundestag, and the Bundesrat participate, and they are passed unanimously.

Each *Fraktion* divides itself topically into working groups or councils, which parallel the Bundestag's committee structure and serve as instruments for crystallizing party policy and developing the expertise of deputies. Indeed, the deputy who does his homework in the party group to which he is assigned—showing leadership, skill, forensic ability, and mastery of subject matter—often winds up as an influential member of a corresponding legislative committee and eventually a parliamentary state secretary. The Bundestag also has a differentiated committee system, including standing, investigating, and special committees. Of these, the 23 standing committees are the most important. Comparable to the committees of the U.S. Congress, they and their numerous subcommittees are parliament's workhorses. In the Bundestag, however, committee chairs are shared by all the *Fraktionen* in

proportion to their strength in the chamber as a whole and are allocated on the basis of expertise instead of seniority.

***Members of Parliament***    Typically, having studied law, political science, or economics, members of parliament begin their careers in the youth branch of a political party, frequently assisting established politicians. After fulfilling an apprenticeship in the party apparatus or, as is often the case, in a trade, farm, or labor organization closely linked to their party, they are then, in their late 30s, elected to parliament. They remain there for about 16 years, only to resign in their mid-50s to draw a comfortable pension and to enter the employment of an organized interest group. The careerism and security inherent in this system of political recruitment are not calculated to staff parliament with "movers and shakers," and often to the consternation of reformers insulate deputies against new and evolving trends in society.

Given these circumstances, it is perhaps predictable that not all groups are equally represented in parliament. Yet the Bundestag has made some progress over the past couple of decades in addressing this problem. Consider the issue of women's representation in parliament. By the 1980s, women represented about 15 percent of the membership, more than double the number elected in the 1970s. In the Bundestag of 1998, this figure jumped to 30.9 percent, the highest ever. (The PDS and the Greens had more women than men in their delegations.) Of the 207 women elected to the fourteenth Bundestag, 35.2 and 18.4 percent belonged, respectively, to the SPD and CDU/CSU.

## The Law-Making Process

Bills may be introduced by any member of the Bundestag or by the Bundesrat. As indicated earlier, however, the overwhelming majority of legislative bills originates with the federal government. A bill sponsored by the latter is first submitted to the Bundesrat, which is required to act on the bill within six weeks. If there are any changes, the Bundesrat must return the bill to the cabinet for its approval or disapproval. (Bills originating in the Bundesrat are submitted to the Bundestag by the cabinet after the latter has expressed its opinion on the bill.) The bill is then submitted to the Bundestag, where it is given a first reading. From there it is assigned to the proper committee. If it survives this stage, together with a second and third reading, it is transmitted to the Bundesrat. If the Bundesrat amends the bill, it may be sent to a joint conference committee for mediation. Any changes by the committee again require the Bundestag's approval of the entire bill. The Bundesrat, however, has a suspensive veto over ordinary legislation and an absolute veto over legislation involving the *Länder*—but any such veto can be overridden by the Bundestag. After final approval, a bill is countersigned by the chancellor or appropriate federal minister and then signed by the federal president, whereupon it is promulgated as law in the *Federal Law Gazette*.

The chancellor, federal and *Land* ministries, and representatives of organized interest groups

are the major actors in the law-making process. They work closely with the *Fraktionen* in hammering out legislative policy, though committees play a critical role in filtering legislation for final passage. So successful are the committees in the performance of this role that few bills, once reported out of committee, are the subject of amendment or even debate from the floor. The intense plenary debates in 1979 on energy policy and in 1996 on cutting social benefits—debates stretching over several days—are exceptions to the customary practice of securing broad interparty agreement on most bills that become law.

## Federalism and Bureaucracy

Like the United States, Germany divides power constitutionally between national and state governments. This structure represents a major check on central power. Federalism is in fact one of the unamendable principles of the Basic Law. The 16 *Länder* consist of 13 territorial states and the three city-states of Berlin, Bremen, and Hamburg. Each *Land,* like the national government, has its own constitution based on principles of republican and democratic government. Each has a parliamentary system. A minister president—lord mayor in the city-states—responsible to a one-house popularly elected legislature is the head of government in the territorial states. Historically, however, German federalism differs from the U.S. brand. The crucial distinction is that in the United States both federal and state governments exercise a full range of separate legislative and administrative functions, whereas German federalism confers the bulk of legislative powers upon the national government, with the *Länder* being mainly responsible for the administration of both federal and state laws.

Although federalism has cultural roots in the German past, the boundaries of the *Länder* were drawn without much reference to their ancestral ties. Only Bavaria, Saxony, and Thuringia survived the war with their pre-1945 boundaries relatively intact. In 1952, however, in an attempt to cement its authority, the GDR abolished the *Länder* and replaced them with 14 administrative districts under the control of the central government. These *Länder* were reestablished in July 1990 as one of the conditions of reunification. The *Länder* now range in population from 680,000 in Bremen to 17.3 million in North-Rhine Westphalia, more than eastern Germany's entire population. They also differ vastly in territorial size: excluding the small city-states, they range from Saarland with 2,570 sq km to Bavaria with 70,554 sq km. The largest and richest states, measured in terms of population and geography, are in the west. The eastern *Länder,* by contrast, are relatively smaller and much poorer.

This imbalance between the eastern and western *Länder* has revived proposals to redraw state lines for the purpose of creating larger and more integrated political and economic units. The Basic Law permits the restructuring of the *Länder* so long as the system as a whole remains federal in design. Under the terms of the Basic Law (Article 29), any federal law proposing a state boundary change must be approved by the Bundesrat, and subsequently ratified by referendum in the affected *Länder.* This procedure was first used in 1952 when the states of Baden, Württemberg, and Württemberg-Hohenzollern were consolidated into the single state of Baden-Württemberg. The next change, considered nearly four decades later, was Berlin's incorporation into Brandenburg, but this was rejected by voters.

One possible solution to the enormous disparity among the states in territory and population would be a merger based on the reorganized council of Germany's central bank (Bundesbank). Instead of giving each *Land* a vote on the Bundesbank Council, the system was changed in 1992 to accord representation to nine economically integrated regions that were defined by existing state boundaries but relatively balanced in population and territory. The nine regions consist of Schleswig-Holstein and Mecklenburg-Pomerania; Berlin and Brandenburg; Bremen, Lower Saxony, and Saxony-Anhalt; North Rhine-Westfalia; Hesse; Thuringia and Saxony; Rhineland-Palatinate and Saarland; Bavaria; and Baden-Württemberg. Any such fundamental change in *Land* boundaries, however, would almost surely lack the required popular support and face resistance by political and economic interests favored by the current system.

## The Bundesrat

The Bundesrat, the mainstay of German federalism, was designed to safeguard the vital interests of the *Länder* (see Table 4.12). But it is not a second chamber like the U.S. Senate. First, its powers are not equal to those of the Bundestag; second, its 69 votes are cast by officials who serve at the pleasure of the *Länder.* Thus each *Land* delegation votes as a unit and in accordance with the instructions of its government. How a delegation—or the person appointed to represent the state—votes often depends on the party composition of the *Land* cabinet. Nearly all seats in the Bundesrat are occupied by *Land* minister presidents or their delegates.

To accommodate the interests of the eastern *Länder,* the Unity Treaty amended Article 51 of the Basic Law, changing the allocation of seats in the Bundesrat. As before, each state is entitled to at least three votes, but now states with a population of more than 2 million are entitled to four votes, those with more than 6 million receive five votes, and those with more than 7 million receive six votes. (In the past, the largest states had five votes.) This system favors the smaller states. The five largest states, with two-thirds of the population, have 29 votes in the Bundesrat; the remaining states, with one-third of the population, have 40 votes.

The Bundesrat's consent is required for all federal legislation affecting the administrative, financial, and territorial interests of the *Länder.* With respect to other legislation, it has a suspensive veto, as noted earlier. If the Bundesrat objects to a bill by a majority vote, the Bundestag may override by a majority vote; if the former is by two-thirds, the vote to override must also be two-thirds. Additionally, the Bundesrat is authorized to approve all federal action enforcing national law in the *Länder,* to participate in major legislative decisions taken during a national emergency, and to elect half of the members of the Federal Constitutional Court. This last prerogative is important, for the Bundesrat has a

**TABLE 4.12**

**THE BUNDESRAT, SEPTEMBER 30, 2000**

| Land | Votes | Ruling Coalition | Population (millions) |
|---|---|---|---|
| Baden-Württemberg | 6 | CDU-FDP | 10.51 |
| Bavaria | 6 | CSU | 12.21 |
| Berlin | 4 | SPD–Alliance 90/Greens | 3.38 |
| Brandenburg | 4 | SPD-CDU | 2.60 |
| Bremen | 3 | SPD-CDU | 0.66 |
| Hamburg | 3 | SPD-PRO-FDP | 1.71 |
| Hesse | 5 | CDU-FDP | 6.06 |
| Mecklenburg-W. Pomerania | 3 | SPD-PDS | 1.78 |
| Lower Saxony | 6 | SPD | 7.92 |
| N. Rhine Westphalia | 6 | SPD–Alliance 90/Greens | 18.01 |
| Rhineland-Palatinate | 4 | SPD-FDP | 4.03 |
| Saarland | 3 | CDU | 1.07 |
| Saxony | 4 | CDU | 4.43 |
| Saxony-Anhalt | 4 | SPD | 2.62 |
| Schleswig-Holstein | 4 | SPD–Alliance 90/Greens | 2.79 |
| Thuringia | 4 | CDU | 2.44 |

record of electing judges with strong federalist leanings, thus giving to the upper house an indirect influence in constitutional cases involving the interpretation of federal laws and ordinances.[27]

## An Emerging Instrument of Opposition

In spite of its considerable powers, the Bundesrat largely functioned during its first 20 years in the shadow of the Bundestag, ratifying the latter's policies and those of the government's ruling party or coalition. Its leaders tended to view the Bundesrat as a nonpartisan chamber concerned exclusively with the merits of proposed legislation, an image reinforced by the dominant role of bureaucratic officials in its proceedings.

Since 1969, however, the Bundesrat has risen in political importance and popular awareness. Until then the parties dominating the lower house also controlled the upper chamber. Owing to the distribution of power among the parties within the states, however, the Christian Democrats—the party out of power in the government—enjoyed a 21–20 voting edge in the Bundesrat between 1969 and 1975—an advantage that swelled to 11 votes by 1979—leading to sharp confrontations with the governing parties in the Bundestag.

In the 1990s, however, the tables were turned. The ruling CDU/CSU–FDP coalition in the Bundestag confronted a Bundesrat overwhelmingly controlled by SPD-led coalitions in the *Länder*. Given that all financial legislation and nearly all legislation affecting the administration of federal law require the Bundesrat's consent, this house—contrary to the expectations of the Basic Law's founders—has evolved into a body virtually coequal with the Bundestag. In recent legis-

[27]See Donald P. Kommers, *Judicial Politics in West Germany* (Beverly Hills, CA: Sage, 1976), pp. 128–144.

lation periods, between 50 and 60 percent of all bills passed by the Bundestag required the Bundesrat's consent. The clash between the CDU/CSU-led government coalition was most evident in the twelfth Bundestag. No fewer than 85 government bills had to be taken up by the Mediation Committee, as opposed to 13 in the eleventh and 6 in the tenth Bundestag. Under these circumstances, important policy initiatives cannot be passed into law without considerable give-and-take by the two parliamentary bodies and by the major parties.

## The Legal System and the Judiciary

***Germany's Legal Tradition and the* Rechtsstaat**    The *Rechtsstaat* or "law state" is a key concept in the German legal order.[28] All just states are based on law, of course, but in its original form the German *Rechtsstaat* placed extraordinary emphasis upon legality. Germans viewed the state as a neutral entity entrusted with the resolution of public issues in accordance with objective standards of law, unsullied by the play of selfish interests or the machinations of political parties. The sovereign state—the axis of the law state—was the guarantor of freedom and equality, just as rights and obligations arose from membership in the state. Liberty did not precede law; rather, law defined it, and the judiciary, staffed by a professional class of impartial and apolitical civil servants loyal to the state, existed to enforce the law as written.

Under the Basic Law the *Rechtsstaat* remains a vital principle of German constitutionalism, but not in its earlier nineteenth-century sense. The *law state* would henceforth be limited by constitutionally guaranteed individual rights enforced by the judiciary, just as it would be moderated by the humanity implicit in the constitutional notion of *Sozialstaat* (freely translated, a *socially conscious state*). In legal theory the sovereign is no longer

---

[28]This subsection on law and the courts draws heavily from Donald P. Kommers, *The Constitutional Jurisprudence of the Federal Republic of Germany,* 2nd ed. (Durham, NC: Duke University Press, 1996).

supreme. Article 20 reads: "All state authority emanates from the people," and further, "Legislation shall be subject to the constitutional order; the executive and the judiciary shall be bound by law *and justice*" (italics added). Finally, Article 20 contains this remarkable provision: "All Germans shall have the right to resist any person or persons seeking to abolish [the] constitutional order should no other remedy be possible."

***The Court System***    Germany has a uniform and integrated judicial system. All lower and intermediate courts of appeal are state courts, whereas all courts of final appeal are federal tribunal courts. Federal law specifies the structure of state courts, but their administration and staffing, including the training of judges, is under the control of the *Länder.* The trademarks of the German judiciary are collegiality and specialization. Except for courts of minor jurisdiction, all tribunals are multijudge courts. Most operate in panels of three. In addition to the regular courts, which handle ordinary civil and criminal cases, there are separate judicial hierarchies consisting of labor, administrative, social, finance, and constitutional courts. The federal courts, as shown in Table 4.13, cap these hierarchies.

Justice in the FRG is carried out by more than 20,000 judges, nearly 80 percent of whom serve on the regular courts of ordinary civil and criminal jurisdiction. About one-quarter of these sit on the courts of specialized jurisdiction, while the high federal courts consist of under 500 judges. In addition to these legal professionals, the German courts have more than 4,000 public prosecutors. As might be expected of a *Rechtsstaat,* even the more than 50,000 attorneys practicing law in the FRG are regarded as officers of the courts.

***The Judges***    The training and professional standing of German judges varies from that of their peers in the United States and Britain. In the United States, for example, judgeships are usually awarded to lawyers in their middle years following successful private practice or experience in public office. In Germany, by contrast, lateral mobility of this kind is rare among legal professionals. After six years of study, which

---

**TABLE 4.13**

**COURTS OF THE FEDERATION AND THE *LÄNDER***

| Jurisdiction | Courts of the Federation | Courts of the Länder |
| --- | --- | --- |
| Constitutional | Federal Constitutional Court | 13 constitutional courts |
| Ordinary | Federal Court of Justice | 25 higher regional courts; 116 regional courts; 717 local courts |
| Labor | Federal Labor Court | 19 higher labor courts; 124 labor courts |
| Administrative | Federal Administrative Court | 16 higher administrative courts; 52 administrative courts |
| Social | Federal Social Court | 16 higher social courts; 69 social courts |
| Finance | Federal Finance Court | 19 finance courts |

*Source:* Wolfgang Heyde, *Justice and the Law in the Federal Republic of Germany* (Heidelberg: C. F. Müller Juristischer Verlag, 1994), p. 9.

---

includes practical training in various administrative and judicial capacities, law graduates must make their choice of a legal career. Those deciding to become judges go through still another three-year probationary period. Upon the successful completion of this training, they receive a judgeship with lifetime tenure and security. Judges can expect to ascend slowly in the hierarchy of the judicial establishment if they meet with the approval of the *Land* justice ministry; if they are lucky and know the right persons in Berlin, they may end their careers in one of the high federal courts.

The civil service orientation of the judiciary tends to be reinforced by the narrow social base from which judges, particularly those appointed by the *Länder,* are recruited. Almost half are the sons and daughters of parents who have spent their lives in the civil service. Federal judges tend to be more diversified in social background and occupational experience, largely because of the method by which they are selected. They are chosen by a committee of electors composed of 11 members of the Bundestag together with those *Land* and federal ministries whose authority is similar to the federal court to which a judge is to be named. This mechanism allows interest groups, political parties, state and federal agencies, and the public to participate in the selection process, producing a federal bench somewhat less characterized by professional inbreeding and political conservatism than the state judiciary.

***The Federal Constitutional Court***   The Federal Constitutional Court with its sweeping powers of judicial review is only as old as the Basic Law. To the surprise of many observers, this tribunal has developed into an institution of major policy-making importance. Judicial review was a relatively new departure in German constitutional history. Postwar German leaders were of the opinion that, in the light of Germany's authoritarian and totalitarian past, traditional parliamentary and judicial institutions were insufficient to safeguard the new liberal democratic order. They created a national constitutional tribunal, as well as equivalents at the *Land* level, to supervise the judiciary's interpretation of constitutional norms, to enforce a consistent reading of the constitution on the other branches of government, to resolve conflicts between branches and levels of government, and to protect the basic liberties of German citizens. Thus the old positivist belief separating the realm of law from the realm of politics was abandoned, together with the idea that justice could automatically be achieved through the mechanical application of general laws duly enacted by the legislature.

Structurally, the Federal Constitutional Court is divided into two chambers, called senates, each of which is composed of eight justices chosen for single 12-year terms. Half of the justices are chosen by the Bundestag's 12-member judicial selection committee and the other half by the Bundesrat. A two-thirds vote is required in both electoral organs. This method of selection, together with the requirement that the Bundestag and Bundesrat alternate in the selection of the court's president and vice president, usually means that judicial appointments are the subject of intensive bargaining among the parliamentary parties. No one party has been strong enough to make appointments over the objections of the other parties. Thus the court's membership has reflected fairly well the balance of forces in parliament as a whole.

**Judicial Review in Operation**   The Constitutional Court's jurisdiction includes 14 categories of disputes, nearly all of which the Basic Law prescribes. The Basic Law authorizes both judges and legislators, as well as state governments, to petition the court directly. Judges may initiate a "concrete" judicial review proceeding by asking the court to rule on a constitutional question arising out of a pending case if in their view the law under which a case has arisen is of doubtful validity under the Basic Law. On the other hand, a state government or one-third of the members of the Bundestag may initiate an "abstract" proceeding by petitioning the court to review the constitutionality of a statute. Cases on abstract review tend to draw the judges directly into the arena of political conflict, prompting its harshest critics to deplore what they perceive as the "judicialization" of politics.

Constitutional complaints account for about 95 percent—an average of 5,000 per year—of all cases coming to the court. These cases relate to fundamental rights and freedoms guaranteed by the Basic Law. To encourage Germans to view the constitution as the source of their rights and freedoms, the Basic Law (Article 93 [13]) authorizes ordinary citizens to file complaints with the Federal Constitutional Court in the event that their basic rights have been violated by the state. Such an action involves neither court costs nor even the participation of legal counsel, an ideal situation in which "Hans Everyman" can bring his woes to the attention of the country's highest tribunal.

**The Constitutional Court's Impact**   Public opinion polls continue to show the high regard German citizens have for the Constitutional Court. In this respect, it outranks all other institutions in the nation's public life, including the civil service and the churches. When the court speaks, Germany's "attentive public" listens; what people hear is often an outspoken tribunal reminding them of their constitutional values, their political morality, and their ethical goals as a nation. This attentiveness is by no means surprising, since the court's landmark cases have involved some of the issues most pressing to the ongoing health of Germany democracy. These have included decisions outlawing extremist parties, overturning certain campaign-finance legislation, prohibiting the display of crucifixes in public school classrooms, and declaring unconstitutional a liberal abortion law.

## Thinking Critically

1. How have postwar Germany's laws and institutions contributed to its distinctive record of political continuity and social stability?
2. On balance, have splinter parties served or hindered the cause of building democracy in Germany? Why might these parties and citizen initiatives be important to the good health of any democratic system?
3. Compared to other democracies, how do established political parties play a special role in German politics?
4. What institutional factors reinforce norms of consensus and incrementalism in the FRG? Why do these factors sometimes lead to frustration among German citizens?
5. How does the German electoral system represent an ingenious way of representing interests across the political spectrum?
6. What factors have helped to ensure the routine circulation of elites in the FRG?

## KEY TERMS

abstract judicial review *(233)*
Alliance for Jobs *(220)*
Bundesrat *(229)*
chancellor democracy *(223)*
citizen initiatives *(212)*
constructive vote of no confidence *(223)*
*Fraktion (226)*

Grand Coalition *(217)*
Greens *(207)*
*Neue Mitte (220)*
new middle class *(220)*
overhang votes *(214)*
PDS *(207)*
*Realos (207)*
*Rechtsstaat (231)*
second ballot *(214)*
semisovereign state *(211)*

# *F*URTHER READINGS

Baker, Kendall, Russell J. Dalton, and Kai Hildebrand. *Germany Transformed: Political Culture and the New Politics* (Cambridge, MA: Harvard University Press, 1981).

Blair, Philip M. *Federalism and Judicial Review in West Germany* (Oxford: Clarendon Press, 1981).

Braunthal, Gerard. *The German Social Democrats since 1969,* 2nd ed. (Boulder, CO: Westview Press, 1994).

Burkett, Tony. *Parties and Elections in West Germany* (New York: St. Martin's, 1975).

Cerny, Karl H. *Germany at the Polls: The Bundestag Elections of the 1980s* (Durham, NC: Duke University Press, 1990).

Clemens, Clay. *Reluctant Realists: The Christian Democrats and West German Ostpolitik* (Durham, NC: Duke University Press, 1989).

Dalton, Russell J. *Germans Divided: The 1994 Bundestagswahl and the Evolution of the German Party System* (Oxford: Berg Publishers, 1996).

Doering, Herbert, and Gordon Smith. *Party Government and Political Culture in Western Germany* (New York: St. Martin's, 1982).

Dyson, Kenneth H. F. *Party, State and Bureaucracy in Western Germany* (Beverly Hills, CA: Sage Publications, 1977).

Gunlicks, Arthur. *Local Government in the German Federal System* (Durham, NC: Duke University Press, 1986).

Heyde, Wolfgang. *Justice and Law in the Federal Republic of Germany* (Heidelberg: C. F. Müller Juristischer Verlag, 1994).

Jesse, Eckhard. *Elections: The Federal Republic of Germany* (Oxford: Berg Publishers, 1990).

Johnson, Nevil. *State and Government in the Federal Republic of Germany,* 2nd ed. (Oxford: Pergamon, 1983).

Kommers, Donald P. *The Federal Constitutional Court* (Washington, DC: American Institute for Contemporary German Studies, 1994).

Langguth, Gerd. *The Green Factor in West German Politics* (Boulder, CO: Westview Press, 1986).

Loewenberg, Gerhard. *Parliament in the German Political System* (Ithaca, NY: Cornell University Press, 1966).

Mayntz, Renate, and Fritz Scharpf. *Policy-making in the German Federal System* (Chapel Hill: University of North Carolina Press, 1963).

Padgett, Stephen, and Tony Burkett. *Political Parties and Elections in West Germany* (New York: St. Martin's, 1986).

Padgett, Stephen, and Thomas Saalfeld, eds. *Bundestagswahl 1998: End of an Era?* (Portland: Frank Cass, 2000).

Spath, Franz. *The Federal Presidency* (Washington, DC: American Institute for Contemporary German Studies, 1996).

Thaysen, Uwe. *The Bundesrat, the Länder and German Federalism* (Washington, DC: American Institute for Contemporary Germany Studies, 1994).

# C. PUBLIC POLICY

## CIVIL LIBERTIES: AN ORDERING OF CONSTITUTIONAL VALUES

To understand the distinctive culture of public policy making in the FRG, there is no better place to start than with its constitution. The first part of the Basic Law (Articles 1 to 19) is a charter of fundamental rights and an affirmation of human personhood. It is rooted in the natural law thesis that certain liberties of the individual are antecedent to organized society and beyond the reach of governmental power. As interpreted by the Federal Constitutional Court, the Basic Law has established a value-oriented order based on human dignity. Article 1 is no idle declaration. As the Basic Law's "highest legal value," the idea of human dignity—a concept that was clearly lacking in German politics during the period of Nazi dictatorship—has been employed by the Constitutional Court as the defining standard by which to measure the legitimacy of state actions as well as the uses of individual liberty.

Apart from the freedoms guaranteed by Articles 1, 2, 3, and 5, the Basic Law's fundamental rights include the freedoms of religion (Article 4), assembly (Article 8), association (Article 9), privacy (Articles 10 and 13), and movement (Article 11), together with the right to property (Article 14), the right to choose a trade or occupation (Article 12), and the right to refuse military service for reasons of conscience (Article 12a). Additionally, criminal defendants are accorded most of the rights and privileges nor-mally associated with the Anglo-American notion of due process of law.

These rights, however, have been proclaimed with an important German twist—that is, they are to be exercised responsibly and used to foster the growth of human dignity within the framework of the political and moral order ordained by the Basic Law. In this sense, Article 2 is a paradigm of Germany's special approach to basic rights. While individual liberty and personal autonomy are jealously guarded values of the legal order, they are also constrained by the equally important values of political order and social morality. Thus, the right to develop one's personality is limited by the moral code, just as the right to freedom of speech is limited by the inviolability of personal honor. As the Constitutional Court noted in a famous case on communications privacy: "The concept of man in the Basic Law is not that of an isolated, sovereign individual: rather, the Basic Law has decided in favor of a relationship between individual and community in the sense of a person's dependence on and commitment to the community, without infringing upon a person's individual value."[29]

With regard to the polity as a whole, the Basic Law creates what the Constitutional Court refers to repeatedly as a "militant democracy." This means that certain forms of speech and behavior

---

[29]Walter F. Murphy and Joseph Tanenhaus, *Comparative Constitutional Law* (New York: St. Martin's, 1977), p. 660.

---

A CLOSER LOOK

4.5

### ARTICLE 65 OF THE BASIC LAW—THE CHANCELLOR

The Federal Chancellor shall determine, and be responsible for, the general policy guidelines. Within the limits set by these guidelines, each Federal Minister shall conduct the affairs of his department autonomously and on his own responsibility. The Federal Government shall decide on differences of opinion between Federal Ministers. The Federal Chancellor shall conduct the affairs of the Federal Government in accordance with rules of procedure adopted by it and approved by the Federal President.

described as anticonstitutional—activities that would probably be protected under prevailing U.S. constitutional doctrine—may be legally punished. The Basic Law predicates political freedom on the acceptance of certain principles of political obligation. Freedom of association, for instance, is guaranteed, but associations "the purposes or activities of which … are directed against the constitutional order" are prohibited (Article 9). Similarly, political parties "whose aims … seek to impair or abolish the free democratic basic order" may be declared unconstitutional (Article 21). These provisions are not accidental. They spring from the conviction of the FRG's founders, who drafted the Basic Law in the aftermath of Weimar's collapse and Hitler's totalitarianism, that a democracy cannot be an unarmed society but has the right—so long as the rule of law is preserved—to dissolve organizations and prohibit activities aimed at the destruction of republican government.

## ASYLUM AND CITIZENSHIP

A portrait of the FRG's civil liberties record, like that of other advanced constitutional democracies, would reveal much light but also some shadows. At various points during the 1990s, the shadows included attacks on asylum seekers and foreign residents by youthful gangs and other acts of aggressive nationalism. Western observers have applauded the government for cracking down on the most xenophobic of these groups, but they also find mixed signals about the FRG's commitment to absorbing the immigrant population into the mainstream of society. As examples of this lack of commitment, they point to German policies on asylum and citizenship.

Until 1993, Article 16 (2) of the Basic Law granted the right of asylum to all persons persecuted on political grounds, a powerful expression of the FRG's constitutional morality in the light of Germany's Nazi past. The policy behind Article 16 (2) was extremely generous. Any person arriving on German soil who claimed asylum on the ground of a well-founded fear of political persecution could have that claim adjudicated, during which time the claimant would be entitled to free housing and other benefits under German law.

In the early 1990s, however, following the influx of over a million asylum seekers, parliament introduced a constitutional amendment to limit the right of asylum. The ensuing debate took place as extreme right-wing parties won seats in a number of *Land* parliaments by pandering to popular antiforeign sentiments. However, mainstream politicians as well were concerned about the strain asylum seekers were placing on the nation's welfare system and the presumed threat to the security of job-seeking Germans in the face of rising unemployment. In the end, parliament reincorporated the right to asylum into the first paragraph of a new Article 16a, but added qualifying paragraphs that some critics thought would seriously vitiate that right.

According to the new article, which parliament ratified in June 1993, aliens may not claim a right to asylum if parliament has designated their country of origin as safe from political persecution (Article 16a [3]). In addition, aliens may not claim a right to asylum if they come to Germany overland from a member state of the European Union or from a third country statutorily defined as politically safe (Article 16a [2]). If such persons fail to seek asylum in the safe country through which they pass en route to Germany—by land or by air—they forfeit their right to apply for asylum in Germany and thus can be summarily turned back at the border or at an international airport. Finally, aliens claiming asylum from a country of origin that has been declared safe will not have their asylum claims heard unless they can overcome the presumption that they will not suffer political persecution or inhumane treatment upon their return.

Article 16a and its implementing statutes had their intended effect, reducing asylum applications to a fraction of their previous number. However, unsuccessful asylum seekers from Ghana, Iran, Iraq, and Togo challenged the constitutionality of the new policy's most controversial features—i.e., parliament's definition of safe countries of origin, the "third state rule," and the possibility of instant deportation at German airports. In a 234-page opinion handed down on May 14, 1996, the Constitutional Court sustained the validity of each of these practices, claiming that they did not violate the Basic Law's guarantee of political asylum in that the petitioners were afforded the opportunity for asylum in secure third countries.

The asylum controversy of the 1990s was part of a larger debate over immigration and citizenship policy. The influx of refugees and the presence of millions of permanent foreign residents and their families, many of whom had lived and worked in Germany for decades, triggered demands to make it easier for resident aliens to acquire citizenship. Under the Nationality Act of 1913, which remains the law today, citizenship is based on the principle of *jus sanguinis* (i.e., by right of blood or descent rather than by *jus soli* or place of birth). Because of this policy, it has been easier for non-German-speaking ethnic Germans from Eastern Europe to acquire German citizen-

ship than for a third-generation resident alien who is fluent in the language and thoroughly privy to German ways but whose ancestors came from Turkey.

In reality, the FRG is a country of immigrants. Foreign residents make up 8.5 percent of the population, more than in any other European nation (see Figure 4.2). In some large cities, foreign residents exceed one-fourth of the total population. Yet these residents are not permitted to vote or run for public office, they experience discrimination in housing and education, and they are subject to deportation on specified legal grounds. Despite the de facto presence of a large immigrant population and the long-term need for such residents in light of the low native

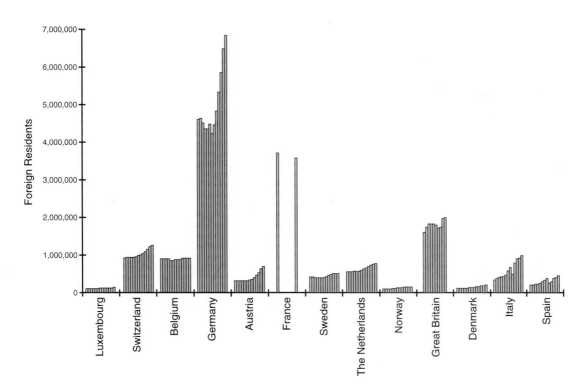

**Figure 4.2 FOREIGN RESIDENTS IN SELECT EUROPEAN STATES, 1981–1996**

*Source:* Adapted from "Statistiken zur Migration und Integration von Migranten," *http://www. uni-bamberg.de/~ba6ef3/ds118a_d.htm.*

birthrate,[30] the FRG continues to understand itself in ethnocultural terms, one reason for Germany's low rate of naturalization.

In 1999, the Schröder government successfully passed legislation to ease the terms under which some foreign residents—especially German-born citizens—can obtain citizenship, and the waiting time for many applicants has been shortened. However, in the wake of recent upheavals in the Balkans and elsewhere in Eastern Europe, even the most liberally minded Social Democrats have had to admit that the FRG cannot afford to meet the needs of all immigrants who wish to cross its borders. Some, like the outspoken minister of the interior and former Green, Otto Schily, have gone so far as to advocate draconian measures for keeping additional foreigners out.

## PUBLIC ADMINISTRATION: DECENTRALIZED FEDERALISM

There are five levels of public administration in Germany, organized mainly on a spatial or territorial basis.[31] The first is the national level. But here (except for those few functions administered directly by the national government), the various ministries are engaged mainly in formulating general policy. Under Article 65 of the Basic Law, each federal minister is in complete control of his or her department, though it must be run within the limits of the chancellor's policy guidelines. The command hierarchy includes the federal minister, the parliamentary state secretary (the ministry's chief spokesperson in the Bundestag), and the permanent state secretary—a career civil servant who, along with aides, plays a significant rule in the policy-making process. Finally, under-secretaries head the major departments of each ministry, which in turn are divided into sections, offices, or bureaus.

The ministries work out their programs in accordance with the guidelines and political predispositions of their top executives. Yet the ministries do not shape policy by issuing central directives from on high any more than they shape it from the bottom up on the basis of purely professional considerations. The planning units of the various ministries weave their program recommendations out of clientele demands, the expertise of bureaucrats, and the politics of top executives. In general, policy planning is more of an interactive process, following what some scholars have described as a "dialogue model" of policy making,[32] involving a good deal of discussion and bargaining within and among bureaucracies.

*Land* governments are the next level of administration. In addition to administering federal law, they enact laws in certain areas within the framework of national policy guidelines and in areas of their exclusive jurisdiction. Public policies at the *Land* level are carried out by *Land* ministries, various functional *Land* agencies, and several self-governing corporations. The last three levels of administration are the administrative district, counties and county-free independent cities, and municipalities. The administrative district, found in the six larger *Länder,* "is a general purpose regional *Land* institution of administration."[33] The county, at the lowest level of *Land* administration, carries out functions delegated to it by state governments. Finally, municipalities or associations of local governments, whose independence is guaranteed by the Basic Law, are responsible, within the framework of *Land* law, for the provision of local public services.

## SOCIAL AND ECONOMIC POLICY

### Fiscal Policy

The fiscal articles of the Basic Law (Articles 104a through Article 115l) mandate a system of rev-

---

[30]See Rainer Münz and Ralf E. Urich, "Depopulation after Unification? Population Prospects for East Germany, 1990–2010," *German Politics and Society* 13 (1995), p. 1–48.
[31]Arthur B. Gunlicks, "Administrative Centralization in the Making and Remaking of Modern Germany," *Review of Politics* 46 (1984), pp. 336–340.

[32]Ibid., p. 100.
[33]Gunlicks, p. 336.

enue sharing among the federation, *Länder,* and local governments, the administration of which requires close cooperation among levels of government. Total tax revenue in 1993 amounted to DM 748.8 billion, of which federal and state shares were each 42.5 percent and that of municipalities 15 percent. The federal government derives its tax revenues mainly from corporate and personal income taxes, the value-added tax, the turnover tax on imports, and selected excise taxes. The main source of *Land* revenue is from taxes on property, automobiles, beer, and inheritance, whereas local governments depend primarily on real estate and business taxes. In addition, *Land* and local governments draw a portion of their tax revenue from income, turnover, and value-added taxes.

The goal of German fiscal policy is to bring about a "unity of living standards" in the various *Länder* and throughout the FRG. This is the reason for the detailed revenue-sharing provisions of the Basic Law. Income, corporate, and turnover taxes are among the tax receipts shared between levels of government. Federal and state governments have an equal claim to these funds after local governments have received their share. In addition, federal and state governments are constitutionally bound to help each other financially. Under so-called vertical equalization procedures, the federal government redistributes a given proportion of its revenues to the poorer states, just as equivalent horizontal procedures require the wealthier states to share a portion of their revenues with poorer *Länder.*

The new eastern *Länder* did not participate in the revenue-sharing scheme until 1995. The Unity Treaty exempted the new *Länder* from the fiscal provisions of the Basic Law for five years, during which time it was hoped that their deficient economies and substandard social structures could be repaired. In the interim, federation and *Länder* agreed to establish an off-budget plan known as the "German Unity Fund." Under this plan, billions of DM were transferred annually to the eastern *Länder,* 80 percent of which was raised in capital markets and the rest supplied from the federal budget. In one form or another, such special subventions of the east have been maintained.

## General Economic Policy

The FRG is noted for its *Sozialmarktwirtschaft* or "social market economy" (SME), a system of free enterprise guided and supported by the strong hand of government and undergirded by a comprehensive scheme of social welfare. In this way, Germany has managed to avoid the extremes of a pure laissez-faire economy and centralized state control.

German federalism has made its own distinctive contribution to the growth of the SME. As Christopher Allen notes, *Land* governments encouraged banks to adjust "their investment and loan policies to improve the competitive position of key industries in various regions" and to "invest heavily in vocational education to provide the skills so necessary for high quality manufactured goods" capable of competing in world markets.[34] *Land* governments also worked closely with business and organized labor, not only to encourage the development of a modern, competitive economy but also to shape the framework of cooperation among trade unions, corporations, banks, and educational institutions, a process of coordination matched at the national level by such major policy initiatives as the Economic Stabilization Act of 1967 and the Codetermination Act of 1975.

***The Codetermination Act***   The issue of codetermination offers an excellent example of the unusual pattern of politics and policy in postwar Germany, one that encourages bargaining and mutual partisan adjustment among state agencies, private groups, and political parties. Codetermination has roots far back in German history. Already in the 1840s workers were demanding a voice in shaping the conditions of their labor. Their influence was gradually solidified and augmented through a series of acts in the late 1800s and the first few decades of the 1900s, so that by 1922 employees were legally

---

[34]"Corporation and Regional Economic Policies in the Federal Republic of Germany: The 'Meso' Politics of Industrial Adjustment," *Publius* 19 (1989), pp. 156–157.

entitled to at least one representative on factory management boards. The progress of workers' rights received a brief setback under the Nazi regime. But following the war all the German *Länder* reestablished work councils—employee groups designed to offer proposals to management—and gave them varying degrees of influence in determining company policies relating to production and operating methods.

Current codetermination policy is based on the Works Constitution Act of 1952 and its successor, the Works Constitution Act of 1972. The 1952 act established one-third employee representation on the management boards of all private industries employing between 500 and 2,000 workers (a principle that was later extended to the public sector), and its 1972 replacement authorized every factory or business with more than five employees to elect a work council to bargain with plant managers over issues not dealt with in collective bargaining agreements.

Finally, in 1976, after four more years of struggle and compromise among various parliamentary groups, an overwhelming majority of the Bundestag passed the Codetermination Act, underscoring the consensus achieved over years of negotiation. This act extended the principle of numerical parity, requiring equal representation of workers on company supervisory boards, to include all enterprises with more than 2,000 employees, affecting about 7 million workers in more than 500 firms. It did this by providing for 12- to 20-member supervisory boards, depending on the size of the plant, with an equal number of shareholders and representatives from the workforce, the latter to include delegations elected separately by blue-collar, white-collar, and managerial staff.

Although the unions were not entirely pleased with the allocation of seats on the boards or with the provision that allows the chairperson—usually a shareholder—to break a tie vote, the act nevertheless gave them a significant foothold in industrial decision making. Not long after the act's passage, it was challenged in the Federal Constitutional Court on grounds that it violated the Basic Law's rights to property, association, and entrepreneurial freedom. But the court cautiously upheld the act, suggesting that codetermination is a

legitimate application of the constitutional ideal of a "social federal state" (Article 20).

This example of codetermination illustrates the institutionalized process of bargaining among various interests that create policy in the FRG, a process requiring extensive cooperation, consultation, and compromise. This filtering process means that a large degree of consensus is necessary before any real movement in public policy can be achieved. This is why policy change in the FRG has been aptly described as *incremental* rather than *large-scale,* even in the face of major shifts in electoral politics.

***Economic Stabilization Act***    Until the mid-1960s, German economic policy contained a strong antiplanning bias. With the adoption of the Economic Stabilization Act, however, long-term fiscal planning became a vital element of the FRG's economy. Influenced in part by Keynesian economic theory, the act authorized the federal government to (1) coordinate the budgetary policies of state and national governments, (2) change, temporarily, rates of taxation on personal and corporate incomes without prior parliamentary approval, (3) stimulate the economy during periods of recession by public expenditures up to specified amounts, and (4) harmonize general fiscal policy with monetary policy.

Here, too, as with codetermination, an enormous amount of cooperation was required within and among governmental and nongovernmental bodies to make the Stabilization Act work. A Fiscal Planning Commission (FPC) consisting of federal and state representatives, as well as representatives from the Federal Bank (Bundesbank), business, and the political parties, was formed to coordinate budgetary policy between the national government and the *Länder.* Over the years, the FPC has contributed to the development of fiscal policy in a number of ways: drawing up draft budgets for national and state governments, setting guidelines for economic growth, coordinating tax policy with cuts in expenditures, and ensuring that federal and state policies complement rather than contradict each other.[35]

---

[35]See Eric Owen Smith, *The German Economy* (London: Routledge, 1994), pp. 61–62.

## A CLOSER LOOK 4.6

### GERMANY'S SOCIAL CODE

1. Purposes of the Social Code

(1) The provisions of the Social Code are intended to provide for social benefits, including social and educational assistance, with the object of making social justice and social security a reality. Its aim is to contribute to ensuring an existence worthy of human beings; providing equal opportunities for the free development of the personality, especially for young persons; protecting and encouraging the family; enabling persons to derive a livelihood through freely chosen activity; and averting or compensating for special burdens in life, *inter alia,* by helping persons to help themselves.

*Source:* Social Code (*Sozialgesetzbuch*), Federal Minister of Labor and Social Affairs, Bonn, 1981; BGBl., I, 1975, 3015.

## Social Welfare Policy

Germany has typically spent more than a third of its GNP on social services—among the highest in Western Europe. Social policy expenditures on all governmental levels amount to nearly one-half of total governmental expenditures. As seen in earlier sections, this social welfare system draws upon a long tradition of state-supported social policies. The current system includes generous programs of health insurance, unemployment compensation, industrial accident insurance, pensions, housing benefits, and youth welfare programs. Old-age pensions, the largest of these programs—they typically account for one-third of the social budget—are financed by contributions from the insured and their employers. Adjusted to inflation and other economic indicators, social security payments have increased nearly every year since 1957, and they are extraordinarily generous. The system also includes a number of other benefits: relief payments for the needy, child benefit allowances, rent subsidies, nursing care for the aged, and special reparations for former prisoners of war and persons who suffered losses under Nazism because of their race, religion, or political beliefs.

After unification, the FRG's social policy, like other economic programs, was extended to the new eastern *Länder.* Social benefits, however, particularly unemployment pay and retirement pensions, were adjusted to eastern economic standards and would not reach western levels until the east achieved economic parity with the west. Even so, these benefits resulted in significant increases in pensions for East Germans who were, as in the west, given the option of retiring at 57 years of age at 75 percent of their former gross pay. West Germany would bear most of the social costs for health and welfare, although some advantages associated with the GDR's old system, such as 20 weeks of paid leave for women after giving birth, were phased out. The costs of these programs were met in part by large transfers of public funds from the federal and state governments.

Yet as might be expected in times of economic austerity, the German government has found it steadily more difficult to supply its citizens with such high levels of well-being. This problem has become particularly acute with the FRG's demographic shift, as Berlin struggles with the challenge of financing the health costs and other retirement needs of an aging population. This factor, combined with the continuing task of modernizing the eastern German economy, has caused the Schröder government to consider a variety of cost-cutting measures and the elimination of some marginal programs.

## Summary

As noted earlier, social welfare policy in postwar Germany has been the product of consensus politics, as well as a long historical tradition. The CDU, SPD, business organizations, and labor unions can all take some credit for Germany's extensive system of social insurance and welfare benefits. The system represents not only a long-standing accord between these groups but also a social compact between the generations. At times, there have been conflicts among these groups, as some threaten to cross the invisible boundary lines of this consensus. This was the case in 1966, when the CDU/CSU–FDP coalition proposed substantial cuts in corporate taxes and social spending in order to spur economic growth, facilitate the creation of jobs, and reduce a public debt aggravated by reunification. In response, union leaders organized a massive protest demonstration in Bonn and attacked the "savings package" as an assault on the social market economy and a threat to the time-honored consensus between labor, management, and government.

Whatever adjustments are made in the delicate balance of interests governing the FRG's social economy, the German model will continue to be less centralized than the French or the British, while still much more sensitive to social concerns than the American. Government ownership of industry and intervention in the market supply of goods and services are still other features of the social market economy, although by the 1990s, the government had begun to divest itself of ownership in areas such as transportation, the postal services, and communications. In addition, although the German government is unusual in owning stock in hundreds of private companies, here too it has begun to denationalize some of them. At the same time, showing that generalizations about Germany's social economic policy are always risky, several state governments continue to subsidize certain industries, either for the purpose of reviving them or to keep them from moving their plants to other states or countries.

## FOREIGN POLICY, NATIONAL UNITY, AND THE ROAD TO NORMALCY

### Resolving the "German Problem"

Germany's foreign policy since 1945 may be summarized as having three foundations. The first is the state's rootedness in the security and common values of the Atlantic Alliance, especially its close ties to the United States. The second is its membership in the European community of states, which was founded on the need to end long-standing tensions with France and has now reached its highest point in the FRG's major economic and political contributions to the European Union (EU). Yet the third leg of the FRG's postwar policy—the need to resolve the "German problem"—for decades prevented the country from fully assuming the functions of a "normal" state.

This problem was the fulcrum of the East-West conflict in post–World War II Europe. First of all, the FRG's hostile relationship with the GDR carried over into all of its relations with Eastern Europe. Additionally, West German rearmament within the North Atlantic Treaty Organization (NATO), coupled with the refusal under a succession of Christian Democratic governments to recognize the Oder-Neisse line as a permanent boundary between Poland and Germany, was viewed by the Soviet Union as a dangerous threat to peace in Central Europe. The city of Berlin represented still another component of the German problem. Cleft by concrete and barbed wire and later by the infamous Wall, the city became the most poignant symbol of German separation and Cold War confrontation.

There clearly could be no resolution of the German problem without a relaxation of tension in Central Europe. Moscow was the key to any such resolution. It is significant that both Adenauer and Brandt journeyed to the Soviet Union—the former in 1955, the latter in 1970—in search of "normalized" relations between Bonn and Moscow. For Adenauer, however, normalization meant not only the reestablishment of

diplomatic relations with the Soviet Union, which he accomplished, but the reunification of Germany, which he failed to achieve. In his Moscow talks, he spoke of the "abnormality" of Germany's division, leaving his Soviet hosts with the message that "there can be no real security in Europe without the restoration of German unity." A decade and a half later, with Germany still divided, Willy Brandt sought to define the *initial* steps to normalization. He announced that it was time "to reconstitute our relationship to the East upon the basis of the unrestricted, reciprocal renunciation of force, proceeding from the existing political situation in Europe."

Brandt's eastern policy (*Ostpolitik*) was designed to achieve this result. The cornerstone of the new policy was the Soviet–West German treaty on the renunciation of the use of force, signed in Moscow in August 1970. The Warsaw Treaty, signed in November of the same year, rounded out this foundation. Essentially, both treaties recognized existing boundaries in Europe. Another stone in Brandt's rising edifice of detente was the 1971 Quadripartite Agreement on Berlin. In fact, Brandt conditioned Bonn's ratification of the Moscow and Warsaw treaties upon progress toward settlement of the Berlin question. Pledging to resolve their disputes by peaceful means, the four powers reaffirmed their individual and joint responsibility for Berlin.

The capstone of detente was the Basic Treaty between East and West Germany, signed in December 1972. The FRG and GDR both agreed to develop regular ties with each other on the basis of equal rights. The concept of "two German states in one nation," which the FRG urged on the GDR, was conspicuously left out of the treaty. Instead, the right of both German states to "territorial integrity" and "self-determination" was affirmed. In addition, the two states agreed that "neither … can represent the other in the international spheres or act on its behalf." In supplementary protocols both states also agreed to settle their frontier problems, to improve trade relations, and to cooperate in scientific, technological, medical, cultural, athletic, and environmental fields.

## Gorbachev and *Glasnost*

The advent of the reform Communist Mikhail Gorbachev in the Soviet Union and the associated policies of *glasnost* (openness) and *perestroika* (restructuring) placed East-West relations in a new light and encouraged many Germans to dream about the prospects of German reunification within a unified Europe. GDR leaders, however, remained adamant in viewing the Basic Treaty as a step toward a fully sovereign and independent GDR—an interpretation the FRG had never accepted. Unlike Poland and Hungary and the Soviet Union itself, the GDR refused to move toward democracy or free markets. The hard-liners in charge of the regime—most of them old men—brooked no opposition to the socialist system of their creation. Yet we have seen that by 1989 this stand was no longer realistic. As thousands of young East Germans fled to the FRG by way of Hungary in search of freedom and employment, GDR leaders seemed increasingly isolated in their own backyard. They accused Hungary of violating various legal treaties and denounced the FRG for encouraging the exodus, but these charges were seen for what they were: feeble attempts to hide the fragility of a regime deeply in trouble in the face of a "new order" emerging in Eastern Europe.

The GDR was caught on the horns of an excruciating dilemma. It could either loosen up the regime and allow its people to move freely in and out of their country or continue its present course. The first option would lead to greater contact between East and West Germans and could undermine its authority. The second option—keeping a tight grip on its people—would lead to another crisis of legitimacy and the continued flight of its most productive citizens. With the collapse of the hardline Communist regime in October 1989, a hastily reassembled government under younger and more pragmatic leadership chose the first option. In the following weeks, events unfolded with dizzying speed, surprising even close observers of German affairs. By the end of the year the Communist Party had disavowed its leading role, promised to hold free elections, and exposed the corruption of

its longtime leaders as an angry and outspoken citizenry demanded their prosecution. In the meantime, the Brandenburg Gate was opened, GDR citizens waved FRG flags in the streets, and East and West German leaders began to talk about a new relationship.

## The Progress and Politics of German Unity

The story of German unity is a fascinating tale. On the one hand, the story seems to show that the forces of history, once unleashed, cannot be stopped. On the other hand, unity would not have come about without the cooperation of the Allied powers, especially the United States and the Soviet Union, and the intense negotiations between the GDR and FRG. Although the FRG held most of the trump cards in these negotiations, the GDR managed to extract significant promises from the FRG, including some changes in the Basic Law. The negotiations between the GDR and the FRG, and those between Britain, France, the Soviet Union, and the United States, did not proceed on separate tracks. They were conducted—in coordinated fashion—over many months; hence, they were known as the *two-plus-four* talks. This mix of international and domestic politics, with its interplay of constitutional law and public policy, made the new Germany possible.

Several months earlier, Chancellor Kohl had proposed a ten-point plan for Germany's eventual union. He had envisioned the development of a *contractual community* in which the two Germanys would establish "confederative structures" leading first to social, monetary, and economic union and eventually, perhaps in a few years, to political union. Events, however, overtook him, as well as those East German reform groups who merely wanted to humanize socialism in the GDR. The "bloodless coup" occurred on March 18, 1990, when East Germans voted in their first free election since Hitler was named chancellor in 1933. Unity *now* was their unmistakable message. Fired up, and with Kohl at the controls, the unity train roared toward its destination. One possible route to unity was the formation of an all-German government under the terms of a new constitution ratified by all Germans. Instead, East Germany agreed to become part of the existing FRG under the simple procedure of accession laid down in Article 23 of the Basic Law.

Four landmarks paved the way to reunification. These are the State Treaty on Monetary, Economic, and Social Union (May 18, 1990), the All-German Election Treaty (August 3, 1990), the Unity Treaty (August 31, 1990), and the Treaty on the Final Settlement with Respect to Germany (September 12, 1990). The GDR and the FRG negotiated the first three treaties, though in consultation with the Allies; the last was the product mainly of the two-plus-four negotiations.

### A CLOSER LOOK 4.7

### AN INDIVISIBLE NATION

On the night of October 2–3, 1990, East and West Germans came together on the *Platz der Republik,* the great lawn before the Reichstag, to celebrate their reunification. Many of them flew the black-red-gold flag of the FRG, which had been the tricolor of the two previous German democracies as well (1848 and 1918). Germany was felt to be reclaiming the best elements of its common past. At the same time, a good number of European Community flags were also in evidence, with the circle of 12 gold stars on a field of blue, seeming to reflect the often-stated aim of the two societies to work together henceforth—not for a "German Europe" but for a "European Germany."

***The State Treaty***    The State Treaty united the social, economic, and monetary systems of East and West Germany.[36] It effectively extended the FRG's social market economy eastward, installing in all of Germany an economy based on private ownership, competition, and the free movement of goods and services. As of July 2, 1990, the West German deutsche mark became the official currency of the GDR. Under the terms of the treaty, all "[w]ages, salaries, grants, pensions, rents and leases" were to be converted at a rate of one East German mark to one West German mark. All other claims and assets were to be converted at a rate of two to one. One effect of the currency union was to increase the importance of Germany's central bank, already renowned for its control over monetary policy in the FRG.[37] The bank would now take responsibility for all of Germany and sorely test its capacity to fight inflation in the face of price rises that were surely to occur from the transfer of billions of deutsche marks into the east.

The State Treaty covered other areas such as intra-German and foreign trade, agriculture environmental protection, social and health insurance, budgetary planning, and tax policy. For each of these areas, the treaty required the GDR to adopt laws consistent with policies prevailing in the FRG. In some instances, however, transitional arrangements were worked out to ease the pain of the legal and structural changes the GDR would have to make. One of these temporary arrangements was the establishment of an arbitration tribunal to resolve disputes arising under the treaty.

***The All-German Election Treaty***    The GDR election of March 18, 1990, set the stage for the all-German election of December 2, 1990. The March election resulted in an impressive victory for the CDU-led Alliance for Germany and thus for German unity. The new parliament went on to create a grand coalition consisting of the Alliance for Germany, the SPD, and the Federation of Free Democrats under the leadership of Lothar de Maizière (CDU). This coalition negotiated the unity treaties with West Germany's CDU-FDP coalition government, one of which was the All-German Election Treaty. The GDR, which had a system of pure proportional representation, objected to the FRG's 5 percent clause, arguing that it would keep smaller parties out of the all-German parliament. Negotiations led to an agreement that would retain the 5 percent clause for all of Germany but permit smaller parties and groups in the GDR to field candidates in alliance with other, larger parties in the west. This plan, however, favored some small parties at the expense of others. In response to petitions by the PDS, Greens, and the far-right Republicans, the Federal Constitutional Court held that the election agreement discriminated against these parties, and it went on to recommend that for this first all-German election, the 5 percent clause should be adopted separately in both east and west. An amended election law followed this recommendation.

***The Unity Treaty***    The historic Unity Treaty—a massive document consisting of 433 printed pages—provided for the GDR's accession to the FRG and the application of the Basic Law to all of Germany. Its 45 articles, annexes, and special provisions touched almost every aspect of German public policy. The treaty's "Special Provisions on the Conversion to Federal Law" appeared in 19 chapters that dealt with the laws, procedures, and institutions subject to the jurisdiction of the various federal ministries. While extending FRG law immediately to numerous policy areas in the eastern *Länder,* these special provisions also contained transitional and interim measures to accommodate special conditions in the ex-GDR.

***Constitutional Amendments***    The Unity Treaty amended several provisions of the Basic Law. First, the preamble was amended to delete all

---

[36]Treaty between the Federal Republic of Germany and the German Democratic Republic Establishing a Monetary, Economic and Social Union (New York: German Information Center, 1990 [official translation]).

[37]For a study of the role of the Bundesbank in the FRG's political system, see Ellen Kennedy, *The Bundesbank* (New York: Council on Foreign Relations Press, 1991).

## THE PATH TO GERMAN UNITY

### 1989

| | |
|---|---|
| July–September | GDR citizens flee to the FRG by way of Hungary. |
| October 9 | 100,000 people demonstrate in Leipzig to the chant, "We are the people." |
| October 18 | Erich Honecker is removed as head of the GDR. |
| November 7 | GDR government resigns after 1 million people demonstrate in Berlin. |
| November 9 | Berlin Wall is breached. |
| November 28 | Chancellor Kohl announces his Ten-Point program for unity. |
| December 1 | GDR constitution amended to end the SED's monopoly of power. |

### 1990

| | |
|---|---|
| March 18 | First free election in GDR. Overwhelming victory for parties allied with Kohl's CDU. |
| April 12 | GDR legislature elects first democratic government. CDU's Lothar de Maizière elected prime minister. |
| May 18 | State Treaty on Monetary, Economic, and Social Union. |
| July 22 | GDR legislature reestablishes its five constituent *Länder.* |
| August 3 | All-German Election Treaty signed. |
| August 31 | Unity Treaty signed. |
| September 12 | Treaty on the Final Settlement with Respect to Germany signed. |
| October 3 | Day of German unity. GDR ceases to exist. |
| October 4 | First all-German legislature meets in the Berlin Reichstag building. |
| October 24 | Five eastern *Länder* elect new parliaments. |
| December 2 | First all-German Bundestag elections. |

references to the goal of reunification, for "Germans in [the sixteen *Länder*] have [now] achieved the unity and freedom of Germany in free self-determination." Importantly for the FRG's neighbors, this new language effectively froze Germany's present borders, making it legally impossible for Germany to claim other territories lost as a result of World War II. Second, the treaty repealed Article 23—the very provision under which the GDR acceded to the FRG. In short, no "other parts of Germany" were left to be incorporated into the FRG by accession. Third, the treaty added the following italicized words to Article 146: "This Basic Law, *which is valid for the entire German people following the achievement of the unity and freedom of Germany,* shall cease to be in force on the day on which a constitution adopted by a free decision of the German people comes into force." Fourth, Article 135a was amended to relieve the FRG of certain liabilities incurred by the GDR or its legal entities. Finally, the treaty changed the number of votes allocated to the states in the Bundesrat under the terms of Article 51.

In addition to these amendments, the Unity Treaty inserted a new article—Article 143—into the Basic Law. The new article allowed the all-German government to deal flexibly with issues that might otherwise have slowed down or even stopped the unity train. Abortion, property rights, and intergovernmental relations were among these issues. The eastern *Länder,* for example, were unable to abide by the revenue-sharing provisions of the Basic Law or other obligations growing out of its scheme of federal-state relations. There appeared to be no constitutional objection to this particular deviation clause.

*Abortion*    The deviation clause of Article 143 (1) was another matter. Its incorporation into the Unity Treaty represented a compromise between east and west over abortion. In 1975, the Federal Constitutional Court had struck down West Germany's liberalized abortion law, holding that it violated the right to life within the meaning of Article 2 (1) of the Basic Law as well as the state's duty to protect human dignity under Article 1 (1). In so ruling, the court obligated the state to make abortion a crime at all stages of pregnancy, subject to exceptions specified by law. The GDR, on the other hand, permitted abortion on demand within the first three months of pregnancy. The effect of Article 143 was to allow East and West Germany to follow their respective policies on abortion. The FRG conceded this much to the GDR. But the treaty also required the Bundestag to enact an all-German policy on abortion by the end of 1992 "to ensure better protection of unborn life and provide a better solution in conformity with the Constitution of conflict situations faced by pregnant women" (Article 31 [4]). This was the GDR's concession to the west.

These concessions, however, raised a difficult constitutional issue, for Article 143 bans deviations from the Basic Law in violation of Articles 19 (2) and 79 (3). The first flatly prohibits any encroachment on a basic right; the second bars amendments that contravene principles laid down in Articles 1 (human dignity) and 20 (enshrining the rule of law). The constitutional issue was whether the deviation clause encroached upon the principle of human dignity with respect to abortion. In addition, some wondered whether a treaty could suspend the application of a court ruling. These questions remained unanswered in 1991 as the Bundestag heatedly debated a number of abortion reform proposals. In the end, a compromise law was passed that decriminalized abortions performed during the first trimester of pregnancy, although in a subsequent ruling the Constitutional Court required women contemplating abortions to submit to pro-life counseling before making their final decision.

*Property*    The deviation clause of Article 143 (1) was also designed to deal with the problem of property rights. On June 15, 1990, the GDR and FRG governments signed a Joint Declaration on the Settlement of Open Property Issues. This agreement provided that property illegally taken by the GDR's Communist government between 1949 and 1989, including expropriated businesses and property placed under state administration, was to be returned to its rightful owner. Compensation would be paid in the event that property could not be returned. The treaty contained some exceptions to this policy of restitution. Expropriated property would not be returned to their former owners if needed for investment purposes—a rule applied mainly to factories and large businesses—if innocently acquired by third parties, or if incapable of being returned in its original form.

The most controversial part of the property settlement was its exclusion from restitution of property expropriated by the Soviet Union in eastern Germany between 1945 and 1949. The Soviet Union had seized all landholdings over 250 acres and distributed most of them to small farmers. Prime Minister de Maizière refused to undo these acts on the grounds that the return of these millions of acres to their former owners would cause enormous social unrest in the east. Yet the right to property, the rule of law, and equality under law are core values of the Basic Law. Accordingly, former owners of land in the east challenged the 1945–1949 exclusion in the Constitutional Court. In this instance, however, the achievement of unity—one of the Basic Law's highest values—outweighed the right to property in the form of its restoration. Further, the court declared that the 1945–1949 takings occurred before the Basic Law entered into force.

*Other Treaty Provisions*    The Unity Treaty provided for the creation of a special trust agency (*Treuhandanstalt*) charged with privatizing East German businesses and industries, and revised the constitutional formula for intergovernmental revenue sharing. Several additional provisions dealt with the status or continuing validity of GDR treaties, court decisions, and administrative rulings, most of which were to remain in effect unless incompatible with the Basic Law or federal statutes. GDR school certificates, university degrees, and titles were to retain their validity, although only in the eastern *Länder,* whereas judges and civil servants were required to submit to recredentialing procedures. The treaty also required the former GDR to adopt regulations in conformity with EU standards, to maintain the church tax, and to decentralize cultural, educational, and athletic institutions. The German government took responsibility for "[rehabilitating the] victims of the iniquitous SED regime," obliging it to pay compensation for their suffering. In this connection, and at the insistence of the GDR the 6 million files of the disbanded state security police (*Stasi*) were to remain in the ex-GDR until an all-German parliament could enact a law regarding their storage and access. GDR officials were interested in keeping control of the files and allowing public access to them, in part to expose the crimes of human rights violators.

### Treaty on the Final Settlement with Respect to Germany

After seven months of negotiation, the four wartime Allies and the two Germanys signed the treaty that finally closed the books on World War II.[38] As part of the treaty—known as the Two-Plus-Four Treaty—the Allied powers relinquished all their occupation rights and restored full sovereignty to a united Germany. Under the treaty, the new Germany (1) accepted its present boundaries and guaranteed the border with Poland, (2) renounced aggressive warfare as well as the production and use of biological, chemical, and nuclear weapons, and (3) agreed to reduce its armed forces to 370,000 and to finance the return of Soviet troops to their homeland by 1995. Germany also agreed to ban any NATO presence in the east while Soviet troops remained there, but Moscow's greatest concession was to allow the FRG to choose its military alliance.

Finally, in a supplementary letter to the Allied foreign ministers, Foreign Minister Hans-Dietrich Genscher and Prime Minister de Maizière noted that Germany would abide by the agreement excluding property expropriated between 1945 and 1949 from the general terms of the Unity Treaty. They pledged on behalf of Germany to preserve monuments to war victims erected on German soil and to maintain war graves. The two German politicians also declared that in united Germany "the free democratic basic order will be protected by the Constitution." It provides the basis, they underscored, "for ensuring that parties which ... seek to impair or abolish the free democratic basic order as well as associations which are directed against the constitutional order or the concept of international understanding can be prohibited." This language was taken directly from Article 21 of the Basic Law, which authorizes the prohibition of antidemocratic parties. In this fashion, reunited Germany would remain a "fighting democracy."

## Post-Unification Foreign Policy

When novelist Günter Grass opposed reunification, he did so by arguing that "we Germans would become, once again, something to be feared" because a "reunited Germany would be a colossus loaded with complexes, standing in its own way and in the way of European integration."[39] Yet the reality has been quite different. The FRG's political leaders immediately reassured their eastern neighbors that Germany would honor all treaties respecting its present boundaries and obligations to the European Union. This reassurance was underscored in March 1991 by a treaty between the FRG and the USSR, reaffirming the two countries' "respect [for] each other's sovereign equality, territorial integrity and political independence." Most important, both powers declared their unqualified adherence to the territorial integrity of all

---

[38]The Treaty on the Final Settlement with Respect to Germany (New York: German Information Center, 1990).

[39]*Two States—One Nation?* trans. by Krishna Winston and A. S. Wensinger (New York: Harcourt Brace, 1990), p. 13.

European states and pledged to have no territorial claims whatsoever.

The FRG has adhered to these principles in the face of the Warsaw Pact's dissolution, the breakup of the Soviet Union, and the collapse of Communism in Eastern Europe. In some ways, as its own situation has become normalized with the restoration of national unity, the FRG has even begun to play a more active role in both Atlantic and European affairs. This was nowhere more apparent than in the decision of the SPD-Greens government in 1999 to fly combat missions in support of NATO's air war in the Kosovo campaign. This was a starting reversal of German military policy, because previous governments, including that of Helmut Kohl, had argued that the Basic Law barred the use of German troops outside of NATO, even for peace-keeping purposes. Yet thanks to a July 12, 1994, decision by the Federal Constitutional Court which freed the way for such deployments, a new generation of German leaders, including the former peace activist and new foreign minister Joschka Fischer (Greens), was able to rationalize a new role for the FRG. The use of the military for restoring peace and preventing massive human rights abuses, they argued, was not only consistent with the lessons of the past; it was a moral obligation for Germans to combat dictators and overcome oppression. Fischer and his colleagues appealed to the same rationale to support the deployment of German troops to Afghanistan in December 2001.

This is not to say that Germany thereby became a more aggressive power or, in Grass's words, a "colossus." If anything, as demonstrated in the country's active role in the EU, the FRG of the early twenty-first century is defining its priorities less in terms of a narrow national self-interest than within the context of a broader and more inclusive "European house." There was a time when many Germans—and the Bundesbank in particular—were among the greatest skeptics of the benefits of European monetary integration, largely for fear of losing a pillar of the FRG's postwar economic miracle: the deutsche mark. Moreover, of all of Germany's parties, the SPD had for years been the most outspoken proponent of Euroskepticism. Yet as the German people accepted the introduction of a new currency to their economy in 2002, their attitudes had clearly changed. They were now supporters of the euro, while many of the Bundesbank's previously formidable powers were passed on to a common European Central Bank. Furthermore, in 2001, Germany's Social Democratic chancellor Gerhard Schröder was once again demonstrating his capacity to be a man for all seasons. He endorsed even more ambitious plans than his neighbors for regional integration, such as a stronger European parliament that would eventually lay the foundations for a continental "federation."

These developments did not mean that the FRG would have no occasion in future years for serious differences with either its Atlantic or its

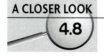

## A CLOSER LOOK 4.8

### FOREIGN POLICY: A SPECIAL RESPONSIBILITY TO HISTORY

"At the beginning of the new century, the 'never again,' the lesson to be learned from our history, remains the basic principle in German politics and policies: within our country, in Europe, towards Israel and the Jewish communities, in our commitment to peace and respect for human rights around the world. That is the moral obligation, as well as the firm political will, of the generation of those who must shoulder responsibility for the heavy burden of German history."

*Source:* Joschka Fischer, German Foreign Minister, New York, September 11, 2000.

European allies. Nor did they imply that Germany's leaders were oblivious to their own domestic interests as they underscored the importance of political and economic cooperation in an era of globalism. They did suggest, however, that the Germany that had once been a cause of so many of the world's problems in the first half of the twentieth century had been fundamentally transformed.

# CONCLUSION

The portrait of German policy making presented in this chapter is of a polity that has functioned effectively and, in the process, brought about a high measure of stability and prosperity. The Federal Republic of Germany also appears to have come of age politically. Its people are committed to democratic values, its party system is open and competitive, and its policy-making institutions are responsive to public opinion. For all intents and purposes, the transition to democracy has been completed in the eastern *Länder*, although the region must still catch up with the west economically.

Institutionally, the FRG remains a decentralized state marked by a system of administrative federalism, a fragmented bureaucracy, autonomous federal ministries, and a powerful Bundesrat capable of blocking parliamentary action. These institutions, like the political parties and parliament itself, are closely linked to social and economic groups in the private sector, producing a notable politics of compromise and consensus. The Federal Constitutional Court, another independent center of power, watches over this system, keeping the major organs of government within their proper spheres of competence while safeguarding individual rights and liberties. Finally, having regained full sovereignty under the Two-Plus-Four Treaty of 1990, and increasingly confident of its ability to influence world events, Germany can be expected to be a major international actor in the years to come, both within the framework of the Atlantic Alliance and in an expanding European Union.

## Thinking Critically

1. What does it mean to say that the FRG is a "militant democracy"? What are the advantages of this type of democratic politics?
2. Overall, how would you assess the FRG's citizenship policy? Is this policy fair to immigrants, asylum seekers, and other non-Germans living in the FRG?
3. What crucial role does "decentralized federalism" play in the German system? What are its advantages in comparison with more centralized democracies?
4. How is "codetermination" an essential feature in the making of German social and economic policy?
5. Did reunification solve the age-old "German problem"? Should the legacies of injustice committed by the National Socialist and communist regimes in the twentieth century continue to concern Germany's leaders in the twenty-first century?

## KEY TERMS

abortion compromise *(247)*
Article 16a *(236)*
Article 143 *(246–247)*
codetermination *(240)*
decentralized federalism *(238)*
Economic Stabilization Act *(240)*
"German problem" *(242)*
German Unity Fund *(239)*
Lothar de Maizière *(245)*
militant democracy *(235)*
monetary union *(245)*
*Ostpolitik (243)*
Two-Plus-Four Treaty *(249)*
vertical equalization procedures *(239)*

## FURTHER READINGS

Braunthal, Gerard. *Political Loyalty and Public Service in Germany* (Amherst: Massachusetts University Press, 1990).

Bulmer, Simon, ed. *The Changing Agenda of West German Public Policy* (Brookfield, VT: Gower Publishing, 1989).

Garton Ash, Timothy. *In Europe's Name: Germany and the Divided Continent* (New York: Random House, 1993).

Hancock, Donald M., and Helga A. Welsh, eds. *German Unification: Process and Outcomes* (Boulder, CO: Westview Press, 1994).

Hanrieder, Wolfram P. *Germany, America, Europe: Forty Years of German Foreign Policy* (New Haven: Yale University Press, 1989).

Katzenstein, Peter J., ed. *Industry and Politics in West Germany* (Ithaca, NY: Cornell University Press, 1989).

Kommers, Donald P. *The Constitutional Jurisprudence of the Federal Republic of Germany,* 2nd ed. (Durham, NC: Duke University Press, 1996).

Markovits, Inga. *Imperfect Justice* (Oxford: Clarendon Press, 1995).

McAdams, A. James. *Judging the Past in Unified Germany* (New York: Cambridge University Press, 2001).

Schweitzer, C. C., et al., eds. *Politics and Government in Germany, 1944–1994* (Oxford: Berghahn Books, 1995).

Smith, Eric Owen. *The German Economy* (London: Routlege, 1994).

Swenson, Peter. *Fair Shares, Unions, Pay, and Politics in Sweden and West Germany* (Ithaca, NY: Cornell University Press, 1989).

Thelen, Kathleen. *Union in Parts: Labor Politics in Postwar Germany* (Ithaca, NY: Cornell University Press, 1991).

# WEB SITES

## Political Development

www.democ.uci.edu/democ/germany.html
Superb source of information and sites on all aspects of German politics and society.

www.mathematik.uni-ulm.de/de-news/
Compilation of the latest news from Germany.

www.germany-info.org/fgic/index.html
The German embassy in Washington, DC.

www.germany-info.org/relaunch/business/business.html
Background information on the role of business in German society.

www.usembassy.de/
American perspective on German affairs, provided by the U.S. Embassy to the Federal Republic.

## Political Processes and Institutions

www.constitution.org/cons/germany.txt
Germany's constitution, or Basic Law (*Grundgesetz*).

eng.bundesregierung.de/frameset/index.jsp
The official Web site of the German government.

www.bundestag.de/htdocs e/index.html
Up-to-date information about Germany's parliament, the Bundestag.

www.destatis.de/e home.htm
Useful source of official statistics on the German economy and people.

## Public Policy

www.eng.bmi.bund.de/
Germany's Ministry of the Interior, addressing such controversial topics as immigration policy and citizenship.

www.bma.de/
Federal Ministry of Labor and Social Affairs, dealing primarily with labor relations and social security issues.

www.aicgs.org/index.shtml
Analyses of German public policy and decision making, provided by the premier center on Germany in the United States, the American Institute for Contemporary German Studies.

www.foothill.fhda.edu/divisions/unification/
Stimulating teaching guide on the triumphs and perils of German unification.

www.rferl.org/nca/special/10years/germany2.html
Information on the first ten years of German unification.

europa.eu.int/
Official site of the European Union.

www.democ.uci.edu/democ/gread.htm
Further readings on German history, society, economics, and politics.

# CHAPTER 5

## THE GOVERNMENT OF
# Italy

*Giuseppe Ammendola*

## INTRODUCTION

**Background:** Italy became a nation-state in 1861 when the city-states of the peninsula, along with Sardinia and Sicily, were united under King Victor Emmanuel. An era of parliamentary government came to a close in the early 1920s when Benito Mussolini established a Fascist dictatorship. His disastrous alliance with Nazi Germany led to Italy's defeat in World War II. A democratic republic replaced the monarchy in 1946 and economic revival followed. Italy was a charter member of NATO and the European Economic Community (EEC). It has been at the forefront of European economic and political unification, joining the European Monetary Union in 1999. Persistent problems include illegal immigration, the ravages of organized crime, corruption, high unemployment, and the low incomes and technical standards of southern Italy compared with the more prosperous north.

### GEOGRAPHY

**Location:** Southern Europe, a peninsula extending into the central Mediterranean Sea, northeast of Tunisia

**Area:** 301,230 sq km

**Area—comparative:** slightly larger than Arizona

**Land boundaries:** 1,932.2 km

*border countries:* Austria 430 km, France 488 km, Holy See (Vatican City) 3.2 km, San Marino 39 km, Slovenia 232 km, Switzerland 740 km

**Climate:** predominantly Mediterranean; Alpine in far north; hot, dry in south

**Terrain:** mostly rugged and mountainous; some plains, coastal lowlands

**Elevation extremes:** *lowest point:* Mediterranean Sea 0 m *highest point:* Mont Blanc (Monte Bianco) 4,807 m

**Geography note:** strategic location dominating central Mediterranean as well as southern sea and air approaches to Western Europe

## PEOPLE

**Population:** 57,679,825

**Age structure:** *0–14 years:* 14.17% (male 4,209,102; female 3,964,765)

*15–64 years:* 67.48% (male 19,375,742; female 19,546,332)

*65 years and over:* 18.35% (male 4,368,264; female 6,215,620)

**Population growth rate:** 0.07%

**Birthrate:** 9.05 births/1,000 population

**Sex ratio:** 0.94 males/female

**Life expectancy at birth:** 79.14 years

*male:* 75.97 years

*female:* 82.52 years

**Nationality:** *noun:* Italian, Italians

*adjective:* Italian

**Ethnic groups:** Italian (includes small clusters of German-, French-, and Slovene-Italians in the north and Albanian-Italians and Greek-Italians in the south)

**Religions:** predominately Roman Catholic with mature Protestant and Jewish communities and a growing Muslim immigrant community

**Languages:** Italian (official), German (parts of Trentino-Alto Adige region are predominantly German speaking), French (small French-speaking minority in Valle d'Aosta region), Slovene (Slovene-speaking minority in the Trieste-Gorizia area)

**Literacy:** *definition:* age 15 and over can read and write

*total population:* 98%

## GOVERNMENT

**Country name:** *conventional long form:* Italian Republic

*conventional short form:* Italy

**Government type:** republic

**Capital:** Rome

**Administrative divisions:** 20 regions (*regioni,* singular—*regione*)

**Independence:** 17 March 1861 (Kingdom of Italy proclaimed; Italy was not finally unified until 1870)

**Constitution:** 1 January 1948

**Legal system:** based on civil law system; appeals treated as new trials; judicial review under certain conditions in Constitutional Court; has not accepted compulsory ICJ jurisdiction

**Suffrage:** 18 years of age; universal (except in senatorial elections, where minimum age is 25)

**Executive branch:** *chief of state:* President Carlo Azeglio Ciampi (since 13 May 1999)

*head of government:* Prime Minister (referred to in Italy as the president of the Council of Ministers) Silvio Berlusconi (since 10 June 2001)

*cabinet:* Council of Ministers nominated by the prime minister and approved by the president

*elections:* president elected by an electoral college consisting of both houses of Parliament and 58 regional representatives for a seven-year term

**Legislative branch:** bicameral Parliament or Parlamento consists of the Senate or Senato della Repubblica (315 seats elected by popular vote, of which 232 are directly elected and 83 are elected by regional proportional representation; in addition, there is a small number of senators-for-life including former presidents of the republic; members serve five-year terms) and the Chamber of Deputies or Camera dei Deputati (630 seats; 475 are directly elected, 155 by national proportional representation; members serve five-year terms)

**Judicial branch:** Constitutional Court or Corte Costituzionale (composed of 15 judges: one-third appointed by the president, one-third elected by Parliament, one-third elected by the ordinary and administrative Supreme Courts)

## ECONOMY

**Overview:** Italy has a diversified industrial economy with roughly the same total and per capita output as France and the United Kingdom. This capitalistic economy remains divided into a developed industrial north, dominated by private companies, and a less developed agricultural south, with more than 20% unemployment. Most raw materials needed by industry and more than 75% of energy requirements are imported. Since 1992, Italy has adopted budgets compliant with the requirements of the European Monetary Union (EMU); wage moderation agreements by representatives of government, labor, and employers have helped to bring Italy's inflation into conformity with EMU requirements. Italy's economic performance, however, has lagged behind that of its EU partners and it must work to stimulate employment, promote labor flexibility, reform its expensive pension system, and tackle the informal economy.

**GDP:** purchasing power parity—$1.273 trillion

**GDP—real growth rate:** 2.7%

**GDP—per capita:** purchasing power parity—$22,100

**GDP—composition by sector:** *agriculture:* 2.5%
  *industry:* 30.4%
  *services:* 67.1%

**Labor force:** 23.4 million

**Labor force—by occupation:** services 61.9%, industry 32.6%, agriculture 5.5%

**Unemployment rate:** 10.4%

**Currency:** Italian lira (ITL); euro (EUR)
  *note:* on 1 January 1999, the EU introduced the euro as a common currency; it will replace the local currency for all transactions as of 2002

# A. POLITICAL DEVELOPMENT

Italy is a fascinating country both culturally and politically. The value of its artistic treasures is estimated by many to be half of the world's total. It is the land of music giants like Vivaldi, Rossini, Verdi, Puccini; eminent painters and architects like Leonardo and Michelangelo (both actually much more than that); illustrious poets like Dante, Petrarch, Leopardi; inspiring writers like Boccaccio and Ariosto; great scientists like Galileo and Volta. Together with countless others, these names evoke the enormous impact of Italian culture across the centuries and across the world.

Politically, early systems of government like that of the *comune* (commune), the *signoria,* and the *principato* had immense political influence, providing useful models of study to, among others, the drafters of the American and French constitutions. Other factors of a political nature have had a considerable impact outside Italy across the years and have stimulated interest in the study of Italian politics. Such factors include the movement of Italy from political fragmentation to unification and independence, its imperial ambitions, its involvement in the two world wars of this century, the birth and demise of Fascism, Italy's strategic role during the Cold War, the high turnover rate of its coalition governments, the large presence of the state in the economy, and its transformation into one of the world's largest markets, with a GDP at times larger than Great Britain's. Moreover, as in the case of other major Western European countries, many of Italy's public policy issues and concerns in areas such as health, education, public finance, immigration, crime, and foreign policy led to courses of action (and inaction) whose analysis can shed much light on the problems currently facing the United States.

Political development and change continue. Since the early 1990s, Italy has been in the midst of a political revolution that finds no equivalent in magnitude and scope anywhere else in Western Europe. This revolution originated from a cleanup operation started at the beginning of 1992 by some determined judges against corrupt public officials. Political behavior, political institutions, and processes as well as the conduct of public policy have undergone significant modifications. Changes in the areas of elections, political parties, local administration, and elite replacement and recruitment had already been so substantial by the mid-1990s that they led many observers to talk of the creation of a Second Republic even in the absence of any major reform of the institutions of the present Republic. While with the beginning of the new millennium the sense of impending extraordinary institutional change had probably abated, there can be little doubt of the mutable nature of the Italian political system. It is its mix of old and new that makes the study of current Italian politics so bafflingly complex, yet so challenging and intellectually rewarding.

## THE LAND

Italy extends over a surface of 116,000 square miles, approximately the areas of Georgia and Florida combined. The total length of its sea-coasts is over 4,500 miles. Across an arc spanning over 600 miles, the Alps provide the natural boundaries to Italy's neighbors—to the northwest France, to the north Switzerland and Austria, and to the northeast the Republic of Slovenia. The Apennine chain extends into the Mediterranean Sea for over 700 miles. It is the peninsula's spine and delimits, together with the Alps and the Adriatic Sea, the Po valley which constitutes 71 percent of Italy's lowlands, only one-fifth of the territory, the balance being hills and mountains. Most of the rest of the plains are located along or near the coastline and are the result of alluvial deposits from the Apennine rivers and from large works of reclamation across the centuries.

The marked differences in elevation observable throughout the peninsula and in the two main islands of Sicily and Sardinia are matched by equally substantial climatic differences which also defy neat categorization.

## A CLOSER LOOK
### 5.1

### THE COMMUNE ("*IL COMUNE*")

The commune, substantially influenced by ancient republican Rome's politics, was based on an assembly of free citizens, the parliament, which decided on the most important laws; on the consuls, holding executive powers of a legal, political, and military nature; and on the councils, whose elected members had consultative powers. The most powerful active participants in political life were the *magnati* who were the noblemen from the city proper; later the former feudal lords joined their ranks. Later still the very rich members of the bourgeois class obtained nobility status through imperial bestowal. Below them was the bourgeoisie, which was divided into *il popolo grasso*—bankers, industrialists, and professionals—and *il popolo minuto*—artisans and shopkeepers. The *plebe* comprised all types of salaried workers who had no political rights. Class-based divisions were a considerable source of conflict, with the noblemen frequently joined among themselves by links of kinship and the bourgeoisie organized along professional categories (the guilds).

The earlier period of dominance by the consuls was followed in the twelfth century by the *podestá*, who was usually a professional man coming from another city or sometimes from outside Italy and thought of as capable of rising above the contending factions. The *podestá* extended the sphere of influence of the city over neighboring urban centers. Thus the commune, essentially a democratic or semidemocratic regime, evolved into a *signoria*, a form of dictatorship of oligarchic or monarchic nature where the *signore* (the lord), frequently supported by foreign mercenaries, transformed his office into a hereditary one. In the fifteenth century with the official papal and imperial recognition of the lord's hereditary chain and his sovereign powers, the *signoria* became a *principato*.

## HISTORICAL DEVELOPMENT

The historical process leading to the creation of the nation-state of Italy was long and complex. Political unification was achieved through the determined efforts of elites. Only a minority of the population could be said to have a sense of Italian national identity, which led prominent statesman and writer Massimo D'Azeglio to say "We have made Italy; now we must make the Italians." Thus the political leaders in the kingdom of the new state, in order to unify the country and meet the challenges of nation building, opted for policies of very strong centralization and substantially limited local autonomy.

The country was at first (1861–1876) ruled by the political Right (*destra*). Internal tariffs throughout the country were removed, decisive action was undertaken to reduce the budget deficits, exports increased, the economic infrastructure was improved, and military readiness strengthened. The Left (*sinistra*) during its time

of control of Parliament (1876–1891) broadened suffrage, reduced the weight of taxation on the poor, further diminished privileges of the clergy, improved the lay public school system, and increased decentralization of government. In 1877, under pressure from northern agrarian and industrial groups combined with southern latifundists (large estate owners), the government erected very controversial protective tariffs.

The political differences between Left and Right subsided in the early 1880s with the beginning of the *trasformismo,* under which parliamentary majorities were created on the basis of political deals rather than ideological positions and party affiliation. *Trasformismo* was partially attributable to concern by many about the growing power of the extreme left parties and the turmoil in the countryside, where the agrarian crisis pushed large masses to emigrate from the south to the Americas.

In foreign policy, Italy started to expand in the Horn of Africa, occupying Eritrea and Somalia. Italy also established a protectorate over

## THE MAKING OF ITALY

| | |
|---|---|
| Seventh Century B.C.E. | Rome founded. Many different ethnic groups, cultures, and political systems are brought together. |
| First Century B.C.E. | Unification of Italy; complex system of checks and balances along different functional and geographical lines among the Senate, Emperor Augustus, and various classes of elected and unelected public officials. Growth of Roman law. |
| 476 C.E. | Collapse of the Western Roman Empire from barbaric invasions; end of unity. Church provides continuity. |
| 1000 C.E. | Feudalism starts giving way. Conflict between the Papacy and the German emperors. The growth of cities or communes like Milan, Pavia, Lucca, Florence favored by the rising power of the merchant class. Cities on the coastline like Genoa, Pisa, Amalfi, Venice benefiting as commercial centers from the Crusades and later from the advances in ship design and navigation techniques. In the south, the cities did not blossom as independent commercial centers. |
| Sixteenth Century | Italy is divided into several major states—the republics of Florence and Venice, the Duchy of Milan, the papal state—and a few smaller ones. Humanism and Renaissance bring blossoming of all forms of art. Machiavelli's desire for Italy of a prince who, even with ruthless methods, could unify the country and make it independent from Church and foreign influences. Spanish domination on the peninsula (1559–1704). The Papal States had very little desire for autonomy from Spain, which was holding in check the expansion of Protestant ideas in Italy and the Turks' threats against Europe. Turkish control of commercial routes to the Orient; shift of world trade away from the Mediterranean. |
| 1700–1861 | The War of the Spanish Succession (1701–1704) marked the end of Spanish and the beginning of Austrian hegemony over Italy. Napoleon (1796–1815) centralized and unified legislation and administration and instituted an Italian army, extending directly or indirectly his hegemony over the entire peninsula. The Congress of Vienna in 1815 reestablished the pre-Napoleonic order but divine right to govern of rulers no longer unquestioned. |
| 1860–1870 | Unification of the country. In 1859 Franco-Piedmontese troops won Lombardy over from Austria. The One Thousand, a small voluntary army headed by Giuseppe Garibaldi, landed in Sicily and started to climb up the boot, joining with local volunteers to defeat in battle after battle the Bourbon troops. The King of Savoy, wanting to avoid the invasion of Rome (fearing France's reaction) and to make Garibaldi's victories his own, invaded the Papal States in Marche and Umbria and gained the whole south with popular referendums confirming the annexations. Turin Parliament proclaimed Vittorio Emanuele II King of Italy (1861). Austria defeated by the combined forces of Italy and Prussia (1866); Austria cedes Venice to Italy. Collapse of Napoleon III's empire (1870) following Prussia's attack; pope lost France's protection; Italian troops enter Rome. As with Venice, a popular referendum further legitimized annexation obtained through force. The process of unification of Italy completed. |

Abyssinia, but the 1896 defeat at Aduwa put an end to it. Italy would afterwards maneuver between the European power blocs, one led by Great Britain and France and the other by Germany and Austria. Italy could thus both satisfy its ambitions in northern Africa on the one hand and those in the Adriatic (where Austria still controlled Trieste) and the Balkans on the other.

## THE NEW CENTURY

It started with a bang. In 1900 an anarchist killed King Umberto, who had been seen as supportive of the antiunion and antidemocratic government repressions of 1898. There were very substantial political divisions in the country. Within the bourgeoisie there were agro-industrial interests (largely of a protectionist nature) which supported a very strong limitation of the rights of free association and strike, while other interests—largely entrepreneurial and professional—were

supportive of much more democratic and liberal policies. Within the socialist movement, divisions existed between those who believed in a gradualist and reformist approach to improving the conditions of workers and those who believed in the necessity to achieve change through violent means. The Catholic movement was also divided between a right wing and a left wing.

These conflicts among political forces were mediated in Parliament by the liberal leader Giovanni Giolitti. In this period of uneasy coalition governments, several major pieces of legislation were approved: nationalization of the railways, legalization of the unions, regulation of the working conditions for women and children, and the introduction in 1912 of universal male suffrage. On the economic front, links between the banking and industrial sectors became stronger, concentration of ownership of enterprises increased, and protection of the steel, sugar, and cotton industries continued, though these changes met with strong opposition. Italy during the Giolitti

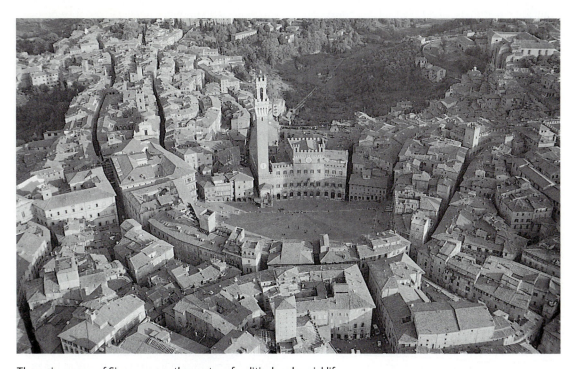

The main square of Siena: as ever the center of political and social life.

era also resumed its expansionist policy by waging war against Turkey and annexing Libya, Rodi, and the Dodecanese Islands.

At the beginning of World War I in 1914, a debate in Italy took place between those who wanted to intervene in the war on the side of France and Britain and those, mostly socialists and Catholics, who favored neutrality. The interventionists won and when the war was over, Italy obtained border gains from Austria but did not achieve what had been promised by France and Great Britain at the London conference of 1915. These two powers successfully supported Yugoslavia in its dispute with Italy over Dalmatia.

## THE RISE OF FASCISM

The end of World War I in 1918 marked the beginning of a period of great economic, political, and social turmoil. The economy was beset by large budget deficits, substantial increases in prices, and unresolved labor and land issues. Liberals, socialists, and Catholics coexisted uneasily and the coalition governments that they formed were unstable.

In 1921, Benito Mussolini, a former revolutionary socialist leader who had supported intervention in the war, founded the Fascist Party. Exploiting popular discontent over the "mutilated victory" stemming from French and British policies denying Italy promised territory, the sense of malaise generated by the high level of unemployment and underemployment among war veterans, the concerns of industrialists and landowners over the growing claims for redistribution by the Left and over the events in Russia, and the rivalry between blue-collar and white-collar workers, Mussolini built substantial support for his movement in a very short time. In October 1922, he felt strong enough to guide his paramilitary organization, the black shirts, to a march on Rome. Prime Minister Luigi Facta wanted to declare a state of siege, which would easily have disposed of Mussolini's ragtag militants, but the king refused to sign the decree and invited Mussolini to become prime minister and form a new government. Mussolini almost immediately organized the black shirts into a militia personally accountable to him,

thus trying to legitimize their continued physical attacks against unions and newspapers.

## Mussolini in Power

The elections of April 1924 were conducted under a new electoral law granting a two-thirds majority to the winning list. The victorious coalition led by Mussolini included some prestigious names of the moderate right and the (Catholic) Popular Party, which contributed to confer on it a certain cloak of respectability. By the end of 1926, through a combination of militia violence, governmental action, and legislative activity, Mussolini had dissolved all parties except his own, reintroduced the death sentence, created a special tribunal for crimes against the state and a special secret police, both of which were under his firm control, while basically abolishing the parliamentary regime.

The Fascist Party became the central institution of the country and evolved during 20 years from a purely political entity to a propagandistic, educational, and welfare organization under the direct control of its leader *il Duce,* who was also the head of the government. The king remained as the nominal sovereign of the nation but all the power lay in the hands of Mussolini, assisted in a de facto consultative capacity by the Great Council of Fascism. The Parliament took decisions that basically were a rubber stamp of Mussolini's decrees.

The Fascist regime organized workers and employers into fascist unions, prohibited strikes and closeouts, instituted a special court system for labor controversies, and created a pension system and a 40-hour work week. The regime also discouraged urbanization and land laborers' flight from the countryside. Economic self-sufficiency became an important goal after the beginning of the depression following the 1929 crisis.

State intervention in the economy increased with the creation of agencies for the provision of long-term financing (IMI) and for the ownership and control of banks and industries (IRI) as well as the enactment of legislation requiring government authorization for major plant renewal expenditures and of measures aiming at meeting the growing demands of the military.

The Lateran Pacts (or Concordat) signed between Italy and the Vatican in 1929 recognized the legitimacy of the Italian state (as well as Fascism) and Rome as its capital, while Catholicism became officially the state religion, its teachings made compulsory in all schools, and Catholic marriages were granted complete legal recognition. Catholic bishops would pledge allegiance to the Italian state and priests' access to civil service jobs was regulated, while Italy compensated the Vatican monetarily for the territorial losses suffered decades earlier.

## Aggressive Foreign Policy

In foreign policy proper, Mussolini made it clear that the Peace Treaties of 1919 had to be revised and pursued a policy of friendship with various Balkan states to isolate Yugoslavia. In 1935, following some months of attempted mediation by France and Great Britain, Italy invaded Ethiopia. The League of Nations enacted economic sanctions against Italy, which were largely ineffective since raw materials and industrial products continued to come in from the United States and Germany. The ties with Germany were further strengthened by the agreement with Adolf Hitler to support General Francisco Franco in the Spanish Civil War. Having tolerated Germany's annexation of Austria, and emboldened by Hitler's dismemberment of Czechoslovakia and his demands on Poland in April 1939, Mussolini sent his troops to Albania, where since 1925 Italy had exercised a protectorate, and conquered the country in the name of King Vittorio Emanuele III.

## WORLD WAR II

The entrance of Italy into World War II occurred in June 1940. Mussolini—in spite of the opposition to the war by large portions of the public, his own party, and the king—was determined to sit at the winners' table to extract territorial concessions for Italy. The low level of Italian military preparedness soon became evident. In July 1943, Allied troops landed in Sicily and started to move northward. As a result of Italy's military defeats, Mussolini was dismissed by the king.

Within weeks Italy became divided in two: in the north, the Republica Sociale Italiana, a Fascist puppet state headed by Mussolini and under the control of German forces; in the south the Marshall Badoglio government and the king under the control of the Allies. The resistance movement in the north carried out actions of guerrilla warfare that were often met with German reprisals on the civilian population. In the south it operated openly and organized a National Liberation Committee (CLN), grouping together the major antifascist parties. When in June 1944 the Allied forces entered Rome, the parties of the CLN were asked by the king's son Umberto to form a new government.

The partisans in the north operated clandestinely through the winter of 1944–1945 until April 1945, when a coalition of American, British, French, Polish, and regular Italian troops broke through the German line and invaded the Po valley. Mussolini was executed by the partisans on April 28 in a political climate in which the antifascists carried out actions of summary and oftentimes brutal justice against their former oppressors. Within the next few days the Germans surrendered completely and on all fronts.

## AFTER THE WAR

The peace treaty signed in February 1947 deprived Italy of all colonies. Most of the Istrian Peninsula went to Yugoslavia and two small cities to France. The territorial losses paled in comparison with the human casualties, almost 450,000.

Italy faced substantial problems of reconstruction after the war. Considerable damage had been inflicted on building structures (dwellings, plants, schools, hospitals) and on the transportation sector. Industrial and agricultural production were a fraction of their prewar levels, and inflation was rampant. The country needed a new constitution. In June 1946, elections were held to decide whether Italy should remain a monarchy or become a republic and also to select the members of a Constituent Assembly. With northern and central Italy massively voting in favor of it, the republican form of government carried the day. Christian Democrats, Socialists, and Communists were victorious at the elections and the new constitution would reflect a compromise among the different views and values of the three parties.

The constitutional system proved to be in the next decades less and less adequate. While the country experienced high economic growth rates and increasing standards of living, the Italian government coalitions were unstable. There were also serious problems in the areas of bureaucratic efficiency, the ethics of public officials, and public order. By the beginning of the 1990s these factors led to widespread consensus about the need for a new institutional system.

## THE RELEVANCE OF HISTORY

A number of factors embedded in history have been influential in shaping contemporary Italy. Among the most prominent are language, the Church, secularism, Fascism, centralization, and *trasformismo*.

### Language

Italians are a complex people. Across the centuries there have been many foreign influences, whether through invasion, exertion of various forms of political control, or commercial and cultural interaction by land and sea. Combined with the fact that Italy is a geographically diverse country with many natural enclaves, these influences have led to great linguistic variety. On Italian soil 13 "lesser" languages of the European Union are currently spoken, and there are at least 14 major dialects very different from each other and from Italian.

Use of the Italian language has become much more widespread since the beginning of the era of mass TV ownership in the 1950s, which went beyond the impact exerted, during Fascism, by the radio and the newsreel. Language has been frequently used by politicians to impress the electorate, to hide underlying inter- and intraparty squabbles over the sharing of the governmental pie, and at times to disguise a lack of technical expertise. This situation has changed

abruptly since the late 1980s in the wake of the popular support reaped by Umberto Bossi, the leader of the Northern League, the party advocating autonomy for the north. He achieved this popularity through his use of language, which was frank though abrasive. The other parties had to follow suit and their leaders abandoned the use of excessively ornate prose. Concision of expression and immediacy of message is obviously an important dimension of any electoral campaign, and at the general elections of 2001 there was a distinct difference between the posters of center-left leader Francesco Rutelli and his center-right opponent Silvio Berlusconi's: the former used more words than the latter. Supporters of Rutelli defended the higher level of specificity of his messages and defined Berlusconi's as slogan-like, but there can be little doubt that the latter were more effective. This left vs. right dichotomy in the level of prolixity can arguably be noticed in elections elsewhere in Europe and the world.

### The Church, Secularism, and Socialism

The influence of the Church on Italian society since 1945 has been extremely important. The Catholic mind-set of fatalism and acceptance of the status quo described in other contexts by Max Weber has most likely affected negatively the work ethic and, especially in the south, has probably contributed to the continuation of feudal and patronage-like relationships.[1] The Church has also helped maintain the unity of the Italian family, and Italy has one of the lowest divorce rates in Europe. It has also supported a vision of solidarity among its followers that has favored the growth of the welfare state and later the acceptance of immigrants, among whom the Catholic hierarchies may have also seen possibilities for conversion and clergy recruitment. The Church leaders directed their opposition against Marxist

---

[1]Max Weber's theory can be found in his *The Protestant Ethic and the Spirit of Capitalism* (New York: Scribners, 1958).

ideology, and the parties supporting it, and acted to weaken that sense of national identity, which, in countries like France and Great Britain, among others, has contributed to the development of a more decisive foreign policy.

Secular forces have also been very significant, frequently exerting an influence countervailing that of the Church. Thus, much of today's entrepreneurial spirit traces back to the commercial and financial classes' activities across the centuries since the end of feudalism. Similarly humanism and the Renaissance, with their magnificent artistic and cultural achievements, celebrated earthly life and human creativity. The idea that man could have a large influence over the world he lived in was further strengthened by the arrival in Italy of the Enlightenment and the political principles of liberty and equality that Napoleon was instrumental in spreading. The ethos of the quest for national unity was mostly secular.

Socialist thought has exerted possibly a more visible influence than the above-mentioned secular ideas, both in its reformist and revolutionary variations. Grafted onto Catholic principles of solidarity, socialist ideas were instrumental for the development of the welfare state, workers' rights, and more recently, a benign attitude toward immigration and negative stands against globalization and military involvements. Socialist thinking provided also some of the ideological underpinnings for the terrorism of the Left in the 1970s until the mid-1980s. Socialist ideas, already somewhat incorporated in the center-left coalition governments that appeared since the 1960s, got tested when the former communists finally reached power in the second half of the 1990s.

## Fascism and Centralization

Fascism left a very significant political heritage. Most prominently, the centralization of powers survived the regime, as the Republic's slow devolution of powers to the regions attests. The large state-owned enterprises also survived and thrived under the Christian Democrat–led governments, which considered them their own patronage plums. Fascism is also responsible for

fostering among the average citizens subservience to hierarchies and reluctance to take personal initiatives. This would have damaging effects on entrepreneurship especially in the south and would help develop a mind-set among civil servants of respect for formalism and not for results. Recent attempts to reform the civil service and make it more accountable and oriented toward results are trying to change this.

Until the early 1980s, the Fascist era represented for a small but not insignificant percentage of Italians a period of law and order for which they felt nostalgic. Against the great social and economic transformations of the 1960s and 1970s, such opinions encouraged some branches of the government and the secret services gone astray to consider the possibility of carrying out a right-wing coup and, as it was believed by many, to pursue a "strategy of tension" that would be at the basis of "black" terrorism in those years. While the Italian democracy was and is still young and the tradition for authoritarian solutions across Italian history very substantial, the ideas and experiences of tolerance, solidarity, and above all democratic participation are sufficiently ingrained in the Italian people that the successful fight waged against terrorism in previous decades was not accompanied by any meaningful limitation of civil rights. Furthermore, the imperial ambitions of Mussolini and the defeat in World War II made Italians also very leery of nationalist policies and symbols and poorly inclined to spend money on their armed forces. The crisis in the Balkans has brought back some sense of national and almost militaristic pride, which may be further bolstered in the years to come by the fight against international terrorism.

### Trasformismo

Another important historical phenomenon that carried over from an earlier era was that of *trasformismo*. The practice of forming coalition governments that tend to blur the political differences between parties, and especially between government and opposition, took different forms since the mid-1960s, when the Italian Communists started to participate more actively in lawmaking through parliamentary commissions, and later in the 1970s when they started to share more substantially in the patronage system overseen by the Christian Democrats. While positive in terms of dampening the disastrous effects that a major polarization of political forces could have had in those years, *trasformismo* also distorted the principles of a well-functioning democracy, which require a vigilant opposition.

## THE REGIONS

Though Italy is a unitary state, the constitution provides for its division into 20 regions. The profound cultural, social, and political differences that exist among them originate from the country's complex history and the highly fragmented nature of the territory.

Powerful centralizing forces have operated against local interests since the end of the war. First, education has been a strong homogenizing force, with nationwide curricula and standards making inroads among larger percentages of children than ever before across a longer number of years of schooling. Television has also contributed immensely to the consolidation of a national cultural identity, especially in light of the monopoly enjoyed by state-owned broadcasting until the 1970s. The expansion of weekly journals with nationwide circulation and the equally important nationwide nature of advertising campaigns have also contributed immensely to the development of a single consumption-oriented culture.

The fact that the establishment of most regions as administrative subunits with their own elected councils was delayed about 25 years, and the very limited powers that decision-making units other than those located in Rome have wielded, also contributed to these unifying trends. At the same time, the separatist movements based in Sicily and Trentino have been successfully contained and are dormant now, as a result in no small measure of the autonomy granted to these regions since the early postwar years and the politics of compromise pursued by

the Italian central government. On the regional question at present, for analytical purposes the divide between north and south figures prominently. The dichotomy stems mainly from the general perception that public services and things in general function well or at least adequately in the north and poorly in the south.

The south comprises eight regions, which constitute about 40 percent of the country's territory, 35 percent of its population, and have an average GDP per capita which is 54 percent of that in the north-center regions.[2] In the three regions of Campania, Calabria, and Sicily, the perception of inefficiency and waste is the most widely held. In Abruzzi, Molise, and Apulia, all three on the Adriatic Sea, there is more efficiency and higher levels of entrepreneurship, which could probably be attributed to the prevalence of Venetian influences over Roman. Basilicata and Sardinia are somewhere in between. Unemployment levels are much higher than in the north, and the quality of public services in the areas of health, water, transportation, telecoms, and energy is unequivocally inferior.

### The Southern Question

From the unification of the country onward the southern question, the persistent underdevelopment of the south vis-à-vis the north, has been at the center of intense debate. The feudal structure of land ownership, the backwardness of agricultural methods, the poor road network, the pervasiveness of absentee landlords, the poverty of farmers, the high levels of illiteracy, all caused problems. Their solution would have required replacement at high political and administrative levels of the pre-unification landed gentry with elements from a middle class capable of promoting among the lower socioeconomic classes a sense of allegiance toward the new state. This did not happen and the industrialization process that materialized in Italy from the beginning of the present century up to World War II left the south

---

[2]Calculated by author from ISTAT data.

unaffected. After the war, land reform, huge grants, loans, and tax incentives given to foster private investment in the area would not prove to be sufficient to bridge the large gap in standard of living between south and north. This gap in quality of life, however, is mitigated in the south by the presence of large numbers of public employees, the application of national wage contracts for the better-unionized private jobs, and the very large government transfer payments which act as substantial forms of income support.

Resistance to the transfer of resources from the north to the south that these policies entailed coalesced around Umberto Bossi and the Northern League who railed against government inefficiency and corruption, the welfare system, and its southern beneficiaries. This helped create a climate hostile to Rome and its political ruling class that saw the beginning of "operation clean hands" by the Italian magistrature in 1992 to end corruption. Moreover, it has powerfully initiated a debate over decentralization, fiscal federalism, and the welfare state that was long overdue and that will continue to be central to Italian political life for years to come.

## Crime and Punishment

One aspect of the southern question that has raised much concern in recent years is the Mafia and the problem of organized crime. The Mafia and other regional criminal organizations exert their influence on a vast gamut of criminal activities taking place in certain specific areas of the south (the control of territory) and on the trade of illicit substances (the control of products). Violent crimes, whether or not associated with organized crime, are not on the whole a bigger problem in Italy than in other major Western countries. However, in areas where the Mafia and other criminal organizations are strongest, the GDP growth rate is the lowest, a testimonial to their sapping effect on entrepreneurship and rates of return.

Organized crime's ability to control votes to secure the election of friendly candidates to public office has typically been traded for politicians'

protection against zealous law enforcement officials and judges and channeling of public works contracts toward areas under criminal control. However, the power of corrupt politicians has been substantially reduced since the early 1990s by the much more aggressive attitude of the magistrature and the police, supported by the press and public opinion alarmed at the expansion of criminal activities.

In 1992, the Mafia, in an attempt to intimidate the magistrature, killed the two most prominent Sicilian judges, Giovanni Falcone and Paolo Borsellino. The assassination of the two judges was met with a popular backlash of unprecedented strength, even greater than that following the killing 14 years earlier by the Red Brigades of Aldo Moro, the former leader of the Christian Democrats and prime minister. Rallies against the Mafia and all forms of organized crime occurred across the entire country. Giuliano Amato's government in 1992 introduced the first witness protection program and relegated the most prominent Mafia bosses to island prisons, from where controlling their interests back home would become much more difficult.[3] By 2001, over 1,200 mafiosi, faced with the threat of very long prison sentences, had turned state's evidence. Many witnesses to Mafia crimes came forward, and tips on where to find Mafia bosses who had eluded capture proved to be ruinous for the organization. By 2001, people imprisoned for organized crime would number in the thousands and it had also become apparent that "Mafia Inc." was facing significant financial difficulties. Most law enforcement officials would state though that the battle against these illegal organizations is not over yet.

The immigration waves of the last few years, permitted by a coastline too long and difficult to control, have also brought in some individuals who have engaged alone or in organized ethnic-based groups in a multitude of illegal activities with or without the help of local criminals. This

---

[3]Ugo Stille, "The Fall of Caesar," *The New Yorker,* September 11, 1995, pp. 68–83.

## REVIEW 5.2

### PROFILE OF ITALY

#### POPULATION

- 57.6 million; 36 percent live in south.
- Foreign residents: 573,000 (1993), 1,270,000 (2000).
- Life expectancy 75.8 for men, 82.0 for women (1999, est.); men are 48.5 percent of population.
- Literacy rate 98.3 percent; 99 percent U.S.
- Infant mortality rate 5.9 per 1,000; 6.8 U.S.
- 6.5 hospital beds per 1,000; 4.0 U.S.
- One doctor for every 182 inhabitants (highest percentage of doctors in the world).
- Labor force 21 million (28 percent self-employed, 10.6 percent unemployed).
- Unemployment rate north 4.7 percent; center 8.3 percent; south 21 percent.

#### SOCIAL INDICATORS

- Rates per 1,000 persons:
  - Daily newspaper circulation 104 (U.S. 212).
  - Radio receivers 880 (U.S. 2,116); TV receivers 528 (U.S. 806).
  - Telephone main lines 462 (U.S. 661); cellular phone subscribers 528 (U.S. 312); personal computers 192 (U.S. 511); cars 539 (U.S. 486).
  - 19 percent of private consumption on food, 6.4 percent on leisure.
  - Teacher/student ratio (primary school) 10.1.
  - Foreign prison inmates as percentage of total: 25 percent (1998); 17 percent(1996).

#### ECONOMIC INDICATORS

- Gross domestic product $1,124 billion; GDP per capita $19,500; across 1990s, GDP growth was 1.3 percent, against 2.2 percent EU average and 3 percent in U.S.
- Trade surplus $10.7 billion; main trading partner Germany.
- 2.4 percent inflation rate (est. 2001).
- 10-year government bond 5.1 percent.

*Sources:* ISTAT, *Statistical Abstract of the United States,* IMF, *The Economist, Eurispes.*

---

in no uncertain terms has contributed to the rise of anti-immigrant feelings, which were practically nonexistent a few years ago. The number of people in jail in Italy nowadays is slightly lower than in 1950. When one takes into account the increase in population since then and the attending increase in crime levels, not unlike other Western democracies, one can foresee the growth of support among the general population for harsher and more effective policing, prosecutorial, judicial, and legislative measures against crime.

## The Third Italy

Another concept crucial to understanding the regional realities of the country is that of *Terza Italia* (the Third Italy). While the industrial triangle—the area comprised within Milan, Turin, and Genoa—has traditionally epitomized the large industrial aggregates of the northwestern area of the peninsula, the Third Italy is characterized by the small industrial districts specializing in similar types of products that have flourished in the northeast and center of the country. Developing since the early 1970s out of the need for large Italian enterprises to downsize and farm out part of their production to smaller and less unionized entities, the Third Italy accounts in large part for Italy's impressive economic performance in terms of exports, productivity, investment, and output growth in the 1980s. Most of the enterprises constituting this second economic miracle, which led Italy's GDP to hover in size around that of Great Britain's, are family owned, very flexible, and quickly capable of responding to market shifts in demand. Many of these enterprises, while fiercely competing with each other, are also capable of sharing technological information and pooling together resources to create buying cartels. Thus, cooperation is frequently seen as better for the common good.

## SOCIAL CLASSES

The economy of Italy is postindustrial. Since the end of World War II, the number of persons employed in agriculture has decreased substantially and, largely through urbanization, the ranks of those employed in industry have increased considerably. Furthermore, especially since the early 1970s, there has been a substantial growth of those employed in the service sector, growth that has made this the largest sector of the economy, a phenomenon not dissimilar in nature to that observable in other advanced Western countries (see Table 5.1).

Today farmers, who number approximately 1.12 million, account for 5.5 percent of all workers and for 2.5 percent of national income. Nearly 60 percent of farmers are independent

**TABLE 5.1**

**OCCUPATIONS IN ITALY (PERCENTAGES)**

| Year | Agriculture | Industry | Services |
|------|-------------|----------|----------|
| 1951 | 42.2 | 31.3 | 26.5 |
| 1971 | 17.2 | 42.0 | 40.8 |
| 1991 | 8.5 | 32.0 | 59.5 |
| 2000 | 5.5 | 32.1 | 62.6 |

owners, compared to 22 percent in industry and 28 percent in the service sector. There are relatively few farms managed professionally and less than 10 percent of farms account for more than two-thirds of agricultural production. In the last few years, immigrants (from Africa especially) have appeared in increasing numbers on Italian farms; not unlike other sectors of the economy, they take those jobs not particularly palatable to natives, and at lower wages.

Blue-collar workers have decreased in number since the early 1980s. The interaction of factors such as greater decentralization of the productive process, greater mechanization, the emergence of new types of work in professional areas of support, the lower employment opportunities themselves, and the changing international competitive climate has reduced the power of traditional unions and with it the sense of class consciousness that characterized the working class 25 years ago. This sense of alienation from other workers and from the reality of the factory floor is much greater among younger workers, who tend to have less secure jobs.

The growth in size of the service sector is at the basis of the growth of the middle class, which now is thought of as comprising half of the active population. The middle class is composed of artisans, shopkeepers, teachers, technicians, clerks, and professionals like lawyers and doctors, who are viewed alternatively by some as members of the upper class, especially when very successful financially.

The blue-collar workers have tended to vote for the parties of the Left, the middle class has voted for the center parties and particularly for the Christian Democratic Party (DC), and the farmers have traditionally been dividing evenly the bulk of their votes between the DC and the parties of the Left.[4]

The upper class is composed occupationally of high-level managers of state-owned enterprises, who frequently owe much of their career to political connections, and entrepreneurs, who have often benefited from policies aiming at reducing their tax burden and their competition from abroad. The Christian Democrats and center parties have traditionally drawn a large proportion of votes from these professional categories.

At the pinnacle of the economic pecking order, the influence that a few prominent families and the groups linked to them are capable of exerting on Italian governments is clearly evidenced by the very high levels of concentration of ownership existing in the stock market and the lack of effective antitrust legislation.

At the bottom of the economic ladder are the poor, who tend to be the unemployed, the divorced or separated, the young, and the old. Not surprisingly, 70 percent of the poor reside in the south, where 36 percent of the population lives. The poor in Italy have the same problems of alienation, of feeling left out, of living day-by-day, and of not being in control of their destiny that all people in their condition experience in the rest of the world. The existence of a social safety net and strong family ties mitigates their situation, however.

## Standards of Living and Status

Italy has become more affluent than ever. Across the whole spectrum of Italian society, consumption levels have grown immensely since the end of the war. In the 1980s, in the wake of the economic expansion and influenced in their behavior by the trends coming from America, ever larger numbers of Italians started to purchase luxury items, such as consumer electronics products, designer apparel, and jewelry, and to undertake activities in their leisure time such as

skiing and traveling, especially abroad, where the elements of status and immediate self-gratification have been very conspicuous.

The professions which require massive training carry with them substantial status because of the importance that Italians attach to education. Education, which is free (and of very good quality on the whole) throughout high school and low cost afterwards, is seen by Italians as the best way to achieve intra- and inter-generational mobility. Such mobility, or the perception thereof, is fairly low compared to that in a country like the United States but possibly not much dissimilar from that of other Western European countries. Another perception, in Italy as elsewhere in the European Union, is that a neat dichotomy exists between those who are "in" and those who are "out"—those who have jobs that provide good benefits, and these who are either unemployed or underemployed and in conditions of much lesser job security. The existence of powerful equalizers in the standards of income such as inexpensive education and socialized medicine has somewhat lessened the impact of this dichotomy, which, however, once again tends to separate the south with its high youth unemployment from the rest of the country.

## THE FAMILY

The family has traditionally been considered by many observers, at home and abroad, as the central element of Italian society as well as one of its most enduring and solid institutions. In a much quoted study, Edward Banfield, analyzing a southern village, called "amoral familism" the absolute allegiance toward one's family over any other type of group or institution. This allegiance is typically accompanied by distrust of the state. Such distrust was in no small part fueled by the Catholic Church, which, deprived of its temporal claims after the unification of the country, saw the family as its most natural preserve. Even the signing of the Concordat in 1929 never completely resolved the tension existing between church and state in this area, and during the

---

[4]Paolo Farneti, *The Italian Party System (1945–1980)* (New York: St. Martin's, 1985), pp. 90–101.

Fascist era, Catholic organizations coexisted in some form of uneasy competition with the regime's official associations.

The Italian family has not been immune from the broader influences that have been affecting other countries in the Western world. Starting in the mid-1960s, with the access to better education and to new centers of socialization such as the factory floor and schools, an era of greater emphasis on consumption and much less delayed gratification was ushered in. The extensive presence of the television in Italian households made them aware of different behavioral realities in other Western countries. Marriage as an institution started to be seen as not the only inevitable or most desirable option for individual adults. Sexual freedom acquired growing levels of legitimacy. Following the cultural pattern in the United States, parents' judgment came under increasing attack by their children. The young started to abandon the limiting confines of their family not just by generally criticizing "the system" to which at some levels the family web of relationships belonged as well, but also by actively engaging in politics. This tide of activism among the younger generations would largely benefit the parties of the Left and especially the Italian Communist Party. Catholic youth organizations, mainly connected to the Christian Democrats, trailed behind substantially in the ability to adjust their message to these changing realities. These new social trends were soon to be reflected in important legislative measures, which would indeed affect the relationship between state and family.[5]

Many of the reforms were passed against the opposition of the Church, which was also strongly critical of the Italians' increasing secularization and obsession with consumption, which it viewed as promoting a lowering of moral standards and the erosion of family values. But the pressure brought to bear on the Christian Democrats in Parliament by the Italian Communist Party, in alliance with the socialist and lay parties, was too powerful. The general trend of secularization in Italian law culminated in the 1984 revision of the Concordat between state and church, which among other things ended the principle of state religion. The reforms aimed at carrying out a state policy toward the family were part of the general establishment of the welfare state which was taking place in the 1970s. However, social programs, several of them with an emphasis on the family, such as family planning, have been uneven in efficiency and quality.

## The Family since the 1980s

The 1980s represented a return to family ties and a lessening of involvement in politics. The disappointment generated by the failures of the historic compromise between the DC and the Communists, the movement toward more pragmatic and more cynical and power-acquisitive strategies by the Socialist Party under Bettino Craxi, the exposure to the ideas of Thatcherism and the Reagan revolution, together with the above-mentioned malaise materializing in the welfare state—all militated toward discouraging large segments of the population from active participation in politics. Since the late 1970s, the young especially have become less enthusiastic and optimistic over their ability to be active promoters of positive change in Italian society and politics and more interested in the pursuit of individual self-interest and gratification.

Italian families stand out in Europe on account of the extremely low birthrates, the low divorce rate, the low percentage of unwed mothers, the later and fewer marriages, the prolonged stays with the family, and the low rates of cohabitation between unmarried members of the opposite sex.

Several explanations, at times working at cross purposes, are offered to explain this set of characteristics. Thus, in the case of the low birthrate, some emphasize the fact that children may represent for their parents a hindrance for their careers, their acquisition of consumption goods, and the full enjoyment of their leisure time. Others mention the excessive burden placed on women who frequently have to juggle family and work without being capable of relying too much on their men for help with household

---

[5]See Paul Ginsborg, *A History of Contemporary Italy* (London: Penguin, 1990), especially pp. 248–249.

REVIEW

5.3

## THE FAMILY: POLITICS AND PUBLIC POLICY

| 1968 | State kindergarten system set up. |
| 1970 | Legalization of divorce. |
| 1971 | Communal day-care centers created. |
| 1974 | Referendum to repeal divorce defeated. |
| 1975 | Family consultation centers to advise on all areas of family planning and legal counseling; broad overhaul of family law (complete legal parity of husband and wife, recognition of children born out of wedlock and their completely equal treatment to that of their legitimate brethren when inheriting, the regime of common property for the spouses, and a significant expansion of the judges' role in the family life). |
| 1978 | Legalization of abortion; creation of the national health service. |
| 1981 | Referendum to repeal abortion defeated. |
| 2001 | Abolition of the inheritance tax. |

chores. Others still talk about parents' rejection of the Fascist preference for large families and their passing it on to their children. More convincingly still, Italian parents might be motivated in their reproductive choices by the desire to offer their children a standard of living present and future that is better than or at least equal to theirs. In this sense, another child might represent an obstacle to the desired upward intergenerational mobility. Such a view is bolstered by polls suggesting that Italians consider top priorities to be the education of their children, their health, and owning a house, in that order.

## Closeness in the Family

Having absorbed fully their parents' belief that parenting truly never ends, and seeing the ongoing support they receive from their own families, young Italians are undoubtedly intimidated by the large responsibilities that having children entails. The negative images of the outside world that Italian parents tend to offer their children do not help much either and promote their stay in the safe family cocoon. The tolerance that parents have developed for their children's individual needs and lifestyles has made the prolonged intergenerational cohabitation easier.

The lower rates of unwed motherhood and divorce, while stemming from concern for the children's future, are also rooted in lingering religious and social stigmas (incidentally, Italians are particularly tolerant toward political leaders' private lives). The perceived "right" way to start a family is often, especially among the middle class, to own a house, and the families of both newlyweds frequently offer financial support. Interestingly, in the decision on where to locate their home, proximity to their parents' dwelling plays a large role, with a preference for nearness to the bride's parents (what sociologists call "matrilocal residence").

The desire to live with their parents or near them stems from the strong emotional bonds that exist between generations. Italians enjoy free or low-cost medical care, subsidized public transportation, and free or subsidized schooling at all levels, but they do not receive much financial assistance in terms of income maintenance to the young and those never employed. Thus, generally speaking, parents tend to provide their children with financial support with their often relatively generous pensions and with free babysitting for the grandchildren. Italians are also much more likely to ask their parents for financial assistance than Americans, British, Germans, and Aus-

**REVIEW
5.4**

### FACTS ABOUT THE ITALIAN FAMILY

- Italy's family size: 4.3 members (1936); 3.6 (1961); 2.8 (1991). Italy has one of the lowest fertility rates in the world: 1.18 children per woman; birthrates lowest in the north.

- Marriages, rate per 1,000 population: 7.9 (1961); 4.8 (1991).

- Number of divorces per 1,000 population: 0.6 (United States 4.5; France 2.0; Germany 2.3; United Kingdom 3.3; Japan 1.7).

- 80 percent of families live in owned housing.

- In 1975 the average age of a woman giving birth for the first time was 25; in 2001 it is 29.

- Italians tend to get married later: four out of five individuals between 15 and 29 years of age live at home with their parents.

- Fewer cohabiting unmarried couples than in most European countries.

- A century ago an Italian could expect at birth to live approximately 35 years, now 79 years.

*Sources:* ISTAT, *Statistical Abstract of the United States, The Economist.*

tralians.[6] In turn, they may provide the older generation with present or future nursing care. This level of intergenerational solidarity accounts in large part for the relatively small numbers of nursing homes and homeless and for the young's fairly widespread reluctance to relocate away from their families of origin.

## GENDER ISSUES

The women's movement, which started at the same time as the socialist and union movements in the 1880s, was interrupted by the rise of Fascism. Once Fascism rose to power, the role that women had carved out for themselves in the area of providing public assistance, earlier recognized by legislation, expanded considerably. Fascist women's organizations were given the task to administer winter assistance, gifts to children, and summer and year-round camp programs.

[6]The research was conducted by Eurisko. See "Mondotrends," *Il Mondo,* April 1994, p. 137.

During the World War II, women's role in the resistance movement was not completely appreciated and had to conform anyhow to the political differences that existed within the National Liberation Committee. At the end of the war, having gained for the first time the right to vote, women coalesced in organizations centered on the political parties represented in Parliament. This political link, especially with the parties of the Left, would be one of the most distinguishing features of Italian feminism and only in the 1970s would women's organizations start to move in more independent directions.

For an outside observer especially, it is quite remarkable how the Italians' outlook and legislation in the areas of women's rights have changed since the latter part of the 1960s. The Italian feminist movement was instrumental in the passing of legislation that would permit divorce and abortion and in the victory against those referendums supported by the Church aiming at repealing them. The Church's Madonna imagery in relation to women contributed across the centuries to the development of the essentially matriarchal nature of Italian society, which arguably came to be the foundation whence the feminist ideas that mushroomed across the Western world could be adapted in Italy. In any event, distinctly authoritarian patriarchal postures had become basically much less acceptable before the 1970s and even more so since then.

Women's condition in Italy at the beginning of the twenty-first century is not basically dissimilar from that of women in other advanced industrial countries. Some general points need stressing, however. Women have increased their levels of participation in the Italian workforce since the early 1970s. Most significantly, between 1980 and 1990, female employment has grown by 20 percent while male employment has barely budged. In 1999, women represented 38.2 percent of the total workforce, up from 37.1 percent in 1991 and 36.1 percent in 1987. Among managers, younger women (up to 40 years of age) are far more represented than older classes of age. Barring their hitting the "glass ceiling," this means that in the future women's presence at the highest levels of decision making in both private and public sectors should increase. There is some anecdotal evidence that in private jobs women are being denied promotion or pay raises for reasons such as marriage status, which would be considered by an American court discriminatory. Women working in the public sector are much better protected. There is also significant evidence that women are paid less than men across various job classifications and income levels, in spite of the fact that women are at least as well educated as men. For instance, the number of women students in Italian universities is greater than that of men, and graduation rates of females also exceed those of men.

The most striking characteristic of the Italian feminist movement is its emphasis on protection of women rather than on strict equality. For instance, Italian women enjoy one of the best maternity leave treatments in Western Europe and can go into retirement several years earlier than men. Many argue, along the prevailing view in the United States, that such protection is not desirable since it acts as a deterrent for the hiring of women.

The general stagnation in employment growth that had materialized in Italy in the early 1990s, a phenomenon not dissimilar to that observable elsewhere in Western Europe, had slowed down considerably the trend toward the greater representation of women in the workforce. Later, between 1995 and 1999, however, it became evident that women's growth rate in employment was again much faster than men's. The continuation of this trend in the next years will most likely be linked to the economy's ability to generate new jobs. In any event, the general thrust toward a more service-oriented economy should continue to exert a positive impact on women's employment levels.

In the political sphere, as elsewhere in Western democracies, women are underrepresented. For instance, at the 2001 elections, they constituted 9.8 percent of the total membership of the Chamber of Deputies and 7.8 percent of the Senate. The Constitutional Court in 1995 struck down the new electoral law requiring that 50 percent of party candidates for the proportional list be women. At the end of 2001, one could note that women's access to politics was being fostered by legislation on public financing of electoral campaigns, and that as a part of the reform on devolution, regional electoral laws would have to promote parity of access. In terms of the political alliances across the parties represented in Parliament, women elected officials from all parties worked together in the 1994 legislature to change the laws against rape and make them much more severe.

## Thinking Critically

1. Would you agree that Italy is essentially divided between a North and a South?
2. What factors explain the rise of Italian nationalism?
3. Has the influence of the Catholic Church on Italian citizens declined in recent years?
4. Did the Italian Republic inherit anything from the Fascist regime?
5. What have been the main effects of class divisions on Italian life?

# KEY TERMS

amoral familism *(268)*
Fascism *(260)*
feudalism *(257)*
industrial triangle *(267)*
Lateran Pacts *(261)*
secularism *(263)*
southern question *(264)*
*trasformismo (257)*
unification *(257)*

# FURTHER READINGS

Almond, Gabriel, and Sidney Verba. *The Civic Culture: Political Attitudes and Democracy in Five Nations* (Boston: Little, Brown, 1965).

Banfield, Edward C. *The Moral Basis of a Backward Society* (Glencoe, IL: Free Press, 1958).

Bethmont, Jacques, and Jean Pelletier. *Italy: A Geographical Introduction,* trans. Eleanor Kofman (London: Longman, 1983).

Birnbaum, Lucia. *Liberazione della Donna: Feminism in Italy* (Middletown, CT: Wesleyan University Press, 1986).

Bobbio, Norberto. *Ideological Profile of Twentieth-Century Italy* (Princeton, NJ: Princeton University Press, 1995).

Cassese, Sabino, ed. *Ritratto dell'Italia* (Bari: Laterza, 2001).

Chubb, Judith. *Patronage, Power, and Poverty in Southern Italy* (Cambridge: Cambridge University Press, 1982).

Clark, Martin. *Modern Italy: 1871–1982* (New York: Longman, 1984).

De Felice, Renzo. *Interpretations of Fascism,* trans. B. H. Everett (Cambridge, MA: Harvard University Press, 1977).

Eurispes. *Rapporto Italia 2001* (Rome: Eurispes). Annual.

Mack Smith, Denis. *Italy: A Modern History* (Ann Arbor: University of Michigan Press, 1969).

Putnam, Robert. *Making Democracy Work: Civic Traditions in Modern Italy* (Princeton, NJ: Princeton University Press, 1993).

# B. POLITICAL PROCESSES AND INSTITUTIONS

## ELECTIONS

The electoral system created between 1946 and 1948 reflected the anti-Fascist ideology of its drafters, who tried to limit concentration of power in only one party. It was (and is) also a system where voter registration is the responsibility of local authorities, who send the voting card automatically by mail to eligible voters. This fact helps explain the high voter turnout at Italian elections. The electoral system, moreover, extended universal suffrage to women for the first time in its history and was highly proportional in both the Chamber of Deputies and the Senate.

Before the changes introduced in the 1990s, for the elections of the Chamber of Deputies, the 630 seats were divided among 32 districts, according to their population. In each district, each party would present a list of candidates. Voters in casting by secret ballot their votes for a list could also express their preferences for up to four candidates within the list, by writing the names or number on the party list. The distribution of the seats among the parties that competed in the district reflected the percentage of the total votes cast, and the seats were assigned to the candidates with the highest number of preference votes. About one-tenth of the seats (and the votes) could not be mathematically divided among the parties and were pooled together in a nationwide district, which permitted smaller parties exceeding 300,000 votes nationwide to achieve parliamentary representation.

The voting system for the 315 Senate seats was characterized by the parties' choice of a single candidate to support in each senatorial district and was de facto proportional, too. The distribution of seats was made according to the number of votes that each party's list obtained on a regional basis. The electoral system resulted in a fairly high correlation between the votes obtained by a party nationwide and the number of seats it won in both chambers and was in this sense highly representative of the electorate's political opinions. Unfortunately, by making it

easy for relatively small organized groups to win parliamentary seats, it promoted the growth of a large number of parties. This, in turn, reduced the governability of the country, since it was difficult to form stable coalition governments. Moreover, Italian voters could never know in advance who their future prime minister was going to be, since he is chosen by the president of the Republic and must meet with the approval of the coalition parties' secretariats before receiving the vote of confidence by the chambers. Knowing in advance the government's composition and programs was also nearly impossible for voters, given the ambiguous nature of party platforms and the compromises that would take place in the formation and running of the government.

The electoral system that was introduced in 1993 and has been used in the 1994, 1996, and 2001 elections is a mixed majoritarian-proportional system. At present 75 percent of deputies are elected in uninominal districts with the first-past-the-post method. The remaining 25 percent of the seats are attributed proportionally among those parties which have obtained at least 4 percent of the votes nationwide. This threshold aims at reducing the proliferation of small parties. Thus voters cast two different ballots: one for the majoritarian 75 percent of the seats and the other for the 25 percent proportional share.

In the Senate the distribution of the seats on a regional basis in proportion to the population has been maintained. At present three-fourths of the Senate seats are located in uninominal districts, while the competition for the remaining one-fourth is on the basis of the proportional vote obtained by party lists regionwide. As we shall see later, in order to improve the stability of Italian governments, many advocate that the voting system be changed again, possibly with the introduction of a double ballot and even greater reliance on a majoritarian criterion.

Change of the electoral system came about through the other means that Italians have to express directly their political views on a nationwide basis—the referendum. The constitution provides for two types of referendums: one to repeal existing laws, and the other to revise the constitution. The former type can be proposed by 500,000 petitioners or five Regional Councils. The constitution does not allow referendums on laws in the areas of tax and budget, amnesty, and authorization to ratify international treaties. The latter type of referendum has been used only once, in connection with the 2001 constitutional reform on devolution.

The legislation enabling the holding of referendums did not materialize until 1970. The proreferendum movements, with the exception of the fights against nuclear plants in 1987, were not particularly successful at first. In 1990 when three more referendums supported by the environmental groups failed to reach the needed majority at the polls, many thought that referendums could not be relied on to effect change. The results at the 1991 and 1993 referendums and their impact on electoral legislation changed this perception considerably. By late 2001, however, after a raft of referendums held in 1997 and 2000 did not even reach the necessary quorums, their role as agents of change was again deemed unlikely.

The 1991 referendum on the elimination of preference voting (which many claimed reduced the secrecy of voting and thus permitted vote buying) and the April 1993 referendum to reform the Senate electoral system forced Parliament to act. In the summer of 1993, Parliament enacted its reform of the electoral law which, as we have seen, made the system more majoritarian and hopefully more stable. The April 1993 referendum to abolish the public financing of political parties also forced Parliament to introduce legislation profoundly affecting electoral campaigns. At present, political candidates and parties have fairly rigid campaign expenditure ceilings, and reporting and control procedures have improved. The new legislation has also tried to regulate access to public and privately owned media and has created a supervisory authority. The presence on the political scene of a player like media tycoon Silvio Berlusconi makes the issue of the equitable access to media time particularly controversial.

# POLITICAL PARTIES

Italy has a multiparty system. Italian parties, not unlike those of other Western European parliamentary democracies, are powerful and on the whole disciplined (although less so since the early 1990s).[7] Citizens vote primarily for parties, not for their individual candidates. The party labels are very important to candidates, since a party legislator who antagonizes the party leadership by taking positions contrary to those of the official party line risks being expelled from the party. This results in the impossibility for him or her to get reelected on the party slate. This explains the much higher level of party discipline existing in Italy than in the United States, where the individual representative has a greater need to pay attention to interest groups and to please the electorate in his or her district. Party affiliation is also important when it comes to the assignment of jobs, since it gives more legitimacy to the patron-client relationship.

Italian parties have traditionally reflected the divisions existing in Italian society. The class, religious, and center against periphery and urban-rural cleavages have found, each in different ways and degrees, representation in the parties. Moreover, the Italian parties, especially the larger ones, have established subsidiary organizations engaging in social, cultural, and recreational activities to a degree that is unimaginable in the United States.

Italian political parties tend to display profound differences not just over policy issues but also in ideological terms. At least until recently, Italians did not just vote Christian Democrat, Communist, Socialist, or Liberal but they *were* Christian Democrat, Communist, Socialist, or Liberal. Internally, Italian parties also display a level of fragmentation and polarization greater than that of other Western parliamentary democracies. The patterns of voting along the left-right spectrum were established early on, and for nearly five decades the voting support received by each individual party did not change much, as

[7]Michael Gallagher et al., *Representative Government in Western Europe* (New York: McGraw-Hill, 1992), p. 29.

Table 5.2 shows. However, developments occurring since the early 1990s are changing this and many of the elements outlined so far.

## The Individual Parties

*Christian Democratic Party and the Popular Party*    The Christian Democratic Party (DC), founded while the country was still divided in two during World War II, has dominated the Italian political system since the 1946 elections. Until 1992, the DC always obtained the largest number of votes and governed either alone or in coalitions headed in almost all cases by a prime minister from its parliamentary ranks. The quintessential catchall moderate-center party, it drew support not only from staunch Catholics but also across class and regional lines. It had an extensive organization built on political patronage somewhat similar to the erstwhile American urban political machines, and it was highly factionalized. The DC Party Congress displayed the ever shifting balance of power among these factions.

In 1993, in the midst of an apparently endless series of corruption probes by the magistrature, it changed its name to the Italian Popular Party (PPI), as it was known before the advent of Fascism. At the 1994 elections there were three lists of candidates emerging from what had been the DC: the PPI, the group headed by reformer Mario Segni, and the Democratic Christian Center (CCD), which joined the coalition headed by Silvio Berlusconi. At the elections of 1996, a splinter group from the PPI, the Unitary Democratic Center (CDU), joined the Berlusconi-led Alliance for Freedom, while the rest of the PPI joined professor Romano Prodi's Olive Tree coalition. At the elections of 2001, the PPI joined other small Catholic-inspired groups, the Democrats, the Udeur, and the Dini-led Italian Renewal to form a coalition party named *Margherita* (Daisy). Gianfranco Rutelli, the head of this new coalition party, would also become the leader of the Olive Tree. The CCD and the CDU, after some defections and additions, joined forces and ran

### TABLE 5.2

#### 1948–1992 ELECTION RESULTS FOR THE CHAMBER OF DEPUTIES (PERCENTAGE OF VOTES CAST)

| Year | PCI/PDS | PSI/PSU | PSDI | Greens | PR | PRI | DC | Northern League | PLI | MSI-DN |
|------|---------|---------|------|--------|-----|-----|------|------------------|-----|--------|
| 1948 | 31.0[a] |         | 7.1  |        |     | 2.5 | 48.5 |                  | 3.8 | 2.0 |
| 1953 | 22.6    | 12.7    | 4.5  |        |     | 1.6 | 40.1 |                  | 3.0 | 5.8 |
| 1958 | 22.7    | 14.2    | 4.6  |        |     | 1.4 | 42.3 |                  | 3.5 | 4.8 |
| 1963 | 25.3    | 13.8    | 6.1  |        |     | 1.4 | 38.3 |                  | 7.0 | 5.1 |
| 1968 | 26.9    | 14.5[b] |      |        |     | 2.0 | 39.1 |                  | 5.8 | 4.5 |
| 1972 | 27.1    | 9.6     | 5.1  |        |     | 2.9 | 38.7 |                  | 3.9 | 8.7 |
| 1976 | 34.4    | 9.6     | 3.4  |        | 0.8 | 3.1 | 38.7 |                  | 1.3 | 6.1 |
| 1979 | 30.4    | 9.8     | 3.8  |        | 3.4 | 3.0 | 38.3 |                  | 1.9 | 5.3 |
| 1983 | 29.9    | 11.4    | 4.1  |        | 2.2 | 5.1 | 32.9 |                  | 2.9 | 6.8 |
| 1987 | 26.6    | 14.3    | 2.9  | 2.5    | 2.6 | 3.7 | 34.3 | 0.5              | 2.1 | 5.9 |
| 1992 | 16.1    | 13.6    | 2.0  | 2.8    | 1.2 | 4.4 | 29.7 | 8.6              | 2.9 | 5.4 |

[a]PCI and PSI together
[b]PSI and PSDI together
PSDI = Social Democrats
PRI = Republicans
PR = Radical Party; since 1992 Pannella list
PLI = Liberals
MSI-DN = Neo-Fascists

together as the Biancofiore list with the center-right coalition, the House of Freedoms.

### The Communist Party and the Democratic Party of the Left

The second largest party since the end of the war, the Italian Communist Party (PCI) was born in 1921 from a split within the Socialist Party. A most powerful force in the Resistance movement, the PCI was always banned from entering the DC-led governments by opposition from the United States and the Church. Its loyalty to Moscow was severely tested with the invasion of Hungary in 1956 and of Czechoslovakia in 1967, which caused many of its members to defect to join the socialists.

The PCI drew its most substantial electoral support from the industrial areas of the north and the "red" regions in the center of the country. While receiving its core support from industrial workers, the party received votes from all segments of Italian society. The PCI, following the collapse of the USSR, changed its name at the 1991 Party Congress to the Democratic Party of the Left (PDS), so as to show that it would henceforth pursue more moderate policies. A core of Marxist holdovers founded the alternative Refounded Communism (RC).

At the election of 1994, the PDS was the strongest force within the defeated center-left coalition, the Progressive Alliance. At the elections of 1996, the Progressive Alliance, now reborn as Olive Tree, won, and the PDS obtained the largest number of votes. Refounded Communism increased its votes by 43 percent from 1994, and its support became crucial to the formation of the new center-left government. At the elections of 2001, Refounded Communism did not agree to pre-electoral agreements with the rest of the Olive Tree while an RC splinter faction, the Pdci, did. The PDS ran with the new name of *DS,* Democrats of the Left.

### The Italian Socialist Party

The Italian Socialist Party (PSI) was founded in 1892. Up to the early 1960s, the PSI played junior partner to the PCI at the opposition. When the PSI joined the government in 1963, the party's agenda for social reforms rapidly gave way to the desire to get its share of patronage. Under the strong lead-ership of Bettino Craxi, since 1976, interfaction rivalries were reduced, and the party moved much more toward the center and aggressively attacked the PCI, whose voters it actively sought. The PSI never exceeded 15 percent of the total votes cast for the Chamber of Deputies. The party lost almost all its support as a result of the 1992 corruption scandal.

At the elections of 2001, a PSI reincarnation, the New PSI, ran under the banner of the Berlusconi-led House of Freedoms. Another reincarnation of the PSI ran with the Olive Tree Coalition.

### The Social Democratic Party

What would become known after 1952 as the Social Democratic Party (PSDI) came to life in 1947. It was founded by a faction that detached itself from the PSI and which was very strongly pro-American and opposed to a policy of a national front with the Communists. It never got more than 6 percent of the votes, and in 1968 when it temporarily reunited with the PSI, the result was unsatisfactory for both. The PSDI upheld the interest of the petit bourgeoisie and claimed to be in the mainstream of European social democracy, a claim also made by Bettino Craxi. The PSDI's participation in many coalition governments and in the patronage system made it also a prime object of the magistrates' inquiries, and the scandals swept it away.

### The Republican Party

Resurrected after the end of Fascism, the Republican Party (PRI), just like the PSDI and the Liberal Party, was a secular party. It started with centrist positions in the governments under De Gasperi and then moved toward center-left positions. Drawing its support from middle-class professionals and businesspeople, the PRI never exceeded 5 percent of the votes. A party involved in many postwar governments, it was less touched by the bribery scandals than the two other lay parties, but it was nevertheless decimated by the scandals.

### The Liberal Party

The Italian Liberal Party (PLI) was resurrected while World War II was still going on. The PLI represented the interests of the large entrepreneurs, wanted little state intervention in the economy, and was strongly anti-Communist. It never obtained more than 7 percent of the votes and was also brought down by the bribery scandals that started in 1992.

### The Social Movement and the National Alliance

The Italian Social Movement (MSI) was born after the war to pull together those forces that the collapse of Fascism had dispersed. Always ostracized by the other parties, it never obtained more than 8 percent of the votes. At the March 1994 elections, it became the National Alliance and obtained excellent results, in no small measure on account of its not having been tainted by the scandals that had hit the DC and its coalition partners. The results also showed that by 1994 many Italians thought that the Fascist component of National Alliance, toned down skillfully by its new leader Gianfranco Fini, was no longer a threat to democracy. At the elections of 1996, National Alliance did not increase its electoral support by as much as its leader had expected. The presence of candidates from the extreme Right, running independently under the newly created banner of the Flame, played a role in the disappointing performance by siphoning off some crucial votes in several districts.

### The Radicals and the Greens

Even less important in terms of size than the lay parties, the Radicals and the Greens represented a significant core of ideas maintained by some of the Italian people. The Radicals originated in the 1950s from a split within the PLI and have held throughout a very libertarian position, spearheading political battles that through the sponsoring of referendums have had substantial political and social impact. At the election of 1994, only very few representatives were elected, under the banner of the Forza Italia–led Alliance for Freedom.

The Greens have been inspired by the environmentalist efforts of the homonymous party in Germany. Despite their small size, their agenda has influenced that of all other parties. The major example of their influence has been their support of a 1987 referendum that has de facto reduced Italy's reliance on nuclear energy to zero. At the 1994 election, they joined the PDS-led Progressive Alliance. At the 2001 elections, the Greens

joined forces with some holdovers of the Social Democratic Party and ran under the name Girasole (Sunflower) in the Olive Tree Coalition.

### The Northern League

Born at the end of the 1980s from the fusion of regional northern parties, the Northern League under the guide of sharp-tongued Umberto Bossi has attacked corruption in government, the misuse of tax revenues raised in the north, and the inefficiency of a bureaucracy predominantly staffed by southerners, and it has pursued a policy of federalism that has occasionally invoked downright secession. Only marginally affected by the scandals, it scored a great victory in the 1992 elections and gained control of many cities at the fall 1993 local elections. At the 1994 elections, the Northern League joined forces with Forza Italia and the National Alliance, in the Alliance for Freedom/for Good Government, which was victorious. The League's withdrawal from the winning coalition at the end of 1994 provoked the collapse of the Berlusconi government. While Berlusconi and Fini went to the opposition, Bossi supported the Dini government. Then, dissatisfied that the Dini government had not done anything to promote federalism, in the election campaign of 1996 the League emphasized its independence from Rome and any other political formation. The result obtained at the elections went beyond most expectations and made Bossi's threats of secession sound more real than at any other time. At the 2001 elections, the League formally joined the Berlusconi-led alliance.

### Forza Italia

The political party created in the fall of 1993 by media magnate Silvio Berlusconi, Forza Italia, made excellent use of the business network of its leader and, critics argue, of his TV networks. It created in a few weeks an extensive network of "clubs" across the country which led him to victory at the 1994 elections on a populist platform stressing anti-Communism and free markets. At the 1996 elections, Berlusconi's party retained its electoral strength, but the defeat of the coalition he headed meant that he would be relegated to the opposition. At the 2001 elections, Forza Italia emerged as the strongest party in the country.

***The Olive Tree***   The Olive Tree is a new center-left coalition of parties and political forces which at the elections of 1996 comprised the PDS, various groups inspired by the Christian Democratic, Republican, Socialist, and Liberal ideologies, a moderate group headed by Lamberto Dini, and the Greens. Headed by the unassuming economics professor and former head of IRI, Romano Prodi, it was established at the beginning of 1995. Prodi tried to avoid the mistakes of the 1994 coalition of the Left, the Progressive Alliance, by reassuring moderate voters. The Olive Tree's victorious platform at the 1996 elections supported the simplification of the current tax system, the fight against tax evasion, the maintenance of a strong independent judiciary, and public education. In 2001, without its leader Prodi, who was in Brussels heading the EU commission, the coalition lost to the Berlusconi-led coalition House of Freedoms.

***Alliance for Freedom***   The Alliance for Freedom, a center-right coalition, which was set up shortly before the elections of 1994, comprised Forza Italia, National Alliance, the Northern League, and various of the same center forces (Catholics, Republicans, Socialists, and Liberals) that can also be found on the center-left coalition. Running in 1996 without the Northern League, the Alliance for Freedom proposed a program advocating tax cuts, the reduction of the powers of the investigating magistrates, and the support of private schools. At the elections of 2001, the center-right coalition changed its name into House of Freedoms and ran with the League as a full partner.

# CHRISTIAN DEMOCRATS AND POST–WORLD WAR II POLITICS

The Christian Democratic Party (DC) started to play a pivotal role in the postwar Italian political system with its victory at the June 1946 elections for the Constituent Assembly. The party program supported freedom of education, universal suffrage, private property, and obviously Catholic values. The cooperation between the DC and the Communists in governing the country, which had started as the war was still going on, continued throughout 1946. In May 1947, concerned over the high inflation rate, the not-too-favorable conditions of the Peace Treaty signed by Italy, the poor results for his party at the regional elections of April 1947 in Sicily, the imposition of Soviet-backed governments in much of Eastern Europe, encouraged by the ousting of the Communists from the French government, but above all continuing to feel the anti-Communist pressure from a United States dominated by Truman's doctrine and from an ever more intolerant Catholic hierarchy, Alcide De Gasperi, the leader of the DC, resigned as prime minister. De Gasperi was given again the task of forming a new government, and he relied this time exclusively on parties of the center. The Communists and the Socialists were out. What was thought of by many as just a temporary exclusion would, in the case of the Communists, become a permanent one.

The new constitution was approved by the Constituent Assembly with a very large majority (88 percent) and was deeply influenced by different strands of thought. Christian Democrats borrowed from traditional liberal-democratic principles (such as equality of all citizens as holders of rights preceding the creation of the state, and protection of civil rights and of the right to property). They also borrowed from the Catholic-democratic tradition (protection of the family, freedom of setting up private schools, promotion of local autonomies—regions, provinces, communes—and full incorporation of the Lateran Pacts). The PCI and the PSI participation in the writing of the new constitution is reflected in its emphasis on social justice, equality, and workers' rights.

## The Elections of 1948

The elections of June 1948 marked a real watershed in the history of Italy. The electoral campaign was incredibly intense and polarized. The Marshall Plan, with its funding of public projects and convoys of food and medicine, was buying a lot of goodwill among the Italian people, and the Christian Democrats, with the help of Washington, succeeded in portraying themselves as the best friends of the United States.

The Catholic Church intervened directly in the political fray and warned Catholics that voting for anti-God parties, or even nonvoting, was a mortal sin (which helps explain Italy's high voter turnout). The DC appealed to the largest possible gamut of Italian professions and economic and social interests (industrialists, workers, farmers, shopkeepers, as well as housewives and retirees). The results of the April 1948 election represented a landslide victory for the DC and marked the beginning of the DC's hegemony over Italian political life.

The new government of the DC and three small moderate parties had soon to confront a major crisis. On July 14, 1948, the Communist leader Palmiro Togliatti was shot by a right-wing extremist. There were two days of great street violence between rearmed partisans, workers, the unemployed, and the police, especially in the north. Togliatti, when he regained consciousness, strongly urged Italian workers to surrender all arms and the crisis was over.

The crisis revealed how the right wing of the DC was ready to exploit through harsh police measures the fears of collapse of law and order among the middle and upper classes. It also showed that the PCI leadership feared the anti-Communist leanings of the armed forces and the police and the Americans' almost certain military intervention against any violent attempt at seizing power made by the Left. The DC also had factions which, in the name of the Catholic tradition, believed in a socially just world. In the area of agriculture, for instance, the DC decided in 1950 to pass legislation aiming at achieving land redistribution, especially in the south. The redistribution benefitted frequently those farmers who had some links with the DC and led to the excessive fragmentation of the land. The creation in 1950 of the Cassa per il Mezzogiorno, a major state-owned development bank for the south, would further reinforce the DC control of the patronage system in the area of the country that had already proved to be its most important reservoir of votes.

## Less Stable Majorities

The local elections of 1952 saw a marked decline in DC votes, attributable in no small part to the party's incapacity to meet the electoral promises of 1948 as well as the growth of the monarchical and neo-Fascist parties, also a result of the increased concern over Communism. The DC leadership pushed forth an idea that could serve it well: the coalition that would obtain 50 percent plus one of the votes would get 65 percent of the seats. Parliament transformed this proposal into law (dubbed by its opponents the "swindle law") before the June 1953 elections for the new Parliament took place. Against all expectations, the coalition of DC and lay parties obtained slightly less than 50 percent of the votes. It would be the end of De Gasperi's career and of a group of leaders who had been at the helm of the country in the years preceding Fascism.

In the period of the second legislature (1953–1958), the DC leaders were mostly men of the Catholic left whose overall strategy was to enhance the influence of the party through the increased control of universities, mass media, unions, and employers' organizations and by an even tighter grip on the large network of state-owned enterprises (the IRI) created under Fascism, which were further expanded. During this period and that of the next legislature (1958–1963) governments were either coalitions led by the DC or were single-party (called *monocolore*), exclusively composed of DC ministers with the support, through their abstention from voting, of parties at the center and right of the political spectrum. These years have been viewed as a period of "immobilization" where the main preoccupation of the DC was to manage these not-too-stable governments characterized by slim majorities rather than governing the country itself. The 1950s were not, however, years of economic stagnation as we shall see.

## The 1960s: The Socialists out of Quarantine

Powerful forces of change were at work. Some of these were the DC's desire to increase the stability of its governments, some Socialist leaders' increasingly uneasy relationship with the Communists in the wake of Hungary's invasion by Soviet troops, and most importantly, a shift in the position of the DC's two main allies. The first,

Pope John XXIII, had completely different views from those of his predecessor, supporting a reduction in East-West tensions and in general the Church's adaptation to modern times through dialogue with society's different groups and forces. The second, U.S. President John F. Kennedy, shared the views of many in the Italian business elite who saw the need to drive a wedge between Socialists and Communists. Thus in February 1962, a new tripartite government of the DC-PSDI-PRI was formed, supported by the PSI's abstention.

The new government presented a program whose objectives were the nationalization of the electric power industry, the reform of the school system, the reform of public administration, the establishment of national economic planning, and the reform of urban planning. With the exception of the first two, by the end of 1962, the most conservative elements in the government had blocked or delayed considerably all the others. At the elections of 1963, the DC lost votes, a result of its disappointing both moderate voters and its more left-leaning voters because of its timid approach toward social and economic reforms. The DC would never resolve this tension between these opposing forces within the party.

### The Center-Left Governments

The new era of center-left governments that started in 1963, in which the DC accepted the PSI as a full partner, is viewed by many also as a period of immobilization. The DC prime ministers repeated constantly to their coalition partners that the need to improve the overall performance of the economy should take precedence over social and redistributive reforms. The only concession to the Socialists were the *leggi ponte* (bridging legislation), essentially stopgap measures to alleviate the most urgent problems.

While the DC grip on state-owned industry and its penetration of the bureaucracy through patronage hirings and appointments was continuing, the broad changes occurring in Italian society since the mid-1960s were eroding the Church's position and a substantial portion of the Christian Democrats' traditional ideological message lost its effectiveness.

In the 1960s, various schemes to subvert the democratic institutions were uncovered. At the center of these plots there was typically some intricate connection among high-level members of the military, the police, the secret services, various secret extreme right-wing organizations or groups, and the government and parties of the center and right, including the DC. Most of these plans appear to have been not too well organized and some may have never existed at all, but they nevertheless raised widespread concern.

### Politics as Usual

At the elections of 1968, the DC made small gains and afterwards formed several governments in which, as usual, it continued to have the prime ministership and the lion's share of the cabinet posts. Legislation was passed creating the regions as a new territorial and administrative subdivision. At the 1970 regional elections, the first ones ever held, no major movement in terms of voters' preferences occurred. But what the DC feared came about. The regional councils of Emilia-Romagna, Toscana, and Umbria were won by the parties of the Left. Another major legislative reform was the passing of the Statute of the Workers, a law very protective of workers' rights, even by Western European standards.

At the election of 1972, the DC campaigned as the only political force capable of fighting the "opposite extremisms" of the Right and Left and held its own. The DC formed a new center-right government with the liberals (PLI) and the Social Democrats (PSDI), the first in several years. It lasted only one year, swept away by the economic crisis that was also affecting the other Western countries. The succeeding governments also had to grapple with the unpleasant economic situation, and the DC's stewardship did not prove too convincing.

### Historic Compromise: Enter the Communists

The next general elections, held in 1976, were the most arduously fought since 1953. There was great concern about *il sorpasso* (the "overtake"), the fact that the PCI might get more votes than the DC. A famous journalist encouraged the Italians to "hold their noses and vote DC," an obvious reference to the need to vote for the only party capable, because of its size and despite its penchant for favoritism and corruption, to be an effective barrier against Communism.

The elections represented a victory for the PCI which, however, did not succeed in making *il sorpasso.* The DC held its own and Republicans, Socialists, and Liberals lost votes to the main contenders. The Left found itself with 47 percent of the votes. But the Communist leadership decided that in a climate of great economic crisis, with great inflation and budget deficits, and of great tension arising from "red" and "black" terrorist attacks, attempting to form a coalition government of the Left was too risky. Thus the PCI supported indirectly the newly formed government of Giulio Andreotti by abstaining from voting. It would be a government where abstentions would exceed favorable votes. This government would fold in January 1978 and Andreotti's newly formed *monocolore* (single-party, DC) government left the PCI dissatisfied and threatening to give a no-confidence vote. The kidnapping of DC notable Aldo Moro by the Red Brigades would put an end to the crisis.

Moro was the most important DC leader to be in favor of Communist participation in the government of the country. The Communists immediately acted by voting in favor of Andreotti's *monocolore,* as a show of resolve against any threat to the public order. After the killing of Moro by his captors, a referendum held in June to repeal a tough public order law saw DC and PCI together recommending to their supporters to vote against the repeal. The law remained intact. A very important referendum repealing the law providing for public financing of political parties also saw the successful cooperation of DC and PCI, together with other major parties, to convince their voters to maintain the status quo.

## The End of the DC-PCI Cooperation

The government of "national solidarity" with the support of the PCI ended at the beginning of 1979. The United States had remained very much opposed to any entrance of the Commu-

nists into the government, scoffing at the notion of "eurocommunism" whereby there could be a way for the Communist parties of Western Europe to participate in the governments of the region in a manner completely independent of Moscow. The PCI, on the other hand, became concerned that its association with the Andreotti government could be very damaging to its image. In point of fact, the PCI was no longer perceived as the completely clean and principled party of only a few years before. Its partaking in the *lottizzazione,* a patronage system with jobs divided up among parties according to their electoral strength, while enabling it to lure a more moderate electorate, deeply disenchanted many idealistic youths and blue-collar workers.

The elections held in June 1979 saw the DC and the PSI holding their own, while the PCI lost votes. The new government of DC-PSDI-PLI plus some PSI-linked "technicians" continued to try to grapple with the problems of terrorism, increasing drugs and Mafia violence, and a very difficult economic situation. Terrorism would be almost completely defeated by the end of 1983, thanks to some defections in the ranks of the terrorists among those thinking that the violent means had gone too far and also thanks to a system of giving partial or total immunity to those who would turn state's evidence.

## The 1980s: The Rise of the Socialists

One major departure from the traditional game of musical chairs which kept more or less the same people in the government occurred when the prime ministership went for the first time in 1981 to a non-DC politician, the Republican Giovanni Spadolini. He headed the first two of a new formula of government coalitions, the *pentapartito* ("five parties"), comprising DC, PSI, PRI, PSDI, and PCI.

The elections of 1983 showed clearly the dissatisfaction of the electorate against the Christian Democrats and left the door wide open to a government headed by the very ambitious Bettino Craxi, the secretary of the PSI. Craxi would be premier from August 1983 to March 1987, giving Italy its de facto longest government ever. Craxi benefitted from favorable international economic conditions. The domestic economy, although beset by budget deficits, inefficient public services, and very rigid labor rules, witnessed lower inflation, substantial GDP growth, and a buoyant stock market. The Craxi government came to an end in April 1987, when the DC leadership asked him to step down to leave his premiership to a Christian Democrat, according to an agreement reached a year before. Craxi refused to do this and new elections, once again before the end of the legislature, were held.

The elections of 1987 saw some improvement for the DC, partly the result of perceived progress in eliminating its most scandal-tainted leaders. The PSI progressed, gaining votes over the other lay parties while the Communist Party, hurt by Gorbachev's *glasnost,* lost 3 percent of the votes. One trend continued from 1983: an increasing number of unmarked ballots, evidence of the voters' growing sense of dissatisfaction about their political leaders. This dissatisfaction would also be highlighted by the strengthening of protest parties such as the Radicals or the surfacing of others such as the Greens and, more importantly, the Northern regional parties, which shortly thereafter coalesced into the Northern League.

In general, the DC-led coalition governments of those years continued to face inter- and intra-party divisions. Policy making was almost always the result of carefully crafted compromises informed by considerations of self-interest and very seldom efficiency and effectiveness. The political system that the DC had been at the center of, however, was about to change permanently and in a most dramatic way.

## The 1990s: Referendums, Judges, and the Northern League

Mario Segni, a Christian Democratic deputy with a particularly limpid political history, became the promoter of a major referendum for the elimination of preference voting, an important piece in the system of "selling" votes that bred substantial corruption. The ruling majority leaders scoffed at the referendum, suggesting to their voters to ignore it and stay at home. On June 9, 1991, an astounding majority of 96 percent of

the votes cast went to repeal preference voting. The parties at that point could not ignore the massive will of the people and, not to be outdone by one another, started to introduce proposals for institutional reforms. But a far greater shock to the system would soon materialize.

In February 1992, Magistrate Antonio Di Pietro, soon to become a living legend, incarcerated the Socialist manager of a public retirement home, accusing him of forcing firms that were bidding for cleaning contracts to pay a bribe. The manager at first refused to cooperate, hoping for some political intervention which would have put the overambitious judge in his place. Di Pietro and his colleagues, however, enjoyed the support of most of the press and public opinion and the manager caved in, starting to give out the names of his higher-up accomplices. It was an investigative pattern that would be repeated with many other suspects, climbing very high on the Italian political and business ladders. The magistrates uncovered a system of contributions to political parties in exchange for the granting of government contracts (called by the press *tangentopoli,* literally "bribesville"), which also permitted some individuals to amass large personal fortunes. It involved all the government parties, with the DC and the PSI taking the lion's share.

At the elections of April 1992, voters showed clearly their dissatisfaction with the traditional parties. The DC went for the first time below 30 percent of the votes. The Communists, now running under two different labels, jointly lost over 4 percent of the votes, still feeling the brunt of the worldwide rejection of the Soviet political and economic model. The PSI and the PSDI lost some votes, just as did the neo-Fascists. The protest vote was reflected in the small gains of the Greens and in the dramatic success of the Northern League, which went from a single seat in 1987 to 55.

## THE END OF THE TRADITIONAL POLITICAL SYSTEM

The government that emerged from the 1992 elections was a DC-PSI-PSDI-PLI coalition. The new prime minister, Socialist Giuliano Amato, was a sophisticated intellectual with a firm grasp of the problems facing the country. During his ten-month term, he tried to handle the immense public debt problem and the thorny question of preparing for greater integration in the European Union. He also dealt substantial blows to the Mafia.

The DC experienced a great many defections. Segni went his way, to pursue the electoral and institutional reforms that the country needed. Other groups defected, seeking distance from the old party bosses. In a climate of economic uncertainty, evidenced also by the exit of Italy from the European monetary system, Italians saw day in and day out on their evening news a parade of party leaders, businessmen, and heads of state enterprises getting arrested. The public at large relished the humbling of these powerful men and women who were perceived as responsible to a very large degree for the huge public deficits.

At the beginning of 1993, the inquiries had started to reach the highest political levels, involving former premiers Craxi and Andreotti, and some people even in the Amato government. On March 5, 1993, the Amato government prepared a decree which would have decriminalized political bribes if the recipients returned the sums received. The Italians, outraged, took to the streets, the press thundered against the decree, and President Scalfaro refused to sign it. Amato lost immense political capital and would stay in power only one more month, so as to permit the holding of a referendum on electoral law reform. With a turnout of 77 percent, 83 percent of those who went to the polls voted to replace the system of proportional representation with a majority system. Italians wanted clear majorities, tired of the backroom haggling of political power brokers and patched-up coalition governments that lasted only a few months. Italians' disapproval of political parties was also evident in the 90 percent favorable majority obtained in the referendum to end the public financing of political parties.

In April 1993, Carlo Azeglio Ciampi, until then governor of the Bank of Italy, formed a new government, composed of technicians not affiliated with any party and some of the most competent and untainted politicians of the DC, PSI, and PLI. This was the first time in the history of the Republic of Italy that the prime minister

formed a viable government without consulting the leaders of the political parties. It would be a government marked by very good results in the area of economic management.

At the local elections of June 1993, held under new rules providing for the direct election of the mayor, the Northern League obtained a landslide victory in the north, while the DC continued to lose votes throughout the country. The new "moderate" Communist Party, the PDS, running together with other progressive forces, obtained good results also. In other local elections held in the fall of 1993, the DC and the PSI would almost disintegrate. Under the combined interaction of factors as diverse as the end of the Cold War, the referendum movement, the Northern League's vehement accusations, and the inquiring magistrates' ever broader probes, the traditional government parties were basically swept away.

The good electoral results of the MSI notwithstanding, many thought that, after nearly 50 years of political exile, the Communists, relying on the alliances with other leftist and "progressive" forces, would be the winners at the 1994 political election. This was something that Silvio Berlusconi, entrepreneur turned politician, set out to prevent, mounting in a few weeks an extraordinarily successful campaign that would see him victorious. He syphoned off moderate votes from the largely defunct lay parties and from the most prominent splinter group of the former DC, the Popular Party. Berlusconi also took full advantage of Mario Segni's indecisiveness in using the political capital he had gained thus far.

## THE ELECTIONS OF 1994

The campaign leading to the March 1994 elections was intensely fought. The PDS created a coalition of forces of the Left called the Progressive Alliance that ran on a very moderate platform aiming at reassuring center-leaning voters of its break away from the past. However, the presence in its coalition of the extreme left-wing Refounded Communists with their support for old-guard state interventionism highlighted the contradictions within the Alliance. At the center, the PPI (the former Christian Democrats) and the

Segni Pact coalesced in the Pact for Italy and tried their traditional pitch for middle-of-the-road voters. On the Right, Berlusconi's Forza Italia made in the north a strategic alliance with Bossi (Alliance for Freedom) and in the south with National Alliance (Alliance for Good Government). Berlusconi succeeded—with a message of deregulation, privatization, promises of new jobs, more than a dollop of anti-Communism and some entrepreneurial optimism—to present himself as a new person, totally removed from the party system under which (or, as his supporters would say, in spite of which) he had made his fortune.

Interpreting the election results is complicated. The new electoral system provided for three-quarters of the seats in both houses to be elected according to a first-past-the-post system, with the remaining seats distributed proportionally on the basis of nationwide results. Strategic agreements among the partners of each coalition on the candidates to be supported in the single-member districts make it difficult to assess exactly the real strength of each political group (see Table 5.3).

In essence, the Berlusconi-led coalition was very successful in both the north and the south, leaving the four traditionally "red" regions of the center to the Progressives. It seems that the victorious Berlusconi coalition got many of the former DC, PSI, and PSDI votes.

The small parties on the Left were penalized by the 4 percent threshold in the proportional vote, which however served Segni and the PPI well. In the Senate the Left fared better, especially in the south. Contrary to expectations, as it would become clearer in the months to come, because of the internal disagreements among the winning coalition partners, no truly stable majority would come out of the elections.

## A NEW PARTY SYSTEM?

The party system has been undergoing great change since 1992. Small parties—the Liberals with their emphasis on the free market; the Republicans emphasizing efficient administration; and the Social Democrats with their desire to imitate their Northern European brethren, who always puzzled domestic and foreign observers for their inability to unify and thus constitute a viable alternative to the DC—have been swept away. The PSI and the DC have disappeared as well. The vacuum that these parties have left is being filled by others, new or reconstructed.

**TABLE 5.3**

**1994 ELECTIONS FOR THE CHAMBER OF DEPUTIES**

| Leftist Parties | % of Votes[a] | Seats[b] |
|---|---|---|
| *Progressive Alliance* | | |
| Democratic Alliance | 1.2 | 18 |
| Greens | 2.7 | 11 |
| The Network | 1.9 | 6 |
| PDS (Democratic Party of the Left) | 20.4 | 109 |
| PSI (Italian Socialist Party) | 2.2 | 14 |
| RC (Refounded Communism) | 6.0 | 39 |
| Others | | 14 |
| Total | 34.4 | 213 |
| **Center Parties** | | |
| *Pact for Italy* | | |
| Segni Pact | 4.6 | 13 |
| PPI (Italian Popular Party) | 11.1 | 33 |
| Total | 15.7 | 46 |
| **Rightist Parties** | | |
| *Alliance for Freedom/ for Good Government* | | |
| National Alliance | 13.5 | 109 |
| Forza Italia | 21.0 | 99 |
| Northern League | 8.4 | 117 |
| Former Radicals | 3.5 | 6 |
| Christian Democratic Center | | 29 |
| Others | | 6 |
| Total | 46.4 | 366 |
| **Others** | 3.5 | 5 |

*Source:* Adaptation of Ministry of Interior data.
[a]Calculated from proportional portion of vote
[b]Includes both single-member districts and proportional seats

These new political formations have been trying to develop their positions on the electorate's old and emerging concerns, and they are doing so with a language that is much more accessible to voters than it has ever been. Moreover, while relying on some of the organizational structures of the defunct parties and displaying their same propensity for bickering with their partners in a government coalition, the new parties all claim to represent a break from the past.

The complex and uncertain nature of the situation as it has been evolving since 1992 is highlighted by several factors. The decreased influence of the Church and the unions means that the level of *automatic* support that the DC and the PCI enjoyed will not for the foreseeable future be experienced by any party. Ideological loyalties seem destined to continue to lose their importance, and the Italian electorate seems to have become much more volatile and unpredictable. As a matter of fact, the party of the uncommitted voters has unquestionably grown, and so has that of the nonvoters.

Parties no longer have the firm grip on cultural, social, and recreational associations they used to have. Nonprofit organizations independent from the political parties have mushroomed in the last ten years. Many traditional party power brokers who had turned their districts into personal fiefs are no longer around. With television conferring instant visibility upon those who are more telegenic and master more effectively the soundbite, new political personalities can surface at any time. In turn, politicians will probably much more overtly assert their individual support for a specific interest group or position. In Parliament, the influence that parties exert has also diminished. In turn, this has engendered the expansion of the visibility and power of the president of the Republic, the presidents of both chambers, certain judges, and more recently still, mayors and presidents of regions.

## THE ELECTIONS OF 1996

The results of the elections of 1996 seem to point to a possible reduction in the uncertainty sur-

rounding Italian political life, since, contrary to most expectations, a clear majority emerged from the polls (see Table 5.4).

The coalition of the center-left headed by Romano Prodi, the Olive Tree, was the clear winner at the elections of April 1996. The results represented a victory for the strategic vision of the PDS's D'Alema, who, in order to reassure moderate voters, has moved since 1994 much closer to positions similar to those of the main European social democratic parties.

The Program of the Olive Tree had probably appeared to the voters as more credible and focused than that of the Berlusconi's Alliance for Freedom. For instance, Berlusconi's promises of tax cuts may for some have seemed unrealistic in

### TABLE 5.4

### 1996 ELECTIONS FOR THE CHAMBER OF DEPUTIES

| | % of Votes[a] | Total Seats[b] |
|---|---|---|
| **Center-Left Parties** | | |
| *The Olive Tree* | | 284 |
| PDS (Democratic Party of the Left) | 21.1 | |
| Prodi Group | 6.8 | |
| Dini List | 4.3 | |
| Greens | 2.5 | |
| RC (Refounded Communism) | 8.6 | 35 |
| **Center-Right Parties** | | |
| *Alliance for Freedom* | | 246 |
| AN (National Alliance) | 15.7 | |
| Forza Italia | 20.7 | |
| CCD-CDU | 5.8 | |
| Others | 1.9 | — |
| **Other Parties** | | |
| Northern League | 10.1 | 59 |
| The Flame | 0.9 | — |
| Others | 1.6 | 6 |

*Source:* Ministry of Interior data.
[a]Calculated from proportional portion of vote
[b]Includes both single-member districts and proportional seats

view of the objectives of European integration. In order to rule, the government headed by Prodi, with a convincing majority in the Senate, had to rely on the votes of the Refounded Communists in the Chamber of Deputies. Prodi had thus to try to please the RC without disappointing the Olive Tree moderate supporters. As we shall see, he was not successful at that.

The good results of the Northern League validated to some extent Bossi's secessionist pronouncements and forced the Olive Tree governments to address the issue of federalism, which they did with a constitutional reform which was approved through a referendum held in the fall of 2001 when the new Berlusconi government was in power.

## THE ELECTIONS OF 2001

On May 13, 2001, for the first time ever, Italians found themselves in a position to decide between an incumbent coalition government and an opposition ready to rule. There was definitely a record that could be looked at. The Olive Tree coalition could point to its having brought the country successfully into the Euro area as a founding country, achieved significant improvements in the economy, and managed to complete the whole natural term of the legislature of five years. The House of Freedoms disputed strongly the claim that the country's economic numbers revealed a much improved reality over five years before. The Berlusconi-led coalition also added that the governments after Prodi's (D'Alema I and II, and Amato II) were not the result of an electoral mandate and that the poor results of the Olive Tree parties at the European elections of June 1999, the regional elections of April 2000, and at various referendums showed the dissatisfaction of the electorate with its "illegitimate leaders."

Some elements of these elections stand out. First, when elections are perceived as important (and these were), Italy continues to be among the Western developed countries where voters' participation is the highest (over 80 percent). Second, the numbers show that the victory of Forza Italia, Berlusconi's party, has been

outstanding and that the trend toward the increasing personalization of Italian politics is pretty clear (see Table 5.5). With the exception of the leader of the defeated coalition, the telegenic Francesco Rutelli, all the other political figures came out much downsized, which attests also to the increasing benefits enjoyed by the heads of the coalitions, an evident sign of the increasing bipolarization of Italian political life. It seems that Berlusconi was perceived as better than Rutelli in terms of intelligence, strength, and ability to persuade, while the

### TABLE 5.5

### 2001 ELECTIONS FOR THE CHAMBER OF DEPUTIES

|  | % of Votes[a] | Seats[b] |
|---|---|---|
| **Center-Left Parties** | | |
| *The Olive Tree* | | 242 |
| DS (former communists) | 16.6 | |
| Pdci | 1.7 | |
| Margherita | 14.5 | |
| Girasole | 2.2 | |
| **Center-Right Parties** | | |
| *House of Freedoms* | | 368 |
| AN (National Alliance) | 12.0 | |
| Forza Italia | 29.4 | |
| Biancofiore (CCD-CDU) | 3.2 | |
| Northern League | 3.9 | |
| New PSI | 1.0 | |
| **Other Parties** | | |
| RC (Refounded Communism) | 5.0 | 11 |
| Lista Bonino | 2.3 | |
| Lista Di Pietro | 3.9 | |
| Dem. Europea | 2.4 | |
| The Flame | 0.9 | |
| Others | 1.6 | 1 |
| Olive Tree-Svp | | 8 |

*Source:* Ministry of Interior data.
[a]Calculated from proportional portion of vote
[b]Includes both single-member districts and proportional seats

former mayor of Rome was perceived as more even-handed and simpatico.[8]

The House of Freedoms fared better with those above 65, especially among women, possibly by finding consensus in the reservoir of votes that had been the defunct DC's. The Olive Tree did better among those aged between 45 and 54, the left-oriented generation of the late 1960s. Those between 25 and 34, more inclined toward market-based solutions, preferred the center-right Berlusconi coalition. Berlusconi's conflict of interests issues, the unresolved question of the blind trust and his personal legal problems, seemed to have been important for the voters of the center-left but minor to those who voted for him. Arguably, by strongly advocating tax reduction and, more importantly, a tougher immigration and anticrime stand, Berlusconi proved more in touch with ordinary people's concerns. Last, but not least, the House of Freedoms appeared to be a more united coalition. The Olive Tree seemed mired in internal squabbles and could no longer count on the special electoral agreements it had with RC in 1996, and it lost some consensus for the presence of other groups such as those headed by former magistrate Di Pietro, former union leader D'Antoni, and radical leader Bonino, which siphoned off votes. All these small groupings were seriously beaten, further unequivocal evidence of the bipolarization of Italian politics now underway.

## INTEREST GROUPS

Since the end of World War II, Italian political parties have played so strong a role that they have not just occupied the state but also have had a particularly strong grip on Italian society. Against the backdrop of ideological polarization, political parties worked to prevent the growth of associations and organized interests that would cut across the political divides. Former resistance fighters' groups, feminist groups, youth organizations, and all sorts of recreational entities were affiliated to parties such as the DC or the PCI but also to other left, center, and right parties. Shopkeepers belonged to an association linked to the DC or to one linked to the Left, and the same happened for farmers. The Confindustria, the main umbrella organization for business, divided along territorial and functional (that is, sector) lines, was fairly close to the small lay parties. Yet, since there was no other force capable of standing up to the PCI, it continued to support the DC. The connection between political parties and interest groups was particularly strong with unions where, for instance, even career moves to party positions and parliamentary seats were very common.

## The Unions

Trade union organizations have grown in Italy since the end of the nineteenth century, developing links with socialist and later Catholic political parties. With Fascism, all free unions were eliminated. After World War II, the now legal and unified union, the Italian General Confederation of Labor (CGIL), entered an agreement with the Confindustria on minimum wage, piecework, and equal pay for women. The agreement introduced the *scala mobile,* a system of wage indexation to the cost of living. The highly political nature of Italian unions, which goes beyond working conditions and wage demands, soon emerged in 1948 when, following the attempt on PCI leader Togliatti's life, part of the CGIL directorate decided to proclaim a general strike, which was opposed by the union leaders not linked to the PCI.

The rift within CGIL led in 1950 to the creation of two other unions, the Italian Union of Labor (UIL)—which included sympathizers of the PSI, PSDI, and PRI—and the Italian Confederation of Workers' Unions (CISL), which was close to the DC. The other two unions siphoned off members from the CGIL, benefitting from the anti-Communist climate of the 1950s. An agreement signed in 1972 would never lead to complete unity because of enduring political suspicions.

The ability of unions to negotiate against employers' organizations was limited through-

---

[8]Giacomo Sani, "Berlusconi ha vinto perché . . ." *Il Mulino,* no. 4, 2001, p. 620.

out the 1950s, due to the high unemployment levels. The situation would start to change in the early part of the 1960s when some labor shortages started to materialize and workers' desire to share in the expanding pie could be more easily met.

By 1968, unions had grown dissatisfied with the inability of the center-left governments to introduce social reforms. The workers' and students' movements took to the streets with massive protests. From the "hot autumn" strike wave of 1969 to the mid-1970s, unions, displaying a particularly united front, scored many victories. In addition to getting wage increases that outstripped those in productivity (a dramatic reversal from the 1950s), the unions obtained the passing of the Statute of the Workers in 1970, which, among other things, made laying off workers very difficult, protected student workers, and supported pro-union activities on the job. The contracts won contained very favorable cost of living provisions. Their downside was that they tended to put a cap on the increases on the higher salaries, thereby negatively affecting the specialized blue-collar and most white-collar workers. Down the road, this would prove very divisive within the membership and reduce internal consensus.

## Unions' Waning Power

The economic crisis of the early 1980s and fundamental changes the Italian economy was undergoing, such as the downsizing of firms forced by foreign competitors and the expansion of the service sector, were also weakening the three unions' positions. In the political arena, in 1985 a referendum was held over the abolition of a decree issued by the Craxi government, which had set limits to *scala mobile* automatic cost of living increases, and it was defeated. The PCI and most of CGIL, which had promoted the referendum, lost a most important battle, both substantively and symbolically. The weakening of the Communist ideology and later the disappearance of the PSI, PSDI, and PRI meant the loss of important political support, as the negative results of the June 1995 referendums on union activities confirmed. At present, the percentage of the workforce in the private sector which is unionized has gone down from the late 1970s, and retirees and unemployed workers are about 50 percent of the membership.

The increase in the number of rival unions—especially in several state sectors like health care, education, and rail transportation—and their growing membership of 6 million against the CGIL-CISL-UIL's nearly 11 million bespeaks more complicated and possibly conflictual industrial relations in the years to come.

## Interest Groups since the 1990s

Unions are not the only interest groups affected by the crisis of the traditional party system. Business interest groups never had a completely amicable relationship with parties, and when "operation clean hands" started, the newspapers controlled by the employers' organizations supported the inquiring magistrates and steered pubic opinion against the politicians. Italian businessmen were no longer willing to support their very expensive political class which presided over a bureaucracy that provided them and their workforce with poor services. It stands to reason that the need to be competitive within and without Europe will continue to push business interest groups to demand from the political class better public services.

The traditional grip that political parties have held on other interest groups has been loosened as well. In the last ten years, there has been a growth of voluntary organizations not linked to political parties in areas as diverse as environmental protection and consumer advocacy. Disenchantment with the welfare state has also led to the birth of organizations not affiliated with any party that offer services such as drug rehabilitation programs, or associations whose members are united by a common claim to specific rights, such as the disabled. While not as extensive as in countries like France or Germany, these organizations are growing in number and visibility, and their recognition by the law and the courts is on the rise. They reflect the higher levels of education and disposable income, and the greater amount of free time that Italians have been experiencing in recent years.

The emerging trend of greater personalization of Italian politics, if it continues, will translate in individual elected officials' sponsoring of organized interests, thereby replacing the role traditionally performed by parties. In the same vein, lobbying techniques will continue to become more similar to those observed in the United States.

## THE PARLIAMENT

The Italian Parliament is composed of two houses (or chambers): the Chamber of Deputies and the Senate (see Figure 5.1). There are 630 deputies and 315 senators directly elected, with five more senators appointed for life by the president of the Republic. At present, two former presidents of the Republic are ex-officio members. The two chambers basically have the same powers and both are elected for five years, which is the regular length of a legislature. During each legislature there can be more than one government and the Parliament can be dismissed by the president before the completion of the five-year term. Each of the two houses controls its own staff, finances, disciplinary system, and security system. Members of Parliament have complete immunity from civil, penal, and administrative action for the votes and opinions expressed while carrying out their functions. Parliamentary committees are organized by functional areas fairly close to the corresponding government ministries. Committee members are designated by their parliamentary groups, which are the organizational form taken by political parties in Parliament. The groups' presidents are their spokespersons, and are very visible on the evening news shows. Many complain that the groups' system as it is currently designed runs counter to the logic of rewarding the winning coalition, as for instance with the regulations on filibustering and parliamentary quorums.

In the last fifteen years, reforms of the Parliament's rules have almost eliminated secret voting, and the government has seen its powers to

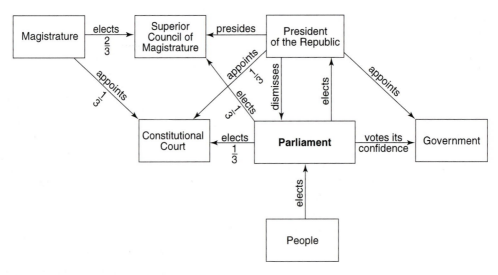

**Figure 5.1** ITALY'S MAIN POLITICAL INSTITUTIONS

The Italian Constitution provides for overlapping and balance among the various powers of the state, and not a rigid separation. The people elect their representatives to Parliament. The government, the president of the Republic, the Constitutional Court, and the Superior Council of the Magistrature receive, at least partially, their powers from Parliament. The Magistrature is autonomous. *Source:* Chamber of Deputies.

pass legislation through decrees (until 1996) and its ability to set the legislative agenda substantially increased. The overall ability of the government to act with less interference from the whole Parliament has thus increased, and this has meant a reduction in the opportunities given to opposition parties to share in decision making. However, until the April 1996 general elections, following the third dissolution of Parliament in four years, this had not resulted in an increased stability of government coalitions.

## Lawmaking

The Parliament's main responsibility is to pass laws. The procedure starts with the initiative, the power to submit bills to Parliament. Such power is attributed by the constitution first and foremost to the government, which uses it to achieve the objectives of its program, on the basis of the support of the majority which originally gave it its confidence vote. Bills can also be introduced by individual members of Parliament or parliamentary groups, by 50,000 voters through a petition, by the Regional Councils, and by the National Council on Economics and Labor.

Once introduced, the bill has to be examined, debated, and voted upon. There are two main procedures to do this. In brief, the ordinary procedure requires that the committee competent in terms of subject matter submit to the floor of the house the bill (with modifications, if any) plus a report on it. The assembly then votes on the individual articles of the bill and on the whole text again. There is also a special procedure. The competent committee can act in a *deliberante* (deliberating) capacity: the bill is examined and voted upon by the committee without ever reaching the floor. If, however, the government or one-tenth of the members of the chamber or one-fifth of those of the committees objects, the ordinary procedure has to be used. This usually happens when those objecting believe that the issue needs a broader debate on the floor. After final approval, the bill is transmitted to the other chamber.

In order to be transmitted to the president of the Republic for the *promulgazione* (promulga-

tion), the texts of the bill passed in the Chamber of Deputies and the Senate must be exactly alike. In case the second house makes modifications, the bill will go back and forth until it meets the equivalence criterion or is killed in one of the chambers. There is no conference committee as in the U.S. Congress to hammer out differences in the texts passed by the two chambers.

## Other Powers

The Parliament also performs the function of approving the budget presented by the government, to which it can attach amendments. Parliament's "guidance-control" of government extends to the ratification of international treaties, with the government's role proving to be predominant.

With regard to legislation of the European Union (formerly the European Community), laws passed in the late 1980s have put an obligation on the government to adequately inform the Parliament about planned EU activities, a dimension further strengthened by legislation passed in the late 1990s. Pursuant to the treaties signed by Italy with its EU partners, EU laws are "directly applicable" when they are "self-executing" (that is, specific and complete). In other cases, Parliament's intervention to add specificity to them is needed to make them implementable domestically.

Parliament's control over government is exerted also through the important tool of the confidence vote, which is given by each chamber after the cabinet is first appointed by the president of the Republic. Such a vote is given on the basis of the government's composition and program. Parliament can submit questions to the cabinet on its activities. Parliament can also initiate inquiries on matters of public interest and issue resolutions to pressure the government to act in a certain way.

A government can be brought down by a vote of no confidence. The motion must be presented by at least one-tenth of the members of one chamber. In practice, there has been only one no-confidence vote actually passed (in 1998, putting an end to the Prodi government) on any of the governments that have been formed since 1948. The resignation of such governments has always been associated with political disagreement among the political parties forming the coalition. In general, these conflicts have stemmed from either policy differences or from clashes among parties over the distribution of ministerial posts.

Parliament has also the very important power to revise the constitution. The procedure requires two votes of each chamber to approve the changes, with an interval of time between each voting session of at least three months. These revisions, unless passed by a majority exceeding two-thirds of the members of each chamber, may have to be approved through a popular referendum if so requested by one-fifth of the members of a chamber, 500,000 voters, or five regional councils.

## A Changing Parliament

Of the three major political elections following the collapse of the traditional parties in the early 1990s, the one held in 1994 saw a truly unprecedented number of new members entering Parliament. In the Chamber of Deputies over 70 percent of members were freshmen, a clear indicator of the general distrust toward professional politicians. The wave of renewal was slightly smaller in the center of the country, where the PDS's traditional core electoral support helped its incumbents. As expected, the National Alliance and the PDS, basically untouched by the scandals and "running against Rome," managed to be the parties with the highest number of incumbents reelected. True to the party's image, Forza Italia's elected entrepreneurs and managers were nearly 30 percent of the party's representatives, a percentage four times as high as that of the other parties. Another sign of the mistrust toward professional politicians was that trustworthy figures from the world of culture and entertainment and members of the magistrature were elected in higher numbers than in the past. The inclusion of figures of high profile in all party lists continued in 1996 and 2001 and will most likely continue in future elections as parties try to capture an electorate much less committed to ideological beliefs and more susceptible to charismatic personalities.

## THE GOVERNMENT: THE PRIME MINISTER AND THE COUNCIL OF MINISTERS

The government of the Italian Republic, headed by the prime minister and the organ he presides over, the Council of Ministers (or cabinet), carries out the main executive functions. A new government commences to operate effectively when, after having received the mandate from the president of the Republic, the prime minister designate presents formally the list of ministers and they are sworn in before the president (see Table 5.6). Then the government has to present its political program before each chamber and receive a confidence vote. The prime minister, or president of the Council of Ministers as he is officially designated, directs and is responsible for the general policy-making functions of the government and promotes and coordinates the activities carried out by the ministers. The prime minister, until the early 1980s, has always been a Christian Democrat and until now, with the exception of Carlo Azeglio Ciampi and Lamberto Dini, has always been a member of Parliament.

Such was the dominance of the party system that many considered the position of prime minister less important than that of the secretary of the DC. This started to change with the lay governments of the 1980s which, aware of public opinion's disapproval of the frequent collapses of government coalitions, maneuvered to strengthen the powers of the government against the parties and Parliament.

The prime minister participates in the formulation of those individual ministers' public statements which may have a bearing on the whole government's program. He represents the Council when he explains the government's program to the chambers and sets the agenda for the Council's meetings. The prime minister has also some exclusive powers in some sectors such as regional, EU, and information policy. He has a staff of 3,000–6,000 (depending on the

**TABLE 5.6**

**ITALIAN GOVERNMENTS, 1948–2002**

| Legislatures | Coalition Parties | Prime Ministers |
|---|---|---|
| *First Legislature* (1948–1953) | | |
| May 1948–Jan. 1950 | DC+PSDI+PRI+PLI | De Gasperi |
| Jan. 1950–July 1951 | DC+PSDI+PRI | De Gasperi |
| July 1951–June 1953 | DC+PRI | De Gasperi |
| *Second Legislature* (1953–1958) | | |
| July 1953 | DC | De Gasperi |
| Aug. 1953–Jan. 1954 | DC | Pella |
| Jan. 1954 | DC | Fanfani |
| Feb. 1954–June 1955 | DC+PLI+PSDI | Scelba |
| July 1955–May 1957 | DC+PSDI+PLI | Segni |
| May 1957–June 1958 | DC | Zoli |
| *Third Legislature* (1958–1963) | | |
| July 1958–Jan. 1959 | DC+PSDI | Fanfani |
| Feb. 1959–Feb. 1960 | DC | Segni |
| Mar. 1960–July 1960 | DC | Tambroni |
| July 1960–Feb. 1962 | DC | Fanfani |
| Feb. 1962–May 1963 | DC+PSDI+PRI | Fanfani |
| *Fourth Legislature* (1963–1968) | | |
| June 1963–Nov. 1963 | DC | Leone |
| Dec. 1963–June 1964 | DC+PSI+PSDI+PRI | Moro |
| July 1964–Jan. 1966 | DC+PSI+PSDI+PRI | Moro |
| Feb. 1966–June 1968 | DC+PSI+PSDI+PRI | Moro |
| *Fifth Legislature* (1968–1972) | | |
| June 1968–Nov. 1968 | DC | Leone |
| Dec. 1968–July 1969 | DC+PSI+PRI | Rumor |
| Aug. 1969–Feb. 1970 | DC | Rumor |
| Mar. 1970–July 1970 | DC+PSDI+PSI+PRI | Rumor |
| Aug. 1970–Jan. 1972 | DC+PSDI+PSI+PRI | Colombo |
| Feb. 1972 | DC | Andreotti |
| *Sixth Legislature* (1972–1976) | | |
| June 1972–June 1973 | DC+PLI+PSDI | Andreotti |
| July 1973–Mar. 1974 | DC+PSDI+PRI+PSI | Rumor |
| Mar. 1974–Oct. 1974 | DCI+PSI+PSDI | Rumor |
| Nov. 1974–Jan. 1976 | DC+PRI | Moro |
| Feb. 1976–Apr. 1976 | DC | Moro |

*continued*

**TABLE 5.6  (continued)**

**ITALIAN GOVERNMENTS, 1948–2002**

| Legislatures | Coalition Parties | Prime Ministers |
|---|---|---|
| *Seventh Legislature (1976–1979)* | | |
| July 1976–Jan. 1978 | DC | Andreotti |
| Mar. 1978–Jan. 1979 | DC | Andreotti |
| Mar. 1979 | DC+PSDI+PRI | Andreotti |
| *Eighth Legislature (1979–1983)* | | |
| Aug. 1979–Mar. 1980 | DC+PSDI+PLI | Cossiga |
| April 1980–Sept. 1980 | DC+PSI+PRI | Forlani |
| Oct. 1980–May 1981 | DC+PSI+PSDI+PRI | Forlani |
| June 1981–Aug. 1982 | PRI+DC+PSI+PSDI+PLI | Spadolini |
| Aug. 1982–Nov. 1982 | PRI+DC+PSI+PSDI+PLI | Spadolini |
| Dec. 1982–April 1983 | DC+PSI+PSDI+PLI | Fanfani |
| *Ninth Legislature (1983–1987)* | | |
| Aug. 1983–June 1986 | PSI+DC+PRI+PSDI+PLI | Craxi |
| Aug. 1986–Mar. 1987 | PSI+DC+PSDI+PRI+PLI | Craxi |
| Apr. 1987 | DC (minority government) | Fanfani |
| *Tenth Legislature (1987–1992)* | | |
| July 1987–Mar. 1988 | DC+PSI+PSDI+PRI+PLI | Goria |
| April 1988–May 1989 | DC+PSI+PSDI+PRI+PLI | DeMita |
| July 1989–Mar. 1991 | DC+PSI+PSDI+PRI+PLI | Andreotti |
| April 1991–April 1992 | DC+PSI+PSDI+PLI | Andreotti |
| *Eleventh Legislature (1992–1994)* | | |
| July 1992–Apr. 1993 | DC+PSI+PSDI+PLI | Amato |
| Apr. 1993–Jan. 1994 | Government formed without consulting parties | Ciampi |
| *Twelfth Legislature (1994–1996)* | | |
| May 1994–Dec. 1994 | Forza Italia, Northern League, National, Alliance, others | Berlusconi |
| Feb. 1995–Dec. 1995 | "Nonpartisan" government | Dini |
| *Thirteenth Legislature (1996–2001)* | | |
| May 1996–Oct. 1998 | Olive Tree coalition | Prodi |
| Oct. 1998–Dec. 1999 | | D'Alema |
| Dec. 1999–April 2000 | | D'Alema |
| May 2000–April 2001 | | Amato |
| *Fourteenth Legislature (2001–)* | | |
| June 2001– | House of Freedoms | Berlusconi |

*Note:* Each new general election follows the dissolution of Parliament by the president and starts a new legislature. The outgoing prime minister stays on in a caretaking capacity until his successor forms a new government and receives a vote of confidence. All prime ministers have been Christian Democratic parliamentarians except Spadolini, Craxi, Amato, Ciampi, Berlusconi, Dini, Prodi, and D'Alema.

estimates), not comparing unfavorably to the White House's Executive Office of about 4,000.

The Council of Ministers is the organ which determines the general course of government policy making as well as its administrative thrust (we will discuss public administration later). It has important powers of appointment of top officials of government agencies and state-owned enterprises, exerts its control over laws passed by the regions and their activities, and plays a determining role in the setting of foreign policy. Individual ministers are at the same time members of the Council of Ministers and the heads of their departments or ministries. The ministries are established by law and cover specific areas such as foreign affairs, justice, treasury, defense, health, and environment.

## Government's Legislative Powers

Parliament can authorize government to legislate, specifying the parameters government has to conform to in issuing its legislative decrees. In cases of "extraordinary need and urgency," the constitution (Article 77) states that the government can issue laws without Parliament's previous authorization. These decree-laws have to be converted into law by Parliament within 60 days, otherwise they lose their validity. Increasingly, decree-laws were being issued on the most diverse and important subject matters. The very frequent use of the decree-laws arose mostly from the necessity to circumvent the slow and cumbersome nature of the ordinary legislative procedure in Parliament. The growth in the number of decree-laws, from a few dozens in the first legislatures to hundreds from the eighth to the twelfth, was viewed as further reinforcing a system in which too many laws are being written and possibly too many of them enacted only for the benefit of specific interest groups. In 1996, the Constitutional Court struck down the practice at the basis of such increase, by declaring unconstitutional the ongoing rolling over of decree-laws. Since then their number has decreased considerably. The government, taking advantage of the firmer majorities that have materialized after the elections of 1996 and 2001, uses more

frequently the delegation it receives from Parliament to legislate.

The recent increase of government's powers in the political, legislative, and regulatory arenas has been the result of the greater demands put on it by the changed nature of policy making, just as it has happened in most industrial countries. It has also been made easier by the public's desire for greater efficiency and a climate in which the traditional parties, having lost a lot of legitimacy, have left a significant political vacuum.

## THE PRESIDENT

The president of the Italian Republic is the head of state and represents its national unity. He is elected by a joint session of Parliament with the addition of three representatives for each region. He must be at least 50 years old and cannot hold any other position. His term lasts for seven years and, in case of temporary incapacity, his functions are carried out by the president of the Senate. The president of the Republic cannot be held responsible for actions pertaining to the exercise of his functions except for high treason and violation of the constitution.

The president announces new elections for the chambers and the holding of referendums. He can call for extraordinary meetings of the chambers and can dissolve one or both of them. He can send messages to the chambers, bringing attention in a public way to the country's needs. The president appoints five outstanding citizens as senators for life. He also signs the laws and thus makes them effective and publishable as such in the *Gazzetta Ufficiale* (Official Journal of Notices). He does the same for decree-laws, government regulations, and ministerial decrees. The president can also veto a law, sending it back to Parliament for reexamination. However, if the chambers reapprove the law, he cannot oppose it.

The president appoints the prime minister and the ministers he proposes. Once he has appointed the prime minister, the president cannot dismiss him unless the government has been the subject of a no-confidence vote. The president is the head of the armed forces and presides over the Supreme Defense Council, ratifies international treaties, and promotes the establishment of peaceful relations with other states. The president presides over the Superior Council of the Magistrature (CSM), the body that guarantees the independence of the judges. He can also grant pardons.

Italian presidents have nearly always kept a very low profile in Italian political life, leading most observers to consider this position as little more than a ceremonial job. Socialist President Sandro Pertini (1978–1985) started to break away from this mold, decrying political corruption and supporting a firm stance against terrorism. His successor, Francesco Cossiga (1985–1992), became most outspoken in the last two years of his term. He clashed with the CSM, which he formally headed, over the expansion of its powers. Later, Cossiga sent a message on institutional reforms to Parliament, advocating a change of the constitution from Parliament-based to presidential. His prescription, however, was judged risky by many because it could promote the rise to power of authoritarian individuals. Cossiga was also criticized on the grounds that as the defender of the constitution, it was not up to him to propose changes to the makeup of its institutions. Socialists, liberals, and the MSI sided with the president in a debate that became very heated on the Parliament's floor and even more so on the air waves. After the end of his presidential term, Senator-for-life Cossiga created a new party, the UDR, which he later left, and offered much publicized pronouncements over Italian politics which stirred much controversy for, among others, their polemic tone and his nonelected position.

## Presidents Scalfaro and Ciampi

Cossiga's successor, Oscar Luigi Scalfaro, handled his responsibilities in a very active way. His appointment as prime minister of Socialist Giuliano Amato in 1992 and of nonpoliticians Carlo Azeglio Ciampi and Lamberto Dini are generally regarded as very adroit. Scalfaro's refusal to sign a decree issued by the Amato government to depenalize the crime of illicit financing of public parties received strong approval by the public, the press, and the inquiring magistrates.

Scalfaro skillfully jockeyed between his role of defender of the constitution as it is presently designed and the impetus for change that emerged from the 1991 and 1992 referendums on electoral laws. His support for international alliances, the European Union, peace, the principles of freedom and legality, and for the indivisible nature of the country (in open contrast with the Northern League) have been manifested through his 1994 correspondence with Silvio Berlusconi. Scalfaro also urged Berlusconi to avoid conflicts of interest with his business activities and vetoed the appointment of the industrialist's lawyer to the Ministry of Justice. Berlusconi's unwillingness to restrain his fellow ministers from launching personal attacks on the

---

**REVIEW**

**5.5**

## PRESIDENTS OF THE REPUBLIC

| | | | |
|---|---|---|---|
| Enrico De Nicola | 1948 (temporary head of state since 1946) | Giovanni Leone | 1971–1978 |
| Luigi Einaudi | 1948–1955 | Sandro Pertini | 1978–1985 |
| Giovanni Gronchi | 1955–1962 | Francesco Cossiga | 1985–1992 |
| Antonio Segni | 1962–1964 | Oscar Luigi Scalfaro | 1992–1999 |
| Giuseppe Saragat | 1964–1971 | Carlo Azeglio Ciampi | 1999– |

president's past as interior minister contributed to a strong climate of tension between the tycoon and the professional politician.

Scalfaro's appointment of Dini in 1995 reflected the president's concern over the financial recovery of the country.[9] In the course of the year, as Dini, much to the dismay of the Right, was discreetly expanding his caretaking mandate, he found a powerful ally in the president. At the end of 1995, Scalfaro, much to the chagrin of Berlusconi's supporters, explained his reluctance to dissolve Parliament on account of the beginning in January 1996 of the Italian semester of EU presidency. Moreover, Dini's position (and many others') that new elections would not give to the country the stable majority it needed had also been shared by the president. After the 1996 elections, Scalfaro also raised much controversy by letting it be known beforehand that even if the Prodi government collapsed (which it did, two years later), he would not dissolve Parliament, a stance which the center-right coalition led by Berlusconi viewed most unfavorably. The current president, Carlo Azeglio Ciampi, was elected on May 1999 on the first ballot, a sign of bipartisan support. Never elected to Parliament, he spent nearly 50 years at the Bank of Italy, at whose helm he was for 14 years. In 1993, in the midst of the corruption scandals, he was appointed prime minister and served in this capacity until the elections of 1994. He acquitted himself well and his government transformed into law the electoral reform along majoritarian principles which voters had supported in a 1993 referendum. In 1996 he joined the Prodi government as treasury minister, playing a pivotal role in bringing the country into the Euro area and stayed on also in the D'Alema government. President Ciampi is well regarded internationally and is a staunch supporter of European integration. In large measure because of his long tenure at one of the most efficient and independent institutions of the country, the central bank, he has a

very strong sense of the state, akin to that of a high-level French bureaucrat. Catholic in his personal life and secular in his public dimension, he is widely regarded as nonpartisan in outlook (unlike his predecessor) and the right man to mediate controversies and to shepherd along the needed institutional reforms. Whatever developments will ensue in the next few years, there can be little doubt that the relationship among government, Parliament, and presidency will continue to be subject to ongoing change.

## THE PUBLIC ADMINISTRATION

The public administration is the set of organs which are entrusted with the implementation of the laws so as to meet the citizens' needs. At its pinnacle we find the Council of Ministers, headed by its president, what we would call using British terminology the prime minister. Each of the ministries is responsible for a functional area, has its own internal administrative and disciplinary bodies, and its Central Accounting Office (in turn, part of the General Accounting Office attached to the Ministry of Treasury) to control the legitimacy and the merit of expenditures. Ministers can rely on ad hoc consulting bodies for specific expertise, and for legal representation and advice on the General Advocate of the State, which extends its services to the whole public administration of the state.

The prefetto, who heads each one of the 103 areas in which the nation is divided for administrative purposes, oversees all the various ministerial offices of the province, regardless of their size or functional competence. To improve coordination of the various organs of public administration at provincial and regional levels, respectively, the central government increased its presence with the Provincial Committee of Public Administration and the Commissary of the Government. The legislation creating these two bodies, which was passed in 1988 and 1991, should be seen as part of the government's ongoing effort to deliver services more effectively to the citizens. The devolution of state powers to the regions and other local territorial subunits is

[9]Robert Graham, "Old versus New," *Financial Times,* May 14, 1994, p. 9; Sergio Romano, "Troublesome Technocrat," *Financial Times,* September 5, 1995, p. 14.

changing on an ongoing basis these institutional and functional configurations.

## A Large State Presence

Italy is a country where the presence of the state in the economy is far greater than that of the federal government in the United States. Various types of public enterprises carry out economic activities in Italy. Among these are the Autonomous Enterprises (*Aziende Autonome*), which are formally ministerial organs with their own budget (for example, Tourist Office), and the Public Corporations (*Enti Pubblici*), which have a legal identity separate from that of the state (or region or other territorial subunits). Public Corporations reflect in their high level of heterogeneity the historical tendency of the state to enter into spheres that an American would view as typical of the nonprofit voluntary organization, and this is the case with the Italian National Olympic Committee, the Red Cross, and some professional bodies. Public Corporations may have public powers and operate in areas such as park management, foreign trade promotion, disability prevention, or they may carry out more commercial-oriented activities, often under special obligations of a public nature, and enjoy some advantages versus their private competitors (for example, state universities and port authorities). Frequently, as in the case of the public banks and many state-owned enterprises, the corporations operate under conditions of some parity with their private-sector competitors. This entire sector is in great flux because of the trends toward downsizing government, privatization, and decentralization.

In recent years, in order to improve control over the public administration, Parliament has set up independent administrative authorities and agencies which enjoy considerable autonomy from the government. Examples of these are the CONSOB (roughly the equivalent of the U.S. SEC), the National Agency for the Protection of the Environment, and various commissions on competition, radio, TV, and publishing, and on the access to public documents.

## The Auxiliary Organs

The Constitution provides for three "auxiliary organs" which perform various functions of support to both Parliament and government and which are regulated in detail by ordinary law. The National Committee on Energy and Labor (CNEL) is a consulting body composed of 122 members, mostly drawn from the private and public sector unions and employers' organizations. It offers opinions and may conduct studies, solicited or not, that are submitted to Parliament, the government, or the regions in the areas of the economy and labor markets. It can also prepare legislation in these areas. The Council of State, composed of about 120 administrative magistrates, acts as a consulting body on legal and administrative issues in terms of both legitimacy and merit for the public administration and, as an adjudicating body, as a court of appeal for the sentences rendered by the regional administrative tribunals. The Court of Accounts is the highest organ of control of the public administration and the highest magistrature in the public accounting sphere. The control can be exerted ex ante and ex post, while the adjudicating function is evolving into one of appeal since recent legislation has created lower courts of accounts tribunals in each region.

## Regions, Provinces, and Communes

The Italian state is divided and organized into three kinds of territorial subunits: the regions, the provinces, and the communes (*Comuni*). There are 20 regions, of which five have "special autonomy": Sicily, Sardinia, Trentino-Alto Adige, Friuli Venezia Giulia, and Valle D'Aosta. The majority of the Italian regions enjoy an "ordinary autonomy." The organs of the Italian regions mirror to a large degree those of the state. Thus the Regional Council, the Giunta, and the president of the region (this latter elected directly by the people since November 1999) are somewhat modeled after, respectively, the Parliament, the government, and the president of the Republic. The constitutional reforms enacted in October 2001 define the areas where the state has exclusive legislative powers. Among these are foreign policy, defense, customs, financial markets regulation, public order, immigration, judicial system, social security, environmental protection, statistics collection coordination, and state tax system. Among the legislative powers to be shared with the regions (with the state establishing the principles and the detailed legislation to be issued by the regions) are international relations (including those with the EU), foreign trade, the main elements of the country's infrastructure, the local banking system, scientific research, education, health protection, emergency services. Most importantly and innovatively, all the areas not explicitly mentioned among these two categories are subject to the legislative authority of the regions, with the limitations inherent in the constitution, EU, and international obligations.[10]

In the administrative arena, regions can operate in the same functional areas in which they have legislative powers. The financial autonomy that regions enjoy was limited, since the tax-levying system is highly centralized. The constitutional reforms of October 2001 give much expanded resources to regions, provinces, communes and metropolitan cities. Along dimensions that will be defined by future laws and which will undoubtedly be much discussed and analyzed in the years to come, all these territorial units will have their own revenue-raising powers, participate in the general state revenues originating in their territory, and participate in a redistribution fund designed to assist poorer areas. The five "special autonomy" regions differ from the other 15 most notably in that they enjoy somewhat greater independence.

The provinces and the communes are political entities which, pursuant to state legislation that started to appear in the early 1990s and to the constitutional reforms of 2001, have a similar organizational outlook. They have, respectively, a Provincial and Communal Council, which acts as the organ for political and administrative

policy setting and control. The president of the province and the mayor have strong executive powers and share day-by-day management responsibilities with the Giuntas (provincial and communal, respectively), and report to their respective councils. The communes' powers have been expanded by the 2001 reforms, and their main administrative focus is in the areas of delivery of social services, urban and territorial planning, and economic development, where they also have regulatory powers.

## Demand for Efficiency

The trend toward trying to meet the public's desire for greater efficiency and accountability has manifested itself also in the area of local government. Legislation passed in 1993 has made the mayor and the president of the province directly electable and increased their powers substantially. The direct election of the president of the region conforms to this logic as well.

Indeed, much needs to be done at all levels of government. Italians spend too much time when interacting with the public administration whether through the mail or the telephone, relying extensively on face-to-face contact arrived at after waiting in lines that are largely not regulated. The average time to initiate and conclude any administrative procedure or request is six months. The delivery of many services is also uneven geographically, with certain areas served better than others.

## THE CONSTITUTIONAL COURT

The Constitutional Court has jurisdiction over controversies concerning the constitutionality of laws. It also decides on the conflicts originating from the constitutional assignment of powers within the state, on controversies between the state and the regions, on those among the regions, on the impeachment of the president of the Republic, and whether the holding of a referendum repealing a specific law is constitutional. The Court is composed of

---

[10]Beniamino Caravita, "Prime osservazioni di contenuto e metodo sulla riforma del Titolo V della Costituzione," *www.federalismi.it*.

15 judges, of whom five are elected by joint session of Parliament, five elected by the highest courts of the land, and five appointed by the president of the Republic. The judges serve a nine-year nonrenewable term and must possess high professional qualifications. The Court enjoys substantial financial, administrative, and self-regulatory independence.

The jurisprudence of the Court has gone through at least three phases. In the first one, which went from 1956 (when the Court became operational) to the late 1960s, the Court attacked those aspects of the Italian legal system inherited from the Fascist era that most glaringly limited civil and political freedoms. In a second phase, from the late 1960s to recent years, the Court has promoted sweeping reforms in the areas of the tax system, family law, and penal and civil procedures. In the last few years, the Court has moved more decisively toward the support of equal rights. In the future, the Court will probably address the redefinition of the welfare state and its compatibility with budgetary constraints, the ever-evolving relationship between EU and national legislation, the admissibility of more referendums, constitutional reform and its limits, and the conflicts among legislative, executive, and judicial powers and those among levels of government. The impact of the Court's decisions on the governability of the country could thus be extraordinary indeed.

## THE JUDICIAL SYSTEM

The Italian judicial system comprises ordinary and special jurisdictions. The former is exercised by ordinary judges (civil and penal), while the latter by administrative (regional administrative tribunals, Council of State), accounting (Court of Accounts), tax (Tax Commissions), and military magistrates.

The ordinary magistrature is competent to decide on the basis of subject matter and territorial criteria established by law. Both civil and penal jurisdictions have at a first level both individual (the Justice of Peace and the Judge *monocratico*) and collegial bodies, like the Tribunals.

At the appellate level, Courts of Appeal are always collegial bodies. At the pinnacle of the Italian judicial system is the Court of Cassation, which decides on questions of law and never on the merits of a case.

The career of Italian magistrates starts after having obtained a law degree and passed a very rigorous competitive entrance exam. The magistrates' independence from outside interference is guaranteed by the constitution. This independence is defended by the Supreme Council of the Magistrature (CSM), which is responsible for the promotion, transferral, and discipline of magistrates. The CSM is composed of the president of the Republic, who presides, two high magistrates of the Court of Cassation, ten members chosen by joint session of Parliament, and 20 elected by all magistrates. In such elections, the political groupings in which the judges' professional association—the National Association of Magistrates—is divided mirror, not too overtly and with much less conflict, the left-right spectrum that exists in Parliament. Proposals have been put forth by the Berlusconi government in 2001 to change the way these elections are held by creating a single list of candidates, and more importantly, to separate the careers of prosecuting and adjudicating magistrates. The opposition parties and the judges themselves have voiced very strong objections to these proposals.

From the unification of Italy throughout the Fascist era, the judiciary never enjoyed independence from the executive power. With the end of the war and the new constitution, the judges were guaranteed this independence and the two careers of adjudicating and prosecuting magistrates became intertwined, with the possibility for judges to switch between them. In 1958 the CSM became operational, but it would not be until the late 1960s that the magistrature would start to display greater independence from the executive power. Some judges in the early 1970s would thus begin to abide by the constitutional mandate to take action against all illegal acts. They actively began to investigate corrupt politicians belonging to parties of the majority coalition as well as the secret services' slow-moving inquiries into some major terrorist bombings.

The growing independence of the CSM, the existence of a strong left-wing opposition, and the greater automaticity of careers for the magistrates sheltered considerably—albeit not completely—investigating judges from political interference. The growing independence of the judges was a thorn in the side of government parties and especially of the PSI, which spearheaded efforts in the mid-1980s to limit the independence of the prosecutors, justifying it on the basis that they had become completely unaccountable and were mostly tilting at windmills. At the beginning of the 1990s, the climate seemed conducive to introduce laws aiming at subjecting the inquiring judges to greater government control. And then everything changed.

## Operation Clean Hands

The referendum movement, the Northern League's growing success and visibility, the beginning of "operation clean hands" by the Milan judges, and the very negative results at the political elections of April 1992 sent the political parties into a crisis of immense proportions. As the inquiries progressed, and as the political vacuum left by the political parties kept on expanding, the Italian judges' visibility and standing increased to a degree that finds no equivalent in the Western world. Many would claim that this increase in standing was also attributable to the huge legality vacuum created by a political ruling class not capable of self-policing for decades. This augmented stature is also the result of the judges giving frequent television and newspaper interviews. These have been instrumental in rallying the people's support to prevent the Amato government in March 1993 and the Berlusconi government in July 1994 from achieving, through decree legislation, the derailment of their inquiries. The magnitude of the inquiring judges' activities is indeed extraordinary, and thousands of individuals have been investigated and prosecuted.

An unfortunate downside of the aura of near infallibility surrounding the prosecuting judges has been the damage done to the rights of the individuals subpoenaed, who, in the courts of public opinion, have already been condemned. At the same time, Italians cannot be blamed for wanting to see those who have pillaged the public coffers have their heads roll. Many fear this desire may go partially unfulfilled because of the slowness of Italian justice and the possibility that many of the crimes might go into prescription before the trials can start.

Even taking into account Italians' great thirst for justice, the power vacuum that the collapsing party system has created can only temporarily be filled by the judiciary. The good functioning of a modern industrial democracy needs an efficient legislature and executive sustained by strong popular support, where the judiciary is not in the limelight nor should it be forced to be to protect its inquiries.

## *Thinking Critically*

1. Have Italian governmental institutions worked satisfactorily?
2. How would you explain the emergence and evolution of Italy's multiparty system?
3. What has caused the decline of the Christian Democrats?
4. How significant has been the role of pressure groups in Italy?
5. Does Italy have a system of checks and balances?

## KEY TERMS

center-left *(281)*
confidence vote *(291)*
decree-laws *(295)*
Eurocommunism *(282)*
historic compromise *(281)*
*monocolore (280)*
operation clean hands *(301)*
opposite extremisms *(281)*
*pentapartito (282)*
referendum *(275)*
*il sorpasso (282)*
spoils system *(282)*
*tangentopoli (283)*

# FURTHER READINGS

Di Palma, Giuseppe, *Surviving without Governing: Italian Parties in Parliament* (Berkeley: University of California Press, 1977).

Farneti, Paolo. *The Italian Party System (1945–1980)* (New York: St. Martin's, 1985).

Germino, Dante, and Stefano Passigli. *The Government and Politics of Contemporary Italy* (New York: Harper and Row, 1968).

Ginsborg, Paul. *A History of Contemporary Italy: Society and Politics, 1943–1988* (London: Penguin, 1990).

*Ideazione.* Una certa idea dell'Italia. Special Issue. November 2001.

Kogan, Norman. *A Political History of Italy: The Postwar Years* (New York: Praeger, 1983).

Leonardi, Robert. *Italian Christian Democracy: The Politics of Dominance* (New York: St. Martin's, 1989).

Mammarella, Giuseppe. *Italy after Fascism: A Political History 1943–1965* (Notre Dame, IN: University of Notre Dame Press, 1966).

Mershon, Carol, and Pasquino Gianfranco, eds. *Italian Politics: Ending the First Republic* (Boulder, CO: Westview Press, 1994).

Nanetti, Raffaella, and Raimondo Catanzaro. *Italian Politics: A Review* (New York: Pinter, 1990).

*Politica in Italia.* (Bologna: Il Mulino, 2001). Annual.

Spotts, Frederick, and Theodore Wieser. *Italy: A Difficult Democracy. A Survey of Italian Politics* (Cambridge: Cambridge University Press, 1986).

# C. PUBLIC POLICY

## THE POST–WORLD WAR II YEARS: BETWEEN MARKET AND STATE

At the end of World War II, Italy found itself in a difficult economic predicament. The war had wrought substantial damage to the stock of housing in the large cities, and the rail and road networks were in considerable disarray. The Italian merchant marine was less than one-seventh of what it had been in 1938. In 1945 agricultural production was 69 percent of what it had been in 1938, while the corresponding figure for industrial production was down 29 percent.

The damage to manufacturing plants was less than what the production figures suggest, since the much more industrialized north had not been a major theater of hostilities and was relatively unscathed. As a matter of fact, by the end of 1946 the capabilities of Italian industry were estimated to be approximately equivalent to those of prewar 1938. Thus, the low levels of productivity stemmed from other factors such as the negative impact of the hobbled transportation system on both sourcing and distribution, together with the more fundamental scarcity of raw materials, fuel, and foreign exchange.

To these problems, one has to add runaway inflation. The situation in terms of unemployment and underemployment was serious as well, affecting several millions of individuals. Confronted with this host of problems, the economic policy makers of the time broke into two very distinct camps: those who thought that the reconstruction effort and the ensuing development had to be centrally planned and directed by the state, and those who favored a market-oriented solution, leaving to the free interplay of market forces the most optimal allocation of resources. The former policy posture was favored by the parties of the Left, which somewhat paradoxically wanted to use the interventionist economic tools inherited from Fascism. They supported the continued rationing of food in order to even out somehow the standards of living among the population and the change of all the currency in circulation so as to identify and tax the holders of large amounts

of capital, who in many cases had profited through speculation from the war. The Left also favored very strict controls over foreign exchange transactions and a program of nationalization of the largest industrial groups, connected also to an effective antitrust policy supporting smaller enterprises.

### The Free-Market Choice

Supporters of policies of economic liberalization included prominently those who wanted the total dismantling of all administrative controls, and the curbing of public spending, which they saw as the sole source of the rampant inflation. They opposed as well the change of the currency for its possible negative impact on depositors' confidence and on the management of monetary policy. While accepting the need for expanded debt financing and greater taxes on the largest holders of wealth, they staunchly supported workers' wage freezes.

Within the governments of national coalition, those in favor of the removal of restrictions to economic activity progressively imposed their views. Exchange rate transactions became less burdened by administrative controls, public spending was limited, and proposals for the change of banknotes never came to pass. The Confindustria succeeded in reasserting managerial control over individual factories through centralized collective bargaining with the unified unions, regained the right to lay off workers, while granting to unions the *scala mobile*. The actual layoffs would only start to take place substantially once the Left was ousted from government, in the second half of 1947.

The new DC government, whose economic ministries were all headed by supporters of free markets, immediately tackled the problem of inflation, increasing considerably bank reserve requirements. The reduction in liquidity and the fall in demand that ensued had also unpleasant though unavoidable effects on the employment level. The country plunged into a recession that would last until 1950.

## The Western Choice

The economic crisis was somehow lessened by UN-administered aid and more significantly by the Marshall Plan. The subdued inflation also enabled the Italian government to comply with its IMF membership requirements of greater liberalization and stability of the exchange rate. Thus, the free-market-oriented domestic policies dovetailed with international economic choices. Other such important choices were the full adherence to the Bretton Woods system of exchange rates in 1947, a lowering of tariff barriers, and the joining of the Organization of European Economic Cooperation in 1949, the entrance into the European Payments Union in 1950, and Italy's participation as a founding member in the European Coal and Steel Community in 1951. This last event marked unequivocally the beginning of the European integration process, which received the blessing of the United States, since Washington saw in it the opportunity to build a great bastion against the formidable enemies beyond the Iron Curtain.

## Economic Intervention in the South

The reconstruction years also saw the attempts on part of the state to try to address the "southern question." The need for action was heightened by the demographic pressure associated with the return of Italians from the former colonies and territories lost in the peace treaties and to the increase in birthrates in the wake of the reconstruction climate and the return of the veterans. On the agricultural front, land expropriation and redistribution policies aiming at increasing the electoral support for the DC in the south resulted in the creation of an excessively large number of small properties. Their dimension and nonspecialization, while responding to centuries-old desires of self-sufficiency, represented a marked contrast with the trends toward economies of scale and mechanization in agriculture observable in the typically much larger farms of other advanced industrial countries. The Cassa per il Mezzogiorno, the huge state development bank for the south, reflected in its activity the policy biases of the early years. It devoted until 1960 more than 50 percent of its funds to agricultural projects, with the balance largely going to infrastructural projects such as roads, water and sewage systems, schools, and hospitals. Other special state banks provided low-cost credit and grants for industrial purposes, but on the whole, industrial policy would never be particularly effective in the south.

## The Economic Miracle

The 1950s saw marked improvements in the economic conditions of the country as well as substantial changes in the structure of the economy. Between 1951 and 1958, the GNP grew yearly in real terms by 5.3 percent, in 1959 and 1960 by 6.6 percent and 6.3 percent, respectively, and in 1961 its growth reached 8.3 percent. Between 1952 and 1963, per capita income almost doubled to reach $970. The percentage of workers engaged in agriculture would go from 42.2 percent in 1951 to 29.1 percent in 1961, while by 1961 the percentage of workers engaged in the industrial sector would exceed 40 percent, up from 32.1 percent in 1951. The percentage of workers in the service sector would increase as well from 25.7 percent in 1951 to 30.3 percent in 1961. The change of Italy into an industrial country is also highlighted by the production figures of the decade, which for the industrial sector revealed growth rates close to 10 percent yearly, while the agricultural sector hovered around 3 percent.

The 1950s, and especially the period between 1955 and 1963, were the years of the "economic miracle," in which the above-mentioned economic growth was accompanied by price stability, high rates of investment, and lack of imbalances in the external accounts. Geographically the growth was not evenly distributed since it was concentrated in the industrial triangle of Genoa-Turin-Milan in the northwest. It was an area that became the point of arrival of many emigrants from the south. Between 1951 and 1961, the population of Milan increased by 24.1 percent, while that of Turin grew by an even more impressive 42.6 percent. In the years between 1958 and 1963, more than 900,000 individuals emigrated from the south to other regions of Italy.[11] With large masses relocating to the north, the supply of labor became swollen and the bargaining power of unions was considerably diminished. Italy thus experienced in those years an export-led boom which was in no small measure based on its low labor costs.

## Trade and Europe

In terms of the markets toward which Italy exported, there could be no choice: with the disappearance of trading opportunities in Eastern Europe, the limited access to Latin America (under U.S. influence) and North Africa (under French and British influence), the economies of what in 1957 would become the European Common Market represented the natural outlet for Italian industry. In turn, these rich economies' demand for goods of mass consumption of an upscale nature pushed Italy to develop its mechanical and chemical industries. At the same time, specialization in those labor-intensive products in which the country had a comparative advantage because of its large labor supply was neglected.

The economies of scale and the greater efficiency in production of their export-oriented sectors made it easier for Italians to buy television sets, washing machines, and automobiles, since these goods were in relative terms less expensive than more basic items such as food and clothing. This imbalance in the composition of private consumption highlighted a basic contradiction existing in the economic development of those years. The sectors which were subject to external competition experienced great productivity increases, substantial and growing profits, and high reinvestment rates. Those sectors sheltered from foreign competition, such as textiles and food, on the other hand, were characterized by much lower productivity increases. In terms of plant size, the former tended to be much larger and with a higher level of capital invested per worker,

but it was in the less-efficient sector that the greater absorption of workers occurred.

## Investments in the South

Sizeable industrial investments started to appear in the south toward the end of the 1950s. In the period between 1958 and 1963, they reached an unprecedented 25 percent of the national total for new plants. In the wake of legislation requiring the state to grant at least 30 percent of its contracts to southern enterprises and the state-owned or co-owned enterprises to locate at least 40 percent of their new investments in the south, the first very large steel, chemical, and refinery plants were being set up on the coasts of the south. This logic of creating industrial nuclei around which ancillary enterprises and employment would flourish would in later years be heavily criticized on the basis of these plants' minimal contribution to employment and their substantial contribution to pollution. Critics coined for these large industrial complexes the label "cathedrals in the desert" and decried government parties for using them as a vehicle for patronage.

## THE 1960S AND ECONOMIC PLANNING

The 1960s witnessed important changes from the previous decade. The entrance of the Socialists into the government meant that the debate over economic planning became more intense. The electricity-producing industry was nationalized, and concern over possible additional nationalizations across the Italian economy, the introduction of a withholding tax on dividends and one on real estate profits, and the creation of a National Commission on Economic Planning engendered substantial fear among Italian entrepreneurs. Such fears were compounded by the changed reality of the workplace, where a situation of near full employment had materialized in many segments of the manufacturing industry, thereby strengthening the bargaining power of unions. The single

---

[11]Ginsborg, p. 220.

most important element of competitive advantage for the Italian export-oriented industry, its low salaries, was evaporating.

## The End of the Miracle

Higher salaries put pressure on the profit margins of Italian enterprises. In those sectors which entered into direct competition with foreign manufacturers, raising prices was not an available option. In those sectors less subject to foreign competition, prices were indeed raised and, in the presence of the increased consumption stemming from the salary concessions and the rising tide of investments, inflation surged substantially. In the climate of fixed exchange rates of those years, with the unlikelihood that the international monetary authorities would allow a devaluation of the lira, the increases in domestic demand and the inability to increase production in the short term led to a growing deficit in the balance of trade. To stem the growing capital flight, the Bank of Italy decided to carry out a very restrictive monetary policy in the summer of 1963. Investments, which had already begun to falter because of the changed conditions, collapsed.

At the same time, the integration of the new immigrants from the south into the north's urban settings was not proceeding easily and was imposing heavy burdens on existing public services. The famous "great reforms" in areas as diverse as housing, transportation, regions, schools, and economic planning, so dear to the Socialist leaders, were shelved on account of their excessive costs. Soon the PSI started to shift its interest away from the reforms and toward strengthening its hold over government positions. The party justified this shift to its members and voters on the grounds that doing otherwise might have rendered republican institutions more susceptible to the risks of coups, or some other type of authoritarian development.

The negative impact on the competitiveness of Italian enterprises of problems underlying the end of the economic miracle was compounded by the firms' need to confront the country's low levels of investment in research and development. Not as well-endowed with capital as their larger-sized private foreign counterparts in the richest industrial countries and stymied by a government comparatively less supportive of cutting-edge research, Italian enterprises found it difficult to focus on product development. Instead, they concentrated on the best ways to improve productivity through ongoing efforts at upgrading and rationalizing production processes, the so-called process development. This was a business strategy that would be followed to this very day.

## European Integration

In the latter part of the 1960s, the increasing levels of integration of Italy into the world economy and the European Community became more evident. The country experienced growing levels of imports and exports, and the balance of current account remained firmly positive as a result of emigrants' remittances and tourism receipts. Yet the EC agricultural policy's aim to achieve food self-sufficiency through protection and price supports in grains and meats was not beneficial to Italy. Fruits and vegetables did not receive the same protection and the south of Italy, a major producer of such staples, bore the brunt of such a policy of neglect, while the nation as a whole was forced to feed itself through purchases on the Community's market, the most expensive agricultural market in the world.

## Stronger Unions

Toward the end of the decade, during what was labeled the "hot autumn" of 1969, a massive wave of industrial unrest began. The number of hours lost to strikes in 1969 came to exceed 200 million in the manufacturing sector, against the previous record in 1962 of 113 million. Labor rights and conditions, work shifts, limitations on the use of piecework and overtime became more important issues, even more so than salary increases, whose benefits had all too frequently been eroded by inflation. Workers also took to the streets together with students and retirees to protest the slow carrying out of the reforms in housing and social and public services, as well as to take a stand against the terrorist attacks and bombings that would plague the country for over a decade henceforth.

In terms of labor conditions and rights, the results of the strikes were impressive. In 1970, Parliament acceded to most workers' demands by enacting the Statute of the Workers. In 1970, salary increases adjusted for inflation exceeded 13 percent, and in the next two years 4 percent. Italian industrial wages came much closer to those of the richer nations of Western Europe.

## THE INFLATIONARY 1970s

The 1970s saw events that profoundly altered the nature of the world economy. The impact of such events on Italy was enormous and bears testimony to the high levels of interdependence and integration that the Italian economy had reached

by then. The end of the Bretton Woods system of fixed exchange rates in August 1971 and the start of the era of floating exchange rates in the beginning of 1973 were accompanied by substantial increases of the prices of raw materials. Most notably, following the unilateral declarations of the oil-producing countries in the fall of 1973, the price of oil quadrupled. Italian industry thus found itself squeezed between the higher costs of raw materials and intermediate goods on the one hand, and the loss of its comparative advantage in labor costs on the other. This latter factor became particularly evident around that time because of the emergence of the newly industrializing countries (NICs). These countries were selling products in those same noninnovative sectors as Italy did, and they had very low labor costs. Products from the likes of Taiwan, South Korea, Hong Kong, and Singapore, because of the

The small family firm: lean and flexible manufacturing.

advances of these countries in process development, had also become of much higher quality and started to invade the markets of the West at very competitive prices.

To cope with these problems, the Italian economic authorities adopted in the exchange markets a two-pronged strategy. With regard to the dollar, they tried to keep the exchange rate stable or even to have the lira appreciate against the dollar, since 50 percent of the Italian imports were invoiced in dollars. As to the deutsche mark, the aim was to have the lira depreciate against it, since that was the most important export market for Italy.

## Entrepreneurial Choices

Italian enterprises responded in two ways to the challenges represented by escalating costs, very protective labor laws, and their 1975 acceptance of the unions' demands for complete inflation adjustment to wages. First, sheltered by the general climate of growing inflation and the exchange rate policies, Italian entrepreneurs foisted on domestic consumers major price hikes. Second, through a massive process of subcontracting to much smaller companies, less subject to labor regulations, the cost of labor was brought down and workers' flexibility increased.

Many of these new smaller enterprises, located in the northeastern and the central regions, are at the core of the "Third Italy." These enterprises are frequently also part of that submerged economic sector spread all over the country in which there is substantial tax evasion and loose compliance with labor safety and environmental regulations. The unions found it very difficult to respond to these attacks to their power since these companies used segments of the workforce such as women, the aged, and the very young, who are very abundant in terms of supply and difficult to unionize because their workplaces are small and decentralized. The freedom of movement of the unions was further limited in the second half of the 1970s by the fact that the PCI was de facto part of the government coalition. Concerned over the threat to political institutions that terrorist attacks represented and

over its image as a responsible democratic party, the PCI pressured the union movement to limit their demands and industrial action.

## A Postindustrial Society

In the 1970s, Italy also experienced societal changes that, following from those observed during the 1960s, attested to its entrance into a postindustrial phase. In spite of some years of economic difficulties, Italians continued to experience growing standards of living and consumption levels. The 1981 census showed a country markedly different from what it was in 1951. The percentage of workers in agriculture further declined to 11.2 percent of the population. The corresponding figure for the manufacturing sector was 39.8 percent, down from 44.3 percent in 1971, an unmistakable sign of the increase of workers in the service sector. Mostly as a consequence of the large waves of internal migration of the 1960s, the percentage of Italians living in cities with more than 50,000 inhabitants grew from 28 percent in 1951 to 37 percent. The percentage of the population which was illiterate went down to 3 percent with growing numbers of individuals accessing all levels of education, a result in no small part attributable to the reforms of the early 1960s.

The major wave of reform legislation that materialized in the 1970s in labor rights (and a very costly workers' redundancy scheme—the Cassa Integrazione), public financing of political parties, and access to medical and hospital care, among others, led to a level of government intervention and presence that would soon reveal itself as being among the highest in the Western world. This would be, as we shall soon see, at the basis for large public deficits.

## THE 1980s

### Changing Labor Relations

In the 1980s, the substantial contradictions characterizing the Italian economy and society came powerfully to the fore. In the early part of the

1980s, not unlike the rest of Europe, Italy fell victim to the recession largely induced by the oil price hikes of 1979. Industrial production by 1983 was 7.3 percent lower than the 1980 level, and GDP at constant prices registered minuscule growth rates in 1981 and 1982 and was only 1 percent in 1983. Consumer prices grew at 21.2 percent a year in 1980, and the rates of increase went down to only 19.5, 16.5, and 14.7 percent in the following three years. Wages grew 24 percent in 1981, 17 percent in 1982, and 15 percent in 1983.[12] Trying to break the link between wage indexation and inflation, the government issued a decree in February 1984 that reduced the cost of living adjustments. Large segments of the union movement went along, understanding the difficulty of the moment. However, the largest part of the CGIL and the PCI vehemently opposed the decree, and the 1985 referendum, failing to repeal the legislation, was perceived by many as a major blow to organized labor.

## Less Participation

In terms of collective ethics, changes in values with regard to redistribution and social justice would soon become apparent. The increasing secularization of Italian society, the greater levels of consumption, the increase in leisure time (ironically in no small part attributable to unions' activities) reduced interest in political participation and labor activism and ushered in a rediscovered sense of individualism. There could be nothing more emblematic of this shift than the events of 1980.

Following massive layoffs announced by Fiat to meet the crisis affecting the car industry, the unions organized a general strike and occupied the carmaker's factories with the blessing of the PCI. Many were expecting the beginning of another "hot autumn." Three weeks later, however, 40,000 middle-level managers, employees, supervisors, and specialized blue-collar workers marched through the streets of Turin protesting the continued occupation of the factories and

clamoring for a return to work. This display of support strengthened Fiat's hand at the negotiating table and the unions had to accept the layoffs and call off the strike. This episode marked the beginning of an era of deterioration of Italian confederal unions' power. Possibly stymied in their decision making by an excessively bureaucratized staff of 16,000, the unions had made the critical error of promoting wage demands that did not reward different levels of skills and responsibility. This progressively led to a flattening of salary differences that would not and could not sit well with the most specialized segments of the Italian workforce.

Unions were also being weakened by the ongoing downsizing of firms, increasing automation, the increasing importance in the economy of the less easy to unionize service workers, and the growing numbers of foreign workers (especially since the second half of the 1980s). The increasing acceptance among most segments of Italian society since the early 1980s of the Thatcher- and Reagan-inspired ideas on entrepreneurship and risk taking, which throughout the 1970s would have been met with disapproval bordering on ridicule, also reflected the changed times.

## A Second Economic Miracle?

The second half of the 1980s saw a much improved economic picture. The cost of raw materials and most notably that of oil went down. Inflation went down to 10.8 percent in 1984 and has turned into a single-digit reality ever since. GDP growth resumed at a satisfactory pace. In 1986 the national statistics office, ISTAT, declared that, if one would take into account the informal economy, Italy had just overtaken Great Britain, thus becoming the fifth economy in the world in GDP size. The role played in this economic renaissance by the "Terza Italia" enterprises of the central and northeastern regions was very significant. The signing of the Single European Act and the approach of the magic year 1992 had in the latter part of the 1980s a very beneficial effect on the Italian economy, not unlike that on other EC countries.

---

[12]Calculations of the author from IMF data.

Some problems would remain unresolved, however. The south continued to have a lower level of growth than the north and a much higher level of unemployment, especially among the young and women. The service sector—in addition to being composed of advanced segments in the areas of education, information technology, accounting, finance, and research—was also composed of less well paying jobs in, say, domestic work, street vending, dining, and tourism. Increasing numbers of immigrants came in the second half of the 1980s to fill these latter types of positions, with growing problems of integra-

tion for the years to come. Public deficits continued to rise, cynicism over the political class kept on growing, and the level of quality of public services continued to be considered inadequate to meet the competition with the rest of the EC.

After the entrance of Italy in the European Monetary System in 1979, the two-pronged maneuver described earlier became very arduous to carry out because of the appreciation of the dollar in the first half of the decade and, even more importantly, the gradual revaluation of the lira against the deutsche mark. More specifically, with the transformation in 1987 of the EMS into a de

---

**REVIEW**

**5.6**

## HIGHLIGHTS OF ITALIAN FINANCE

- From 1970 to 1993 public expenditures grew by 24 percentage points of GDP, while revenue growth was only 18 percent.

- In 1980 Italy's public expenditures were 4 percentage points of GDP lower than EU average; in 1993 they were 5 percent higher.

- Public investment was 3.7 percent of GDP in 1985; 3.3 percent in 1990; 2.1 percent in 1995 (the low point); 2.4 percent in 2000.

- Public expenditure on education is 4.7 percent of GDP; public expenditure on health is 7.3 percent of GDP.

- Interest costs were in 1992 12 percent of GDP, almost twice the EU average; in 2000 they were 6.5 percent.

- High technology products as a share of total exports of manufactures: 8 percent for the last 10 years. EU average went from 13 to 19 percent; U.S. from 26 to 29 percent.

- Foreign direct investment into Italy as a percentage of GDP: 0.2 (1996); 0.4 (1999). EU average 1.3 (1996); 3.1 (1999).

- 8 million self-employed.

- Net investment position: positive, 4 percent of GDP.

- Underground economy: 25 percent. Other major Western democracies' does not exceed 14 percent.

- Debt-GDP ratio in 1995 was 124 percent; Great Britain's was 54 percent; France's 52 percent; Germany's 59 percent; Belgium's 135 percent. Debt-GDP ratio now 110 percent.

- Deficit-GDP ratio in 1995 was 7.8 percent; Great Britain's was 4.2 percent; France's 5.4 percent; Germany's 3.6 percent. All of them are now below 3 percent.

- In 1991 stocks and mutual funds ownership combined were 27 percent of households' financial wealth, in 1999 50 percent.

---

*Sources:* OECD, ISTAT, EU, Franco Reviglio *Piu' Stato Meno Mercato* (Milan: Mondadori, 1994), Andrea Monorchio and Luigi Tivelli, *Viaggio Italiano* (Milan: Mondadori, 2001), EIU.

facto fixed exchange rate system among European currencies, the Italian currency could no longer be devalued against its main European trading partners for competitive purposes. This resulted in substantially negative current accounts balances, which would lead by 1992 to a net debtor position rapidly approaching 200,000 billion lire.

## POLICY COURSES SINCE WORLD WAR II

Looking back to the end of World War II, the policies pursued by the Italian economic authorities in the monetary and fiscal arenas seem to have gone through fairly distinct phases. The inflation of the early years was heavily fought through substantial restrictions on credit. Since deficit spending was avoided and economic conditions improved, the debt-GDP ratio got better: while over 90 percent in 1945, the ratio did not exceed 33 percent in all the following years. Interestingly, Italian leaders' fiscal conservativeness was even considered excessive by the Marshall Plan administrators.

Throughout the 1950s up until 1963, Italians experienced buoyant growth rates, stable prices, high investment rates, and a rapid industrialization. Starting in 1953, budget revenues exceeded expenditures, with the result that by 1963 the debt-GDP ratio had gone down to 24 percent. In 1963, which marks the end of the economic miracle, the great growth in consumption led to a sudden acceleration in price growth and to a worsening of the balance of current accounts. Not unaffected by the thinking from the United States, where deficit-spending advocates had arrived in Washington as presidential advisers, and also by Great Britain's example, Italian monetary and fiscal authorities took a more activist stance. They started to carry out "stop and go" policies of contraction and expansion to offset the increasing oscillations in the business cycle.

### The Center-Left

From a fiscal point of view in the period between 1966 and 1974, the center-left-supported governments increased expenditures substantially,

without however raising taxes. Thus the debt-GDP ratio went up, reaching 34 percent in 1970. It would climb rapidly to 40 and 43 percent in the following two years. Moreover, in the year preceding the 1973 oil shock, Italy had a deficit-GDP ratio of 7 percent while that of the other major industrial countries was negligible or nonexistent, largely on account of their greater reliance on taxation.

The beginning of the 1970s saw the unequivocal shift toward policies aimed at supporting the employment level rather than price stability and informed by short-term considerations over long-term ones. In those years it also became common practice for the government to assist domestic enterprises with low-cost access to credit, tax incentives to investments, and the partial or total absorption by the state of social security charges. With the onset of the recession induced by the oil shock in 1973, raw materials and energy were made available at much reduced or no cost to many enterprises to prevent them from folding, while in case of layoffs, substantial and prolonged unemployment benefits maintained the households' income levels. Government takeovers of troubled private enterprises to safeguard employment were also very common and contributed further to the expansion of the already inefficient state-owned sector.

### Consociational Politics

Government coalitions and the main opposition party, the PCI, were basically practicing a very economically dangerous form of consociational politics, which would last in some of its most nefarious forms up until 1992. Unwilling and unable to say no to the organized interests pressing them, political parties traded electoral support for all sorts of handouts. These transfers to enterprises and individuals were all the more substantial in the periods preceding elections, following a pattern also observable, albeit with slightly different modalities, in other industrial countries like the United States.[13]

---

[13]Edward R. Tufte, *Political Control of the Economy* (Princeton, NJ: Princeton University Press, 1978).

The accommodating stance extended on the whole to monetary policy as well, and real interest rates in the period 1974–1979 were the lowest among the major industrial countries. Moreover, no longer restrained by the Bretton Woods fixed-rate system, monetary authorities let the lira depreciate to increase the competitiveness of Italian-made goods. Things would soon change.

## The Fight against Inflation

The beginning of very decisive anti-inflationary policies in the United States at the end of the decade took the U.S. prime rate above 18 percent by 1981. European rates had to follow suit to prevent even more massive capital outflows to the United States. The Bank of Italy could follow the other European central banks on this restrictive path because since the 1981 "divorce" from the Treasury Department, the Bank was no longer obligated to purchase all unsold Treasury securities. Thus, in the 1980s, real interest rates became positive and higher than those of the other industrial countries. High interest rates proved to be for Italy the right medicine to fight inflation and, as we have seen, by 1985 growth of consumer prices had reached a single-digit level and would continue to decrease in the following years.

Additional limits on Italian monetary authorities came from the ever greater European integration. Even given the greater leeway that it had obtained by participating in a wider exchange rate band in the European Monetary System, Italy was forced to follow fairly closely the anti-inflationary path of Germany. No longer capable of relying on the acquiescence of the Bank of Italy, politicians, unwilling to ask Italians to tighten their belts for fear of electoral retribution, let public expenditures soar.

## The Public Deficits

While in 1970 and 1980 Italy's public expenditures were still 4 percentage points of GDP lower than those of the European Community average, by 1993 they were greater by a 5 percentage point margin. The main reason for this discrepancy does not lie in expenditures on education, health, or defense. It stems from Italy's far more costly social security system, early retirement policies, disability benefits, and subsidies to several public services. These expenditures, which skyrocketed in the 1980s, are the natural outgrowth of consociational politics and are now difficult to roll back. Moreover, with the debt-GDP ratio going from 34 percent in 1970 to 52 percent in 1980, and reaching 100 percent in 1990, the interest bill became big and painful to pay. The growing budget deficits also stemmed from Italy's low fiscal pressure. Only in the early 1990s would Italy basically have tax revenues as a percentage of GDP in line with those of the other EC members (about 40 percent), and this has occurred in large measure because of the pressures created by European integration. It was in fact the signing of the Maastricht treaty of December of 1991 that made the adjustment no longer postponable.

The Amato government, which started its tenure in June 1992, set out to tackle the huge problems of the public deficits and debt and enacted a very substantial series of tax raises. In July the agreement between the Confindustria and the unions on controlling the cost of labor and the Bank of Italy's confident reduction of the discount rate seemed to some to show that the country was on the right course. The international capital markets, however, did not think that the criteria of convergence would be met and, taking advantage of the risk-free speculation that a system of near fixed exchange rates permitted, attacked the lira vehemently. Between the end of August and September 16, 1992, the Bank of Italy stepped up the already very costly intervention to prop up the currency, but to no avail.

## Out of the ERM

On the dawn of September 17, 1992, Italy had to drop out of the European Exchange Rate Mechanism (ERM), a fate that had befallen the United Kingdom a few hours earlier. A few days later, in the face of total costs to defend the lira amounting to $48 billion and the risks of not being capable of selling treasury securities, the Amato government proposed the most massive tax package ever imposed on the country. Between almost equally split revenue increases and expenditure reductions, the package would be a huge 5.8 percent of GDP. The measures, although belated, were the kind of tough medicine that received strong approval from international monetary authorities. Albeit somewhat watered down in Parliament, the measures, an integral part of the budgetary law, did pass. The unpopular aspects of the yearly budgetary law, compounded by the "corrective" revenue-raising laws needed several times a year, was lessened this time by the Amato government's legislation on the confiscation of the assets of corrupt politicians and bribing citizens. The Ciampi government in 1993 also enacted stringent fiscal measures. Later on, the Berlusconi and Dini governments pursued less decisive fiscal policies, affected respectively by the tycoon's personal troubles with the Milan judges and the technocrat's not-too-firm majority in Parliament.

## Into the EMU

The Prodi government emerging from the victory of the Olive Tree coalition at the elections of 1996 had to confront head on the harsh realities of meeting the criteria for entry into the European Monetary Union (EMU). Debt-GDP and deficit-GDP ratios were much higher than those of most European countries, and so were the inflation rate and the rates on long-term bonds. Armed with a significant level of popular and business groups' support "not to be left out of Europe," Prodi succeeded in overriding the party squabbles within the coalition and pass the harsh budgetary measures (taxation levels reached 44 percent of GDP in 1997) needed to enter the EMU club. When this happened in May 1998, it soon became evident that the very reluctant support that the Refounded Communists had been providing was coming to an end. The budget for 1999 was deemed by them too effete in fighting unemployment and helping the poorest segments of the population. With the RC vote against Prodi,

the heretofore second-longest-lived government since World War II was brought to an end.

## The Former Communist in Power

The Olive Tree coalition regrouped and Massimo D'Alema, by many believed to be the inspirer of the RC coup against Prodi, in October 1998 became the prime minister of the 56th postwar government. It was the first time that a leader of what was once the communist left was at the helm of the country. It soon became evident that D'Alema's freedom of movement in terms of spending was no greater than Prodi's. The existence of the constraints deriving from the EU's Stability Pact confined the country to deficit-GDP ratio objectives not to exceed 2 percent. Further, it soon became obvious that the better relations that the Left had traditionally held with the unions were of little aid in securing their cooperation on pension reform, where they were essentially unmoved from their previous positions.

D'Alema also attempted to table with the Berlusconi-led opposition discussions on constitutional reform and electoral reform. The idea was to respond to the needs of governability of the country. D'Alema's desire to reach an agreement with Berlusconi on these issues, according to many, explains his reluctance to tackle vigorously the issue of the conflict of interests between government leaders' business and political activities—something strongly resisted obviously by the Alliance for Freedom's leader. The failure to reach an agreement on constitutional and electoral reforms, and the personalization of the conflict with Berlusconi with regard to the ill-fated regional elections (where not for the first time national themes dominated), led in April 2000 to D'Alema's resignation from the premiership.

## Amato Is Back

President Ciampi accepted D'Alema's resignation and conferred on April 21, 2000, the mandate to nonparliamentarian Giuliano Amato. The president wanted to reduce the criticism from the Alliance for Freedom that, just like the two immediately preceding governments headed by D'Alema, this government was not a direct emanation of the popular will. So Ciampi stressed the need that the Amato government be economically responsible and avoid passing a budget of an expansionary nature for electoral aims; enact an electoral reform; and limit the number of ministers. Amato accepted, and his government would last basically until the end of the natural life of the legislature, a little over a year.

With regard to the electoral reform, the three sages that he appointed to the task were unsuccessful in building the political consensus needed to achieve results. The budget was the first one in years where some resources were available for redistribution and where no new taxes had to be levied. The redistribution to the neediest households, to pensioners, and to enterprises was not as controversial as some of the clauses inserted in the budget, which the opposition vehemently accused of favoring specific constituents of the center-left coalition.[14]

When it came to the selection of the front runner to oppose to Silvio Berlusconi, the party notables within the coalition that supported Giuliano Amato decided that, in spite of his abilities, he was too much of a man of the past. The choice fell thus on the mayor of Rome, Francesco Rutelli. The not too happy incumbent prime minister acquiesced, and the following months of his lame duck government saw the telegenic contenders Rutelli and Berlusconi fight their campaign on the airwaves, in the press, in the mail, and on billboards.

## The Economic Policies of the Olive Tree

The five years of government of the Olive Tree (1996–2001) were first and foremost characterized by economic policy making aiming at entering and staying in the Euro area. Italians have been among the greatest supporters of European

integration, not in small measure because of their weaker sense of national identity and because their most enlightened elites believe that adherence to European standards could provide the needed outside discipline to undertake otherwise unpopular economic measures. The former Communists, part of the center-left coalition, thus found themselves instrumental in bringing Italy even closer to an institution, the EU, which years before they looked at with great suspicion as an elite club with a basic antiunion bias. They followed in this change of ideological course and embraced the ideas of Romano Prodi and Carlo Azeglio Ciampi. It is also arguable that the stringent fiscal and incomes policies that were enacted in the second half of the 1990s were easier to handle for a center-left government, capable of a less confrontational relationship with the unions and perhaps more aggressive against tax dodgers, than that of a center-right government.

The large deficits and debts and the very high level of interest rates meant a huge interest payments bill. Then Treasury Minister Ciampi fully realized that the high level of interest rates in turn was the result of high inflation and an unfavorable country-risk perception.[15] With the incentive provided by the fact that a decrease in interest of one percentage point saved the country a whopping $10 billion, the budget for 1997 provided for sizeable cuts in expenditures and very large tax increases. The aim of that budget and of those enacted thereafter, plus various ad hoc corrective revenue-raising measures, was not just to meet the criteria for European convergence and those of the Stability Pact, but also to improve the image of the country, so that the risk component of the interest costs could be reduced. On this front the Olive Tree governments undoubtedly scored good results. Inflation went from 3.9 percent in 1996 to less than 2 percent in the following three years, to inch upward to 2.5 in 2000, in large measure on account of the higher oil prices.[16] Most remarkably, the

---

[14]Gianfranco Pasquino, "Premiership e leadership da D'Alema a Amato e oltre" in *Politica in Italia,* Edizione 2001, p. 63.

[15]Dino Pesole, *I conti in regola* (Milan: Il Sole 24 Ore, 2001), p. 153.

[16]Data from the Economist Intelligence Unit.

deficit-GDP ratio went from 6.5 percent in 1996 to 1.5 percent in 2000, while the debt-GDP ratio went from over 120 percent to 110 percent during the same period.[17]

On the negative side, GDP growth, which reached 2.9 percent in 2000, was nevertheless for the five preceding years the slowest in the Eurozone. Further, unemployment, which remained stubbornly high throughout the period, went down from its 11.8 percent peak in 1998 only to 10.5 percent at the end of 2000, largely because of the policies of somewhat greater flexibility on part-time and temporary work introduced. The balance of current account showed a steady deterioration from a surplus of $40 billion in 1996 to a deficit of $6.1 billion in 2000, very revealing of the overall reduction in competitiveness of Italian firms, no longer sheltered by devaluations of the lira. One unfortunate aspect of the need to curtail government expenditures has been the great decline in public investments as a percentage of the GDP, which reduces obviously the quality of the country's infrastructure. Further, foreign direct investment into the country lagged in the period 1996–1999, considerably behind the EU average, hardly a vote of confidence by the international investment community.

## Enter Berlusconi

In his electoral campaign, Silvio Berlusconi emphasized the most negative aspects of the economic performance of the Olive Tree governments. Further, he accused the professional politicians and professors who had guided the country in the past five years of not having done anything on issues such as reforming the pension system, the labor markets, the constitution, and the electoral system, among others. Berlusconi committed himself in a document called "contract with the Italians" to lower taxes, reduce crime, raise the minimum pension levels,

create one and half million new jobs, and effect a major public works program. The soon-to-be prime minister declared also that if he failed to achieve specific targets in at least four of these five objectives, he would not run again at the next elections.

Shortly after the Berlusconi government took office in the weeks following the victorious elections of May 2001, his economy minister Giulio Tremonti launched a scathing attack on the budget that he had "inherited" from the previous administration. Identification of significant revenue shortfalls at the beginning of a new administration occurs pretty frequently in most democratic governments of the world. It makes the preceding government look bad, enables you to backtrack on overly generous campaign promises, and gives you more of a political cushion for future problems. Obviously, the recently ousted center-left economic policy makers disputed vehemently the numbers. In any event, at the end of 2001, after six months in power, against the backdrop of a slowing world economy, the substitution of the lira for the euro, and the worldwide emergency on terrorism, the Berlusconi government passed the yearly budget that would in its view permit Italy to meet the targets of the EU Stability Pact. The areas in which the new government has taken action, or declared that it will, or should in any case act upon are many. Let us look at some of the most important of them.

## THE ROAD AHEAD

### European Economic Integration

Many current public policy problems will continue to be around for the next few years and in most instances well beyond that. In the first place there is the process of European economic integration and continued participation in what is now a single currency area. The need for economic convergence before entry into the Eurozone and for meeting on an ongoing basis the Stability Pact targets afterwards have obviously provided Italy with the needed external discipline

---

[17]James Blitz, "Budget deficit pledge gives early problem in Italy: A Survey," *Financial Times,* June 5, 2001, p. II.

against fiscal profligacy. Further, at the beginning of 2002, with the lira being phased out for the euro within weeks, the convergence of the inflation rate toward the Eurozone average seemed basically accomplished. However, one caveat is in order. The stringent limits to the running of budget deficits (there is a hard-to-meet commitment for a balanced budget in 2003) strongly constrain the ability of the country to put in effect countercyclical policies. In other words, in the presence of a prolonged recession, it becomes very difficult to run deficit-spending policies aiming at getting the economy going again. If one adds to this that monetary policy is now carried out by the European Central Bank, which could under such a scenario continue to pursue a non-inflationary policy pursuant to its mandate, one can easily see how unpopular the until now virtuosity-inducing European integration process could become.

The debate over the role of the ECB, a body of nonelected bankers working in Frankfurt, and the continued adherence to very stringent fiscal criteria with attendant reduction in economic sovereignty will most likely continue in the months and years ahead and will become particularly heated in case of truly difficult economic times. No Eurozone country is and will be immune from it. Further, in the case of Italy, the presence for the first time of some vocal Euroskeptics in government will mean that the pursuit of national economic self-interest (for instance in the area of agriculture or regional assistance) will play a much bigger role in its dealings with Brussels.

## Privatization and Capital Markets

Another area of great importance is that of the ongoing downsizing of the largest state-owned system of enterprises in the Western world through massive privatizations. The privatization program, started in earnest in the 1990s after some dithering in the 1980s, had brought into the public coffers over $50 billion between 1992 and the beginning of 2001. At the beginning of the Berlusconi government, the Italian state maintained a controlling interest over ENEL

(electricity), ENI (oil and gas), Finmeccanica (aerospace, defense, electromechanic production), Alitalia airlines, and RAI (TV and multimedia). If one considers that the Italian state still owns among others the Postal and Railways systems, and that there are over 1,200 firms under the control of local public territorial entities, and that the public presence in the banking sector is still strong, it is evident that the privatization process will continue for the next few years and more. It is difficult to estimate the value of all these enterprises. One estimate puts the potential amount that could be raised from an aggressive privatization program at no less than $200 billion. More important than the amounts and their impact on debt reduction are the benefits that should arise in terms of the greater efficiency with which the privatized entities will operate. The process is made more difficult, as the fall 1995 sale of shares in energy giant Ente Nazionale Idrocarburi (ENI) has shown, by small shareholders' reluctance to buy when they suspect that their rights may sooner or later be trampled on by large domestic investment groups—or as we have seen after the worldwide debacle in high-tech stocks in the spring of 2000, when the markets are in a bearish mood.

This is related to another major challenge. Italy needs to expand its capital markets, since it ranks by far lowest among the four major EU members for number of companies in the top 500 list. In March 2001, Italy's stock market capitalization was 62 percent of GDP, similar to Germany's but much less than Spain's and France's at 89 and 103 percent respectively. To achieve the needed expansion, in addition to better protection through effective anti-insider trading enforcement, transparency has to improve further, and the small shareholder, who in the past few years has indeed moved fairly rapidly toward an equity culture, must receive more fiscal incentives. Institutional investors such as mutual funds and banks have similar needs.

The entrepreneurs in Italy are also responsible for this state of affairs, since even when they do have the size to go public, they may for cultural reasons resist the visibility and questioning of their management that being listed on the stock exchange entails. The individualism and desire for independence found in many small family-owned concerns are indeed at the basis of the high flexibility and responsiveness to market needs observable in so many Italian entrepreneurial success stories. Unfortunately, capital cannot always be generated internally, and on the whole, Italian enterprises, to compete effectively (which means also meeting their competitors' research budgets), must accept venture capital as a source of funds. Thus, in order to foster a culture of risk among investors and entrepreneurs to attract foreign capital and prevent capital flight, major legislative changes will have to be enacted to regulate effectively all Italian financial markets.

## Deregulation and Antitrust Legislation

Italy has many heavily regulated areas of business in which entrepreneurship is suffocated and in which deregulation is badly needed. Such is the case, for instance, of telecommunications, electricity, and energy. Another problem is that several markets are controlled by a few families or interest groups and could use more effective antitrust legislation and enforcement. One such major sector is that of automobiles. Fortunately, adapting to EU legislation will go a long way toward improving these two problem areas. Adopting and enforcing European standards will also be very beneficial to the country in the area of consumer protection.

## Unemployment

Dealing with Italy's high unemployment rates will prove a formidable task. By one middle-of-the-road estimate, the rate in the north and center of the country is 8 percent, while in the south it is 21 percent. It is also highest among the young and women. Not unlike other European countries, the high unemployment level is attributed in large measure to the rigidity of labor markets. Significantly, dismissing employees is harder and costlier than it is for other European countries, and the exemptions available to enter-

prises with fewer than 15 employees must account substantially for Italy's higher percentage of firms of this size compared to the EU average. Hence, the process of liberalization of the labor market, which started in the mid-1980s, must be accelerated and regulations on overtime and part-time work have to be further eased. Predicting the role of the unions, traditionally resistant on these issues, is difficult and their waning strength should not be overemphasized. For instance, with regard to pension reform, the Dini government found it necessary to compromise with them in order to avoid the unproductive open conflict that befell the Berlusconi government in the fall of 1994.

The negotiations among unions, employers' organizations, and the government over the terms for employee dismissals and pensions appeared at the beginning of 2002 particularly confrontational and will constitute undoubtedly a major test for the Berlusconi government. The challenges deriving from a rapidly aging population, longer life expectancy, a very low labor participation rate (the percentage of the population either working or looking for a job), and the need to move from a system of defined benefits to one of defined contributions make pension reform a truly daunting task. Solutions will have to center on extending the length of the working life. Further, given the higher birthrates among immigrants, future debates on intergenerational solidarity will likely acquire interethnic, interracial, and perhaps even interreligion dimensions. The ability to offer the new arrivals, and especially their children, good education and training as part of effective and balanced integration policies leading to their espousal of the vision of intergenerational solidarity that has characterized the pension system thus far will be crucial to reduce societal conflict years from now. While perhaps more acute in Italy, these issues have to be addressed in basically all the Western world.

## The South

The south must also be on top of decision makers' agenda. Public investments, which have dwindled in the past few years, must resume vigorously. The challenge for governments will be to set up in the south a virtuous cycle by which the improvements in the infrastructure will be accompanied by more private investment. In turn, more investment will do much to reduce some of the cynical resignation that one can all too frequently find among job seekers and potential entrepreneurs. A change in political and economic climate, carried out also through a significant attack on tax evasion (this one nationwide) and through substantial reform reducing the cost of hiring, will also have a very positive impact on the fight against organized crime. Many hold, convincingly, that once the state is no longer perceived as a distant entity, and unemployment goes down, the fertile ground for the growth of criminal activities will disappear.

Two additional points are worth noticing. First, the Berlusconi government's agenda of public works expenditures has undoubtedly appealed to many in the south and across the country, contributing to his victory. Second, the underground economy estimated at 25 percent of GDP, against an EU average of 14, is particularly present in the south, and government has to do everything possible to make it emerge by reducing the fiscal burden and labor regulations on this segment of the economy. However, any aid to southern enterprises has to be structured so as to not be distorting competition, otherwise it will run afoul of EU regulations.

## Public Administration

Public administration will have to continue to be reformed. The quantity and especially the quality of public services offered are frequently inferior to those of other European countries. This reduces considerably the competitiveness of Italian enterprises, hobbled by inefficient postal, transportation, and health services, and by the need to receive a panoply of authorizations from the public administration to comply with a gigantic legal system comprising 150,000 laws (the corresponding figures for France and Germany are 5,600 and 7,300, respectively). Many entrepreneurs claim that their managerial effective-

ness is significantly stymied by the lack of legal certainty on applicable legislation, and that they risk inadvertently infringing even penal laws and being subpoenaed and perhaps prosecuted as a result. Public administrators are said to be fearful of unwittingly infringing some law when soliciting bids for public contracts. Steps have to continue to be taken to improve the conforming of public administration to principles of efficiency, simplicity, transparency, and publicity. For instance, compilation of well-organized codes on various subject matters is a must and so is the explicit repeal of previous laws.

Fortunately since the early 1990s, the bureaucracy's emphasis on procedures and punctilious respect for the law has been slowly giving way to greater stress on actual results. Public employees can be more easily transferred from one location to another, and their contracts have been made more similar in nature to those in the private sector. In the wake of foreign experiences such as those in the United States and Great Britain, a "Public Services Charter" listing users' rights was circulated by the government in early 1994. Reforms aiming at greater accountability for high-level bureaucrats have been passed, but this is an area in great legislative and judicial flux and a controversial one because of the need to define the boundaries between political appointees and career bureaucrats, their terms of service, and conditions for removal.

## Decentralization

Decentralization of power to regions and other territorial subunits will have to be effectively implemented, following the constitutional reforms of 2001. Decentralizing some of the revenue raising should lead to greater accountability of local administrators, who at present spend mostly funds not raised locally, and to greater citizens' involvement and control. This is indeed a major point raised by the Northern League, and the issue of transfer of resources from rich to poor regions will continue to be hotly debated.

A reform of the school system passed during the tenure of the Olive Tree was being at the beginning of the Berlusconi government substantially changed. In addition to providing for an expansion of private school resources much resisted by the Left, it will entail a very controversial transfer of power to the regions. Two considerations are in order. One, a much decentralized school system could result in larger differences in the quality of education in various parts of the country and prove detrimental to the continued development of a sense of national unity and solidarity in the nation. Two, recent complaints about a higher college dropout rate in Italy than in the rest of Europe shows a sensibility imported from the United States. Regrettably, just as here, few understand how little such statistics mean because of the large role played by promotion policies entailing the lowering of standards. Thus, while the Italian school system at all grade levels should be improved (for instance with better access to new technologies and with the introduction of German-style vocational schools), on the whole it is pretty good. This leads to the major point that while at times Italians have like other Europeans a certain smugness with regard to their abilities stemming from their great cultural past, they can also be excessively critical of themselves even when they have little cause to be.

The reforms passed in the early 1990s and during the years of the Olive Tree, which have set up and kept on modifying the national health care system, present the same kind of public versus private dichotomy with regard to the status of doctors and the organizational structures they are connected to. They also present and will continue to present significant funding problems heightened by the devolution process.

The workings of a domestic Stability Pact introduced for the first time in 1999, aiming at involving territorial subunits in the process of conforming to the fiscal objectives set in Brussels, will be interesting to watch in the years to come. Since the European Union views transfers of public resources to enterprises which locate in the south as infringing competition rules, but supports regional development policies for infrastructural purposes, national and local administrations will have to upgrade their heretofore insufficient ability to present in a timely fashion projects worthy of receiving European regional support.

## The Justice System

Difficulties in many policy areas will be eased by the upgrading in the efficiency of the justice system. Inquiring magistrates have proven particularly active since 1992 at investigating dishonest politicians, entrepreneurs, and public officials. They have worked just as actively with mafiosi. Where the problem lies is in actually trying the suspects. On account of the large backlog of cases, many of these individuals are in jail waiting for a trial. True, in almost all instances there is a large body of evidence to go from indictment to conviction, but the successful prosecutions of some of the alleged crimes is affected by the statute of limitations. To serve justice well, substantial resources and much organizational effort will have to be devoted to clearing the backlog. Perhaps more importantly, the backlog is far greater in the civil arena, where a case can last from six to ten years. This is tantamount to denying justice and acts as a powerful deterrent to entrepreneurship, which to grow healthy also needs a climate of legal certainty. Thus the choice will be either increasing the resources available to the justice system or creating private regulatory entities and a private justice system in many substantive areas along with appropriate criteria. All these changes will need to be extensively debated and analyzed.

Matters are much complicated by the controversy that the Berlusconi government has engendered since its onset in this policy area. The first measures passed—a law significantly reducing the penal and civil responsibilities for false accounting, a new cross-border cooperation law making it more difficult to admit as evidence foreign documents, as well as the opposition to a EU-wide arrest warrant (withdrawn with reserve after major criticism from other European countries)—have been considered by the center-left opposition particularly self-serving. Its claim and that of many in the judiciary is that they are all directed at making life easier for Berlusconi's attorneys in the several trials for false accounting and corruption of public officials in which he is a defendant. Further, while legislation against violence at sports events and strong antiterrorist laws have been basically supported by the opposition, the measures aiming at fostering the repatriation of illegally exported (as long as not illegally gained) capital have been criticized by many of his adversaries as designed to help his richest constituents.

Berlusconi's supporters maintain that the several cases brought against the prime minister and still pending (there have also been acquittals and instances where the statute of limitations applied) are all politically motivated. People in Mr. Berlusconi's economic position, it is argued, also because of the general climate of corruption in which businessmen operated in Italy especially before 1992, inevitably have cases brought against them. The decision of prosecuting judges to investigate and prosecute him rather than

other prominent businessmen would in this pro-Berlusconi view be explained by some magistrates' left-wing political leanings and their desire to punish him for having entered politics. Berlusconi's supporters further point out that when he was elected in what amounted to a landslide victory for his party, voters were essentially accepting his campaign claims that he was the object of political persecution and demonization. Thus, by prosecuting him with such zeal (and for so many years without success), magistrates would be in direct confrontation with the will of the people. These points are rebutted by many in the judiciary and the center-left opposition who argue that nobody is above the law and that, when a judge is aware of a crime, he has a constitutional duty to investigate.

The controversy is further heightened by the Berlusconi government's desire to reform the career paths of magistrates, dividing the adjudicating ones from the prosecutors, just as it is in

Silvio Berlusconi, standing.

the United States and in so many Western democracies. Thus, the prosecutors would be responsible to the executive, the Ministry of Justice. This proposal for reform is seen by most in the judiciary and the center-left as a blatant attempt at limiting the independence of the inquiring magistrates, who are in turn viewed by the Berlusconi supporters as an arrogant life-tenured caste which has accumulated a huge backlog of cases and picks and chooses its targets. In any case, there can be little doubt that any reform should not compromise the independence of the judiciary, since the country needs more and not less legality, albeit not of the kind that unduly stifles entrepreneuship.

## Institutional and Electoral Reforms

Prior to the Olive Tree ascendancy to power in 1996, the weakness of the Italian coalition governments with their frequent reshufflings and collapses leading to nonconclusive elections had really tired Italians. Even before the unsuccessful attempt by D'Alema (he himself had to rely on a slightly different set of parties in the second consecutive government he headed) in the late 1990s, the desire for better governability had led to the creation of several ill-fated commissions aiming at drafting the necessary changes to the constitution. Among the issues whose resolution was deemed necessary for the creation of less volatile governments were federalism, the functions and powers of the president and those of the prime minister, their direct electability by the voters, and the further transformation of the electoral system through the introduction of the double ballot and an even greater use of the winner-take-all system.

One improvement has been the enactment of a devolution-type of reform that, in spite of the dissatisfaction expressed by the Northern League, in large part incorporates many of its favorite positions. More importantly, the emergence of a de facto bipolar system at the elections of 1996 and even more so in 2001, with clear choices and stronger majorities than in the past, has made the whole issue of electoral and institutional reforms appear less urgent.

Gianfranco Fini of the National Alliance.

## FOREIGN POLICY

At the end of World War II, Italy found itself a vanquished power, all its colonies lost, and with Anglo-American troops on its soil. Italy's position made it of crucial strategic importance in the emerging bipolar world order and, following the landslide victory of the DC in 1948, the choice of the Western camp was in most respects obligatory. It would bring the country to join NATO in 1949 and also, with the blessing of the United States, to be at the forefront in the process of European integration.

The less tense climate following the death of Stalin, the end of the Korean War, and the subsiding of the McCarthy-inspired witch hunt in the United States saw the emergence of a more independent foreign policy in the mid-1950s, with Italy trying to gain greater influence among the oil-rich countries of the Mediterranean Sea and the Middle East and then President Gronchi supporting the neutrality of Germany and a more equidistant relationship between the blocs. Gronchi's declarations, at variance with the much more pro-American views expressed in general by the Italian premiers and foreign affairs ministers of the time, are reflective of some of the undercurrents that would characterize Italian foreign policy thinking in the decades to come. Thus, strands of neutralism, pacifism, and (at times contradictorily) nationalism originating in the parties of the Left, part of the DC, and even the Right would find expression in declarations in favor of the Palestinian cause, the decolonization process in all its forms, and against the Vietnam War. On the whole, however, large segments of the DC, all the center lay parties, and later ever more frequently the Right were nearly always in line with the U.S. position. Such views would be prevailing as the general policy stance of the country and in those truly critical moments of testing Western cohesiveness, such as the placement of Jupiter missiles in 1958, that of Cruise missiles in 1979, and the joining of the multilateral force in 1991 against Saddam Hussein.

The end of the bipolar world has generated in Italy, as elsewhere in the European Union, substantial concern, and the current and future debates on Italian foreign policy will be connected to the broader discourse on the future of NATO and the trade relations between the United States and the European Union. Affected by its uncertain domestic politics, Italy has never carried out a foreign policy with an impact commensurate to its weight in the world economy. The Somalia, former Yugoslavia, and East Timor crises, where Italian military forces participated in various types of peace-keeping activities, bear testimony to the unpredictability and volatility of the new world configuration. In light also of possible future security problems in the Mediterranean, it stands to reason that Italy can no longer afford not to have a greater level of military readiness and a more incisive posture in foreign affairs.

Table 5.7 reflects the respective military expenditures of Italy and other industrialized nations. The ongoing peace-keeping activities in

**TABLE 5.7**

**MILITARY EXPENDITURES**

|  | % of GDP |
|---|---|
| United States | 2.9 |
| Great Britain | 2.4 |
| France | 2.6 |
| Germany | 1.5 |
| Italy | 2.0 |
| Japan | 1.0 |

*Source:* Author's computation from *The Military Balance 2001–2002,* ISS.

the former Yugoslavia and in other hot spots in the world, and much more importantly, the involvement since 1997 in Albania, where Italy has had the primary responsibility under a UN mandate for helping the local government to maintain law and order and where the presence of its financial aid, non-profit humanitarian organizations, and entrepreneurs (attracted by the low labor costs) has been truly significant, are signs that the country has been moving in the last years in a direction of greater activism. The abolition of the draft and the shift toward a professional military force has to be viewed as conforming to this new way of thinking.

Much will also depend on the developments that security and foreign policies will undergo in Brussels. The Berlusconi government has shown in its first months in office the propensity for a more assertive policy with regard to the EU, which has raised some eyebrows in various European capitals, accustomed to an Italy not too vocal or effective in pursuing its self-interest, and which probably has contributed to some pillorying of its leader in the foreign European press. In terms of its relations with the United States, this is likely to be the most clearly pro-American government since World War II, as its strong support for antiterrorism actions such as Operation Enduring Freedom (which has enjoyed the backing of sizeable portions of the opposition as well) confirms.

# CONCLUSION

Despite the list of challenges ahead, there is no doubting the economic success of Italy. Italian products can be found all over the world and their design wins high praise. Italian small enterprises continue to be the subject of business school case studies for their flexibility in meeting world market demands. Any U.S. soldier going back after over 55 years from the end of World War II would marvel at the sense of prosperity that buildings, paved roads, residential dwellings, and cars convey. This same aged visitor would see that Italians are very well fed and dressed, enjoying restaurants, movies, and resort areas just as their counterparts in any of the other wealthy countries of the West. Our visitor would easily realize that Italians, who enjoy a decent safety net provided by the state and the family, have access to very inexpensive health care, education, and rail and bus transportation. Yet the large pockets of inefficiency and poor quality in the delivery of some public services are undeniable. The markets for goods and services offer a good range of choices but they could function better, since they are all too often too rigidly regulated. EU integration and the global economy make policies promoting competition and competitiveness unavoidable and nonpostponable.

Many attribute the responsibility for these and the other problems besetting the country to its political class and would talk about economic and social progress achieved in spite of it. Certainly, Italians have had a political class for the past 50-plus years that has not been capable of providing the leadership necessary to enable the whole country to reach its potential. Italians know this and they will keep on asking for more stable governments while trying to select through voting a better class of representatives. To achieve both, it is necessary to create through electoral and institutional reforms a system that promotes bipolarism and stable coalitions. This is difficult to achieve because of the unpredictable consequences that all operations of electoral and constitutional engineering can have and also because of the fears that each political

party has that a specific change of the rules of the game may reduce its power.

Even in the absence of reforms, however, since the elections of April 1996, the country has experienced a form of bipolarism that has increased the stability of its governments. True, the Olive Tree legislature has experienced conflict within its coalition among the very left-wing agenda of Refounded Communism, the more socialist-oriented one of the Democrats of the Left, and the more moderate centrist parties harking to the Catholic and lay parties' tradition. But their lack of cohesion and capability of leadership in setting a course for the future has cost them. The Berlusconi-led coalition in May 2001 was victorious exactly because of its unity of purpose and sense of direction of where the country should go. Certainly, the new government has to reconcile the pro-market, essentially pro-EU, single-leader dimensions of Forza Italia with the decentralizing, anti-EU, anti-immigrant posture of the Northern League, with the nationalist, essentially state-interventionist, Euroskeptic soul of the National Alliance. While the entrepreneurship and leadership abilities of Silvio Berlusconi have given him a can-do aura, the months and years ahead will severely test them.

Silvio Berlusconi has the opportunity to lead the country for the full five years of the legislature and enact many of the difficult measures needed. It is to be hoped that he can attend to the task without undue obstructionism from his opponents, which could damage the country and their standing with public opinion as well. Matters are made more complicated by Berlusconi's conflict of interests (for which a solution should be found), but his majority seems solid and the Italians have voted him to get change. At the beginning of 2002, his popular support was even higher than eight months before, a result in no small measure attributable to his ease in front of the cameras and his outspokenness and decisiveness. Italians are not accustomed to seeing these traits in a government leader, and they obviously consider the change refreshing.

The opposition in the months following the defeat at the May 2001 elections appears disjointed and capable of criticizing (too often even with tiresome relentlessness) but not of proposing policy courses. Much hinges on the capabilities of the Margherita to develop greater cohesiveness and of the DS to shed the last remnants of a market-adverse heritage. Italy needs a parliamentary opposition which is strong, united, and clear and comprehensive in its policy prescriptions. The reemergence in the future of centrist coalitions, or worse, governments in which the center parties detached from the currently opposing coalitions join forces, would not be good for the country. The reconstitution of a center that swings its support in either direction and thus becomes the absolute arbiter of Italian political life would re-create the situation of domination without alternation that existed under the DC.

Two key parties of the two opposing coalitions, the DS and National Alliance, because of their noncentrist nature, stand much to lose from this scenario. It is to be hoped the Massimo D'Alema (DS) and Gianfranco Fini (AN) together with the emerging leaders in both their parties will continue on their road of moderation and push for reforms promoting a clear-cut bipolarism. The loser of the round of elections following such reforms could look at getting his chance the next time around, and the cycle of alternation that the country needs thus will continue on firmer footing.

## Thinking Critically

1. Explain why Italy was at the forefront of European integration.
2. What are the biggest economic challenges facing Italy?
3. What are the biggest political challenges facing Italy?
4. Have the policies of the center-left governments since 1996 been affected by the different members of the coalition?
5. How is each major coalition partner in the Berlusconi government likely to affect policy making?

## KEY TERMS

economic miracle *(304)*
great reforms *(306)*
privatization *(316)*
process development *(306)*
product development *(306)*
reconstruction *(303)*
*scala mobile (303)*
*Statuto dei Lavoratori* (Statute of Workers) *(307)*
"stop and go" policies *(311)*
submerged economy *(308)*
*Terza Italia* (the Third Italy) *(309)*

## FURTHER READINGS

Allen, Kevin, and Andrew Stevenson. *An Introduction to the Italian Economy* (New York: Barnes and Noble, 1975).

Baldassarri, Mario, ed. *The Italian Economy: Heaven or Hell?* (New York: St. Martin's, 1994).

Bank of Italy. *Annual Report.*

Bianchi, Andrea, et al. *The Italian Commonwealth* (Washington, DC: CSIS Press, 1999).

Bufacchi, Vittorio, and Simon Burgess. *Italy since 1989: Events and Interpretations* (New York: St. Martin's, 1998).

Burnett, Stanton H., and Luca Mantovani. *Italian Guillotine: Operation Clean Hands and the Overthrow of Italy's First Republic* (Lanham, MD: Rowman and Littlefield, 1998).

Caracciolo, Lucio, and Michel Korinman, eds. *What Italy Stands For* (Washington, DC: CSIS Press, 1997).

Cento Bull, Anna. *Social Identities and Political Cultures in Italy* (New York: Berghahn, 2000).

Cento Bull, Anna, and Mark Gilbert. *The Lega Nord and the Northern Question in Italian Politics* (London: Macmillan, 2001).

Gilbert, Mark. *The Italian Revolution: The End of Politics, Italian Style?* (Boulder, CO: Westview, 1995).

Lutz, Vera. *Italy: A Study in Economic Development* (London: Oxford University Press, 1962).

Newell, James L. *Parties and Democracy in Italy* (Burlington: Ashgate, 2000).

Partridge, Hilary. *Italian Politics Today* (New York: Manchester University Press, 1998).

Podbielski, Gisele. *Italy: Development and Crisis in the Post-War Economy* (Oxford: Clarendon Press, 1974).

Sassoon, Donald. *Contemporary Italy* (London: Longman, 1986).

Sechi, Salvatore, ed. *Deconstructing Italy: Italy in the Nineties* (Berkeley: University of California Press, 1995).

Tambini, Damian. *Nationalism in Italian Politics: The Stories of the Northen League, 1980–2000* (New York: Routledge, 2001).

# Web Sites

www.quirinale.it/
Site of the presidency of the Republic.

www.parlamento.it/
Site covering Parliament's two chambers.

www.palazzochigi.it/
Site of the prime minister.

www.cortecostituzionale.it/
Constitutional Court.

www.italia.gov.it
A portal by the Department for Innovation and Technology designed to assist Italian citizens in accessing government services.

www.forza-italia.it
Forza Italia.

www.perlulivo.it/
Olive Tree Movement.

www.casadelleliberta.net/
House of Freedoms.

www.dsonline.it/
Site of DS, Democrats of the Left.

www.alleanzanazionale.it
Site of National Alliance.

www.leganord.org/
Site of Northern League.

www.comunistiitaliani.it/
Site of the Pdci, Party of the Italian Communists.

www.rifondazione.it/
Site of Refounded Communism.

www.cdu.it/
Site of one of Christian Democrats' offspring.

www.federalismi.it
Site on federalism.

www.istat.it/
National Institute of Statistics; very useful.

www.bancaditalia.it/
Italy's Central Bank.

www.corriere.it/
One of Italy's main centrist newspapers; good archive.

www.repubblica.it/
Major Italian newspaper, more on the left than *Il Corriere*.

# Note

For this second edition, the author has relied almost exclusively on material in the Italian language not easily available in the United States and on numerous interviews with leading political scientists, economists, sociologists, legal scholars, journalists, and entrepreneurs.

# THE GOVERNMENT OF
# Spain

*Thomas D. Lancaster*

## INTRODUCTION

**Background:** Spain's powerful world empire of the sixteenth and seventeenth centuries ultimately yielded command of the seas to England. Subsequent failure to embrace the mercantile and industrial revolutions caused the country to fall behind Britain, France, and Germany in economic and political power. Spain officially remained neutral in World War I and II but suffered through a devastating Civil War (1936–1939). In the second half of the twentieth century, Spain became fully integrated into the Western European community of democratic countries.
Continuing concerns are large-scale unemployment and the Basque separatist movement.

### GEOGRAPHY

**Location:** Southwestern Europe, bordering the Bay of Biscay, Mediterranean Sea, North Atlantic Ocean, and Pyrenees Mountains, southwest of France

**Area:** 504,782 sq km

   *note:* includes Balearic Islands, Canary Islands, and five places of sovereignty *(plazas de Soberania)* on and off the coast of Morocco: Ceuta, Melilla, Islas Chafarinas, Penon de Alhucemas, and Penon de Velez de la Gomera

**Area—comparative:** slightly more than twice the size of Oregon

**Land boundaries:** 1,917.8 km

   *border countries:* Andorra 63.7 km, France 623 km, United Kingdom (Gibraltar) 1.2 km, Portugal 1,214 km, Morocco (Ceuta) 6.3 km, Morocco (Melilla) 9.6 km

**Climate:** temperate; clear, hot summers in interior, more moderate and cloudy along coast; cloudy, cold winters in interior, partly cloudy and cool along coast

**Terrain:** large, flat to dissected plateau surrounded by rugged hills; Pyrenees in north

**Elevation extremes:** *lowest point:* Atlantic Ocean 0 m

*highest point:* Pico de Teide (Tenerife) on Canary Islands 3,718 m

**Geography note:** strategic location along approaches to Strait of Gibraltar

## People

**Population:** 40,037,995

**Population growth rate:** 0.1%

**Birthrate:** 9.26 births/1,000 population

**Sex ratio:** 0.96 males/female

**Life expectancy at birth:** 78.93 years

*male:* 75.47 years

*female:* 82.62 years

**Nationality:** *noun:* Spaniard, Spaniards

*adjective:* Spanish

**Ethnic groups:** composite of Mediterranean and Nordic types

**Religions:** Roman Catholic 99%, other 1%

**Languages:** Castilian Spanish 74%, Catalan 17%, Galician 7%, Basque 2%

**Literacy:** *definition:* age 15 and over can read and write

*total population:* 97%

## Government

**Country name:** *conventional long form:* Kingdom of Spain

*conventional short form:* Spain

**Government type:** parliamentary monarchy

**Capital:** Madrid

**Administrative divisions:** 17 autonomous communities (*comunidades autonomas,* singular—*comunidad autonoma*)

**State Creation:** 1492 (expulsion of the Moors and unification)

**Constitution:** 6 December 1978, effective 29 December 1978

**Legal system:** civil law system, with regional applications

**Suffrage:** 18 years of age; universal

**Executive branch:** *chief of state:* King Juan Carlos I (since 22 November 1975)

*head of government:* President of the Government (prime minister) José Maria Aznar Lopez (since 5 May 1996); First Vice President Juan José Lucas (since 28 February 2000) and Second Vice President (and Minister of Economy) Rodrigo Rato Figaredo (since 5 May 1996)

*cabinet:* Council of Ministers designated by the prime minister

*elections:* the monarch is hereditary; prime minister proposed by the monarch and elected by the National Assembly following legislative elections; vice presidents appointed by the monarch on proposal of the president

**Legislative branch:** bicameral; General Courts or National Assembly or Las Cortes Generales consists of the Senate or Senado (259 seats—208 members directly elected by popular vote and the other 51 appointed by the regional legislatures to serve four-year terms) and the Congress of Deputies or Congreso de los Diputados (350 seats; members are elected by popular vote on party lists by proportional representation to serve four-year terms)

**Judicial branch:** Supreme Court or Tribunal Supremo, Constitutional Court

## Economy

**Overview:** Spain's mixed capitalist economy supports a GDP that on a per capita basis is 80% that of the four leading Western European economies. Its center-right government successfully worked to gain admission to the first group of countries launching the European single currency on 1 January 1999. The Aznar government has continued to advocate liberalization, privatization, and deregulation of the economy and has introduced some tax reforms to that end. Unemployment has been steadily falling but remains the highest in the EU at 14%. The government intends to make further progress in changing labor laws and reforming pension schemes, which are key to the sustainability of both Spain's internal economic advances and its competitiveness in a single currency area. Adjusting to the monetary and other economic policies of an integrated Europe—and further reducing unemployment—will pose challenges to Spain in the next few years.

**GDP:** purchasing power parity—$720.8 billion

**GDP—real growth rate:** 4%

**GDP—per capita:** purchasing power parity—$18,000

**GDP—composition by sector:** *agriculture:* 4%
*industry:* 31%
*services:* 65%

**Labor force:** 17 million (2000)

**Labor force—by occupation:** services 64%, manufacturing, mining, and construction 28%, agriculture 8%

**Unemployment rate:** 14%

**Currency:** euro (EUR)

# A. POLITICAL DEVELOPMENT

While experiencing the change from the twentieth to the twenty-first century, students of comparative politics have witnessed the dominance of democratic principles as the acceptable norms for political change. Countries in Eastern Europe, Latin America, and Asia are making the difficult change to democracy. Although the paths of democratic development are as varied and uneven as the countries themselves, the case of Spain stands out in the eyes of many as the very model for a peaceful transition to democracy. The "Spanish model" is frequently invoked in discussions about political reforms in many parts of the world.

The basic events in Spain's transition to democracy are now part of the historical record: the long dictatorship of General Francisco Franco following a bloody civil war (1936–1939); Franco's death in November 1975; the restoration of the monarchy several days later; King Juan Carlos I's behind-the-scenes encouragement of the peaceful dismantling of the old system; passage of the Law of Political Reform and its subsequent approval by referendum in December 1976; the first parliamentary elections in June 1977; the finalization and approval of the Constitution of 1978; new elections; and the peaceful alternation of power when the Spanish Socialist Workers Party (PSOE) won the October 1982 general elections. The broader historical, social, and economic contexts of this transition to democracy, however, are not as well known; espousal of the Spanish model necessitates a fundamental understanding of the relevant individuals, groups, organizations, and institutions that played a part in this transition and that have since become vital to Spain's democratic political system.

This introduction to the Spanish polity should help provide students with such an understanding. It proceeds in three parts. Section A gives a historical overview of Spanish politics, economics, and society. While introductory, it presents enough basic background to place later discussion of Spain's democratic institutions and processes in their broader context. Section B presents a general discussion of the contemporary Spanish political system. Besides political parties and voting, emphasis is placed here on the groups and political actors seeking a voice in Spain's democracy and the public institutions and structures within which their interests are articulated. Section C focuses on outcomes, both in terms of intended policy and unresolved problems and other challenges facing Spain's relatively new democratic system.

Taken as a whole, this analysis of Spain's democracy emphasizes two thematically related points. One prompts the student to question whether the uniqueness of the Spanish transition to democracy is something that can be emulated. Are the events and processes of the Spanish case unique and therefore nonreplicable in other countries? Second, despite being a country study, this chapter emphasizes the similarities of Spain's democratic polity with the other European political systems presented in this volume. Many of Spain's historical influences, political institutions, and social problems are, either explicitly or implicitly, considered comparatively. While democratic Spain is frequently raised as a model for successful political transitions, students should not miss the fact that in terms of crafting democracy, Spain has probably learned as much from other countries as it has passed on. Students should thus remain sensitive to similarities—they are at the heart of the comparative study of European politics. Comparative analysis seeks to discover similarities in patterns of political behavior in several countries, especially regarding basic issues in political developments.

## HISTORICAL BACKGROUND

Modern Spanish political affairs find their roots deep in the history of the Iberian peninsula. While certainly not the only place to begin, the year 1492 has an almost magical ring. Drilled in important milestones in Western civilization, students immediately think of Christopher Columbus and his explorations in the New World. The travels of Columbus and the Conquistadores fundamentally affected Spain's development. They embarked Spain on the building of an empire whose political, economic, and emotional impact dominated Spanish leaders for hundreds of years. Images of national grandeur did not rapidly leave Spain's collective psyche. They resurfaced at different times and through different individuals, and always with political consequences.

The year 1492 also marked three other important events in Spanish history. As with nostalgic memories of the Spanish empire, all three can be considered part of the search for Spanish unity. The Reconquest ended in 1492. The year thus marked the culmination of the belligerent removal of the Moors from the Iberian Peninsula. With a final victory early in the year, the Christian monarchs completed their protracted campaign against the Moors who had conquered most of the peninsula in 711 A.D. The Moors' presence for more than seven centuries influenced all aspects of society. Examples abound. Architecturally, marvelous mosques and other stylistic influences are at the heart of southern Spain's culture. Socially, the lighter complexions prevalent in northern Spaniards and darker complexions in the south physically help mark even today the general north-to-south pattern in the Reconquest's military campaign. Linguistically, the Moorish influence can be heard daily on the lips of all Spaniards. The Arabic language enriched modern Castilian Spanish with many words such as "Ojalá" meaning "if only . . ." or "I hope . . ." but etymologically derived directly from "if Allah (God) so wishes."

The final military victory of the Reconquest coincided in 1492 with the beginning of another cultural and religious quest for national unity—the Inquisition. This prolonged official pursuit of religious and cultural uniformity included the forced expulsion of all Jews who refused to convert to Christianity. During the Inquisition, the authorities tolerated little deviation from accepted interpretations of Catholicism.

Finally, the marriage of Ferdinand of Aragon and Isabella of Castile in 1492 politically united the Spanish state. This union brought together all the regions of Spain under the same administrative authority. Such state unity, combined with the attempts at cultural and religious uniformity, made Spain a superpower in the sixteenth century, along with France and England.

The year 1492 thus saw the emergence of a unified country led by skillful and ambitious monarchs who created one of the first modern states. Its building blocks included the institution of the monarchy—served by military, diplomatic, and bureaucratic staffs—and a unified and highly centralized organizational scheme despite many confederal components. These same elements—with their inherent advantages, tensions, and problems—remain a fundamental part of the modern Spanish political system.

## Modern Political History

Spain's military, economic, and political power of the sixteenth and seventeenth centuries left many Spaniards with a nationalistic sentiment that subsequent political reality could not fully satisfy. The eighteenth and nineteenth centuries were difficult times for Spain. For many, the country's past was greater than its prospects for the future. Poverty and economic hardship were difficult to accept, given the squandered fortunes and missed opportunities for a constructive use of the economic benefits reaped by the empire. For many, the eighteenth and nineteenth centuries meant an inward turn to romanticism, pessimism, and other "isms" that found expression in literature, art, and politics.

As with earlier times, broader trends in European politics influenced Spain's nineteenth-century development. Napoleon's forces conquered the country toward the end of the eighteenth century. This French occupation had two important consequences. First, most of Spain's overseas colonies, especially those in South America, learned they could administratively manage alone just fine. Following Spain's expulsion of the French from the peninsula, reassertion of administrative authority aggravated colonial relationships. Within a relatively short period, most of Spain's South American colonies gained their independence. Second, the war to remove

REVIEW

6.1

## KEY EVENTS IN SPANISH HISTORY

| | |
|---|---|
| Fifth century A.D. | Collapse of Rome, followed by three centuries of rule in Spain by Visigoths. |
| 711 | Moorish conquest of most of Iberian Peninsula. |
| 1492 | End of the Reconquest. Marriage of Ferdinand and Isabella, unification of Spain. Columbus's first trip to America. Beginning of the Inquisition. |
| 1580–1640 | Unification of Spain and Portugal. |
| 1588 | Defeat of the Spanish Armada by England. |
| 1705–1713 | War of Spanish Succession. Conflict ends with the establishment of Bourbon dynasty in Spain. |
| 1808 | French troops invade Spain, Joseph Napoleon placed on Spanish throne. |
| 1812 | Constitution of Cádiz. |
| 1833–1840 | First Carlist War. |
| 1870–1875 | Second Carlist War. |
| 1873–1874 | First Republic. |
| 1875 | Second Bourbon Restoration. |
| 1879 | Founding of Spanish Socialist Workers' Party (PSOE). |
| 1888 | Founding of General Union of Workers (UGT). |
| 1895 | Founding of Basque Nationalist Party (PNV). |
| 1898 | Defeat in Spanish-American War, loss of few remaining colonies. |
| 1902 | Alfonso XIII assumes Spanish throne. |
| 1923–1931 | Dictatorship by General Primo de Rivera. |
| April 1931 | Municipal elections won by Left. Alfonso XIII voluntarily leaves Spain. |
| 1931–1936 | Second Republic. |
| 1936–1939 | Spanish Civil War. |
| 1939–1975 | Dictatorship of General Francisco Franco. |

Napoleon's brother, Joseph Bonaparte, from power—referred to as the War of Independence in Spain and as the Spanish War in France—crystallized Spain's feeling of nationality. The earlier creation of a modern state was now complemented with the fulfillment of a sense of commonality, the two basic elements of the modern nation-state. Spain's defeat in the Spanish-American War of 1898, and the loss of its remaining possessions of Cuba, Puerto Rico, and the Philippines, produced an introspective questioning, much reflected in the literature of the early twentieth century. Following military defeat, Spain was left with only itself to worry about politically.

In most respects, the modern history of Spanish democracy begins with the proclamation of the Constitution of 1812 by the Cortes of Cádiz. This was the first genuinely Spanish constitution. Fernando VII abolished the Constitution of 1812 upon his return to Spain two years later. He ended Spain's first attempt at superimposing the principle of national sovereignty on the ancien régime. More importantly, it set the political tone for the nineteenth and the twentieth centuries: major political upheavals centered on the split between those supportive and those opposed to specific constitutions. While not following exact progressive-liberal and conservative-reactionary cycles, these confrontations generally arose from fundamental political questions. Specifically, they involved different answers to concerns about the ultimate source of sovereignty: the people in the liberal sense or the monarchy in a traditional sense. A politics of conflict and conspiracies characterized both the periods of constitutional rule based on the notion of popular sovereignty (the constitutions of 1812, 1837, 1869, and 1931) and those of joint sovereignty between the Crown and the Cortes (1834, 1845, and 1876).

Modern Spain's polemic between democratic and monarchical principles is best demonstrated by the fact that the constitutions based on popular sovereignty lasted only 20 years compared to 72 years for those dominated by monarchs (see Table 6.1). While fairly typical of the constitutionalism of continental Europe, the dominance of monarchical power led to cyclical periods of crises, violence, and changes of political regimes. It is within this context that one should view the Spanish Civil War of 1936–1939, the Franco regime, and the contemporary democracy.

### The First Republic

In 1868, a revolution overthrew Isabel II. It followed the degeneration of a classic *pronunciamiento,* an attempt by the military to take political power. A provisional government drafted the Constitution of 1869, establishing a constitutional monarchy. The monarchy of Amadeus of Saboya, however, commanded little support in this period of high political mobilization. Following his abdication, the Spanish First Republic was proclaimed on February 11, 1873. It survived only until December 29, 1874, when the monarchy was restored under Alfonso XII (Isabella II's oldest child). The First Republic's emphasis on federalism and socialism introduced Spain to concepts to which it would later return. In the meantime, a pattern of military involvement in politics continued.

Historically, the Spanish military has taken a direct and active role in politics. It usually starts with a *pronunciamiento,* the Spanish version of a coup d'état. Spain's tradition of the *pronunciamiento* is frequently misunderstood. While led by military forces, a *pronunciamento* has not tended to be particularly violent. In Spain it has served to lessen political conflict without a great deal of blood being spilt. As a matter of fact, in modern Spanish history, *pronunciamientos* tend to force the changing of the government without a shot being fired. This was essentially the case when the army seized power in 1923 under General Miguel Primo de Rivera. His authoritarian regime openly admired that of Mussolini's in Italy. Unfortunately for his sake, King Alfonso XIII too closely supported the ill-managed Primo de Rivera governments.

### The Second Republic

An overwhelming victory for republican candidates in the local elections of February 1931 ended the dictatorship of Primo de Rivera. Alfonso XIII left the country and the Second Republic was proclaimed. Following general elections, a new constitution was drafted and approved.

The Second Republic's constitution made Spain one of the most democratic European countries of its time. The preamble stated,

---

**TABLE 6.1**

**CONSTITUTIONS OF MODERN SPAIN**

| Constitution | Source of Authority | Orientation | Longevity (in years) |
|---|---|---|---|
| 1812 | Popular sovereignty | Progressive | 5–6 (nonconsecutive) |
| Royal Statute of 1834 | Monarch | Conservative | 3 |
| 1837 | Popular sovereignty | Progressive | 8 |
| 1845 | Monarch and Parliament | Conservative | 24 |
| 1869, First Republic (1873–1874) | Popular sovereignty | Progressive | 4 |
| 1876 | Monarch and Parliament | Conservative | 47 |
| 1931, Second Republic (1931–1939) | Popular sovereignty | Progressive | 8 |

"Spain is a democratic Republic of workers of all classes that is organized in a free and just system. All power comes from the people. The Republic constitutes an integral State, compatible with the autonomy of its municipalities and regions." The Second Republic thus institutionalized a democratic, secular, and decentralized set of governing principles. Its emphasis on religious, intellectual, and personal freedom clearly reflected its leftist orientation.

The political history of the Second Republic might be thought of in three distinct periods. The first (1931–1933) was led by leftist governments that pushed reform policies in agriculture, decentralization in Catalonia (Catalunya in the Catalan language, Cataluña in Castilian Spanish) and the Basque country (Euskadi), and reform of education and cultural policies. However, religious and military tensions rose. The second period (1933–1936) began with right-wing victories in municipal and general elections. Clashes occurred during this period over the suspension of the Agrarian Reform Law, the granting of amnesty to the rebels of an August 1932 abortive coup, a serious confrontation between the central government and Catalonia's Generalitat (regional parliament), and the army's brutal suppression (directed by Franco) of the October 1934 revolution in Asturias. With the Popular Front's victory in the February 1936 general elections, the Second Republic entered its third, and last, phase. This government, which included various parties of the Left including Socialists and Communists, swung back the policy pendulum. It resumed the agrarian reforms and the regional statutes for Catalonia, the Basque country, and ultimately Galicia. Violence escalated to the point that when a key leftist military figure was killed on July 12, 1936, the soldier's own troops retaliated and killed the rightist politician Calvo Sotelo, the conservative leader of the parliamentary opposition. Spain's civil war began five days later.

### The Spanish Civil War

Literally thousands of books have been written on the Spanish Civil War. Students interested in finding out more about the war can readily locate more books on the topic than any one person could possibly read. Those interested in the civil war from a military perspective might start with Hugh Thomas's classic *The Spanish Civil War.* For political and social background, read Gerald Brenan's *The Spanish Labyrinth*. Students with stronger literary interests might enjoy George Orwell's *Homage to Catalonia* and Ernest Hemingway's *For Whom the Bell Tolls.*

The Spanish Civil War began in July 1936 when military opponents of the Second Republic put into action a long-planned military coup. While conceived of in the Spanish tradition of a *pronunciamiento,* the events of 1936 and the subsequent civil war proved a historical aberration. The initial events demonstrated how the direction of an insurrection can be highly unpredictable once a military becomes politically mobilized. In 1936, generals throughout Spain led the initial rebellion: Mola in Navarre, Pamplona, and Saragossa; Queipo de Llano in Seville; Goded in the Balearic Islands; and Franco in the Canary Islands and Morocco. General Yagüe moved through Extremadura, and Mola took Irún. On September 29, 1936, Franco became commander of all the Nationalist forces and head of government. With the help of crucial military assistance from Nazi Germany and Fascist Italy, the Nationalist army made rapid advances against the Republican army. By the end of 1936, the Nationalists controlled most of southern, northwestern, and north-central Spain.

Following these early successes, the confrontation turned into a prolonged war of attrition. During this time, the Spanish Civil War became an international rallying cry, with the International Brigades and the Soviet Union supporting the Republicans, the Western nations including Great Britain and the United States maintaining a military embargo on both sides, and Mussolini's Italy and Nazi Germany assisting the Nationalists. Most fighting was concentrated in northern Spain in 1937. The following year the Republican zone was divided at Castellón. The Nationalists then won the bloody Battle of the Ebro, splitting the Republican forces and exhausting their resistance. Many Republicans began fleeing into France. Catalonia fell on February 10. Madrid surrendered on March 28. General Franco officially declared a Nationalist victory on April 1, 1939.

In placing the Spanish Civil War in its proper context, students should remember three general points. First, the Spanish Civil War was a domestic conflict in that it reflected the clear division of Spanish politics and society into camps of the Left and Right. This division began early in the nineteenth century. Compromise had become increasingly elusive. The lack of a political solution unfortunately led Spaniards to the barracks and battlefields. Second, the civil war was an international affair. Coming when it did in the 1930s during the height of Fascism in Europe and immediately prior to World War II, both belligerents found support and aid from beyond Spain's borders: the Nationalist forces under Franco received aid from Fascist regimes; the Republican government, while subject to the arms embargo, received aid from the Soviet Union and the International Brigades. In many respects, the Spanish Civil War was a trial run for World War II. Third, the war's extraordinary costs in human and physical terms left a deep scar on Spain's collective psyche.

Estimates of the civil war's cost vary widely. The validity of any set of figures of casualties and destruction depends on many factors, including which side collected them. Perhaps more importantly, the civil war took an enormous psychological toll. When the war's military events stopped, the hatred and bitterness did not. Partisans on both sides remained quick to recall the thousands of executions and other killings carried out behind the military lines against, and frequently by, the civilian population. The victor's harsh political repression after the war and the economic hardship all Spaniards had to endure did not ameliorate such sentiments. Yet the people's sheer exhaustion following the war partly explains their passivity to the subsequent Franco regime. The division of society, and the severe price paid by all in human terms, cast a heavy shadow on the Franco regime for the next 35 years.

The memory of the civil war was so strong that some four decades later it clearly framed negotiations during the transition to democracy. Following Franco's death in 1975, everyone sought to avoid a repetition of the tragedy of the Spanish Civil War, regardless of ideology. A painful collective memory unquestionably guided members of the political elite who directed the country's transition to democracy. The price for failure in political reforms was obvious to all. The country knew too well the cost borne for the demise of Spain's previous attempt at democracy.

***The Franco Government***    Characteristic of many right-wing authoritarian systems, the Franco regime fundamentally overlapped the executive, the legislature, and the judiciary. Equally indicative of the regime's dictatorial nature, Franco served as both head of state and head of government until June 1973, when he appointed Admiral Luis Carrero Blanco as prime minister. Even after this, and until his death in November 1975, Franco clearly dominated governmental affairs. Throughout his rule, emphasis on the concept of "the unity of Spain" institutionally centered around him. As Caudillo, all powers ultimately resided in him. Those in other executive, legislative, or judicial positions were eventually accountable to him and only him.

In 1969 the Franco regime approved an Organic Law of the State regarding questions of leadership succession. This law created some institutional diffusion of power toward the end of Franco's life. Yet even after 1969 and prior to his death, Franco still used reserve powers to govern by decree when he did not wish to go through his Council of Ministers. Nevertheless, the Organic Law of 1969 made institutional adjustments that later proved instrumental to the manner in which the transition to democracy unfolded. These included limited choice in electing members from certain "families" to an organic parliament, the Cortes.

***Franco's Parliament***    Students of comparative politics frequently misunderstand the nature of authoritarian regimes. Sensitivity to the different varieties of nondemocratic political systems is important. For example, one should give attention to the notion of representation in many authoritarian regimes like Franco's. While clearly limited, the Cortes did contain an element of representation. Reflective of Franco's distrust of liberal democracy, representation was consistent with the corporatist philosophies of the 1930s witnessed in Mussolini's Italy. Cortes members came from various sectors of Spanish society. Frequently viewed in terms of vertical divisions of society—that is, the Church, syndical labor organizations, professional groups, and so on—such representation was based more on the principles of "organic democracy."

As a consequence of the regime's selection and screening process, the Cortes in fact served to rubber-stamp Francoist policies. It had no power of parliamentary control over the government, it rarely debated, and certain topics such as foreign policy and the maintenance of public order were off limits. In considering Franco's authoritarian regime, however, students should nevertheless ask why a dictator would bother to go through the motions of establishing such a legislature.

## The Transition to Democracy

As Franco grew older, many Spaniards accepted the notion that significant change would have to wait until after his death. The price one would have to pay to oppose him directly, the slowing of the regime's inertia, and Franco's advancing age suggested time itself was key to any changes in Spain's political system. Events in Francoist Spain, however, did not stand still. Two of the most important include the 1969 Law of Succession and the assassination of Carrero Blanco.

The succession of a dictator is always a tricky issue. If the appointment is made by the dictator himself, he runs the risk of creating his own rival. If the decision is postponed until after his death, a succession crisis often ensues, with power struggles by competing groups and individuals that destabilize the system. The problem of succession can be even more formidable when one adds the question of the monarchy, as was also the case in Italy and Greece after World War II.

The Nationalist forces fought the Spanish Civil War with a strong rightist vision of the unity of the nation. While heavy in rhetoric and emotion, the most institutionalized expressions of this vision could be found in the army itself, the Church, and the state. The last of these most importantly included questions about the monarchy. As a symbol of the unity of Spain since 1492, Spain's throne had remained unoccupied since

1931 when Alfonso XIII left the country (he never officially abdicated) and the Second Republic was proclaimed. Early in his rule, Franco promised a full restoration of the monarchy. The problem, however, was that Alfonso XIII died while in exile and his son, Don Juan, was known to have a liberal orientation. He was thus not compatible with Franco's vision for Spain.

Throughout much of his authoritarian regime, Franco strategically avoided naming a successor. As he grew older, however, it was apparent to all that such an important decision could not be avoided forever. Franco finally proposed in 1969 that the Cortes should restore the monarchy upon his death, but by skipping over Don Juan and making Don Juan's son Juan Carlos the next King of Spain. Thus from 1969 until 1975, Juan Carlos, the grandson of Spain's last reigning king, became "Prince of Spain" (not the normal "Prince of Asturias") and waited until Franco's death to become King.

A second critical, but often overlooked, event in the chronology of Spain's transition to democracy occurred on December 20, 1973. Admiral Luis Carrero Blanco, who as prime minister was probably Franco's handpicked successor for governmental affairs, attended church. As he left in his automobile, a powerful bomb placed under the street exploded, blowing the car over the church into a nearby courtyard. The Basque nationalists of Basque Homeland and Freedom (ETA) carried out this assassination. Gruesomely violent, this killing altered the course of events in Spain. Carrero Blanco had been committed to carrying forward Franco's traditions. His successor as head of government, Carlos Arias Navarro, proved more reformist-oriented, although possibly from a position of weakness. When Franco died in November 1975, Arias Navarro's government had managed to advance a series of important moderate reforms for political liberalization, including the legalization of "political associations," which passed the Francoist Cortes in December 1974.

These events, along with the world's condemnation of Franco following the execution of ETA members in 1970 after the Burgos trials, played a central role, in retrospect, in the direction of Spain's political reforms. Franco's death on November 20, 1975, however, clearly proved to be the watershed of post–civil war Spanish political history.

Two days after Franco's death, Juan Carlos became King of Spain, taking an oath of allegiance before the Cortes of the Francoist regime. Juan Carlos then adroitly utilized the Francoist laws to engineer fundamental changes. An early and critical step came in July 1976. He named Adolfo Suárez prime minister (president of the government) after successfully maneuvering to get Suárez's name placed on the Cortes's short list of candidates. Suárez, a virtual political unknown in Spain at the time, had been the general secretary of the Francoist political movement. With the King's endorsement, he worked behind the scenes to choreograph the delicate political reforms that would make Spain a democracy.

In October 1976 the most amazing event occurred in Spain's transition and, at the time, was unique in the history of democracy. By a vote of 424 to 15 with 13 abstentions, the Francoist Cortes approved Adolfo Suárez's Law on Political Reforms. Among other things, this law established a new bicameral parliament and provided for free elections. In passing the bill, the Francoist Cortes peacefully committed collective suicide by voting itself out of existence. As explained by Paul Preston in *The Triumph of Democracy in Spain* (1986), this vote was "based on the ingrained habits of obedience to authority, an inflated sense of patriotism and, above all, tempting promises whispered in the ears" (p. 101). In a December 1976 referendum, the Spanish people approved the Law on Political Reform by an overwhelming majority. Steps toward democratic reform came rapidly after this.

In February 1977, the Council of Ministers administratively legalized most political parties by issuing a decree replacing the registration process of the Francoist single-party system. In March, it approved an election law for Parliament. In April, after some judicial considerations, the Suárez government surprised many, and upset others such as the High Army Council, by legalizing the Spanish Communist Party (PCE). The government then called elections. On June 15, 1977, Spain held its first democratic elections since 1939. As discussed below, Prime Minister

Suárez's own right-of-center coalition of parties, the Union of the Democratic Center (UCD), won.

The new parliament's primary task was to write a new, democratic constitution. This was done with a great deal of hard work and key compromises between the UCD and the largest parliamentary opposition party, the Spanish Socialist Workers Party (PSOE). In a popular referendum, the Spanish people approved the Constitution on December 6, 1978. With its goal accomplished, Suárez dissolved Parliament and called for new elections. On March 1, 1979, Adolfo Suárez and the UCD were reelected as the first government under Spain's new democratic constitution.

***Reform by Agreement***    The legal transformation of the Franco regime into a Western European–style parliamentary democracy made Spain's transition to democracy unique at the time. A new democratic system emerged with the essential approval, even if by acquiescence, of the Francoist establishment. The transformation clearly involved negotiations and compromises between the successors of Franco and the democratic opposition. This style of change came to be known as reform by agreement (*reforma pactada*) or breakthrough by agreement (*ruptura pactada*), depending on one's point of view. Amazingly, the entire process essentially entailed the rejection of the Francoist past, a stepping aside willingly or the entering into a new set of (democratic) rules of the game by most of the Francoist elite, and the replacing of the victors of Spain's bloody and bitter civil war with those that ideologically sided with the losers. The amazing aspect of this change was that it occurred peacefully.

Unquestionably, Spain's transition to democracy would not have been as peaceful or successful without the key role played by Juan Carlos. As Franco's designated successor, he clearly guided the country in a direction different from the one Franco anticipated or desired. He legitimized the negotiated transition and democracy itself. He asserted his democratic principles both publicly and privately in elite negotiations at critical junctures in the process. Equally important, his presence neutralized the military by maintaining its loyalty to him and the institution of the monarchy.

## KEY EVENTS IN DEMOCRATIC SPAIN

| | |
|---|---|
| November 20, 1975 | Francisco Franco dies. |
| November 22, 1975 | Juan Carlos sworn in as King of Spain. |
| December 1975 | Carlos Arias Navarro, prime minister under Franco, forms new government. |
| July 3, 1976 | King Juan Carlos I requests Adolfo Suárez to form government. |
| December 15, 1976 | Referendum on Law on Political Reform approved overwhelmingly. |
| June 15, 1977 | First general elections, won by UCD. |
| July 6, 1977 | Adolfo Suárez forms UCD government. |
| December 6, 1978 | Constitution approved in national referendum. |
| March 1, 1979 | Second general elections, won by UCD. |
| August 8, 1979 | Granting of autonomy to Catalonia. |
| February 23, 1981 | Taking of the congress, military coup attempt. |
| February 25, 1981 | Leopoldo Calvo Sotelo becomes prime minister following Suárez's resignation. |
| June 1981 | Enactment of divorce law. |
| December 1981 | Parliamentary approval of Spanish membership in NATO. |
| August 1982 | Adolfo Suárez quits the UCD. |
| October 1982 | Third general elections, overwhelmingly won by PSOE; Felipe González becomes prime minister. |
| June 1985 | Spain and Portugal sign Treaty of Adhesion to the European Community. |
| November 20, 1985 | Tenth anniversary of Franco's death; major demonstrations by rightists in Madrid; anti-NATO demonstrations. |
| January 1, 1986 | Spain and Portugal officially become members of the European Community. |
| January 30, 1986 | Felipe, Prince of Asturias, sworn in as heir apparent to Spanish throne; act reaffirms the continuation of Spain's constitutional monarchy. |
| March 12, 1986 | NATO referendum; yes vote wins by small margin. |
| June 22, 1986 | Fourth general elections; PSOE retains majority. |
| December 2, 1986 | Manuel Fraga resigns as leader of AP. |
| November 10, 1987 | Spain informs United States that agreement on U.S. bases will not be extended. |
| January 15, 1988 | U.S. promises to remove F-16 fighter planes from Spain to preserve remaining military presence in country. |
| February 22, 1988 | Julio Anguita elected PCE leader, succeeding Geraldo Iglesia. |
| December 14, 1988 | General strike led by UGT and CCOO against PSOE government; country paralyzed. |
| January 22, 1989 | Popular Alliance reorganized as Popular Party. |
| April 12, 1989 | New ETA attacks end three-month truce; breakdown of ETA-government talks in Algiers. |
| September 4, 1989 | José María Aznar, personal choice of Manuel Fraga, chosen as PP candidate. |
| October 29, 1989 | Fifth general elections, PSOE victorious again, gains exactly half of Congress's seats. |
| November 12, 1989 | Dolores Ibárruri dies. |
| December 17, 1989 | Former PP leader Manuel Fraga elected leader of regional government in Galicia. |
| November 11, 1990 | PSOE formally breaks ties with UGT at party conference. |
| May 27, 1991 | Adolfo Suárez resigns as CDS leader. |
| April 1992 | Seville Expo '92 opens. |
| May 28, 1992 | General strike against PSOE government. |
| July–August 1992 | Twenty-fifth Summer Olympic Games held in Barcelona. |

(continues)

REVIEW

6.2

### KEY EVENTS IN DEMOCRATIC SPAIN, (continued)

| | |
|---|---|
| November 25, 1992 | Parliament ratifies Maastricht Treaty establishing the European Union. |
| April 1, 1993 | Don Juan de Borbon, father of King Juan Carlos, dies at age 79. |
| June 6, 1993 | Sixth general elections, PSOE forms minority government with support from CiU. |
| April 19, 1995 | ETA blast slightly wounds José María Aznar, saved only by armor plating of car. |
| October 25, 1995 | Proposed PSOE budget defeated following CiU withdrawal of support. |
| December 15, 1995 | Madrid holds European Summit at end of six-month EU presidency. |
| February 14, 1996 | ETA assassinates former head of Constitutional Court, Francisco Tomás y Valiente. |
| March 3, 1996 | Seventh general elections, PP's José María Aznar becomes prime minister. |
| November 4, 1996 | Supreme Court decides not to press ETA-related "Dirty War" charges against former PSOE Prime Minister Felipe Gonzalez and two others. |
| June 22, 1997 | Joaquín Almunia elected as PSOE new leader. |
| October 6, 1997 | Trial begins against leadership of Herri Batasuna (HB), charged with collaborating with ETA. All 23 member of executive committee later imprisoned. |
| May 25, 1998 | "Dirty War" trial begins. Former PSOE ministers charged with kidnapping Basque business leader. Several later sentenced to ten years in prison. |
| September 16, 1998 | ETA begins new cease-fire. Talks with government fail when ETA's demand for self-rule referendum rejected. ETA resumes violence shortly thereafter. |
| February 2, 2000 | PSOE and IU form alliance for upcoming general elections. |
| March 12, 2000 | Eighth general elections. PP wins outright majority. Aznar remains prime minister. |
| July 23, 2000 | José Luis Rodríguez Zapatero elected new PSOE leader. |
| October 16, 2001 | ETA announces its violence campaign has failed, claims it will search for political solution. |

Section B of this chapter contains a more in-depth discussion of the Spanish political system following the transition to democracy. It also elaborates some points relevant to contemporary Spain's political affairs touched upon thus far in this brief historical discussion. Prior to this discussion, however, we turn to some basic physical, social, and economic facts about Spain.

## SOCIETY AND THE ECONOMY

### Physical Characteristics

Spain occupies about 84 percent of the Iberian Peninsula, and additionally includes the Balearic Islands to the east, the Canary Islands off the northwest coast of Africa, and the two tiny North African enclaves of Ceuta and Melilla.

Several features dominate Spain's geography. Its location in Europe's extreme southwest corner does not make it one of the continent's crossroads. This isolation influenced much of Spain's history. Its geographical position, however, presents some important advantages, such as principle North Atlantic maritime routes. Spain's extensive coastlines, on both the Atlantic and the Mediterranean, have given it a strong maritime orientation. Economically, fishing and shipbuilding have traditionally been important.

Physically, the land of the Iberian Peninsula contains at least two sharp contrasts. Spain is an extremely mountainous country, with an average altitude exceeded in Europe only by Switzerland. Its mountains have added to the country's isolation. The Pyrenees in the north cut Spain off from the rest of Europe at the isthmus. The Betica mountain range in the south and the Cantabrian and Galician ranges in the west and north separate it from the sea. These mountains form walls that remind many of a fortress. The interior of the peninsula is, in contrast, dominated by the vast Meseta Plateau. This tableland is Spain's cultivation area for the typical Mediterranean agricultural trilogy of wine, wheat, and olives. Other grains and livestock are also produced. Throughout much of its history, the Meseta essentially served as the border for the Kingdom of Castile. This fact is central to Spanish history, given Castile's extension of political and cultural control to the rest of the country.

## The Regions

The geographical features of the Iberian Peninsula and its relative isolation produced through the centuries many "different Spains" or a "Spain of regions." Knowledge of these different regions is fundamental to appreciate fully Spain's contemporary political system. The old Kingdom of Castile shaped different historical regions on the Meseta: León and Old Castile in the northern Meseta; New Castile, including La Mancha in the center; and Extremadura to the southwest. Murcia was part of Castilian expansion toward the Mediterranean Sea. The vast region of Andalusia in southern Spain has long rivaled the Meseta in agricultural production and is best known for its wines and sherries. It, like the region of Valencia to the east, also produces vegetables and fruits, especially oranges. The rugged area of Galicia, north of Portugal, is Spain's and one of Europe's most important fishing regions. Adjacent to Galicia, Asturias and Cantabria, given their mountainous terrain, were essential to the early years of the Reconquest. Asturias holds Spain's most important coal deposits. It also produces an excellent fermented apple cider. Between the Meseta and the Pyrenees are Navarre and Aragón. Navarre, with Pamplona as its major city, was formed from the ancient Kingdom of Vasconia. Aragón, like Navarre, has historically had important military significance. Passing through it were the routes between the Meseta and the French Midi, the Road of Saint James (used by European religious pilgrims on the way to Santiago de Compostela in Galicia) and roads heading eastward to the Mediterranean and Central Europe through Catalonia.

In the Iberian Peninsula's north-central part, at the western end of the Pyrenees separating Spain and France, is the Basque country (Euskadi). Since the early nineteenth century, Euskadi has been an economic engine of growth for Spain: Basque iron, cooperatively produced with Asturian coal, provided the base for a powerful iron and steel industry. At the other, eastern, end of the Pyrenees lay Catalonia. Its agricultural production has long coexisted with the other of Spain's most prosperous manufacturing and industrial regions. Catalonia, with Barcelona as its major urban area, possesses large textile and chemical industries and produces many consumer goods. Given Catalonia's early industrial development and its proximity to the rest of Europe, Barcelona has long been considered Spain's most international city, one exposed earliest and strongest to all major European political influences. Allied with Catalonia, Aragón conquered and occupied Valencia and the Balearic Islands, which formed the heart of the Kingdom of Aragón.

## The Societies: Nationalism and Language

For students of European politics, the importance of regional diversity in Spain is more social and political than geographical. The distinctiveness of Spain's regions, with all their political implications, are most readily noticeable in terms of the multinational nature of Spanish society. Directly stated, the Spanish state includes many different nations of people.

Linguistics play an important part in the politics of Spain's multinationalism. The contemporary peoples of the Iberian Peninsula speak a rich variety of languages. Castilian is what most people think of as Spanish. Via politics, government, and coercion, the peoples of the Meseta have linguistically come to dominate much of the rest of the peninsula. Besides Portuguese, however, many other languages and dialects have survived. Euskera, the Basque language, and

Catalan are the most distinctive. Gallego, Valencian, and Mallorcan in the Balearic Islands are also spoken. Many dialects, including Andalusian, are distinctive but linguistically fall into one of the other groups.

As seen in our later analysis, the politics of the regions, the politics of language, and all other types of polities are impossible to separate in democratic Spain. During the Franco years, the public speaking of non-Castilian languages, especially Euskera, was repressed. In contrast, democratic Spain greatly facilitates, and to the dismay of some, even encourages the use of these other languages in many aspects of public life. How and why such language usage and other expressions of cultural distinctiveness have occurred is discussed in several places in this chapter.

## The Population

Spain has a population of about 40 million people. (There are approximately 82 million in Germany, 59 million in the United Kingdom, 59 million in France, 57 million in Italy, 10.6 million in Greece, and 10 million in Portugal.) The population has doubled since 1910. The greatest impact from changes in the distribution of Spain's population has come in rural-to-urban migration. Such movement has altered the country's social and political fabric. For example, the provinces of Barcelona and Madrid accounted for 9.8 percent of Spain's total population in 1900. This has grown to 17.2 percent in 1940, 26.3 percent in 1970, and 28.3 percent in 1991. That this dropped back to 24.5 percent by 1998 suggests the growth of other urban areas as well. Such rural-to-urban migration was typical for many European countries in the twentieth century. For Spain, however, it reflects a fundamental shift from an agricultural-based society to a much more urban one.

## The Economy

Spain has traditionally possessed an agricultural-oriented economy. As mentioned earlier, the agricultural basis of the economy varies from region to region. Many of the products are well known, particularly given their export value: the fruits and vegetables of regions like Andalusia, Valencia, and Catalonia dominated by the Mediterranean climate; the wines of places such as La Rioja and the sherries of southern Spain; and the olives and grains of much of the peninsula. Along with the fishing of Galicia and other coastal areas, such agricultural strengths characterized the Spanish economy for many centuries and provided a fundamental base to sustain its people.

Europe's industrialization, however, impacted Spain in the same manner as in many other countries—unevenly. While Spain's rural areas generally remained virtually unchanged until only a few decades ago, the country's urban parts have long been heavily industrialized, urbanized, or both. Of particular note is Catalonia, especially Barcelona, with its textile and machine industries, the Basque country with its heavy industry such as steel production and shipbuilding, and much more recently, the financial and government-driven economy of Madrid. As in many other European countries, modern economics is frequently an economics of the cities. Increasingly Spain's economy has followed this pattern. It is also why the country now finds a very large percentage of its working population in the service sector.

Spain has thus long possessed two economies, one agricultural and the other "modern." The real story of the Spanish economy, however, is its rapid move from one to the other. During the twentieth century, Spain went in an extremely short period of time from being a third world economy to one of the world's largest. Its development into one of the ten largest economies in the world requires a discussion of political economy.

## Francoist Economic Policy

Following the civil war, the Franco regime embarked on an inward-looking policy of economic development known as autarky. Borders were closed to foreign goods, services, and capital. Based on the assumption that Spain had enough resources for self-provision, autarky as an economic policy also matched the conditions Spain found itself in internationally. The Western world isolated Spain diplomatically following World War II, given its affinity with the losing countries of Nazi Germany and Fascist Italy, even though Spain officially remained neutral during the war. Strong state intervention supplemented the policy of economic protectionism. The Francoist state set prices as well as interest rates. It organized most industrial development through a huge public holding company, the National Institute of Industry (INI). The obvious failures of the autarkist policies forced Franco to rethink his economic polices by the late 1950s. Despite the change of economic course marked by the Stabilization Plan of 1959, many of the institutional features of this period of autarky remained in place, some such as the INI (now called SEPI) even to this day.

Franco's reform of his economic policies, while leaving the political system as repressive as ever, ushered in what came to be known as "the Spanish economic miracle." During the 1960s and into the 1970s, the Spanish economy grew faster than that of any other European country. The economy boomed, employment opportunities induced changes in many people's lives, and consumer possibilities began to bring Spain up to European standards.

Many of these reforms of economic liberalization emulated France. They opened Spain's borders to foreign goods and capital. Increased trade spurred rapid growth in production. Increased imports, caused in part by increased national income, reflected the country's acute need for capital and raw materials and the Spanish economy's low competitiveness. While paralyzing balance-of-trade deficits were always a problem, Spain avoided them through its appeal as a favorite tourist destination, remittances sent home by Spanish guest workers in Europe's more developed countries, and foreign investment.

Despite these reforms, the Spanish economy remained a heavily state-centered economy. High custom tariffs remained to protect many domestic industries from foreign competition. The national economy remained rigid. State economic paternalism and protectionist policies minimized and frequently distorted market forces. State planning, development, and financing emphasized the industrial sector—primarily steel and shipbuilding as well as traditional textiles and footwear. Comparative advantage and competitiveness were based on cheap labor and the suppression of worker unrest. The latter policies were aided by Spain's large workforce, especially the increase in women and the many unskilled workers who had left agriculture for the cities. Even with the enormous growth of Spain's service sector and strong emigration during the 1960s, Francoist Spain could not maintain full employment. As mentioned below, the unemployment picture has at times grown even darker in contemporary Spain.

Several problems converged on the Spanish economy in the mid-1970s. One was international in origin. The world energy crises of 1973–1974 and 1979 and the subsequent economic recession jolted Spain's economy, given its almost total dependence on foreign petroleum and strong need for outside capital. Another problem was structural. The Francoist economic system with its protective and state-centered characteristics simply did not possess the flexibility to adjust to this newest shock. The third problem was political. Franco died in November 1975. Spain was thus in the middle of an economic crisis when the country embarked on its difficult transition to democracy. While painful to many, Spain's political concerns took precedence over the economic problems.

## The Moncloa Pacts

One of the most significant events in the transition to democracy came in the area of macroeconomic policy. Highly indicative of Spain's policy-making style during the transition, political, economic, and governmental leaders signed a series of broad agreements in 1977 at the Moncioa Palace, the prime minister's official residence. These "Pacts of Moncloa" signaled elite-level agreement between the political parties, employers' associations, and trade unions on wage increases and income policies, among other things, in exchange for limits on labor union work stoppages, commitments to initiate structural reforms, a moderately restrictive monetary policy, and a devaluation of the peseta. While directed at the economic conditions Spain faced, the Pacts of Moncloa were generally more important politically than economically. They bought basic economic and social peace and postponed Spain's needed economic adjustments. This delay permitted more focused attention on the political task at hand—the consolidation and institutionalization of democracy. This example of politics before economics is why the Pacts of Moncloa proved to be only the first in a series of such elite agreements. Others included the Acuerdo-Marco Interconfederal in 1980, the National Employment Agreement in 1981, and the Economic and Social Agreement in 1984 (see Table 6.2).

# CULTURE: SOCIAL AND CIVIL

Spain's economic and political changes in the twentieth century fundamentally altered society. Three areas in which these changes had the greatest impact are in the areas of education, religion, and the press.

## Education

Extensive reform characterizes the structure and administration of formal education in Spain since the transition to democracy. Prior to 1970, preschool education was extremely limited, primary school was far from universal, secondary education primarily private and elitist, and only

## TABLE 6.2

### SOCIAL-ECONOMIC PACTS IN DEMOCRATIC SPAIN

| Year | Pact | Signatories |
|------|------|-------------|
| 1977 | Moncloa Pacts | Political parties in Congress |
| 1980 | Interconfederal Framework Agreement (AMI) | UGT, CEOE |
| 1981 | National Employment Agreement (ANE) | Government, CEOE, UGT, CCOO |
| 1983 | Interconfederation Agreement (AI) | CEOE, CEPYME, UGT, CCOO |
| 1984 | Economic and Social Agreement (AES) | Government, CEOE, CEPYME, and UGT |
| 1994 | Interconfederal Agreement to Regulate Labor Ordinances & Regulations | CEOE, CEPYME, CCOO, and UGT |
| 1996 | Tripartite Agreement for Extra-Judicial Resolution of Labor Conflicts (ASEC) | Government, CEOE, CEPYME, CCOO, and UGT |
| 1996 | Tripartite Agreement on Professional Training | Government, CEOE, CEPYME, CCOO, and UGT |
| 1997 | Interconfederal Agreement for Employment Stability (AIEE) | CEOE, CEPYME, CCOO, and UGT |
| 1997 | Interconfederal Agreement on Collective Bargaining (AINC) | Government, CEOE, CEPYME, CCOO, and UGT |
| 1997 | Interconfederal Agreement on Coverage Gaps (AICV) | Government, CEOE, CEPYME, CCOO, and UGT |
| 1997 | Agreement over Part-Time Work | Government, CCOO, and UGT |
| 2000 | Third Agreement on Continuous Training | Government, CEOE, CIG, CCOO, and UGT |
| 2001 | Second Social Agreement on Extra-Judicial Resolution of Labor Conflicts | CEOE, CCOO, and UGT |
| 2001 | Interconfederal Agreement for Collective Bargaining 2002 (ANC 2002) | UGT, CCOO, CEOE, CEPYME |

a privileged minority could enter a university. Changes began to occur with the economic expansion of the 1960s. The General Law on Education (LGE) of 1970 overhauled Spain's educational system. In democratic Spain, the Law on University Reform (LRU) in 1983, the Organic Law of Rights to Education (LODE) in 1985, and the more extensive 1990 Education Law (LOGSE) all fundamentally changed Spanish education. The last of these, the Organic Law for the General Structuring of the Education System, established a new system that has recently been implemented.

Spain now has four basic levels of education: preschool (to age 6); general basic education (EGB)/primary education; secondary education/pre-university (BUP) and technical training; and university. One part of the most recent reforms increased compulsory education from age 14 to 16.

Indicative of Spain's spectacular educational expansion of the last 30 years or so, preschool and compulsory education are now virtually universal. Secondary and pre-university education reaches about 65 percent of the eligible youth. University education has clearly reached the level of mass education, enrolling more than 1.5 million students, some 30 percent of that age group.

Politically, education policy at all levels is deeply embedded in Spain's regional question. The Constitution of 1978 outlines governmental responsibilities for education. Spain's central administration retains control of matters such as basic legislation, basic standards of quality and organization, and certification and degrees. Remaining responsibilities and administrative tasks are increasingly being devolved to the autonomous communities (Spain's system of regional government). These include the universities and lower-level schools that instruct in non-Castilian languages—in Catalonia, the Basque country, Galicia, Valencia, the bilingual parts of Navarre, and the Balearic Islands. Local governments provide for the maintenance of preschools and elementary schools.

The Popular Party's clear majority in the 2000 general election permitted it to end a long-standing political deadlock in higher educational reform. The PP government's strong majority enabled it to pass a reform law in December 2001 that seeks to modernize university administration, devolve more responsibilities to the regions, and address the universities' chronic shortage of funding. Highly controversial, the law also seeks to reform two of Spanish universities' most dominant characteristics. First, it hopes to alter the pattern in which about of one-third of the students never graduate and many repeat courses simply to delay entry into a tight labor market. Second, it proposes to end traditional clientelistic recruitment practices for faculty by which key professors hire their own institutions' favorite graduates, who then serve as the professors' assistants. The law outlines a system of national tests and a central applicant pool from which universities will choose their faculty.

The Spanish educational system is thus in a period of rapid change. Many different influences account for this. Spain's rapid social and economic growth during the 1960s and 1970s placed increased pressure on governmental authorities for greater access to formal instruction. The transition to democracy prompted concerns about the equality of educational opportunities, the incorporation of the teaching of democratic values, and the elimination of discrimination and inequality in a multilingual and multicultural state. Thus, as will be discussed later, the autonomous communities have increasingly taken on greater responsibilities in providing education, including its financing. Simultaneously, the Catholic Church has solidified its position in the Spanish education system. Approximately one-third of all nonuniversity education in Spain is private, with Catholic education counting for about one-fifth of the entire system. Finally, in terms of influences on Spanish education, the European Union has established certain European-wide educational standards and goals. It has also facilitated the exchange of educational material and established exchange programs for both students and teachers.

One final comment needs to be made about education. Spanish women have greatly benefited from the rapid enlargement of the country's education system. The growth rate reflects women's greatly increased access to secondary and higher education. As a matter of fact, female students outnumber males at both the secondary and university levels. (A slightly higher percent of male students receive technical education.) The role of women in Spanish society is slowly changing. Aspects of "machismo" clearly still remain, since societies tend to change slowly. As seen in education, however, the state has taken a leading role in pushing for a greater degree of gender equality. This also applies to such areas as hiring for the state bureaucracy, the government's promotion of Spain's divorce law in 1981, and the encouragement of positive images and role models. While Spain clearly has room for improvement, its democratization and Europeanization has greatly altered the role of women in this Iberian country.

## Religion and the Church

Spain is a Catholic country. There are, however, two ways to consider the Catholic Church in Spain. One is the Church as a social and religious institution. The other is the Church as a political actor. Both are important for a full understanding of the history, culture, and politics of Spain.

As a religious institution, the Church clearly influences the people of Spain. Because of its involvement in births, baptisms, marriages, and funerals, most Spaniards maintain at least nominal affiliation with the Church. The Church's role in education, including four Catholic universities (there are 48 public and 12 private ones), has also been strong. As with most other European countries, the secularization of Spanish society has greatly diminished the impact of the Church on people's daily lives. Services tend to be sparsely attended and primarily by the elderly. As in many European countries, comments can frequently be heard about the increasing "irrelevance" of the Church and its problems of being "out of touch" with the people. This is especially true with younger Spaniards.

Politically and historically, the Church played a central role in the polarization of Spanish society in the nineteenth and twentieth centuries. For several centuries, the Church supported nondemocratic forces in Spain; it has historically aligned itself with the authoritarian Right and traditionally stood firm against anticlerical liberals and the Left. The Church strongly supported Franco's Nationalist forces during the civil war; it openly favored a new regime led by Franco over the government of the Second Republic. This is, nonetheless, only the most recent example of how the Church long provided legitimacy to antidemocratic forces in Spain.

Throughout the Franco period, the Church wielded power as one of Spain's "real powers," along with the military and the financial and banking system. The longevity of the Franco regime affected Church-regime relations. As the years passed, the Spanish Church's embrace of Franco's authoritarian regime increasingly came to be questioned by significant numbers of the Spanish clergy, and even Rome itself. The liberalization of the Roman Catholic Church under the papacy of John XXIII moderated the Spanish Church's stance in political and social affairs.

To its credit, the Church generally supported the most recent transition to democracy. Moderation of its anti-Marxism, combined with a similar softening by the Spanish Communist Party, helped prevent the polarization characteristic of the past. While generally supporting democratic reforms, the Church hierarchy, through the Episcopal Conference, has spoken out against specific social policies, for example arguing strongly against a liberalized divorce law. Nevertheless, the Church's shift in position during the contemporary democracy has aided in the healing of one of Spain's most persistent social and political cleavages.

## The Press

Freedom of speech and the free circulation of ideas is a central part of all definitions of liberal democracy. The mass media are therefore crucial to any country's newly acquired exercise of democracy. In Spain, the media reflect many of the country's recent political trends.

The press was strongly repressed during the Franco dictatorship. For many years this included severe censorship. Following the 1966 Law of Press and Printing, state control of the press relied more on a system of fines, suspensions, and occasional closures. The effects, however, were the same. Criticism of the Franco regime and issues it stood for, such as religious and social conservatism, quickly drew the authorities' attention. Repression of the press ended with the transition to democracy.

In most respects, the Spanish press today resembles that found in other Western European democracies. To reach this condition following such a long period of state repression meant a great deal of rapid growth. The Madrid-based newspaper *El País* is the greatest success story. It was founded in the very early days of the transition as a progressive daily, and its high quality quickly established it as Spain's most widely circulated newspaper. It is also well-received around the world. As seen in Table 6.3, a strong competitor is the conservative *ABC*, a daily also published in Madrid. *La Vanguardia* and *El Periódico* are published in Barcelona. They are most frequently read in Catalonia. Other daily newspapers abound in Spain, with approximately 145 currently publishing. Most are local or regional papers. In Spain, the majority of newspapers experience their strongest sells on weekends. *El País*'s Sunday edition, for example, sells about one million copies. Sports dailies such as *Marca* and *AS* are also quite successful, and economic newspapers and supplements to existing papers are increasingly doing well.

By European standards, Spain's statistic of newspapers sold per capita is quite low. Two factors help explain this, both with political implications. One is that each copy tends to be read by many people, estimated at between four and five persons per issue. This suggests Spaniards tend to share more among family members and circles of friends than citizens of Great Britain, France, and Germany. Second, reader loyalty is high. Spaniards tend to read a single paper consistently, one that mirrors their political ideology and social values. Such a political link to information gathering unquestionably affects attitudinal formation in Spain.

Changes in radio and television also reflect Spain's political transformation. Radio's initial

### TABLE 6.3

#### MAJOR DAILY NEWSPAPERS IN SPAIN, 1999

| Paper | Circulation |
| --- | --- |
| El País | 450,176 |
| Marca | 417,456 |
| ABC | 302,013 |
| El Mundo del Siglo XXI | 272,299 |
| El Periódico (Cataluña) | 230,724 |
| La Vanguardia | 212,202 |
| AS | 140,378 |
| El Correo Español/El Pueblo Vasco | 133,032 |
| Sport | 121,015 |
| La Voz de Galicia | 105,533 |
| El Mundo Deportivo | 102,480 |
| El Diario Vasco | 95,061 |
| Heraldo (Aragón) | 65,851 |
| Diário de Navarra | 62,489 |
| Expansión | 59,021 |
| Levante-El Mercantil Valenciano | 55,751 |
| Las Provincias | 55,652 |
| La Nueva España | 54,979 |
| La Verdad | 42,351 |
| Información | 41,391 |

*Source:* Oficina de Justificación de la Difusion (OJD)/Circulation Adit Office, 1999.

surge in worldwide popularity in the 1930s corresponded with Spain's political upheavals in the Second Republic and the civil war. The Franco regime further paralyzed radio's development by outlawing news broadcasts on anything other than the government-controlled Radio Nacional de España (RNE) or, after 1960, by requiring other licensed stations to carry simultaneously RNE's news broadcasts. Such severe restrictions and strong government control ended with democracy. The 1977 Decree on Information and Freedom and the issuance of FM station licenses initiated a period of rapid growth in Spanish radio. Today the state-owned Radio Nacional de España owns more than 250 stations of all types—AM, FM, and short wave, and both national and local ones—but the private SER network has more listeners. COPE, owned by the Catholic Episcopal Conference, is the second largest private radio network, and Onda Cero with over 170 stations is owned by the National Organization for the Blind (ONCE). Most regions have radio stations that broadcast for local and regional audiences, including broadcasts in the area's language. Thus, in a relatively short period, Spanish radio has gone from a system controlled by the state to a highly competitive one with over 2,000 stations.

Despite the obvious technological constraints that make it different from radio, Spanish television has experienced some of the same changes. From its first broadcast in 1956, the Franco regime treated television as a public service. As with radio, state control was important politically. However, television was and is even more politically important because Spaniards watch it a great deal; some 90 percent of all Spaniards watch television on a daily basis. Spanish Television and Radio (RTVE, now just TVE) established the country's second channel in 1965. As with other media, the Franco regime strictly controlled broadcast content on both channels (this is one reason Spaniards watched so many old John Wayne movies).

All this began to change in democratic Spain for two reasons. Specific to Spain, in the 1980s public television created nine regional networks in addition to TV1 and TV2, the two countrywide channels. New regional networks included numerous stations in Catalonia, the Basque country, Madrid, and Valencia. The regionalization of Spanish television grew out of the need to address regional issues and questions of language that had again become politically important. Second, and generalizable to all modern countries, in the 1990s cable and satellite technologies provided private television companies increased opportunities to take advantage of the elimination of the state monopoly in television. Several private TV networks began operations in Spain in the 1990s. These include Antenna 3, Tele 5, and Canal Plus.

## Thinking Critically

1. What physical, social, and economic characteristics have placed the concept "the unity of Spain" at the center of Spanish political history? How did this concept manifest itself politically in the twentieth century?
2. Even though historically separated by four decades of the Franco regime, how did the Spanish Civil War influence the country's transition to democracy? What is the role of social and political memory in political development in a country like Spain?
3. While making their own transitions to democracy, what aspects of the "Spanish model" are other countries most likely to emulate?
4. How has political and economic development coincided in Spain? What is the relationship between political change and economic development?

## Key Terms

autarky *(341)*
Caudillo *(335)*
Conquistadores *(331)*
Inquisition *(331)*
National Institute of Industry (INI) *(342)*
Nationalists *(334)*
*pronunciamento (333)*
Reconquest *(331)*
Republicans *(334)*

## Further Readings

Beiberg, Marianne. *The Making of the Basque Nation* (Cambridge: Cambridge University Press, 1989).

Bonime-Blanc, Andrea. *Spain's Transition to Democracy* (Boulder, CO: Westview Press, 1987).

Brassloff, Audrey. *Religion and Politics in Spain: The Spanish Church in Transition, 1962–96* (New York: St. Martin's, 1998).

Brenan, Gerald. *The Spanish Labyrinth: An Account of the Social and Political Background of the Spanish Civil War* (Cambridge: Cambridge University Press, 1960).

Carr, Raymond. *The Spanish Tragedy: The Civil War in Perspective* (London: Weidenfeld and Nicolson, 1977).

Carr, Raymond, and Juan Pablo Fusi. *Spain: Dictatorship to Democracy* (London: Allen and Unwin, 1979).

Díez Medrano, Juan. *Divided Nations: Class, Politics, and Nationalism in the Basque Country and Catalonia* (Ithaca, NY: Cornell University Press, 1995).

Gunther, Richard, ed. *Politics, Society, and Democracy: The Case of Spain* (Boulder, CO: Westview Press, 1993).

Gunther, Richard. "Spain: The Very Model of the Modern Elite Settlement," in John Higley and Richard Gunther, eds., *Elites and Democratic Consolidation in Latin America and Southern Europe* (Cambridge: Cambridge University Press, 1992).

Hemingway, Ernest. *For Whom the Bell Tolls* (New York: Scribner's, 1943).

Lancaster, Thomas D., and Gary Prevost, eds. *Politics and Change in Spain* (New York: Praeger, 1985).

Orwell, George. *Homage to Catalonia* (London: Secker and Warburg, 1986).

Pérez-Díaz, Victor M. *The Return of Civil Society: The Emergence of Democratic Spain* (Cambridge, MA: Harvard University Press, 1993).

Preston, Paul. *The Triumph of Democracy in Spain* (London: Methuen, 1986).

Preston, Paul. *Franco: A Biography* (London: HarperCollins, 1993).

Share, Donald. *The Making of Spanish Democracy* (New York: Praeger, 1986).

Thomas, Hugh. *The Spanish Civil War,* rev. ed. (New York: Harper and Row, 1977).

# B. POLITICAL PROCESSES AND INSTITUTIONS

Contemporary Spain's democratic system can best be described as a constitutional monarchy with a parliamentary form of government. Spelled out in the Constitution of 1978, the overall system has many similarities with other Western European polities. Thus in discussing and analyzing the institutional arrangements of democratic Spain, we should bear in mind its European context. Drawing similarities with other countries such as the United Kingdom, Germany, and Italy is necessary for a complete understanding of the Spanish political system.

The King of Spain—currently Juan Carlos I—is the head of state. Spain's monarchy carries essentially the same responsibilities as the British monarchy. Spain's King symbolizes the unity of the country, reflects the centrality of the state, and embodies the essence of the Spanish people. With several important distinctions discussed below, powers and concerns for everyday public affairs rest not with the King but with his prime minister, the head of government.

In its institutionalization of a parliamentary democracy, the Constitution of 1978 placed Spain within the norm of contemporary European polities. As in Great Britain and Germany, executive powers in Spain are vested in the prime minister (President of the Council of Ministers). In classic parliamentary fashion, the prime minister chooses the members of his cabinet. This "government" is then approved by Parliament. Becoming prime minister generally depends on the ability to muster the support of a majority of Spain's lower house of Parliament, the Congress of Deputies.

## THE SPANISH PARTY SYSTEM

Any student of European politics should immediately recognize the importance of political parties. Unlike in the United States, most political recruitment, issue development, and policy formulation occurs through well-organized political parties. In Europe, political parties are central to the functioning of liberal democracy. The devel-opment of Spain's democratic system is in many respects synonymous with the development of its party system. The party system clearly reflects the major social cleavages of the country.

## Social and Political Cleavages

Two dominant and one historically based cleavages are important to an introductory understanding of the Spanish political system. The two dominant cleavages are the traditional left-right ideological orientation and a central-regional split. The other, a secular-religious division, can still be found in contemporary Spanish politics but has become less pronounced since the end of the Franco regime. It is also partially subsumed by the left-right cleavage.

*Ideology*   Despite the end of the Cold War and the extensive changes in European party systems it brought about, the traditional left-right ideological scale remains a useful—even if not always totally precise—manner to generalize about European party systems. This applies to Spain as well. Few would question the placement of the United Left on the ideological left. Besides its very name, the Communist Party of Spain (PCE) remains the most important party within the United Left. Similarly, the Popular Party is consistently referred to in the Spanish press as a moderate-right party. While more difficult to place, given its ideological movement toward the middle and its strong liberal economic policy orientation, the Spanish Socialist Workers Party (PSOE) is generally referred to as a moderate-left party.

*Central-Regional Cleavage*   Spain is a multinational country. Multinationalism strongly influences the politics of democratic Spain in many ways. This is certainly true of the party system. Many of Spain's historical regions have produced political parties reflecting interests of that area. For example, the Basque National Party (PNV) is a moderate-right party from the Basque country, and the Convergence and Union Party (CiU) is in some respects its counterpart in

Catalonia. In contrast, the Popular Party and the PSOE tend to be more centrally based, desirous of an electoral base as broad as possible throughout Spain. The central party headquarters of these two nonregional parties are, symbolically and logistically, located in Madrid.

***Party Descriptions*** As with any new democracy, and certainly witnessed in the early 1990s in Eastern Europe, Spain's party system went through an initial shaking-out period. Many parties participated in the elections of 1977 and 1979, but many did not gain lasting support. Many "parties" that contested the elections were in fact little more than a name and someone's telephone number. We will limit our discussion to parties that have gained entry into the Spanish Parliament.

Two sets of parties constitute the party system in Spain. The "centralist" parties are those that are generally directly comparable to the better-known parties of other European polities. Primarily based in Madrid, they tend to represent the traditional left-right cleavage found in most European political systems. Spain's "nationalist" and regional parties reflect the country's central-regional cleavage as well as the more generalizable left-right divisions. The existence of both sets of parties makes Spanish politics complex and intriguing. Unless one is careful, it also makes it somewhat difficult to fully appreciate.

The essence of Spain's party system can graphically be captured along two dimensions. Figure 6.1 depicts this two-dimensional variation in Spain's party system. The precise placement of each party in any political system is always open to question. Parties also change over time. The general point here, however, is that Spain contains both a central party system and many regional party systems, yet all compete at the many different levels of electoral competition.

## The Central Parties

### *The Democratic Center Union and the Social and Democratic Center Parties*
As suggested throughout this chapter, the name Adolfo Suárez is key to the story of Spain's transition to democracy. As the King's choice as

prime minister in 1976 to establish democracy, Suárez headed a government that legalized political parties. Its eventual calling of elections in 1977 produced for Suárez a need to form his own political base. Prime Minister Suárez thus founded the Union of the Democratic Center (UCD) as his vehicle to engage in competitive party politics. Despite being a loose grouping of 13 or so small parties ranging from moderate-left social democrats to moderate-right economic liberals, and with christian democrats covering this entire ideological span, the UCD served its purpose and produced victories for Suárez in the new democracy's first two general elections. Always on the verge of splitting apart, the party found that the holding of government power provided a certain degree of cohesion. Suárez's UCD formed minority governments after each of these two elections and proved instrumental in giving Spain's democratic system the moderate, centrist orientation it has today.

The UCD, along with the Socialist Party as the main opposition in Parliament after the 1977 and 1979 elections, dominated the writing of the 1978 Constitution. However, as with many top-down-created parties, such as the various Gaullist-inspired parties in France, numerous internal differences within the UCD continually resurfaced despite the allure of being in power. The UCD started a rapid decline when Suárez surprisingly resigned as prime minister in 1981 and shortly thereafter left the UCD. Leopoldo Calvo Sotelo served the remainder of Suárez's term as prime minister. As seen in Table 6.4, the UCD feebly competed in the 1982 general elections and received only 6.8 percent of the vote as the incumbent party. Without the coherence that Suárez provided as leader, the UCD disintegrated shortly after this election. Its members either joined other parties or simply left politics. Never before in the history of European politics had a party gone so rapidly from being the incumbent party to leaving politics for good.

The reasons for Suárez's leaving the UCD and his position as prime minister are still not totally clear. Most probably they can be attributed to the UCD's internal problems, since Suárez almost immediately founded another party—the Social and Democratic Center Party

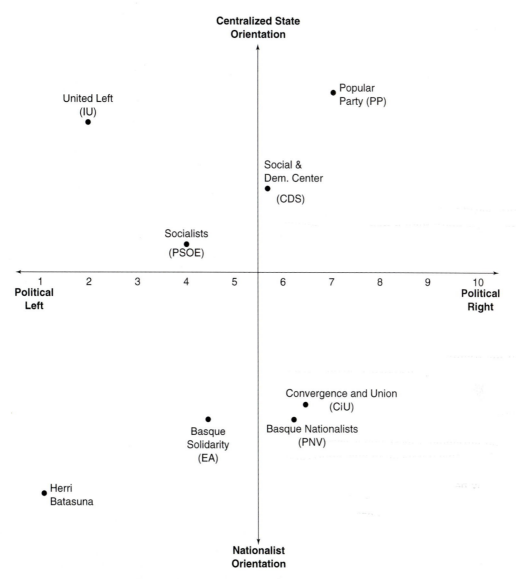

**Figure 6.1 IDEOLOGICAL POSITIONS OF THE SPANISH PARTY SYSTEM, ON TWO IMPORTANT DIMENSIONS**

(CDS). This new party competed against the UCD and the other parties in the 1982 general elections, winning 2.9 percent of the vote. It also provided Suárez with a seat in Parliament. With the UCD's demise, the CDS took advantage of its centrist position to do relatively well, by small-party standards, in the 1986 and 1989 general elections. Given the CDS's social democratic orientation, Suárez's party might have made an attractive coalition partner for the Socialist Party—much like the position the Free Democrats have played in government formation in the

**TABLE 6.4**

**SPANISH GENERAL ELECTIONS, 1977–2000 (PERCENTAGE OF VOTE AND NUMBERS OF SEATS)**

| Year | Popular Party | UCD/CDS | PSOE | PCE/United Left | CiU | PNV | Others |
|------|--------------|---------|------|-----------------|-----|-----|--------|
| 1977 | 8.4 | 34.8 | 30.3 | 9.3 | 2.8 | 1.7 | 12.7 |
|      | (16) | (165) | (118) | (20) | (11) | (8) | (12) |
| 1979 | 6.5 | 35.0 | 30.5 | 10.8 | 2.7 | 1.7 | 12.8 |
|      | (9) | (168) | (121) | (23) | (8) | (7) | (14) |
| 1982 | 26.5 | 6.8+2.9 | 48.4 | 4.1 | 3.7 | 1.9 | 5.7 |
|      | (106) | (12)(2) | (202) | (4) | (12) | (8) | (4) |
| 1986 | 26.1 | 9.2 | 44.3 | 3.8 | 5.1 | 1.5 | 10.0 |
|      | (105) | (19) | (184) | (7) | (18) | (6) | (11) |
| 1989 | 25.4 | 7.8 | 39.6 | 9.2 | 5.3 | 1.3 | 11.4 |
|      | (107) | (14) | (175) | (17) | (18) | (5) | (14) |
| 1993 | 34.8 | 1.8 | 38.7 | 9.6 | 5.0 | 1.2 | 8.9 |
|      | (141) | (—) | (159) | (18) | (17) | (5) | (10) |
| 1996 | 38.9 | — | 37.5 | 10.6 | 4.6 | 1.3 | 7.1 |
|      | (156) | (—) | (141) | (21) | (16) | (5) | (11) |
| 2000 | 44.6 | — | 34.1 | 5.5 | 4.2 | 1.5 | 11.1 |
|      | (183) | (—) | (125) | (8) | (15) | (7) | (12) |

*Note:* Congress of Deputies has 350 seats.

Federal Republic of Germany—had the PSOE not won an outright majority in the 1982 elections.

Suárez's retirement from active politics in the early 1990s along with that of several other key party leaders placed the CDS in the same unfortunate position as the UCD in 1981—as a party unable to survive beyond the departure of its founder. The CDS also miscalculated when it formed a local and autonomous communities pact with the Popular Party in June 1989. The Socialist's electoral victory that year highlighted the CDS's strategic misjudgment. The other insurmountable problem was the continued drift toward the ideological center by both the Popular Party from the right and the Socialist Party from the left.

***The Popular Party***  As the largest and most important party on the ideological right, the Popular Party demonstrates how political parties can adapt under democratic pressures. Founded in

1977 as the Popular Alliance (AP), the Popular Party (PP) initially provided a political home for many former Francoist officials and other conservatives who sought to remain engaged in public affairs in the new democracy. Manuel Fraga, a Francoist Minister of Information and Tourism, founded the Popular Alliance and was its first leader. While the party claimed to adhere to democratic principles, the political background of many of the party's leaders raised questions with potential voters about its commitment to the new system. AP's policies reinforced its image as a party on the Right, but clearly not as far right as Francoist pretenders like Blas Piñar and his New Force Party. Attracting much attention but few votes, Blas Piñar's party openly advocated a continuation of the nondemocratic past.

Popular Alliance struggled in its early years to leave behind the questions about its commitment to democracy. As seen in Table 6.4, the Popular Party fared poorly in Spain's first two democratic elections. However, by 1982 the PP had successfully made some inroads with its strategy of advocating moderate-right positions on many issues. In that year the PP also benefited from the demise of the UCD, drawing former UCD activists and voters from the moderate right. With the PSOE victory that year, the PP became Spain's main opposition party in Parliament. In this role, the PP increasingly moderated its position, transforming itself into the moderate-center party it is today, fulfilling a role in the Spanish party system similar to that of the Conservative Party in Great Britain and the Christian Democratic Party in Germany. The party's leadership changes, from Manuel Fraga to Antonio Hernández Mancha and then to José María Aznar as its present leader, suggests the PP's concerted efforts to leave behind all association with the Francoist past and successfully compete in Spain's democracy as a mass party on the moderate right. This strategy has clearly worked, as the party has steadily gained in electoral success.

The Popular Party emerged from the March 1996 general elections as Spain's largest party. Shortly thereafter, José María Aznar became contemporary democratic Spain's fourth prime minister. Under his leadership, the Popular Party formed a minority government with the support of several key regional parties. In the March 2000 general elections, this government won a strong vote of confidence from the Spanish people when it won an outright parliamentary majority. As discussed below, such a majority makes it much easier for Aznar and his Popular Party to govern without first making significant political compromises.

The contemporary Popular Party encourages market-oriented solutions to Spain's economic problems. As a strong advocate of privatization of many public services and companies, the party draws strong support from organized business and small-business people and entrepreneurs. It also increasingly appeals to a new generation of younger Spaniards who have politically matured during the years of PSOE government. Oriented toward fiscal conservatism, the PP advocates a lowering in the amount of taxes Spaniards must pay. As a strong defender of the Spanish state, it appeals to nationalist Spaniards on questions of foreign affairs, pro-military policies, and more centralist regional developments. Given the absence of a formidable christian democratic party in Spain, the Popular Party appeals to conservative social and religious Spaniards.

### The Spanish Socialist Workers Party

Unlike the PP and the UCD or the CDS, the Spanish Socialist Workers Party (PSOE) predates the current democratic system. Founded in 1879 by Pablo Iglesias, the PSOE is one of Spain's oldest parties. It thus has a long and rich history that can be drawn on in difficult times. With some interesting historical parallels with the German Social Democratic Party, the PSOE grew from Marxist inspiration. Its leftist orientation before and during the Second Republic—advocating land reform, workers' rights and control, and social progress—brought it into direct conflict with the historic forces of the Spanish right—the military, the Church, and the economic elites. Nationalist forces under Franco targeted PSOE activists during the civil war. Many were killed in combat and others were executed. The PSOE and most other parties were outlawed by the Franco regime. Many of PSOE's surviving leaders remained in exile during the most repressive periods of his rule. Other, frequently younger, members such as Felipe González clandestinely worked for the party within Spain.

The PSOE's historical legacy presented the party certain organizational advantages as the Spanish party system reconstructed itself in 1976–1977. The youthful nature of the party's leadership also helped—the length of the Franco regime prevented much continuation in PSOE leadership from the Second Republic. Felipe González became PSOE's secretary general in 1974. On behalf of his party, González was thus in position to take advantage of the political events following Franco's death in 1975.

As seen in Table 6.4, the PSOE emerged from the 1977 general elections as Spain's second largest party, thus making it the main parliamentary opposition party to the UCD government. Under González's leadership, the PSOE used this position to formally modify the party's ideological orientation, to make pragmatic proposals for democracy's development,

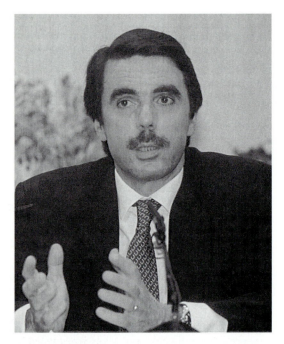

José María Aznar, prime minister of Spain since 1996 and leader of the Popular Party.

and to leave behind the party's Marxist roots. Such modifications brought the PSOE in line with most other major socialist parties in Western Europe, such as the French Socialist Party, the British Labour Party, and the German Social Democratic Party.

These ideological changes had three important consequences. First, the PSOE moved toward the political center. Its responsible behavior in leading the parliamentary opposition between 1977 and 1982 attractively projected it as an alternative government. The PSOE electoral victory in 1982 and the subsequent alternation of power from the UCD to the PSOE was a significant event in twentieth-century Spanish political history: The losers in the civil war peacefully replaced a UCD government full of members who started their political careers as Francoists. Second, the PSOE's position on the center-left in Spain's party system facilitated the preservation of the Spanish Communist Party on the Left while

helping to squeeze out smaller centrist parties. Third, as with most mass parties, such ideological and policy changes maintained several competing currents within the party. Throughout the PSOE governments from 1982–1996, two main groups of party activists were found in the PSOE: supporters of González and the direction in which he has taken the party, and followers of PSOE's "number two" person, Alfonso Guerra. The Guerristas believe the party has abandoned too many of its historic roots in the quest for power. A similar ideological schism, discussed below, exists in the socialist labor union, the General Union of Workers (UGT).

The PSOE's electoral defeat in the March 1996 returned the party to the parliamentary opposition for the first time in 14 years. As is often the case with European political parties following an extended period in power, the PSOE has gone through a difficult period of adjustment in the post-González period. Elected as the party's new general secretary in June 1997, Joaquím Almunia opted, among many other leadership decisions, to challenge Prime Minister José María Aznar and his Popular Party in the March 2000 general elections in a coordinated manner with Spain's other major party on the left, the United Left. This electoral strategy proved unsuccessful. This defeat prompted the party to question again its leadership. In July 2000, the PSOE elected José Luis Rodríguez Zapatero as its new secretary general and Manuel Chaves as its president.

Despite these leadership changes, the Spanish Socialist party continues to represent a moderate social democratic philosophy. It has pressed forward on issues of social and individual rights, including equal rights for women, and has made considerable progress on structural and political solutions to Spain's regional question. While in government from 1982–1996, the PSOE made Spain a loyal and trusted member of the community of democratic nations in Europe. Its embrace of many liberal economic policies, however, simultaneously prompted many people to question its socialist label. While in government the PSOE was also increasingly accused of corruption. Although the party was clearly tainted by political scandals during its later years in power, many Spaniards would nevertheless agree that the PSOE's long period in power greatly facilitated Spain's sinking of deep democratic roots.

### The Spanish Communist Party

The Spanish Communist Party (PCE) began as a splinter party of the PSOE in 1921 following the Second International's breakup. As a small party, the PCE remained eclipsed by the PSOE throughout much of its early history. The PCE remained active during the Second Republic as a key part of the political left during this period of ideological polarization, including participating in the 1936 Popular Front government.

With the outbreak of the civil war, the significance of the Spanish Communist Party far surpassed what its electoral strength and number of members would suggest. This occurred for several reasons. First, in the absence of U.S. and British assistance, the Soviet Union became the Republic's primary source of military aid. Stalin made sure this aid was funneled locally through the Spanish Communist Party. This control over supplies placed the PCE in a highly advantageous position relative to other competing interests within the Republican forces. Second, unlike the anarchists (particularly strong in Catalonia) and even the socialists, the PCE called for a postponement of the Marxist revolution in Spain in order to defend the Republic. Such a position reflected Moscow's broader-based foreign policy interests and its influence on the PCE. Third, the Spanish Communist Party was the Second Republic's best organized anti-Nationalist resistance force, in a manner similar to Marxist parties in other countries such as the French Communist Party during the heyday of the French Resistance to the Nazis. The PCE successfully organized the defense of Madrid during the civil war's early years. Santiago Carrillo, the PCE's long-standing secretary general, played a leading role in organizing Madrid's defense, and Dolores Ibárruri—known as "La Pasionaria"—provided much needed inspiration to the anti-Fascism forces.

Following the Civil War, PCE activists who managed to survive either lived in exile in places such as France and the Soviet Union or maintained very low profiles within Spain. During the Franco years, the PCE slowly and clandestinely developed an impressive organizational base despite being outlawed. Most activities occurred through the Workers Commissions (CCOO), the communist labor union that secretly grew up within Franco's official labor syndicates. As PCE secretary general, Santiago Carrillo provided crucial leadership from exile in Paris, including taking the party in a Eurocommunist direction, much like the Italian Communist Party under Enrico Berlinguer. In terms of party orientation, the PCE's adoption of Eurocommunism meant pursuing distinctive national adaptations of Marxism, dropping its revolutionary orientation, and severing direct ties with Moscow.

Legalized in 1977 shortly before the first general election, the PCE generally took conciliatory positions regarding Spain's democratic developments, including acceptance of the monarchy as an important defender of its right to operate legally as a party. The 20 PCE representatives elected in this first election generally cooperated in passing the 1978 Constitution, even supporting Article 15, which mentions the Catholic Church. The importance of the PCE's helping to avoid extreme ideological polarization at this critical juncture and to consolidate Spain's democracy cannot be overemphasized.

At its Ninth Congress in April 1978, the PCE dropped the terms "Leninist" and "hegemony of the working class" from its self-description. Such moderation was not accepted by all PCE members. Intraparty conflict continued to boil over when the powerful and autonomous Catalan wing of the party—the Unified Socialist Party of Catalonia (PSUC)—rebelled against what it perceived as Carrillo's authoritarian manner. As seen in Table 6.4, such internal ideological and leadership division seriously hurt the party in the 1982 and 1986 elections. The PSOE's victories in these elections also drew away some of the PCE's support.

Following this difficult period and under new leadership, first Gerardo Iglesias and then Julio Anguita, the party rebounded. During the centrist-moving PSOE governments of 1982–1996, the PCE firmly established itself as a moderate-left alternative. Similar to other Eurocommunist parties such as the Italian Communist Party (now the Democratic Party of the Left), the PCE responded to the changes following the collapse of the Soviet Union by altering how it presented itself. The PCE contested the 1989 election with other leftist parties—the Socialist Action Party (PASOC) and the Independent Republican Left (IR). This association was then made permanent, as the PCE is now integrated into, and remains the largest party within, the United Left (IU).

As mentioned above, the IU entered into an electoral coalition with the PSOE for the 2000 general elections. As seen in Table 6.4, this proved an electoral disaster. The IU lost almost half its support from the previous election, dropping from 10.6 to 5.5 percent of the vote. Partly as a consequence, Julio Anguita stepped down as the General Coordinator of the IU and the Secretary General of the Spanish Communist Party. Under the leadership of Francisco Frutos, who replaced Julio Anguita in both positions in October 2000, the IU has returned to its goal of providing voters on the Left an alternative to the PSOE. Given its ability to attract a small but loyal group of voters, the IU should be viewed as one of Spain's three largest central parties along with the PSOE and the Popular Party.

## The Nationalist Parties

***The Basque Nationalist Party***    Sabino Arana founded the Basque Nationalist Party (PNV) in 1895 to promote the Basque language and culture. Until the current democratic system, the PNV was the only party available for the political expression of nationalistic sentiment in the Basque country. The PNV is a conservative Catholic party with a strong nationalistic orientation. During Spain's contemporary period of democracy, it has pushed hard for greater autonomy for the Basque provinces within the Spanish state. During negotiations on the 1978 Constitution, the PNV worked to have the Spanish state explicitly recognize the rights of the Basque people and to provide for greater autonomy from Madrid. As a moderate-conservative party, the PNV expresses its nationalism without arguing for independence from Spain. During the

1985–1986 period, one part of the party split over issues about relations with Madrid and the role of the Basque government in Vitoria. This new party took the name Eusko Alkartasuna (EA), which means Basque Solidarity.

***Euskal Herritarrok***    The left-wing nationalist party Euskal Herritarrok ("We Basques") earlier went by the name Herri Batasuna ("Basque United People"). The change in name reflects the party's dubious suggestion that it is no longer the direct political arm of Euskadi Ta Askatasuna (Basque Homeland and Freedom). This violent organization is better known by the initials ETA. In some respects analogous to the relationship between Sinn Fein and the Irish Republican Army (IRA), Euskal Herritarrok clearly advocates an independent Basque state, specifically a socialist one. Founded in 1978 as Herri Batasuna, Euskal Herritarrok has done quite well in general elections and in contests at the autonomous community level. Such support clearly signals that some people seriously question the basic legitimacy of the Spanish state, even with its current system of democracy. Interestingly, and another sign of the party's orientation, Herri Batasuna/ Euskal Herritarrok deputies who have been elected to the Congress in Madrid have generally refused to take their seats there. Several highly publicized events have centered on these deputies' refusal to take the parliamentary oath because it includes a swearing of allegiance to the Spanish constitution.

***The Convergence and Union***    The Catalan equivalent to the Basque Nationalist Party is the Convergence and Union Party (CiU). The CiU is in fact two parties. The most dominant of these is Democratic Convergence of Catalonia (CDC). The current President of Catalonia, Jordi Pujol, founded it in 1974. The other party incorporated into the CiU is the Democratic Union of Catalonia. The UDC is a product of the Second Republic, having been founded in 1931. The CiU initially coalesced prior to the 1979 general election. The CiU has its roots, more ideologically than structurally, in the first Catalan nationalist party, the Catalan Regionalist League. Like the

CiU, this earlier party pushed issues important to the Catalan business community. The CiU has nevertheless appealed to Catalan voters from all walks of life. As a moderate party, it has long controlled the Catalan regional government. This has helped the CiU develop an image of a modern mass party capable of effective and efficient government. The absence of a radical Catalan nationalist party has given the CiU more political room for maneuver. The CiU has nevertheless remained a staunch defender of Catalan interests, but all the while maintaining good relations with Madrid.

The CiU has governed the Autonomous Community of Catalonia since 1980 under the leadership of Jordi Pujol. It has thus been quite successful in regional and local elections. Like the PNV in the Basque country, the CiU has also contested general elections but frequently finishes behind some of the centralist parties running in Catalonia. Despite this and the fact that it is a regionally based party, the CiU attracts enough voters in general elections to be Spain's fourth strongest party. As seen in Table 6.4, the CiU has frequently passed the PCE/IU as the third largest party group in the Congress of Deputies. This position enhances the CiU's position in Madrid-based politics, most importantly as a possible coalition partner in central government. The CiU supported the PSOE minority government from 1993 to 1995 and the PP minority government from 1996–1999. As an indication of the regional party's importance in central state politics, its withdrawal of this support was the major reason for the PSOE government's calling of early elections in March 1996.

***Other Nationalist Parties***   Many other nationalist parties compete in general, regional, and local elections. Their strength and support varies greatly from region to region and from election to election. Many frequently do better in local elections and those to select representatives for the parliaments of the autonomous communities. In more recent general elections, nationalist parties that have gained representation in the Congress of Deputies in Madrid, besides those already mentioned, include the Republican Left of Catalonia (ERC); Eusko Alkartasuna (EA), which broke from the Basque Nationalist Party; Euskadiko Ezkerra (EE), which after internal problems merged with the Socialist Party of Euskadi (PSE-PSOE); the Canary Coalition (CC) from the Canary Islands; the Andalucian Party (PA); the Valencian Union (UV); and the Argonese Party (Par). While many of these parties are small, the numbers of nationalist parties, including those that do not win seats in Madrid, strongly suggest the importance of the centralist-nationalist dimension in Spain's party system.

## THE ELECTORAL SYSTEM

As in other democracies, Spain's electoral system has had a profound impact on its party system and the very nature of representation. In general elections, Spain uses a modified version of proportional representation (PR). Voters cast ballots for their preferred party's list of candidates, as is the case with all European systems of proportional representation. Each voter casts one ballot. In this closed-list electoral system, no preference votes or other means of altering the parties' predetermined ordering of individual candidates on the list is permitted. Parliamentary seats are then allocated proportionally according to the percentage of total votes a given party receives. Spain's constituencies are many and very small, which makes Spain different from other countries such as those in Scandinavia that also use proportional representation.

Spain's 50 provinces serve as the country's electoral districts. Thus, in any general election, a major party will have 50 different party lists (plus others in Ceuta and Melilla). According to Spain's election law, no province/electoral district can have fewer than three representatives. Of the Congress of Deputies's 350 seats, 150 are determined in a manner that distorts the overall proportionality of votes cast. The remaining 200 seats use a province's population as the criteria for determining the magnitude (number of seats per district). The combination of the province as the basic unit for a constituency and the relatively small size of the Congress of Deputies means that the Spanish electoral system facilitates a multiparty system yet does so in a rather distorted way. As can be seen in Table 6.4, this disproportionality tends to benefit parties with supporters regionally concentrated and Spain's largest central parties.

## Frequency of Elections

General elections must be held in Spain at least once every four years. As in other parliamentary systems such as Great Britain's, the government of the day has the power to call elections. Elections may come very close to the end of the parliamentary term, as is generally the case in Germany. They may, however, also come earlier in the session if the government so chooses. For example, the Suárez government called early elections in 1979, only two years after the last general election. Suárez's UCD government sought an expression of political legitimacy following the constitution's ratification in 1978. It also thought, and correctly so as we can now see in retrospect, that it would win. Felipe González also called an early election for March 3, 1996, given the loss of support by CiU for his minority PSOE government. With the exception of Adolfo Suárez's first government, other governments in Spain have generally come close to completing their full terms.

One other note must be added about the frequency of elections. Elections for local and regional assemblies, institutions discussed below, are generally not held on the same electoral cycle as the Madrid-based central government. For example, a general election was held in June 1993 while many municipalities and 13 of Spain's 17 autonomous communities held elections in May 1995. Interpretation of these elections makes for interesting discussion. The outcomes of such elections depend a great deal on local and regional politics. They are also frequently used as an indicator of the direction in which broader political winds are blowing. A prevalent argument is that such regional elections in Spain can be viewed in a manner similar to by-elections in Great Britain: as an indicator of the popularity of the country's current central government.

## Electoral Performances

Spanish general elections should be viewed essentially in three stages. The first stage—"the consolidation of democracy"—included the 1977 and 1979 elections. In these two elections the UCD emerged as the largest single party. A UCD government was formed following each of these two elections. The second stage—"alternation of power/Socialist control"—saw the PSOE win the 1982 election. As the party of government, the Socialists repeated this victory in the 1986, 1989, and 1993 general elections. Each election, however, brought a narrower victory for PSOE, including the 1993 election in which, while remaining the largest party, it failed to gain a majority of parliamentary seats. Following this 1993 election, the PSOE government of Felipe González managed to remain in power only as a minority government. While not formally included in the cabinet, the Catalan CiU supported this post-1993 government. The third stage of Spain's current democratic system occurred with a shift of power to the right after the election on March 3, 1996. As seen in Table 6.4, the Popular Party won the election as expected but without an outright majority. While now returning to a role as the main parliamentary opposition party, the PSOE did better than most expectations.

José María Aznar became Spain's newest prime minister on May 5, 1996, following nearly two months of intense negotiations between the Popular Party and several nationalist parties. Following individual agreements, Aznar's investiture by the Congress of Deputies was voted for by deputies of his own Popular Party and those of the Catalan CiU, the Basque Nationalist Party (PNV), and the Canary Coalition. These nationalist parties' support for Aznar's minority government had several important consequences. First, despite its minority status, Aznar's PP government proved to be quite stable throughout the 1996–2000 term. Second, the regional parties' support gave the government the parliamentary strength to implement policies it needed to move Spain toward meeting the criteria for European monetary integration. Third, regional party support encouraged the PP to continue with many important structural reforms regarding Spain's regional system of governance, including some of the autonomous communities' financial arrangements with Madrid. Finally, Aznar's minority government proved popular enough to win an outright parliamentary majority in the March 2000 general elections. Throughout his second term, Prime Minister Aznar has the political strength to implement the Popular Party's agenda without the support of other parties.

Besides general elections, local, regional, and European elections are held in Spain. Understanding and analyzing these should be thought of in their broader European context. Such elections clearly include debate about issues specific to each of these levels. The fact that such elections are generally not held at the same time as general elections, however, means they tend to reflect Spaniards' attitudes about the central government at that particular point in time. Regional variations in Spain add some interesting twists to such election results, especially in Catalonia and the Basque country. The Spanish press and private conversations tend to link these election results to Madrid-based politics even if such interpretations do not actually capture the complete meaning of these local, regional, and European elections.

*Referendums*   One other type of election has proved important to Spanish democracy. A referendum is a direct consultation via the ballot box of the citizens of a country on a specific issue. Some Western European countries frequently use referendums: Switzerland is the classic example, but countries such as Italy also frequently use them. Germany and Great Britain never or infrequently do. (The Federal Republic of Germany has never held a national referendum and Great Britain had a national referendum on maintaining membership in the European Community).

Spain's use of the referendum falls somewhere in the middle. While still relatively young as a democracy, it has held several state-wide referendums. These include the Referendum on Political Reform in 1976, the ratification of the Constitution in 1978, and the referendum on Spain's membership in NATO in 1985. As seen in Table 6.5, referendums were also held within

| TABLE 6.5 | | |
|---|---|---|
| **REFERENDUMS IN CONTEMPORARY SPAIN** | | |
| Year | Issue | Type |
| 1976 | Law on Political Reform | National |
| 1978 | Ratification of Constitution | National |
| 1979 | Autonomy, Basque country | Regional |
|  | Autonomy, Catalonia | Regional |
| 1980 | Autonomy, Galicia | Regional |
|  | Autonomy, Andalusia | Regional |
| 1981 | Autonomy, Andalusia | Regional |
| 1986 | NATO membership | National |

many of the regions on the question of regional autonomy (in various years). While we can leave the debate to others if the use of the referendum lessens the power, prestige, or centrality of parliament, it is clear that this act of voting on specific issues has been an important instrument for the legitimation of democracy in Spain.

## INTEREST GROUPS

Characteristic of liberal democratic systems, Spain witnessed the development of a variety of interest groups following its transition to democracy. As in other pluralistic democracies, many organized interests reflect individual and group concerns with the environment, social issues such as advancement of the welfare state and women's rights, and other issues. For example, one of the strongest and certainly best-funded is the National Organization for the Blind in Spain, well known by its acronym ONCE. This organization, created during the Franco period and given an early position within the lottery market, has used its enormous financial surplus to invest in many traditional business ventures.

### Economic Organizations

Organized labor and business interests are the most important pressure groups, given their role in the government's implementation of economic policy. The Spanish Confederation of Employers'

Organization (CEOE) brings together more than 90 percent of Spain's businesses. Founded in 1977, the CEOE emerged over its rival organizations—the Spanish Confederation of Small- and Medium-Sized Firms (CEPYME) and the Union of Small- and Medium-Sized Firms (UNIPYME)—to act as business's primary representative organization. All of these organizations reflect a relatively new tradition of employers' organizations in Spain. Despite its very decentralized structure, the CEOE has grown over a relatively short period into an effective instrument for the representation of business interests. It serves as the umbrella organization for 165 different individual employers' organizations. About one-third of these are intersectorial (meaning they cross into different types of business activities) and regionally based. The other two-thirds come from specific economic activities such as construction, banking, steel making, and so on. The CEOE claims to have over 1.3 million members representing 80 percent of the nongovernmental labor force. Students should nevertheless be aware that small- and medium-sized firms characterize the Spanish economy. This explains why CEPYME did not integrate into the CEOE until 1980 and, even today, maintains a special status within it.

The CEOE speaks on behalf of Spanish business as a whole, especially where national and international issues are involved, such as in Spanish business-labor pacts and within the European Union. The CEOE thus represents business in national-level negotiations on pay and working conditions. Negotiations on collective agreements are, however, left to the individual associations.

***Labor Unions*** Unlike business organizations, the Spanish labor union movement played a highly visible and tumultuous role throughout twentieth-century Spain. Many unions, including the anarchist-oriented National Confederation of Labor (CNT), the socialist General Union of Workers (UGT), and the Union of Basque Workers (ELA-STV), were active during the Second Republic. They were subsequently declared illegal in 1937 and strongly repressed during the civil war and the early Franco years. Many members, especially the leaders, were killed, imprisoned, or went into exile.

Franco replaced these unions during his early years with an official system of vertical syndicates. Twenty-eight syndicates represented different types of production. The Franco regime sought to use these syndicates to combine all producers, employers, and employees into a system of state corporatism. Reflecting the regime's authoritarian nature, strikes were illegal, wages were centrally determined, and membership was compulsory. The system's rigidity nevertheless was relaxed over the years. Labor milestones during the Franco years included the 1958 Law on Collective Agreements, the economic growth of the 1960s that changed attitudes of both employers and employees, and the Union Law of 1971. The Communist-oriented Workers' Commissions (CCOO) was the key labor organization to emerge and gain a foothold during this time.

As with so much else in Spanish politics, Franco's death and the subsequent transition to democracy profoundly changed the nature of labor's aggregation and political articulation. The Constitution of 1978, the Workers' Statute of 1980, and the Organic Law on Trade Union Freedoms in 1984 together fundamentally brought Spanish workers' rights up to the standards of those in other European democracies. Such rights include the freedom to organize, to democratically elect union representatives, and to engage in collective bargaining.

Democratic Spain's two major labor unions are the Workers' Commissions and the General Union of Workers. The former tends to be concentrated in the public sector and the latter consolidated its position in small- and medium-sized firms.

***The General Union of Workers*** The UGT is a socialist-oriented union, historically but now informally associated with the PSOE. Founded in 1888, it has returned to its pre–civil war strength and position in Spain's contemporary democratic system despite its severe repression under Franco. Organizationally the UGT's congress meets every three years and elects an executive committee to govern the union. The executive committee also constitutes part of the confederal committee, along with general secretaries of the industrial federations (production-specific groupings) and the provincial and regional unions (the aggregation of the local unions). Such organization essentially makes the UGT a union of local unions, one in which the local unions maintain a high degree of independence. This autonomy includes the power to call a work stoppage.

Ideologically the UGT, similar to most Western European unions, has gone through a period of questioning its direction. Much of this has been caused by the loss of members and broader antiunion sentiments. A dominant concern for many leaders and rank-and-file members has been the UGT's relationship to the Socialist Party. This relationship became increasingly strained after 1982 once the PSOE came to power. The basic question was how much to distance itself from the González government when the UGT's leadership, under Secretary General Cándido Méndez, disagreed with important labor-oriented policies. The UGT's support of several general strikes against the Socialist government suggested the PSOE-UGT relationship was an uneasy one—yet almost a family matter. The UGT's relationship with the PSOE has been less contentious since the Popular Party came to power in 1996. Oppositional politics has emphasized the UGT's and PSOE's common orientations to labor, economic, and related policies.

### The Workers' Commissions

The CCOO was founded during the Franco years as a series of workers' councils. They initially flourished in the early 1960s as a reaction to Franco's official corporatist syndicates. At first tolerated and later, in 1967, outlawed and repressed, the workers' commissions benefited greatly from their decentralized organization and their strong links to the Spanish Communist Party.

Today organized much like the UGT, the CCOO is a federation of workers in similar areas of production that are, in turn, linked as confederations in territorial congresses. The CCOO's national congress meets biannually. Between congresses, the confederal council manages the unions. Fifty federation representatives, 50 territorial confederation representatives, the general secretary, and the executive committee constitute this confederal council. Compared to the UGT, the CCOO tends to be a more centralized union with a top-to-bottom policy style.

The Workers' Commissions, like the UGT and PSOE, also struggle in their relationship to the most closely identified political party—the PCE/IU. Marcelino Camancho had a long history as CCOO general secretary. His leadership style maintained a certain confrontational direction for the union but his critical sector of the union eventually lost control within the union. First under the leadership of Antonio Gutiérrez and now under that of Secretary General José María Fidalgo Velilla, the CCOO has greatly modified the earlier confrontational style of the defense of Spanish workers.

### Other Unions

The relative strength of the UGT and the CCOO might lead one to forget that several other unions represent Spanish workers. This is compounded by the fact that Spanish law gives only the larger unions a position at tripartite negotiations with business and the government.

Among the smaller unions, the Workers' Syndical Union (USO) rose, like the CCOO, in authoritarian Spain in reaction to Franco's official unions. In its early years, the USO had a strong Catholic base of support. Another union, the National Confederation of Labor (CNT), has its roots in nineteenth-century anarchosyndicalism. Both historically and in contemporary Spain, the CNT has been the strongest in Catalonia. Rejecting "bourgeoise democracy" and thus any type of political party affiliation, the CNT has generally boycotted democratic Spain's labor union representative elections. Table 6.6 presents the results of some of these elections. Finally, geographically based unions such as the Basque ELA-STV, which is closely linked to the Basque Nationalist Party (PNV), and the Federation of Unions in Galicia (INTG) also play an important role in the political economy of their respective regions.

## The Church

The Catholic Church's role in Spanish politics has evolved considerably over the last 50 years. This change is yet another strong indicator of the

**TABLE 6.6**

**LABOR UNION ELECTIONS (PERCENTAGE OF REPRESENTATIVES ELECTED)**

| Year | UGT | CCOO | USO | ELV-STV | INTG | Unaffiliated | Others |
|------|-----|------|-----|---------|------|--------------|--------|
| 1978 | 21.7 | 34.5 | 3.8 | 0.9 | — | 18.1 | 20.8 |
| 1980 | 29.3 | 30.9 | 8.7 | 2.2 | 1.0 | 14.6 | 12.2 |
| 1982 | 36.7 | 33.4 | 4.6 | 3.3 | 1.2 | 12.1 | 8.7 |
| 1986 | 40.9 | 34.5 | 3.8 | 2.9 | 1.2 | 7.6 | 10.0 |
| 1990 | 42.0 | 36.9 | 2.9 | 3.2 | 1.4 | 3.8 | 7.1 |
| 1995 | 34.9 | 37.8 | 3.7 | 3.6 | 1.8 | 3.3 | 22.1 |
| 1999 | 36.8 | 37.7 | — | — | — | — | — |

*Source:* Spanish Ministry of Labor and Social Security, and the CCOO. (I also gratefully acknowledge the assistance of Sebastián Royo.)

dynamic nature of the foundation of Spanish politics. During the Second Republic, the Church had a tumultuous relationship with the democratically elected governments. As with several other key issues, clashes between Church supporters and adherents of strong anticlerical beliefs led to a severe polarization of political attitudes. During and after the civil war, the Church was one of the Nationalists' fundamental institutional allies. The Church's loyal support gave the Franco regime an important source of early legitimacy. This church-state relationship was formalized in a treaty with the Vatican, the Concordat of 1953.

During the regime's later years, Franco lost the Church's uncritical support. Changes within the Church, specifically growing out of the Second Vatican Council and the leadership of Pope John XXIII, and the modernization of Spanish society led to open conflict with the regime. Spaniards on the Right viewed this as a betrayal of traditional Spanish Catholicism; sceptics on the Left saw the Church maneuvering for a position of influence within a changing political landscape.

Given Vatican II, the Spanish Church essentially went through a period of modernization some ten years before the political system. The Church thus had a stronger effect on Spanish politics than democracy did on the Church. By the time of the democratic transition, the Catholic Church was independent enough to defend its interests and values in a manner similar to the churches in other pluralistic European societies.

Several laws and treaties clarify church-state relations in Spain. In July 1976, the Vatican and King Juan Carlos agreed on a set of issues, including that the monarch would no longer appoint bishops to the Church. For its part, the Vatican renounced the Spanish clergy's exemption from the application of Spanish law. Issues such as the Church's legal position were also resolved.

The Constitution of 1978 formalizes the Church's independence from the Spanish state. Specific mention of the Catholic Church in the document also clearly signals its important role in traditional Spanish society. Characteristic of the constitution's general vagueness, it states: "The public powers will take into account the religious beliefs of Spanish society and will maintain the consequent relations of cooperation with the Catholic Church and other confessions." The Church thus received special recognition but within a set of guarantees of individual religious freedom.

The Catholic Church remains a fundamental institution representing traditional society within Spain. It engages in public discourse as a vital part of a modern functioning democracy in a manner similar to other actors with interests and views to defend. But because of its internal changes prior to democracy, the Church no longer speaks as a monolithic institution, certainly not to the extent it did during the early Franco years. Voices within the Church can be heard from many political persuasions.

As an institution, the Church has established since the end of the Franco regime a clear pattern of political independence from the state and has demonstrated its cooperation in political-societal negotiations. It played an active role in the transition to democracy. Many of the changes at the time involved broad questions of political, social, and religious matters. During the consolidation of democracy, the Church often publicly articulated its interpretation of important issues facing the country. Today, the Church frequently takes clear stands on such fundamental issues as church-state relations, education, divorce, and abortion. Long some of the most difficult issues in church-state relations, questions about the state's financial support of the Church and the Church's role in education continue to receive attention. The Church maintains a strong institutionalized influence in Spanish education.

While ongoing reforms in the Spanish educational system are based on other European models, the Catholic Church remains extensively involved in pre-university education. Approximately one-third of all pre-university education in Spain is private, generally being tied to the Catholic Church, and 95 percent of Spain's primary education linked to the Church is publicly financed. While public educational standards and curriculum must be maintained in these Catholic schools, private schools can establish their own religious orientation.

The Spanish Catholic Church has also been forthright in entering the public debate on other issues such as divorce and abortion. Despite being part of intense political discussions, such position-taking has occurred within an open debate within Spain's remarkably tolerant democratic system. Fortunately, democratic Spain has not reproduced the Second Republic's violent anticlericalism and polarization of political attitudes.

The Church's political independence can be found in many places, including the party system. Democratic Spain has no clerical party. Unlike Germany, it doesn't even have a significant christian democratic party. No single political party is either directly or indirectly tied to the Church. Within any given party, the Church is only one of many voices seeking to be heard. While the Church naturally has an ideological affinity with parties on the Right, the Church's independent role characterized its relationship to the UCD during the transition's early years as well as its current preference for the Popular Party and some of the regional parties.

## The Military

Historically, the armed forces have been actively involved in Spain's politics. The Spanish military has frequently taken direct control of the state. Examples of such military intervention during the last century include the dictatorships of General Miguel Primo de Rivera (1923–1930) and General Francisco Franco (1936–1975). Therefore, a central question during the early stages of Spain's most recent transition to democracy was how to keep the military out of politics. Given that fears of a military coup are now minimal, Spain's handling of its political-military relations are a success story worthy of emulation.

The Spanish military contains numerous branches: the army, the navy, the air force, the marines, the Civil Guard, the National Police, and the Coastal Civil Guard. Military academies are maintained at Saragossa (army), Martín (navy), and San Javier (air force).

The most distinctively Spanish of these military branches is the Civil Guard. Well known for their green uniforms and tricornered black leather hats, this proud force dates back to 1844. As an instrument of the central government in Madrid, its primary responsibility has traditionally been in the nonurban areas outside the capital. As an internal security force, the Civil Guard has been susceptible to being used as an apparatus of repression, especially by dictatorships such as the Franco regime. Consequently, the Civil Guard has long been viewed negatively by many. This is especially true in the Basque country, where during the early years of the transition cries were frequently heard of the Civil Guard being "Madrid's occupation force."

One event in democratic Spain epitomizes the delicate nature of political-military relations, especially as they were in the early critical years of the transition. On the night of February 23, 1981, Colonel Antonio Tejero Molina and some 200 members of the Civil Guard charged into a packed session of the Congress of Deputies. Firing shots into the ornate chamber's ceiling, Colonel Tejero and his men took all the members hostage. His timing was well calculated. The Congress was full. Three weeks earlier Prime Minister Adolfo Surárez had resigned and, on that night, the outgoing cabinet was present to witness the investiture of Leopoldo Calvo Sotelo's new incoming UCD government. While almost all deputies huddled under their desks, the conspirators manhandled the liberal Deputy Prime Minister Manuel Gutiérrez Mellado, a retired army general. General Gutiérrez was one of the few parliamentarians to offer any sign of resistance.

While announcing they were waiting for orders, but never identifying from whom, Colonel Tejero and his men held the entire Parliament hostage for about 18 hours. News of the coup attempt spread instantaneously, since this important meeting of Parliament was being televised. In Valencia, the commander of that military region sent tanks into the streets. Other commanders waited. All eyes quickly turned to King Juan Carlos. This was the critical moment for Spain's new democracy. The King met the challenge. He acted decisively and with great courage. He quickly created a "governmental commission" of ministerial undersecretaries to assume civilian government responsibility for those being held captive. He skillfully convinced

Coup attempt, February 1981: Colonel Tejero of the Civil Guard holding the Congress of Deputies captive.

General Alfonso Armada, his own military tutor, mentor, and adviser—and one of the highest-ranking plotters in the conspiracy—that any termination of democracy would have to mean killing the King. Convinced of the King's sincerity, General Armada was then dispatched by Juan Carlos to convey this to the plotters in the Parliament. Then, utilizing personal contacts in the military from his own days of training, Juan Carlos persuaded key military leaders to remain uninvolved, including keeping the tanks of the elite Brunete armed division off the streets of Madrid. Via telephone, the King convinced the generals in charge of Spain's nine military districts to remain loyal to him.

Having essentially isolated Colonel Tejero and his men, King Juan Carlos then went on national television at 1:15 A.M., in full military regalia and with symbols of Spain and the monarchy visible behind him, to announce that "the crown, symbol of the permanence and unity of the nation, cannot tolerate, in any form, actions or attitudes attempting to interrupt the democratic process." Following this, the coup attempt quickly fizzled out. Colonel Tejero peacefully surrendered the next morning. Democracy had survived but the events provided an important lesson on its highly fragile nature.

The attempted coup of February 23 reemphasized the delicate balance between civilians committed to democratic government and conservative military authorities. Several key steps helped maintain this balance and preserve democracy. Early in the transition, the civilian government carefully removed the military from control of the National Police and gave it to the civilian Minister of the Interior. The Civil Guard was also placed under civilian control, as was the military. Later, Spain's civilian government tightened its control over the military by making a single Chief of Defense responsible to the Minister of Defense, by reducing the high number of generals in the Spanish army, and by reducing from nine to six the number of military regions.

Civilian authorities also sent a clear message about the price one would pay for challenging democracy's primacy. A year after the February 23 coup attempt, its leaders were tried and sentenced, including Colonel Tejero and General Milan del Bosch, the person responsible for sending tanks into the streets of Valencia. Each received 30 years in jail.

Catering to the pride of the military, concerted efforts were made to modernize and streamline the army. Better equipment was produced, pay was raised by 25 percent, and tougher stands were taken on issues deemed important to the military, such as Spanish claims to Gibraltar, Ceuta, and Melilla. The debate over Spain's eventual membership in NATO should also be considered here.

While each of these steps has significantly decreased the likelihood of future military interventions into Spanish politics, such intrusions have a long history in Spain. As in many other European countries, such as France, the military remains a conservative force with a strong interest in the political directions the country takes.

## MAJOR STATE INSTITUTIONS

The Constitution of 1978 institutionalized Spanish democracy in a manner consistent with the classic parliamentary model. The Spanish political system thus contains many similarities with its Western European counterparts (see Figure 6.2). It does, however, deviate from this model in several important ways. Like all systems, it contains some interesting differences in several key institutions of the state.

### The Monarchy

Spain is a constitutional monarchy with a parliamentary form of government. In this respect, Spain institutionally resembles Belgium, the Netherlands, Sweden, and the United Kingdom. All of these countries have a monarch who serves as the country's head of state. Spain's King Juan Carlos I, however, serves more than a ceremonial role. As demonstrated by his critical role in the coup attempt of February 23, 1981, Juan Carlos and the institution of the monarchy have played a central role in Spain's transition to democracy and its consolidation.

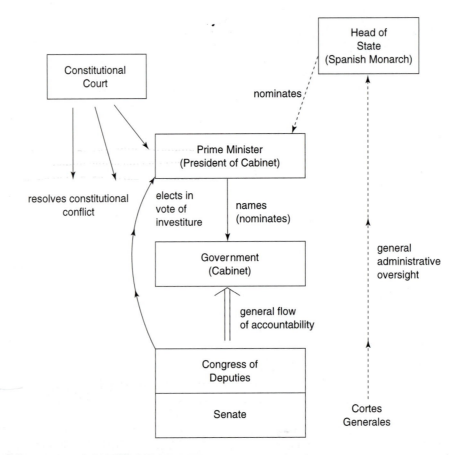

**Figure 6.2** SPAIN'S PARLIAMENTARY SYSTEM

King Alfonso XIII left the country in 1931. The Second Republic was proclaimed shortly thereafter. As a republic, this earlier attempt at democracy contained strong antimonarchical tendencies. During and after the Nationalists' success in the Civil War, Franco promised to restore the monarchy. This restoration, however, did not come without questions. The Caudillo postponed naming his own successor as long as possible; this left the question of the restoration in some doubt for a long time. Between the end of the civil war in 1939 and Franco's passage of the Law on Succession in 1969 when he officially designated Juan Carlos as Spain's next king, the questions about the monarchy and Franco's successor were left unresolved.

Franco was not totally content with the possibilities. The royal family lived in exile in Italy during the civil war. Following Alfonso XIII's death in 1941, his son Don Juan, Count of Barcelona, lived in exile in Portugal throughout the Francoist period. That Franco detested Don Juan's liberal political orientations is well known. Franco saw other choices: Alfonso Borbón y Dampierre, Juan Carlos's cousin who had married Franco's granddaughter; Carlos-Hugo de Borbón-Parma, the Carlist pretender to the throne; and, of course, the possibility of not restoring the monarchy at all despite Franco's earlier promises. Many Spaniards favored at the time this later option. Following their authoritarian experiences, Italy and Greece abolished their monarchies through referendum, replacing them with a republican form of parliamentary democracy.

Franco opted to bypass Don Juan's claim to the throne and instead chose his son Juan Carlos. Almost as an apprenticeship, Juan Carlos was educated in Spain after the age of 10, served in all three branches of Spain's armed forces, worked in various aspects of government service, and increasingly appeared publicly at Franco's side prior to the official nomination in 1969. Juan Carlos's marriage in 1962 to Princess Sofía of Greece, the sister of former Greek King Constantine, also enhanced his royal credentials. He was crowned King of Spain before the Spanish Cortes two days after Franco's death.

Juan Carlos's future role as the champion of Spanish democracy was not readily apparent. He had remained publicly silent about such matters for years prior to Franco's death and was harshly criticized and ridiculed by many for this. Nevertheless, as Spain's new king, he faced several options: to perpetuate Franco's authoritarian regime; to reform the country's political system; or to give in to those who opposed the monarchy as an institution or disliked Juan Carlos for his close association to the Franco regime. Besides his constant support of democratic principles, at least three events or actions are important to understand why public opinion polls today consistently indicate that the Spanish monarch is the country's most popular public institution.

First, in 1976 Juan Carlos chose the relatively unknown and young Francoist official Adolfo Suárez as his prime minister. Juan Carlos had identified Suárez as a "closet democrat" within the Francoist ranks. As history proved correct, the King saw in Suárez the political skills necessary to dismantle legally and peacefully the Francoist regime and replace it with a new democracy. Second, Juan Carlos proved his own skill and courage to the country in February 1981. During the coup attempt by the military and the Civil Guard in which the government and the entire parliament in Madrid was held overnight, Juan Carlos adroitly exercised his constitutional powers and moral persuasion to face

The Spanish royal family.

down the rebels and preserved the young democracy in its most threatened moment. Third, and less noticed, Juan Carlos has ensured the survival and legitimacy of the Spanish monarchy by his own acts and the careful grooming of his son Felipe, Prince of Asturias, to become Spain's next king. Both the behavior of King Juan Carlos and his son Felipe has been well received by the Spanish public.

The Spanish monarch's constitutional powers are similar in most respects to those of the head of state in other European parliamentary systems. The King serves many symbolic functions in areas such as international relations (representing Spain during trips abroad, receiving official visiting dignitaries including resident ambassadors and diplomats), judicial and administrative matters (acts are symbolically carried out in his name), and social, cultural, and scientific affairs (he is patron of royal academies, encourages charitable acts, etc.). Governmentally, the King collaborates in the carrying out of executive and legislative activities. When requested by the government or its president—the prime minister—the King calls parliamentary elections, convenes and dissolves Parliament, promulgates laws, and appoints and dismisses ministers of the government. What is constitutionally clear about these powers is that they serve as moderating functions: All such acts emanate from the people and their representatives. The King is, in fact, only countersigning decisions taken by either the government or the Parliament. As in Great Britain, any attempt by the monarch to act independently would send the country into a constitutional crisis, one that most likely would end with the abolishment of the institution of the monarchy.

Despite constitutional limitations, the Spanish monarch can exercise some discretional powers. At least two can be identified. Both are quite limited. One is characteristic of many other European heads of state; the other has a distinct Spanish flavor.

The normal procedure following an election or the fall of a government is that the King consults the leaders of all political parties represented in the Cortes prior to calling on the leader of the largest party to form a new government.

Thus far in democratic Spain's short history, this has been a rather straightforward matter. However, when a coalition government is needed, the King's influence might prove decisive in giving important political direction. One can see such discretionary power periodically exercised by Italy's head of state. The same potential exists in Spain, but would likely come to pass only in a period of coalition governments.

Spain's own twist on the head of state's discretionary powers involves the fact that the Spanish monarch is the commander in chief of the armed forces. Nominally, this is the norm for most European heads of state; the military nevertheless remains effectively under the civil control of the government. In Spain, however, King Juan Carlos has openly and consistently utilized his own military background and authority to remind the armed forces of their constitutional role in a democratic society. It was no accident that on the night of February 23, 1981, in the middle of the attempted military coup, King Juan Carlos wore his military uniform during the television broadcast in which he commanded the soldiers to return to their barracks. Less dramatically, Juan Carlos annually uses the military festivities of *Pascua Militar* (January 6) to remind the country's military of its mission in a democratic Spain.

In sum, as Spain's monarch, Juan Carlos performs the ceremonial duties of a European head of state. Given his personal role in Spain's transition to democracy, however, he is much more than a figurehead. He remains above day-to-day political affairs but, to the surprise of many earlier doubters, has played a fundamental role in the preservation of Spanish democracy.

## The Government

Although Spain's governing institutions and procedures are generally similar to those of other Western European parliamentary systems, several important differences can be found in the functioning of the Spanish executive and its relationship to other state institutions. Among others, these include (1) government formation with its separate election of the prime minister and his government, (2) the constructive vote of no confidence, and (3) the nature of government coalitions.

***Government Formation***    Unlike the British parliamentary system, the investiture of a new government in Spain's Congress of Deputies is essentially a two-step process. Following the King's consultation with the leadership of all political parties represented in the Congress, the prime minister designate negotiates to secure promises of support. If his party won a parliamentary majority in the last general election, finding such support is a straightforward matter. A formal "vote of investiture" follows in the Congress of Deputies on the prime minister alone. Characteristic of other parliamentary systems, the decision rule is majority. On the first vote an absolute majority is required; a simple majority will suffice on the second and any subsequent rounds. Upon a successful investiture, the new prime minister then has several days to present his cabinet and program to the Parliament. Following extensive debate, a second vote takes place. This dual selection procedure serves to reinforce a growing trend in European parliamentary systems toward the personalization of the executive. Such a presidential style in Spain is similar to "chancellor democracy" in Germany and "prime ministerial democracy" in the United Kingdom. Increased reliance on television and other forms of mass media has also intensified this personalization of government.

***Constructive Vote of No Confidence***    In a classic parliamentary system like Great Britain's Westminster model, a prime minister and his or her cabinet—the government—can be removed from power with a majority vote *against* it. This is called a "vote of no confidence." In some parliamentary systems such as contemporary Italy, the French Third and Fourth Republics, and Weimar Germany, such votes of no confidence were frequent. Governments came and went at an amazing rate of speed. A basic political problem in such systems is that it is easier to find a negative majority against a sitting government than to maintain a positive majority in support of one. Parliamentarians, like many people, find it easier to vote negatively than to create a government with a more positive outlook. Certain changes in parliamentary rules have sought to address such behavioral tendencies and the resultant government instability.

Spain's Constitution of 1978 borrowed the "constructive vote of no confidence" from the Federal Republic of Germany. Essentially the "constructive vote" means that in order to vote a government out of power (the classic vote of no confidence), a new majority must simultaneously be found as its replacement. In other words, in parliamentary systems like Spain's with the constructive vote of no confidence, a prime minister and his government are removed from power only upon the election of their replacement. While still too early to assess fully the consequences, this variation in the classic Westminster model has probably helped add a degree of governmental stability to Spain's democracy. The need to find a replacement for a sitting government helped prolonged the minority governments of Adolfo Suárez from 1977 to 1979 and Felipe González from 1994 to 1996.

***Coalition Government***    In great part attributable to its election law, four of Spain's elections have produced majority governments despite the fact that no party has won a majority of the popular vote. In part given the role played by the constructive vote of no confidence, minority governments can remain remarkably viable. Recent Spanish governments have tended more toward the British style of single-party government than the Italian or even the German pattern of government coalitions of several parties. When the electorate gave no single party a parliamentary majority in Spain, minority governments managed to survive with support from other parties not participating directly in the government (for example, the CiU's support for Felipe González's PSOE government from 1994 to 1995, and the CiU's, PNV's, and other regional parties' support of Aznar's PP government from 1996 to 1999). If in the future governments turn to formal coalitions—when neither the PSOE or the PP are able to form governments alone—Spain will then more likely follow the German model of government coalitions than that of Italy.

# The Parliament

As with most parliamentary systems, the legislature institutionally expresses the people's sovereignty. The Spanish Parliament, generally referred to as the Cortes, is bicameral. The lower house—the Congress of Deputies—meets in the historic Palacio del Congreso. The upper house—the Senate—has a modern home in Madrid's Palacio del Senado. As with Great Britain's House of Commons, Spain's Congress has precedence in most matters, including the most important role of supporting or removing the government. Occasionally both houses meet in joint sessions. Called the Cortes Generales, such meetings constitutionally address issues about the monarchy.

***The Congress of Deputies***    In most respects, the lower house of the Spanish Parliament looks and operates much like the legislatures in other Western European parliamentary systems. Constitutionally, the Congress of Deputies can vary in size from 300 to 400 representatives. In fact, since 1977 it has had 350 members, making it smaller than its counterparts in Great Britain, Germany, and Italy. Besides its normal roles in Spain's bicameral system, the Congress of Deputies constitutionally holds some specific powers. These deal primarily with the Congress's relationship to and control over the government. These powers include the investiture of the prime minister, the holding of a vote of confidence on the government at the prime minister's request, and the conducting of censure motions against the government. Other powers specifically given to the Congress of Deputies by the Constitution of 1978 include the ratification of decree-laws, the authorization of states of emergency, and dealing with treasonable offenses by members of the government.

***Organizations and Functions***    Most European parliaments determine their own internal organization and procedures through standing orders. Spain is no different in this regard. Such standing orders cover many specific topics. Our discussion will focus on the presidents of the Cortes, the creation of parliamentary party groups, the Council of Party Spokesmen, and the legislative process.

***The President of the Chamber***    Both houses of the Spanish Cortes elect a president. The President of the Congress of Deputies is equivalent to the Speaker of the House in Great Britain. The primary responsibility of the President of the Congress and the President of the Senate is to supervise the general operations of their respective houses of Parliament, maintain the norms of fair debate, facilitate effective representation, and protect the proper relations of members to each other and the Spanish state itself. The presidents of the Cortes possess the power to impose discipline within their chambers. They also represent their respective house of Parliament in relation to other state institutions. For example, the president of the Congress is officially the one to whom the King proposes a candidate for prime minister. Constitutionally, he must also be consulted prior to the calling of general elections and must countersign the decree convening these elections.

***Party Groups***    As elsewhere in Europe, parliamentary party groups are the key to understanding legislative operations in Spain. They conduct the bulk of parliamentary business. Generally, membership in a party group extends logically from which party list the member was elected to Parliament in the previous general election. In other words, parliamentary groups tend to consist of legislators from the same political party or electoral coalition. For example, the PSOE, the PP, and other large parties each form their own parliamentary group Spain's Congress of Deputies requires at least 15 deputies and the Senate requires at least 10 members to form a party group. The Congress also permits the formation of a parliamentary group with as few as five members if they won at least 15 percent of the vote in the areas where that party fielded candidates—a rule mostly utilized by the Basque Nationalist Party (PNV). Parliamentary members of political parties not meeting these criteria join the "mixed group."

Parliamentary groups are important to individual members as well as to the functioning of the two chambers of the Cortes. First, members are seated by party groups in the plenary meetings of their respective chambers, in the traditional left-right manner. Second, parliamentary groups determine speaking and debate time for

Front view of the Congress of Deputies, the lower house of the Spanish parliament.

members. Third, committee membership is determined by size of parliamentary groups. Fourth, the elected spokesman of each group represents that group on the Council of Party Spokesmen.

***Council of Party Spokesmen***   In both the Congress and the Senate, the president of the chamber presides over the meetings of the Council of Party Spokesmen. Other officials such as at least one vice president, one secretary, and the general secretary also attend. The council is the decision-making body for the operation of legislative activities. It sets the agenda for the full meetings of the parliamentary chamber as well as its committees, establishes the order of debate, and determines the overall length of each parliamentary session. The council normally meets on Tuesdays prior to plenary sessions.

***The Passage of Laws: The Legislative Function***   As with any democratic legislature, the leg-islative function of the Spanish Cortes is of fundamental importance. Spain has several types of laws, which vary in their degree of overall importance. Hierarchically, Spain's categories of laws include (1) constitutional laws, (2) organic laws of the state, (3) ordinary and basic laws, (4) decree-laws, and (5) different types of regulations. Each of these will be briefly dealt with in turn.

Reform of the constitution may be initiated by the government, the Congress, the Senate, or the autonomous communities. They must be approved by a three-fifths majority of each house of Parliament, with some modified legislative paths if the two houses disagree. Following parliamentary approval, if 15 parliamentarians request, the constitutional change must be ratified in a countrywide referendum. Total reform of the Constitution or partial reform of some key sections requires a two-thirds vote in each house; dissolution of Parliament and new elections, a two-thirds majority again in each of the two newly elected houses of Parliament, and then a final ratification in a national referendum.

Organic laws address basic institutional and procedural questions of the state. Imitating the 1958 Constitution of the French Fifth Republic, Spain's organic laws tend to fill out basic constitutionally created institutions and procedures such as election rules, royal succession, the council of state, the constitutional court and the development of rights and liberties, states of emergency, and international treaties. They also deal with the transfer and delegation of powers to the autonomous communities and the creation of regional police forces. Following the ratification of the 1978 Constitution, debate and passage of such organic laws have been essential to the institutionalization of Spanish democracy. Given this centrality, only the Cortes has the power to approve, modify, or repeal organic laws. Approval is required by an absolute majority of the Congress and a simple majority in the Senate.

Ordinary laws are the most common type of law in Spain. Following plenary and committee scrutiny, ordinary laws require a simple majority of both parliamentary chambers. This classification of law can be found at the central as well as the regional level. Similar to ordinary laws, basic laws are where the parliamentary representatives delegate legislative power to the executive in specific areas. Such delegation of the legislative function must be clearly, expressly, and purposely stated in both principle and criteria. Similarly, framework laws delegate legislative functions to the autonomous communities, and basic legislation outlines the shared responsibilities between the central state and the autonomous communities.

As increasingly used and abused in contemporary Italy, the issuance of decree-laws is prevalent in Spain. While decree-laws cannot deal with the basic institutions of the state or individual rights, the government can issue decree-laws without immediately consulting the Parliament. Decree-laws have the immediate power of law throughout the entire country "in situations of extraordinary and urgent necessity" (Article 86 of the 1978 Constitution). The key here is what constitutes "extraordinary" and "urgent." While such decree-laws must be submitted to the Congress within 30 days, the fact is that very few are then repealed. Such decree-laws increase the government's role in the legislative function and tend to place the Congress in a react-only mode.

Finally, as in any other liberal democracy in an increasingly bureaucratized world, many types of regulations carry the power of law. In Spain, these include royal decrees, orders from the government's delegated committees, ministerial orders from individual ministries of the Madrid-based government, resolutions from regional ministries, and circulars and instructions issued by ministries at the central and regional level.

## The Legislative Process

Legislation in Spain can be initiated by the government, members of either house of Parliament, or the autonomous communities' assemblies. A government-initiated proposal is called a *proyecto de ley* (government bill). A draft law initiated by the Parliament or submitted directly by a regional legislature is referred to a *proposición de ley* (proposed law). As with private-member bills in Great Britain, proposed laws in Spain have a much more difficult time and a treacherous parliamentary path than government bills. The power of the government, its parliamentary majority, and the functioning of the parliamentary party groups are generally not behind them. Nevertheless, while government bills take priority over proposed laws, some important laws in Spain such as the Basic Law on Employment and the Ombudsman Law began as proposed laws.

Reflecting the government-centered nature of Spain's parliamentary democracy, and reinforced by the overlapping importance of the political parties, the majority of ordinary laws passed in Spain begin as government bills. Thus, as seen in Figure 6.3, the first step in the legislative process is with the government. The government initiates the bill and a preliminary version is drafted by the relevant cabinet member or members with the technical assistance of

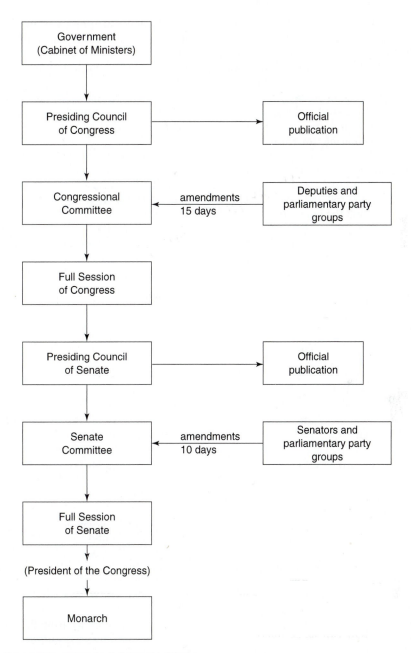

**Figure 6.3** BASIC LEGISLATIVE PROCESS IN SPAIN

the appropriate departments within the ministries. After discussions and changes, the Council of Ministers gives its final approval. Second, the government bill is then submitted to the presiding council of the Congress, who publishes it in the lower house's version of the *Office Bulletin of the Cortes*. The third step in the passing of a law in Spain is the committee stage. Following consideration of proposed amendments and changes to the bill by a working group and a report on proposed improvements, the modified bill is debated in committee, article by article. Fourth, if rejected, the bill can start the entire process over again from the beginning. If the bill receives committee approval, it is taken up for debate in a plenary session of Congress. At this stage, the bill is initially introduced by an appropriate government member who defends its logic and rationale.

Following debate, a bill can be sent back to committee for further consideration. If approved by a majority in the Congress, the bill enters the fifth stage. Here the entire process is repeated in the Senate. Reflecting its secondary status in Spain's bicameral Parliament, the Senate has two months to approve the bill. Following majority approval and the bill's return to the Congress of Deputies, the President of the Congress submits it to the King. The King has 15 days to ratify the approved bill. Following promulgation, it is published as a new law in the *Official Bulletin of the State*.

**The Senate**   The parliamentary balance of power in Spain tilts heavily toward the lower house, the Congress of Deputies. Senate powers are much more limited. For example, the Congress can override a Senate veto of an entire parliamentary bill with an absolute majority or, after two months, with a simple majority. Senate amendments require only a simple majority for the Congress to override. Even more limiting, a bill the government or the Congress considers urgent reduces the Senate's ability to delay it to only 20 days.

The current Spanish Senate thus serves only as a "house of second thoughts" much like the House of Lords in the United Kingdom. It is not as powerful as the German Bundesrat. Senate amendments or other perceived improvements in legislation ultimately depend on the will of the Congress. Current discussions about reform, however, may lead to important changes in the role the Senate plays in Spain's democratic system. As discussed below, such changes would reflect the increasingly federalized nature of the Spanish polity.

**The Congress of Deputies**   In all parliamentary systems, government formation rests with the legislature. How the parliament holds the government accountable also varies from system to system. In Spain, such powers reside in the Congress of Deputies. Legislative control of the Spanish government, as in other parliamentary democracies, includes votes of confidence and censure motions, budgetary and fiscal control, the right to approve or reject decree-laws, and different means of daily control.

The day-to-day parliamentary control of the Spanish government takes several forms. One, question time, borrows from the popularity of this instrument in the British House of Commons. Question time in Spain is normally held on Wednesday afternoons. Inquiries may take the traditional form of questions, requesting either an oral or written response by a member of the government, or "interpellations," which may also be formulated by parliamentary groups. This latter type tends more to question matters of general policy and frequently requires a full debate after being formulated as a motion. Other forms of parliamentary control exist in Spain in the right of either house of the Cortes or their committees to demand the testimony of government members before them. The power to require the prime minister and his government to speak before the legislature clearly symbolizes the government's ultimate accountability to Parliament. These same bodies also have the right to information and assistance from the government, the ministries, or any state authority.

## The Regional System of Government

A fundamental tension has long existed in the Spanish state over the question of centralization or decentralization of decision-making power.

Centralization tendencies dominated during the sixteenth and seventeenth centuries, that is, during the building of the Spanish state itself. More recently, such unifying tendencies were especially prevalent during the nineteenth century. Administrative centralism also dominated much of the twentieth century, especially during the Franco regime. In such periods, governmental power flows from Madrid, as the center of state authority and the country's capital. In contrast, decentralization tendencies stem from the traditional kingdoms in Spain and, more recently, from the nationalist diversity of the country. Decentralization, or devolution, has politically been expressed both in terms of Carlism, which among other things sought from a traditional perspective a legal recognition of the special rights of the kingdoms that existed prior to the Spanish state, and during periods of liberal democracy such as the Second Republic and the current system. The rise of nationalism in the early twentieth century, primarily in the Basque country and Catalonia, motivated the push for political devolution in Spain's most recent attempts at democracy.

During the short-lived Second Republic, regional reforms were initiated to grant autonomy to the municipalities and regions. These reforms were never completed, given the Second Republic's defeat in the civil war. Only Catalonia achieved such autonomy. During the civil war, the Basque country gained self-government, and a similar process started in Galicia. The Nationalist's victory abruptly ended this experiment in political devolution. Authentic decentralization and Franco's authoritarianism were fundamentally incompatible. Not only was Spanish politics Madrid-dominated during this period, but the Franco regime openly persecuted the expression of regional nationalism, whether it took a symbolic, linguistic, or political form.

In contrast, the contemporary Spanish state possesses four levels of governance: the central administration, the regional authorities (the autonomous communities), the provinces, and the municipalities. We will focus our discussion only on the first two of these, since they possess the most basic legislative and decision-making power. The latter two—the provinces and the municipalities—primarily tend to administer policies made by the central and regional authorities.

The Constitution of 1978 protects the indissoluble nature of the Spanish state yet recognizes its multinational nature. Constitutionally Spain thus walks a politically delicate line between the institutionalization of centralized authority and the constitutionally protected system of regional governments. The implementation of Spain's system of autonomous communities (ACs) situates Spain somewhere between the unitary nature of Norway, Sweden, and the devolving Great Britain and a fully federal system like Germany or Austria.

As seen on the map at this chapter's introduction and listed in Table 6.7, Spain currently has 17 autonomous communities. As with the German *Länder,* each of Spain's autonomous communities elects its own legislature which in turn, and consistent with the parliamentary model, chooses its own AC government. In Spain, regional elections must be held at least every four years.

While the central state guarantees basic individual rights and retains normal central state powers such as the maintenance of the military, the conducting of international relations, and monetary authority, the autonomous communities can exercise functions not exclusively reserved, constitutionally speaking, by the central state. The autonomous communities assume executive functions in areas such as health, social security, and basic administrative procedures. Through the AC parliaments, legislative powers also build upon basic legislation passed by the central government. Autonomous community laws have the same force as those of the central state. When conflicts arise over the exercise of power, the Constitutional Court serves as arbiter.

Spain's regional system of government is an excellent example of the developmental nature of a new democracy. The system of autonomous communities is relatively new, not fully determined, and thus still evolving. For example, discussions are underway to reform the Spanish Senate, the central state's upper house of Parliament, to more directly represent Spain's system of autonomous communities, possibly in a manner similar to the relationship of the German

**TABLE 6.7**

**AUTONOMOUS COMMUNITIES OF SPAIN**

| Autonomous Community | Province | Autonomous Community | Province |
|---|---|---|---|
| Andalusia | Almería | Catalonia | Barcelona |
| | Cádiz | | Girona |
| | Córdoba | | Lleida |
| | Granada | | Tarragona |
| | Huelva | Valencia | Alicante |
| | Jaén | | Castellón |
| | Málaga | | Valencia |
| | Seville | Extremadura | Badajoz |
| Aragón | Huesoa | | Cáceres |
| | Teruel | Galicia | La Coruña |
| | Saragossa | | Lugo |
| Asturias | | | Orense |
| Balearic Islands | (Baleares) | | Pontevedra |
| Canary Islands | Las Palmas | Madrid | |
| | Santa Cruz de Tenerife | Murcia | |
| Cantabria | | Navarre | |
| Castile-La Mancha | Albacete | Basque Country | Alava |
| | Ciudad Real | | Guipúzcoa |
| | Cuenca | | Vizcaya |
| | Guadalajara | | |
| | Toledo | | |
| Castile and León | Avila | | |
| | Burgos | | |
| | León | | |
| | Palencia | | |
| | Salamanca | | |
| | Segovia | | |
| | Soria | | |
| | Valladolid | | |
| | Zamora | | |

Bundestag and the *Länder.* Spain's current system of regional governments is a product of historical developments mixed with new institutional creations. Clarification of what powers reside where, central or AC governments, is frequently debated and often requires the intervention of other institutions such as the Constitutional Court.

The structure of the ACs overlaps with the regional and nationalist tendencies in Spain's party system. Many parties, such as the Basque Nationalist Party (PNV) and the Convergence and Union (CiU) of Catalonia are, almost by definition, minority parties in the Spanish Cortes in Madrid but are frequently the largest party in the parliament of their respective autonomous community.

In sum, Spain's system of autonomous communities exists in great part as a response to the regional cleavages that have long characterized the country. With an eye to the future, it additionally places new issues on Spain's political agenda and fundamentally alters the institutional setting within which politics is played out.

## The Judicial System

Many introductory analyses of comparative political systems tend to neglect the role of the judiciary. In the Spanish case, failure to consider the judiciary would lead the student to miss crucial, even if generally less visible, institutional arenas of public policy decision making. Different types of courts have impacted Spain's democratic performance. Similarly, of course, democratic reforms have also affected the judiciary's conduct and operations. While summary in nature, the following discussion focuses on three different aspects of the Spanish judiciary: the normal courts, the Constitutional Court, and the Defender of the People.

***The Legal System*** Similar to most continental European countries, the Spanish legal system is essentially based on civil law traditions. In contrast to the British and U.S. common law systems, civil law is codified law. Two hundred years of direct Roman rule initiated Spain's legal development along the same path as Roman legal traditions. Throughout the centuries, local codes have incorporated local law and customs with Roman-based law. Napoleon's invasion of Spain in 1808 marked the beginning of the modern period of Spanish law. Spanish law as we know it today was codified under the French influence.

***The Normal Courts*** During the nineteenth and twentieth centuries, the structure of Spain's ordinary courts, meaning general civil and criminal courts, has generally remained unchanged despite the shifts between monarchy, dictatorship, and democracy. As with most other European legal systems, the student should think of a hierarchical system, with the Supreme Court at the apex. Created in 1812 and situated in Madrid,

the Supreme Court is the country's highest appellate court. Its different specialized chambers decide appeals brought to it from the lower courts. Most appeals reach the Supreme Court either because one contends a lower court has misapplied a legal doctrine previously issued by the Supreme Court or the appeal is based on a procedural or formal issue. In the former, the Supreme Court issues a new sentence in the case; in the latter, the case is returned to the lower court for resentencing. Generally recognizing "general principles of law" in the Spanish civil code, the Supreme Court tends not to "make law" through its decisions, leaving that power to the legislature. The concept of legal doctrine, however, does present a certain degree of legal precedence, somewhat analogous to that of the U.S. and British systems.

Spain's lower courts provide the source of appeals for the Supreme Court. Working hierarchically from the top down, appeals from the regional Superior Courts of Justice and the Provincial Audiences go directly to the Supreme Court. The National Audience was created in 1977 while the other two have a longer history under previous regimes. The Superior Courts of Justice replaced earlier territorial courts that geographically covered Spain's original kingdoms. The Superior Courts reflect Spain's territorial division into autonomous communities. The Provincial Audiences help spread the case workload across the population. In civil matters, the Superior Courts of Justice and the Provincial Audiences serve as appellate courts for regional and municipal courts as well as Courts of First Instance. In serious criminal matters, they serve as trial courts.

In terms of judges, the Superior Courts of Justice and the Provincial Audiences are collegial, with three-judge panels. In civil matters, they also play a rather minor role, in part because arguments tend to be written more than oral. In criminal cases, these courts follow the continental European accusatory style rather than the English and American adversarial format. Similarly, Spanish judges direct much of the pretrial investigation. As in the grand jury system in the United States, the discovery of sufficient evidence at this level leads to trial in the Provincial Audience.

Judges at all levels are recruited by a judicial corps of nonpolitical civil servants, initially gaining entry through performance on nationwide competitive examinations. Judicial assignments, promotions, discipline, and issues of regulation and administration are made by the General Council of the Judiciary, the administrative organ of the Spanish judicial corp.

During Spain's reforms from the Franco dictatorship to democracy, the tasks and procedures of Spain's ordinary court system did not fundamentally change, except in increased workloads. Under all types of political systems, courts tend to work on normal, day-to-day human conflict. Generally speaking, Franco's abuse of the Spanish judiciary remained fairly focused, occurring primarily in special tribunals of military courts, where even crimes such as armed robbery committed by civilians were heard, and the Court of Public Order. The latter, created in 1963, dealt with cases of "subversion." The 1978 Constitution abolished this overtly political court and limited military jurisdiction to military matters and personnel.

### The Constitutional Court

While Spain's ordinary courts changed little, Spanish democracy brought some major judicial innovation. The creation of the Constitutional Court is the most obvious, and the most important. Borrowing heavily from the examples of Germany and Italy, the 1978 Constitution created the Constitutional Court as an institution of public law. Confusing to American students because functionally the United States Supreme Court serves as two distinct courts—the country's ultimate appellate court as well as serving as a constitutional court—the Spanish Constitutional Court decides three basic types of cases.

First, it determines the constitutionality of, in order of importance, all statutes, organic laws, ordinary laws, laws of the autonomous communities, and executive orders. Many of these cases are raised as "unconstitutionality appeals," which request the law's annulment. Unlike the U.S. Supreme Court, with its appeals by individuals, the Spanish Constitutional Court can only be accessed through petition by one of the fol-

lowing: the prime minister, 50 members of either house of Parliament, the Defender of the People, the head of government of an autonomous community, and, if applicable, the AC parliaments. Unlike in France where appeals must be made before parliament's passage of the bill, unconstitutionality appeals in Spain can be made up to three months after the law's publication in the *Office Bulletin of the State.*

Second, the Constitutional Court hears appeals known as a *recurso de amparo.* Specific to Hispanic law, the *amparo* appeal is central to the protection of constitutional guarantees of fundamental individual rights. It seeks to stop the application of an act or decree; it does not challenge the law itself. The Court's decision applies only to the specific case. The Court's decision is not generalizable.

The third type of case heard by the Constitutional Court involves conflicts between state institutions. At the central level, such conflict might involve the gray areas between the government, the Congress, the Senate, and so on. With the regions, disputes may occur between a specific autonomous community and the central state or between different autonomous communities.

As with all judicial systems, politics envelope Spain's Constitutional Court. One entry of politics into what might initially appear a rather straightforward interpretation of constitutional law is through the recruitment process. The Court has 12 judges, serving nine-year terms. According to the 1978 Constitution, nominations are rotated every three years, with the Congress of Deputies proposing four members of the court, then the Senate four, and then two each by the government and the General Council of the Judiciary. The eight members nominated by the Cortes require a three-fifths majority in the respective assembly. This high decision rule has several important effects: (1) it makes the nomination process a partisan battle; (2) it tends to produce allocations of the four seats among both the government and opposition parties; and (3) it frequently slows down the nomination process to the point that court seats are often left unfilled for long periods.

A second manner in which the Constitutional Court is directly involved in the politics of the day comes from the type of cases it decides. Many of the cases are extremely high-profile. Decisions are frequently front-page headlines. Cases involving the autonomous communities have, for example, been both numerous and highly visible. In the opinion of many, the single greatest contribution the Constitutional Court has made to the new Spanish democracy is in the area of conflict resolution pertaining to the institutionalization of the system of regional government.

Third, the Constitutional Court has increasingly become politicized because of the very nature of Spain's parliamentary system. Political parties in the parliamentary opposition have frequently used their right to bring cases before the Court after losing in Parliament. Frustrated by majority decision making, many members of opposition parties have turned for help to other state institutions. In this manner, the Spanish Constitutional Court has increasingly taken the role of *"La Tercera Camara"*—the Third Legislative Chamber.

***The Defender of the People***    The Constitution of 1978 provided an institutional innovation in the area of the protection of individual rights by creating a Spanish version of an ombudsman—the Defender of the People. The Defender's essential task, however, frequently carries this institution into the world of judicial politics.

An ombudsman protects fundamental rights and freedoms, especially given the growth of the size and power of the modern state in Western democracies. Following the Scandinavian tradition, the ombudsman's primary concern is protection of the individual from unjust or illegal application of the law by administrative or legislative authorities. In Spain, the Defender of the People serves as such an administrative watchdog. This ombudsman-like position serves as a high commission of the Spanish Parliament. Appointed by the legislature, with the possibility of removal for failure to fulfill the job, and required to submit an annual report of actions to the Cortes, the Defender maintains an autonomous position to initiate inquiries and has the power to investigate in all offices of public administration, which means the right to obtain documents and data and to conduct interviews.

Following an investigation, the Defender has several options. He can recommend changes to the public administration authority relevant to the case. Second, and if not satisfied with the first, he can make the appropriate ministry and even Parliament itself aware of the situation. Third, in other areas, the Defender may bring to the Constitutional Court appeals of unconstitutionality and *amparo* appeals. It is through the Defender of the People that an individual in Spain can bring a case to the Constitutional Court.

Given the relative newness of Spain's Defender of the People, an ombudsman tradition has only begun to develop. Regardless, most public opinion polls consistently report that, after King Juan Carlos and the monarchy, the Defender of the People is the most favorably viewed public institution in democratic Spain.

## Thinking Critically

1. Institutionally speaking, what is the classic model of a parliamentary democracy? How has Spain adapted this model to fit its particular needs? How has Spain been especially creative in terms of institutional innovation?
2. How does the head of state differ from the head of government in a parliamentary system? What are the advantages and disadvantages of this institutional duality?
3. Is a constitutional monarchy such as the King of Spain an anachronistic institution? Why and how did Juan Carlos play such an important role in Spain's transition to democracy?
4. What are the major social and political cleavages that differentiate the many political parties in Spain?
5. What role does the judiciary play in the operation of the Spanish political system? Why is it important to consider judicial institutions and processes in analysis of a political, and not just a legal, system?

# KEY TERMS

autonomous communities *(375)*
civil law *(377)*
collective bargaining *(360)*
common law *(377)*
Constitutional Court *(378)*
devolution *(375)*
minority government *(369)*
ombudsman *(379)*
Senate *(374)*

# FURTHER READINGS

Gibbons, John. *Spanish Politics Today* (Manchester: Manchester University Press, 1999).

Gunther, Richard, Giacomo Sani, and Goldie Shabad. *Spain after Franco: The Making of a Competitive Party System* (Berkeley: University of California Press, 1988).

Heywood, Paul. *The Government and Politics of Spain* (New York: St. Martin's, 1995).

Lancaster, Thomas D., and Micheal Giles. "Spain" in Alan N. Katz, ed., *Legal Traditions and Systems: An International Handbook* (New York: Greenwood, 1986).

Merino-Blanco, Elena. *The Spanish Legal System* (London: Sweet and Maxwell, 1996).

Newton, Michael T., with Peter J. Donaghy. *Institutions of Modern Spain: A Political and Economic Guide* (Cambridge: Cambridge University Press, 1997).

Penniman, Howard R., and Eusebio M. Mujal-Léon, eds. *Spain at the Polls, 1977, 1979, and 1982* (Durham, NC: Duke University Press and AEI, 1985).

Powell, Charles. *Juan Carlos of Spain: Self-Made Monarch* (London: Macmillan, 1996).

Royo, Sebastián. *From Social Democracy to Neoliberalism: The Consequences of Party Hegemony in Spain, 1982–1996* (New York: St. Martin's, 2000).

Share, Donald. *Dilemmas of Social Democracy: The Spanish Socialist Workers' Party in the 1980s* (New York: Greenwood Press, 1989).

Wiarda, Howard J. *Politics in Iberia: The Political Systems of Spain and Portugal* (New York: Longman, 1993).

# C. PUBLIC POLICY

The very nature of Spain's transition to democracy and its consolidation has in many respects dictated the essentials of Spanish public policy. Many questions of policy have revolved around fundamental issues of how to implement democracy itself. Issues such as the creation and adoption of a constitution, the establishment of a basic institutional framework for public affairs, and the elaboration and filling out of such initial frameworks have consumed a great deal of time and energy. Related to such policy issues essential to democracy's developments have been concerns important to other Western European countries as well. Analytically, these issues can be grouped into two categories that reflect a remarkable set of disconvergent patterns in a Europe in the early years of the twenty-first century—the process of European integration and regional decentralization.

European integration is bringing citizens in many different nation-states closer together in ways formerly thought impossible. Common policies applied in all member states of the European Union are at the heart of this integration process. Such movement toward "supranational" integration, however, is occurring simultaneously with a process of greater decentralization or devolution within the existing nation-states, including Spain. Pushing this process is the fact that regions and territorially concentrated ethnic and linguistic groups are seeking, and often receiving, increased control over public affairs in that area. Reorganization of fundamental state structures are involved in both these processes: the passing of sovereignty in certain policy areas to the European Union centered in Brussels in terms of supranational integration and the granting of powers to regional or other authorities in the devolution process. Spain is an excellent example of this public policy phenomenon in Western Europe of "pulling in two directions." Understanding these two simultaneous processes should greatly assist in understanding the politics of public policy in democratic Spain.

## REGIONAL POLITICS

One of the most important public policy issues confronting democratic Spain during its early years involved decisions of whether or not to create certain public institutions and, if so, how. The regional system of what became the autonomous communities was one of the most salient. The question of the very existence of a layer of decision-making institutions between the Madrid-based central authorities and the provincial and local authorities has been polemic throughout modern Spanish history. Devolution of Madrid's power to a regional level has been more favorably viewed during periods of liberal democracy, such as Spain's Second Republic (1931–1939) and the contemporary period. In contrast, during periods of authoritarian rule such as the Franco regime, concentration of power in Madrid has been the norm. Ideology and conceptualization of how the Spanish state should be organized thus underscore the politics of regionalization in Spain.

The map at the beginning of this chapter shows the 17 regions or autonomous communities (ACs) of Spain. Three are generally referred to as "historic" regions: Catalonia (Cataluña or Catalunya), the Basque country (Euskadi), and Galicia. The other 14 autonomous communities vary considerably in size, population, diversity of peoples, language usage, and so on. For example, regions like Valencia keep afresh linguistic debates about the relationship of Valenciano to Catalan—whether the former is a separate romance language or a distinct dialect of the latter. Two of the ACs are island groups—the Canaries and the Balearic Islands. The AC of Madrid reflects the very social, economic, and political weight of this metropolitan area in terms of its unique problems of public policy. The contrast of the eight-province ACs of Andalusia and Castile-León and the one-province autonomous community of Murcia reflects the political nature of the very creation of the ACs themselves.

Such unevenness complicates a general discussion of regional politics in Spain. So does the ongoing developmental nature of this process. Nonetheless, several examples of public policy should help illustrate the nature of regional politics in Spain. These include the issues of fiscal policy, the institutionalization of regionalism and regional representation (the Senate and the role of the Constitutional Court), the political impact regionalization can have, and the problem of political violence.

## Fiscal Policy

A primary reason unitary countries like France and Italy raise devolution as an issue is a desire to bring decisions about the raising of revenues (taxes) and the spending of public monies closer to "the people." In some federal systems, the subcentral entities such as the *Länder* in the Federal Republic of Germany account for most public spending. In Spain, much debate has occurred over what policy areas should be transferred to the ACs along with the relevant spending. Particularly in the historic regions of the Basque country (Euskadi) and Catalonia, policy areas such as education and culture were, early in the process, obvious top priorities. Issues of language usage cannot be separated from these. Other powers tend to be region-specific. For example, the transfer of police authority to Euskadi has been completed, and questions about the management and use of water are important to Andalusia and Extremadura.

The AC's power to spend public monies leaves untouched the public issue of central-regional questions of public policy—the power to tax. The politics behind this fundamental power is polemic in Spain. This is due, in part, to the related issues of how central authorities view issues of economic redistribution, territorially speaking, perceptions of possible imbalances in the ratio of amounts of revenue raised in a region and the amount spent there, and political issues of who should ultimately control public finance and at what level of the state. Spain's system of autonomous communities has clearly provided an institutional means for the devolution of cer-

tain policy areas. The independent raising of revenue has not involved the raising of revenues outside the historic regions. For the most part, the making of taxation policy has remained centered in Madrid. Intense political conflict can be found in the regions in Spain where regional authorities wish to control some aspects of this side of fiscal policy.

## Institutionalization of Regionalism

Spain's process of devolution of powers to the autonomous communities has been uneven. It has fluctuated over time, varied among the regions, and faced many political obstacles. While much can be said about this process, two issues might help one better understand the institutionalization of Spanish democracy described earlier. The politics of regionalism in Spain have involved the exercise of powers of at least two other key institutions: the Constitutional Court and the Senate.

As described above, Spain's Constitutional Court is a new institution. The Constitution of 1978 outlined its role as a defender of constitutional principles. Consistent with this role, one of its functions is to resolve disputes between institutions of the state. This includes a clarification of powers between central and regional institutions as well as between the autonomous communities. Creation of Spain's current quasi-federal system has naturally produced a need to resolve critical issues of institutional conflict and clarification of questions of power. As a consequence, the Constitutional Court has played a key role in the development of Spain's regional political system and in the process of the devolution of powers from Madrid. Many of its decisions have involved cases involving the institutionalization of regional policy in Spain. While the government-parliamentary process at the central level remains the most important stage for setting the agenda for regional policy, the Spanish Constitutional Court has had a significant impact on its long-term development. For example, the Constitutional Court's declaration of unconstitutionality of key components of the Organic Law for the Harmonization of Autonomy Process (LOAPA) in 1983 demonstrated both the Court's ability to reverse a politically determined direction for regional policy and to frame the longer-term nature of regional policy in Spain. LOAPA had been enacted by the Cortes in June 1982 as a way to rationalize and make more uniform the development of regional governments.

The Senate—the upper house of the Spanish Parliament—is a second institutional arena that serves as an important indictor of regional policy in Spain. As discussed earlier, the Senate is not a "chamber of the regions" like the Bundesrat in the Federal Republic of Germany or the Senate in the United States. Instead, the Constitution of 1978 created an upper house based on the provinces in a manner that has left open political questions about what is and should be the Senate's role and representative base. The central point here is that reform of the Senate is currently being discussed but the direction of any changes is not yet clear. One possibility is to have the Senate serve as the center of parliamentary representation for Spain's 17 autonomous communities. Such reform would clearly integrate democratic Spain's central state institutions with its developing regional policy.

## Political Terrorism

The most visible manifestation of the Spanish state's inability to resolve fully regional issues is the continuation of political violence. The most perplexing problem facing democratic Spain is the killing and other acts of violence that continue over the status of the Basque country. This region's political and governmental relationship to Madrid has historically been extremely strained and turbulent. Early Castilian monarchies governmentally gained political peace by granting *foros*—locally based rights of self-government. (The current devolution process should be viewed within a broader historical context of the blowing of similar political winds.) At other times, Madrid-based authorities sought to dominate the Basque country. The Franco regime serves as the last example of this tendency, most violently demonstrated during the civil war in the bombing of Guérnica, the historic and symbolic center of Euskadi.

Given such historic vacillation in center-regional governmental relations, a small section of Basque society remains unconvinced that any solution other than a complete separation and independence from Madrid is acceptable. One such sector contains supporters of ETA-militar and Herri Batasuna/Euskal Herritarrok, the political party related to it. Beginning during the Franco regime, ETA-militar has carried out many political assassinations and other attacks. These attacks tend not to be random acts of violence against the civilian population. Most of the violence has been directed against the politicians, businessmen, and members of the military and security forces. One early and highly visible attack was the 1973 assassination of Prime Minister Carrero Blanco, Franco's political heir apparent. His assassination altered the course of the political transition that began following Franco's death in 1975.

Many people optimistically hoped that ETA's struggle was one directed only against the authoritarianism of the Franco regime. Its continued campaign of assassinations and kidnappings throughout the present democratic regime has clearly revealed the organization's fundamental colors—that of an independence group to its supporters and a terrorist organization to others. This political violence remains democratic Spain's most intractable problem. Other violent groups such as GRAPO (Groups of Antifascist Resistance, First of October) have also existed, but ETA remains the single most visible threat. Government policies have included hard-line stances, concerted efforts to work with moderate political forces within the Basque community, and attempts at coordination of policy on an international basis, especially with France. Furthermore, accusations have been made of counter-assassination organized by government leaders during the Socialist government of Felipe González. Beyond specific details, the issue of political violence as a consequence of the country's central-regional cleavage remains a troubling issue in democratic Spain.

Spain's regional politics and its devolution process follow a pattern found in other Western countries. As the twenty-first century begins, a

Artful graffiti in the Basque country: propaganda for Herri Batasuna, the political party linked with the Basque terrorist group ETA.

clear pattern can be witnessed in the preferences held by many democratically governed peoples to territorially disaggregate governmental decision making and public administration. Whether motivated by a desire to bring government "closer to the people" or as a reaction against the growth in the state, the fact is that similar trends in devolution can be found throughout the world. Spain, in this regard, is no exception.

## THE POLITICS OF EUROPEAN INTEGRATION

Spain is simultaneously part of another large pattern involving the internationalization of Europe and the world. The country's democratic transition facilitated membership in international organizations key to contemporary Europe. Most prominent of these are the European Union (EU) and the North Atlantic Treaty Organization (NATO).

## The European Union

Membership in the European Union (EU), earlier the European Community (EC), cannot be separated from Spain's transition to democracy. As a supranational organization, the EC required member countries to be liberal democratic systems, which is why Franco's application in 1962 never received a formal response and why the former socialist countries of Eastern Europe are now lining up for membership. The EC would only take seriously applications for membership from democratic countries.

Thus, on July 28, 1977, little more than a month after Spain's first democratic election, Prime Minister Adolfo Suárez submitted Spain's formal application for membership to the European Community. Official discussion, however, did not begin until February 1979. Negotiations were difficult and protracted. Issues such as state subsidies to agriculture and the sheer size of the Spanish fishing fleet slowed the many agreements required. The PSOE government formed after the October 1982 elections gave a new impetus to the negotiations. Major progress was made in the June 1983 Stuttgart Summit and from the end of 1984 to March 1985. When agreement on all aspects of membership was finally reached between Spain and the Community, the Accession treaty was signed on June 12, 1985. As with other new members, this treaty formally and legally linked Spain to the European Community (and the European Community for Atomic Energy—EURATOM). While making membership effective on January 1, 1986, it also spelled out a series of progressively integrative stages that would bring the Spanish economy fully into Europe's. This complex transition period culminated on January 1, 1996.

Spain's membership in the European Community, now the European Union, occurred without a great deal of domestic controversy. According to public opinion polls, most Spaniards supported EC membership. So did most groups active in the public arena. Unlike Portugal's Communist Party, Spain's largest political parties were willing to accept the Community's liberal economic orientation. Similarly, Spain's major economic and social entities, such as the largest trade unions, business organizations, and other prominent interest groups, supported integration. In contrast to Greece (which joined in 1981) and Portugal (which joined simultaneously with Spain), little domestic political friction came with Spain's bid for EC membership.

In the short term, Spain's push for European membership appeared to have placed politics before economics. The most frequently advanced argument in favor of membership contended that membership would stabilize democracy in Spain. The reasoning here was that integration with the

other European liberal polities would add an additional pillar to support Spain's budding democracy. Besides seeing membership as strengthening the country's democratic institutions and traditions, Spaniards remembered that the Franco dictatorship had long excluded Spain from the Community's collection of democratic countries. The argument thus suggested EC membership might also give the other European countries a vested interest in preserving Spain's democracy.

On the other hand, the short-term economic price of Spain's membership was taken by many as a given. The opening of Spain's domestic economy forced a great deal of structural adjustment, especially because of the lingering high protective tariffs and import substitution policies of the Franco era. State subsidies to key industries, long established monopolistic practices, the lack of standard regulations in such areas as the environment, and an antiquated fiscal system of revenue generation meant EC membership would shake the Spanish economic system hard. Acknowledging these economic hardships, Spain's leadership knew that the country's future rested with the integration process of the other European democracies.

Since Spain joined the European Union in 1986, Spanish foreign policy is difficult to separate from that of the rest of Europe. Membership in the process of European integration now fundamentally dictates the nature and direction of Spanish foreign policy. As a full and active member of the European Union, Spain is politically and economically linked to Europe's path. Study of Spain's international relations must thus be understood within the broader context of the European Union. As Europe goes, so goes Spain. The years of Spain's international isolation, particularly from Europe, are clearly over.

## NATO

Contemporary foreign relations and their relationship to domestic politics can be symbolized in many respects by why and how Spain joined the North Atlantic Treaty Organization. American military bases were established in Spain in the mid-1950s. These and Spain's membership in the United Nations were the other half of a deal negotiated between Franco and President Eisenhower in which the United States ended its embargo against Spain and diplomatically recognized the Franco regime. Such events and decisions must be placed in their proper context within the Cold War. This same East-West division still dominated international politics during Spain's transition to democracy. Thus, one of the early debates following the institutionalization of democracy centered on the question of Spain's joining the West's military alliance.

Domestically, the issue of NATO membership split the emerging party system down the ideological middle. The Left, especially the PCE and the PSOE, argued against membership. Preferring a neutral position, they reminded the people of Spain's official neutrality in both world wars. More centrally, and in some ways similar to the French position at the time, they feared joining an essentially American-dominated military club. On the other hand, the Right, especially the UCD and the PP, favored NATO membership. Proponents of membership highlighted democratic Spain's new responsibilities in the West's important international organizations, the need to stand united against the Communist-dominated East, and internal issues like the professionalization of the Spanish military.

While clearly not ideologically as tidy as this, the issue of Spanish membership in NATO was an early topic indicative of how politics was to be played in democratic Spain. First, consistent with the general elite nature of Spain's democratic transition, the UCD government brought Spain into NATO with a simple parliamentary vote in 1981, about a half year after the abortive coup of February 23. This was perfectly legal within the constitutional framework, but the Left sensed both the political weakness of Calvo Sotelo's UCD government (Adolfo Suárez had resigned earlier) and that public opinion seemed opposed to this entry. As the 1982 general election approached, the PSOE smelled power. Regarding the NATO question, the PSOE argued for the withdrawal of Spain from the Western Alliance. More importantly,

and in a populist appeal, they argued that such an important issue should be resolved by the people themselves in a referendum. The 1982 electoral victory thus committed Felipe González's PSOE government to a NATO referendum within four years, that is, prior to the next general election. This timing became more important as the years passed because the PSOE government slowly changed its position to one favoring Spain's remaining in NATO. Increasingly the González government saw the issue of NATO membership as one step in improving civilian-military relations and in a broader international context that included European Community membership. While neither formally nor legally linked, the NATO question and Spain's pending membership in the European Community began to overlap. Both issues were cast as part of democratic Spain taking its "proper" role within Europe.

In an adroit set of political and leadership maneuvers, Felipe González managed to keep Spain in NATO and to effectively resolve the issue for good. First, he postponed the NATO referendum as long as possible. It wasn't held until June 1985. Second, he embarked on a skillful campaign to convince the Spanish people that NATO membership was in the country's best interest over the long term. Third, he produced a wording for the referendum question that, in a rather complex statement, never referred specifically to NATO (only the "Atlantic Alliance") and that sought to leave Spain in NATO but not as part of the military command structure (much like France at the time). Finally, he indirectly made it an issue of confidence in his government and leadership. Despite public opinion polls to the contrary up until the actual vote, the referendum passed 53 percent in favor of Spain remaining in NATO and 47 percent against.

The referendum politically resolved the issue of Spain's membership in NATO. Domestically, the way in which the NATO question was resolved clearly showed the effect of elite decision making in Spain. Rhetoric to the contrary, leadership matters. The peaceful resolution of the NATO question also demonstrates a general underlying consensus that exists in democratic

Spain. The relatively uncontroversial participation of Spain in multinational military forces in Bosnia, and Afghanistan after September 11, 2001, clearly demonstrates this consensus.

# ECONOMIC POLICY

Spain's consensus model of a transition to democracy can clearly be seen in the area of economic policy making. Both as a consequence of Franco's policies and the energy crises of the 1970s, Spain's transition to democracy unfolded simultaneously with a worldwide economic slowdown. Inflation was high, unemployment increased, and economic growth slowed. The political elite directing Spain's transition clearly followed the strategy that politics had to come before economics, that the difficult but necessary economic decisions would have to be postponed until after the difficult political decisions were made. To tackle these intransigent economic problems without consensus on most elements of the new democracy's foundation would doom the political transition. A strategy of consensus and compromise thus dominated economic policy making until democracy had been secured.

This strategy of consensus in economic policy making came in the form of a series of social-economic agreements among key political and economic actors. Many of the agreements tended to have a tripartite nature, including the government, business, and labor. Some involved political parties representing their affiliated interests such as business and labor, and others involved key interest organizations: the CEOE (the business umbrella organization) and the UGT and the CCOO (the two largest labor unions). While not always signed by the same participants, these agreements bought economic peace in order to reach agreement on the solidification of democracy. The agreements tended to focus on key economic areas such as wage restraints, employment creation, industrial restructuring, and social security. Their existence permitted early democratic governments to postpone difficult economic decisions until Spain's political house was in order, democratically speaking.

The Pacts of Moncloa were the first of these agreements. They were signed in the prime minister's official residence in 1977 after the first democratic elections. In them, all major political parties agreed to limitations on wage increases and dealt with issues of prices and monetary policy, tax reform, social security, employment, housing, and many more issues. They also established an important pattern for future agreements between business, labor, and the government.

Table 6.2 lists these and subsequent pacts that characterized Spain's elite-level and peak association policy-making style during the early years of democracy. While all were not legally binding, they suggest the strong degree of cooperation between business, labor, and the government. Many of the economic goals were not met, but the fact that agreement could be found and attempts at implementation made nevertheless proved remarkable, especially given that the CEOE is much more coherently organized than the trade unions and that the trade unions only account for about 15 percent of the Spanish workforce. The Economic and Social Agreement of 1984 shows that such pact-making carried beyond the first UCD governments and into the first years of Felipe González's time in power. Such pact-making, however, then stopped rather abruptly—the PSOE governments pursued other leadership styles in economic policy making and labor relations, as indicated by their strained relationship with the socialist-oriented UGT. Since the Popular Party came to power in 1996, Spain has returned to a pact-making style similar to its early years of the transition. Negotiations and agreements between Spain's business association, the labor unions, and the government appear central to José María Aznar's approach to macroeconomic policy making.

## Macroeconomic Policy Making

The macroeconomic management of a country's economy generally targets two broad goals: economic growth and the balancing of unemployment and inflation. In turn, economic policy can generally be viewed in two parts: fiscal and monetary policy. The latter most directly involves central bank decision making. Monetary policy tends to utilize instruments such as management of the money supply, interest rates, reserve ratios, and the regulation of credit to target an acceptable level of inflation while maintaining growth in the economy. Fiscal policy, on the other hand, primarily involves government spending on the expenditures side and taxation in terms of revenue generation. Like monetary policy, macroeconomic fiscal management tends to focus on economic growth. However, fiscal policy also places prime consideration on distributive consequences and specific policy programs that would increase or decrease public spending. While both the instruments and targets of monetary and fiscal policy overlap, the following discussion maintains these normally accepted distinctions to analyze economic policy in democratic Spain.

## Monetary Policy: From the Bank of Spain to the Euro

Like all other European central banks, the Bank of Spain found itself throughout the 1990s in the interesting position of working to put itself out of business. The Bank's larger economic goals were framed by the criteria laid out in the European Union's Maastricht Treaty to bring all member state's currencies in line to achieve European monetary union. Throughout the last decade of the twentieth century, the goal of replacing the Spanish peseta with the euro constrained Spain's economic policy. The European Union's standards for monetary convergence, including inflation, public debt, and so on, were determined at the supranational level. Spain successfully met these standards. With European monetary union, and the introduction of the euro into circulation on January 1, 2002, the Bank of Spain lost to the European Central Bank in Frankfurt, Germany, the power to determine Spain's monetary policy. The fact that so many other European central banks underwent the same process suggests how far Spain has come to resemble the other democ-

ratic countries of Europe in the area of economic policy.

The powers and responsibilities of the Bank of Spain are a useful indicator of how economic policy making has changed in Spain since the transition to democracy. First, no introduction to Spanish political economy, however brief, can avoid mentioning the importance of monetary policy, certainly in a country such as Spain, where economics and politics go hand in hand. Second, the Bank of Spain long served as the country's central bank, meaning it was the public institution responsible for day-to-day operations of the monetary system and for supervision of the country's overall banking system. Third, the Bank can serve as an institutional indicator of change in democratic Spain, given the banking system's economic importance during the Franco regime. Finally, as already mentioned, the Bank of Spain played a determining role as Spain and the other member countries of the European Union completed the steps toward monetary integration in 2002.

While the Bank of Spain has now given up most of its powers in monetary policy making to the European Central Bank, it still maintains many fundamental responsibilities within Spain's banking system. A close reading of the importance of the Bank of Spain in the history of Spanish monetary policy will help show what all students should learn about the European Central Bank—because it now controls monetary policy for Europe in much the same manner as the Bank of Spain did for so many years for Spain. In addition, despite the recent historical changes in some of the Bank of Spain's most important functions, it did play an important role in recent Spanish political and economic history.

With a history similar to the central bank of many other European countries, the Bank of Spain began in the eighteenth century as a private bank and grew in importance. It changed its name in 1856 to the Bank of Spain to reflect its new role as the country's central bank. The Bank was officially nationalized in 1962. Until the introduction of the euro, the Bank of Spain as a modern central bank was the sole issuer of legal tender, handled the government's financial business including servicing the public debt, managed Spain's foreign currency reserves, supervised the functioning of the banking system by maintaining commercial and other banks' legally required reserves and utilizing a system of control and inspection, and centrally coordinated the collecting and reporting of financial data.

The political and economic context for these operations changed greatly over the years, and not just with the most recent adoption of the euro. During the Franco regime, the banking system played center stage to economic development and financial activities. The authoritarian regime stifled financial sector competition by preventing nonbank and other alternative sources of finance, by forbidding foreign banks, by preserving the privileged status of certain domestic banking groups through a severe limitation of entry of new domestic banks into the domestic market, and by permitting these privileged banking groups to control a significant portion of Spanish industry. Such economic policies placed the Bank of Spain at the head of an inflexible and inward-looking financial system.

Reforms that increased the system's openness began in the 1970s and paralleled many political changes. Banks received greater freedom to expand, fix interest rates, and seek new ways to attract funds. Beginning in 1978, foreign banks were permitted to operate in Spain. The Bank of Spain, too, received more powers to manage monetary policy, control liquidity, and assert itself in its supervisory capacity.

The key question about any central bank, certainly for political science students, should be this: to what degree does a central bank possess independence in decision making from elected officials, particularly the government? The Bank of Spain was traditionally politically dependent on the government through the Ministry of Economics and Finance. Both under the Franco regime and in the first decade or so of democracy, the Bank followed government directives. This changed, however, in 1994 when the Bank of Spain gained independence. The legislation granting this was a major and required step in Spain's participation in European monetary integration.

Behind Spain's highly visible shift from use of the peseta to the euro is the institutional transfer of power for monetary power from the Bank of Spain to the Central European Bank. The Bank of Spain is now clearly subordinate to the European Central Bank in terms of monetary policy. Understanding this institutional change in monetary policy is fundamentally important to a full understanding of Spanish macroeconomic policy. It should, however, be viewed in a manner similar to institutional change in other parts of the Spanish political system. Like the many public institutions of contemporary democratic Spain, the initial steps have been taken but long-term consequences must be carefully observed. Institution-building as a central part of political development often has many unforeseen consequences.

## Fiscal Policy

The politics of fiscal policy in any country fundamentally involve governmental leadership. In democratic Spain, fiscal policy directs our analytical attention to the prime minister, the cabinet, and the Parliament. Who has been in power and the constraints under which this power has been exercised suggest a great deal about the nature and direction of Spain's fiscal policy. Three aspects of Spain's fiscal policy are considered here: reforms in taxation, the ubiquitous task of minimizing budget deficits, and the persistent unemployment problem.

*Taxation*    Democratic Spain inherited the Franco regime's macroeconomic policies and structures. Unlike in Eastern Europe, where the transition to democracy simultaneously involved change from a socialist command economy to one more oriented to free-market capitalism, the changes in Spain were primarily political. As suggested earlier, during the heady days of the transition, economics generally took a back seat to politics: decisions by Suárez's UCD governments tended to suggest a strategy of consolidating democracy first and postponing difficult economic decisions. Reform of the Francoist system of taxation was one such difficult item on the country's fiscal policy agenda.

The Franco regime possessed a regressive and generally inefficient system of taxation and other forms of revenue generation. While relying primarily on indirect taxes that placed the heaviest burden on those least able to pay, the inefficient state bureaucracy made revenue collection of all types a relatively expensive undertaking. Politically, taxation systems tend to be judged by their distributional consequences. Economically, however, they should also be evaluated in terms of the ratio of the amount spent to collect revenue and the total amount of revenues actually collected. In both areas, a general consensus existed among Spain's new liberal democratic leadership that taxation reform was badly needed. But what type of reform? The problem with debate over any tax reform is that, regardless of country, it mobilizes many political actors and interests. It also draws rather rigid lines of confrontation between competing groups.

Spain's fiscal policy response to this politicized question about tax reform rested with the European Union. As already mentioned, immediately following the transition to democracy, a general political consensus existed within Spain on the desirability of joining the EC. Politics came first: EC membership, it was argued, would help reinforce the fledgling democracy. One price for admission generally not discussed, however, was the requirement that all members adopt the value added tax (VAT), a policy directed at harmonizing fiscal policy. The question of Spanish membership in the EC contained an understanding that taxation reform would be part of the package.

The VAT is an indirect tax on products. Generally speaking, it functions much like a sales tax. Utilized throughout Western Europe, the VAT's built-in reporting mechanism gives it the advantage of being relatively inexpensive to collect, it fluctuates with economic activity, and it is somewhat invisible politically speaking. For Spain, the advantage of the VAT meant all parties could claim that tax reform was out of their hands. External constraints, especially desired EC membership, thus removed most controversy from the politics of tax reform. The value added tax became law in Spain and its most important means of revenue generation, on January 1, 1986—the day Spain officially joined the European Community.

As a major step in fiscal reform, Spain's adoption of the VAT also served as a catalyst for many other important changes in fiscal policy. While fundamentally important, VAT's adoption did not break Spain's tradition, along with that of other Mediterranean countries, of relying heavily on indirect taxes. In the 1980s Spain pushed farther on fiscal reform and significantly broadened its system of taxation. New laws on personal income tax expanded the state's revenue base, more in line with countries like Germany, Austria, and the Benelux countries. Increased reliance on income taxes helped add a more progressive flavor to Spain's overall system of taxation. More recently, a great deal of political discussion has focused on greater fiscal devolution to the regions, including taxation powers.

## Budget Deficits

As with monetary policy and some aspects of taxation policy, membership in the European Union has served to constrain many aspects of Spain's fiscal policy. Specifically, the EU's move toward monetary integration, as spelled out in the Treaty of Maastricht, required certain directions for member states' fiscal policy. Similar to most Western European countries, Spain struggled throughout the 1990s to keep its budget deficits and overall national debt within the guidelines set forth in Maastricht. As monetary integration occurred, Spain's record on deficit spending placed it somewhere near the median of EU members. It was thus able to meet Europe's criteria on budget deficits.

Having to operate with the EU's framework will continue to impose fiscal discipline on Spanish governments. Most people will focus on two major political and economic pressures on maintaining such fiscal discipline. One involves a pattern of rapidly growing spending by the relatively new autonomous communities. The other is the persistent problem of unemployment in Spain.

## Unemployment: The Persistent Problem

What should be clear from the previous discussion is that EU membership has increasingly harmonized Spain's monetary and fiscal policies with those of other Western European countries. Fiscal and monetary convergence is unquestionably shifting the location of political debate over such questions. However, while the goals of macroeconomic policy are increasingly determined at the supranational level of the European Union, many of the ways of achieving them and their consequences continue to reside at the nation-state level. Simply stated, each EU country continues to possess some unique economic issues. For Spain, the most persistent problem is the dubious distinction of maintaining the highest rate of unemployment in Western Europe.

As seen in Figure 6.4, Spain's official rate of unemployment was higher than 20 percent of the active workforce throughout most of the 1990s. It reached as high as 24.2 percent in 1994. Such

a rate well surpasses unemployment in the United States during the worst period of the Great Depression. While recent trends are encouraging, the perplexing problem for Spanish authorities is that high unemployment is not a short-term problem. Throughout most of the country's current democratic experience, Spain's rate of unemployment has been a blemish on its record. Unemployment seems permanently stuck in the 10–25 percent range. Such figures clearly suggest a fundamental structural flaw in the Spanish economy. Students of politics will readily note that this unemployment problem has persisted regardless of which party is in power in Madrid. Addressing Spain's serious unemployment problem has been at the foremost of macroeconomic policy for democratic Spain's early moderate UCD government, the long years of PSOE rule, and rule by the moderate-right Popular Party since 1996.

Many explanations can be given for democratic Spain's most perplexing economic problem. Given its earlier corporatist orientation,

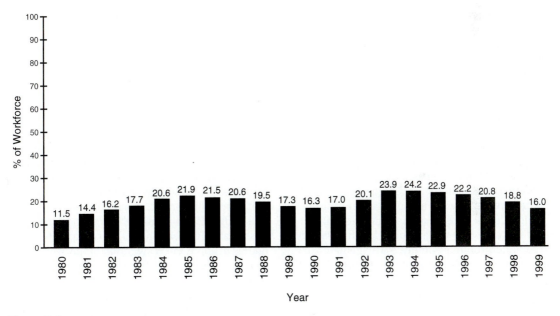

Figure 6.4  UNEMPLOYMENT IN SPAIN

the Francoist economic system inherited by democratic Spain was full of market inefficiencies, including the labor market. Dismissing workers has been extremely difficult. State support of key industries—frequently through the state holding company, the National Institute of Industry (INI)—added to these distortions in the labor market. The PSOE governments' increased liberalization of the economy—one reason its relationship with the trade unions has been strained—included privatization policies that facilitate the elimination of labor redundancies. The various PSOE governments of Felipe González additionally appeared to have leaned more toward fighting inflation than combating unemployment, in the classic Phillips curve tradeoff. González's commitment to Spain's increased reliance on market forces has, of course, also come within the context of EU membership.

Spain's joining the EU has had many beneficial economic effects, including a boom in growth in the late 1980s, but market integration and policy harmonization such as constraints on deficit spending have made it more difficult for any quick fixes to the unemployment problem. Since coming to power in 1996, the Popular Party has strongly pushed a liberalization of the economy as a long-term solution. Under Prime Minister Aznar, the PP government has strongly pushed for a greater privatization of all aspects of the Spanish economy. This included a major liberalization package in June 2000 with reforms in many economic sectors, including competition policy, telecommunications, electricity, natural gas and oil distribution, retail distribution, and pharmacies.

One final explanation of Spain's high level of unemployment focuses on an argument that the problem is not as bad as the figures might initially indicate. For years, Spain has had a very large underground economy. Many people work in a cash-only economy, with both employers and workers seeking to avoid taxes and other regulations. While many people continue to draw various types of state assistance targeted for the unemployed, some proportion of the officially unemployed continue to work. While such

a black-market economy is difficult to measure, some estimates argue that it accounts for about one-third of those in Spain officially registered as unemployed.

## CORRUPTION AND SCANDALS

We began our analysis suggesting that the dominant question about the Spanish political system concerned the nature, direction, and survival of the transition to democracy and its consolidation. Similarities of the Spanish system with other Western European democracies have been emphasized throughout this discussion. For believers in the principles of democracy, such comparisons are encouraging for an evaluation of the long-term prospects of this form of system in Spain.

Unfortunately, not all similarities are positive. As appears so endemic in Italy and periodically witnessed in places widely recognized as successful democracies, Spain regrettably experienced throughout the 1980s and 1990s a series of public affairs involving accusation of political corruption, financial improprieties, abuse of power, and negligence in administration. The list of such accusations is quite long: the Toxic Syndrome case in which hundreds of Spaniards died terrible deaths from contaminated cooking oil in 1981 and the subsequent inability to bring to justice those responsible, even as late as trials in April 1992; the "Guerra affair," in which the brother of then Vice Prime Minister Alfonso Guerra appeared to have enriched himself by using his family ties and government offices to win government contracts and buy public property at extraordinarily low prices—accusations that eventually forced Guerra to resign in March 1991; the "Renfe scandal" involving land purchases and fabrication of VAT receipts that ultimately brought the resignation of the Minister of Health in January 1992; the "Filesa affair," in which accusations were disclosed in April 1993 that this group of consulting companies had billed banks and companies for work not performed and then channeled the money to the PSOE for its 1989 election campaign; lax enforcement efforts in policing corruption when in November 1993 Luis Roldán, the head of the Civil Guard from 1986 to 1993, was arrested on charges of diverting large amounts of public funds to secret bank accounts and then, while permitted out of jail on bail, fled the country; the arrest in December 1994 of Mário Conde, the former chair of the Banesto banking group, and nine members of the board for embezzling $53 million, then when the Bank of Spain took control of Banesto, the former director of the central bank from 1984 to 1992 was arrested and accused of violating insider trading laws by passing on confidential economic information; the Cesid case, which revealed in June 1995 that Spain's military espionage service had conducted secret wiretappings of conversations by many political and business leaders including King Juan Carlos—revelations that brought the resignation of the PSOE government's minister of defense and Vice Prime Minister Narcís Serra, who was defense minister at the time; and the GAL case (Antiterrorist Liberation Group) in which former Interior Minister José Barrionuevo and others were accused of forming and operating death squads in the fight against terrorism, specifically against ETA.

The PSOE governments of Felipe González drew most of the political fire for this long string of scandals. They unquestionably help account for the PSOE defeat in the March 1996 general elections. Interestingly given the success of Spain's consolidation of democracy, many observers argued that the basic underlying problem was the very longevity of PSOE's democratic control of power. Certainly fewer scandals have emerged since the Popular Party has been in power. Did these scandals occur in Spain given a certain complacency by PSOE in holding power, similar to arguments made in Italy about the corruptive effects of any real alternation of parties in power there? Or should the very awareness of these scandals be viewed as the positive effect of the ability of democracies to bring to light the weaknesses of corrupt individual officials? Whatever the answer, the very reason for such debate suggests that the Spanish democratic system has moved beyond questioning its initial develop-

ments. Now, the Spanish polity must face questions unfortunately confronted from time to time by all viable democracies.

## CONCLUSION

This overview of the Spanish political system sought to describe its historical context, many of the key governmental institutions and political actors, and a few of the problems the country faces as it enters the twenty-first century. This analysis of the Spanish political system emphasized two thematic issues. First, it considered the uniqueness of the Spanish transition to democracy, and whether it can be replicated in other countries. Second, we analyzed Spain's current democratic system with an emphasis on its similarities with other European polities. Such similarities include the positive construction of state institutions, arenas of democratic decision making, and avenues for the free expression of individual preferences. They also contain negative features such as democratic Spain's three greatest challenges: the elimination of political terrorism and violence, persistently high levels of unemployment, and signs of institutionalized corruption.

The identification of these similarities should suggest to the reader that Spain's democratic system borrowed heavily from already established democratic systems of Western Europe. Given the fact that other countries traveling the difficult road to democracy have borrowed from Spain and evidence presented here that Spain learned from other democracies reinforces the notion that democratic systems are, by definition, dynamic in nature. They do not develop in isolation. The importance of Spain's democratic system is thus most fully appreciated from a broad comparative perspective.

### Thinking Critically

1. What policy issues are specific to Spain and which are typical questions of governance for all European political systems?

2. How has the process of regionalization affected public policy in the Spanish political system? Which areas in this "output" side of governance appear the most heavily intertwined with the regionalization process?

3. European integration in general, and membership in the European Union specifically, has had a significant impact on Spanish public policy. Where has this impact been the strongest? In which policy areas has EU membership affected the making and implementation of public policy in Spain?

4. How is Spain an example of Europe's "pulling in two directions," in terms of simultaneously under a process of European integration and regionalization? In your opinion, are these two processes related, or are they separate phenomena?

5. What are the links between Spanish political history, as described in Section A, and this section's discussion of policy issues such as political terrorism and NATO membership?

# KEY TERMS

Bank of Spain *(388)*
Catalonia *(381)*
European Union *(384)*
Euskadi *(381)*
*foros (383)*
fiscal policy *(382)*
monetary policy *(388)*
NATO *(385)*
value added tax *(390)*

# FURTHER READINGS

Clark, Robert P., and Michael H. Haltzel, eds. *Spain in the 1980s* (Cambridge, MA: Ballinger, 1987).

Fishman, Robert M. *Working-Class Organization and the Return to Democracy in Spain* (Ithaca, NY: Cornell University Press, 1990).

Foweraker, Joe. *Making Democracy in Spain.* (Cambridge: Cambridge University Press, 1989).

Gillespie, Richard, Fernando Rodrigo, and Jonathan Story. *Democratic Spain: Reshaping External Relations in a Changing World* (London: Routledge, 1995).

Heywood, Paul, ed. *Politics and Policy in Democratic Spain* (London: Frank Cass, 1999).

Martinez, Robert E. *Business and Democracy in Spain* (Westport, CT: Praeger, 1993).

Maxwell, Kenneth, and Steven Spiegel. *The New Spain: From Isolation to Influence* (New York: Council on Foreign Relations Press, 1994).

Mujal-Léon, Eusebio. *Communism and Political Change in Spain* (Bloomington: Indiana University Press, 1983).

Payne, Stanley G., ed. *The Politics of Democratic Spain.* (Chicago: Chicago Council on Foreign Relations, 1986).

Smith, W. Rand. *The Left's Dirty Job: The Politics of Industrial Restructuring in France and Spain* (Pittsburgh: University of Pittsburgh Press, 1998).

# WEB SITES

**www.electionworld.org/spain.htm**
General site leading to others
**www.sispain.org**
General site with links
**www.members.tripod.com/spainresources/ governme.htm**
General site with links
**www.casareal.es**
Monarchy
**www.congreso.es**
Congress of Deputies
**www.senado.es**
Senate
**www.la-moncloa.es**
Prime Minister (President of Government)
**www.tribunalconstitucional.es**
Constitutional Court
**www.cgpj.es**
General Council of the Judiciary

**www.bde.es**
Bank of Spain
**www.pp.es**
Popular Party
**www.psoe.es**
Socialist Party
**www.izquierda-unida.es**
United Left

**www.convergencia-i-unio.org**
Catalan National Party (CiU)
**www.eaj-pnv.com**
Basque National Party (PNV)
**www.ccoo.es**
Workers Commissions (CCOO) trade union
**www.ugt.es**
General Union of Workers (UGT)

THE NETHERLANDS

NORTH
SEA

West Frisian Islands

Leeuwarden

GRONINGEN

Groningen

FRIESLAND

Den Helder

Assen

DRENTHE

NORTH
HOLLAND

Northeast
Polder

FLEVOLAND

Zwolle

Flevoland
Polder

OVERIJSSEL

Haarlem

Amsterdam

Enschede

Apeldoorn

GELDERLAND

The Hague

SOUTH
HOLLAND

UTRECHT

Utrecht

Delft

Arnhem

Rotterdam

Dordrecht

Nijmegen

GERMANY

Breda

NORTH
BRABANT

Middelburg

Tilburg

ZEELAND

Eindhoven

LIMBURG

BELGIUM

Maastricht

0      25      50 Miles

0   25   50 Kilometers

# THE GOVERNMENT OF THE
# Netherlands

*Ken Gladdish*

## INTRODUCTION

**Background:** The Kingdom of the Netherlands was formed in 1815. In 1830 Belgium seceded and formed a separate kingdom. The Netherlands remained neutral in World War I but suffered a brutal invasion and occupation by Germany in World War II. A modern, industrialized nation, the Netherlands is also a large exporter of agricultural products. The country was a founding member of NATO and the EC and participated in the introduction of the euro in 1999.

### GEOGRAPHY
**Location:** Western Europe, bordering the North Sea, between Belgium and Germany
**Area:** 41,526 sq km
**Area-comparative:** slightly less than twice the size of New Jersey
**Land boundaries:** 1,027 km
   *border countries:* Belgium 450 km, Germany 577 km
**Climate:** temperate; marine; cool summers and mild winters
**Terrain:** mostly coastal lowland and reclaimed land (polders); some hills in southeast
**Elevation extremes:** *lowest point:* Prins Alexanderpolder –7 m
   *highest point:* Vaalserberg 321 m
**Geography note:** located at mouths of three major European rivers (Rhine, Maas or Meuse, and Schelde)

### PEOPLE
**Population:** 15,981,472
**Age structure:** *0–14 years:* 18.38% (male 1,501,925; female 1,436,017)
   *15–64 years:* 67.9% (male 5,518,575; female 5,333,442)
   *65 years and over:* 13.72% (male 899,052; female 1,292,461)

**Population growth rate:** 0.55%

**Birthrate:** 11.85 births/1,000 population

**Sex ratio:** 0.98 males/female

**Life expectancy at birth:** 78.43 years

*male:* 75.55 years

*female:* 81.44 years

**Nationality:** *noun:* Dutchman(men), Dutchwoman(women)

*adjective:* Dutch

**Ethnic groups:** Dutch 91%, Moroccans, Turks, and other 9%

**Religions:** Roman Catholic 31%, Protestant 21%, Muslim 4.4%, other 3.6%, unaffiliated 40%

**Languages:** Dutch

**Literacy:** *definition:* age 15 and over can read and write

*total population:* 99%

### GOVERNMENT

**Country name:** *conventional long form:* Kingdom of the Netherlands

*conventional short form:* Netherlands

**Government type:** constitutional monarchy

**Capital:** Amsterdam; The Hague is the seat of government

**Administrative divisions:** 12 provinces (*provincien,* singular—*provincie*)

**Dependent areas:** Aruba, Netherlands Antilles

**Independence:** 1579 (from Spain)

**Constitution:** adopted 1814; amended many times, last time 17 February 1983

**Legal system:** civil law system incorporating French penal theory; constitution does not permit judicial review of acts of the States-General; accepts compulsory ICJ jurisdiction, with reservations

**Suffrage:** 18 years of age; universal

**Executive branch:** *chief of state:* Queen Beatrix (since 30 April 1980)

*head of government:* Ian Peter Balkenande (since 22 July 2002)

*cabinet:* Council of Ministers appointed by the monarch

*elections:* none; the monarch is hereditary; following Second Chamber elections, the leader of the majority party or leader of a majority coalition is usually appointed prime minister by the monarch; vice prime ministers appointed by the monarch

**Legislative branch:** bicameral States-General or Staten Generaal consists of the First Chamber or Eerste Kamer (75 seats; members indirectly elected by the country's 12 provincial councils for four-year terms) and the Second Chamber or Tweede Kamer (150 seats; members directly elected by popular vote to serve four-year terms)

**Judicial branch:** Supreme Court or Hoge Raad (justices are nominated for life by the monarch)

### ECONOMY

**Overview:** The Netherlands is a prosperous and open economy depending heavily on foreign trade. The economy is noted for stable industrial relations, moderate inflation, a sizable current account surplus, and an important role as a European transportation hub. Industrial activity is predominantly in food processing, chemicals, petroleum refining, and electrical machinery. A highly mechanized agricultural sector employs no more than 4% of the labor force but provides large surpluses for the food-processing industry and for exports. The Dutch rank third worldwide in value of agricultural exports, behind the United States and France. The Dutch were among the first 11 EU countries establishing the euro currency zone on 1 January 1999.

**GDP:** purchasing power parity—$388.4 billion

**GDP—real growth rate:** 4%

**GDP—per capita:** purchasing power parity—$24,400

**GDP—composition by sector:** *agriculture:* 3.3%

*industry:* 26.3%

*services:* 70.4%

**Labor force:** 7.2 million

**Labor force-by occupation:** services 73%, industry 23%, agriculture 4%

**Unemployment rate:** 2.6%

**Currency:** euro (EUR)

# A. POLITICAL DEVELOPMENT

A preliminary comment is needed before introducing an account of the government of the Netherlands. Until recently, despite its importance within Europe and the European Union, the Netherlands has not enjoyed wide coverage by political scientists. The Dutch political system, however, is inherently interesting, even fascinating, because it combines a unique geometry with monumental stability. These characteristics will be a central theme of this survey of the evolution and operation of contemporary politics in the Netherlands.

## THE SETTING

Since its inception as a state in the late sixteenth century, the Netherlands has been important both as the commercial gateway to northwestern Europe and as a world trading power. Its territory is small even by European standards, equaling that of Denmark and Switzerland, but less than a tenth the size of France or Spain. Its population, however, at 16 million, is out of scale with its limited area, which gives it the highest density of habitation in Europe. It is also remarkable for being one of the flattest countries on the planet, since nowhere is it more than a few hundred feet above sea level and a quarter of the land surface is below sea level. Crisscrossed with rivers and canals, and with scores of historical towns, the Dutch landscape is highly distinctive.

Dutch culture has crystalized over four centuries of independence, resulting in the contemporary Dutch language (also spoken by 6 million in Belgium) and marked by an impressive tradition in the visual arts and a strong, though unaggressive, identity. Since the end of World War II, the Netherlands—also known as Holland, after its former leading province—has become an extremely prosperous postindustrial society. Its gross domestic product per capita is above the average for the European Union (see Table 7.1), and its volume of exports ranks seventh in the world, at the remarkable figure of 40 percent of the U.S. total for external trade.

## HISTORICAL BACKGROUND

### Origins of the State

The Low Countries—a term which covers both Holland and Belgium—are located in the northwestern corner of Europe between France and Germany. As such, they have been a political fault line since the end of the Roman Empire and a battleground for neighboring powers. Unified

**TABLE 7.1**

**THE NETHERLANDS: SOME COMPARISONS**

| Country | Area (1000 sq km) | Population (millions) | Population Density (per sq km) | GDP per Capita Netherlands = 100 |
|---|---|---|---|---|
| Netherlands | 41 | 16 | 390 | 100 |
| Denmark | 43 | 5 | 121 | 106 |
| Switzerland | 41 | 7 | 170 | 145 |
| European Union | 3,235 | 377 | 90 | 87 |
| United States | 9,372 | 262 | 29 | 124 |
| Japan | 378 | 121 | 333 | 98 |

*Source:* Compiled from *The Netherlands In a European Perspective*, S.C.P. The Hague, 2001.

An historic canal in Amsterdam.

by the Dukes of Burgundy in the fifteenth century, they came under Spanish rule early in the 1500s. There followed a protracted struggle against Spain—political, military, and religious—which eventually created a new state north of the Rhine River, initially called the United Provinces. The seven original provinces combined to form a confederal republic with its capital and governing assembly in The Hague, which has remained the center of government.

By far the leading province was Holland with its great port of Amsterdam, which gave the new state a strongly maritime character. By the early seventeenth century the Dutch Republic was a world power with a first-class shipping fleet, some heroic naval exploits to its credit, and a constellation of trading settlements in Africa, Asia, and the Americas. All this was accomplished with a tiny population of around 2 million and a highly decentralized, almost invertebrate political system.

Ostensibly a country with a representative government, power was effectively in the hands of a few hundred families in western Holland whose heads, known as regents, controlled the nation's commerce and its external politics. Nevertheless, the provinces prized both their autonomy and their nonautocratic institutions. In a period when most of Europe experienced so-called absolute monarchy, the United Provinces was a rare case of a patrician republic, with no kings (though they supplied England with one in 1689) and no princes. A minor nobility did survive into the nineteenth century and its residue is still visible (elevation to aristocratic rank was not formally ended until 1953), but the successful Amsterdam and Rotterdam merchants did not seek noble titles. Earned material rewards were sufficient, reinforced by a predominantly Calvinist faith which saw signs of grace in wordly achievement but condemned vanity and ostentation.

## Religion

A conspicuous item in the revolt against Spanish rule was the effect of the Christian Reformation on the Dutch Provinces. In the early sixteenth century, first Lutheran and later Calvinist preachers had challenged the Catholic establishment. As the Dutch revolt gathered strength, it increasingly acquired a Protestant complexion. After independence, therefore, the dominant religious force was the Calvinist faith, in the form of the Dutch Reformed Church.

Many citizens remained Catholic, however, and in the seventeenth century when the two southern provinces were conquered, the Catholic population became as numerous as the Calvinist. This balance has persisted until the present, although the decline of church adherence since the 1960s has now blurred its significance. Until the mid-nineteenth century, Catholics were generally regarded as second-class citizens. But in the 1850s civil and political rights were granted to them. Thereafter, both Catholic and Protestant churches became a focus for democratic political organization. This form of political mobilization based on religion was a prime feature of twentieth-century Dutch politics.

## Republican Virtues

From 1579 until 1795, the United Provinces was the only European republic other than Venice and the Swiss Confederation. Contemporary American observers were impressed by its qualities, even though its economic performance had declined during the eighteenth century. Since the republic had few national institutions, political life revolved around the towns and the provinces. Gradations of rank, wealth, and authority existed as elsewhere, but social distances were at least conceptually less than in neighboring aristocratic societies. Although there was political conflict and violence, an atmosphere of communal solidarity struck foreign visitors as exemplary.

This cooperative energy was most vividly deployed in the recovery and protection of the great tracts of agricultural land that are below sea level. In this eternal struggle against flood, industry was praised, idleness castigated, mod-

esty enjoined, and sobriety commended. It would not be fanciful to cite this historic conditioning when referring to some of the more abiding qualities of Dutch behavior—like thrift, diligence, reliability, tolerance, and social calm.

During the 1790s, in the fallout from the French Revolution, the Dutch Republic was extinguished and Holland became a French possession until the defeat of Napoleon. In 1813, a monarch was installed, largely on the initiative of the victorious allies, and the Netherlands became a kingdom, which it remains.

## The New Kingdom

The installation of William I as king of the United Netherlands had two precedents. One was that in each province under Spanish rule, a governor or *stadholder* acted for the Spanish king. This office had become largely hereditary and a famous stadholder—William the Silent—had played a major role in Dutch independence. The other was that Napoleon had made his brother Louis king of Holland from 1806 to 1810.

The new monarch, like his distinguished stadholder predecessors, was from the House of Orange. He ruled not only Holland or the northern Netherlands, but also the south—which had formerly been Austrian and would later become Belgium. William I inherited a political system which under the French had become far more centralized than anything the old republic had tolerated. Provincial autonomy was already a thing of the past. A new national bureaucracy had started to regulate trade and customs, and a national assembly had, briefly, replaced the ancient States-General which served as the republic's parliament.

The new constitution reflected both republican features—the Lower House of Parliament would be elected by provincial assemblies—and the more recent experience of executive government. Later an Upper House was added, composed of members directly appointed by the king. Ministers were also appointed and dismissed by the king, an act which gave the government a predominantly royal flavor. Popular elections were held only for the provincial assemblies, not the national Parliament. The electorate, both north and south, amounted to 15 percent of adult males (much higher than in England at the time), though there was no party system to focus the concerns of voters.

Whatever the merits of the new settlement, it failed to convince the elite in Brussels, the chief city of the southern provinces. In 1830, riots were followed by a separatist demand for a Belgian state. Dutch military intervention met French resistance (the more affluent southern provinces were French-speaking) and by 1831 the Netherlands was trimmed back to the nine northern provinces. Henceforth, Holland would be entirely Dutch, and the Low Countries would be divided into two states.

The loss of Belgium fed back into changes in political practice in The Hague. Ministers gradually acquired more independence from the crown. In 1840 William I abdicated, and under his son, William II, government became more parliamentary in style. Social reforms and fresh approaches to economic management went along with the new liberal atmosphere. Freer trade, Catholic emancipation, and in November 1848 a revised constitution inaugurated the modern era of politics and society in the Netherlands.

## PARLIAMENTARY GOVERNMENT

The constitutional revision of 1848 was a victory for liberalism, and it mirrored the social, political, and economic forces that were asserting themselves throughout Western Europe. The word "liberal," coined in the eighteenth century, had by the mid-nineteenth century come to mean a whole family of doctrines based on the notion of freedom from prescriptive authority.

In the Netherlands, the liberals who carried out the constitutional change and implemented it in government were known as "The Doctrinaires." Led by a law professor, J. R. Thorbecke, they represented the professional and commercial middle classes whose values were progressive, in terms of economic modernization, and secular. This last meant that they supported both freedom *for* all religious confessions and freedom

*from* religion in determining government policy. The more fundamental Calvinist churchgoers—the Anti-Revolutionaries—were opposed to the liberal program. But the Catholic churches understandably supported it.

Under the new political arrangements, the king and his advisers retained some influence in foreign affairs and in military and colonial matters. The appointment of ministers and the summoning and dissolution of Parliament were also formally under the royal aegis. But there were three vital provisions which made the break with monarchical government. The first was that ministers were now to be responsible to Parliament. This crucial step is, in the European context, the paradigmatic shift from royal authority to popular sovereignty. It means that the composition of the political executive, in the shape of the Council of Ministers or Cabinet, is essentially determined by the pattern of support in the popularly elected House of Parliament.

Its corollary is, of course, the institution of direct elections to the effective chamber, which was the second of the key constitutional provisions. At this point in democratic development, universal adult suffrage was not on any European agenda.[1] The new Second Chamber was to be elected by only one in ten adult males—those who paid a fairly high rate of tax. Parliamentary government was initiated, therefore, by some 75,000 electors, out of an adult population of about 1.5 million.

However, under the third set of provisions, Parliament secured two vital areas to its jurisdiction: the state budget and education. The first now required the approval of the directly elected Second Chamber. The new Upper House would no longer be filled with life-tenured royal appointees but would be elected by the provincial assemblies (as the Second Chamber had for-

---

[1]Universal suffrage began in the United States in the 1820s with the dropping of property qualifications for male voting in New Hampshire, Maryland, and Connecticut (Russell Nye and J. E. Morpurgo, *History of the United States,* London: Penguin, 1955). In Europe, universal voting rights were delayed until the twentieth century.

merly been). The second area, education, would be the subject of enormous debate, inside and outside Parliament for the next two generations.

The model for future parliamentary development had thus been set in the year of popular ferment throughout Europe. Outside the Netherlands, many of the aspirations of 1848 remained unfulfilled, but in Holland there was no retreat from the form and style of popular government. The electorate would enlarge as wealth increased, assuming tax levels reflected increased prosperity, and the executive would become more precisely related to popular sentiment as a national party system emerged.

## The Liberal Era

For almost a century after the inauguration of parliamentary government, up to the end of World War II, Holland may be fairly described as a classic European liberal polity. This meant that politics reflected the most influential interests in society and sought to provide an appropriate arena for their reconciliation. In policy terms it meant that the perpetual agenda consisted of four main items: (1) trade, which included colonial policy; (2) education, which involved the churches and strategies affecting religion; (3) social improvement, a concern which accelerated in the 1890s; and (4) increased citizen participation in politics. In the Dutch case it also meant a commitment to peaceful relations with neighboring countries, neutrality in relation to European conflicts, and except in the colonies, nonmilitary solutions to problems.

These key issues were not approached in a prescriptive way. Nor, until the time of World War I, were radical solutions either proposed or adopted. The tenor of social life was overwhelmingly conservative, but the liberal agenda was slowly fulfilled by the evolution of political expression on the part of newly enfranchised groups: the Catholics, lower-class Calvinists, primary producers—farmers and fishermen—and, from the 1880s on, the emergent industrial working class in the growing cities.

There were certainly groups, like the great merchant families and trading corporations, who sought to hold on to power and influence. But the liberal tide in Holland washed away even the word "conservative" as a political label. In 1888 only one of the hundred elected members of the Second Chamber of Parliament called himself a conservative (see Table 7.2). The presence of only a vestigial nobility contributed to a lack of entrenched resistance to social reform. Also the Calvinist tradition frowned upon conspicuous consumption by the upper classes. The poor were intensely poor up to World War II. But revolutionary fervor was virtually nonexistent. The slow rise of the socialist movement reflected that absence, alongside the massive competition for working-class votes from the Catholic and Reformed Calvinist political parties.

### TABLE 7.2

#### PARTY MEMBERSHIP IN THE SECOND CHAMBER OF PARLIAMENT, 1850–1888

| Party | 1850 | 1860 | 1878 | 1888 |
|---|---|---|---|---|
| Liberal | 44 | 40 | 51 | 45 |
| Conservative-Liberal | 8 | 10 | — | — |
| Conservative | 13 | 18 | 8 | 1 |
| Anti-Revolutionary (Calvinist) | 3 | 4 | 10 | 27 |
| Catholic | — | — | 17 | 26 |
| Socialist | — | — | — | 1 |
| Total seats in Chamber | 68 | 72 | 86 | 100 |

*Source:* Th. van Tijn, in J. Bromley and E. Kossman, eds., *Britain and the Netherlands*, vol. 4 (The Hague: Macmillan 1971).

Quiet street in Haarlem.

## Development of Modern Politics

The century from 1848 to 1945 can be presented as a series of steps toward the emergence of a latter twentieth-century democratic polity. The first stage in this process was the crystallization of a national pattern of popularly organized political parties. Parliamentary rule began with a small electorate and representatives, who were mostly notable figures, chosen by local election committees. In the 1870s this system was jolted by the formation of the Anti-Revolutionary Party, based on a Calvinist breakaway from the official Dutch Reformed Church. By 1888 this group of parliamentarians, in coalition with mainstream Catholics, was able to forge the first government to which the title "confessional," that is, religious, can be applied.

The creation of Calvinist/Catholic coalitions quickly became a central feature of parliamentary politics. The alliance of the two principal Christian denominations was a marriage of convenience, designed to deliver nonsecular policies, above all in the provision of state funds for religious schools. In social affairs the confessionals soon had to compete with the Social Democratic Workers Party, founded in 1894, as well as reform-minded liberals. From the 1890s to 1918, liberal governments pioneered a progressive income tax, a wealth tax, compulsory education up to age 13, workmen's compensation, and a public health service.

These measures were, of course, in line with similar welfare and educational provisions elsewhere, notably in Holland's giant neighbor, the German Empire. They were a start, but for two

REVIEW
7.1

### CHIEF FEATURES OF THE 1917 PACIFICATION

- Universal male suffrage, and provision for female suffrage.
- National proportional representation (PR).
- Equal state funding for secular and denominational schools.
- Compulsory attendance at the polls (abolished in 1970).
- Equal qualifications for entry to both chambers of the parliament.

generations they remained inadequate to deal with the problems of unemployment and social distress resulting from industrial development and urban growth.

Alongside social problems, dislocation in the political process became apparent by the turn of the century. Electoral competition had been organized in localities, with one or two representatives serving a geographical constituency. As more political groups contended for the legislature, majorities became impossible to deliver. Also the franchise was a continuing bone of contention.

All these items confronted the last cabinet dominated by liberals, which was formed in 1913. Within a year Europe had exploded and World War I was unleashed. Holland, unlike its neighbor Belgium, managed to remain neutral. Dutch politicians spent the middle years of the war compiling a constitutional package that would fix the key political arrangements for the rest of the twentieth century. The package was christened "the Pacification" to signal the achievement of a firm consensus between the major political forces.

## THE PACIFICATION AND ITS SEQUEL

Just as 1848 was a landmark in parliamentary terms, 1917 is a landmark in representational terms because of the changes brought about by the Pacification. The franchise law—extended to females in 1919—gave all males over 25 the right to vote in elections to the Lower House of Parliament. (The voting age was lowered to 23 in 1946, 21 in 1967, and 18 in 1972.) The provision for equal funding of state and religious schools settled a controversy that had simmered, if not raged, for half a century (and which took another 40 years to settle in Belgium). But the most distinctive formulas were the introduction of national proportional representation (PR) and compulsory voting. (Both will be elaborated on in Section B). The effects of these two devices transformed the mechanics of electoral competition and the perception of their democratic consequences. The consequences for the major political forces, both immediate and longer-term, are set out in Table 7.3.

**TABLE 7.3**

**THE SECOND CHAMBER BEFORE AND WITH PR**

|  | 1913 (pre-PR) | 1918 | 1937 |
|---|---|---|---|
| Liberal (all shades) | 39 | 20 | 10 |
| Calvinist (both wings) | 21 | 20 | 25 |
| Catholic | 25 | 30 | 31 |
| Socialist | 15 | 22 | 23 |
| Communist | — | 2 | 3 |
| Other | — | 6 | 8 |
| Total seats in Chamber | 100 | 100 | 100 |

The most vivid results of allocating seats in exact proportion to party votes nationally affected the liberals and the socialists. Until PR, liberals in various guises had managed to win enough constituencies, usually by a plurality, to constitute a major grouping in Parliament. The new mass electorate, however, reduced these elite formations to a marginal role, while augmenting the socialist camp to around a quarter of the chamber. The new rules also confirmed the position of the major confessional parties—Catholic and Calvinist—as a dominant grouping when acting in concert, as they almost invariably did.

So the geometry of parliamentary politics was significantly reshaped by the Pacification. From 1918 on, the religious parties would monopolize the formation of governments. Usually they were prepared to include a few liberal ministers in their cabinets, but the premier, up to World War II, was always a religious party figure. The Left, despite its strength, was excluded from the interwar cabinets except for the all-party coalition formed in 1939, a few months before the German invasion.

## THE PILLARS OF SOCIETY

Reference has already been made to the religious division of society between Catholics and Protestants, and to the importance of this division in the latter nineteenth century as a basis for political mobilization. Those are two dimensions of an extremely complex phenomenon, which is rendered in Dutch by the word *verzuiling* and in English as "pillarization." In a previous work I summarized this concept and its realization as follows:

> Originating in the 1880s when the Confessional movements sought to mobilise their followers into self-conscious communities, this process became in the 1920s the dominant and most conspicuous feature of social organisation. Trade unions, educational bodies, welfare schemes, cultural associations, employers organisations and the media, all became

orchestrated on the basis of would-be hermetic pillars topped by political parties.[2]

There is, however, much debate about the nature and significance of pillarization. Its importance is now largely historic, since most commentators regard it as waning in the latter 1960s and becoming residual in the 1970s. But few would question its centrality in any analysis of post–World War I politics and society. There can be little doubt that many of its political and organizational offspring survive in the contemporary Netherlands. The two most far-reaching of these legatees are the system of elite accommodation known as *consociationalism* and the method of interest articulation usually described as *corporatism*.

*Verzuiling,* or pillarization, was essentially a twin phenomenon. It described both the separation between the religious and secular subcultures, and their respective superstructures, whose networks and associations embraced their members. The separation was partly geographical in that the southern provinces, predominantly Catholic, were the heartland of the Catholic pillar. Friesland, and the cities of Amsterdam and Rotterdam, were strongholds of the Socialist pillar, while the northeast was a Calvinist redoubt. The exclusiveness of the pillars was not, however, accompanied by any literal apartheid, or by any legal discrimination.

A graphic picture of the operation of the Catholic pillar, the most cohesive and comprehensive of all, is given in a recent work by two political scientists at Leiden University.[3] It portrays the likely experience of a Catholic child in the 1950s who would have been born in a Catholic hospital, would attend a Catholic school, and would hope to go to a Catholic university. His or her father would belong to a Catholic labor or professional union, would read a Catholic newspaper, sing in a Catholic choir if musical, and lis-

---

[2]Ken Gladdish, *Governing from the Center* (De Kalb: Northern Illinois University Press, 1991), p. 28.
[3]Rudy Andeweg and Galen Irwin, *Dutch Government and Politics* (London: Macmillan 1993), pp. 27–29.

ten nightly to the Catholic radio and TV channels. All of this was, of course, voluntary. Some 20 percent of practicing Catholics in fact espoused the Socialist pillar. But the vast majority of mass-goers complied with the social norm of pillarized life and, as the crucial political top-dressing, voted for the Catholic People's Party.

This biographical sketch may appear relatively simple and straightforward. But much controversy surrounds the precise form and salience of the pillars. One fundamental issue is whether the pillars reflected a deeply divided society, or alternatively whether the cultivation of subcultures was the source of social divisions. To an extent, this question revolves around the ostensible origins and objectives of the pillars. Some commentators see the networks as having a long historical ancestry, whereas others regard them as deliberate creations by late nineteenth-century social and political elites, in order to fence off whole segments of the population for electoral and resource-staking purposes. There is also argument about the exact configuration of the arcade which the pillars composed. The Catholic subculture was the clearest, and most unified. Protestants had several strands within their much broader spectrum and, unlike the Catholics, access to two mainstream political parties—the Anti-Revolutionary and the Christian Historical. The Socialists had no church as a focus for their

adherents. Also there were small parties to their left, notably the Communists, which operated independently of the Social Democrats (the postwar Labor Party). Finally, there are uncertainties about how concrete the existence of a liberal or center-right secular pillar actually was.

## CONSOCIATIONAL DEMOCRACY

The credit for the coining and exploration of the concept of consociation is usually accorded to a Dutch political scientist, Arend Lijphart, since the 1970s a professor at the University of California. In a strikingly original book—*The Politics of Accommodation,* first published in 1968—he expounded the theory that the Netherlands, and certain other states, experienced a particular form of democratic government which could be labeled "consociational."

To reduce a book-length thesis to a paragraph risks massive oversimplification. But Lijphart himself provides a summary of the concept in the form of a model with two factors and two variables. One factor is the political culture—here equivalent to the makeup of society—which can be either "homogeneous" or "fragmented." The other factor is the prime characteristic of elite behavior, which can be either "coalescent" (consensus-seeking) or "competitive" (see Figure 7.1). In the Dutch case,

**Political Culture**

|  |  | Homogeneous | Fragmented |
|---|---|---|---|
| **Elite Behavior** | Coalescent | Depoliticized | Consociational |
|  | Competitive | Centripetal | Centrifugal |

Figure 7.1 DEMOCRACY IN THE NETHERLANDS

he discerns a culture fragmented by pillarization, and elites who accommodate this disunity by making pacts and compromises in order to deliver stable democratic government. The elites also distribute resources in proportion to electoral support for the pillars and exercise a mutual veto, thus ensuring that only consensual decisions are taken.

This analysis was issued at a point when the system of pillars had begun to crumble, though that hardly invalidated a diagnosis applied to a century and more of political experience. The debate about the theory, which has not died down in political science, centers upon two key questions. One is the precise degree to which Dutch society could plausibly be regarded as fragmented or disunited. The other is how far consociational democracy is a political arrangement that has wide and ongoing relevance within the world of states.

The first question refers back to the status of the pillars, and focuses particularly on how far their role in social and political behavior either offset or gave rise to deep divisions. To an observer from outside, Dutch society can seem remarkably uniform and nonconflictual, since 93 percent of the population is of Dutch ancestry, and all but recent immigrants are native Dutch speakers. Even when pillarization was in its fullest bloom, the separate networks still provided an extremely homogeneous sense of nationality and culture. One could, of course, attribute much of that similarity to the efforts of elites to defuse conflict and transcend latent diversity.

What is undeniable is that the main political parties from the start of democratization until the final third of the twentieth century were underpinned by distinctive subcultures. Nevertheless, a very high degree of consensus was achieved in political decision making, certainly at the level of national elites.

## WAR AND RECONSTRUCTION

The hope that the Netherlands could remain neutral during World War II was shattered by the German invasion in 1940. For five years the country was under military occupation. Resistance was brutally suppressed and most of the Jewish population was deported and murdered. This appalling experience, however, served to unify political groups that had previously differed in their views of state and society.

In the prewar political environment, adherents of the mainstream religious parties broadly accepted the status quo, not unnaturally since they largely constituted it. Liberals, reflecting the values of the secular upper classes, had been somewhat aloof, but on the Left there had long been deep criticism of the way the country was run, especially during the depression of the 1930s. In the latter war years, an active underground operated to defend Dutch life against the occupiers. In this, politicians of different stripes worked closely together, some ending up in Nazi concentration camps. So when the war ended, there was a disposition to tackle the problems of reconstruction on a concerted basis.

The scale of destruction and deterioration resulting from the war was immense. Industry and the infrastructure had been devastated, and up to 20 percent of the population needed urgent rehousing.[4] A provisional government was formed from surviving politicians to take emergency measures. From the outset it was decided to proceed by planning and close consultation between the major economic actors. The machinery which implemented the reconstruction went under the heading of "corporatism."

## THE CORPORATIST PACKAGE

The pedigree of European corporatism is of mixed repute. One source is the late nineteenth-century papal encyclical *Rerum Novarum,* which prescribed the resurrection of employer and worker guilds. Another strand was brandished in Italy under Mussolini and in Portugal under Salazar. The essence of corporatism is the systematic rec-

---

[4]See P. W. Klein, "The Foundations of Dutch Prosperity," in Richard T. Griffiths, ed., *The Economy and Politics of the Netherlands since 1945* (The Hague: Martinus Nijhoff, 1980), pp. 1–12.

onciliation of the interests of capital and labor, and in postwar Holland this was built into the provisions for managing economic and social policy.

Overall economic forecasting was carried out by a prestigious Central Planning Bureau. Employers and workers came together in a Foundation of Labor. Other bodies served the needs of particular industries and, of course, agriculture. In 1950, the structure was completed with the setting-up of the Social and Economic Council. The council was a high policy trio of government, employer, and labor representatives, whose proposals went straight onto the cabinet agenda. On paper this looked like a model of technocracy, and there was criticism that the whole system bypassed Parliament and the democratic system. Nevertheless, corporatist institutions presided over two decades of recovery, growth, and social harmony, with full employment, equitable wage awards, and the highest rate of industrial investment in Western Europe.

Corporatism needs to be distinguished from consociationalism, though the two share some ingredients at least in the forms adopted in Holland. The latter term covered the accommodation of the different subcultures, whereas the former was an official strategy of reconciling different *producer* interests. Dutch corporatism, unlike in fascist regimes, was not deployed to subdue labor unions; indeed, it promoted them to high status as "social partners." Nor, despite criticisms, did it seek to replace normal democratic representation with some "functionalist" sham in which trades replaced citizens in the legislature.

## THE CRUMBLING OF THE PILLARS

Both on the Left and the secular Right, there were concerns about and moves toward a change of operational style after the war. But they were not realized in any radical way, largely because the mainstream religious parties retained their grip on their supporters. There were, however, some important changes in the secular parties, notably the formation of a new "Party of Labor" (the PvdA) in 1946 to replace the Social Democrats, and the creation of a sin-

gle liberal force, the Party of Freedom and Democracy (VVD) in 1948.

Above all, the democratic Left, in the shape of the new Labor Party, became a major player in government. From 1946 until 1958, cabinets consisted of a combination of Labor and the mainstream confessionals under a celebrated wartime leader, Willem Drees. This was a profound shift in the balance of political forces because the Left had played no part in prewar governments. But it did not affect the basic geometry of the system, which remained poised upon the traditional pillars, that is, until the mid-1960s when they began to crumble. The disintegration of the pillars was essentially a decline of adherence both to religious networks and to the mainstream parties that had capped the subcultures. The reasons for the decline are still a matter of debate. Western Europe as a whole experienced a cultural sea change during the 1960s, which is sometimes presented as a revolt of the younger generation against a social conservatism that had survived World War II.

This revolt was particularly graphic in the Netherlands, where society and politics had displayed a surprising continuity since World War I. The forms of change were both individual and institutional. Churchgoing became less comprehensive. Citizens no longer felt obliged to stay within the bounds of the subcultural associations. They began to read other newspapers, listen to other radio programs, and watch other TV channels. Cross-pillar mergers took place, such as the amalgamation of the Socialist and Catholic labor federations. Indeed, it was the Catholic pillar which crumbled most dramatically, centered upon a 30 percent fall in attendance at mass between 1966 and 1977.

But it was not only the religious pillars which suffered. The Socialist network lost support and its leaders were challenged by new groups and new parties. The clearest manifestation of political change was the results of the 1967 election to the Second Chamber (see Table 7.4). Between them, Labor and the Catholic People's Party suddenly lost 14 seats in a Chamber of 150. The Catholics went on losing seats until, in the mid-1970s, they settled for a merger with the two

**TABLE 7.4**

**PILLARED AND NONPILLARED PARTIES IN THE SECOND CHAMBER, 1946–1972**

| Pillared Parties | 1946 (Total Seats 100) | 1952 | 1959 (Total Seats 150) | 1967 | 1972 |
|---|---|---|---|---|---|
| Catholic | 32 | 30 | 49 | 42 | 27 |
| Anti-Revolutionary | 13 | 12 | 14 | 15 | 14 |
| Christian Historical | 8 | 9 | 12 | 12 | 7 |
| Labor | 29 | 30 | 48 | 37 | 43 |
| Liberal | 6 | 9 | 19 | 17 | 22 |
| Total seats | 88 | 90 | 142 | 123 | 113 |
| **Nonpillared\*** | | | | | |
| Communist | 10 | 6 | 3 | 5 | 7 |
| Minor Calvinist | 2 | 2 | 3 | 4 | 5 |
| Other | — | 2 | 2 | 18 | 25 |
| Total seats | 12 | 10 | 8 | 27 | 37 |

\*Parties outside the main blocs of the *verzuiling* system.

main Calvinist parties to form the Christian Democratic Appeal. This merger was the showpiece of depillarization.

## POST-PILLARIZATION POLITICS

Pillarization was neither a formal nor an official mechanism. The concept of a pillared society was arrived at by social scientists, not by constitutional draftsmen. As such, it was susceptible to infinite interpretation. Writing in the 1980s, its chief propounder, Arend Lijphart, insisted that the loosening of individual ties to the pillars did not mean they had disappeared. This view is countered by other commentators, writing in the 1990s, who maintain that most authors have overemphasized the importance of pillarization.[5]

So far as the operation of the political system, however, it is beyond question that the 1960s saw the start of a switch away from politics that were fueled by long-term adherence

to either a religious denomination or a secular ideology. Thereafter, allegiances would become less fixed, parties would become less committed to doctrines, and the style of government more pragmatic.

In the early 1970s, the Labor Party, now recovered under a dynamic leader, Joop den Uyl, tried to take advantage of the sea change to both secularize and polarize the party contest. It formed a "progressive alliance" with two new parties—the Democrats (D'66) and the Radical Party (PPR)—in the hope of winning a parliamentary majority. This bid, which might have restructured the political arena, was unsuccessful, though Labor did become the major partner in the 1972–1977 government.

The amalgamation of the Catholic and the two main Calvinist parties managed to stem the tide of confessional losses, so that by 1977, the new Christian Democratic Appeal (CDA) was able, in coalition with the Liberals, to restore the hold of the religious parties over cabinets. CDA-Liberal coalitions then ruled the Netherlands—with a brief interlude from 1981 to 1982—until 1989. That year's parliamentary election gave

[5]Andeweg and Irwin, p. 45.

the two parties only the barest majority in the Second Chamber, and the partners had anyway already fallen out. From 1989 to 1994, the CDA therefore switched from the Liberals to a coalition with Labor. But the 1994 election changed the picture dramatically.

In 1989, the CDA and Labor had won, together, two-thirds of the popular vote (see Table 7.5). The Liberals and D'66, the other two significant formations, jointly received only a fifth of the poll. Five years later, the two governing parties experienced huge losses of support,

### TABLE 7.5

#### ELECTIONS TO THE SECOND CHAMBER, 1982–2002

| Party | 1982 | | 1986 | | 1989 | | 1994 | | 1998 | | 2002 | |
|---|---|---|---|---|---|---|---|---|---|---|---|---|
| | % | Seats | % | Seats | % | Seats | % | Seats | % | Seats | % | Seats |
| PvdA | 30.4 | 47 | 33.3 | 52 | 31.9 | 49 | 24.0 | 37 | 29.0 | 45 | 14.9 | 23 |
| CDA | 29.3 | 45 | 34.6 | 54 | 35.3 | 54 | 22.2 | 34 | 18.4 | 29 | 28.2 | 43 |
| VVD | 23.1 | 36 | 17.4 | 27 | 14.6 | 22 | 19.9 | 31 | 24.7 | 38 | 15.3 | 23 |
| D'66 | 4.3 | 6 | 6.1 | 9 | 7.9 | 12 | 15.5 | 24 | 9.0 | 14 | 5.3 | 8 |
| PPR | 1.6 | 2 | 1.3 | 2 | — | — | | | | | | |
| CPN | 1.8 | 3 | 0.6 | — | 4.1[a] | 6[a] | 3.5[a] | 5[a] | 7.3[a] | 11[a] | 7.0 | 10 |
| PSP | 2.2 | 3 | 1.2 | 1 | — | — | | | | | | |
| EVP | 0.7 | 1 | 0.2 | — | — | — | | | | | | |
| SGP | 1.9 | 3 | 1.8 | 3 | 1.9 | 3 | 1.7 | 2 | 1.8 | 3 | 1.7 | 2 |
| GPV | 0.8 | 1 | 1.0 | 1 | 1.2 | 2 | 1.3 | 2 | 1.3 | 2 | CU* 2.5 | 4 |
| SP | — | — | — | — | — | — | 1.3 | 2 | 3.5 | 5 | 5.7 | 9 |
| AOV/55+ | — | — | — | — | — | — | 3.6 | 7 | 0.5 | — | — | — |
| RPF | 1.5 | 2 | 0.9 | 1 | 1.0 | 1 | 1.8 | 3 | 2.0 | 3 | See CU* | |
| CD | 0.8 | 1 | 0.4 | — | 0.9 | 1 | 2.5 | 3 | 0.6 | — | — | — |
| | | | | | | | | | | | LPF* 17.1 | 26 |
| | | | | | | | | | | | LB* 1.6 | 2 |
| Total turnout | 80.6 | | 85.7 | | 80.1 | | 78.3 | | 73.2 | | 78.9 | |

[a]Joint list as "Green Left"

*Abbreviations:*

| | | | |
|---|---|---|---|
| PvdA | Labor Party | GPV | Reformed Political Union (Calvinist) |
| CDA | Christian Democratic Appeal | PSP | Pacifist Socialist Party |
| WD | People's Party for Freedom and Democracy (Liberals) | RPF | Reformed Political Federation (Calvinist) |
| D'66 | Democrats '66 | SP | Socialist Party |
| SGP | Reformed Political Party (Calvinist) | AOV/55+ | Pensioner Groups |
| PPR | Radical Party | EVP | Evangelical People's Party (Calvinist) |
| CPN | Communist Party of the Netherlands | CD | Center Party (Ultra-right) |
| CU* | Christian Union (RFP + GPV) | LPF* | List Pim Fortuyn |
| LB* | Liveable Netherlands | | |

to fall well below 50 percent of the seats in the chamber. A new coalition needed to be built. This time, the first occasion since 1918, it was formed without the Christians.

Despite the desertion of a quarter of its voters, Labor emerged as the largest party and was able to take the pilot role in assembling a new coalition with the Liberals and D'66. It was styled "purple" because it blended the red of the Left with the blue of the Right. This was a departure from both custom and political geometry, because the major left and right secular parties had only once before briefly served together in government. The mid-1990s thus saw a new era in the dynamics of political cabinet making. This continued in 1998 when the parties in the purple coalition increased their majority and formed a further government for the next four years.

## QUALITY OF LIFE

In 1986, a survey of human rights reported that in the Netherlands, "The individual was respected. Government was answerable to the people. There was a prosperous economy, a free press, and a cohesive society"; in sum, it was "a country very committed to human rights causes."[6] This verdict certainly corresponds both to the deep impression of decency and fairness which almost all visitors to Holland sense, and to the traditional reputation for tolerance and justice which goes all the way back to the republic. The Pilgrim fathers, let us remember, were ousted from England but were able to take refuge in Leiden from 1609 to 1620, before they sailed for America.

It is therefore not surprising that the survey awards the Dutch, along with only four other nations, the highest human rights rating on the planet. The rating is 98 percent. The gap of 2 percent is ascribed to three areas that are less than perfect: political and legal equality for women, social and economic equality for women, and social and economic equality for ethnic minorities.

The Dutch experience of ethnic minorities has three main tributaries. The stream with the longest history derives from the East Indian empire, most specifically the influx, after 1949, of those whose ties were with the Dutch colonizers rather than with the Indonesian legatees. The vast majority of the 250,000 migrants from the East Indies were Asian by birth. But they mostly spoke Dutch and, with the exception of an irredentist group from the Moluccas, are generally reckoned to have been successfully absorbed into Dutch society.[7] This does not, of course, mean that they are among the social or economic elite, merely that their integration has been relatively undramatic.

The second wave of postimperial immigrants hails from the Caribbean. These incomers either entered Holland after the independence of Surinam in 1975, or continue to drift over from the still-dependent Antilles. The total population of West Indian origin in 2000 was some 400,000.[8] The record of successful integration here is decidedly mixed, and there are problems which anti-immigrant groups choose to highlight.

The third significant category of immigrants has no imperial source. It consists of foreign workers, predominantly from Turkey and Morocco, though also from Southern Europe, who have arrived as economic migrants. These, by definition, are not settlers, although some are now second-generation residents. Their numbers are substantial—around 800,000 in 2000 (5 percent of the total population) and growing.[9] Mostly they qualify only for low-grade jobs, which explains the caveat about their equality with Dutch citizens.

The Netherlands, in common with other highly prosperous European countries like Germany, is experiencing high levels of immigration. This reflects both its economic attractions and its relatively tolerant entry policy. Paradoxically, migrants drawn into successful economies tend to

---

[6]*World Human Rights Guide,* compiled by Charles Humana (London: PAN 1987), p. 189.

[7]W. Brand, "The Legacy of Empire," in Richard T. Griffiths, ed., *The Economy and Politics of the Netherlands since 1945,* pp. 251–275.

[8]Netherlands Planning Office, *Social and Cultural Report 1994,* p. 44, table 3.9.

[9]Ibid.

experience high rates of unemployment, which creates both socioeconomic and political problems.

## WOMEN'S POLITICAL PARTICIPATION

The concern about women's rights in the 1986 survey was not, of course, peculiar to Holland. Indeed, the status of Dutch women is probably as high as anywhere in the world, and high even by first world standards. In 1992, an opinion poll recorded that 86 percent of those sampled (men and women) rejected the notion that it was "unnatural for women to exercise leadership over men in a business."[10] Although this shows an impeccable attitude toward women in business, the reality is that most businesses are run by men. The same is true of political parties, of Parliament, and of the cabinet, though here again the Dutch record is probably superior to that of most of its European counterparts. The position is summarized in Table 7.6.

To evaluate the Dutch scores for women's participation at the highest political levels would require elaborate comparisons with other cases. Intuitively, however, the picture looks relatively bright. The number of women holding posts in the political executive is particularly impressive; parliamentary participation is encouraging, and only the political parties themselves appear not

---

[10]*Social and Cultural Report 1994*, p. 508, table 11.28.

to have opened up many top leadership positions to women.

### *Thinking Critically*

1. For what reasons is the Netherlands regarded as a highly liberal state?
2. The Netherlands has been both a republic and a monarchy. Can you relate this to any aspects of its political arrangements?
3. Why has religion not been a conflictual issue in the modern Netherlands?
4. What were the main effects of World War II on Dutch party politics?
5. Why has the Netherlands been styled a consociational democracy?
6. What were the pillars? Why did they crumble?

### KEY TERMS

accommodation *(407)*
Anti-Revolutionaries *(402)*
Calvinists *(401)*
Catholics *(401)*
Christian Democrats *(410)*
confederal republic *(401)*
confessionals *(404)*
consociational democracy *(406–408)*
corporatism *(406, 408–409)*
monarchy *(401–402)*
pacification *(405)*

---

### TABLE 7.6

#### WOMEN IN THE NATIONAL POLITICAL ELITE, LATE 1990s

| Position | Total | Number of Women | Women as Percentage |
|---|---|---|---|
| Cabinet members | 15 | 4 | 27% |
| Junior ministers | 11 | 5 | 46% |
| First Chamber | 75 | 20 | 26% |
| Second Chamber | 150 | 54 | 36% |
| European Parliament | 41 | 10 | 24% |
| Party chairs (of parties in Parliament) | 12 | 2 | 17% |
| Parliamentary floor-leaders | 12 | 1 | 8% |

parliamentary government *(402–403)*
pillarization *(406–408)*
reconstruction *(408)*
regents *(400)*
secularism *(409)*
Social Democrats *(407, 409)*

# *F*URTHER READINGS

Blom, J. C. H., and E. Lamberts, eds. *History of the Low Countries* (New York: Berghahn Books, 1999).

Daalder, Hans. "The Netherlands: Opposition in a Segmented Society," in Robert A. Dahl, ed., *Political Oppositions in Western Democracies* (New Haven, CT: Yale University, 1966), pp. 188–236.

Gladdish, Ken. *Governing from the Center: Politics and Policy-Making in the Netherlands* (De Kalb: Northern Illinois University Press, 1991), chs. 1–4.

Gladdish, Ken. "Opposition in the Netherlands," in Eva Kolinsky, ed., *Opposition in Western Europe* (London: Croom Helm, 1987), pp. 195–214.

Griffiths, Richard T., ed. *The Economy and Politics of the Netherlands since 1945* (The Hague: Martinus Nijhoff, 1980).

Israel, Jonathan. *The Dutch Republic* (Oxford: Clarendon Press, 1995).

Kieve, Ronald A. "Pillars of Sand: A Marxist Critique of Consociational Democracy in the Netherlands," *Comparative Politics,* no. 3 (1981), pp. 313–337.

Kossman, E. H. *The Low Countries, 1780–1940* (Oxford: Clarendon Press, 1978).

Lijphart, Arend. *The Politics of Accommodation: Pluralism and Democracy in the Netherlands,* 2nd ed. (Berkeley: University of California Press, 1975).

Parker, Geoffrey. *The Dutch Revolt* (London: Pelican, 1979).

Scholten, Ilja, ed. *Political Stability and Neo-Corporatism,* (Beverley Hills, CA: Sage, 1987).

Vlekke, B. H. M. *The Evolution of the Dutch Nation* (New York: Roy, 1945).

Warmbrunn, W. *The Dutch under German Occupation, 1940–45* (Stanford, CA: Stanford University Press, 1963).

Windmuller, John P. *Labour Relations in the Netherlands* (Ithaca, NY: Cornell University Press, 1969).

# B. POLITICAL PROCESSES AND INSTITUTIONS

In all political systems, processes and institutions are in a continual state of interaction. In liberal democracies above all, institutions are being constantly refined by the pressures of participation acting upon events. There is always, therefore, a "chicken and egg" dilemma when presenting the development of institutions and the growth of participatory mechanisms.

As a general rule in European systems, the democratization of *institutions* has tended to precede and thus trigger the emergence of comprehensive interest aggregation and articulation by political parties. This reflects the fact that the prime dynamic of institutional democratization has been the shift from monarchical to parliamentary authority.

From the vantage point of the start of the twenty-first century, however, democratic politics can be, and by the media mostly are, seen as essentially a contest between the major participatory forces. The reason for this is that in most Western European countries the institutional reforms which yielded representative legislatures and responsible executives were completed several generations ago.

The Netherlands is no exception here, having experienced the prime institutional shift to parliamentary government in the mid-nineteenth century, and having enjoyed continuous progress toward fuller participation since then. In this progression, as elsewhere, provision for elections came before and were a necessary catalyst of the formation of national mass political parties.

## PROPORTIONAL REPRESENTATION

### Elections Before PR

Direct elections to Parliament, that is, to the effective Second Chamber, came with the constitutional revision of 1848. As with the previous system of indirect elections via provincial councils, the qualification for voting remained extremely narrow. Only male owners of substantial property who were over the age of 25 could vote. This confined the electorate to around 80,000 citizens, or 6 percent of the adult population.[11] In 1850 there were only 68 seats in the Lower House, so that on average little more than 1,000 voters were entitled to compete for the choice of each member of Parliament.

It goes without saying that the great proportion of members elected by this tiny voting elite were notables from an upper-class or

---

[11]For the growth of the electorate, see Gladdish, *Governing from the Center,* pp. 16, 71, 95, and 98.

Holland's capital—The Hague—at the dawn of the republic.

upper-middle-class background. In the years before national parties emerged—the first was the Anti-Revolutionary Party in 1879—members were selected as candidates by local committees. Until the 1880s, most candidates were some variant of liberal in that they supported secular constitutional reform. In 1888, however, confessional members—Catholic and Calvinist—were able to secure a slender majority and form the first "Christian" coalition government (see Table 7.2).

By this time the electorate had grown—through both lower property qualifications and greater prosperity—to a quarter of the adult males. The Second Chamber had also grown to a total of 100 seats. A reform of 1897 extended the vote to half the males over 25, by which time the country was divided into single-member constituencies, with provision for runoffs, or second ballots, so that the eventual choice would reflect a majority of votes.

There was, however, a growing problem by the turn of the century. Constituencies could be fought over by candidates from four or more different political segments (see Section A) so that there were often no "natural" majorities. Electoral alliances sought to deal the cards so that contests would not be chaotic, but it was clear that locality representation was unlikely to be the solution to an increasingly multiparty system. This issue became a major thread in the 1917 Pacification (see Section A). The outcome was the introduction of a strictly proportional electoral formula that translated votes—wherever cast throughout the Netherlands—into seats in the Second Chamber. At the same time the vote was extended to all males over 25 and soon after to women on the same basis. So universal adult suffrage came about alongside national proportional representation.

## Meticulous Proportionality

Proportional representation (PR), which was devised in the mid-nineteenth century as elections began to be about the construction of party governments, had become by the early twentieth century a progressive cause. The basic thinking behind PR was that all subdivisions of a national electorate distorted the mobilization of party support. This was particularly acute in single-member constituencies (as in Great Britain and the United States) where votes were recurrently "wasted," because they did not result in, nor affect, actual representation.

Although a relatively small country, Holland possessed as much local identity as anywhere else. But when it came to the compilation of a national parliament, then, given the subcultural pattern in the Netherlands, it seemed vital that the distribution of seats should reflect the total support for each pillar. It is of course true that other European states, the Scandinavian countries for example, adopted regional PR in the early twentieth century without having pillared societies. But the Dutch case appeared to its political leaders to require a more extreme form of proportionality.[12]

This amounted to a decision to regard the entire country as one vast constituency, in which parties would compete on a national basis and voters would vote primarily for parties, rather than for individuals. The results of each parliamentary election would be arrived at by adding up the total votes for each party and then distributing seats in proportion to those totals. Given a legislature consisting of 100 members (the size of the Second Chamber in 1917), a party that won 25 percent of the overall national poll would be awarded 25 seats. Votes—wherever cast—would thus be translated directly into seats on a strictly proportional basis. The same rule applied to local government elections. The formula was clear, symmetrical, and instantly intelligible. But, of course, it had to be enacted in a practical way, and although easy to summarize, the actual mechanics turn out to be rather complex.

In the first place, the country is not operated as a single polling unit but is divided into electoral districts, currently 19. Also, one consequence of the system is that voters are presented with long lists of names, and there are elaborate

---

[12]For a fuller account, see Hans Daalder, "Extreme Proportional Representation: The Dutch Experience," in Sam E. Finer, ed., *Adversary Politics and Electoral Reform* (London: Wigram, 1975), pp. 223–248.

rules to regulate this procedure. For example, no more than 30 names may appear on each party list, unless a party holds more than 15 seats in the chamber. In that case parties may list names up to twice the number of seats they hold, up to a maximum of 80.

The rules that govern the actual distribution of seats to named candidates are also complicated. The process is based on the calculation of an electoral quota. In 1998, 8.6 million votes were cast in the election of members to the Second Chamber. The chamber contains 150 seats, and the total vote divided by the number of seats to be filled provides the electoral quota. The quota in 1998 was 57,460. The most successful party in that election was Labor, which collected a total of 2.5 million votes over the whole country. This meant that on the application of the electoral quota, Labor was awarded 45 seats (see Table 7.7).

Despite the need for some elaborate arithmetic on polling night, the system works smoothly and always delivers a proportional outcome which all accept. This does not mean there has been no interest in alternative systems since its adoption in 1918. But national PR, with some refinements of detail over the years, has survived thus far. Two other features of the system should be noted. One, compulsory voting no longer applies, having been abolished in 1970. It was introduced because it was thought that full democratic participation required all to vote, or at least attend the polling station. This produced very high turnouts and Holland is still notable for the high percentage of electors who actually vote for members of Parliament (80.3 percent in 1989 and 73.2 percent in 1998 for the Second Chamber). The other feature is the absence of a threshold, which means that small parties can gain representation merely by accumulating the electoral quota without any

---

### TABLE 7.7

#### ELECTION TO THE SECOND CHAMBER, MAY 1998

| | | | |
|---|---|---|---|
| Electorate | 11,742,000 | Seats | 150 |
| Votes cast | 8,604,207 | Electoral quota | 57,460 |
| Turnout | 73.2% | | |

**Votes and Seats by Parties**

| Position | Party | Votes | % of Total Votes | Seats |
|---|---|---|---|---|
| 1 | Labor (PvdA) | 2,493,911 | 29.0 | 45 |
| 2 | Liberals (VVD) | 2,122,472 | 24.7 | 38 |
| 3 | Christian Democrats (CDA) | 1,580,650 | 18.4 | 29 |
| 4 | Democrats '66 (D'66) | 773,464 | 9.0 | 14 |
| 5 | Green Left (GL) | 625,170 | 7.3 | 11 |
| 6 | Socialist Party (SP) | 303,483 | 3.5 | 5 |
| 7 | Calvinist Federation (RPF) | 175,370 | 2.0 | 3 |
| 8 | Calvinist Party (SGP) | 153,153 | 1.8 | 3 |
| 9 | Calvinist Union (GPV) | 108,625 | 1.3 | 2 |
| 10 | Others | 169,149 | 1.9 | 0 |

The position of the parties will be their list number at the next election.

**Outcome**

| | | |
|---|---|---|
| Coalition Cabinet | PvdA/VVD/D'66 | Total 97 seats |

## THE 2002 ELECTION

The parliamentary election of May 15, 2002, took place in the shadow of two grim events. The first was the final report of the enquiry into the massacre at Srebenica in Bosnia in 1995. The government took responsibility for criticisms of the performance of the Dutch troops and resigned a month before polling day. The second was the murder of a populist politician—Pim Fortuyn—whose group had stormed ahead in Rotterdam in the local elections in March. Fortuyn's assassination, an unprecedented act in Holland, curbed the campaign and almost deferred the election. His platform was essentially anti-immigrant and aroused passions rarely voiced in Dutch political discourse.

Because of these precursors, the election outcome was unusually difficult to forecast; much depended on how far Fortuyn's campaign and his violent death would change the standard pattern of party support. Turnout was nearly 80 percent and there was a distinct shift to the right. But the sudden burst of support for anti-immigrant policies changed the right-of-center map. Instead of the Liberals (VVD), Fortuyn's makeshift list had become the second largest party in the Chamber, and the Christian Democrats had moved into first place, their best result since 1989. As one prominent daily newspaper observed, this was "a strange reward for years of impotent opposition and decades as a symbol of the established order."

On the Left only the Socialists, a minor party, made ground. Labor (PvdA), a major player in government since 1989, was deserted by almost half its 1998 voters. Democrats '66 suffered an identical fate and there was no prospect of the previous coalition—PvdA, VVD, and D'66—resuming office. But what could its successor be? The traditional center-right alliance, Christians and Liberals, had insufficient seats for a majority in the Lower House. Minority government was not a Dutch option. So it looked as though the scratch team picked by the late Fortuyn, reputedly on the basis of five-minute interviews, would somehow have to be represented in cabinet. Since ministers do not need to be and cannot be members of parliament, this was perhaps less alarming than might be the case.

A new coalition government was constructed rather more rapidly than usual. A three-party cabinet was inaugurated on July 22 consisting of six CDA ministers, four ministers from the List Pim Fortuyn, and four ministers from the VVD.

---

further barrier. This has served to keep the party system and the legislature open to new and minuscule contenders.

## Parties and PR

Given an electoral system as unusual as the one just described (only Israel has a comparably open and national form of PR), how do the political parties operate it, and what are the costs and benefits to both parties and voters? One vivid difference from constituency systems is that in Holland, ordinary candidates do not need to present themselves to the voters. In any parliamentary election, of the hundreds of candidates listed by the various parties, only the leaders will participate in meetings or more commonly in radio and TV broadcasts. Since there are no constituencies, the likelihood of a candidate being elected depends first on his or her party and second on his or her position on the list. National leaders will appear at the head of the list in all districts, and the higher positions will go to notables within the party. Most candidates do not get elected because the legislature is small and even the largest parties contain only a few dozen parliamentarians.

Candidates are elected if their position on a list is within the number of electoral quotas gained by their party. If, therefore, a party wins 300,000 votes for its list in, say, the Leiden electoral district, then on a quota of 60,000, the first five candidates on that list would be elected. Party managers will have anticipated this when compiling the list, and there is little doubt that the selection of candidates in a national list system tends to be a centralized operation. This can, of course, ensure that the ticket is balanced by so many women, so many representatives of important interest groups, and so on. Major parties are well versed in list politics. Minor parties have the incentive that if they manage to assemble, from all over the Netherlands, a mere 0.67 percent of the total vote, they will get a party representative in Parliament. In 1998, 23 parties submitted lists in all electoral districts, and four of these won seats with less than 4 percent of the poll.

So who misses out in the national electoral competition? There is some evidence that it may be the voters.[13] That voters have no role in the selection of candidates is a feature of many, if not most, parliamentary systems, where there is normally no provision for primaries. But in Holland there is little scope for voters to meet candidates or get to know much about them, unless candidates happen to be national celebrities. The situation worsens after Parliament is elected because, since there are no constituencies, voters have no individual member to represent them. Studies of relations—in so far as they exist—between voters and parliamentarians strongly suggest that Dutch MPs do not fulfill the tasks of grievance-monitoring, or of consultation about issues, or even of access to government.

If the electoral system meticulously reflects the pattern of party support within the nation, it does so at the cost of anonymity on the part of many candidates, and the absence of any form of locality representation. This is well understood by Dutch commentators and analysts, and periodically proposals are made for the introduction of some element of regional representation. But the system is probably now too entrenched for

---

[13]For more detail on this, see Ken Gladdish, "The Netherlands," in Vernon Bogdanor, ed., *Representatives of the People? Parliamentarians and Constituents in Western Democracies* (Aldershot, UK: Gower, 1985), pp. 135–148.

change to be likely, unless there are radical shifts within other elements of the political system.

## THE PARTY UNIVERSE

The first national mass party was formed in 1879 by a clergyman, Abraham Kuyper, to unify and mobilize the adherents of the more strict Calvinist churches. Within a decade the Anti-Revolutionaries—so named because they were opposed to the secular doctrines of the French Revolution—held a quarter of the seats in the Lower House of Parliament. This provided the basis for a coalition with Catholic members, also a quarter of the chamber, to form the first confessional, or religious, government in 1888.

By that stage, after a remarkably short period of high political acceleration, a party system was in place. In addition to the two religious blocs, Catholic and Calvinist, it consisted of Liberals (almost half of the Parliament up to 1900) and an embryonic Socialist movement. This last became a full-fledged party in 1894, under the title Social Democratic Workers (SDAP).

The party system that was forged in the final decades of the nineteenth century has in some essentials at least survived until the present (see Figure 7.2). Accordingly, the party configuration at the election of May 1998 can be related, without too elaborate translation, to the results of the election of 1897. The main actors in the party arena have thus been surprisingly long-lived since the onset of mass mobilization 120 years ago.

Of the cleavages around which competitive party systems may be constructed, the Netherlands possesses only two: religion and class. There were no ethnic or linguistic divisions within the population at the outset of democratization. Nor were there any great convulsions, such as civil war or decolonization, which might have created conflicting traditions. Religion as a cleavage assumed early on a somewhat strange but enduring character. There were various forms of Christianity to which people could attach themselves, but there was little active competition between the churches. The Calvinists were subdivided into a relatively tolerant mainstream—the Dutch Reformed Church—and

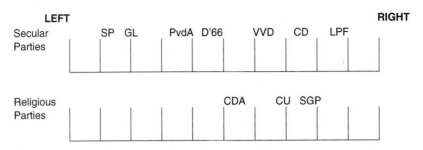

**Figure 7.2   THE CURRENT PARTY SPECTRUM—IDEOLOGICAL POSITIONS**

a more militant sect, "the Re-reformed." The Catholics were monolithic, under an episcopal hierarchy restored in the 1850s.

Although the different denominations were the armatures of separate pillars, they tended to ally rather than clash in the political arena. This reflected a cleavage that went deeper than the interconfessional: between the devotees of church-based politics and those who supported secular parties.

The second major cleavage was predicated on social class. But this again has to be qualified in important respects. In the nineteenth century, the class structure was made up of a minute residual nobility, a substantial mercantile and professional middle class in both town and country, and a working class of primary and secondary producers, from fishermen and ship builders to canal bargees and factory hands. Upon this familiar pattern of social stratification, the churches projected their appeal to newly enfranchised voters. Their call was for support in the protection of Christian values and institutions, above all in the field of education. Within a generation, starting in the 1870s, roughly half of the politically active population had been won over to a religious view of politics. These then became, and their successors remained, largely immune to the lure of secular politics promoted by nonreligious parties.

Class divisions had thus been blanked off by the confessionals so far as their supporters were concerned, and half the electorate had been decommissioned so far as appeals to class interests went. The confessional parties had therefore to take account, within their network and policy platforms, of both employers and employees, landowners and farm laborers, ship owners and seamen. This was because the success of their attention to the whole range of social and economic interests within their camp determined how far they could head off more starkly phrased interest group politics.

In fact, even among the proportion of the population who chose to see politics as a secular realm, class remained a much weaker feature than religion in determining party allegiance. Table 7.8 shows the virtually complete convergence between church attendance and voting habits on the part of Catholics and militant Calvinists. Under class-based voting, however, not only did one-fifth of declared secularists vote for religious parties, but more middle-class voters preferred Labor to the Liberals, who, in economic terms, were to the right of the center.

This last point reflects a variety of factors, including social mobility and the institutional distance between the Labor Party and organized labor. Among secular working-class voters, the majority adherence to Labor is clear. The figures for class-based voting have changed very little since the mid-1950s. In 1986, 60 percent of working-class electors voted Labor, and 29 percent of middle-class electors voted Liberal.

Twenty-three parties submitted lists in all districts in the 1998 parliamentary election. Of the nine that won seats (see Table 7.7), five can be regarded as major parties. The remainder can be subdivided into minor ideological groupings, minor religious parties, and ephemerals. Summaries of the parties' aims and origins follow.

**TABLE 7.8**

**TRADITIONAL VOTING BEHAVIOR, MID-1950s**

| Religion-Based Support | Catholic Party (KVP) | Main Calvinist Party (ARP) |
|---|---|---|
| Catholics regularly attending mass | 97% | |
| Re-reformed Calvinists regularly attending church | | 99% |

| Class-Based Support | Labor (PvdA) | Liberals (VVD) | Mainstream Religious Parties |
|---|---|---|---|
| Secular lower-class voters | 68% | 5% | 17% |
| Secular middle-class voters | 44% | 32% | 19% |

*Source:* Compiled from references summarized by Galen A. Irwin and J. J. M. van Holsteyn, in Hans Daalder and Galen Irwin, eds., *Politics in the Netherlands* (London: Cass, 1989). pp. 21–41.

## Major Parties

*Christian Democratic Appeal*    The Christian Democratic Appeal (CDA) was formed during the 1970s as a consortium of the three formerly separate mainstream religious parties: the Catholic People's Party, the Calvinist Anti-Revolutionaries, and Christian Historicals. Amalgamation had first been mooted in 1967, shortly after the Catholics had suffered a sharp reverse at the polls. After 1972 when the Christian Historicals lost ground, the strategy of a merger appeared the only way to stem the tide. A single list was presented in the 1977 election, and in 1980 the three parties were fully incorporated in the CDA.

By 1986 the formula of merger seemed to have worked. In that year's election, and again in 1989, the Christian amalgam recovered to become the country's leading party. But in 1994 disaster struck. The popular CDA leader and Minister President (Prime Minister) Ruud Lubbers stepped down, and the party lost more than one-third of its previous votes. Even more crucially, it was excluded from the government coalition—the first time since 1918 that a cabinet had been formed without the confessional bloc. Further losses followed in 1998, when support fell to below 20 percent of the total poll and the party was again left out of government.

The regaining of support in the mid-1980s signaled a change in the character of the party. Until then, it had attracted adherents of the mainstream churches. In the late 1980s and early 1990s, however, it began to win support as a nondenominational center grouping. The major confessionals had always governed from the center, because although broadly conservative on social and ostensibly moral issues, their components covered the whole socioeconomic range of interests. Also, because of the parliamentary arithmetic, since no coalition could be formed without them, they were able to dominate the middle ground. From there they could determine whether cabinets would be center-left (by including Labor) or center-right (by allying with the Liberals).

After 1982, however, there was competition in the center of the political arena, both from the major secular parties—Labor and Liberal—who sought to maximize votes, and from the new movement, Democrats '66. As the CDA broadened its approach, it risked losing both its character and its purpose. But in 2002 the CDA made impressive gains and emerged as the largest single party with 43 seats.

*Labor*    Labor's origins go back to 1894 when the Social Democratic Worker's Party (SDAP) was founded. Initially Marxist, at least in vocabulary, its nonrevolutionary character was confirmed when the Communists broke away. But because of the confessional challenge, the SDAP failed either to mobilize more than a minority of workers or to enter government before 1940.

After World War II, its leaders sought to create a wider movement. In 1946 the Labor Party (*Partei van der arbeid*) was launched and became the key player in successive coalitions with the confessionals during the reconstruction period. From 1958 until 1989, however, Labor had only one significant spell in office—during the 1970s. In 1977 and again in 1986, it managed to attract one-third of the voters. But in 1994, after a period in office with the CDA, it slumped badly yet still emerged as the leading party because of the wide distribution of votes. Its cabinet leader, Wim Kok, then became prime minister of a three-party coalition. Labor's popularity recovered in 1998 when the mandate for the purple coalition was renewed, but its support fell away in 2002 after 13 years in government.

Both in 1945 and during the early 1970s, Labor strove for a polarization of politics which would marginalize the religious parties. This called for a clear ideological definition, always a problem because of the party's middle-class support (see Table 7.8). By the 1980s it seemed that Labor would best enhance its fortunes by moving nearer the center ground. Like all European parties of the Left, the PvdA has had to acknowledge the backlash against welfare, redistribution, and public ownership which has fueled the marketeers and antiegalitarians during the past decade and a half.

**Liberals**    The contemporary party normally referred to as "Liberal" dates only from 1948, but the liberal tradition is the oldest in modern Dutch politics. The first government to which the label can be attached was formed by J. R. Thorbecke in 1849. But the foundation of a political party, or rather parties, came in the 1890s when three liberal strands were represented in Parliament. Between the wars, liberals and radicals together occupied 10–15 percent of the seats in the Lower House. Finally, postwar liberals were united in a new party—the People's Party for Freedom and Democracy (VVD).

The liberal tradition in Holland is secular, constitutionalist, and elite, and is associated historically with the tolerant, patrician style of the mercantile bourgeoisie. Given the two dimensions of party space—religion and class—the confessionals tended to occupy the right of center on social issues, making the liberal place in the spectrum different from that of European conservatives. The VVD is, however, the main force to the right of center in terms of economic policy and reflects the employer interests on most questions of taxation and welfare.

Over its half-century, the VVD has had two distinct periods of electoral performance: weak, at around 10 percent of seats and votes, until 1972; then more impressive with peaks of over 20 percent in 1982 and 1994. The party was in government as the CDA's partner from 1977 to 1989. It returned to office in 1994 in a coalition with Labor and Democrats '66. At the 1998 election, the VVD became the second largest party and continued in office in the succeeding purple cabinet. Despite losing seats in 2002 it remained in government, in coalition with the CDA and the List Pim Fortuyn.

**Democrats '66**    As the name implies, the Democrats '66 (D'66) arose in the mid-1960s out of the challenges to the politics of accommodation. Its initial thrust was a bid to modernize the political arena through constitutional and operational change. Formed by a group of young intellectuals with one or two seasoned politicians—mostly from the Liberals—it set out its program in an appeal to Dutch citizens. At the heart of the appeal was deep frustration with the working of the political system, in particular its lack of accountability to voters: "You, the voter, have no influence whatsoever on [cabinet] formation, no influence with regard to the composition of the government, no influence on its program."

To remedy these defects the party called for: (1) the direct election of a prime minister, who would form a cabinet from supporting parties, and (2) the reintroduction of locality representation, in the form of multimember electoral districts. These two measures should, it was thought, produce something close to a two-party system, which would be more directly responsive to the electors than the traditional system. Neither measure has been adopted, and the survival of D'66 as a significant party has surprised many writers, including this one. Its performance over the 30 years since its formation has fluctuated from a mere 4 percent of the vote in 1972 and 1982 to 15 percent in 1994. It did less well in 1998 but managed to retain three ministers in the second purple cabinet. The 2002 election, however, saw it drop to 8 seats, its worst performance for 20 years.

Part of the explanation for its survival is its value as a changeover point within a multiparty system. In 1986 for example, there was substantial traffic in votes between D'66 and Labor as voters moved either slightly left or slightly right of their former positions.[14] D'66 has tended to occupy a space between CDA and Labor, and in 1994, apart from attracting a large number of new voters or former nonvoters, it drew a third of its 12-seat gains from previous supporters of those two parties.

*Green Left*   In the 1989 elections for the European Parliament, four parties which had formerly been independent produced a combined list of candidates under the label "Rainbow Coalition." The quartet was certainly multicolored, since it consisted of the following parties:

1. The Communist Party, formed in 1918.
2. The Pacifist Socialist Party, a breakaway from Labor in 1957.
3. The Radical Party, a confessional breakaway dating from 1968.
4. The Evangelical People's Party, formed by left-wing Anti-Revolutionaries after the confessional merger in 1980.

For the 1989 parliamentary election, the grouping changed its name to Green Left. This was a successful maneuver which netted six seats, and shortly afterwards the component parties were dissolved. In 1994 the new formation did slightly less well with only 3.5 percent of the vote and five seats. But in 1998 it made impressive gains, doubling its proportion of the vote. The party acts as a left-wing outrider to Labor and its title has so far headed off mass support for the more committed ecological movement—the Green Federation.

---

[14]See Ken Gladdish, "The Centre Holds: The 1986 Netherlands Election," *West European Politics* 10(1) (January 1987), pp. 115–119.

## Minor Parties

*Calvinist Parties*   Formed in 1918 as a breakaway of strict Calvinists from the Anti-Revolutionaries, the Calvinist Party (SGP) relies on a small but steady group of voters, regularly gaining two or three seats in the Lower House. The most extreme of the minor religious parties, it has long opposed the participation of women in politics.

For the 2002 election, two formerly separate parties—the Calvinist Union (GPV) and the Calvinist Federation (RPF)—formed a single list under the title Christian Union, and won four seats.

Although the Calvinist parties have often acted as a bloc, none has ever served in government and only rarely are they considered as potential cabinet members. They may be regarded as relics of the confessional era, since they are almost entirely sectarian and not part of the increasingly open market for votes which the other parties comprise.

*Socialist Party*   The recent success of the Socialist Party exemplifies two recurrent features of Dutch politics. One is the spring of dissident left-wing opinion that bubbles away at the fringe of the mainstream parties. The other is the capacity of tiny parties to win seats in the open climate of the voting system. The party began as a small local movement. In 1989 it submitted its first national list of candidates and in 1994, with only 1.3 percent of the poll, it won two seats. By 1998 it had mobilized over 300,000 voters and risen to five seats in the Lower House, plus representation in the Upper House and the European Parliament. In 2002 its support soared to new heights, returning nine members to the Second Chamber.

## Party Programs

The breakdown of the *verzuiling,* or pillared structure of politics, has changed the nature of Dutch parties over the past 30 years. Until the mid-1960s, they could rely on their faithful adherents turning up at the polling station, a compulsory act of devotion up to 1970 (see Section A). As that certainty diminished, parties were forced to compete in a manner more typical of European electoral contests, by persuading voters that their programs were desirable. One consequence was the increasing length and detail of election manifestos. These inventories of positions and intended policies are, of course, merely responses to the circumstances surrounding each election. They are underpinned by statutes which define the essential aims and purpose of each party and by periodic statements of principle on issues such as NATO, abortion, or social welfare.

There is, therefore, a whole geology that underlies any account of the programs of individual parties. At the deepest level lie propositions such as: "The party regards holy scripture as the guide for political action," Article 1 of the statutes of the CDA. At the visceral level lie the attitudes of party activists on basic issues (see Table 7.9). At the manifesto level there will be specific views and positions on every conceivable matter, from the percentage of GDP to be devoted to overseas aid, to maximum automobile speeds and obligatory AIDS tests.

These stances, so far as the major parties are concerned, are not solely designed as bait for voters. Immediately after the election is over, they become bargaining positions in the game of coalition forming. Each cabinet comes into office having agreed, among the participating parties, on a governing program. The drafting of the election manifesto is a contribution to the auction for office which will follow the election results, and this is firmly in the mind of party planners.

Manifestos are, therefore, tailored to the realities of maximizing votes and the subsequent coalition negotiations. At the same time they nor-mally reflect the character and role of each party within the spectrum. Table 7.10 summarizes the main points in the programs of the major parties in the 1989 parliamentary election campaign. They show where the parties stood relative to each other at the end of the 1980s, even though the differences between their proposals may seem slender.

The CDA has moved slightly to the right on defense and the economy since the 1960s. But its distrust of commercialism survives, along with the concern for human dignity. Labor's traditional concerns are well displayed in points 1–4, but point 5 is a concession to public anxiety about rising crime. This is contrary to the party's general position on security, which is that it has a lower priority than welfare.

For the Liberals, defense has been a long-term preoccupation, and the party has consistently advocated the retention of nuclear weapons by NATO. On the other issues, the Liberal center-right approach to socioeconomic policy is nicely balanced by compassion. In terms of the attitudes of party supporters, D'66 was closest to Labor on cardinal issues during the 1980s, as Table 7.9 demonstrates. This is borne out by points 1 and 2 of the D'66 program, and indeed by point 5, given Labor's position on police expenditure. Points 3 and 4 suggest an identification with a middle-class business constituency.

Broadly, the Left looks to government to spend in order to provide public services and benefits, while the Right seeks to achieve a higher ratio of private to public spending. But the

---

## TABLE 7.9

### ATTITUDES OF PARTY ACTIVISTS ON CARDINAL ISSUES (PERCENTAGE)

| In favor of | VVD | CDA | D'66 | PvdA |
|---|---|---|---|---|
| Implementation of sex equality | 95 | 99 | 98 | 99 |
| Increase of military spending | 71 | 35 | 7 | 1 |
| More control of multinationals | 33 | 71 | 83 | 99 |
| Less control of private firms | 86 | 48 | 27 | 8 |
| Reduction of income differences | 23 | 72 | 82 | 99 |
| Development of nuclear energy | 87 | 68 | 37 | 17 |

*Source:* Documentation Centre for Dutch Political Parties, University of Groningen, 1982.

## TABLE 7.10

### PARTY PROGRAMS, 1989 PARLIAMENTARY CAMPAIGN

**CDA**

1. Raise defense budget by 0.6 percent
2. Reduce social welfare taxes
3. Raise public housing rents
4. Restrict commercial broadcasting
5. Prohibit trade in human organs

**Liberals**

1. Raise defense budget by 1 percent
2. Reduce social welfare taxes by 0.5 percent
3. Promote private housing, but give tenants right to buy
4. Compel unemployed to retrain, but require employers to hire disabled
5. Raise police budget, but by less than Labor's amount

**Labor**

1. Reduce defense budget by 4 percent
2. Maintain health insurance premiums
3. Mix public and private housing
4. Fix working week at 35 hours
5. Raise law and order budget by 3 percent

**D'66**

1. Freeze defense budget
2. Maintain tax levels, but increase child benefit
3. Allow tax relief for home maintenance
4. Allow commercial broadcasting
5. Raise police budget by 5 percent

permanence of coalition government dilutes party programs. This was the more evident from 1994 until 2002, when the new Left and Right parties went together in office.

## Party Membership and Resources

Looked at from the standpoints of staffing and finance, political parties in the Netherlands—though vital to the fluency of the political system—are extremely modest organizations. They have no special legal recognition and are treated like any other voluntary association, except in the context of elections, which are carefully regulated by the electoral law.

All parties are made up of individual members, without any corporate affiliations, such as trade unions or employer federations. Membership requires simply allegiance and a small fee, and is open to anyone, Dutch or foreign, living in Holland. Dutch parties have never had mass memberships. The highest levels were probably reached in the 1960s at around 10 percent of the electorate. Since then numbers have declined to 2.5 percent, as set out in Table 7.11.

## TABLE 7.11

### NATIONAL PARTY MEMBERSHIP, 1990s

| Party | Numbers | As % of Voters |
|---|---|---|
| CDA | 112,000 | 6.0 |
| Labor | 75,000 | 3.5 |
| Liberal | 54,000 | 3.0 |
| SEP | 24,000 | 16.0 |
| GPV | 14,000 | 12.0 |
| Green Left | 14,000 | 4.5 |
| D'66 | 13,000 | 0.9 |
| Others | 15,000 | 1.0 |

| **Totals** | | |
|---|---|---|
| **Year** | **Numbers** | **As % of Electorate** |
| 1998 | 294,000 | 2.5 |
| 1994 | 321,000 | 2.8 |
| 1960 | 750,000 | 8.3 |

*Source:* Adapted from Ruud Koole, "The Specifics of Dutch Political Parties," *Netherlands Journal of Social Sciences* 29(2) (1993).

Various reasons have been offered for the low membership of the major parties (note that the highest proportion of members to voters occurs in the sectarian minor Calvinist parties). Under conditions of high pillarization—though memberships were greater then—it was not crucial that voters should be mobilized by party activists, since other organizations, from churches to pillared radio channels, defined and stimulated supporters. There was not even any need to turn out the faithful on polling day, because until 1970 voting was a legal obligation upon all citizens.

Another consequence of pillarization was that parties were "cadre" rather than "mass" in character, meaning that they were operated by small elites and did not require huge numbers of recruits. The absence of corporate membership, already noted, further contributes to low numbers. Finally, since there is no spoils system in the Netherlands, party membership is not a prerequisite (unlike in Belgium) of acquiring rewards and privileges.

Modesty in party numbers is paralleled by modesty in party finance.[15] Political operations in Holland are distinctively low-budget. Until the 1960s, the need for party coffers was indeed minimal, since campaigns were almost surreally low-key—again an effect of pillarization and compulsory voting. A slight gearing-up occurred with the decline of the pillars, and in 1971 the first state subsidies were introduced, though only for research institutes. This was later extended to educational and youth work.

In the 1990s, a royal commission recommended more comprehensive state aid but this has not so far been implemented. Accordingly, annual budgets range from Labor's $6 million (U.S.) to $4 million for the CDA, $2.5 million for the Liberals, and less than $1 million for D'66 (in 1989 figures). From a comparative standpoint, it is interesting that, since business donations to parties are frowned upon, the party most likely to appeal to business—the Liberals—has a much lower income than the Labor Party.

## Party Organization

Although parties naturally vary in their internal arrangements, there is a general pattern to which most conform. The two principal national organs are the party congress and the party executive. The congress is a large assembly of delegates from all sections of the movement which meets, usually annually, to debate policy and make proposals. The executive, as its name implies, is the instrumental part of the policy process. Much smaller and more frequently convened than the congress, its members exercise a continuous control over party matters.

The relationship between congress and executive is clearly a linchpin of effective operations over time. But even more important strategically is the link between the executive and the parliamentary group or *fractie*. The nature and status of Parliament as the summit of political legitimacy means that parliamentary groups are sovereign in respect of their legislative decisions. Indeed, the Dutch tradition of remote Cabinet-Parliament relations formerly conferred on the *fracties* an unusual degree of autonomy in the context of European governance.

One pervasive effect of this autonomy on party dispositions and decision making has been the creation of a multipolar situation. Party members look upward to the national executive, headed by the party chairman. Voters, however, regard the *fracties* as the deliverers of party policy, and the floor-leaders in the Second Chamber as the oracles of party stances on the issues of the day. If a party happens to be in government, a third level of command emerges in the form of ministers. So how party policy is settled will depend first on the nature of the issue—whether short- or long-term, profound or trivial, urgent or postponable. Second, it will hinge on whether it is a major party, since smaller parties tend to settle more matters outside Parliament. Third, it will reflect whether or not the party is in the cabinet.

A further factor to complicate party management is the demands of the electoral system.

[15]See Ruud Koole, "The 'Modesty' of Dutch Party Finance," in H. E. Alexander, ed., *Comparative Political Finance in the 1980* (Cambridge: Cambridge University Press, 1989), pp. 209–219.

Party lists compiled on a national basis mean that elaborate mechanisms are needed to handle the selection of candidates. Here regional party organs come into the picture, along with national sections that deal with women, youth, and special groups. Dutch parties are, or endeavor to be, run with some attention to democratic participation by their members. This inevitably leads to much organizational complexity.

## Party Support

Firms need customers; parties need voters. What sorts of voters do the various parties in Holland attract? The basic cleavages of religion and class have already been discussed. It is, however, worth pointing out here that over the past 30 years, Dutch political scientists have recurrently looked for signs that the crumbling of the pillars has "de-aligned" voters from traditional patterns of behavior (up to the 1960s) and "re-aligned" them in terms of other more recent criteria. So far, however, there is no convincing evidence that this has happened to any conclusive extent. In a study of the mid-1990s it was found that "the combination of social class and religion still explained much of the voting behaviour of the Dutch in the nineties."[16] It was certainly the case in the 1980s that these two hoary variables continued to dominate the picture.

---

[16]Peer Scheepers, Jan Lammers, and Jan Peters, "Religious and Class Voting in the Netherlands," *Netherlands Journal of Social Sciences* 30(1) (1994), pp. 5–24.

Table 7.12 conforms surprisingly well both to the lineaments of the traditional pattern and the emphases of party programs throughout the postwar period. The Christian Democrats' distribution of voters almost exactly matches the overall distribution, as it has since 1918, which precisely reflects the appeal of the religious mainstream to religious voters in all classes. The Liberals, by contrast, clearly confine their attraction to the middle and upper-middle segments, as indeed do the Democrats '66. The sole anomaly, but one which was manifest back in the 1960s (and already discussed), is Labor's appeal to middle-class voters.

Table 7.13 shows how the 1986 vote went in terms of religion and is interesting on several counts. For the first time since their inception in the mid-1970s, the Christian Democrats succeeded in attracting measurable support from secular voters. Also worth noting is the preponderance of Catholic voters in the CDA poll. The three other major parties mirror in their support the distribution of religious, or nonreligious, affiliation in the population at large. This corresponds to the way, in Table 7.12, the Christian Democratic voters reflected the overall pattern of social stratification.

Apart from class and religion, voting support can be identified in terms of other variables such as gender, age, education, and geography. Are any of these further variables significant in the Dutch case? Gender as a discriminator is generally considered to be of little value in analyzing electoral outcomes. There are some detailed studies, but none suggest that women and men

## TABLE 7.12

### VOTING BY CLASS IN THE 1986 PARLIAMENTARY ELECTION (PERCENTAGE)

| Class | Distribution of Voters | CDA | Labor | Liberal | D'66 |
|---|---|---|---|---|---|
| Upper middle | 19 | 15 | 10 | 41 | 29 |
| Middle | 46 | 53 | 39 | 48 | 45 |
| Upper working | 11 | 10 | 15 | 7 | 9 |
| Working | 24 | 23 | 37 | 4 | 17 |

*Source:* 1986 National Election Study, The Hague, S.D.U.
*Note:* Each voter's class was self-ascribed. This may have inflated the upper categories.

**TABLE 7.13**

**VOTING BY RELIGION IN THE 1986 PARLIAMENTARY ELECTION (PERCENTAGE)**

| Denominations | Distribution of Voters | CDA | Labor | Liberal | D'66 |
|---|---|---|---|---|---|
| Catholic | 32 | 51 | 23 | 29 | 23 |
| Dutch Reformed (Calvinist) | 15 | 20 | 12 | 12 | 14 |
| Re-reformed (strict Calvinist) | 6 | 11 | 1 | 2 | 4 |
| Other | 4 | 3 | 4 | 5 | 0 |
| No church | 43 | 16 | 60 | 51 | 60 |

*Source:* 1986 National Election Study, The Hague, S.D.U.

respond differently to the general framework of political mobilization.

Age is better than gender in showing variations of response to individual parties. In the 1986 national election study, support for Labor came closest to the overall age pattern of the voters. Support for the Christian Democrats was lower among young voters than with other major parties, while Democrats '66, the newest major party, had the lowest proportion of voters over 60. But age has little predictive value compared with either churchgoing or class. The same is true of education. Here again, Labor conforms best to the overall national pattern in which two-thirds of voters have completed secondary education and one-fifth higher education. But the only marked correlation is that voters who did not complete secondary education (and are mostly old) are unlikely to vote either for the Liberals or for D'66.

Finally there is geography. Given that religious denominations, and religion itself, have provided major cleavage lines within the political universe, it would be surprising if there were no territorial consequences. Certainly up to the 1970s, the Catholic Party was dominant in the southern provinces of Limburg and North Brabant. Likewise the Anti-Revolutionaries had their concentrations of support in the north and the east. The merging of the confessional parties superseded this pattern, though in 1994 the CDA peaked in Limburg and Overijssel (formerly a Calvinist stronghold).

Labor's strength, and to some extent Liberal's, has rested in the cities, which are mostly in the west. Of the 24 principal urban areas in 1998, Labor showed strong backing in Amsterdam, Groningen, and Rotterdam while the Liberals did particularly well in Haarlemmermeer (a suburban district) and The Hague, a traditional bastion. Green Left was also best supported in the cities, especially Utrecht and Nijmegen. D'66 had its best results in Leiden, Amsterdam, and Utrecht.

These findings are, however, more of sociological than psephological interest, since when calculating results the electoral system irons out all geographical variations. Regional and locality party support does nevertheless feed into the recruitment of party elites and affects the choice and listing of parliamentary candidates.

## INTEREST GROUPS

"The past was more statist, and the present is more corporatist than is often assumed."[17] The overriding reason for this view is that in Holland interest groups are more embedded in the policy process than the term "interest" usually implies. There is also the complication that major interests—most obviously the "social partners," that is, employer and labor organizations—were heavily pillarized under the ancien regime. So their inclusion in the corporatist arrangements

---

[17]Andeweg and Irwin, p. 173.

reflected not merely interests, but also religious and political connections.

The "social partners" exemplify this complexity. In the case of organized labor, three separate "pillared" federations emerged during the initial phase of mobilization: one Calvinist, one Catholic, and one Socialist. Each survived until the 1970s, when the latter two combined to form the Federation of Dutch Trade Unions (FNV). Despite the amalgamation of the political camps into the CDA, the smaller Calvinist Federation (NV) chose to carry on. Of the 6 million or so employees in Holland, only a quarter are currently organized into labor unions. Of this number, two-thirds belong to the FNV and a fifth to the CNV.

Employer organizations also stem from the pillared society, though their residual pattern reflects it differently from the case of the labor unions. An umbrella grouping, the Confederation of Netherlands Industry (VNO-NCW), covers the larger employers. It now includes the Netherlands Federation of Christian Employers (NCW), an amalgam of former Catholic and Calvinist organizations.

Other professional, educational, media, and agricultural bodies exert pressure on public decision making as elsewhere in Europe. Many are, however, formally part of the policy process and, as members of "advisory organizations," work within ministries as policy prompters.

## THE CONSTITUTION

The Netherlands is a constitutional state, governed according to a constitution first issued in 1814 on the creation of the monarchy. The constitution is a document of some 40 pages in the English version published by the Ministry of Home Affairs. Its eight chapters cover fundamental rights, the institutions of national government, the legislative process, the administration of justice, and procedures for constitutional revision.

Nevertheless, the Dutch Constitution does not have the sacrosanct character enjoyed by its American counterpart. It is not that it is ignored; its provisions are scrupulously addressed. But its status is not that of a document outside and beyond the normal legislative process. Indeed, the entire constitution stems from a principle which effectively overrides its autonomy. The principle is that of parliamentary supremacy. As an official digest puts it, "Strictly speaking there is little difference between the constitution and any other act of parliament."[18]

The key lack of difference is one of status, because the procedure for constitutional amendment is more complex than for ordinary legislation. Amending bills have to be approved both before and after a parliamentary election, the second time by a two-thirds majority in both chambers. But this usually presents little difficulty, updates are quite frequent, and the result is not open to judicial review. Article 120 states unequivocally: "The constitutionality of acts of parliament shall not be reviewed by the courts." So although the Netherlands, unlike Great Britain, has a comprehensive written constitution, what it contains, not unlike in Great Britain, is what Parliament thinks it should contain. The Dutch Constitution is, however, a useful document in that it sets out, with admirable clarity, the rules of government and the citizens' rights.

It also contains certain policy commitments, which have been added to and refined over the years. For example, Article 19 requires "the authorities" (both local and national) "to promote the provision of sufficient employment", while Article 20 makes it a "concern" of government "to secure the means of subsistence of the population and to achieve the distribution of wealth." Other articles deal with the environment, health, living accommodation, education, privacy, and even culture and leisure. It is perhaps not surprising, given the breadth of these aspirations, that judges are not offered the opportunity to decide whether or not they have been fulfilled.

## THE MONARCHY

The role, status, and constitutional position of the Dutch monarch are similar to those of European

---

[18]"The Constitution," Ministry of Foreign Affairs, 1985.

counterparts. The title is hereditary and, under the constitution, passes to the senior of the legitimate descendants of the previous monarch. Since 1890, these descendants have been female. The present monarch, Beatrix, who succeeded her mother Juliana in 1980, is the third successive queen. Assuming that both the monarch and her eldest son—Willem-Alexander—survive, the Dutch should have a king around 2010, since both previous queens abdicated in their later years.

The Dutch monarch is the head of state and has certain formal "powers" but no direct power. Indeed, it would be more accurate to call his or her powers tasks, because under the constitution there is no option not to carry them out. The monarch appoints ministers, establishes ministries, and co-signs all acts of Parliament, but all on the advice that he or she is given. There is, however, one area in which the monarch can and does contribute in a more than ceremonial way to political events. Each election for the Second Chamber is followed by a prolonged period of negotiation to decide which parties should make up the cabinet. The queen consults all party leaders and then appoints a cabinet-former. As with all other tasks, she receives advice, but in this particular process she is not merely a figurehead; in difficult negotiations, she can exercise some influence at least to avoid a logjam and to move the action along.

The monarchy, by all accounts, is a popular institution. Occasionally there is public dissent, as when the present queen married a German. But the royal family goes back to William the Silent of the House of Orange, a key figure in the independence struggle of the seventeenth century. It is, therefore, a prime symbol of national identity, as it was even in the days of the republic.

## THE POLITICAL EXECUTIVE

The monarch is apolitical. The rest of the government divides between a political executive—the ministers and their deputies, the state secretaries—and a professional executive—the apolitical public service (see Table 7.14). The political executive has evolved continuously since the establishment of the monarchy in 1814. In the preparliamentary phase of government, up to 1848, ministers were appointed and dismissed by the king and held office under the royal prerogative (those powers and duties which came under royal authority). After 1848, ministers became responsible to Parliament and derived their legitimacy from their support in the legislature.

The emergence of a cabinet, or council of ministers, under the chairmanship of a prime minister, or minister president, has been a slow process in Holland. Several factors have inhibited the development of a ministerial team, collectively responsible for national strategy and public policy making. One is the tradition of autonomous ministries which dates from the royal period. A second is the continual need for multiparty coalition governments, which will be more fully discussed in the next section. A third factor has been the very late recognition of a need for a chief minister. Finally, it is only recently that ministers were regarded as the summits of the political hierarchy.

During the present century however, the huge growth in the scope of the state has forced the political executive to conform increasingly to the pattern of modern governments. In 1900 the

| TABLE 7.14 | | | |
| --- | --- | --- | --- |
| **THE POLITICAL EXECUTIVE, 1994–2002** | | | |
| **Cabinet ministers** | **PvdA** | **VVD** | **D'66** |
| 1994–1998 | 5 | 5 | 4 |
| 1998–2002 | 6 | 6 | 3 |
| **Previous Posts** | **1994–1998** | | **1998–2002** |
| Minister | 3 | | 6 |
| Deputy minister | — | | 2 |
| Parliament | 5 | | 2 |
| Public servant | 2 | | 5 |
| Other | 4 | | — |
| | 14 | | 15 |

cabinet comprised a mere eight ministers—for home and foreign affairs, finance, justice, war, navy and the colonies, commerce, and waterways. By 2002 the executive totaled 28 ministers and deputies distributed among 14 ministries. They consisted of

1. General affairs (the prime minister's department)
2. Foreign affairs
3. Home affairs
4. Justice
5. Education, culture, and science
6. Finance
7. Housing and environment
8. Defense
9. Transport and public works
10. Economic affairs
11. Agriculture and fisheries
12. Social affairs and employment
13. Welfare, health, and sport
14. Urban policy and integration

The members of the Council of Ministers normally meet once a week in The Hague, under the chairmanship of the minister president. State secretaries are in effect deputy ministers and hence political not professional appointees. They may attend cabinet meetings if invited on particular issues.

In terms of its agenda, the political executive in Holland is much like its counterparts in other European constitutional monarchies. It deals with proposed legislation; the budget; social, economic, and foreign policy matters; and senior appointments within the realm. Policy is hammered out not only in plenary meetings, but also in cabinet committees. In this sense, the Dutch cabinet is much like its British equivalent. Where the Dutch cabinet is less like most of its opposite numbers is in its method of formation and in its relationship with the legislature. Both of these areas impact the character of the cabinet and the background of ministers.

## Cabinet Formation

Much has been written about the egregious nature of Dutch cabinet formation.[19] Three main questions about it are of interest here: What party coalitions are manufactured after elections? How is the operation carried out? What are the political consequences of the often prolonged delays before a new government is announced? The first question falls within a general category of political analysis, that of coalition theory. A review of coalition making in the neighboring Low Country of Belgium has proposed three possible rationales for party coalitions:[20]

1. The greatest shift in support in the relevant election.
2. The continuing majority of opinion among the voters.
3. The minimal winning combination.

All three possibilities highlight the two problems recurrently thrown up in multiparty systems: First, who has "won" the election? Second, how can this "victory" be translated into a workable government? If we look back to Table 7.5, we can consider these problems in relation to any election result since 1982. In the case of the parliamentary election in May 1994, some of the more obvious dilemmas are immediately visible, for the party that attracted the most votes—Labor— had suffered a massive hemorrhage of support compared with the previous election in 1989. At the same time, Democrats '66 had doubled its poll and its seats in the Lower House, though it lay only fourth in the parties' ranking.

So who "won" the 1994 election? And by which criteria? If the criterion is the greatest shift, then the winner was D'66. If however it is the continuing majority, or rather plurality, then

[19]See Ken Gladdish, "Governing the Dutch," *Acta Politica* (Amsterdam) 25(4) (1990), pp. 389–402; and Richard T. Griffiths, ed., *The Economy and Politics of the Netherlands since 1945* (The Hague: Martinus Nijhoff, 1980), ch. 9, pp. 223–249.
[20]Eric C. Browne and John Dreijmanis, eds., *Governing Coalitions in Western Democracies* (New York: Longman, 1982).

it was Labor. But in either case, the judgment is essentially abstract, because neither party had enough seats to govern, and even the two together still lacked a legislative majority. So far as the third rationale goes, no two parties had enough seats to govern the Netherlands in 1994. The minimal winning three-party coalition would have been CDA, Labor, and Green Left (76/150 seats). But no one would have suggested that combination as a practical solution.

How then is a coalition decided on in Holland? Until 1994, the answer could be simply delivered, though some of the reasoning was complex. It required a distinction to be drawn between "pivotal" and "polar" parties. From 1918 on, the mainstream confessional parties—merged into the CDA by 1977—were pivotal. No coalition could be formed without the Catholics plus one or both major Calvinist groups because they commanded the center ground. Both Labor and Liberals were polar. To gain office they had to woo the confessionals, but the confessionals usually had the choice of which to admit into the cabinet.

This thesis, however, failed to work in 1994. Essentially this was because the main polar parties—Labor and VVD—chose to make a bridge of D'66 in order to oust the CDA as a pivotal formation. D'66 had long seemed to provide some of the ingredients of a secular center grouping, although its philosophy is closer to that of Labor than to VVD. So the long-term geometry of coalition forming suddenly changed, at least for that formation.

## Coalition Negotiations

The formal process of consultation after a parliamentary election is initiated by the monarch. It consists of a series of interviews with party leaders and others. These result in the appointment, by the monarch on advice, of either a mediator, called an *informateur*, or a cabinet-former, called a *formateur*. There are three stages in any cabinet formation:

1. Which parties are going to form the government?
2. What policy program will they adopt?
3. Which ministries will go to which parties?

To complete these stages after an election rarely takes less than two to three months and has taken as long as seven months. The 1994 election was held on May 3. Within a week, the queen had appointed a senior Labor politician as an *informateur*. After a further week he reported that a coalition of Labor, Liberals, and D'66—styled a "purple" coalition (a combination of the left [red] with the right [blue])—was feasible. The three parties then tackled the big issue of how to reconcile their separate and differing election manifestos into a common program.

The main problem was agreement on the level of expenditure cuts. By early June, cuts of 20 billion guilders ($12 billion U.S.) had been agreed on, a long way beyond Labor's proposed 6 billion. But on June 27 bargaining broke down over the social security budget. In early July, a different coalition of CDA, VVD, and D'66 was discussed by the Christian and Liberal leaders. But D'66 would not join it. On August 1, the queen moved the process on by appointing Wim Kok, the Labor leader, as *formateur*. Through August the program was finally agreed on and the ministries were divided up between the parties. On August 22—111 days after the election—a new government of Labor, Liberals, and D'66 was sworn in. This was not a terribly protracted formation period by Dutch standards (the average is around 70 days), especially given the novelty of the coalition.

## The Cost of Delay?

If it takes, on average, two to three months to form a new cabinet after an election, what happens to the operations of government in the interim? Because the previous cabinet will have resigned on election day, is everything then suspended until the new coalition is finalized? The answer is no, the previous cabinet simply carries on as a caretaker. Since 1946, over four years have seen caretaker rule, and on several occasions the caretakers have proposed and enacted the budget.

This fact may seem surprising, but it actually demonstrates a very significant truth about government in Holland. Continuity of the same pivotal formation in office (up until 1994) has bred a degree of stability that is quite remarkable in the European, or perhaps any other, context. There have been no discernible costs arising from the leisurely business of cabinet formation, though maybe in the relatively new context of the omission of the Christian center from 1994 to 2002, this could change in future.

## Executive and Legislative Relations

As in all democracies, the relationship between the political executive and Parliament in Holland is the centerpiece of the entire political system. Nowhere in Europe is there a separation of powers as rigorous as in the United States. But countries vary in the extent to which governments are part of the legislature, as in Britain, or have a separate source of legitimacy, as in France. On this scale the Netherlands, although a fully parliamentary, nonpresidential system, has historically inclined toward distance between the two organs. Over the past quarter century, much of the earlier aloofness between ministers and parliamentarians has abated. But there remain strict constitutional barriers between the two bodies, and there is no sign of these being dismantled.

Until the 1970s, there was much to confirm Lijphart's characterization of the relationship as one of a "semi-separation of powers."[21] Traditionally ministers did not hold or retain seats in Parliament. This position was progressively constitutionalized, so that Article 57 of the present constitution forbids ministers and state secretaries from membership of either House. But the apartness of the two arms of state was more deeply signaled by the different sources of recruitment for each. In a celebrated statistic, Lijphart recorded that "between 1848 and 1958, almost half of all ministers never served in parliament." They were instead drawn from the public service or the professions and were appointed for their experience, not their party credentials.

This division between officeholders and representatives pointed up an evolutionary fact: the source of the government's authority was, at root, the exercise of the royal prerogative, while the entirely distinct source of Parliament's

authority was its status as the representative assembly of the people. Since virtually all European states were originally monarchies, this duality could be applied across the board. But in the Netherlands there has been less fusion of the two bodies in the course of democratization.

Until recently this had the rather surprising consequence that ministerial office was not highly regarded by ambitious MPs. In an interview in 1971, this author was told by the floor-leader of a major parliamentary group that he had never offered to be a minister, since he regarded a cabinet post as less influential and more restricted than the role of a senior parliamentarian.

This attitude of superiority has, however, given way to much greater fluency in relations between parliamentary leaders and the cabinet. To a large extent this expresses a more proactive approach by the political parties toward the exercise of governmental power. It also reflects the demise of *verzuiling,* or pillared politics, in which party leaders managed their pillars while cabinets presided over the technicalities of government.

The effect of this is that cabinets are now tied in much more closely to electoral outcomes. As late as the 1960s, whole coalitions could be dismantled and replaced without consulting the voters. This was largely because governments were regarded as the creations of the major parliamentary "barons," who were the acknowledged voices of the pillars. The collapse of *verzuiling,* in this regard as in others, has undoubtedly contributed toward a certain modernization of government in the Netherlands.

Ministers cannot be legislators. But the conduct of public business requires them to attend Parliament when presenting policy proposals, especially since nine-tenths of all legislation is now drafted in the ministries. Ministers are these days increasingly drawn from the ranks of MPs, past or present. Present members are made to resign their seats if appointed to the political executive. This presents no problem given the electoral system, because the party lists are used to fill any vacancies without further popular voting.

There remains the question of political dynamics in a system where a semiseparated multiparty cabinet confronts a multiparty legislature. As already pointed out, the earlier position

---

[21]Lijphart, p. 135.

was that cabinet unity, and indeed survival, depended very much on the goodwill of the parties which supposedly supported the government, and on their relations with each other. Where cabinet coalitions contained up to five parties, this geometry could be complex. As the posture of parties toward government has changed, the critical linkage has switched from that between floor-leader and minister to that between the parties in cabinet, so that governments since 1965 have tended to fall because of breaks in cabinet unity. But in 1989 a cabinet was still brought down by a party floor-leader, so the capacity to wreck governments from the legislature remains.

## THE PROFESSIONAL EXECUTIVE

Unlike politicians, members of the civil or public service are expected to be rational, educated, incorruptible, and committed to the public interest rather than to private interests. How these expectations are translated into practical provisions varies somewhat from country to country, and the Dutch bureaucracy does have some special characteristics. In comparison with its European neighbors, it is probably most distinctive because it is nonunitary. Recruitment is to particular ministries, and not to a centralized, monolithic national corps of administrators and technocrats.

The reasons for this are, as might be assumed, historical and relate to the traditional autonomy of ministers and ministries. Originally civil servants were hired by a system of personal ministerial patronage. These days, although there are no competitive examinations nor uniform methods of entry, selection is by merit, though each ministry interprets that in its own way. Salaries and pensions are now uniform, but departments each have their own operational styles and what one commentator has called "distinct cultures" which extend to language, dress, and legislative presentation.[22]

Essentially the Dutch public service is apolitical. This is not laid down in the constitution, which specifies merely that Parliament shall regulate public servants' legal status, employment protection, and negotiating machinery (Article 109). Neither is it directly safeguarded by the pattern of pluralism, which could leave senior civil servants open to ministerial influence, given that most spend their whole career in one department. But the service is regarded as being dedicated to functional specialism, so that the perceived needs of, say, the environment or education (not an inherently apolitical area of policy) are the driving imperative.[23]

These needs are attended to within a complex web of policy inputs, which formerly reflected the pillared society and which retain corporatist features (see Section A). In scale, the national bureaucracy compares with its European counterparts. There are currently around 150,000 personnel employed by the ministries (a sixfold increase since World War II) in relation to a population of 16 million. The provinces and municipalities have their own staff (see Subnational Government).

One feature of the Dutch public service is that, although careers within it are often confined to particular policy areas, mobility between the service and politics or business or professional work is relatively common and made fairly easy. This links in with the high mobility and comparatively brief tenure of Dutch MPs, which is discussed in the next section.

## THE PARLIAMENT

References to the Dutch Parliament are indispensable to an account of almost any aspect of the political system. This is because Parliament is the apogee of the representative and party systems, the heart (but not the head) of the legislative process, and the prime source of each government's composition. In its operations, Parliament in the Netherlands parallels the role and scope of its European counterparts, though since it is not fused with the executive, it is more autonomous in character.

---

[22]Andeweg and Irwin, p. 178.

[23]Hans Daalder and Galen A. Irwin, eds., *Politics in the Netherlands* (London: Cass, 1989), p. 8.

In the constitution, Parliament is referred to as the States-General, a term that goes back before the republic to the assembly of feudal estates in the fifteenth century. Chapter 3, Section 1, of the constitution sets out the organization and composition of Parliament. The basic characteristics are:

Parliament is divided between a First and a Second Chamber.

Each chamber is elected for four years (though not on fixed dates).

The First Chamber consists of 75 members, elected by provincial councils.

The Second Chamber consists of 150 members, elected by all citizens over 18 years (except for prisoners and lunatics).

No person can belong to both chambers simultaneously.

Section 2 of the same chapter of the constitution sets out Parliament's procedures. The basic features are as follows:

Sessions will be public (nowadays augmented by radio and TV coverage).

Decisions will be by majority vote.

Members cannot be mandated or instructed when voting (which makes clear they are not delegates).

Ministers and state secretaries, though they cannot be members, are covered by Parliament's freedom from prosecution.

All other matters are for Parliament to decide, including the provisions for elections and the citizens' rights to vote. Since it has already been noted that Parliament is supreme and there can be no judicial review, it follows that it must be self-regulating. Chapter 5 of the constitution—shaped over the years by successive parliaments—does, however, specify briefly the sequence to be followed by legislation. Essentially the steps are:

Bills may be *presented* only by the government or members of the Second Chamber.

Bills can be *introduced* only in the Second Chamber.

Bills can be *amended* only in the Second Chamber.

After *approval* in the Second Chamber, bills go to the First Chamber, which must approve or reject them without amendment.

## Parliament's Functions

From the provisions set out in the constitution, it is clear that the Second Chamber is the effective one. But the First Chamber does from time to time reject bills, and it can sometimes induce amendments by threatening to reject them. With only rare exceptions, legislation nowadays is proposed by ministers, but the Second Chamber submits proposals to careful and detailed scrutiny and has unlimited powers to amend them. An extensive committee structure examines bills, and ministers can be questioned intensively. Up to half of all bills are amended, and the government may be forced to withdraw proposals which the chamber dislikes.

This is, of course, the first and principal task of Parliament—the *legislative* function. It includes, through the power to amend or reject the budget, financial control of the government and the public purse. From this power flows a whole set of *scrutiny* capabilities, which ensure ministerial accountability to the nation's elected representatives. The three specific forms of scrutiny are questions, interpellations, and commissions of inquiry, in that order of significance.

Since ministers attend Parliament (in effect the Second Chamber) only when proposing particular measures, questions on general matters and their answers are normally written. Alongside other activities, there has been a substantial increase over time in the number of questions put to ministers. Interpellations are more elaborate and require ministers to attend and explain their conduct. On average these may be staged once a month when Parliament is in session (see Table 7.15).

The most severe of Parliament's powers to call the executive to account is the commission of inquiry. This is a full-scale investigation and is reserved for major anxieties and scandals. A commission sat from 1947 to 1956 to enquire into the conduct of the Dutch government in

**TABLE 7.15**

**PARLIAMENTARY ACTIVITY**

|  | Bills | Amendments Adopted | Motions Proposed | Interpellations | Questions |
|---|---|---|---|---|---|
| 1963–1964 | 252 | 62 | 9 | 5 | 208 |
| 1973–1974 | 274 | 81 | 196 | 12 | 1,498 |
| 1988–1989 | 305 | 304 | 409 | 9 | 796 |
| 1999–2000 | 246 | — | 970 | 7 | 1,537 |

*Sources:* G. Visscher, "De Staten Generaal," in Hans Daalder and A. Nauta, eds., *Compendium voor Politiek en Samenleving in Nederland 1986,* Tweede Kamer Information Office, 2002.

London during World War II. It was 30 years before the next commission was set up to investigate public subsidies to a private shipyard.

The third function of Parliament is the *deliberative* one, which fulfills the twin tasks of publicity and policy generation. The usual mechanisms here are debates and motions. There has been a huge increase in the number of motions over the past generation.

Finally, but very importantly, Parliament—in the form of the Second Chamber—exercises an *elective* function. This has both positive and negative aspects. National elections are staged in order to decide the party composition of the legislature. But this party configuration also determines the alternative patterns of the executive, and the major parliamentary groups settle which shape the government will assume. That is the positive elective function. Once a cabinet has been formed, its continuation depends on the coalition parties retaining their parliamentary support. If any part of this support is withdrawn, then the government may fall. This is the negative capability.

Until the 1960s, cabinets were not infrequently reconstituted, sometimes with different parties, after a coalition had collapsed. It has since become the convention that at least the Second Chamber must be dissolved when a coalition falls and fresh elections held. Parliamentary group leaders, therefore, know that failure to support the party's ministers will result in mutually assured demise. So there is less temptation than previously to bring down governments, and where coalitions have fallen over the past quarter century, it has mostly been because of dis-

agreements within the cabinet. Nevertheless, the Liberal floor-leader in 1989 was prepared to challenge the CDA-Liberal coalition and the outcome was a dissolution and fresh elections.

## Parliamentary Groups and Members of Parliament

Both chambers of Parliament are made up of parliamentary groups, known as *fracties*. Unlike legislatures where a predominantly two-party system obtains (as in Great Britain and the United States), parliamentary parties in the Dutch context produce a much more complex mosaic. There are currently ten separate groups in the Second Chamber, and nine in the First Chamber (see Table 7.16). Three parties in each chamber—CDA, Liberals, and List Pim Fortuyn—have ministers in the present government. The rest might be considered as being "in opposition," but the Dutch system is not presented as adversarial.

Parliamentary groups range in size from 43 members (2002 figure) to one-person units. They are led by a chairman, and members usually have to master a particular policy area. In this they are helped by professional staffs, the number of which have grown mightily in recent years and now average two staffers per member. The budget for services to members has likewise grown hugely, by a factor of 50 since the 1960s.

Members of both chambers, given the electoral system, have no constituencies, and therefore no constituents. Their representative role is therefore highly generalized and they regard themselves more as policy channels than tri-

## TABLE 7.16

### PARTY COMPOSITION OF THE FIRST CHAMBER

| Party | 1987 | 1991 | 1995 | 1999 |
|---|---|---|---|---|
| VVD | 12 | 12 | 23 | 19 |
| CDA | 26 | 27 | 19 | 20 |
| PvdA | 26 | 16 | 14 | 15 |
| D'66 | 5 | 12 | 7 | 4 |
| GL | 3 | 4 | 4 | 8 |
| SGP | 1 | 2 | 2 | 2 |
| RPF | 1 | 1 | 1 | } 4 |
| GPV | 1 | 1 | 1 | |
| SP | — | — | 1 | 2 |
| Others | — | — | 3 | 1 |
| Total seats | 75 | 75 | 75 | 75 |

bunes of the people. They also tend to see service in Parliament, especially in the Second Chamber, as only part of a career profile. Mobility between Parliament, the public service, and the professions is high and the average tenure of Second Chamber members is about five years. Members can easily dispose of their seats, since under the list system no by-elections are needed.

Historically there has been no direct conduit between Parliament and ministerial posts. In recent years, however, more senior parliamentary figures have tended to enter the cabinet. During the two decades from 1946 to 1967, less than half of all ministers had served in Parliament. In the succeeding period (1967–1986), this figure rose to two-thirds. Although service in Parliament tends to be much briefer in Holland than elsewhere, members of both chambers have high status and are well remunerated. The great majority are university graduates. A survey in 1981 disclosed that only one member of the Second Chamber was the son of a member.[24] The proportion of women members has risen steadily over the past 30 years, from 10 to 36 percent in the Second Chamber, and from 5 to 26 percent in the First.

---

[24]M.C.P.M. van Schendelen, *The Dutch Member of Parliament 1979–80* (Rotterdam: University Press, 1981).

## SUBNATIONAL GOVERNMENT

Until the nineteenth century, the Netherlands was a collage of autonomous provinces with power concentrated in the major maritime cities. Under the monarchy the state became both unitary and more centralized. Like all contemporary democracies however, Holland has an elaborate system of local authorities with directly elected councils which manage subnational affairs.

The two levels of subnational government are the province and the municipality. Although the provinces were historically important and still select the members of the First Chamber of Parliament, the municipalities are nowadays the focus of much greater activity. The 12 current provinces are governed by provincial executives, appointed by and responsible to elected councils. The councils are elected by proportional representation, and invariably executives are party coalitions, as with the national government. Indeed, the four-yearly provincial elections are regarded as a barometer of national party fortunes. Provinces are responsible for planning, transport, and environmental issues plus certain licensing tasks. Provincial executives are headed by a central government appointee, the Queen's Commissioner, whose role has some comparability with a departmental prefect in France.

Municipalities, whose numbers have been whittled down in recent years to some 700, are cities and towns with more than 10,000 inhabitants. Like the provinces, they are governed by elected councils which appoint executives, also usually composed of party coalitions. Municipal mayors or burgomasters are appointed by the central government on the recommendation of the Queen's Commissioner of the province. Mayors are normally party figures. Amsterdam, for example, is a Labor fief, while the Liberals provide the burgomaster in The Hague.

Around a third of total public expenditure is disbursed by the various municipalities, who now derive 90 percent of their revenue from the central government. They are, however, very much controlled in their policies by the ministries which provide the cash for their operations.

# SUPRANATIONAL POLITICS

Since 1957, as a founder-signatory of the Treaties of Rome, the Netherlands has been a loyal and enthusiastic member of a supranational consortium. Originally styled the European Economic Community when the total membership was only six (France, West Germany, Italy, and the Benelux states), this organization now includes 15 countries and has advanced to the status of the European Union.

The reasons Holland signed up for the community will be summarized in the next section under the title European Integration. The inclusion of EU membership under Dutch political institutions signifies how important it is in terms not merely of economic integration, but of its impact on the political process, above all the legislative function. Under the Rome and subsequent treaties, decisions of the Community, now Union, affect virtually every aspect of Dutch life. Indeed, there is no longer a minister responsible for European issues, since all ministries are involved in Union affairs.

Holland's participation in the European Union reflects contrarily both the minor institutional role that smaller states are inevitably accorded, and the importance the Dutch themselves place upon integration. There is only a single Dutch commissioner out of a commission now of 20. The Netherlands deploys only 5 votes out of 87 in the Council of Ministers, and the electorate sends only 31 representatives to the 626-member European Parliament (see Table 7.17). Nevertheless, the proportionate Dutch contribution to the EU budget, at $150 U.S. per head per annum, is currently the second highest in the Union. The proportions of the Dutch presence in the European Union will change with the implementation of the provisions of the Treaty of Nice (2001).

## Thinking Critically

1. What drove the Dutch to adopt extreme proportional representation?
2. Which problems has the electoral system mitigated and which has it exascerbated?

### TABLE 7.17

**ELECTIONS TO THE EUROPEAN PARLIAMENT**

| Party | 1989 | 1994 | 1999 |
|---|---|---|---|
| CDA | 10 | 10 | 9 |
| PvdA | 8 | 8 | 6 |
| VVD | 3 | 6 | 6 |
| D'66 | 1 | 4 | 2 |
| SGP-GPV-RPF | 1 | 2 | 3 |
| GL | 2 | 1 | 4 |
| SP | — | — | 1 |
| Total seats | 25 | 31 | 31 |
| Total turnout | 47.2% | 35.6% | 29.9% |

3. Why have governing coalitions mostly been formed around the center?
4. What factors restricted the expansion of left-of-center parties?
5. How far does the separation of powers go in the Netherlands compared with the United States?
6. Why does it take, on average, 70 days to form a new government after an election, and does this have any adverse consequences?

## KEY TERMS

cabinet *(430)*
coalition *(416, 431)*
Democrats '66 (D'66) *(422-423)*
electoral quota *(417)*
European Union *(438)*
First Chamber *(435)*
*formateur (432)*
Green Left *(423)*
*informateur (432)*
interpellation *(435)*
Labor Party (PvdA) *(421–422)*
Liberal Party (VVD) *(422)*
list system *(418–419)*
municipality *(437)*
Parliament (States-General) *(435)*
parliamentary party (*fractie*) *(436)*

proportional representation (PR) *(416–417)*
province *(437)*
Second Chamber *(415–418, 435–436)*
social partners *(428–429)*
supranational *(438)*

# FURTHER READINGS

Andeweg, Rudy B. "The Netherlands: Coalition Cabinets in Changing Circumstances," in Jean Blondel and Ferdinand Muller-Rommel, eds., *Cabinets in Western Europe* (London: Macmillan, 1988).

Andeweg, Rudy B., and Galen A. Irwin. *Dutch Government and Politics* (London: Macmillan, 1993).

Daalder, Hans. "Extreme Proportional Representation: The Dutch Experience," in S. E. Finer, ed., *Adversary Politics and Electoral Reform* (London: Wigram, 1975).

Daalder, Hans, ed. *Party Systems in Denmark, Austria, Switzerland, the Netherlands and Belgium* (London: Pinter, 1987).

Daalder, Hans, and Galen A. Irwin. *Politics in the Netherlands: How Much Change?* (Totowa, NJ: Frank Cass, 1989).

Eldersveld, Sam, Jan Kooiman, and Theo van der Tak. *Elite Images of Dutch Politics* (Ann Arbor: University of Michigan, 1981).

Gladdish, Ken. *Governing from the Center: Politics and Policy-Making in the Netherlands* (De Kalb: Northern Illinois University Press, 1991), chs. 5–8.

Gladdish, Ken. "Parliamentary Activism and Legitimacy in the Netherlands," *West European Politics* 13(3) (1990), pp. 102–119.

Gladdish, Ken. "The Netherlands," in Vernon Bogdanor, ed., *Representatives of the People? Parliamentarians and Constituents in Western Democracies* (Aldershot, UK: Gower, 1985), pp. 135–148.

Gladdish, Ken. "Dutch Politics at the Turn of the Millennium," *Low Countries Journal* 22(2) (1998).

Irwin, Galen A. "The Dutch Party System," in Peter Merkl, ed., *Western European Party Systems* (New York: Free Press 1980), pp. 161–184.

Koole, Ruud A. "The 'Modesty' of Dutch Party Finance," in H. E. Alexander, ed., *Comparative Political Finance in the 1980s* (Cambridge: Cambridge University Press, 1989), pp. 209–219.

Koole, Ruud A., and Monique Leijenaar. "The Netherlands: The Predominance of Regionalism," in Michael Gallagher and Michael Marsh, eds., *Candidate Selection in Comparative Perspective* (Beverley Hills, CA: Sage, 1988), pp. 190–209.

Swaan, Abram de. "The Netherlands," in Eric C. Browne and John Dreijmanis, eds., *Government Coalitions in Western Democracies* (Harlow, NY: Longman, 1982), pp. 219–236.

# C. PUBLIC POLICY

## POLICY GENERATION

The Dutch, over the past half-century, have created as elaborate a policy structure as any in the developed world. Why this is so requires a look back at pre–World War II Holland, when the ideas that have governed much of the last 50 years were first shaped.

During the 1930s, a barrage of events—mostly adverse—served to influence a whole generation of thinkers, planners, and statesmen. The events were inherently economic, but they had huge political fallout. Most dramatic was the world depression from 1930 on, which elsewhere triggered responses as diverse as the New Deal and an intensification of Soviet five-year plans. The lesson seemed to be that secure economies depended on planning, either directly by the organs of the state or indirectly by a set of deliberative and regulatory agencies.

The second course was the one advocated by Dutch economists. It fitted the circumstances of Dutch society in that a combination of delegation and consensus was the way the pillars had traditionally operated. The pillared organizations thus became the building blocks of a structure which was surmounted by a set of national agencies after 1945. Their emphasis was on statistical information-gathering, the allocation of rewards among the various sectors—business, labor, agriculture—and systematic planning. Each task had its own machinery. For information there was the Central Bureau of Statistics, which had been set up back in 1899. For planning, a Central Planning Bureau was established in 1945. For the oversight of fiscal policy, there was the Central Bank, which was nationalized (taken over by the state) in 1948.

But the most elaborate mechanisms arose in the field of reward allocation. Here from 1950 on, an attempt was made to set up a regulatory network which covered the whole field of production, so that each trade, craft, or manufacture would become self-regulating according to an overall formula. All these guild-type operations would, it was envisaged, be coordinated nationally by a Social and Economic Council, which would preside over wage levels, price levels, profits, economic growth, and the balance between imports and exports.

This was the Dutch style of corporatism (see Section A). Though never fully achieved, its elements functioned with apparent success, in terms of the economic indicators, up to the 1960s. It then began to be challenged by the cultural sea changes of the mid-to-late 1960s, and it was badly holed by the time of the first oil crisis of 1973–1974, when the Organization of Petroleum Exporting Countries (OPEC) raised world oil prices by around 300 percent. But the corporatist strategy was not abandoned. When the oil crisis struck, Holland was being governed by a coalition in which Labor was the major partner. Since Labor had also been a major player in government from 1946 to 1959 when the whole corporatist edifice was assembled, the same levers of control still seemed appropriate.

By the time of the second oil crisis in 1979, the government had changed to a center-right coalition of Christian Democrats and Liberals. But again the old mechanisms were invoked with a wage freeze in 1980, followed by a wage policy with the force of law behind it. Signs of a new approach to policy making, which involved a dilution of corporatist strategies, are evident from 1982 on, under a fresh CDA-Liberal cabinet headed by business-oriented economist Ruud Lubbers. The changed attitude embraced both a bypassing of parts of the corporatist circuit in favor of more executive decision making and a retreat from procrustean tactics such as national wage-fixing.

Broadly, the withdrawal from state-supervised corporatism has continued through the 1980s and 1990s. It has left large areas in which the market winds now blow without statutory mitigation. But this still falls far short of a surrender to an outlook of laissez-faire. The policy statement of the second Kok cabinet in August 1998 made clear that government remained committed to a wide range of prescribed public aims, even though there was no explicit reference to a corporatist approach to them.

In many ways policy generation in the Netherlands is now closer to the methods adopted by its neighbors than in the period from 1950 to 1980, yet differences remain. The corporatist structure has not been dismantled, even if its pillared underpinning is increasingly residual. Also the organization of government itself, with its somewhat autonomous departmental structure, has led to policy generation on a sector-by-sector basis, so that agriculture has its own policy crucible, the environment another, and so on.

One overriding factor in the cultivation of consistent policy goals is the permanence of coalition government. In a study undertaken in the early 1980s, the conclusion was that although parties within government might alter, there was "a basic similarity of response to circumstance within the framework of a high consensus about commitments and priorities."[25] This finding accords with much other evidence about the nature of political consensus in Holland (see Section B).

## ECONOMIC POLICY

The great watershed in the economic development of the Netherlands was the period from the end of World War II up to the early 1960s. During that half generation, a late industrial economy was launched which, like the German recovery, took advantage of high technology. The Dutch outcome was however somewhat vulnerable. Structurally it was top-heavy, with half a dozen multinationals—Shell, Philips, and Unilever being the three largest—controlling over 50 percent of manufactures. Much capital went into overseas investment and trade, which left the economy open to external fluctuations. Until the discovery and exploitation of natural gas in the later 1960s, there were few indigenous fuel resources.

By 1950 the immediate tasks of postwar reconstruction were complete. Thereafter the

Social and Economic Council, which formed the summit of the corporatist framework, formulated a national long-term strategy with five main goals:

1. Full employment.
2. Economic growth.
3. A reasonably equitable income distribution.
4. A balance of trade and payments equilibrium.
5. Price stability.

These aims were known as the "magic pentangle," and for two decades, until the shocks of the early 1970s, they were surprisingly well fulfilled. A key lever in the hands of successive governments was the means for the control of wages. Until the mid-1960s, national wage agreements were achieved by amicable bargaining between employers, labor unions, and governments. Thereafter various unions—especially in the shipbuilding and ship repair industries—began to break ranks, and the cabinet had to resort to wage freezes and statutory controls to hold back rising inflation.

Nevertheless, the record remained impressive into the 1970s. In 1971, economic growth reached 4.5 percent per annum, while unemployment—the specter at the feast of modernization—was a mere 1.5 percent of the workforce. Inflation was by then, however, troublesome, running at 8 percent per annum and rising—thus undermining price stability.

The oil price hike of 1973–1974 drove a deep groove through the economic policy agenda, for not only did the main transport fuel treble in price, but import costs—in a high import economy—rose by over 40 percent within a year. The crisis signaled the twilight of nearly 30 years of ascending affluence. Annual economic growth rates fell from over 4 percent to below 3 percent by the late 1970s, and down to barely 1 percent in the early 1980s. Even worse was the surge of unemployment, up from 2 percent over 1971–1973, to 5 percent by 1978 and 15 percent by 1984.

The postwar set of levers, by which governments carefully managed the allocation of resources through a blend of negotiation and controls, was in clear disarray by the early

[25]Ken Gladdish, "Coalition Government and Policy Outputs in the Netherlands," in Vernon Bogdanor, ed., *Coalition Government in Western Europe* (London: Heinemann, 1983), p. 185.

1980s. New policies were in grave need when Ruud Lubbers succeeded Andreas van Agt as prime minister of a new CDA-Liberal government after the 1982 election.

The overriding task was to get the public finances under control. The budget deficit was due to exceed 10 percent of net national income in 1983 (a Dutch postwar record), and the public sector was absorbing 70 percent of that income. The Lubbers government took steps to reduce expenditure, including a 3 percent wage cut for civil servants, and to promote industrial growth. Fortunately this program coincided with a recovery in the Western economies, so that by 1986 labor costs had fallen, investment had increased, and unemployment had tapered off from its 1984 peak.

In 1986, the CDA-VVD governing coalition renewed its majority and took further measures to impose itself on the economy. These embraced the ending of subsidies to private firms, freezing public salaries, and cutting health costs by increasing charges to patients. When the cabinet fell in 1989, progress on the unemployment and inflation fronts was manifest and social security premiums had been clipped by 10 percent.

Nevertheless the succeeding coalition of CDA and Labor (the last Lubbers administration) faced substantial problems in the familiar areas of the budget deficit, the cost of social security, and the high rate of unemployment. Also annual growth was still under 2 percent and a fresh recession was imminent. The new government did make progress with the deficit, which had been almost halved by 1993. It was less successful in reducing social security costs, and unemployment continued to dominate fiscal planning.

By the 1990s, unemployment in Holland had become more of an iceberg than in other comparable European economies. An official rate of around 10 percent of the workforce concealed some rather deadly statistics showing spectacularly low participation in work and unusually high disincentives to working. Thus in 1994 a quarter of the potential workforce was either in receipt of benefits for not working or on job promotion schemes. More tellingly, of the total population,

from age 16 to 65, only half were engaged in productive employment.

The disincentives to working consist partly of unusually high unemployment benefits, but more remarkably of an inordinately generous provision for disability or invalidity payments. Unemployment compensation averages 50 percent of previous earnings, while disability benefits stand at 70 percent of earnings up to age 65, having come down from 80 percent in 1984. The Netherlands faces here a fundamental dilemma which confronts all Western countries: any stimulation of the demand for employment, by reducing welfare, simply exposes the insufficiency of worthwhile jobs in increasingly high-tech economies.

At the midpoint of the 1990s, Holland disclosed a "basically healthy economy."[26] The currency was strong, interest rates were among the lowest in Europe, and more had been done to reduce the budget deficit than in most other European countries. The prize here, of course, was to qualify for admission to the single currency being established by the European Union. The chief problem besetting the "purple coalition," which came into office in August 1994, remained the high cost of the collective burden of direct taxes and social security premiums.

From 1995 up to 2000, relative prosperity eased the task of paring down welfare benefits. With an average annual growth rate of nearly 3 percent, low inflation, and a steady fall in unemployment, the second Kok government from 1998 to 2002 enjoyed a period of economic good fortune (see Table 7.18).

# THE STATE IN THE MARKETPLACE

Despite the high proportion (about 60 percent in 1994) of the gross national product that is the public sector's share of the economy, the Dutch state has never been an ostentatious entrepreneur. In the mid-1970s, a rare assessment of state

---

[26]*OECD Economic Survey of the Netherlands,* 1994.

**TABLE 7.18**

**MAIN ECONOMIC TRENDS, 1975–2000**

|  | 1975–1979 | 1980–1984 | 1985–1989 | 1990–1994 | 1995–2000 |
|---|---|---|---|---|---|
| Gross domestic product (percentage average annual growth rate) | +2.5% | +0.6% | +2.8% | +1.8% | +2.9% |
| Inflation (percentage average annual change) | +8.6% | +5.5% | +1.5% | +2.5% | +2.2% |
| Unemployment (average annual percentage of workforce) | 3.8% | 7.5% | 14.0% | 8.5% | 5.0% |

*Source:* OECD Economic Surveys.

holdings reported that public enterprises accounted for some 10 percent of total production.[27] The calculation was difficult because the only enterprises that were directly and openly state-owned, and whose operatives were civil servants, were the post office, telecommunications, the mint, and the government printing office.

Effectively however, the railways, the gas industry, and the mines were publicly owned, though classed as ordinary commercial companies. Similarly, nuclear fuels and explosives were run as companies (though under a different heading), while water and electricity were classed as non-profit associations, as was the broadcasting foundation. All these enterprises can be classified as publicly owned in that, whatever their form, they excluded private shareholders. In addition, the state held significant amounts of stock in a number of large companies, such as Royal Dutch Airlines (KLM) and a steel corporation, Hoogovens.

As part of its campaign to reduce the size of the public sector, the incoming Lubbers government announced in 1982 a program of deregulation, decentralization, and privatization. Two tracks were laid out on the privatization front: spinning off the post office, telecommunications, and the printing office, and selling off some of the

Amsterdam houses—two narrow townhouses, one traditional, the other post-modern, stand side-by-side in Amsterdam.

[27]W. Keyser and R. Windle, eds., *Public Enterprise in the EEC, Part VI: The Netherlands* (with H. van der Kar) (Alphen: Samson, 1978), p. 71.

state's shares in semipublic corporations like KLM. This was nothing like as ambitious a campaign of privatization as that embarked on in Britain by the Thatcher government. But the issue of private versus state ownership was not highly charged in Holland, and there was no great ideological or economic motivation toward wholesale privatization.

The modest program charted by Lubbers has proceeded undramatically. The post office has been privatized by stages, though the government retains some shares. Holdings in big corporations have been reduced, and it has been calculated that the treasury had collected some $3 billion U.S. by these means by 1992.[28] Pressure to extend the program seems weak because many of the public enterprises are profitable which, unlike in the British case, has not bred an appetite for selling them off.

## SOCIAL SECURITY

As in all European democracies, the dominant dimension of social policy in the Netherlands is the provision of social security. The history of the Dutch welfare state goes back to the Poor Law devised by Thorbecke's Liberal government in 1854, which inaugurated a "state-directed, national program of public assistance."[29] It was not a lavish program by present-day standards, and it became largely a channel for subsidizing private charities. The development of a pillared society in the late-nineteenth century intensified the grip of the churches and charities on the dispensation of welfare, a fact endorsed by the second Poor Law of 1912.

The move from largely private assistance to uniform state-administered social security began in the 1950s with a national public provision for unemployment benefits and old-age pensions. In the 1960s, health care, family allowances, and income support or national assistance were put on

a firm state footing. In the 1970s, compensation for disability was elaborated and put on the same level as sickness and unemployment benefits.

The methods by which these measures were financed and administered are complex and not easy to summarize. The most signal feature of social security in the Netherlands is that it is based on the principle of insurance. That is to say, benefits are, at least conceptually, linked to regular contributions, either from all citizens or from employers and employees. In practice, levels of benefit are determined by the government, and the various insurance funds are topped up to ensure that all receive their prescribed entitlements.

Since the 1970s, the growing size of the social security budget has been a preoccupation of economists, social administrators, and politicians. Forty years ago, the sparse welfare system cost 5 percent of national income. By 1993, the elaborate network of social protection was costing over 30 percent of national income and had become a key political issue. In the 1994 parliamentary election, all major parties, right and left, proposed substantial reductions in social security expenditure.

The principal anxieties of policy makers are first the enormous resort to disability benefits, which for a long time were almost an alternative to long-term unemployment compensation. Second, rising longevity has pushed up the costs of pensions for the elderly against the backdrop of a declining workforce. These concerns are shared by thoughtful citizens whose attitudes to the adequacy or generosity of work-related benefits has hardened during the 1980s.

In 1993 a survey was undertaken of views on the introduction of "workfare," defined as "a system in which unemployed people and disability benefit claimants are compelled to carry out socially useful work in return for the minimum wage." Supporters of parties in the present government came out from 49 percent (D'66) to 80 percent (VVD) in favor, with Labor adherents registering 60 percent approval.[30]

---

[28]Andeweg and Irwin, p. 201.
[29]Robert H. Cox, "Public Assistance in the Netherlands," *West European Politics* 13 (1990), p. 87.

[30]*Social and Cultural Report,* p. 169.

## FOREIGN POLICY

During the 1970s, Joris Voorhoeve, who would become defense minister in the 1990s, undertook a study of Dutch foreign policy which he shrewdly entitled "Peace, Profits, and Principles."[31] In it he discerns, throughout Dutch history, three consistent threads which have fueled and focused the stances taken vis-à-vis the rest of the world. The first strand is what he calls "maritime commercialism."

This goes all the way back to the foundations of the republic in the late sixteenth century. In that remote period, the Dutch founding fathers and their seagoing contemporaries realized that prosperity, in a small and materially unpropitious country, would depend on trade and investment overseas. That conviction drove the Dutch sea captains to chart routes to all the continents and to establish trading posts from Brazil and the Hudson River to West Africa and the East Indies.

Within a generation, Holland had replaced the Portuguese as the leading world trader. Two generations later Admiral de Ruyter made history by sailing up the Thames estuary and towing away the English flagship. Naval mastery of the oceans however was beyond the resources of a small population, and after the Treaty of Utrecht in 1713, peaceful commerce succeeded the bravura exploits of brave admirals. Successful trade requires international order and enforceable contracts, so treaties, international law, and commercial procedures became key concerns of Dutch foreign policy makers in the eighteenth century.

The Netherlands continued, however, to be drawn into the foreign policy imbroglios of other, larger states. In the 1780s, the Dutch became involved, along with France and Spain, in the war that delivered the United States from British colonial rule. There followed the French (and Dutch) Revolution and 20 years of warfare, which for the Netherlands ended with the inau-

guration of a new kingdom of the United Low Countries—Holland and Belgium. From this point on, the second strand of Dutch foreign policy emerges, that of neutrality and abstention from international conflict.

By the late nineteenth century, the policy of neutrality had created around the Netherlands, as with Switzerland, the aura of a principled haven from disputes between nations. These conditions, which one author has labeled a "peace laboratory,"[32] made The Hague an ideal location for the world's first permanent court of arbitration. After 1919, the Dutch city was chosen as the site for the League of Nation's Court of International Justice, which the UN relaunched after 1945. This third strand—that of international idealism—suited the high-minded Calvinist elite. It also enabled the foreign ministry to steer clear of serious entanglements, notably the buildup to World War I, into which all its neighbors were sucked, including the unlucky Belgians.

However, the Dutch were not quite so pure as the Swiss in their involvement with the rest of the world, because the republic had initiated what eventually became full-blooded colonies. Not all the seventeenth-century trading posts survived to evolve into overseas possessions. But many did, and by the nineteenth century there were substantial Dutch colonies in the East Indies and smaller enclaves in the Caribbean and West Africa (the South African settlements round the Cape of Good Hope had been taken over by the British in 1795). Indeed, the Netherlands was, until after World War II, a significant imperial power, though this is not something which is greatly admired, or even happily referred to in contemporary Holland.

But colonial matters apart, and they remained outside the scope of the foreign ministry, "small power isolationist policy was developed by the Dutch to a point little short of perfection."[33] All this changed dramatically at

[31]Joris J. C. Voorhoeve, *Peace, Profits, and Principles: A Study of Dutch Foreign Policy* (Leiden: Martinus Nijhoff, 1985).

[32]Amry Vandenbosch, *Dutch Foreign Policy since 1813: A Study in Small Power Politics* (The Hague: Martinus Nijhoff, 1959).
[33]Ibid., p. 56.

4:00 A.M. on May 10, 1940, when the German 18th Army marched over the frontier and German planes began bombing Dutch airfields. Over a hundred years of neutrality since the Belgian upset of 1830–1831 had finally failed to deliver security. From now on, the perceptions of foreign policy makers would no longer be based on abstention and neutrality.

The rethinking began during World War II and finally crystallized in the decision to become a founding member of the North Atlantic Treaty Organization (NATO), which was set up in 1949. The military had already been heavily involved in efforts to resist decolonization in the East Indies after the surrender of Japan. But the decision to opt for collective security in Europe, through NATO, was the watershed that set the course of foreign and defense policy for the past half-century.

For Dutch foreign and defense policy makers, the NATO umbrella was first and foremost a guarantee of mutual security under American hegemony. In part this expressed the new postwar realism. The resources, logistics, and fire-power to defend Europe in the late 1940s and beyond were clearly located in the United States. But there were additional dimensions to the Dutch willingness to be the Western super-power's "faithful ally." One was the lack of confidence in the reliability of continental neighbors, and above all a deep hostility toward Germany. Another was the view that somehow the Atlantic alliance preserved the essential high-mindedness of Holland's international reputation. All this is well summed up by Joris Voorhoeve: "The Netherlands . . . preferred the gentle hegemony of a remote Atlantic superpower over . . . less credible leadership but more immediate domination by Britain, Germany, France."[34]

## Defense and Domestic Politics

Only the Communist members of the Dutch Parliament opposed the NATO entry in 1949. From then until the mid-1960s, the official commitment to loyal NATO membership was largely

---

[34]Voorhoeve, p. 118.

Rotterdam after German bombing, May 1940.

backed by parties and public. Holland's contribution to the strategic defense shield was respectable in resource terms, and its military budget was proportionately higher than that of comparable states like Norway, Denmark, and Belgium. In 1957 the Dutch government, under a Labor premier, agreed "without discussion" to the deployment of U.S. tactical nuclear missiles— the first European country to accept them. Even U.S. pressure to evacuate West Irian (a residual Dutch possession in the East Indies) in 1962 provoked no irritation in Holland.

But the later 1960s saw challenges from the Left and from protest groups to both the West-East confrontation in the shape of the Cold War and the war in Vietnam. These pressures were ignored by ministers, although the oil crisis of the 1970s brought about a marked reduction of defense expenditure (18.4 percent of the budget in 1961; 9.7 percent in 1977). Economies in military outlay were now accompanied by criticism of nuclear weapons. The Labor group in Parliament supported a motion calling for a nuclear-free zone in Europe. By the 1980s, a powerful head of popular steam had been raised against the installation of cruise missiles, and the decision of the Lubbers government in 1985 to proceed with deployment took political courage.

These, however, were largely symbolic issues. One practical effect of the Dutch commitment to NATO was the unprecedented introduction of military conscription. By the 1970s, this had produced the most highly paid and best looked after draftees in Europe, with their own labor union and relaxed military discipline. Conscription was eventually ended in 1996 in response to changed strategic circumstances in Europe.

Until the Kosovo campaign of 1999, it was not NATO which led to the deployment of the Dutch armed forces, but Holland's membership in the United Nations, for which there had been, in 1945, far less enthusiasm on the part of Dutch diplomats. One early consequence of UN membership was participation in the Korean War in 1950. Other involvements under UN auspices followed, culminating in the tragic capitulation to the Bosnian Serbs at Srebrenica in July 1995. A Ministry of Defense enquiry into this action

sought to limit the damage to military reputations, but it was a scarring incident.

The collapse of Soviet rule in Eastern and Central Europe in 1989 had obvious repercussions on Western European foreign policies. In Holland it triggered a reappraisal which slowly moved strategic thinking away from a Cold War perspective to renewed ideas about security integration between European powers.

## European Integration

The conviction that, after the German occupation, the Netherlands could no longer rely on isolation prompted a move within the Low Countries as early as 1944. The three exiled governments in London—of Holland, Belgium, and Luxembourg—formed a customs union called Benelux. This can be seen as the precursor of an ascending participation in economic alliances. In 1947 the government responded positively to the formation of the organization for European economic cooperation (later OECD), which grew out of the Marshall Plan for U.S. aid to devastated postwar Europe.

By the time of the formation of the first West European supranational authority—the Coal and Steel Community in 1951—Holland was well attuned to cooperation in regional decision making. So the founding of the European Economic Community (EEC) in 1957, of which the Netherlands was an inaugural member, enjoyed strong support in political circles. Entry to the EEC was opposed only by the Communist Party—now a minuscule parliamentary group—and militant Calvinists who saw it as a predominantly Catholic consortium.

The advantages of the EEC to Holland seemed overwhelming. Because the country was at the mouth of the Rhine, a high proportion of European trade went through Dutch ports, making an association of Germany, France, Italy, and the Benelux a club designed for Dutch commercial prosperity. Also politically, EEC membership gave a medium-sized state a permanent seat at the table of European policy making.

As the European Community grew from six states to the 15-member European Union, Dutch enthusiasm for it, at both elite and mass levels, has not significantly wavered. It was the Dutch government, during its six-month presidency of the Community, that prepared the ground for the meeting at Maastricht in 1992. The resultant treaty was a major step in further economic and strategic integration in Europe.

In 1997 a further treaty, concluded in Amsterdam, took further the arrangements for the European Monetary Union, and in 2001 a summit in Nice laid the framework for enlarging the EU to 27 countries. The Nice Treaty will reduce the relative weight of Holland within the EU (as with other existing members) because of the allocation of voting rights to new members.

## Aid and International Visibility

Two generations back, the Netherlands was a largely silent member of the international community. Over the past half-century, it has become almost hyperactive on the world scene, and not merely within and in relation to Europe. Several factors have converged to thrust Holland into the international limelight, most obviously a new belief in collective action, a positive version of the old Calvinist high-mindedness, and by no means least, substantial and unprecedented affluence.

One vivid illustration of the transformed sense of international responsibility is the program for development cooperation, or aid, to less prosperous countries. The policy of overseas aid became a feature of governmental strategy in the 1960s. By the 1970s an annual sum of 1.5 percent of government revenue was earmarked for the external aid budget, which by the mid-1980s had been boosted to almost 1 percent of GDP. This figure compares with the British, Japanese, and U.S. performances at this point of 0.27 to 0.39 percent of their annual GDP.

Over the past 20 years, the Dutch commitment to promoting development in the third world had been matched only by that of Norway. Recently, as cabinets have looked for ways of reducing public expenditure, the proportion of aid has fallen to about 0.7 percent of GDP. The number of recipients has been reduced, so as to concentrate its impact. Also there has been some redirection of aid toward Eastern and Central Europe since the collapse of the Soviet Empire.

## Thinking Critically

1. How do coalition governments create policy out of different party manifestos?
2. Why did successive governments produce lavish welfare policies from 1960 to 1980?
3. Why did the Dutch drop their traditional policy of neutrality after 1945 in favor of collective security?
4. European integration has been a popular strategy in Holland. What are the main reasons for this?
5. "Peace, Profits, and Principles"—is this a fair summary of Dutch external policy?

## KEY TERMS

Benelux *(447)*
budget deficit *(442)*
Cold War *(447)*
collective burden *(447)*
collective security *(446)*
conscription *(447)*
development cooperation *(448)*
European Community (EC) *(447)*
European Union (EU) *(448)*
neutrality *(445)*
North Atlantic Treaty Organization (NATO) *(446–447)*
oil crisis *(440)*
privatization *(443–444)*
Social and Economic Council *(440)*
social security *(444)*
welfare state *(442)*
workfare *(444)*

## FURTHER READINGS

Abert, J. G. *Economic Policy and Planning in the Netherlands* (New Haven, CT: Yale University, 1969).

Andeweg, Rudy. "Less Than Nothing? Hidden Privatisation of the Pseudo-Private Sector: The Dutch Case," *West European Politics* 11(4) (1988), pp. 117–128.

Campen, S. P. van. "How and Why the Netherlands Joined the Nato Alliance," *NATO Review* 30(3) (1982), pp. 8–12; 30(4) (1982), pp. 20–25.

Deboutte, Jan, and Alfred van Staden. "High Politics in the Low Countries," in William Wallace and William Paterson, eds., *Foreign Policy-Making in Western Europe* (Farnborough, UK: Saxon House, 1979), pp. 56–82.

Dutt, Amitava K., and Frank J. Costa, eds. *Public Planning in the Netherlands* (Oxford: Oxford University Press, 1985).

Everts, Philip, and Guido Walraven, eds. *The Politics of Persuasion: Implementation of Foreign Policy by the Netherlands* (Brookfield, VT: Bower, 1989).

Gladdish, Ken. *Governing from the Center: Politics and Policy-Making in the Netherlands* (De Kalb: Northern Illinois University Press, 1991), chs. 9 and 10.

Gladdish, Ken. "Coalition Government and Policy Outputs in the Netherlands," in Vernon Bogdanor, ed., *Coalition Government in Western Europe* (London: Heinemann, 1983), pp. 169–186.

Putten, Jan van. "Policy Styles in the Netherlands," in J. Richardson, ed., *Policy Styles in Western Europe* (London: Allen and Unwin, 1982), pp. 168–196.

Schendelen M.P.C.M. van, and Robert J. Jackson, eds. *The Politicisation of Business in Western Europe* (London: Croom Helm, 1987).

Vandenbosch, Amry. *Dutch Foreign Policy since 1813: A Study in Small Power Politics* (The Hague: Martinus Nijhoff, 1959).

Voorhoeve, Joris J. C. *Peace, Profits, and Principles: A Study of Dutch Foreign Policy* (Leiden: Martinus Nijhoff, 1985).

## WEB SITES

www.minbuza.nl/english
Ministry of Foreign Affairs.

www.scp.nl/uk
Social and Cultural Planning Office.

www.parlement.nl
Parliament.

www.minocw.nl/english
Ministry of Education.

www.rnw.nl/home/Press
Radio Netherlands.

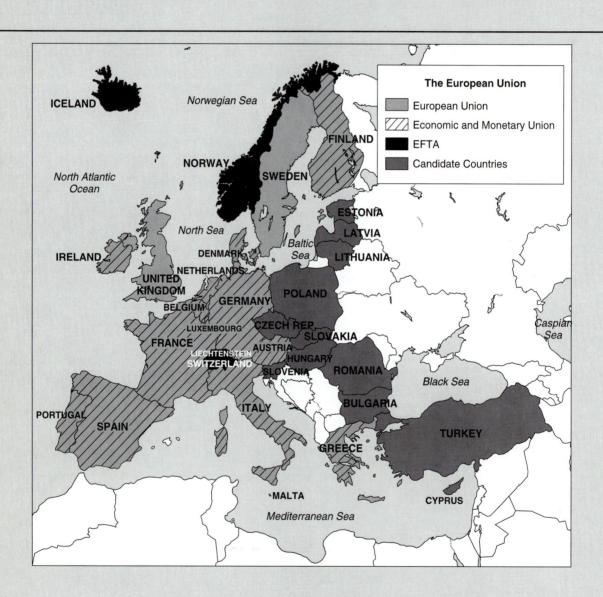

The European Union

- European Union
- Economic and Monetary Union
- EFTA
- Candidate Countries

# THE
# European Union

*Michael Curtis*

## INTRODUCTION

The European Union (EU) is the new name of the organizations engaged in the process of European integration which began in 1952 when the European Coal and Steel Community was established by six member states. Since then it has undergone four enlargements and now consists of 15 member states; another 12 are candidates for accession to the EU. The combined member states give the European Union the third largest population in the world.

### GEOGRAPHY

**Member states:** Austria, Belgium, Denmark, Finland, France, Germany, Greece, Ireland, Italy, Luxembourg, Netherlands, Portugal, Spain, Sweden, United Kingdom

**Area:** 3.2 million sq km

### PEOPLE

**Population:** 375 million

**Age structure:** *0–14 years:* 17%

    *15–64 years:* 67%

    *65 years and over:* 16%

**Sex ratio:** 0.95 males/female

**Life expectancy at birth:** *total population:* 78 years

    *male:* 75 years

    *female:* 81 years

**ECONOMY**

**GNP:** $7,979 billion

**GNP—per capita:** $21,400

**Share of world GNP:** 28.3%

**Share of world trade:** 36.2% imports; 36.7% exports

**Trade as % of GDP:** 12.2% imports; 10.9% exports

**Major imports:** *oil:* 7.9%
*electrical machinery:* 7.8%
*office machines:* 7.6%

**Major exports:** *road vehicles:* 9.2%
*electrical machinery:* 7.5%
*industrial machinery:* 6.0%

**Labor force by occupation:** *agriculture:* highest, Greece 20.8%; lowest, Britain 2.1%
*industry:* highest, Germany 37%; lowest, Netherlands 23.3%
*services:* highest, Netherlands 72.7%; lowest, Greece 55.6%
*high-tech manufacturing:* 7.8%

# HISTORICAL BACKGROUND

The diverse proposals since World War II for some kind of union of Western European countries reflect the complexity and richness of European history and politics. Europe is not a given entity with a single past or tradition. Eastern and Western Europe are both heirs to Roman and Christian traditions, but the Byzantine Empire, Orthodox religion, and Islamic Arabs have made Europe more than a predominantly Romanic and Germanic group of peoples.

After the fourteenth century, the word "Europe," until then rarely used, tended to be identified with "Christendom." But there was never a single political organization for the whole of Christendom or a medieval international order, and Latin and Greek were not really universal languages. In the sixteenth century, the influence of the humanists and the new cartography, which emphasized political authority in territorial areas rather than ecclesiastical rule, began to challenge Europe's identification with Christendom.

European culture cannot be simply defined or described by a single formula. Rationalism, individualism, the devotion to economic activity, industrialism, and the preoccupation with ideals of democracy, communism, fascism, and socialism have all contributed to the pattern of European behavior. Political concepts such as the rule of law and constitutional government, social concerns such as care for the handicapped and the distressed, personal qualities of tolerance and a reliance on persuasion rather than coercion, and shared cultural values exemplify those characteristics still confined largely to European nations or their direct descendants.

The movement for European integration has a long lineage, going back to the Greeks and continuing in various ways throughout history and up to the present. Although the motives have always been complex, the essential reasons have remained largely the same: the preservation of peace, the need for a common defense, the ambition to act as a stronger power bloc, the conservation of a common European culture, the wish to create greater material well-being, and the easing of restrictions on trade.

The development of the European Union has been influenced not only by these same motives, but also by significant external factors. The role of the United States as common friend, supplier of material aid in the immediate postwar years, defensive protector of the West, and now economic competitor, has given an Atlantic dimension to the European story. The fear of Soviet expansion and the threat of Communism to western democracies after 1945 led Western Europe, in association with the United States, to common defense and security arrangements.

The new Europe has been impelled by both positive and negative factors. Europe needed to recover from the devastation and depletion of material resources caused by World War II, and economic growth and social improvements would be advanced by European cooperation. The small, separate European markets compared poorly with the size and economic strength of the United States, as individual countries were politically weaker than before the war, less significant internationally, and obliged to end their colonial empires.

Political factors also spurred the moves toward a more united Europe. Many thought that, after two world wars in one generation, it was imperative to prevent the possibility of further intra-European conflict, especially between Germany and France. (The German problem seemed incapable of solution except within the framework of a larger community.) The economic and military dependence of Western Europe on the United States created a desire for protection against a possible American recession, and inspired awe of American strength. Europe recognized that it was no longer the political center of the world, that apart from Britain and France it did not possess nuclear weapons, and that it would be difficult for it to play an independent political role or act as a third force in world politics. In addition, there was a strong fear of expanding Soviet imperialism, which had reached to Berlin and Prague and had substantial ideological support in the West, where one-third of the Italian electorate and one-quarter of the French had voted Communist.

The interrelation of political, economic, and military factors explains the large spectrum of alternative proposals concerning the new Europe and the various institutions that have been constructed. Politically, the proposals ranged from regular meetings of heads of governments, to regional and functional conferences on specific problems, to a confederal and finally a federal political system. Economic alternatives ran from a tariff and customs community to a full economic union. Possibilities for integration also existed in military alliances among individual sovereign states, collective alliances with common leadership, and integrated defense forces.

## A United States of Europe?

European proposals for integration took account of differing attitudes toward the United States. Some favored an Atlantic alliance, partnership, or community with the United States, whereas others called for an independent Western European political entity, economically sound and militarily strong, capable of acting as a third force without ties to the United States or anyone else.

At the core of the different views toward European integration have been attitudes toward the continued existence of sovereign nation-states. The European nation-state has been a constructive force in the creation of political unity, cultural homogeneity, patriotic feeling, and personal identity. But the destructive twentieth-century wars, partly resulting from militant nationalism, led Europeans to question whether the sovereign nation-state could provide the basis for a peaceful Europe. Some still argue that only the nation-state can be responsible for its own protection and welfare, and that nations should be associated only in some framework of intergovernmental cooperation, with unanimity as the procedure for decision making. This view that sovereign power should largely remain with nation-states was reflected in the policies of Charles de Gaulle and Margaret Thatcher. Others hold that limited cooperation of this kind, while useful, is inadequate for solving problems of peace, order, and economic well-being in modern life. They argue that the solutions will come not from the nation-states but from some form of European integration or unity, or a United States of Europe.

The movement toward European integration was created by intellectuals and political elites rather than by mass demand. The postwar attempt to influence the citizen body and make European integration a popular movement, in fact, hardly lasted after 1949 and the institution of the Council of Europe. All other European organizations have been formulated and organized by elite political groups or key political actors whose dedication to Europe is strong and whose idealism has been tempered by political reality. But even if the integration idea does not enflame millions as communism and nationalism have done, it nonetheless attracts increasing support by the success of these European organizations.

The impetus to European integration began simultaneously in the political, economic, and military fields. In September 1946, Winston Churchill, then leader of the opposition in Britain, talked of "recreating the European family, or as much of it as we can" by building "a kind of United States of Europe." Representatives of a number of organizations aiming at such a result met in The Hague in May 1948 and agreed on the establishment of an assembly of representatives of European parliaments, a European charter of human rights, a European court, an economic union, and the inclusion of Germany into a European community.

During this time the United States, for a number of political and economic reasons, took a historic initiative. In June 1947, Secretary of State George Marshall, in a commencement speech at Harvard, proposed American aid for a Europe still suffering from physical destruction, economic dislocation, and lack of productivity, and suggested "a joint recovery program based on self-help and mutual cooperation." Moscow forced Poland and Czechoslovakia to withdraw their requests to be included among the Marshall Plan recipients, and none of the Eastern European countries, then under Soviet control, accepted the Anglo-French invitation in July of 1947 to join an organization of European economic recovery. The Iron Curtain had effectively divided Europe. In April 1948, after 16 Western European governments agreed that cooperation would continue even after Marshall Plan aid had ended, the Organization for European Economic

Cooperation (OEEC) was established, and a series of bilateral agreements was concluded between the United States and OEEC countries.

Western Europe, meanwhile, was concerning itself with its military defense. In March 1947, the Treaty of Dunkirk was signed by France and Great Britain for mutual protection against any renewed aggression by Germany. As a result of changing international relationships, this pact was extended to include the Benelux countries—Belgium, the Netherlands, and Luxembourg—in the Brussels Treaty Organization (BTO) set up in March 1948. The BTO was set up under Article 51 of the United Nations Charter as a regional organization able to undertake individual or collective self-defense if an armed attack occurred. The Organization was a 50-year alliance based primarily on the principle of collective defense; members agreed to take steps in the event of renewed German aggression and pledged automatic mutual military assistance. The BTO was intended not as a supranational organization, but as an intergovernmental one in which the chief policy organ was the Consultative Council of the five foreign ministers.

The Communist capture of power in Prague raised the possibility of the whole of Western Europe being at the mercy of the Russian forces. With the advent of the Berlin blockade in April 1948, it rapidly became apparent that the BTO was not strong enough to resist the Communist threat. Already in March 1946 Winston Churchill, in a speech at Fulton, Missouri, talked of an "iron curtain" in Europe and called for a military alliance between the United States and the Commonwealth. In April 1948 the Canadian Foreign Minister, Louis St. Laurent, suggested an Atlantic defense system. After the Vandenberg Resolution in the U.S. Senate, which ended the historic American policy of no entangling alliances, the Truman Administration went ahead with negotiations throughout the summer of 1948. On April 4, 1949, the North Atlantic Treaty Organization (NATO), with twelve members—Belgium, Britain, Canada, Denmark, France, Iceland, Italy, Luxembourg, the Netherlands, Norway, Portugal, and the United States—was established.

From the beginning of the discussion on the new Europe, differences existed between the "federalist" and the "functionalist" points of view about the nature of a European political institution. The federalists believed that the best way to encourage collaboration among European nations and deal with the problem of sovereignty was to set up a constitutional convention and a European constitution. The functionalists argued that vested interests, multilingual nations, and diverse customs and traditions prevented such a radical step, and that any new organization must be based on the power of the states. At the same time, however, they recognized the need to subordinate the separate national interests to the common welfare.

The issue was decided with the establishment of the Council of Europe in August 1949. In the debate on the nature of the council the federalists, who argued for an elected bicameral legislature and an executive federal council responsible to the legislature, were defeated. The council has remained an intergovernmental organization.

## European Coal and Steel Community

The first step to a European community came in May 1950 with a proposal for a common market for coal and steel. The proposal was made by French Foreign Minister Robert Schuman, on the suggestion of Jean Monnet, the French public servant often regarded as the inspiration of the European movement. From an economic standpoint, the plan could lead to joint Franco-German control over the Ruhr and assure the French a coke supply, and could end the struggle between the two countries over the Saar's coal and steel. It would also increase the internal market needed for economic expansion. But above all, the motivations were political. National antagonisms could be transcended, and the reconciliation of the two old enemies could lead to a closer European political association. The plan could thus be the first concrete step toward the goal of European unity. For Germany, the plan meant the removal of Allied controls over the German economy; for German Chancellor Konrad Adenauer, it meant the realization of an idea of friendship he had proposed 30 years earlier.

The plan was greeted enthusiastically in some European countries, but Britain refused to participate. After a year of negotiations, the

REVIEW
8.1

## KEY TERMS IN EUROPEAN INTEGRATION

**ACP Countries**—78 African, Caribbean, and Pacific region countries associated with the European Union through the Lomé Agreements

**CFSP**—Common Foreign and Security Policy; a pillar of the EU

**Coreper**—committee of permanent representatives of the states to the EU

**Council of Europe**—founded 1949, located in Strasbourg, now has 43 democratic European states including Russia

**EC**—European Community, incorporates the EEC, ECSC, and Euratom

**ECB**—European Central Bank, in Frankfurt, responsible for monetary policy in the EU countries

**ECJ**—European Court of Justice

**ECOSOC**—Economic and Social Committee composed of employers, employees, and various groups to give advice

**ECSC**—European Coal and Steel Community, founded 1952

**EEA**—European Economic Area, started 1994, includes the 15 EU states and EFTA except Switzerland and provides for free movement of goods, capital, services, and labor across national borders

**EEC**—European Economic Community, set up in 1958 to create a common market

**EFTA**—European Free Trade Association, in Geneva, has agreements with EU to create single market

**EMU**—Economic and Monetary Union

**EP**—European Parliament, directly elected

**EU**—European Union, created 1993 by the Maastricht Treaty

**Euratom**—founded 1965 for common European research on nuclear energy

**Euro**—single currency in effect 2002 in several EU member nations

**Eurocorps**—military unit organized by France and Germany for joint military security, which will be open to other countries

**European Research and Coordinating Agency**—founded 1985 for greater cooperation in research and technology; participants are the EU and EFTA countries and Turkey

**European Social Fund**—the EU unit to finance common social policy, including help and training for unemployed youth, adults, and migrant workers

**Europol**—European police authority, in The Hague, supervises activities against organized crime and narcotics trade

**Maastricht**—treaty on European Union signed 1992

**Nice**—treaty concluded in December 2000 to extend qualified majority voting and prepare for the extension of the EU

**PHARE**—European assistance to countries in Central and Eastern Europe

**Schengen**—border agreements started in 1985 and now part of the EC

**SEA**—Single European Act, in force 1987 to complete the single market

**Subsidiary Principle**—the principle that issues should be dealt with by higher levels of government only if they cannot be handled at a lower level

**WEU**—Western European Union, founded 1954, a European defense organization linked to NATO

---

governments of six countries—France, Germany, Italy, Belgium, the Netherlands, and Luxembourg—signed the Treaty of Paris in April 1951, and in July 1952 the European Coal and Steel Community (ECSC) came into existence, the first European body in which any institution had supranational powers. The six nations set up the ECSC High Authority, a unique institution to which member governments transferred part of their sovereign powers in the area of coal and steel. ECSC had a Council of Ministers, an Assembly (to be renamed a Parliament), and a Court of Justice, and it could act directly on the citizens and businesses of the member states. ECSC achieved quick success with the increase of coal and steel trade among the six countries by 129 percent in the first five years.

Monnet regarded the ECSC as the first of several concrete achievements which would be the building blocks of the new Europe in military, political, and economic matters. Even before ECSC came into operation, another proposal was put forward for a European army, and in May 1952 a treaty for a European Defense Community (EDC) was signed by the six ECSC nations. The EDC would be supranational with common institutions, common armed forces, and a common budget. The six countries also began discussing proposals for an even more ambitious European Political Community (EPC) which would include a European Executive Council, a council of ministers, a court, a bilateral assembly, and an economic and social council. But when the French Parliament refused to ratify the EDC treaty in August 1954, both plans failed.

At this point Anthony Eden, Foreign Minister of Britain—which had refused to participate in EDC or to put its forces under supranational control—proposed that the BTO be enlarged to include Germany and Italy in a new organization, the Western European Union. Britain pledged to keep some forces on the European mainland, and Germany would be admitted to NATO and

supply troops to it. But with the defeat of EDC and EPC, the European integration process had been temporarily checked. Defense policy for the moment would remain a national responsibility. The advocates of European unification then decided that the best policy was to pursue economic integration.

## The European Economic Community

The unsuccessful EPC proposal had included provisions for a common market with free movement of goods, capital, and persons. Two organizations already existed to facilitate trade. On the international level, the General Agreement on Trade and Tariffs (GATT), concerned with reduction of tariffs and quantitative restrictions on goods and setting up a common set of trade rules, was signed by 23 nations in October 1947. A narrower agreement in 1944 by Belgium, the Netherlands, and Luxembourg created a customs union (Benelux), which actually came into operation in 1948. Benelux abolished tariff barriers among the three countries and imposed a common tariff on imports from nonmember countries.

In May 1955 the Benelux countries, aided by Monnet and others, proposed a wider common market and other steps toward European integration. These proposals for organizations to deal with a common market and customs union, and with atomic energy, were discussed by the six ECSC countries, with Britain again refusing to participate. In March 1957 the Treaties of Rome were signed, and on January 1, 1958, the European Economic Community (EEC) and the

---

**A CLOSER LOOK**

**8.1**

### THE COUNCIL OF EUROPE

The Council of Europe was set up in 1949 with headquarters in Strasbourg to foster European cooperation, to protect human rights and fundamental freedoms and the rule of law, and to promote awareness of European cultural identity and diversity. Starting with ten members, in 2002 it has 43 member states. This intergovernmental organization is primarily a forum for discussion by a Council of Ministers, the foreign ministers of the states, and a Parliamentary Assembly. Its main achievements have been the 1950 European Convention on Human Rights, the European Court of Human Rights set up in 1959, and cultural activities.

## THE SINGLE ECONOMIC ACT (SEA)

- Signed in 1986; operative in 1987.
- Amends the Treaties of Rome.
- Qualified majority voting in Council of Ministers on certain subjects.
- Establishes cooperation procedure to give Parliament more input into legislative process.
- Timetables set up to implement a common market by 1992.
- Formal recognition of European Political Cooperation (EPC).

European Atomic Energy Community (Euratom) came into existence. The EEC would merge separate national markets into a single large market that would ensure the free movement of goods, people, capital, and services, and would draw up a wide range of common economic and social policies. Euratom was designed to further the use of nuclear energy for peaceful purposes. In 1965, the three executive bodies of ECSC, EEC, and Euratom were merged into the European Community (EC).

Britain, wanting an organization with no common external tariff or objective for economic or political unification, led the move toward the establishment in 1960 of the European Free Trade Association (EFTA). This body, consisting of Austria, Great Britain, Denmark, Norway, Portugal, Sweden, and Switzerland, was to be concerned with liberalization of trade, not with political objectives. Within two years, however,

Britain changed its mind because of the obvious success of the EEC and applied for membership in July 1961. After being rebuffed twice, Britain became a member of the European Community on January 1, 1973, together with Denmark and Ireland. The government of Norway had also agreed to join, but the parliament refused ratification after the Norwegian electorate voted against accession. Greece joined the EC in 1981, Spain and Portugal in 1986. The Single European Act (SEA), signed in 1986 and operative in 1987, amended the EC treaties and proposed that a single market be established by 1992.

## The Maastricht Treaty

In 1991, the heads of the governments of the 12 EC member states agreed to the Treaty on European Union at Maastricht in the Netherlands. This agreement, known as the Maastricht Treaty,

## THE EUROPEAN ECONOMIC AREA (EEA)

The agreement establishing the European Economic Area (EEA) was signed in 1992 by the EU and three of the four EFTA countries (Norway, Iceland, and Liechtenstein, but not Switzerland) and enforced in 1994. This intergovernmental organization was established to administer the single market—now of 380 million people, accounting for 17 percent of world imports and 20 percent of world exports—and ensure freedom of movement of goods, persons, capital, and services.

## MAJOR FEATURES OF MAASTRICHT

- The EC will now be known as the EU.
- Single currency by 1999, but optional for Britain and Denmark, and transition to an Economic and Monetary Union with a central bank.
- Eventual European defense, but in collaboration with NATO.
- Common foreign policy and security making, and implementation by majority vote.
- Some more legisiative power given to the European Parliament with a veto on some items.
- Common citizenship of European Union: citizens can vote and be candidates in all the countries.
- More majority voting in the Council of Ministers.
- European Social Community accepted by all states except Britain.
- Fund set up to help poorer EC countries in transport and environment.
- Cooperation on justice and home affairs, immigration, drugs, and terrorism.

was signed in February 1992 but ratification was delayed because of a lack of enthusiasm in some of the member states, especially Denmark, France, and Britain. Concessions were made to Britain, which did not accept the Social Charter of the Treaty that will deal with employment, working conditions, social security, and minimum wages.

The Maastrict Treaty came into force on November 1, 1993, creating the European Union (EU). The EU is not founded on a constitution but on international treaties. It can enact rules that directly bind all citizens of the countries in the EU that have relinquished part of their national sovereignty to the EU institutions. The treaty provides the basis for a European citizenship; citizens of a member state can vote and be a candidate for office in any EU country in which they reside.

## THE BASIC STRUCTURE OF THE EUROPEAN UNION

With the signing of the Maastricht Treaty in 1992, the 12 member states of the EC became the European Union. Austria, Finland, and Sweden joined in 1995, bringing the membership to 15 nations. The EU now stretches from the Mediterranean to the Arctic Circle. A number of other countries are candidates for EU membership, the criteria for which are democracy, a market economy, ability to compete in the single market, and ability to apply the laws and treaties of the EU (see Table 8.1). Enlargement of the EU means that it will become more diverse economically, geographically, and culturally (see Figure 8.1).

The EU countries vary widely in population, from Germany with 82 million to Luxembourg with 400,000, and in GDP (see Table 8.1). Some states, Britain and the Netherlands in particular, are more enthusiastic about free trade than others, such as France and Spain.

The EU is not a federal political system, but it is considerably more than an intergovernmental agreement or commercial arrangement. Its objective is integration, not merely cooperation among states, which makes it different from other regional organizations (see Table 8.2). Its institutional structure and procedural rules do not fit easily into any of the categories of political systems discussed in the introduction of this book. It was developed to provide an economic

**TABLE 8.1**

**CANDIDATES FOR EU MEMBERSHIP, 2002**

| Country | Area (thousand km) | Population (millions) | GDP Per Capita (thousand) |
|---|---|---|---|
| Bulgaria | 111 | 8.2 | 4.7 |
| Cyprus | 9 | 0.8 | 17.1 |
| Czech Republic | 79 | 10.3 | 12.5 |
| Estonia | 45 | 1.4 | 7.7 |
| Latvia | 65 | 2.4 | 5.8 |
| Lithuania | 65 | 3.7 | 6.2 |
| Hungary | 93 | 10.1 | 10.7 |
| Malta | 0.3 | 0.4 | 8.8 |
| Poland | 313 | 38.7 | 7.8 |
| Romania | 238 | 22.5 | 5.7 |
| Slovakia | 49 | 5.4 | 10.3 |
| Slovenia | 20 | 2.0 | 15.0 |
| Turkey | 775 | 63.9 | 5.9 |

*Source: Eurostat.*

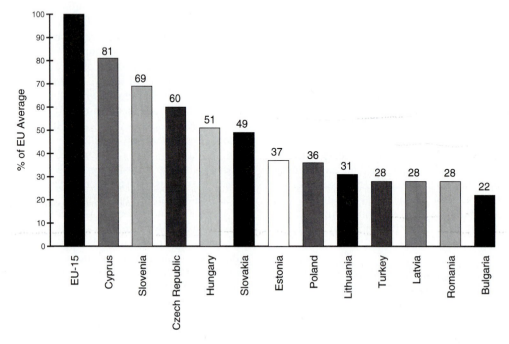

**Figure 8.1  INCOME DIFFERENCES BETWEEN THE EU AND CANDIDATE COUNTRIES**
*Source: Eurostat.*

REVIEW
8.4

## KEY EVENTS IN EUROPEAN INTEGRATION

| | |
|---|---|
| 1947 | Treaty of Dunkirk linked Britain and France |
| | Marshall Plan proposed as joint recovery program for Europe |
| | General Agreement on Trade and Tariffs (GATT) ratified |
| 1948 | Benelux began to operate |
| | Organization for European Economic Cooperation (OEEC) formed |
| | Brussels Treaty Organization set up |
| 1949 | North Atlantic Treaty Organization (NATO) formed |
| | Council of Europe established |
| 1950 | Robert Schuman proposed that coal and steel be put under a common European authority |
| 1952 | European Coal and Steel Community (ECSC) formed |
| 1954 | European Defense Community (EDC) defeated |
| | Western European Union (WEU) formed |
| 1958 | European Economic Community (EEC) and European Atomic Energy Community (Euratom) established |
| 1960 | European Free Trade Association (EFTA) formed |
| | Organization for Economic Cooperation and Development (OECD) replaced OEEC |
| 1962 | Common Agricultural Policy (CAP) adopted |
| 1963 | Yaoundé Convention between EEC and 18 African states |
| 1967 | Merger of Commissions of ECSC, EEC, and Euratom in European Community (EC) |
| 1968 | EEC customs union completed |
| 1973 | Great Britain, Denmark, and Ireland joined EC |
| 1974 | European Council met for first time |
| 1975 | Lomé Convention between EC and 46 African, Caribbean, and Pacific states which gained preferential trading arrangements |
| 1979 | Direct election of European Parliament |
| | European Monetary System (EMS) became operative to achieve exchange rate stability |
| 1981 | Greece joined EC |
| 1986 | Portugal and Spain joined EC |
| | Single European Act signed, became operative in 1987, amended the EC treaties and proposed a European single market by 1992 |
| 1989 | EC countries endorsed a plan for European Monetary Union |
| | EC coordinated Western assistance to Poland and Hungary |
| 1990 | Two intergovernmental conferences on economic and monetary union and on political union opened |
| | Schengen Convention formalized 1985 agreement of five countries introducing freedom of movement for their nationals |
| 1991 | Europe Agreements with Poland, Hungary, and Czechoslovakia to include political dialogue and free trade area |
| 1992 | European Economic Area (EC and EFTA) proposed |
| | Maastricht Treaty on European Union signed |
| 1993 | Single market enters into effect |
| 1994 | EEA comes into force |
| 1995 | Austria, Finland, and Sweden join EU |
| 1997 | Amsterdam Treaty signed, amending Maastricht |

(continues)

**REVIEW**
**8.4**

### KEY EVENTS IN EUROPEAN INTEGRATION (continued)

| | |
|---|---|
| 1998 | Single currency agreed to by 11 of the 15 EU members; European Central Bank established |
| | Accession process to EU starts for 10 applicant states and Cyprus |
| 1999 | Schengen agreements incorporated into EU |
| | Conversion rates fixed for national currencies of 11 countries that will use euro as currency |
| | European Commission resigned after reports of fraud and mismanagement |
| 2000 | Treaty of Nice extended majority voting and preparation for EU expansion |
| | Fifth Lomé Convention signed; Lomé now renamed Cotonou Convention for preferential trading arrangements |
| 2002 | Thirteen countries are candidates for accession to EU |

and monetary union, a common foreign and security policy, and action on common problems of justice and internal affairs.

The EU does not operate on the basis of a clear separation of powers. It is founded on international treaties (of Paris, Rome, and Maastricht) among sovereign nations, not on a constitution. Yet it is more than an international organization because it has power in certain fields to enact laws and regulations that are directly binding and applicable to citizens of the member states, and to adjudicate cases in certain topics in its court. The voting arrangements by ministers, allowing some decisions to be made by simple or weighted majority rather than by unanimity, means qualification of national sovereignty, as does the obligation of members to take specific common actions and decide on common policies. The legislative power of states is limited by their commitment to achieve coordination of economic and monetary policy and harmonization of social legislation. The EU method is to seek communally devised solutions rather than individual or bilateral state action.

In recent years, the EU has said that it operates on the basis of "subsidiarity." This term,

**A CLOSER LOOK**
**8.3**

### THE EUROPEAN COMMUNITIES AND THE EU

There are three European communities governed by separate treaties: the European Coal and Steel Community (ECSC), by the Treaty of Paris, 1951; and the European Economic Community (EEC) and the European Atomic Energy Community (Euratom), by the Treaties of Rome, 1957. The term "European Communities" was used in legal documents to refer to the three bodies, but the generally accepted term was "European Community" (EC). According to the Maastricht Treaty the term "European Union" (EU) is now used.

The European Economic Community (EEC) provided a framework, to which legislation and policies have been added, calling for a customs union, ending cartels and monopolies, guaranteeing free movement of people, services, and capital, and a common policy for agriculture and transport. The treaties have been amended by the Single European Act, signed in 1986, and amplified by case law resulting from determinations made on the basis of the treaties, and by regulations, directives, decisions, recommendations, and opinions.

## TABLE 8.2

### OVERLAPPING MEMBERSHIPS OF THE EU AND OTHER EUROPEAN AND REGIONAL ORGANIZATIONS

| Country | EU | Council of Europe[1] | NATO | OECD[2] | EFTA | WEU | EEA |
|---|---|---|---|---|---|---|---|
| Austria | X | X | | X | | | X |
| Belgium | X | X | X | X | | X | X |
| Denmark | X | X | X | X | | | X |
| Finland | X | X | | X | | | X |
| France | X | X | X | X | | X | X |
| Germany | X | X | X | X | | X | X |
| Greece | X | X | X | X | | X | X |
| Ireland | X | X | | X | | | X |
| Italy | X | X | X | X | | X | X |
| Luxembourg | X | X | X | X | | X | X |
| Netherlands | X | X | X | X | | X | X |
| Portugal | X | X | X | X | | X | X |
| Spain | X | X | X | X | | X | X |
| Sweden | X | X | | X | | | X |
| United Kingdom | X | X | X | X | | X | X |
| Canada | | | X | X | | | |
| Cyprus | | X | | | | | |
| Czech Republic | | | | X | | | |
| Hungary | | | X | X | | | |
| Iceland | | X | X | X | X | | X |
| Liechtenstein | | X | | | X | | X |
| Malta | | X | | | | | |
| Mexico | | | | X | | | |
| Norway | | X | X | X | X | | X |
| Poland | | | | X | | | |
| San Marino | | X | | | | | |
| Switzerland | | X | | X | X | | |
| Turkey | | X | X | X | | | |
| United States | | | X | X | | | |

[1] Council has 43 members.

[2] OECD has 30 members.

drawn from Catholic socioeconomic doctrine, means that the EU is granted jurisdiction and is responsible only for those policies that cannot be handled adequately at the state, national, regional, or local level.

## EU FINANCIAL STRUCTURE

The European communities have been financed in different ways. The ECSC is financed by a levy on the value of coal and steel production paid directly to the EU. The EEC and Euratom were originally financed by differing amounts from the member states, but in 1970 the EC decided to raise its own resources for additional revenue. Its income now comes from a number of sources, levies on imports of agricultural produce, customs duties on other imports from non-EC countries, a small part of the Value-Added Tax (VAT) collected in member states, and contributions based on a proportion of the GNP of the states (see Figure 8.2 and Table 8.3).

The European Commission—the administrative core of the EU—prepares the preliminary budget and presents it to the European Council, which amends and adopts this draft budget. This is then forwarded to the European Parliament (EP), which can propose changes in some areas and can amend it in other areas. The Council then examines it again before the EP adopts the final budget. If the EP and the Council cannot agree, the EP can reject the budget as a whole.

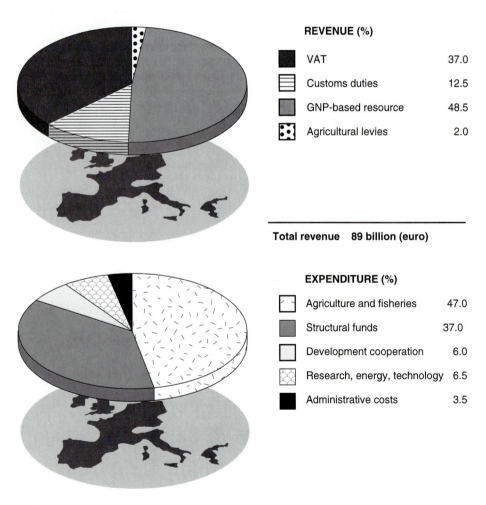

**REVENUE (%)**

| | | |
|---|---|---|
| ■ | VAT | 37.0 |
| ▤ | Customs duties | 12.5 |
| ▨ | GNP-based resource | 48.5 |
| ⁚ | Agricultural levies | 2.0 |

**Total revenue   89 billion (euro)**

**EXPENDITURE (%)**

| | | |
|---|---|---|
| | Agriculture and fisheries | 47.0 |
| | Structural funds | 37.0 |
| | Development cooperation | 6.0 |
| | Research, energy, technology | 6.5 |
| ■ | Administrative costs | 3.5 |

**Figure 8.2** GENERAL EU BUDGET IN 2000

**TABLE 8.3**

**EU, U.S., AND WORLD TRADE, 2000 (IN BILLIONS, U.S. DOLLARS)**

*World Trade (excluding intra-EU Trade)*

|       | Imports | %    | Exports | %    |
|-------|---------|------|---------|------|
| Total | 5,275.0 | —    | 4,974.0 | —    |
| EU    | 959.2   | 18.2 | 855.4   | 17.2 |
| US    | 1,258.0 | 23.9 | 782.4   | 15.7 |

*US Trade*

|       | Imports | %    | Exports | %    |
|-------|---------|------|---------|------|
| World | 1,216.7 | —    | 782.4   | —    |
| EU    | 220.4   | 18.1 | 164.8   | 21.1 |

*EU Trade*

|       | Imports | %    | Exports | %    |
|-------|---------|------|---------|------|
| World | 945.5   | —    | 862.1   | —    |
| US    | 181.9   | 19.2 | 212.9   | 24.7 |

*Sources:* World Trade Organization, U.S. Department of Commerce, and Eurostat.

European Parliament.

## THE INSTITUTIONS OF THE EU

As in the original ECSC, there are four major institutions in the EU: the European Commission, the Council of Ministers, the European Parliament, and the Court of Justice. Other bodies, such as the European Council, the Committee of Permanent Representatives (Coreper), the Economic and Social Committee, and the Court of Auditors, also play roles of different kinds.

## The European Commission

The central institution of the EU is the European Commission, which is both an executive and a civil service as well as the body that prepares and formulates the budget, policy proposals, and legislation for approval. It is the driving force in the legislative process. It is responsible for administering EU policies and for ensuring that decisions are carried out. It has authority to

**A CLOSER LOOK**

**8.4**

### ROMANO PRODI—PRESIDENT OF THE EUROPEAN COMMISSION

Romano Prodi was born in Italy in 1939. He was a professor of economics and industrial politics, a member of the Italian parliament (1996–1999), and prime minister of Italy (1996–1998). In 1999, Prodi was appointed the president of the European Commission.

bring legal action against persons, companies, or states that have violated EU rules. The Commission is the guardian of EU treaties, seeing that the treaties and rules are correctly applied and properly implemented. In addition, its task is to defend the interests of the EU and represent it in international negotiations (see Table 8.4).

There are now 20 commissioners—two each from Britain, France, Germany, Italy, and Spain, and one each from the other ten countries—who are nominated by their governments and approved by agreement of the 15 states for a renewable five-year term. Five of the 20 are women. The European Parliament approves the Commission as a whole but has not yet been given the power to approve individual nominations. The president is chosen from among the commissioners by the governments of the member states subject to approval of the European Parliament.

All commissioners are expected to act in the interest of the EU rather than in defense of national interests, although they have not always followed this rule. The Commission acts in collegiate fashion with decisions made by majority, not unanimity. Each commissioner is assigned a specific policy area or areas of main responsibility, and each has a "cabinet" or small staff of aides. The Commission as a whole has a staff, based mainly in Brussels, of about 13,000 people, a third of whom are employed in translation and interpretation services.

The Commission's chief role as initiator is to propose new policies and regulations to the Council of Ministers; EU decisions can only be taken on the basis of these proposals, which are agreed on by the Commission as a whole at its weekly meetings. The Council of Ministers can accept or reject these proposals, or it can modify

## TABLE 8.4

### THE EUROPEAN COMMISSION

**President 1**

**Vice Presidents 2**

**Members 17**

20 members appointed by common accord of the governments of the member states for a term of five years

| Members | | | Members | |
|---|---|---|---|---|
| 1 | Belgium | | Italy | 2 |
| 1 | Denmark | | Luxembourg | 1 |
| 2 | France | | Netherlands | 1 |
| 2 | Germany | | Portugal | 1 |
| 1 | Greece | | Spain | 2 |
| 1 | Ireland | | United Kingdom | 2 |
| 1 | Austria | | Finland | 1 |
| 1 | Sweden | | | |

| Responsibilities | | | |
|---|---|---|---|
| **Proposing** | **Monitoring** | **Administering** | **Representing** |
| measures for the further development of EU policy | observance and proper application of EU law | and implementing EU legislation | the EU in international organizations |

them by a unanimous vote. The Commission has often amended its own proposals to meet criticism by the Council, but the Single European Act and the Maastricht Treaty have strengthened the position of the Commission in many areas. The Council will be able to make more decisions by majority vote rather than by unanimity, and the Commission always tries to find a consensus.

The Commission also is charged by the Council to negotiate on behalf of the EU in some areas: competition policy, farming, trade policy, and customs duties. It does not have power over fiscal or monetary policies or over central banking, though it has been trying to extend its general authority. Since 1993 it shares in initiatives in foreign policy.

## The Council of Ministers

The main forum for policy making is the Council of Ministers. The Council consists of representa- tives of the 15 states and must approve proposals of the Commission before they can be implemented. The Council, unlike the Commission, is not a fixed group of people. Its membership changes according to the subject being discussed, such as finance, agriculture, transportation, or the environment; the ministers responsible for these activities in the member states will make up the Council. But most often the Council consists of ministers responsible for foreign policy who meet once a month (see Table 8.5).

The Council differs from international organizations that require unanimity to make decisions. The logic of European integration was that the Council would increasingly decide by majority vote. This was stalled by the Luxembourg Compromise of 1966 (a concession to the nationalism of President de Gaulle), which said that the other governments would not overrule a member state that opposed proposals it held to be contrary to its national interest. This veto power by a state has

---

**TABLE 8.5**

**THE COUNCIL OF MINISTERS**

|  |  | Representatives of the Governments of the Member States 15 |  |  |
|---|---|---|---|---|
|  |  | Permanent Representatives Committee (Coreper) |  |  |
|  |  | **LEGISLATION** |  |  |
| **Weighting of Votes** |  |  | **Weighting of Votes** |  |
| 10 | France |  | Greece | 5 |
| 10 | Germany |  | Netherlands | 5 |
| 10 | Italy |  | Belgium | 5 |
| 4 | Sweden |  | Austria | 4 |
| 10 | United Kingdom |  | Denmark | 3 |
| 8 | Spain |  | Ireland | 3 |
| 5 | Portugal |  | Finland | 3 |
|  |  |  | Luxembourg | 2 |
|  |  | Qualified majority: 62 votes out of 87 |  |  |

Members of the Commission of the European Union meeting in Brussels.

rarely been used since 1966, because the Council has generally acted by consensus. Since the Single European Act in 1987, greater use has been made of either simple or qualified majority voting in the Council, though unanimity is still needed for certain matters. Most of the important EU policies are now decided by a qualified majority—approval by 62 of the 87 weighted votes in the Council.

An essential part of the decision-making process has the Committee of Permanent Representatives (Coreper)—the representatives of the member states who hold ambassadorial rank—which meets weekly to prepare meetings of the Council of Ministers. Coreper has played a significant role in coordinating the attitudes of the states with the proposals of the Commission. Most of those proposals go to Coreper before going to the Council, and decisions on some issues have been reached by the states at the Coreper level.

## Other Executive Bodies

Although they have no formal status and were not created by the Treaties of Paris or Rome, two other significant bodies have been acknowledged by the Single European Act. One is the European Council (not to be confused with the Council of Ministers), which consists of the 15 heads of state or govern-ment assisted by their foreign ministers and the president of the Commission. The European Council meets at least once every six months, primarily to discuss foreign policy, defense, and important economic subjects. Since 1993 the European Council is an official body of the EU.

The second body is the European Political Cooperation (EPC), which began in 1970, was acknowledged in the Single European Act, and is now part of the EU institutional arrangements. The EPC is a forum in which the 15 foreign ministers meet regularly to discuss coordination of foreign policy and the political and economic aspects of security. Assisted since 1981 by a small secretariat in Brussels, the EPC has coordinated the policy of the 15 countries at several meetings of the United Nations and on a number of international issues, beginning with the 1980 Venice Declaration on the Middle East.

The EPC, like the Council of Ministers and the European Council, is chaired by one of the states every six months. The overlap between the different executive groups, which are all trying to coordinate the opinions of the national foreign ministries, has sometimes made it difficult to differentiate the working of EPC from that of the European Council. The Single European Act recognized the EPC and suggested it would play an even more important role in the future, a development which may help to resolve the question of who makes foreign policy in the EU. It could also decide whether nonmember states such as the United States should deal with officials from the Commission, the European Council, or the individual 15 countries, a problem that is complicated by the fact that a different country assumes the presidency of the European Council and the EPC every six months. However, the EPC is superseded by the common foreign and security policy.

## THE EUROPEAN PARLIAMENT

The European Parliament, renamed from the Assembly established under ECSC, is composed of 626 members (directly elected in the 15 states for a five-year term) in approximate proportion to the size of the different populations (see Figure 8.3). The Parliament meets one week in each month in plenary sessions in Strasbourg, France, but its committees meet in Brussels and its secretariat of 3,600 meets in Luxembourg. Its members come

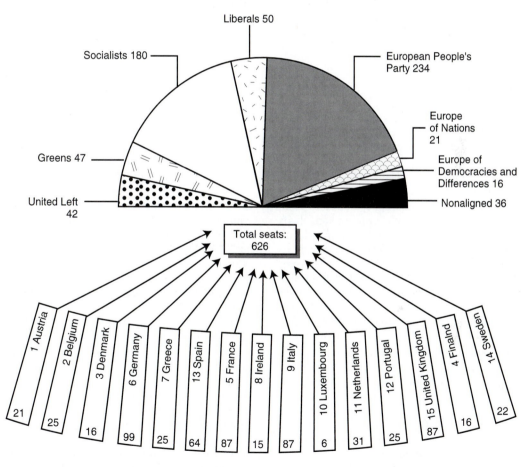

**Political Groups in the European Parliament, 2002**

Liberals 50
Socialists 180
European People's Party 234
Greens 47
Europe of Nations 21
Europe of Democracies and Differences 16
United Left 42
Nonaligned 36

Total seats: 626

| 1 Austria | 2 Belgium | 3 Denmark | 6 Germany | 7 Greece | 13 Spain | 5 France | 8 Ireland | 9 Italy | 10 Luxembourg | 11 Netherlands | 12 Portugal | 15 United Kingdom | 4 Finland | 14 Sweden |
|---|---|---|---|---|---|---|---|---|---|---|---|---|---|---|
| 21 | 25 | 16 | 99 | 25 | 64 | 87 | 15 | 87 | 6 | 31 | 25 | 87 | 16 | 22 |

**Figure 8.3** GROUPS AND NUMBER OF MEMBERS IN THE EUROPEAN PARLIAMENT

## WHO MAKES EU POLICY?

Policy making is shared by the different EU institutions. Ministers of the individual states set long-term policy and request the Commission to deal with certain issues. The Commission has sole initiative in proposing legislation, regulations, and budgetary expenditure.

There are three general kinds of procedure:

1. *Consultation:* now less important than in earlier years. The Commission presents a proposal and consults other EU institutions. Decision is taken by the Council.

2. *Cooperation:* Commission proposal is sent to both the Council and EP, and sometimes to other bodies. Council adopts a common position, which is sent to EP, which either accepts, rejects, or amends. Commission and Council decide after getting EP opinion.

3. *Co-decision:* now the most important procedure. On certain issues (internal market, transport, environment, research) Commission proposal must be approved by both the EP and the Council acting by qualified majority.

from over 60 political parties and almost always come together in political groups—eight in 2002—not in national blocs. They can use any of the 11 official languages of the EU.

The Parliament has been useful as an arena for the discussion of EU matters and as a representative of over 375 million people. But its powers go beyond giving its opinion on draft directives, proposals, and regulations coming from the Commission. The latter may decide to amend its proposals as a result of that opinion. The Parliament has power to dismiss the Commission on a vote of censure by a two-thirds majority, but this has never been done. It also must approve or reject the budget which is prepared with its help by the Commission for decision by the Council of Ministers; it has amended or rejected the draft budget on three occasions. Since 1975 the Parliament has helped the Commission draw up the budget, and can make amendments in limited areas. The Parliament has no formal powers of control over the Council of Ministers. But it is now consulted before governments nominate the president of the Commission, and approve the Commission as a body.

The Single European Act has increased the Parliament's legislative role, allowing it to accept, reject, or amend some legislative proposals. The act has also given it power to ratify new international agreements and even veto some agreements concluded by the Council of Ministers and the admission of new members to the EU. In the complicated process of decision making, the Commission can accept or reject any amendment asked for by the Parliament, and the Council of Ministers can overturn the result only by unanimity. The Parliament is now allowed to question or dismiss members of the Commission and to question the Council.

The Amsterdam Treaty, implemented in 1999, gave more power to the EP in the legislative process and in scrutinizing members of the Commission. This increase in authority was immediately illustrated in January 1999 when a censure motion against the Commission was introduced and only narrowly defeated and when in March 1999 the Commission resigned as a bloc after an independent committee found evidence of fraud and wrongdoing, the same allegations made in the EP.

# THE COURT OF JUSTICE

The European Court of Justice (ECJ), located in Luxembourg, consists of 15 judges—one from each state and the president of the Court—appointed for six years. By the Single European Act, a junior Court of First Instance was set up in 1989 to assist the Court. The Court of Justice differs from two other bodies: the International Court of Justice in The Hague (the World Court), and the European Court of Human Rights, which was established by the Council of Europe in Strasbourg. Member states of the EU must accept the final decisions and judgments of the ECJ but have no legal obligation to accept those of the other two courts, which are not part of the EU.

The essential functions of the ECJ are to ensure that EU law is properly applied and to resolve disputes between governments, EU institutions, and citizens over that law (see Table 8.6). It works by unanimity and thus, unlike the U.S. Supreme Court, no public dissent is registered. All member states are obliged to accept its rulings and its powers which are stated in the Treaties of Paris and Rome. The states have accepted that EU law is now also national law in their countries, that EU law prevails over national law if there is a conflict between them, and that the ECJ's decisions overrule those of national courts. The ECJ has by now laid down a body of law that applies to the EU institutions, states, and citizens. Its decisions are not subject to appeal. It has an increasingly large case load.

**TABLE 8.6**

**THE COURT OF JUSTICE**

|  |  |  |
|---|---|---|
|  | Governments of the member states appoint the 15 judges and 9 advocates general by common accord for a term of six years |  |
|  | **Court of Justice** |  |
|  | Full court of 15 judges 2 chambers with 5 judges 4 chambers with 3 judges |  |
|  | **Types of Proceedings** |  |
| Actions for failure to fulfill obligations under the treaties (Commission vs. member state) Actions by one member state against another | Actions on grounds of failure to act (against Council or Commission) | References from national courts for preliminary rulings to clarify the meaning and scope of Community law Claims for damages against the Community |
|  | **Court of First Instance** |  |
|  | **15 judges** |  |
|  | Staff cases Actions in the field of competition law Actions under antidumping law Actions under the ECSC Treaty |  |

## OTHER AGENCIES

The Economic and Social Committee consists of 222 persons representing employers, workers, and various interests such as consumer groups and professional associations. It meets once a month in Brussels to give its opinion on policies and legislative proposals in certain fields. It has the right to be consulted, but has no right of amendment.

The Court of Auditors, based in Luxembourg, consists of 15 members appointed by the Council of Ministers. It supervises expenditure, checking all EU revenue and spending, and has investigated cases of mismanagement and fraud.

The Committee of the Regions, established in 1993, comprises 222 members, representing local and regional authorities, and is consulted before decisions affecting regional interests are adopted.

The European Investment Bank provides loans in many economic sectors to help less-developed regions of the EU, to modernize enterprises, and to create employment.

## THE SINGLE OR COMMON MARKET

The original objectives of the EC stated in the Treaties of Rome were the development of economic activities, a balanced expansion, greater stability, a higher standard of living, and closer relations between the member states. The members were therefore supposed to establish a common market and to try for similar economic policies.

The first step was a customs union among the original six countries, which meant removing tariffs on internal trade and imposing a common external tariff against nonmember countries. The tariff is paid once on goods entering the EU; the goods then circulate within the EU without further tariff. By 1968 the union had been completed but other barriers to trade continued, preventing the establishment of a real common market. In the late 1980s the EC proposed new measures to eliminate barriers to free trade and movement. These included ending customs checks and border controls within the EC, har-

monization of technical standards, mutual acceptance of professional qualifications and diplomas, a Community market for financial services such as banking and insurance, and approximate taxation rates. The Single European Act, with its important amendments to the EC treaties, has facilitated the implementation of most of these measures to complete the internal market.

The essential objective of the SEA was the creation of a common market in which goods, services, people, and capital can move without obstacles such as frontier delays, fiscal barriers (including Value-Added Tax [VAT] rates and excise taxes), or technical obstructions such as national health and safety regulations. Tariffs and direct trade barriers have been ended since the mid-1960s.

In 2002 the EU is responsible for about 80 percent of all rules on the production, distribution, and exchange of goods, services, capital, and labor in the European market. It has removed barriers to the free movement of goods, put restrictions on state aids to enterprises, and fostered competition. Most of the provisions of the single market have, by the EEA, been extended to Norway, Iceland, and Liechtenstein. The EU has also acted to harmonize existing national standards and set common minimum standards in areas such as health, safety, environment, and consumer protection. Figure 8.4 shows the EU foreign investment flows, revealing the strong relationship between the Common Market and the United States. Figure 8.5 indicates the EU's sizeable share of world trade.

## EU POLICY ISSUES

### A Common Currency

Since 1979 the European Monetary System (EMS), now the EMU, attempted to coordinate economic policies and to stabilize the currencies of the EC countries. The exchange rate mechanism of the EMS obliged member states to limit fluctuations in the value of their currency to small amounts. Central banks of the states ensured that these limits were kept by raising or lowering interest rates, buying and selling

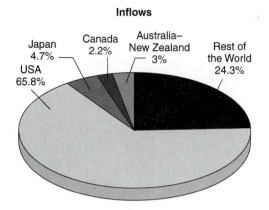

**Inflows**

Japan 4.7%
USA 65.8%
Canada 2.2%
Australia–New Zealand 3%
Rest of the World 24.3%

**Outflows**

Japan 3%
USA 66.1%
Canada 1.3%
Australia–New Zealand 1%
Rest of the World 28.6%

**Figure 8.4** EU FOREIGN DIRECT INVESTMENT, 1999

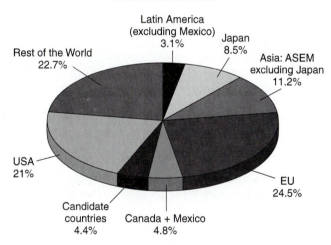

**Commercial Services**

Latin America (excluding Mexico) 3.1%
Japan 8.5%
Asia: ASEM excluding Japan 11.2%
Rest of the World 22.7%
USA 21%
Candidate countries 4.4%
Canada + Mexico 4.8%
EU 24.5%

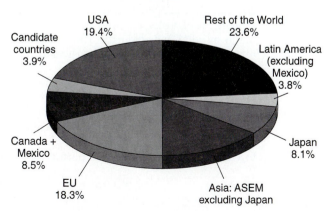

**Goods**

USA 19.4%
Candidate countries 3.9%
Rest of the World 23.6%
Latin America (excluding Mexico) 3.8%
Canada + Mexico 8.5%
Japan 8.1%
EU 18.3%
Asia: ASEM excluding Japan

**Figure 8.5** SHARE OF WORLD TRADE, 1999

*Source: Department of Commerce; World Bank.*

## REVIEW 8.5

### A TALE OF SEVEN CITIES

| City | Signed (and in force) | Number of Countries | Major Decisions |
|---|---|---|---|
| Paris | 1951 (1952) | 6 | Set up ECSC; pooling of some powers; Supranational High Authority |
| Rome | 1957 (1958) | 6 | Set up EEC and Euratom (nuclear energy) |
| Luxembourg | 1986 (1987) | 12 | Single European Act: abolished internal barriers to trade; cooperation procedure for some legislation; extended qualified majority voting |
| Maastricht | 1992 (1993) | 12 | Set up the EU; agreement on monetary union and euro; cooperation in justice and home affairs, and future common foreign and security policies (CFSP); more qualified voting; powers of EP enhanced |
| Amsterdam | 1997 (1999) | 15 | Common strategies in some areas and countries; extended scope of co-decision |
| Helsinki | 1999 | 15 | Summit agreement on rapid reaction force to be established by 2003 with ability to deploy 60,000 troops |
| Nice | 2000 (2001) | 15 | Agreement to prepare EU institutions for future expansion; more scope for qualified majority voting and enhanced cooperation |

currencies, and adjusting fiscal policies. The EMS helped to keep inflation and interest rates low and rates of investment high.

Not until the Maastricht Treaty was a basic plan for a single currency agreed on. A ten year process then began with a European exchange rate control mechanism. In 1999 a virtual currency, the euro, was used in electronic transfers by banks and international businesses, and brokers. The currencies of 12 participating EU countries were pegged to the euro. On January 1, 2002, the euro became the official single currency of those 12 countries, with banknotes and coins replacing the existing individual currencies. Changes of exchange rates are abolished, and money can now move freely across the frontiers between member states. The European Central Bank (ECB) in Frankfurt aims to maintain price stability and to support the EU's general economic policies, and sets interest rates.

The European Monetary Union (EMU) urges that states pursue policies that impose fiscal discipline in order to get balanced budgets.

## Security and Defense

Under the Maastricht Treaty, a common European foreign and security policy is to be decided by the member states by unanimity and intergovernmental cooperation. In certain areas, such as control of arms exports, decisions can be made by qualified majority. The treaty recognized the European Political Cooperation and the Western European Union (WEU).

The EPC is now superseded by the ESDP (CFSP in English), a common foreign and security policy. The ESDP is operational but its planned strong rapid reaction force of 60,000 will not be set up at least until 2003. The ESDP is supposed to complement rather than duplicate NATO. It

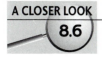

## NO MORE FRANC, NO MORE LIRA—NOW THE EURO

The EU countries using the euro are Austria, Belgium, Finland, France, Germany, Greece, Ireland, Italy, Luxembourg, the Netherlands, Portugal, and Spain.

Euro banknotes are available in denominations of €5, €10, €20, €50, €100, €200, and €500. The official symbol of the euro is €; the official abbreviation is EUR.

Each euro denomination has its own color and size. The higher the value, the larger the banknote.

Pictures of windows and gateways on the front of the banknotes symbolise openness. Pictures of bridges on the back symbolize cooperation.

EURO banknotes. The new money in the EU.

may also foster multinational coproduction of military equipment. The EU also plans to have a 5,000 strong police force as well as crisis management capabilities. The military strength and defense expenditures of the EU member nations are shown in Table 8.7.

## Justice and Home Affairs

Policies in the areas of justice and home affairs, according to the terms of the Maastricht Treaty, are to be decided on an intergovernmental level. They include immigration, asylum, drug trafficking, and other international crimes. The Maastricht Treaty provides for a central police office (Europol).

The Maastricht Treaty was amplified by the Amsterdam Treaty, signed in 1997, in effect in 1999. This pledged the EU members to combat discrimination on the basis of gender, race, religion, age, or sexual orientation. It also called for coordination in policies on unemployment and social matters. The treaty further argued for more shared decision making between the Council of Ministers and the European Parliament; and extended both the scope of qualified majority voting in the Council and the powers of the EP.

**TABLE 8.7**

**EU COUNTRIES AND DEFENSE, 1999**

| Country | Number in Military (thousands) | Defense Expenditure as % of GDP |
|---|---|---|
| Austria | 40.5 | 0.9 |
| Belgium | 41.8 | 1.5 |
| Denmark | 24.3 | 1.6 |
| Finland | 31.7 | 1.4 |
| France | 317.3 | 2.7 |
| Germany | 332.8 | 1.6 |
| Greece | 165.6 | 5.0 |
| Ireland | 11.5 | 0.9 |
| Italy | 265.5 | 2.0 |
| Luxembourg | 0.8 | 0.8 |
| Netherlands | 56.4 | 1.8 |
| Portugal | 49.7 | 2.2 |
| Spain | 186.5 | 1.3 |
| Sweden | 53.1 | 2.3 |
| United Kingdom | 212.4 | 2.6 |

*Source: NATO Review, Autumn 2001.*

## Common Agricultural Policy

In 1950 Robert Schuman said that "Europe will not be made all at once or according to a single general plan. It will be built through concrete achievements, which first create a de facto solidarity." Among the most significant achievements has been the Common Agricultural Policy (CAP).

The objectives of the CAP are to maintain food supplies at stable and reasonable prices, to improve agricultural productivity, and to ensure a fair standard of living for farmers. The CAP initially accounted for about 90 percent and now accounts for about 40–45 percent of total EU expenditure and covers about 90 percent of farm output in the 15 countries. A number of goals underlie the CAP: price guarantees for farmers, common prices for agricultural commodities, variable import levies to raise import prices to the EU level, and subsidies to EU farmers to enable them to export and sell at world prices, which are generally below the internal EU market.

The CAP has been successful and important for the farming community, now a much smaller part of the employed than 30 years ago, but it has also been severely criticized on several grounds. It is expensive, and some argue that it takes too large a part of the EU budget. Prices of agricultural commodities are higher than world market prices. The high prices stimulated production, resulting in surpluses that were very costly to store. These "wine-lakes" and "butter mountains" distorted competition and depressed world prices. Many outside countries, especially the United States, have accused the CAP of being protectionist by preventing or reducing imports. They have called in particular for the elimination of EU subsidies which encourage excessive and inefficient production.

In the mid-1980s, the EC reduced financial support for agricultural products in surplus, and price cuts were made in 1988. Further reforms of the high-cost CAP came in 1992 with sharp price cuts to restrict overproduction and the

## REVIEW
## 8.6

### MAJOR FEATURES OF THE EUROPEAN UNION

#### EUROPEAN COMMUNITY AND SINGLE MARKET

- Democratization of institutions; common European citizenship; qualified majority voting in some issues.
- Enhanced powers of European Parliament.
- Economic and monetary union: single currency; European Central Bank; single monetary policy; economic policy coordination.
- Principle of subsidiarity, decisions taken at lowest possible level.

#### FOREIGN AFFAIRS AND DEFENSE

- Common foreign policy: systematic cooperation; joint positions and actions.
- Common defense policy based on the Western European Union (WEU).

#### JUSTICE AND HOME AFFAIRS

- Enhanced cooperation: customs asylum policy; rules governing the crossing of external borders of the member states; immigration policy.
- Combating drug addiction; combating international fraud.
- Judicial cooperation on crime and terrorism; European Police Office (Europol).

break of the links between price support and production. A system of price guarantees is now combined with direct payments to farmers.

# FOREIGN AFFAIRS

## Trade

The EU is the world's largest trading unit accounting for about 20 percent of world trade. (see Figure 8.5). It therefore played a significant role in GATT and now has an important role in the World Trade Organization. The European Commission, on behalf of the EU, negotiates all external trade arrangements, which are then formally accepted by the Council of Ministers by majority vote.

The United States is the European Union's major trading partner, and the two cooperate on numerous issues, not only on bilateral matters but also an international forums including the UN, WTO, NATO, and the G-8, the major developed countries. The EU and the United States account for over a third of the global economy. Each is the other's largest single trading partner and source of, and destination for, foreign investment.

## Diplomatic Relations and Development Programs

The EU has diplomatic relations with over 140 countries, varied trade agreements with countries throughout the world, and association agreements with others. Two of these external links are particularly interesting. One is the relationship between the EU and the European Free

Trade Association (EFTA), which now includes four countries with a combined population of 12 million. Both the EU and EFTA have abolished customs duties and restrictions on trade in manufactured goods in a free trade area, and in 1991 the two bodies agreed on the creation of a European Economic Area (EEA). This involves a single market with free movement of goods, services, people, and capital, but without EFTA having any vote on EU laws.

A second important link is with the countries of the third world. Since the Yaoundé Convention of 1963, the EU has extended special preferential trading arrangements to the ex-colonies of EU countries. The EU is now linked to 78 African, Caribbean, and Pacific (ACP) countries through a series of Lomé Conventions (now renamed Cotonou) the latest of which was renewed in 2000. The ACP countries are freed from customs duties on almost all their exports to the EU and also receive financial aid from the EU.

Most of the EU's external aid at first was concentrated on former colonies; now much more goes to Central and Eastern Europe. The EU also has multilateral relations with international organizations and with other regional groupings. The EU has been the largest donor of nonmilitary aid to the Palestinians.

Not only is the EU the largest single donor of official development assistance in the world; it now also focuses on the reduction of poverty in third world or developing countries, and on institution building in those countries. The EU is the leading importer of goods from the third world and provides full market access in EU countries for products originating from those countries.

**A CLOSER LOOK**

**8.7**

### CENTRAL AND EASTERN EUROPE

The terms Central Europe and Eastern Europe are used for indefinite groupings of countries. One classification is the following:

*Central Europe:* Poland, Czech Republic, Slovakia, Hungary, Slovenia
*Eastern Europe:* Russian Federation, Ukraine, Romania, Bulgaria

The EU has concluded cooperation arrangements with many other countries, including 12 Eastern and Southern Mediterranean nations, which have been given duty-free access for their industrial exports and agricultural trade and have received financial grants and loans. The EU has also entered into a Euro-Arab dialogue, discussing agricultural, trade, and technical matters with Arab countries.

Since the decline of Communism and the end of Soviet control in Eastern Europe, the EU has become involved in the affairs of Eastern Europe in a number of ways. It coordinated the 1989 PHARE program in which 24 countries sent aid to Poland, Hungary, and other Central and Eastern European countries. It entered into bilateral trade agreements with each of the Eastern European countries and assisted in addressing their environmental problems. This has meant allowing these states a degree of free trade with the EU, granting them aid and loans,

and providing for a number of joint projects, including funds for reconstruction programs and humanitarian aid.

## THE EU'S FUTURE

The European Union has as official objectives the creation of "an organized and vital Europe," laying "the foundations of an ever closer union among the peoples of Europe," and combining together to "contribute to the prosperity of the peoples." The EU has already become an important part of European politics and well-being. Many decisions have been made that affect the states and their citizens in important ways (see Table 8.8).

At this point the nature of the EU has not been clearly defined. It is still a confederation of independent states that have pooled some powers and some aspects of sovereignty in economic

**TABLE 8.8**

**THE STATE OF THE EUROPEAN UNION, 2001**

| | Population (millions) | GDP per capita ($ thousand) | Employment as % of Workforce | | | Sectors as % of GDP | | |
|---|---|---|---|---|---|---|---|---|
| | | | Agriculture | Industry | Services | Agriculture | Industry | Services |
| EU 15 | 377.6 | 20.8 | | | | | | |
| Belgium | 10.2 | 25.0 | 2.0 | 25.0 | 73.0 | 1.4 | 26.0 | 72.6 |
| Denmark | 5.3 | 25.5 | 4.0 | 17.0 | 79.0 | 3.0 | 25.0 | 72.0 |
| Germany | 82.0 | 23.4 | 2.8 | 33.4 | 63.8 | 1.2 | 30.4 | 68.4 |
| Greece | 10.5 | 17.2 | 20.0 | 21.0 | 59.0 | 8.3 | 27.3 | 64.4 |
| Spain | 39.4 | 18.0 | 8.0 | 28.0 | 64.0 | 4.0 | 31.0 | 65.0 |
| France | 59.0 | 24.4 | 4.0 | 25.0 | 71.0 | 3.0 | 26.1 | 70.6 |
| Ireland | 3.7 | 21.6 | 8.0 | 28.0 | 64.0 | 4.0 | 38.0 | 58.0 |
| Italy | 57.6 | 22.1 | 5.5 | 32.6 | 61.9 | 2.5 | 30.4 | 67.1 |
| Luxembourg | 0.4 | 36.4 | 2.5 | 14.3 | 83.2 | 1.0 | 30.0 | 69.0 |
| Netherlands | 15.8 | 24.4 | 4.0 | 23.0 | 73.0 | 3.3 | 26.3 | 70.4 |
| Austria | 8.1 | 25.0 | 3.0 | 29.0 | 68.0 | 2.2 | 30.4 | 67.4 |
| Portugal | 10.0 | 15.8 | 10.0 | 30.0 | 60.0 | 4.0 | 36.0 | 60.0 |
| Finland | 5.2 | 22.9 | 8.0 | 28.0 | 64.0 | 3.5 | 29.0 | 67.5 |
| Sweden | 8.9 | 22.2 | 2.0 | 24.0 | 74.0 | 2.2 | 27.9 | 69.9 |
| Britain | 59.2 | 22.8 | 1.0 | 19.0 | 80.0 | 1.7 | 24.9 | 73.4 |

*Source: Eurostat.*

matters, but that retain their authority to deal internally with law and order, foreign policy, and defense. The EU, however, can act in some areas, including trade, agriculture, competition, transport, research and technology, environment, and education.

Strong differences exist between those calling for more supranational government and more EU impact on citizens and those who think that active cooperation between sovereign states is the best way to build a successful European community, and would be content with little more than an intergovernmental body. Some favor a single market without a political union; others prefer a political union with a wide range of centralized policies. Some want a community focused mainly on deregulation, competition, and capital mobility; others call for a more positive role in world affairs in security as well as economic matters.

Differences on two matters are of great concern to the United States. The first is the dispute about the EU's subsidies on agricultural exports and the degree of European protectionism. The United States claims that these subsidies are unfair and that they distort markets in the rest of the world. The EU in the past, in a dispute now largely resolved, restricted imports of bananas from American companies, and also genetically modified foods produced by American farmers. Yet the EU takes some 20 percent of U.S. exports and accounts for half of all direct foreign investment.

The second issue is that of defense. Some in the European Union believe that there should be a strong European pillar in NATO on which Europe could rely for its defense. Others argue that Europe should be responsible for its own security and defense, and suggest that a European force would be the best organization for this purpose. France and Germany proposed in 1991 a joint military brigade that would be the basis for a European corps.

There are also important disagreements within the EU over questions such as the relative merits of free trade and protectionism; a complete market economy or one with the state intervening to a considerable degree; the cost of the CAP, the cost of regional aid, the extent of welfare systems and of social rights; the enlarge-

ment of the EU to embrace new members, in particular Central and Eastern European states, the weight of voting allotted in the Council to the new states, the number of working languages, and the problem of democratic control over the work of EU institutions. Resolution of these questions will not come easily to a group of states that have had such a long and complex history, and that now must reformulate their attitudes toward the former Soviet Union and Central and Eastern Europe and toward policies on many issues, such as arms control, nuclear proliferation, the Middle East, the United Nations, and the United States. The political dimension of the EU is still to be decided.

That dimension will be affected in a variety of ways. France in 2002 is no longer dominant in the EU with 15 present and more future members and with Germany as a united country. Dramatic international affairs have led to calls for collective European military action, combining joint operations, rationalizing defense and other expenditures, and a European peacekeeping force. New members of the EU have to be incorporated while decision making may be changed, and obtaining a consensus may be more difficult with those countries at different economic levels and different degrees of familiarity with democratic practice. The EU faces an open, interesting, and challenging future for its hybrid structure, which includes some federal features and many intergovernmental ones, and many forms of cooperation in different policy areas, and with sharing power between the institutions of the EU and between those institutions and the member states.

What lies ahead? The EU has been a unique success economically, as shown by its growth in GDP and trade, and by its low tariffs, most of which are expected to end in 2004, its low nontariff barriers to trade, and its open services sector. In return, the EU wants all its trading partners to eliminate or reduce their import duties and barriers such as technical regulations, dumping of goods, subsidies by governments and other public authorities which reduce production costs or costs of exports to the EU, and barriers to a global market in services.

The question now is whether the EU can be an equally potent political and military presence.

It has ambitions to play an important role in world affairs. Javier Solana, currently high representative for the CFSP and secretary general of the Council, as virtual foreign minister is anxious to coordinate the foreign policies of the EU members. Already, the EU has intervened in some global issues; among them are environmental policies, ratification of the Kyoto Protocol, conservation of biodiversity, and emergency assistance and relief to victims of natural disasters or armed conflict outside the EU. It has acted in various international crises, imposing sanctions on the Ivory Coast for rigging the election in 2001, and sanctions on Robert Mugabe in Zimbabwe in 2002 for his expulsion of the EU election observer mission. The EU helped enforce peace in Sierra Leone and Macedonia. It aims at promoting and protecting human rights, developing and consolidating democracy and the rule of law, and combatting discrimination and racism.

To advance progress, a constitutional convention was launched in February 2002 which will propose changes to make decision making in the EU more efficient before the admission of new members. Chaired by former French president Valéry Giscard d'Estaing, this convention of 105 politicians from 28 countries appreciates that the present EU institutions, originally designed for six member states, is inadequate for the larger present and projected membership, which is likely to lead to a more complex and fluid pattern of relationships among the members. Already the EU faces tensions between larger and smaller, between richer and poorer countries.

Is the EU at a crossroads or en route to an "ever closer union"? It will not be easy to resolve the competing views of federalists, wanting stronger powers for the European Commission and Parliament, and those members who are reluctant to increase those powers.

## Thinking Critically

1. Do you think that a Euro-identity is emerging? How might it be affected by immigration into the EU countries?

2. To what extent has the EU diluted the traditional strength of national sovereignty? What does the pooling of sovereignty in the EU mean?

3. Can the EU become a body that can use military force and play a role in foreign policy? Is it time to reinvent NATO?

4. What are the main reasons for EU criticism of the United States?

5. How does the role of the European Commission compare with that of the Council of Ministers in decision making in the EU?

6. Is the EU likely to develop into a federal system? How will the entrance of the present candidate nations into the EU affect this?

## KEY TERMS

Benelux *(455)*
Committee of Permanent Representatives (Coreper) *(468)*
Common Agricultural Policy (CAP) *(476)*
Common Foreign and Security Policy (CFSP) *(474)*
Common Market *(472)*
Council of Europe *(455)*
Economic and Monetary Union (EMU) *(472)*
European Atomic Energy Community (Euratom) *(458)*
European Central Bank (ECB) *(474)*
European Coal and Steel Community (ECSC) *(456)*
European Community (EC) *(458)*
European Economic Area *(458)*
European Free Trade Association (EFTA) *(458)*
European Parliament *(470)*
General Agreement on Trade and Tariffs (GATT) *(457)*
Maastricht Treaty *(458)*
North Atlantic Treaty Organization (NATO) *(455)*
Organization for Economic Cooperation and Development (OECD) *(454)*
Schengen Agreements *(461)*
Single European Act *(458)*
Treaty of Nice *(474)*
Treaty of Paris *(456)*

# FURTHER READINGS

Archer, Clive, and Fiona Butler. *The European Union: Structure and Process,* 2nd ed. (London: Pinter, 1996).

Armstrong, Kenneth, and Simon Bulmer. *The Governance of the Single European Market* (Manchester: Manchester University Press, 1998).

Cram, Laura, et al., eds. *Developments in the European Union* (New York: St. Martin's, 1999).

Dehousse, Renaud. *The European Court of Justice* (New York: St. Martin's, 1998).

Dinan, Desmond. *Ever Closer Union?* 2nd ed. (Boulder, CO: Rienner, 1999).

Duchêne, François. *Jean Monnet: The First Statesman of Interdependence* (New York: Norton, 1994).

Edwards, Geoffrey, and David Spence, eds. *The European Commission,* 2nd ed. (London: Cartermill, 1997).

George, Stephen, and Ian Bache. *Politics in the European Union* (New York: Oxford University Press, 2001).

Guttman, Robert J., ed. *Europe in the New Century* (Boulder, CO: Rienner, 2001).

Hayes-Renshaw, Fiona, and Helen Wallace. *The Council of Ministers* (New York: St. Martin's, 1997).

Lasok, Dominik. *Law and Institutions of the European Communities,* 7th ed. (London: Lexis, 1998).

Laurent, Pierre-Henri, and Marc Maresceau, eds. *The State of the European Union* (Boulder, CO: Rienner, 1998).

McCormick, John. *Understanding the European Union* (New York: St. Martin's, 1999).

Nugent, Neill. *The European Commission* (New York: Palgrave, 2001).

Nugent, Neill. *The Government and Politics of the European Union,* 4th ed. (Basingstoke: Macmillan, 1999).

Peterson, John, and Elizabeth Bomberg. *Decision-Making in the European Union* (New York: St. Martin's, 1999).

Pinder, John. *The Building of the European Union,* 3rd ed. (New York: Oxford University Press, 1998).

Pond, Elizabeth. *The Rebirth of Europe* (Washington, DC: Brookings, 1999).

Rhodes, Carolyn, ed. *The European Union in the World Community* (Boulder, CO: Rienner, 1998).

Richardson, Jeremy, ed. *European Union: Power and Policy-Making* (New York: Routledge, 1996).

Urwin, Derek. *The Community of Europe,* 2nd ed. (New York: Longman, 1995).

Wallace, Helen, ed. *Interlocking Dimensions of European Integration* (New York: Palgrave, 2001).

Wallace, Helen, and William Wallace, eds. *Policy-Making in the European Union,* 4th ed. (London: Oxford University Press, 2000).

Whitman, Richard G. *From Civilian Power to Superpower? The International Identity of the European Union* (New York: St. Martin's, 1998).

Wind, Marlene. *Sovereignty and European Integration: Towards a Post-Hobbesian Order* (New York: Palgrave, 2001).

# WEB SITES

**www.europa.eu.int**
Information on the European Commission.

**www.ue.eu.int**
Information on the European Council of Ministers.

**www.curia.eu.int**
Information on the European Court of Justice.

**www.europarl.eu.int/groups/**
Information on political groups in the European Parliament.

**www.europarl.eu.int**
Information on the European Parliament.

**www.coe.int**
Information on the Council of Europe.

**www.nato.int**
Information on NATO.

**www.weu.int**
Information on the Western European Union.

**www.eurunion.org/infores/euindex.htm**
Index of European Web sites.

# Credits

| PAGE | CREDIT |
|---|---|
| 37 | Steve Benbow/Woodfin Camp & Associates |
| 38 | AP/Wide World Photos |
| 76 | Ken Goff Photos/SIPA Press |
| 93 | John Giles/AP/Wide World Photos |
| 109 | Fievez/SIPA Press |
| 119 | Philippe Laurenson/Reuters/Getty Images |
| 133 | Gregoire Korganow/Getty Images |
| 136 | AP/Wide World Photos |
| 149 | AP/Wide World Photos |
| 173 | Christian Vioujard/Getty Images |
| 185 | Bettmann/CORBIS |
| 200 | Patrick Piel/Getty Images |
| 222 | Michael Urban/Reuters/Getty Images |
| 224 | Kappeler/DDP/SIPA Press |
| 227 | German Information Center |
| 259 | Woodfin Camp & Associates |

| PAGE | CREDIT |
|---|---|
| 307 | Woodfin Camp & Associates |
| 320 | Pizzoli Alberto/Corbis Sygma |
| 321 | Luciano Mellace/Reuters/Getty Images |
| 354 | Daniel Beltra/Getty Images |
| 364 | AP/Wide World Photos |
| 367 | Despotovic Dusko/Corbis Sygma |
| 371 | D. Jenidi/Getty Images |
| 384 | Erica Lansner/Black Star/Stockphoto |
| 400 | Superstock, Inc. |
| 404 | Mike Yamasha/Woodfin Camp & Associates |
| 443 | Christian Sarramon/CORBIS |
| 446 | Bettmann/CORBIS |
| 465 | Isopress/Getty Images |
| 468 | Courtesy European Union |
| 475 | Babyar/SIPA Press |

# Index

Page references followed by *t* and *f* refer to tables and figures respectively.

Abitur, 197, 198
Abortion
  in Germany, 247
  in Italy, 270t
AC. See Autonomous communities
Accession, German, 180, 246
ACP countries, 456t
Act of Settlement (Britain, 1701), 40
Act of Union (Britain, 1707), 34
Adenauer, Konrad, 171, 204, 224,
  242–243, 455
Administrative federalism, 221
Afghanistan, war in (2001), 249
Agence France-Presse, 169
Agence Havas, 169
Agrarian parties, characteristics of,
  20t
Alfonso XIII, King of Spain, 333, 366
Algeria, 123–124, 135, 153
Allen, Christopher, 239
Alliance 90 (Germany), 195t, 208,
  215t, 230t
Alliance for Freedom/for Good
  Government (Italy), 278, 285t
Alliance for Freedom (Italy), 279
  and election of 1996, 286–287, 286t
  partners in, 276
  policies of, 313–314
Alliance for Germany, 245
Alliance for Jobs (Germany), 220
Almunia, Joaquím, 339, 354
Amadeus of Saboya, 333
Amato, Giuliano, 265, 283–284, 294t,
  296, 301, 312–313, 313–314
Amparo appeal, 378
Amsterdam, 400f
Amsterdam Treaty (1997), 110, 470,
  474t, 475
Anarchists, in Italy, 259
Ancien régime, 121, 122, 136
Andalusia, 326f, 341
  autonomy for, 359t, 376t
  language in, 341
Andreotti, Giulio, 282, 284, 293t, 294t
Anglican Church, 51–52, 52t, 68, 89
Anguita, Julio, 338, 355, 356
Anti-Revolutionary Party
  (Netherlands), 402, 403t, 404,
  410t, 416, 419, 421
AP. See Popular Alliance
Arana, Sabino, 356
Archbishops of Canterbury and York,
  51, 52, 89
Argentina, 85
Arias Navarro, Carlos, 336, 338
Aristocracy, in Western Europe, 7
Armada, Alfonso, 364–365
Atlantic Alliance, 242
Attlee, Clement, 60f

Austria
  currency, 475
  defeat by Prussia, 181
  economy of, 478t
  and European Free Trade
    Association, 458
  and European Union, 459
  foreign residents of, 237t
  military in, 475t
  population of, 478t
  regional organization memberships,
    463t
Autarky, in Franco regime, 341–342
Autonomous communities (ACs),
  375–376, 376t
Autonomous Enterprises (Italy), 298
Aznar, José María, 354f
  policies of, 387, 392
  political career of, 353, 354,
    358–359
  support for, 369

Backbenchers, 80t
Bagehot, Walter, 41, 76
Balkans
  profile of, 3
  UN peacekeeping in, 104
Balladur, E., 150, 152t, 154
Baltic states, 3, 5
Banfield, Edward, 268
Bank(s)
  Bank of England, 75
  Bank of Italy, 312
  Bank of Spain, 388–389
  Bundesbank, 229, 240, 245, 249
  Cassa per il Mezzogiorno, 304
  Central Bank (Netherlands), 440
  European Central Bank, 249, 316,
    456t, 474
  European Investment Bank, 472
Baptist Church, 52
Barre, R., 152t, 154
Barrionuevo, José, 393
Basic Law. See Germany, constitution
  (Basic Law)
Basic Treaty (1972), 243
Basque country (Euskadi), 326f, 381
  autonomy for, 334, 336, 359t, 375,
    376t
  economy of, 340, 341
  language of, 340–341
  media in, 347
  nationalist parties in, 349, 356–357
  political terrorism and, 383
  public policy and, 382
  Spanish military and, 363
  unions in, 360, 361
Basque Homeland and Freedom (ETA).
  See Euskadi Ta Askatasuna

Basque Nationalist Party (PNV), 356
  alliances, 358, 369
  in Cortes, 370
  ideology of, 349, 351f
  support for, 352t
Basque Solidarity party (EA), 351f
Battle of the Boyne, 46
Battle of the Diamond, 46
BDA. See Federation of German
  Employers
BDI. See German Federation of
  Industry
Beatrix, Queen of Netherlands, 430
Belgium
  Benelux and, 4
  currency of, 475
  economy of, 478t
  foreign residents of, 237t
  independence of, 402
  military of, 475t
  monarchy in, 6t
  NATO and, 28, 29t
  population of, 478t
  regional organization memberships,
    463t
Benelux countries, 4, 447, 455, 457
Beregovoy, Pierre, 144
Berlin, 189, 213
Berlin blockade, 184, 455
Berlin Wall, 4, 184, 198, 219, 242
Berlusconi, Silvio
  leadership of, 278, 287
  policies of, 316, 318, 319–320, 322,
    323
  political career of, 262, 275, 276,
    284, 296, 314, 315
  as prime minister, 294t, 301
  scandals, 288
Beveridge Report, 101
Biedenkopf, Kurt, 218
Bills of rights
  Britain and, 40, 41, 42, 45, 49, 111
  in German Basic Law, 223, 233,
    235–236
Birth rates
  in France, 116
  in Germany, 178
  in Great Britain, 34
  in Italy, 254, 269–270
  in Netherlands, 398
  in Spain, 328
  in Western Europe, 15t
Bismarck, Otto von, 181
Black Shirts, 260
Blair, Tony, 93f
  background of, 83
  EU and, 110
  policies of, 54, 84, 85, 101, 102, 111
  political career of, 60f, 72, 82

Blanco, Luis Carrero, 335, 336
Blum, Leon, 142
Böll, Heinrich, 201
Bonaparte, Joseph, 332
Bonn, 189
Borselino, Paolo, 265
Bosnia, Srebenica massacre, 418, 447
Bosnia-Herzegovina, 3
Bossi, Umberto, 262, 265
Brandt, Willy, 206, 217–218, 224, 242–243
Bretton Woods system, 304, 307, 312
Britain. See Great Britain
British Commonwealth, 36, 104, 105–108
    member nations, 106f–107f
British National Party, 63
British pound, 35, 37
Brown, Gordon, 85
Brussels Treaty Organization (BTO), 455
BTO. See Brussels Treaty Organization
Bulgaria, 2, 4t, 460t
Bundesbank, 229, 240, 245, 249
Bundesrat. See Germany, legislative branch
Bundestag. See Germany, legislative branch
Bürgerinitiativen, 199–200, 212
Business and industry
    in Franco regime, 360, 392
    in Great Britain, 55–56, 98–100
    as interest group
        in France, 132
        in Germany, 212
        in Great Britain, 74–75
        in Italy, 289–290
        in Spain, 359–360
    in Italy, 306–308, 311, 317
    as political power, 120
By-elections, in Great Britain, 64

Cabinet government systems, 24–25. See also individual nations
Cabinet Office (Great Britain), 85
Callaghan, James, 60f, 83
Calvinism, in Netherlands, 401, 403, 404, 406, 419–420, 421, 428t
Calvinist Federation, 417t, 423, 429
Calvinist Party (SGP), 411t, 417t, 420f, 423, 437t, 438t
Calvinist Union (GPV), 411t, 417t, 423, 425t, 437t, 438t
Calvo Sotelo, Leopoldo, 338, 350, 364, 386
Camancho, Marcelino, 361
Cambridge University, 54–55, 64, 83, 87, 95
Campaign for Nuclear Disarmament, 74
Campaign for Social Democracy, 69
Canada
    GDP of, 187t
    NATO and, 28, 29t
    regional organization memberships, 463t
    trade, 473f
Canary Coalition, 358
CAP. See Common Agricultural Policy

Carey, George, 52
Carlism, 375
Carrero Blanco, Luis, 336
Carrillo, Santiago, 355
Carstens, Karl, 222
Cassa per il Mezzogiorno, 304
Catalonia, 326f, 381
    autonomy for, 334, 338, 359t, 375, 376t
    economy of, 340, 341
    language of, 340–341
    media in, 347
    parties in, 349–350, 355, 356–357
    public policy and, 382
    unions in, 361
Catholic Caritas Association, 198
Catholic People's Party, 407, 409, 421
Catholicism
    in France, 14t, 116, 121, 124, 127–128
    in Germany, 14t, 178, 198–199, 213–214, 219
    in Great Britain, 14t, 44–45, 52, 52t, 68
    in Italy
        in 1990s, 286
        family life and, 268
        Fascists and, 260–261
        Feminist movement and, 271–272
        politics and, 262–263, 279–280
        tensions with state, 268–269
    in Netherlands
        in government, 403t, 405t
        history of, 401
        pillarization and, 406–407
        politics and, 404, 409–410, 419–420, 421t, 427, 428t
    in Spain, 345, 361–363
    in Western Europe, 14, 14t
CCD. See Democratic Christian Center
CCOO. See Workers' Commissions
CDA. See Christian Democratic Appeal
CDC. See Democratic Convergence of Catalonia
CDS. See Centre démocratique et social; Social and Democratic Center Party
CDU. See Christian Democratic Union; Unitary Democratic Center
CDU/CSU
    Bundesrat and, 230–231, 230t
    Bundestag and, 205t
    policies and positions, 217, 220, 242
    support for, 211, 212, 214, 215t, 216, 216t, 217–219, 218t, 221, 223
    women and, 195, 195t
Censure, in France, 159–160
Center Party (Germany), 204
Central Bank (Netherlands), 440
Central Bureau of Statistics (Netherlands), 440
Central Committee of German Catholics, 213
Central Europe
    and decline of communism, 2–5

definition of, 477
    EU aid to, 477, 478
    profile of, 4t
Central Planning Bureau (Netherlands), 409, 440
Centralization. See also Decentralization
    in France, 120–121, 128, 167–168
    in Italy, 263–264
    in Spain, under Franco, 375, 381, 383
Centre démocratique et social (CDS), 141
Centre National des Jeunes Agriculteurs (CNJA), 134
CEOE. See Spanish Confederation of Employers' Organization
CEPYME. See Spanish Confederation of Small- and Medium-sized Firms
CFSP. See Common Foreign and Security Policy
CFTC. See Confédération Française des Travailleurs Chrétiens
CGB. See Christian Trade Union Federation of Germany
CGC. See Confédération Générale des Cadres
CGIL. See Italian General Confederation of Labor
CGPME. See Confédération Générale des Petites et Mayennes Entreprises
CGT. See Confédération Générale du Travail
CGT Force Ouvrière, 131
Chaban-Delmas, Jacques, 136, 140
Chamber of Deputies (France), 155
Charlemagne, 180
Charles, Prince of England, 34, 48
Charles X, King of France, 121, 122t
Chirac, Jacques, 173f
    foreign policy of, 171
    policies of, 147–148, 149–150, 153
    political career of, 137, 140, 141–142, 151, 152t, 154, 155
Christian Democratic Appeal (CDA), 420f, 421
    alliances, 410, 411
    formation of, 410
    membership and resources, 425t, 426
    in parliament, 437t, 438t
    policies of, 424, 424t, 425t
    support for, 411t, 417t, 418, 427, 427t, 428, 428t
Christian Democratic Party
    in France, 127, 141, 143
    ideology of, 20, 20t, 21t
    in Italy (DC), 276–277, 276t
        alliances, 281–282, 283
        corruption and, 282, 283
        decline of, 269, 281, 284, 285
        ideology of, 9–10
        policies of, 263
        postwar dominance of, 279–283
        support for, 267–268, 282
Christian Democratic Union (CDU), 204–205. See also CDU/CSU

allies of, 204, 207
Bundesrat and, 230, 230t
constituency, 219
ideology of, 9–10
policies, 200, 212
reunification and, 245
structure and financing of,
    209–210, 210–211, 210t
support for, 215t, 216, 216t,
    220–221, 221t
women in, 195–196
Christian Historical Party, 410t, 421
Christian Social Union (CSU), 204,
    210t, 215t, 230t. See also
    CDU/CSU
Christian Trade Union Federation of
    Germany (CGB), 212
Christian Union (CU), 411t, 420f, 423
Christianity. See also Catholicism
    in France, 13–14, 14t, 116, 121,
        124, 127–128
    in Germany, 13, 14t, 178, 180,
        198–199, 213–214, 219
    in Great Britain, 13, 14t, 34, 44–45,
        51–52, 52t, 68, 89
    in Netherlands, 13, 14t, 398,
        406–407
        history of, 401, 403, 404, 406
        political parties and, 419–420,
            421, 427, 428t
    in Northern Ireland, 44–45
Church of England. See Anglican
    Church
Churchill, Winston, 8, 60f, 454, 455
Ciampi, Carlo Azeglio
    as president, 313–314
    as prime minister, 284, 292, 294t,
        296, 296t
CIS. See Commonwealth of
    Independent States
CISL. See Italian Confederation of
    Workers' Unions
Citizen initiatives (Bürgerinitiativen),
    in Germany, 199–200, 212
CiU. See Convergence and Union
    Party
Civil Guard (Spain), 363–365, 364f
CNEL. See National Committee on
    Energy and Labor
CNJA. See Centre National des Jeunes
    Agriculteurs
CNPF. See Conseil National du
    Patronat Français
CNT. See National Confederation of
    Labor
Codetermination Act (Germany, 1975),
    239–240
Cohabitation, in France, 154–155, 172
Cold War, 8, 9t
    and decline of Communism, 2–5
    Germany and, 184
    Italy and, 322
    Netherlands and, 447
Commissariat général au Plan,
    168–170
Commissary of the Government, 297
Commissions of Inquiry (Netherlands),
    435–436

Committee of Permanent
    Representatives (Coreper), 456t,
    465, 468
Committee of the Regions, 472
Common Agricultural Policy (CAP),
    476–477, 479
Common Foreign and Security Policy
    (CFSP), 456t
Common law, British, 40
Common Market. See European
    Economic Community (EEC)
"Common Program of the Left," 143
Commonwealth Immigration Act
    (Britain, 1962), 45
Commonwealth Ministerial Action
    Group, 105
Commonwealth of Independent States
    (CIS), 4, 5
Communes (France), 166
Communes (Italy), 257, 299
Communism. See also Communist
    Party
    decline of, Eastern Europe and, 2–5
    Eurocommunism, 21, 282, 355, 453
    in France, 130–131, 145, 453
    unions and, 145
Communist Party
    in France, 120, 126, 137, 139t,
        142–146, 147
    in Germany, 200f
    in Great Britain, 69
    in Italy. See Italian Communist
        Party (PCI); Refounded
        Communism (RC) party
    in Netherlands (CPN), 405t, 410t,
        411t, 423
    in Spain. See Spanish Communist
        Party
    in Western Europe, 16, 20t, 21, 22t
Comte, Auguste, 163
Concordat of 1929, 261, 269
Concordat of 1953, 362
Conde, Mário, 393
Confédération Française des
    Travailleurs Chrétiens (CFTC),
    131
Confédération Générale des Cadres
    (CGC), 132
Confédération Générale des Petites et
    Mayennes Entreprises (CGPME),
    132
Confédération Générale du Travail
    (CGT), 130–132
Confederation of Netherlands Industry
    (VNO-NCW), 429
Conference of Catholic Bishops, 213
Conference of Presidents (France), 157
Confindustria, 288, 312
Congress of Vienna, 181
Conseil National du Patronat Français
    (CNPF), 132
Consensus, in British political system,
    41–42
Conservative-Liberal Party
    (Netherlands), 403t
Conservative Party
    characteristics of, 20t, 22–23, 23t
    in Great Britain

candidates, 42–43, 54, 64–65,
    65t
constituency, 51, 52–53, 58,
    66–68, 69, 75
leadership, 72
organization, 69–72
in Parliament, 72
power in, 73–74, 73t
strength of, 48t, 59, 60f, 61–62,
    61f, 61t, 62t, 63, 69
in Netherlands, 403t
Conservative Policy Forum, 70
CONSOB (Italy), 298
Consociationalism, in Netherlands,
    406, 407–408, 407f
Constitutional Council (France), 156,
    160
Constitutional democracies, 40
Constitutional monarchy, 77
Conventions, in Great Britain, 41–42,
    79–81, 82
Convergence and Union Party (CiU),
    356–357
    alliances, 358, 369
    ideology of, 351f
    as regional party, 349–350
    support for, 352t
Cooperative Party, 70–71
Coreper. See Committee of Permanent
    Representatives
Corn Laws (Britain 1846), 36
Corporatism
    in Germany, 211
    in Netherlands, 406, 408–409, 440
Cossiga, Francesco, 294t, 296, 296t
Cotonou Conventions, 477
Council of Europe, 454, 455, 456t, 457
    member states, 463t
Council of Ministers
    in European Union, 465, 467–468,
        467t
    role of, 457, 466–467, 470, 472,
        475
    voting in, 458, 459
    in France, 154
    in Italy, 292, 297
    in Netherlands, 430–431
        background of ministers, 433
        formation of, 430, 431–433
    in Spain, 337
Council of State (France), 166
Council of State (Italy), 298
Court of Auditors, 472
Court of Cassation, 300
Court of International Justice, 445
Couve de Murville, M., 152t, 153
CPN. See Communist Party, in
    Netherlands
Craxi, Bettino, 269, 277, 282–283,
    284, 294t
Cresson, Edith, 12, 144
Crime, in Great Britain, 55
Croatia, 3
Cromwell, Oliver, 40
CSM. See Supreme Council of the
    Magistrature
CSU. See Christian Social Union
Cyprus, 460t, 463t

Czech Republic, 4t, 460t, 463t
  NATO and, 28, 29t
Czechoslovakia, Soviet Union in,
  145–146

D'66. See Democrats '66
DAG. See German Salaried Employees
  Union
Dahrendorf, Ralf, 182
D'Alema, Massimo, 294t, 313, 321f,
  324
Dawidowicz, Lucy S., 183
D'Azeglio, Massimo, 257
DBB. See German Federation of Civil
  Servants
DC. See Christian Democratic Party, in
  Italy
De Gasperi, Alcide, 279, 280, 293t
de Gaulle, Charles, 136f
  career of, 138–139, 140, 142, 147
  European Union and, 454
  in exile, 123
  and Fifth Republic, 118, 122, 122t,
    124, 134
  foreign policy of, 170, 171
  and presidential power, 136,
    146–147, 150–151, 153–154,
    172–173
  and referendums, 149
  resignation of, 167
de Maizière, Lothar, 245, 247, 248
De Nicola, Enrico, 296t
de Ruyter, Admiral, 445
Decentralization. See also
    Centralization
  in Great Britain, 98–100, 110–111
  in Italy. See Italy, regions of
  in Spain. See Spain, regions of
Declaration of Commonwealth
    Principles (1971), 105–106
Declaration of the Rights of Man and
    the Citizen (France, 1789), 17,
    121
Decree laws (Spain), 372
Decree on Information and Freedom
    (1977), 346
Delors, Jacques, 171
Democracy
  constitutional, 40
  healthy, indications of, 219
  liberal, characteristics of, 16–17
  Spanish transition to, 330,
    336–339, 342–343, 343t,
    364–365, 367–368, 387
  twentieth-century rise of, 330
Democratic Christian Center (CCD),
  276, 286t, 287t
Democratic Convergence of Catalonia
  (CDC), 356–357
Democratic Party of the Left (PDS),
  277, 277t, 284, 285t, 286t, 292
Democratic Union of Catalonia,
  356–357
Démocratie libérale party, 141
Democrats '66 (D'66), 420f, 422–423
  alliances, 410, 412
  in cabinet, 430t

membership and resources, 425t,
    426
  in parliament, 437t, 438t
  policies of, 424, 424t, 425t
  support for, 411, 411t, 417t, 418,
    427, 427t, 428, 428t
Democrats of the Left (DS), 277, 287t,
  323, 324
den Uyl, Joop, 410
Denationalization. See also
    Nationalization
  in Germany, 242, 247–248
  in Great Britain, 98–100, 110–111
  in Italy, 316–317
Denazification, 183–184
Denmark
  economy of, 399t, 478t
  and European Free Trade
    Association, 458
  and European Union, 459
  foreign residents of, 237t
  geography of, 399t
  military in, 475t
  monarchy in, 6t
  NATO and, 28, 29t
  as nordic country, 5
  population of, 399t, 478t
  regional organization memberships,
    463t
Départements (France), 166
Desert Storm. See Gulf War
Deutsche mark, 179, 245, 249
Devolution, in Great Britain, 26,
  44–48, 49, 111
DGB. See German Trade Union
  Federation
Di Pietro, Antonio, 283
Diana, Princess of England, 48
Dicey, A. V., 41
DIHT. See German Chamber of Trade
  and Commerce
Dini, Lamberto, 279, 292, 294t, 296
Dirigisme, 163
Disraeli, Benjamin, 72
The Doctrinaires, 402
Don Juan, Count of Barcelona, 366
Douglas-Home, Alec, 60f
Downing Steet, No. 10, 37f, 85
Downing Street Declaration, 45
Drees, Willem, 409
Dreyfus case, 127
DS. See Democrats of the Left

EA. See Basque Solidarity party
East Germany. See German
    Democratic Republic
Eastern Europe
  and decline of Communism, 2–5
  definition of, 477
  EU aid to, 477, 478
  profile of, 4t
  Soviet Union in, 184
ECB. See European Central Bank
ECHR. See European Convention on
    Human Rights
ECJ. See European Court of
    Justice

Ecole Nationale d'Administration
    (ENA), 164–165
Ecole Normale Supérieure, 126, 165
Ecole Polytechnique, 126, 163, 164,
  165
Economic and Monetary Union (EMU).
    See European Monetary Union
Economic and Social Agreements of
    1984 (Spain), 387
Economic and Social Committee
    (European Union), 456t, 472
Economic and Social Council (France),
  136
Economic Stabilization Act (Germany,
    1967), 239, 240–241
Economy. See also individual nations
    postindustrial
  in Germany, 190–191
  in Great Britain, 45, 50–51
  in Italy, 267, 267t, 308
  in Netherlands, 399
  in Western Europe, 8–9
ECOSOC. See Economic and Social
    Committee (European Union)
ECSC. See European Coal and Steel
    Community
EDC. See European Defense
    Community
Eden, Anthony, 60f
Education Law of 1990 (LOGSE), 344
EEA. See European Economic Area
EEC. See European Economic
    Community
EFTA. See European Free Trade
    Association
Einaudi, Luigi, 296t
EKD. See Evangelical Church in
    Germany
ELA-STV. See Union of Basque
    Workers
Elite. See Political elite
Elizabeth II, Queen of England, 34,
  76f, 77
EMS (European Monetary System). See
    European Monetary Union
EMU. See European Monetary Union
ENA. See Ecole Nationale
    d'Administration
Enabling Act (Germany, 1933), 183
Engholm, Björn, 206
England. See also Great Britain
  elections in, 68
  electoral system in, 58–59
  geography of, 43, 43t
  history of, 6
  in House of Commons, 90
  population of, 43t
  religion in, 51, 52
  stability of, 6
  in United Kingdom, 34
The English Constitution (Bagehot),
  41, 76
EP. See European Parliament
EPC. See European Political
    Cooperation
Equal Pay Act (Britain, 1970), 50
Erhard, Ludwig, 217

Estonia, 2, 3, 460t
ETA (Basque Homeland and Freedom).
    See Euskadi Ta Askatasuna
Établissements publics, 170
Ethnic national parties, platforms of,
    20t
Ethnicity. See also individual nations
    as conflict source, 44, 48
    in Western Europe, 15–16, 15t
Eton, 54, 83, 87
Euratom. See European Atomic
    Energy Community
Euro, 110, 179, 255, 329, 398, 456t,
    475
Eurocommunism, 21, 282, 355, 453
Eurocorps, 456t
Europe. See also Western Europe
    Central
        and decline of communism, 2–5
        definition of, 477
        EU aid to, 477, 478
        profile of, 4t
    culture of, 453
    Eastern
        and decline of communism, 2–5
        definition of, 477
        EU aid to, 477, 478
        profile of, 4t
        Soviet Union in, 184
    history of, 453–454
    and nuclear weapons, 453
    religion in, 453
    women in, 466
European Atomic Energy Community
    (Euratom), 385, 456t, 458, 462,
    464
European Central Bank (ECB), 249,
    316, 456t, 474
European Coal and Steel Community
    (ECSC), 108, 304, 447, 455–457,
    462
European Commission, 464, 465–467,
    466t, 468f
European Community Adaptation Act,
    194–195
European Community (EC), 338, 456t,
    462, 472
European Convention on Human
    Rights (ECHR), 17, 41, 49, 89,
    96, 457
European Council, 464, 468
European Court of Human Rights, 457
European Court of Justice (ECJ),
    109–110, 456t, 465, 471, 471t
European Defense Community (EDC),
    108, 457
European Economic Area (EEA), 456,
    458, 472, 477
    member states, 463t
European Economic Community
    (EEC), 108, 447, 456t, 457–458,
    462, 464, 472
European Exchange Rate Mechanism
    (ERM), 312–313
European Free Trade Association
    (EFTA), 108, 458, 477
    member states, 463t

European Investment Bank, 472
European Monetary System (EMS). See
    European Monetary Union
European Monetary Union (EMU),
    456t, 472–474
    Great Britain and, 110
    Italy and, 310–311, 312, 313
    Netherlands and, 448
European Parliament (EP), 69, 456t,
    464, 465, 465f, 469–470, 469f,
    475
European Payments Union, 304
European People's Party, in European
    Parliament, 469f
European Political Cooperation (EPC),
    458, 468, 474
European Research and Coordinating
    Agency, 456t
European Social Community, 459
European Social Fund, 456t
European Union (EU), 450f, 451–481.
    See also Maastricht Treaty
    agricultural policy, 476–477, 479
    Baltic states and, 3
    challenges facing, 30
    currency, 110, 459, 472–474, 475
    defense and security, 474–475,
        475t, 479
    diplomatic relations and programs,
        477–478
    economic policy, 170
    economies of, 399t, 452, 478t
    establishment of, 29–31
    European Court of Justice (ECJ),
        109–110, 456t, 465, 471, 471t
    financial structure of, 463–464,
        464f
    fiscal policy, 390
    France and, 126, 170–172, 459,
        479
    future of, 478–480
    geography of, 399t, 450f, 451
    Germany and, 242, 248, 479
    Great Britain and, 41, 48, 49, 89,
        108–110
    health spending in, 14t
    history of, 453–459, 461t–462t
    institutions of, 465–469
    Italy and, 314, 315–316
    judicial branch of, 475
    member states, 33, 463t
        candidates for (2002), 460t
    national sovereignty and, 49, 89,
        109–110, 462, 471
    NATO and, 459, 474, 479
    Netherlands and, 438, 447–448
    Nordic countries and, 5
    policies, 470, 472–477
    population of, 399t, 451
    power of, 459, 478–479
    profile of, 451–452
    purpose of, 453, 461–462
    Spain and, 339, 384–385
    Stability Pact of, 313, 315–316, 319
    structure of, 459–463
    taxation by, 109, 390, 464, 464f,
        472, 477–478

trade, 452, 459, 465t, 472, 473f,
    477–478, 479
women in, 466
Europol, 456t, 475
Eurostar train, 109f
Euskadi. See Basque country
Euskadi Ta Askatasuna (Basque
    Homeland and Freedom party;
    ETA), 336, 338–339, 356, 383
Euskal Herritarrok, 356, 383
Evangelical Church in Germany (EKD),
    213–214
Evangelical Lutheran Church, 198
Evangelical People's Party, 423
Executive branch. See individual
    nations

Fabian Society, 71
Facta, Luigi, 260
Falcone, Giovanni, 265
Falkland Islands War, 85, 110
Family
    in Italy, 268–271
    in Western Europe, 10, 10t
Farmers' organizations, in France,
    134
Fascism
    in Italy
        legacy of, 263, 300
        Neo-Fascism, 16, 23
        rise of, 7–8, 260–261
        women and, 271
Fascist Party, 260–261
FDP. See Free Democratic Party
Federal Constitutional Court
    (Germany), 232–233, 232t
    on abortion, 247
    and fundamental rights, 235–237
    gender discrimination and, 193,
        195, 196
    NATO and, 249
    parties and, 209, 210, 214–215,
        245
    and separation of powers, 221
Federal Election Act (Germany), 204
Federal Law Gazette, 228
Federal Republic of Germany (FRG).
    See also Germany
    culture of, 191–193
    economy of, 185–186, 190–193,
        192f, 202
    establishment of, 184
    parties in, 204–211
    political culture in, 199–201
    population of, 188t
    social services in, 193–194
Federal systems, 25–26
Federation for Free Democrats, 245
Fédération Nationale des Syndicats
    d'Exploitants Agricoles (FNSEA),
    134
Federation of Dutch Trade Unions
    (FNV), 429
Federation of German Employers
    (BDA), 212
Federation of Unions in Galicia (INTG),
    361

Felipe, Prince of Asturias, 338, 368
Feminist movement, 7, 9, 11
  in Italy, 271–272
Ferdinand of Aragon, 331
Fernando VII, King of Spain, 332
Fifth Republic (France), 146–161
  business in, 134
  consultation in, 136
  establishment of, 122t, 124, 130
  history of, 16, 118
  imperial tradition in, 122
  parties in, 137, 138
  stability of, 174
Fini, Gianfranco, 278, 320f, 324
Finland
  currency of, 475
  economy of, 478t
  European Union and, 459
  military of, 475t
  as Nordic country, 5
  population of, 478t
  regional organization memberships,
    463t
First Empire, 122t
First Reich, 180–181
First Republic (France), 118, 122t
First Republic (Spain), 333
Fiscal Planning Commission (FPC),
  240
Fischer, Joschka, 171, 249
Five percent clause (Germany), 204,
  206–207, 208, 214, 245
Flame party, 278, 286t, 287t
FNV. See Federation of Dutch Trade
  Unions
Formateur, 432
Foros, 383
Fortuyn, Pim, 418
Forza Italia, 278
  and election of 1994, 285, 285t,
    292
  and election of 1996, 286t
  and election of 2001, 287, 287t
Foundation of Labor (Netherlands), 409
Fourth Republic (France), 16, 118,
  122t, 123–124, 136f
FPC. See Fiscal Planning Commission
Fracties, 426
Fraga, Manuel, 338, 352, 353
Fraktionen, 226–227
France, 114f, 115–175
  ambitions of, 118–121
  bureaucracy in, 120–122, 128,
    152–153, 156, 163–166,
    169–170
    Grands Corps, 164, 165–166
  Center in, 138–141, 140–141
  centralization in, 120–121, 128,
    167–168
  civil service in, 163–166
    Grands Corps, 164, 165–166
  cohabitation in, 154–155, 172
  Communism in, 130–131, 145, 453
  Constitutional Council, 156, 160
  constitutions, 116, 118, 130,
    146–148
  culture of, 120, 128, 163–164, 168

currency of, 475
economy of, 2t, 117, 122, 168–170,
  172, 187t, 478t
  and culture, 124–125, 124f
education in, 116, 126, 128, 163,
  164–165, 164t, 169t
elections, 139t, 150–151
electoral system in, 18, 18t, 138
ethnic groups in, 15, 15t, 16, 116,
  126, 141, 237t
and European Union, 126,
  170–172, 459, 479
executive branch, 116, 146–148
  president, 146–148, 152t,
    153–155
    election of, 150–151
    power of, 148–150, 158–161
  prime minister, 151–152, 152t,
    153–155
  restraints on, 159–160
foreign policy, 170–172
geography of, 2t, 114f, 115–116,
  125–126
government expenditures, 26t, 27
health spending in, 14t
history of, 6, 16, 118–119,
  121–124, 122t
immigration to, 126, 141
interest groups in, 130–137
judicial branch, 117, 161
languages in, 116, 120, 125
Left in, 142–146
legal system, 116
legislative branch, 116, 155–160
  committees in, 158
  deputies to, 161, 161t
  function of, 155–156, 157–158,
    159t
  organization of, 156–157
  power of, 158–161
local government in, 166–168
media in, 168, 169, 170
military in, 322t, 475t
ministerial cabinets, 166
Napoleonic tradition in, 122, 122t
nationalization in, 144, 168–170
NATO and, 28, 29t, 170
in Netherlands, 401
and nuclear weapons, 171
occupation, 119, 145, 147, 169
parties in, 20, 21, 22t, 23, 24, 130,
  137–146
political system in, 25, 116
  consultation in, 136–137
  governmental structure, 152–153
  instability in, 118–121
population and demographics, 2t,
  11t, 116, 124–125, 124t, 478t
president, 146–148, 152t, 153–155
  election of, 150–151
  power of, 148–150, 158–161
prime minister, 151–152, 152t,
  153–155
profile of, 2, 115–117
protest groups in, 135
public sector in, 169–170, 169t
referendums in, 19, 148–149

regional organization memberships,
  463t
regionalism in, 26
religion in, 13–14, 14t, 15t, 116,
  121, 124, 127–128
republicanism in, 123
right in, 138–141
  extreme, 141–142
  and Ruhr, 455, 457
social class in, 7, 126–127
social order of, 124–127
Socialist government in, 132, 135,
  136–137, 143–144, 168,
  169–170, 172
Soviet Union and, 120, 145–146
stability of, 6, 118–121
trade and, 459
United States and, 120
voting rights in, 12–13
women in, 126, 135, 144, 161
  role and status of, 10–13,
    10t–13t
Franchise Acts (Britain), 40
Franco, Francisco
  death of, 330, 338
  Italian support for, 261
  Spanish Civil War and, 334
  Spanish politics and, 363
Franco regime, 330, 335–337
  Catholic Church and, 362
  censorship in, 345–347
  centralization in, 375, 381, 383
  economic policy, 341–342, 391–392
  industry in, 360
  monarchy in, 366–367
  parties in, 353
  religion in, 345
  taxation in, 390
Frankfurt Parliament, 181
Free Democratic Party (FDP), 206–207
  alliances, 206, 216, 225
  Bundesrat and, 230t
  funding of, 209, 210t
  policies, 242
  support for, 204, 212, 215t,
    217–219, 218t, 220, 221,
    221t, 223
  women and, 195t
Free French Movement, 147
Freedom of speech, in Germany,
  235–236
French Communist Party (PCF), 120,
  126, 137, 139t, 142–146
French Revolution of 1789, 7, 119,
  121, 130
French Revolution of 1830, 121
French Revolution of 1848, 121
FRG. See Federal Republic of Germany
Friends of the Earth, 74
Frutos, Francisco, 356
Fulton Committee, 86
Fundis, 207–208

Galicia, 326f, 341, 381
  autonomy for, 375, 376t
  separatism in, 359t
  unions in, 361

GATT (General Agreement on Tariffs
  and Trade)
  European Union and, 457, 477
  France and, 168, 172
Gaullism, 139
Gaullist Party (RPR), 18, 137,
  138–140, 139t
GDP. See Gross domestic product
GDR. See German Democratic
  Republic
General Agreement on Tariffs and
  Trade. See GATT
General Law on Education of 1970
  (LGE), 344
General Union of Workers (UGT), 338,
  360–361, 387
General Workingman's Association,
  205–206
Genscher, Hans-Dietrich, 219, 225, 248
German Chamber of Trade and
  Commerce (DIHT), 212
German Democratic Republic (GDR).
  See also Germany, reunification
  collapse of, 4, 219, 243–244
  culture of, 191–193
  economy of, 186, 189–190,
    190–193, 192f
  education in, 198
  founding of, 184
  Länder of, 228–229
  migration from, 188
  parties in, 208–209
  population of, 188t
  religion in, 198, 213
  reprivatization of, 247–248
  social services in, 193–194
German Federation of Civil Servants
  (DBB), 212
German Federation of Industry (BDI),
  212
German People's Union (Germany), 23,
  23t
"German Problem," 242–243, 453, 455
German Salaried Employees Union
  (DAG), 212
German Trade Union Federation
  (DGB), 212
German Unity Fund, 239
Germanism, 201
Germany, 176f, 177–250. See also
  Federal Republic of Germany;
  German Democratic Republic
  Allied occupation of, 183–184, 455
  cabinet, 224–225, 225t
  chancellor, 223–226
  chancellor's office, 223
  citizen initiatives (Bürgerinitiativen)
    in, 199–200, 212
  civil liberties in, 223, 233, 235–236
  constitution (Basic Law), 178, 184
    asylum rights in, 236
    basic rights in, 223, 233, 235–236
    Bundestag in, 226
    cabinet in, 224
    chancellor in, 223, 235
    and economy, 202
    federal president in, 222

federal system and, 238
  fiscal policy in, 238–239
  gender and, 193
  Länder in, 229
  political parties in, 209
  Rechtsstaat and, 231
  religion in, 213
  reunification and, 229, 245–247
  culture of, 197–202, 201–202, 211
  currency, 179, 245, 249, 475
  denationalization in, 242
  economic policy, 239–241
  economy of, 2t, 179, 185–187, 187t,
    190–193, 478t
  education in, 178, 197–198
  elections in, 196–197, 214, 215t,
    218t, 219–220, 221t
    split-ticket voting, 216, 216t
    trends in, 217–221
  electoral system in, 18t, 19t,
    214–215
    campaigns, 216–217
    reunification and, 245
  ethnic groups in, 15t, 178, 188,
    196–197
  European Union and, 242, 248, 479
  executive branch, 178, 221–226
    chancellor, 223–226
    chancellor's office, 223
    federal president, 221–222
  federal government in, 25, 26, 221,
    223–226
  federal president, 221–222
  federal system, 228–229, 238
  fiscal policy, 238–239
  foreign policy, 242–250, 248–250
  French occupation by, 119, 145,
    147, 169
  geography of, 2t, 176f, 177–178,
    180, 187–189, 189–190
  "German Problem," 242–243, 453,
    455
  government expenditures, 14t, 26t,
    27
  health spending in, 14t
  history of, 6, 7, 180–185, 185–186,
    239–240
  immigration to, 14, 188–189,
    196–197, 207, 213, 236–238,
    237f
  interest groups in, 211–214
  judicial branch and legal system,
    179, 221, 231–233, 232t. See
    also Federal Constitutional
    Court (Germany)
  Länder
    boundaries of, 228–229
    Bundesrat and, 229–230
    federal system and, 25, 26,
      228–229, 238–239
    government of, 228, 238, 239
    legal system and, 231
  language in, 178
  legislative branch
    Bundesrat, 179, 229–230, 230t
    Bundestag, 178–179, 226–228,
      227f

delegates to, 221
  elections for, 204, 205t
  members of, 227–228
  process in, 228
  unions in, 212–213
  women in, 195, 195f
  media in, 197, 217
  military in, 322t, 475t
  NATO and, 28, 29t, 242, 249
  nuclear arms and, 248
  parliamentary state secretaries,
    225–226
  parties in, 20, 21, 22t, 23t, 204–211
    Bundesrat and, 230t
    cabinet and, 225t
    financing of, 209–211, 210t
    organization of, 209
  policy mechanism in, 211, 221–233
  political culture in, 199–201
  political system in, 178
  population and demographics, 2t,
    11t, 13, 178, 187–189, 188t,
    478t
  profile of, 2, 177–179
  protest movements in, 199–200,
    212, 219
  public policy in, 235–250
  regional organization memberships,
    463t
  religion in, 13, 14t, 15t, 178, 180,
    198–199, 213–214
  reunification
    Bundesrat and, 229
    costs of, 186–187
    electoral system and, 214–215, 219
    history of, 180, 184–185, 219,
      242–248
    issues in, 199, 247–248
    Länder and, 228–229
    leaders of, 205
    political parties and, 204
    politics of, 208
    unions and, 213
  and Ruhr, 455, 457
  social class in, 7
  socialization in, 200–201
  and Soviet Union, 242–244, 247
  stability of, 6
  taxation in, 198, 239, 240, 242
  voting rights in, 12–13
  Weimar Republic, 18, 182–183,
    206, 214, 223
  welfare state in, 27, 241–242
  and Western European Union, 457
  women in, 191, 192f, 193–196,
    195f, 200
    role and status of, 10–13,
      10t–13t
Gibraltar, 105, 108
Giolitti, Giovanni, 259–260
Giscard d'Estaing, Valéry
  European Union and, 480
  foreign policy of, 171
  policies and actions, 136, 149, 153,
    154, 160
  political career of, 138, 140, 141,
    143–144, 152t, 173

GL. See Green Left
Gladstone, William, 46
Glastnost, 243–244
Glorious Revolution (Britain), 38
GNP. See Gross national product
Godesberg Platform, 206
González, Felipe
    policies of, 383, 386, 387, 392
    political career of, 338, 353, 354,
        358, 369
    scandal and, 393
Good Friday Agreement (Britain,
    1998), 44, 46
Gorbachev, Mikhail, 3, 184, 243–244
Government, growth of, 26–27
GPV. See Calvinist Union
Grand Coalition (Germany), 217
Grands Corps, 164, 165–166
GRAPO (Groups of Antifascist
    Resistance, First of October), 383
Grass, Günter, 184–185, 201, 248
Great Britain, 25–111, 32f. See also
    England; Northern Ireland;
    Scotland; Wales
    and British Commonwealth, 36,
        104, 105–108
    member nations, 106f–107f
    bureaucracy in, 86–88
    cabinet, 41, 79–82, 87–88
    Cabinet Office, 85
    civil rights in, 40, 41, 42, 45, 49,
        111
    civil service in, 86–88
    constitution of, 38, 38f, 40–41,
        48–49
    crime in, 55
    culture of, 36, 50–54, 56
        political, 41–43, 80t
        socialization process, 42–43,
            54–55
    currency, 35, 37, 48, 110
    denationalization and
        decentralization in, 98–100,
        110–111
    dependent areas, 34
    devolution in, 26, 44–48, 49, 111
    economic planning in, 98, 100–101
    economy of, 50–51, 53–54, 55–56,
        98, 110–111
    employment, 2t, 478t
    European Union and, 109
    overview of, 35, 37
    regional differences in, 49
    education and literacy in, 34, 54–55
    EEC and, 458
    elections in, 62–68
        candidates, 64–65, 65t
    electoral system, 17–18, 18t, 39t,
        58–62, 58t, 64
    empire of, 33, 36, 104, 105–108
    ethnic groups in, 15, 15t, 34, 43,
        52, 52t, 53, 53t, 67–68
    and European Free Trade
        Association, 458
    European integration and, 455–456
    European Union and, 41, 48, 49,
        89, 108–110
    executive branch, 34–35, 37

cabinet, 41, 79–82, 87–88
    Cabinet Office, 85
    Prime Minister, 35, 37f, 39, 41,
        82–86
foreign affairs, 104–110
geography of, 2t, 32f, 33, 43, 43t
government expenditures, 14t, 26t,
    27, 98, 98f, 99t, 100
health spending in, 14t
history of, 7, 33, 36–39
immigration to, 43, 45, 48, 52, 108,
    237t
interest groups in, 74–76, 89
judiciary in, 35, 38f, 41, 95–96, 95t
languages in, 34, 43–44
legal system in, 34, 40, 41–42,
    79–81, 82
legislative branch (Parliament), 35,
    39, 40, 88–95
    House of Commons, 39, 40,
        90–95, 91t
        chamber of, 92f
        elections to, 62–64
    House of Lords, 39, 51, 89–90,
        111
    parties in, 18t, 72, 92–93, 92f
    pluralistic system and, 46, 47
    power of, 42
in Middle East, 104
military in, 104–105
    spending on, 322t
    subordination of, 40
monarchy in, 6t, 7, 34, 41, 42, 48,
    51, 76–77, 76f, 79
National Health Service, 103–104
NATO and, 28, 29t, 63, 104–105
parties in, 39, 59–62, 68–69
    constituencies, 51, 52–53, 66–68
    ideology of, 21, 22t, 23, 24, 54
    leadership, 72–73
    organization, 69–72
    in Parliament, 18t, 72, 92–93,
        92f
    power within, 73–74, 73t
pluralistic system in, 44–48
political development of, 36–56
political problems in, 48–49
political system, 24, 34, 77–79
    conventions, 41–42, 79–81, 82
    as model, 2, 40–41, 369
population and demographics, 2t,
    11t, 34, 43t, 50–51, 478t
Prime Minister, 35, 37f, 39, 41,
    82–86
profile of, 2, 33–35
protest movements in, 74
public expenditure, 37
public policy, 98–111
referendums in, 19, 108
religion in, 13, 14t, 15t, 34, 44–45,
    51–53, 52t
representation in, 40
shadow cabinet, 72, 80t, 81
social class in, 7, 42–43, 51, 54–55,
    66–67
social services in, 42, 53, 101–104
and Spanish Civil War, 334
stability of, 42–43

standard of living in, 58–59
taxation in, 56, 98
trade, 36–37, 55–56, 104, 108, 110,
    458, 459
Treasury, 85
unified system of, 43–44
United States and, 36, 104–105,
    110
voting rights in, 12–13
welfare state in, 27, 42, 53,
    101–104
women in
    employment, 45t, 50
    in government, 63, 65, 65t, 92
    role and status of, 10–13,
        10t–13t
    voting rights of, 39t, 58t
    voting trends for, 67
Greece
    ancient, political system of, 5
    currency, 475
    economy of, 478t
    European Community and, 458
    military, 475t
    population of, 478t
    regional organization memberships,
        463t
Green Federation, 423
Green Left (GL), 420f, 423
    in parliament, 437t, 438t
    support for, 417t, 425t, 428
Green Party, 20t, 23–24
    constituency, 220
    in European Parliament, 469f
    in France, 137, 139t, 146
    in Germany, 207–208
        alliances, 216
        Bundesrat and, 230t
        financing of, 210t
        policies and positions, 210, 217,
            249
        support for, 204, 212, 214–215,
            215t, 218, 218t, 220, 221t
        women in, 195, 195t
    in Great Britain, 39, 63, 69
    in Italy, 278
    reunification and, 245
Greenpeace, 74
Gronchi, Giovanni, 296t, 321–322
Gross domestic product (GDP)
    of East Germany, 187
    of France, 117, 118, 187t
    of Germany, 179, 187t
    of Great Britain, 35
    of Italy, 187t, 255, 256, 309, 315
    of Japan, 187t
    of Netherlands, 398, 399t, 443t
    of Spain, 329
    of United States, 187t
    of West Germany, 187
Gross national product (GNP)
    of European Union, 452
    of Great Britain, 56
    of Italy, 304
Groups of Antifascist Resistance, First
    of October (GRAPO), 383
Grundgesetz. See Germany,
    constitution (Basic Law)

Guerra, Alfonso, 354, 392
Gulf War, 104, 105
Gutiérrez Mellado, Manuel, 364
Gymnasium, 197

Haarlem, Netherlands, 404f
Haas, Evelyn, 196
Habeas Corpus Act (Britain, 1679), 40
The Hague, 400, 415f, 445
Hague, William, 63
Hamm-Bröcher, Hildegard, 222
Hansard, 80t
Harare Declaration (1991), 105–106
Harrow, 54, 83
Hauptschule, 197
Health care
    in Great Britain, 103–104
    in Italy, 266t
    spending, in Western Europe, 14t
Heath, Edward, 60f
Heinemann, Gustav, 222
Helsinki Agreement (1999), 474t
Hernández Mancha, Antonio, 353
Herri Batasuna, 339, 351f, 356, 383,
    384f
Herzog, Roman, 222
Hesse, Hermann, 201
Heuss, Theodore, 222
Hitler, Adolf, 7–8, 182–183
Hohenzollern monarchy, 181
Holland, 399, 400. See also
    Netherlands
Hollande, François, 144–145
Holocaust, 8, 183
Holy Roman Empire of the German
    Nation, 180
Hong Kong, Great Britain and, 104
House of Freedoms (Italy), 277,
    287–288, 287t
House of Lords Act (Britain, 1999), 89,
    90
Human rights. See also Bills of rights
    European Convention on Human
        Rights (ECHR), 17, 41, 49, 89,
        96, 457
    European Court of Human Rights,
        457
    in Germany
        under Basic Law, 223
        in Second Reich, 182
    in Italy
        anti-corruption campaign and,
            301
        anti-terrorism campaign and,
            263
    in liberal democracies, 16–17
    in Netherlands, 412
Human Rights Act (Britain, 1998), 49,
    96
Humanism, in Germany, 201–202
Hungary, 2, 4t, 460t, 463t
    NATO and, 28, 29t

Ibárruri, Dolores, 338, 355
Iceland, 5
    NATO and, 28, 29t
    regional organization memberships,
        463t

trade, 472
Iglesias, Gerardo, 355
Iglesias, Pablo, 353
Immigration Act (Britain, 1971), 45
Imperialism, Western European, 7, 8
Independent Republican Left (IR), 356
Individualism, in France, 125, 130,
    135
Indochina, France in, 123
Industrial Revolution, France and,
    120, 126
Industry. See Business and industry
Infant mortality rates, in Italy, 266t
Informateur, 432
INI. See National Institute of Industry
Inner Freedom, 201–202
Inquisition, in Spain, 331
Interest groups. See individual nations
Internet, in Germany, 190–191, 197
INTG. See Federation of Unions in
    Galicia
Introduction to the Study of the Law of
    the Constitution (Dicey), 41
IR. See Independent Republican Left
IRA. See Irish Republican Army
Iraq, 104, 105
Ireland. See also Northern Ireland;
    Republic of Ireland
    currency, 475
    economy of, 478t
    history of, 34, 46
    military in, 475t
    parties in, 22
    population of, 478t
    regional organization memberships,
        463t
Irish Republican Army (IRA), 44–45,
    46
Iron Curtain, 2, 454–455
Isabel II, Queen of Spain, 333
Isabella of Castile, 331
Islam
    in France, 15t, 127
    fundamentalist, 44, 135–136
    in Germany, 15t, 198, 213
    in Great Britain, 15t, 44, 52, 52t, 53
    in Spain, 15t, 331
    in Western Europe, 14–16, 15t
Italian Communist Party (PCI), 277
    agenda of, 269
    policies, 309, 311–312
    support for, 276t, 279, 281–282,
        284, 453
Italian Confederation of Workers'
    Unions (CISL), 288
Italian General Confederation of Labor
    (CGIL), 288, 309
Italian Liberal Party (PLI), 276t,
    277–278, 283
Italian Popular Party (PPI), 260,
    276–277, 284–285, 285t
Italian Social Movement (MSI), 276t,
    278
Italian Socialist Party (PSI), 269, 277,
    279, 280–281, 282–283, 285,
    285t, 306
Italian Union of Labor (UIL), 288
Italy, 242f, 253–324

centralization in, 263–264
communes and provinces, 257, 299
constitution, 17, 279
    amendment process for, 292
    auxiliary organs in, 298
    regions in, 264
corruption in, 268, 281, 282
    judicial activism against,
        300–301
    lottizzazione system, 282
    reform of, 256, 265, 276,
        283–284, 301, 319–321
    in South, 265
Council of Ministers, 292, 297
culture of, 256, 262, 263, 271–272,
    309
family in, 268–271
currency of, 255, 303, 304, 306,
    307–308, 310–311, 312, 316,
    475
domestic terrorism in, 263, 282,
    306–307
economic policy, 311–315
    reforms needed in, 316–317
economy of, 2t, 187t, 266t, 267,
    267t, 289, 303–311
    government intervention in, 298
    overview of, 255, 478t
    in south, 264–265, 268, 304,
        305, 306, 310, 317–318
    in Third Italy, 267, 308, 309
education in, 254, 264, 266t, 268,
    318–319
elections, 276t
    of 1948, 279–280
    of 1952-1993, 280–284
    of 1994, 284, 285t, 292
    of 1996, 286–287, 286t
    of 2001, 287–288, 287t
    campaigns, 262
electoral system, 18, 18t, 274–275,
    283–284, 323
ethnic groups in, 15, 15t, 254
European Union and, 291, 314,
    315–316
executive branch, 254
    president, 295–297, 296t
    prime minister, 292–295, 295–296
Fascism in
    legacy of, 263, 300
    Neo-Fascism, 16, 23
    rise of, 7–8, 260–261
    women and, 271
foreign policy of, 321–322
geography of, 2t, 252f, 253–254,
    256
government of, 293–295, 293t–294t
    inefficiency of, 299, 323
    legislative power of, 295
    reforms needed in, 315–321
    spending by, 26t, 27, 310t,
        311–312
health care in, 14t, 266t
history of, 6, 256, 257–259, 258t,
    334
human rights in, 263, 301
immigration, 237t
    illegal, 265–266

Italy, *continued*
  interest groups in, 288–290
  judicial branch, 254–255, 300–301
    constitutional court, 299–300
    reforms needed in, 319–321
  language in, 254, 262
  legal system, 254
    reforms needed in, 318, 319–321
  legislative branch, 254, 290–292,
    290f
  media in, 264, 269, 286, 298
  military in, 322, 322t, 475t
  monarchy in, 261
  monetary policy, 304, 306,
    307–308, 310–311, 312–313,
    316
  national debt and deficits, 310, 311,
    312, 314–315, 316
  NATO and, 28, 29t
  organized crime in, 265–266, 284,
    318, 319
  parties in, 20, 21, 22t, 23, 24,
    275–279, 321
    in 1990s, 285–286
    strength of, 288
  political culture in, 263–264, 288
  political system, 254
    revolution in (1990s), 256
  population and demographics, 2t,
    11t, 254, 266t, 478t
  president, 295–297, 296t
  prime minister, 292–295, 295–296
  profile of, 2, 253–255, 266t
  protest movements in, 289,
    306–307
  public administration in, 297–299
    reforms needed in, 318
  public policy in, 303–324
  referendums in, 19, 274–275, 278,
    283, 299
  regional organization memberships,
    463t
  regionalism in, 25–26
  regions of, 264, 281
    government of, 298–299,
      318–319
  religion in, 13, 14t, 15t, 254,
    262–263, 268–269, 286
  separatist movements in, 264
  social class in, 267–268
  south
    crime in, 265–266, 284
    economy of, 264–265, 268, 304,
      305, 306, 310, 317–318
    reforms needed in, 317–318
  stability of, 6, 280, 281, 321, 323
  standard of living in, 266t, 268, 323
  taxation in, 311, 312, 313,
    314–315, 318
  Third Italy, economy of, 267, 308,
    309
  trade, 305, 306
  Trasformismo in, 257, 263–264
  voting rights in, 12–13, 271
  welfare state in, 265, 312
  and Western European Union, 457
  women in, 10–13, 10t–13t,
    269–270, 271–272

    World War II and, 261
      Marshall Plan, 279, 304, 311
IU. See United Left

Jacobins, 121
Japan
  economy of, 187t, 399t
  geography of, 399t
  military spending, 322t
  population of, 399t
  trade, 473f
Jeunesse Agricole Chrétienne, 134
Jews
  emigration from Soviet Union, 213
  in France, 127
  in Germany, 198, 213
  in Great Britain, 39t, 52, 52t
  Nazi regime and, 8, 183
  in Netherlands, in World War II,
    408
  in Western Europe, 13–14
John Paul II, Pope, 198
John XXIII, Pope, 280–281, 345
Joint Declaration on the Settlement of
  Open Property Issues (1990), 247
Jospin, Lionel
  foreign policy of, 171–172
  Greens and, 146
  policies of, 170
  political career of, 137–138, 141,
    144, 150, 152t, 155, 174
Juan Carlos I, King of Spain
  and Church-state relations, 362
  and coup attempt of 1981,
    364–365, 367–368
  installation of, 336, 337, 338,
    366–367
  role of, 349
  and transition to democracy, 330,
    364–365, 367–368
Judicial restraint, in Great Britain,
  95–96
Judicial review
  in France, 160
  in Germany, 232–233
  in Great Britain, 41, 96
  in Italy, 299–300
  in liberal democracies, 16–17
  in Netherlands, 429
  in Spain, 378–379
Juliana, Queen of Netherlands, 430
Junker caste, 7, 181

Katzenstein, Peter, 211
Kennedy, Charles, 73
Kennedy, John F., 281
Kiesinger, Kurt-Georg, 217
Kilbrandon Commission, 47
KLM. See Royal Dutch Airlines
Kohl, Helmut, 185f
  cabinet of, 225
  policies and actions of, 249
  political career of, 196, 205, 206,
    210–211, 217, 218–219, 222,
    223
  reunification and, 184, 219, 244
Kok, Wim, 422, 432, 442
Königsdorf, Helga, 201

Kosovo, UN peacekeeping in, 447
Kristallnacht, 183
Kuyper, Abraham, 419
Kyoto Protocol, 480

Labour Party, in Great Britain
  candidates, 54, 64–65, 65t
  constituency, 51, 52–53, 66–68, 69,
    70, 75–76
  leadership of, 72
  organization of, 69–72, 71f
  in Parliament, 72
  platform of, 54, 100, 101–103, 108
  power in, 73–74, 73t
  strength of, 48t, 59, 60f, 61–62, 61f,
    61t, 62t, 63, 64, 69
  women in, 12
Lafontaine, Oscar, 206, 219
Länder
  boundaries of, 228–229
  Bundesrat and, 229–230
  East German, 228–229
  federal system and, 25, 228–229,
    238–239
  government of, 228, 238, 239
  legal system and, 231
Language. See individual nations
Lassalle, Ferdinand, 206
Lateran Pacts (1929), 261, 269
Latin America, trade, 473f
Latvia, 2, 3, 460t
Law, rule of, 40–41
Law Lords, 80t, 89
Law of Succession (Spain), 336
Law of the Press and Printing (1966),
  345–346
Law on Collective Agreements (Spain,
  1958), 360
Law on Political Reform (Spain), 330,
  337, 359t
Law on Succession (1969), 366–367
Law on University Reform of 1983
  (LRU), 344
LDP. See Liberal Democratic Party
Le Pen, Jean-Marie, 23, 138, 141–142,
  151
League of Nations, 261
  Court of International Justice, 445
Legislatures. See individual nations
Leo XIII, Pope, 127
Leone, Giovanni, 293t, 296t
LGE. See General Law on Education of
  1970
Liberal democracy, characteristics of,
  16–17
Liberal Democratic Party (LDP), in
  Great Britain
  candidates, 64–65, 65t
  constituency, 52–53, 59, 66–68
  platform of, 39
  power in, 73–74, 73t
  strength of, 48t, 59, 61t, 62t, 63, 69
Liberal party(ies). See also specific
  parties
  characteristics of, 20t, 21–22
  in Netherlands, 403t, 405t
Liechtenstein, 6t, 463t, 472
Life expectancy

in France, 10t, 116
in Germany, 10t, 178
in Great Britain, 10t, 34
in Italy, 10t, 254, 266t
in Netherlands, 10t, 398
in Spain, 10t, 328
in Western Europe, 10t, 13
Lijphart, Arend, 407–408, 410
Limbach, Jutta, 196
Lira, 255
List Pim Fortuyn (LPF), 411t, 418
Literacy. See Education under
    individual nations
Lithuania, 2, 3, 460t
LOAPA. See Organic Law for the
    Harmonization of Autonomy
    Process
Local government, in France, 166–168
LOGSE. See Education Law of 1990
Lomé Conventions, 477
London, 49, 78f
Lords of Appeal in Ordinary, 89
Lottizzazione, 282
Louis-Napoleon, 122, 150–151, 401
Louis XIV, King of France, 6–7
Louis XVIII, King of France, 121, 122t
Low Countries, 399–400
LPF. See List Pim Fortuyn
LRU. See Law on University Reform of
    1983
Lubbers, Ruud, 421, 440, 442, 443,
    444, 447
Lübke, Heinrich, 222
Luxembourg
    Benelux and, 4
    currency of, 475
    economy of, 478t
    foreign residents in, 237t
    military in, 475t
    monarchy in, 6t
    NATO and, 28, 29t
    population of, 478t
    regional organization memberships,
        463t
Luxembourg Compromise (1966), 467

Maastricht Treaty (1998), 458–459
    Amsterdam Treaty and, 475
    France and, 149
    Great Britain and, 49, 110
    Italy and, 312
    Netherlands and, 448
    provisions of, 467, 474, 474t
    Spain and, 339
Macmillan, Harold, 60f
Mafia, 265–266, 284, 318, 319
Magic pentangle, 441
Magna Carta, 36, 40
Magnati, 257
Major, John, 54, 55, 60f, 83, 110, 111
Malta, 463t
Mann, Thomas, 201
Marchais, Georges, 143–144
Margherita (Daisy) party, 276, 287t
Marriage, in Western Europe, 10
Marshall, George, 454
Marshall Plan, 454
    Germany and, 185–186

Italy and, 279, 304, 311
    Netherlands and, 447
Marx, Karl, 36
Matignon Accord, 132
May, Erskine, 41
MEDEF. See Mouvement des
    Entreprises de France
Media
    elections and, 62, 63
    in France, 168, 169, 170
    in Germany, 197, 217
    in Great Britain, 77, 84
    in Italy, 262, 264, 269, 286, 298
    in Spain, 345–347, 346t
Medieval period, 5
Méndez, Cándido, 361
Merkel, Angela, 195
Methodist Church, 52
Mexico
    regional organization memberships,
        463t
    trade, 473f
Middle class, rise of, 7
Ministerial cabinets (France), 166
Mitchell, George, 44
Mitterrand, François, 149f
    accomplishments of, 173–174
    policies and actions, 137, 149, 151,
        153, 154, 157, 168
    political career of, 143, 144, 147,
        150, 155, 173
Modernization
    in Great Britain, 36–39
    in Western Europe, 8
Monaco, 6t
Monarchy
    constitutional, 77
    in Germany, 181
    in Great Britain, 6t, 7, 34, 41, 42,
        48, 51, 76–77, 76f, 79
    in Italy, 261
    in Netherlands, 7, 429–430
    in Spain, 6t, 330, 333, 333t, 336,
        337, 349, 365–368, 367f
    in Western Europe, 6–7, 6t
Moncloa Pacts, 342–343, 343t, 387
Le Monde, 168
Money bill, 80t
Monnet, Jean, 168, 455, 457
Moro, Aldo, 265, 282, 293t
Mouvement des Entreprises de France
    (MEDEF), 132–133, 137
Mouvement Occitan, 135
Mouvement Républicain Populaire
    (MRP), 140–141
MSI. See Italian Social Movement
Mugabe, Robert, 480
Multiculturalism, in Great Britain, 53,
    53t
Mussolini, Benito, 253, 260–261

Napoleon I
    in Germany, 181
    in Italy, 258t, 263
    in Netherlands, 401
    policies and ideology of, 119, 121,
        122, 122t, 124, 163, 166
    in Spain, 331

Napoleon III, 119, 122, 122t
National Agency for the Protection of
    the Environment, 298
National Alliance (Italy)
    alliances, 278, 285
    ideology of, 23, 324
    support for, 23t, 285t, 286t, 287t,
        292
National Assembly (France), 155, 156
National Commission on Economic
    Planning (Italy), 305
National Committee on Energy and
    Labor (CNEL), 298
National Confederation of Labor
    (CNT), 360–361, 361
National Democratic Party (Germany),
    207
National Democratic Republicans
    (Germany), 23, 23t
National Economic Development
    Council (NEDC), 100
National Enterprise Board, 100
National Executive Committee (NEC),
    71–72
National Front (France), 18, 23, 23t,
    126, 139t, 141–142
National Health Service (Britain),
    103–104
National Institute of Industry (INI),
    342, 392
National Liberation Committee (CLN),
    261
National Organization for the Blind in
    Spain (ONCE), 347, 359
National Policy Forum (Britain), 74
National Socialist Party (Germany), 183
National Union of Conservative and
    Unionist Associations, 70
Nationalism. See also Regionalism
    in Great Britain, 39, 44–48, 49, 62
    in Spain, 349, 356–357
Nationality Act (Britain, 1981), 45
Nationality Act (Germany, 1913), 237
Nationalization. See also
    Denationalization
    in France, 144, 168–170
    in Italy, 305, 311
NATO (North Atlantic Treaty Alliance)
    Baltic states and, 3
    cost of, 29t
    establishment of, 455
    European Union and, 459, 474, 479
    France and, 28, 29t, 170
    Germany and, 28, 29t, 242, 249
    Great Britain and, 28, 29t, 63,
        104–105
    history and purpose of, 28, 30t
    Italy and, 28, 29t
    member states, 28, 30t, 33, 455,
        463t
    Netherlands and, 28, 29t, 446–447
    Nordic countries and, 5
    Spain and, 28, 29t, 385–387
Nazis, 7–8, 182–183, 240
    Jews and, 8, 183
    Neo-Nazis, 16, 23
NCW. See Netherlands Federation of
    Christian Employers

NEC. See National Executive
    Committee
NEDC. See National Economic
    Development Council
Neo-Fascism, 16, 23
Neo-Nazis, 16, 23
Netherlands, 386f, 397–448. See also
    Benelux countries
  Benelux and, 4, 447
  bureaucracy in, 434
  colonies, 445, 446
  consociationalism in, 406, 407–408,
    407f
  constitution, 17, 398, 429
    amendment process, 429
  corporatism in, 406, 408–409, 440
  culture of, 445
  currency, 398, 475
  economic policy, 409, 441–442
  economy of, 399, 399t, 442, 443t
    employment, 2t, 442, 443t
    history of, 408, 440, 445
    overview of, 398, 478t
  education in, 398, 405
    history of, 402–403
  elections, 411t, 418
  electoral system, 18, 18t, 19t
    proportional representation,
      415–419
      goals of, 415–416
      introduction of, 405–406, 405t
      parties and candidates in,
        418–419
    before proportional
      representation, 415–416
  ethnic groups in, 15t, 398, 412
  European Union and, 438, 447–448
  executive branch, 398
    cabinet (Council of Ministers),
      430–431
      background of ministers, 433
      formation of, 430, 431–433
    legislative branch relations,
      433–434, 437
    political executive, 430–434,
      430t
    prime minister (minister
      president), 430
    professional executive, 434
  foreign policy, 445–448
  geography of, 2t, 396f, 397, 399,
    399t
  government expenditures, 14t, 26t,
    27
  health spending in, 14t
  history of, 6, 399–407, 445–446
    World War II, 408, 445–446,
      446f
  immigration to, 237t, 412–413
    opposition to, 418
  interest groups in, 428–429
  judicial branch, 398
  language in, 398, 399
  legal system, 398
  legislative branch, 398, 434–437
    executive branch relations,
      433–434, 437

  functions of, 435–436, 436t
  parties in, 403t, 405t, 410t, 417t,
    436–437, 437t, 438t
  structure of, 434–435
  military, 475t
    Srebenica massacre, 418, 447
  monarchy in, 6t, 7, 429–430
  NATO and, 28, 29t, 446–447
  parties in
    coalition government and,
      431–433
    history of, 403–406, 403t, 405t,
      409–410, 410t
    ideology of, 22t, 23
    in legislative branch, 403t, 405t,
      410t, 417t, 436–437, 437t,
      438t
    major parties, 420f, 421–423
    membership and resources,
      425–426, 425t
    organization of, 426–427
    platforms of, 423–425, 424t, 425t
    post-pillarization, 410–412, 411t
    proportional representation and,
      418–419
    religion and, 419–420, 421, 427,
      428t
    social class and, 420, 427, 427t
    support for, 427–428, 427t
  pillarization (verzuiling) in, 24,
    406–408
    decline of, 409–410, 410t, 423,
      427, 433
    legacy of, 406, 426, 428–429
  political system
    coalition government in,
      431–433
    evolution of, 402–405
    pacification, 405–406, 405t
  population and demographics, 2t,
    11t, 397–398, 399t, 478t
  prime minister (minister president),
    430
  profile of, 2, 397–398
  provincial and municipal
    government, 437
  public policy in, 440–448
    mechanisms of, 440–441
  quality of life in, 412–413
  regional organization memberships,
    463t
  religion in, 13, 14t, 15t, 398,
    406–407
    history of, 401, 403, 404, 406
    political parties and, 419–420,
      421, 427, 428t
  social class in, 7, 420, 427, 427t
  stability of, 6, 432–433
  trade and, 445, 459
  unions in, 428–429, 441
  voting rights in, 12–13, 404, 416
    compulsory voting, 405, 417
  welfare state in, 27, 404, 444
  women in
    in government, 413, 413t, 437
    role and status of, 10–13,
      10t–13t, 412

  voting patterns, 427–428
Netherlands Federation of Christian
  Employers (NCW), 429
New Force Party, 352
New Steps policy (Britain), 100
NGOs. See Nongovernmental
  organizations
Nice Treaty (2001). See Treaty of Nice
1922 Committee, 72, 93
No confidence vote
  in British Parliament, 93
  in Germany, 217, 223–224
  in Italy, 291–292
  in Spain, 369
Nocturnal Employment case
  (Germany, 1992), 195
Nongovernmental organizations
  (NGOs), women and, 12
Nordic countries, 5
  women in, 12
North Atlantic Treaty Alliance. See
  NATO
North German Confederation, 181
Northcote-Trevelyan report, 86
Northern Ireland
  elections in, 63
  electoral system in, 58–59
  ethnicity in, 16
  geography of, 43, 43t
  in House of Commons, 90
  languages in, 44
  nationalism in, 39, 49, 62
  population of, 43t
  religion in, 44–47, 52
  unrest in, 44–47
Northern League, 278
  and election of 1996, 286t, 287
  policies of, 262, 265, 318–319
  support for, 283, 284, 285t, 286t,
    287t, 301
Norway
  and EEC, 458
  and European Free Trade
    Association, 458
  foreign residents of, 237t
  monarchy in, 6t
  NATO and, 28, 29t
  as Nordic country, 5
  regional organization memberships,
    463t
  trade, 472
Nuclear weapons
  Europe and, 453
  France and, 171
  Germany and, 248
  Great Britain and, 104–105
  Netherlands and, 447
No. 10 Downing Steet, 37f, 85

Oder-Neisse line, 242
OECD. See Organization for Economic
  Cooperation and Development
OEEC. See Organization for European
  Economic Cooperation
Official Secrets Act (Britain), 79
Oil prices
  Italian economy and, 307, 309

Netherlands and, 440, 441, 447
Spanish economy and, 342
Old Catholic Church, 213
Olive Tree coalition, 279
  and election of 1996, 286–287, 286t
  and election of 2001, 287–288, 287t
  partners in, 276
  policies of, 313, 314–315, 318–319
  support for, 277, 321, 323
ONCE. See National Organization for
  the Blind in Spain
Operation Clean Hands (Italy), 301
Ordinary law(s), in Spain, 372
Organic law(s), in Spain, 371, 372
Organic Law for the Harmonization of
  Autonomy Process (LOAPA),
  382–383
Organic Law of the State (1969), 335
Organic Law on Trade Union
  Freedoms (Spain, 1984), 360
Organization for Economic
  Cooperation and Development
  (OECD), member states, 463t
Organization for European Economic
  Cooperation (OEEC), 447,
  454–455
Organization for Security and
  Cooperation in Europe (OSCE),
  30t
Organization of European Economic
  Cooperation, 304
Orléans, Louis Philippe d', 121–122
OSCE. See Organization for Security
  and Cooperation in Europe
Ostpolitik, 184, 217, 243
Otto I, 180
Ottoman Empire, 3
Oxford University, 54–55, 64, 83, 87, 95

Pacification (Netherlands), 405–406,
  405t
Pacifist Socialist Party (Netherlands),
  423
Pact for Italy, 284–285, 285t
Pacts of Moncloa (1977). See Moncloa
  Pacts
El Pais, 346, 346t
Palais Bourbon, 155
Paris, 126
Paris Commune, 123
Parliament Act (Britain, 1911), 88–95
Parliamentary Labour Party (PLP), 71,
  72, 93
Parliamentary Practice (May), 41
Parti Social Français, 140
Party(ies). See also individual nations
  and parties
  two-party system, 2, 17, 40, 59, 69
  in Western Europe, 20–24, 20t
    history of, 7
    religious-based, 14t
    social class and, 9–10
Party of Democratic Socialism (PDS),
  208–209
  Bundesrat and, 230t
  funding of, 210t
  reunification and, 245

support for, 200f, 204, 215, 215t,
  218t, 221t
women in, 195, 195t
Party of Labor (PvdA), 420f, 421–422
  alliances, 410, 411, 412
  in cabinet, 430t
  formation of, 409
  membership and resources, 425t,
  426
  in parliament, 437t, 438t
  policies of, 424, 424t, 425t
  support for, 410, 411t, 412, 417t,
  418, 420, 427, 427t, 428, 428t
La Pasionaria (Dolores Ibárruri), 338,
  355
PASOC. See Social Action Party
PCE. See Spanish Communist Party
PCF. See French Communist Party
PCI. See Italian Communist Party
PDS. See Democratic Party of the Left;
  Party of Democratic Socialism
Pentapartito, 282
People's Party for Freedom and
  Democracy (VVD), 420f, 422
  in cabinet, 430t
  establishment of, 409
  membership and resources, 425t,
  426
  in parliament, 437t, 438t
  policies of, 424, 424t, 425t
  support for, 411t, 417t, 418, 427,
  427t, 428, 428t
Perestroika, 3–4
Persian Gulf War. See Gulf War
Pertini, Sandro, 296, 296t
Pétain, Philippe, 123
Petition of Rights (Britain, 1628), 40
PHARE program, 456t, 478
Pillarization (verzuiling), 24, 406–408
  decline of, 409–410, 410t, 423, 427,
  433
  legacy of, 406, 426, 428–429
Piñar, Blas, 352
Pius X, Pope, 127
Plaid Cymru, 48t, 59, 62, 62t, 63
The Plan (France), 168–169
PLI. See Italian Liberal Party
PLP. See Parliamentary Labour Party
Pluralistic systems, in Great Britain,
  44–48
PNV. See Basque Nationalist Party
Podestá, 257
Poland
  European Union and, 460t
  geography of, 2, 4t
  income in, 460f
  NATO and, 28, 29t
  profile of, 4t
  regional organization memberships,
  463t
Political elite. See also Social class
  in Great Britain, 79
  judges as, 95
Political parties. See Party(ies)
Political Parties, Elections, and
  Referendums Act (Britain, 2000),
  69

Political Parties Act (Germany, 1967),
  209
The Politics of Accommodation
  (Lijphart), 407–408
Pompidou, Georges
  background of, 153
  foreign policy of, 170–171
  policies and actions, 149, 153, 154
  political career of, 136, 140, 152t,
  173
Poor Laws (Netherlands), 444
Popular Alliance (AP), 338, 352
Popular Party
  in Italy. See Italian Popular Party
  in Spain (PP), 352–353
    alliances of, 352
    establishment of, 338
    ideology of, 349, 351f
    policies of, 386, 392
    support for, 339, 344, 352t, 358,
    369
Population. See individual nations
Il populo grasso, 257
Il populo minuto, 257
Portugal
  currency, 475
  EC and, 458
  economy of, 478t
  and European Free Trade
  Association, 458
  military, 475t
  NATO and, 28, 29t
  population of, 478t
  regional organization memberships,
  463t
Postindustrial economy
  in Germany, 190–191
  in Great Britain, 45, 50–51
  in Italy, 267, 267t, 308
  in Netherlands, 399
  in Western Europe, 8–9
Potsdam Conference, 183
Poujade, Pierre, 133
Poujadism, 133–134
Powell, Enoch, 68
PP. See Popular Party, in Spain
PPR. See Radical Party, in Netherlands
PR. See Proportional representation
Prefetto, 297
Presbyterian Church of Scotland, 52
Presidential government systems,
  24–25. See also individual
  nations
PRI. See Republican Party, in Italy
Primo de Rivera, Miguel, 333, 363
Principato, 256
Privy council, 79
Prodi, Romano
  European Union and, 465
  leadership of, 314
  Olive Tree and, 276, 279, 286
  policies of, 313
  as prime minister, 294t
Progressive Alliance
  and election of 1994, 284, 285t
  partners in, 277, 278
Pronunciamiento, 333, 334

Proportional representation (PR)
  in Italy, 284
  in Netherlands, 415–419
    goals of, 415–416
    introduction of, 405–406, 405t
    parties and candidates in,
      418–419
  in Spain, 357
  in Western Europe, 17–18
Proposición de ley, 372
Protestant Diaconal Works, 198
Protestant Methodist Church, 213
Provincial Committee of Public
    Administration, 297
Proyecto de ley, 372–374
Prussia, 180, 181
PSDI. See Social Democratic Party, in
    Italy
PSI. See Italian Socialist Party
PSOE. See Spanish Socialist Workers
    Party
PSUC. See United Socialist Party of
    Catalonia
Public Corporations, in Italy, 298
Pujol, Jordi, 356, 357
PvdA. See Party of Labor

Quadripartite Agreement (1971), 243
QUANGOs (Quasi Autonomous Non-
    governmental Organizations), 75,
    87, 111
Question time
  in Great Britain, 80t, 94
  in Spain, 374

Race. See also ethnic groups under
    individual nations
  as conflict source, 44, 48
  discrimination, in Great Britain, 45
  and party identification, 67–68
Race Relations Act (Britain, 1976), 44
Radical Party, in Netherlands (PPR),
    410, 411t, 423
Radical Party (France), 141, 142, 143
Radical Party (Italy), 278
Radio Nacional de España (RNE),
    346–347
Rainbow Coalition (Netherlands), 423
Rally of the French People, 147
Rassemblement du Peuple Français
    (RPF), 138, 141
Rau, Johannes, 218, 222
RC. See Refounded Communism (RC)
    party
Realos, 207–208
Realschule, 197
Reassemblement pour la République
    (RPR), 140, 173
Rechtsstaat, 231
Recurso de amparo, 378
Red Army Faction, 222
Red Brigades, 282
Referendums
  in France, 19, 148–149
  in Great Britain, 19, 108
  in Italy, 19, 274–275, 278, 283, 299
  in Spain, 337, 359, 359t
  in Western Europe, 19

Reform by agreement, 337–339
Reformation, 180, 401
Reformed Political Federation (RPF),
    411t, 417t, 423
  in parliament, 437t, 438t
Refounded Communism (RC) party,
    277, 284, 285t, 287t, 313, 323
Regional Development Agencies (Great
    Britain), 49
Regional parties, characteristics of, 24
Regionalism
  in France, 26
  in Italy, 25–26, 298–299, 318–319
  in Spain, 375–376, 376t, 381–384
    institutionalization of, 382–383
  in Western Europe, 25–26
Registration of Political Parties Act
    (Britain, 1998), 68–69
Reichstag, burning of, 183
Reign of Terror, 123
Religion. See also Catholicism;
    Christianity; Islam; individual
    nations
  as conflict source, 44–45
  in Western Europe, 13–16
Renaissance, 5–6
Renault, 169, 170
Representation, in Great Britain, 40
Republic of Ireland, 44, 45
Republican Party
  in France, 141
  in Italy (PRI), 276t, 277, 281, 282
Republicanism, in France, 123
Republikaner party, 207
Rerum Novarum, 408–409
Right wing parties, characteristics of,
    20t, 23
Rights. See Bills of rights; Human
    rights
RNE. See Radio Nacional de España
Rocard, Michel, 144
Rodríguez Zapatero, José Luis, 339,
    354
Roldán, Luis, 393
Roman Empire, 5, 258t
Romania, 2, 4t, 460t
Rotterdam, Netherlands, 446f
Royal Arsenal, 70
Royal Dutch Airlines (KLM), 443–444
RPF. See Rassemblement du Peuple
    Français; Reformed Political
    Federation
RPR. See Gaullist Party;
    Reassemblement pour la
    République
Rugby, 54
Rule of law, 40–41
Russia. See Soviet Union
Rutelli, Francesco, 262, 287, 314
Rutelli, Gianfranco, 276

St. Laurent, Louis, 455
Saint-Simon, 163
San Marino, 463t
Saragat, Giuseppe, 296t
Scalfaro, Oscar Luigi, 284, 296–297,
    296t
Scharping, Rudolf, 206, 217

Scheel, Walter, 222
Schengen agreements, 456t
Schily, Otto, 238
Schlink, Bernhard, 201
Schmidt, Helmut, 171, 218, 223,
    224–225
Schröder, Gerhard, 220, 238, 241, 249
Scotland
  devolution of power to, 26, 39
  elections in, 62, 62t, 63, 68
  electoral system in, 58–59
  ethnicity in, 16
  geography of, 43, 43t
  in Great Britain, 34
  in House of Commons, 90
  languages in, 44
  nationalism in, 44–48, 49, 62
  parliament of, 47, 48t
  population of, 43t
Scottish National Party (SNP), 18, 47,
    48t, 59, 62, 62t, 63
SDAP. See Social Democratic Workers
    Party
SDP. See Social Democratic Party
SEA. See Single European Act (SEA)
Second Empire (France), 122, 122t
Second Reich, 181–182
Second Republic (France), 118, 122t
Second Republic (Spain), 333–334
  devolution in, 381
  monarchy in, 366
  regional reforms in, 375
  religion in, 362
SED. See Socialist Unity Party
Segni, Antonio, 296t
Segni, Mario, 276, 283, 284, 293t
Segni Pact, 284–285, 285t
Senate (France), 156
Separation of powers
  in Europe, 433
  in Germany, 226
  in Great Britain, 79
Serra, Narcís, 393
Sex Discrimination Act (Britain, 1975),
    50
SGP. See Calvinist Party
Shadow cabinet, 72, 80t, 81
Shuman, Robert, 455
Siena, Italy, 259f
Signoria, 256
Sikhism, in Great Britain, 52, 52t
Le Sillon, 127
Singapore, 104
Single European Act (SEA)
  bodies created by, 468–469, 471
  European Commission and, 467
  European Parliament and, 470
  Italy and, 309
  provisions of, 456t, 458, 458t, 462,
    472, 474t
Single-member constituencies (SMC),
    17–18
  in Italy, 284
Slovakia, 2, 4t, 460t
Slovenia, 3, 4t, 460t
SMC. See Single-member
    constituencies
SME. See Social market economy

Smith, Ian Duncan, 72
SNP. See Scottish National Party
Social Action Party (PASOC), 356
Social and Democratic Center Party
    (CDS), 350–352, 351f, 352t
Social and Economic Council
    (Netherlands), 409, 440, 441
Social and Liberal Democrats (SLDs),
    69
Social class
    in France, 7, 126–127
    in Germany, 7
    in Great Britain, 7, 42–43, 51,
        54–55, 66–67
    in Italy, 267–268
    in Netherlands, 7, 420, 427, 427t
    in Western Europe, 7, 9–10
Social Code (Germany), 241
Social Democratic Party
    in Germany (SPD), 204–206
        alliances, 207, 216, 216t
        Bundesrat and, 230–231, 230t
        cabinet posts (2001), 225, 225t
        constituency, 219
        financing of, 209, 210t
        platform of, 220
        policies of, 249
        reunification and, 245
        structure of, 200, 209, 212
        support for, 204, 205t, 211, 212,
            215t, 217–219, 218t, 221t
        women and, 195, 195t
    in Great Britain, 39, 59, 69
    ideology of, 20–21
    in Italy (PSDI), 276t, 277, 281, 282,
        283
Social Democratic Workers Party
    (SDAP), 404, 419, 421
Social engineering, in France, 163
Social market economy (SME),
    186–187, 206, 239–241, 242
Socialist Party
    in European Parliament, 469f
    in France, 130–132, 135, 137, 138,
        139t, 141, 142–145, 147, 150,
        173–174
    in Italy. See Italian Socialist Party
    in Netherlands, 403t, 405t, 411t,
        417t, 420f, 423, 437t, 438t
    platform of, 20–21, 20t
    in Spain. See Spanish Socialist
        Workers Party
Socialist Unity Party (SED), 204, 208
Socialization
    in Germany, 200–201
    in Great Britain, 42–43, 54–55
Solana, Javier, 480
Sovereignty, European Union and, 49,
    89, 109–110, 462, 471
Soviet Union
    collapse of, 1, 2–3, 8
        Netherlands and, 447
        Spanish Communist Party and,
            356
    and Communist Party in Europe, 21
    in Czechoslovakia, 145–146
    Eastern Europe and, 184
    European fear of, 453, 455

France and, 120, 145–146
Germany and, 242–244, 247
imperialism of, 453, 455
and Iron Curtain, 454–455
Jewish emigration from, 213
Prussia, annexation of, 180
Spanish Civil War and, 334–335,
    355
Spadolini, Giovanni, 282, 294t
Spain, 326f, 327–394
    autonomous communities in,
        375–376, 376t, 381. See also
        regionalism and regions
        below
        devolution and, 375–377, 376t,
            381–383
        institutionalization of, 382–383
    budget deficits in, 390
    colonies of, 331–332
    constitution(s), 332–333, 333t
    Constitution of 1978, 17, 337, 344,
        349
        amendment provisions, 371
        Congress of Deputies in, 370
        Constitutional Court in, 382
        constructive no confidence in,
            369
        decree laws in, 371
        Defender of the People in, 379
        passage of, 355
        political system in, 365
        regional government in, 375
        religion in, 362
        unions and, 360
        writing of, 350
    corruption and scandals in,
        392–393
    Council of Ministers, 337
    culture of, 343–347
        regional, 340–341
        religion and, 363
    currency, 329, 388, 475
    Defender of the People, 379
    economic policy, 387–392
    economy of
        employment and, 2t, 391–392,
            391f
        European Union and, 385
        history of, 341–342, 387
        overview, 328–329, 478t
    education in, 328, 343–345, 363
    elections, 352t
    electoral system, 18, 18t, 357–359
    ethnic groups in, 15, 15t, 328
    European integration and, 381,
        384–387, 458
    European Union and, 339,
        384–385, 390
    executive branch, 328, 366f
        Council of Ministers, 337
        monarchy's function in, 366f, 368
        prime minister, 349, 366f
    fiscal policy, 382, 388, 389–390
    geography of, 2t, 326f, 327–328,
        339–340
    government of
        characteristics of, 368–369
        coalitions in, 369

constructive no confidence and,
    369
formation, 369
spending by, 14t, 26t, 27
health spending in, 14t
history of, 6, 330–339, 332t
    Civil War, 261, 330, 333,
        334–335, 362
    Franco regime. See Franco
        regime
    transition to democracy, 330,
        336–339, 342–343, 343t,
        354, 364–365, 367–368,
        387
immigration to, 237t
interest groups in, 359–365
judicial branch, 328, 366f, 377–379
    Constitutional Court, 366f,
        378–379, 382–383
    Court of Public Order, 378
    Supreme Court, 377
language in, 328, 331
legal system, 328, 377
    types of laws, 371–372
legislative branch (Cortes), 328,
    366f, 370–372, 374
    Congress of Deputies, 370–372,
        371f, 374
    Council of Party Spokesmen, 371
    party groups in, 370–371
    President of the Chamber, 370
    Senate, 370, 374, 383
legislative process, 372–374, 373f
    types of laws, 371–372
media in, 345–347, 346t
military in, 363–365, 475t
    Civil Guard, 363–365, 364f
    political intervention by, 333,
        334, 363, 364–365, 364f
monarchy in, 6t, 330, 333, 333t,
    336, 337, 349, 365–368, 367f
    function of, 366f, 368
monetary policy, 388–389
NATO and, 28, 29t, 385–387
in Netherlands, 400, 401
parties in, 22t, 23, 24, 349–357
    Cortes and, 370–371
    history of, 337
    regional, 349–350, 351f
    regional government and,
        376–377
political system of, 349, 365, 366f
    as model, 330
    reform by agreement in,
        337–339
political terrorism in, 383–384
population and demographics, 2t,
    11t, 328, 341, 478t
prime minister, 349, 366f
profile of, 2, 327–329
public policy, 381–393
    regionalism and, 381–384
referendums in, 337, 359, 359t
regional organization memberships,
    463t
regionalism in, 26, 375–376, 376t,
    381–384
    institutionalization of, 382–383

Spain, *continued*
  regions of, 340, 381
    government, 374–377, 376t
    parties and, 349–350, 351f
    public policy and, 381–384
  religion in, 13, 14t, 15, 15t, 328,
      331, 345
  politics and, 361–363
  stability of, 6
  taxation in, 342, 382, 389–390
  trade and, 459
  unions in, 360–361, 362t, 387
  voting rights in, 12–13
  women in, 344–345
    role and status of, 10–13,
      10t–13t
Spanish Communist Party (PCE), 337,
    355–356
  NATO and, 386
  support for, 349, 352t
  survival of, 354
  Workers' Commissions and, 361
Spanish Confederation of Employers'
    Organization (CEOE), 359–360,
    387
Spanish Confederation of Small- and
    Medium-sized Firms (CEPYME),
    360
Spanish model, 330
Spanish Socialist Workers Party
    (PSOE), 353–355
  alliances, 338, 339, 369
  European Union and, 385
  NATO and, 386
  policies of, 349, 350, 351f, 387, 392
  scandals, 393
  support for, 338, 352, 352t, 358
  transition to democracy and, 330
  unions and, 360–361
SPD. See Social Democratic Party, in
    Germany
Srebenica massacre, 418, 447
Stabilization Plan of 1959 (Spain), 342
Statute of Rhuddlan (1284), 34
Statute of the Workers (Italy), 281
Stuttgart Summit (1983), 385
Suárez, Adolfo
  democracy and, 337, 338, 350, 367
  European Union and, 385
  parties affiliation of, 350–351
  policies of, 389
  political career of, 337, 338, 358
  retirement of, 352, 364
Subsidiary Principle, 456t, 462–463
Supreme Council of the Magistrature
    (CSM), 296, 300
Sweden
  economy of, 478t
  and European Free Trade
      Association, 458
  and European Union, 459
  foreign residents of, 237t
  military, 475t
  monarchy in, 6t
  as Nordic country, 5
  population of, 478t
  regional organization memberships,
      463t

Switzerland
  economy of, 399t
  and European Free Trade
      Association, 458
  foreign residents of, 237t
  geography of, 399t
  population of, 399t
  referendums in, 19
  regional organization memberships,
      463t
Syndicalists, 130

Taxes
  European Union and, 109, 390,
      464, 464f, 472, 477–478
  in Germany, 198, 239, 240, 242
  in Great Britain, 56, 98
  in Italy, 311, 312, 313, 314–315,
      318
  in Spain, 342, 382, 389–390
Tejero Molina, Antonio, 364, 364f
Terrorism
  Basque country and, 383
  France and, 126, 135–136
  Great Britain and, 56
  Islamic fundamentalism and,
      135–136
  in Italy, 263, 282, 306–307
  in Spain, 383–384
  war on, 85, 104
Terrorism Act 2000 (Britain), 56
TGV train, 191f
Thatcher, Margaret
  European integration and, 109,
      110, 454
  ideology of, 60f
  policies of, 54, 55, 56, 87, 100, 101,
      111
  political career of, 12, 82, 83
Third Reich, 183. See also Nazis
Third Republic (France), 118, 122t,
    138, 155
Thiry Years' War, 180–181
Thorbecke, J. R., 402, 422
Tocqueville, Alexis de, 130
Togliatti, Palmiro, 280
Toleration Act (Britain, 1689), 39t
Tomás y Valiente, Francisco, 339
Totalitarianism, 7–8. See also Fascism;
    Nazis
Trade
  Canada, 473f
  European Free Trade Association,
      108, 458, 477
    member states, 463t
  European Union, 452, 459, 465t,
      472, 473f, 477–478, 479
  France, 459
  Great Britain, 36–37, 55–56, 104,
      108, 110, 458, 459
  Iceland, 472
  Italy, 305, 306
  Japan, 473f
  Latin America, 473f
  Mexico, 473f
  Netherlands, 445, 459
  Norway, 458, 472
  Portugal, 458

Spain, 459
Sweden, 458
Switzerland, 458
United States, European Union and,
    465t, 472, 473f, 477, 479
Trade unions. See Unions
Trades Union Congress (Britain), 50,
    70, 75
Trasformismo, 257, 263–264
Treaties of Rome (1957), 438, 457,
    458, 462, 471, 472, 474t
Treaty of Dunkirk (1947), 455
Treaty of Nice (2001), 438, 448, 456t,
    474t
Treaty of Paris (1951), 455–456, 462,
    471, 474t
Treaty of Utrecht (1713), 445
Treaty of Westphalia (1648), 198
Treaty on European Union. See
    Maastricht Treaty
Treaty on the Final Settlement with
    Respect to Germany, 248
Tremonti, Giulio, 315
Truman, Harry S., 455
Turkey
  European Union and, 460t
  income, 460f
  NATO and, 28, 29t
  regional organization memberships,
      463t
Two-party system
  in Great Britain, 2, 40, 59, 69
  in Western Europe, 17
Two-plus-four talks, 244
Two-Plus-Four Treaty, 248

UCD. See Union of the Democratic
    Center
UDF. See Union pour la Démocratie
    Française
UGT. See General Union of Workers
UIL. See Italian Union of Labor
UK Independence Party, 63
Ulster. See Northern Ireland
Umberto, King of Italy, 259
UMP. See Union pour la Majorité
    Présidentielle
Union de Défense des Commerçants et
    Artisans, 133–134
Union Law of 1971 (Spain), 360
Union Nationale des Etudiants de
    France, 132
Union of Basque Workers (ELA-STV),
    360, 361
Union of the Democratic Center (UCD),
    337, 338, 350, 352t, 358, 386,
    389
Union pour la Démocratie Française
    (UDF), 18, 138, 141, 150
Union pour la Majorité Présidentielle
    (UMP), 140
Union pour la Nouvelle République
    (UNR), 139, 140
Union Sacrée, 142
Unionist Party (Northern Ireland), 62
Unions
  in Basque country, 360, 361
  communism and, 145

in France, 130–132, 133f, 145
in Germany, 212–213, 242
in Great Britain, 50, 56, 68, 70, 73,
    75–76, 89, 100, 101
in Italy, 286, 288–289, 306–307,
    308–309
in Netherlands, 428–429, 441
in Spain, 360–361, 362t, 387
in Western Europe, 9
women and, 50
Unitary Democratic Center (CDU), 276,
    286t, 287t
Unitary vs. federal systems, 25–26
United Kingdom. See also Great
    Britain
    definition of, 80t
    GDP of, 187t
    military, 475t
    regional organization memberships,
        463t
United Left (IU), 351f, 352t, 356, 361
United Nations
    European Union and, 468
    in Kosovo, 447
    Security Council members, 33
    self defense and, 455
United Provinces, 400, 401
United Socialist Party of Catalonia
    (PSUC), 355
United States
    economy of, 399t
    and Europe, relationship with, 453,
        454
    European Union and, 465t, 472,
        473f, 477, 479
    foreign policy, 455
    and France, 120
    GDP of, 187t
    geography of, 399t
    and Great Britain, 36, 104–105,
        110
    and Italy, 279, 282, 311, 312,
        321–322
    military spending, 322t
    NATO and, 28, 29t
    and Netherlands, 446, 447
    population of, 399t
    regional organization memberships,
        463t
    and Spain, 334, 338, 386
    trade, European Union and, 465t,
        472, 473f, 477, 479
Unity Treaty, 229, 245–248
UNR. See Union pour la Nouvelle
    République
USSR. See Soviet Union

Value added tax (VAT), European
    Union and, 390
van Agt, Andreas, 442
Vandenburg Resolution, 455
Venice Declaration (1980), 468
Versailles Treaty, 182, 183
Verzuiling. See Pillarization
Vichy regime, 119, 122t, 123, 140
Victor Emmanuel, King of Italy, 253
Vittorio Emanuele III, King of Italy,
    261

VNO-NCW. See Confederation of
    Netherlands Industry
Voltaire, 128
Voorhoeve, Joris, 445, 446
Voting rights
    in France, 12–13
    in Germany, 12–13
    in Great Britain, 12–13
    in Italy, 12–13, 271
    in Netherlands, 12–13, 404, 416
        compulsory voting, 405, 417
    in Spain, 12–13
    of women, 12–13
        in Italy, 271
VVD. See People's Party for Freedom
    and Democracy

Wales
    assembly of, 47, 48t
    devolution of power to, 26
    elections in, 62, 62t, 63, 68
    electoral system in, 58–59
    ethnicity in, 16
    geography of, 43, 43t
    history of, 34, 47
    in House of Commons, 90
    languages in, 43–44
    nationalism in, 39, 44–48, 49, 62
    population of, 43t, 50–51
    religion in, 51, 52
Walser, Martin, 201
War of the Roses, 38
War of the Spanish Succession, 258t
Warsaw Treaty (1970), 243
Wehner, Herbert, 206
Weimar Republic, 18, 182–183, 206,
    214, 223
Weizsäcker, Richard von, 222
Welfare state
    in Germany, 27, 241–242
    in Great Britain, 27, 42, 53,
        101–104
    in Italy, 265, 312
    in Netherlands, 27, 404, 444
    in Western Europe, 27–28
        government growth and, 26–27,
            26t
West Germany. See Federal Republic
    of Germany
West Lothian question, 47
Western Europe. See also Europe
    defense of, 30t, 455. See also NATO
    definition of, 2
    economy of, 8–9
        employment, 2t, 8–9
    electoral systems in, 17–19
    ethnic groups in, 15–16, 15t
    geography of, 2, 2t
    immigration to, 15–16
    importance of, 1
    integration of, 28–31. See also
        European Union
        Great Britain and, 455–456
        Spain and, 381, 384–387, 458
    marriage and family in, 10, 10t
    monarchy in, 6–7, 6t
    parties in, 20–24, 20t
    political consensus in, 25

political systems in, 16–17, 24–26
    history of, 5–8
    politics in, 9–10
    population and demographics, 2,
        2t, 11t, 13, 27
    religion in, 13–16
    social class in, 7, 9–10
    standard of living in, 8
    women in, role and status of,
        10–13, 10t–13t, 466
Western European Union (WEU), 30t,
    456t, 457, 474
    member states, 463t
Westminster Abbey, 36
Westminster model, 2, 40–41, 369
WEU. See Western European Union
Whips, 80t
Whitehall, 80t, 86
Wilde, Oscar, 36
William I, King of United Netherlands,
    401, 402
William II, King of Netherlands, 402
William the Silent, 401
Wilson, Harold, 60f
Winchester, 54
Women
    employment, 50, 95
        in Germany, 191, 192f, 193–196
        in Italy, 272
        in Western Europe, 9, 10–12,
            10t, 11t
    Feminist movement and, 7, 9, 11
        in Italy, 271–272
    in France, 126, 135, 144, 161
        role and status of, 10–13,
            10t–13t
    in Germany, 191, 192f, 193–196,
        195f, 200
        role and status of, 10–13,
            10t–13t
    in government, 92
        in Europe, 466
        in France, 161
        in Germany, 195–196, 195f
        in Great Britain, 63, 65, 65t
        in Italy, 272
        in Netherlands, 413, 413t, 437
        in Western Europe, 12–13, 12t,
            13t
    in Great Britain
        employment, 45t, 50
        in government, 63, 65, 65t, 92
        role and status of, 10–13,
            10t–13t
        voting rights of, 39t, 58t
        voting trends for, 67
    in Italy, 10–13, 10t–13t, 269–270,
        271–272
    life expectancy, 10t
    in Netherlands
        in government, 413, 413t, 437
        role and status of, 10–13,
            10t–13t, 412
        voting patterns, 427–428
    in Spain
        education and, 344–345
        role and status of, 10–13,
            10t–13t

Women, *continued*
  and unions, 50
  voting rights of, 12–13
    in Great Britain, 39t, 58t
  voting trends for, 13
    in Great Britain, 67
    in Netherlands, 427–428
  in Western Europe
    employment, 9, 10–12, 10t, 11t
    role and status of, 10–13,
      10t–13t, 466
Workers' Commissions (CCOO), 355,
  360, 361, 387
Workers' Statute of 1980 (Spain), 360
Workers' Syndical Union (USO), 361

Works Constitution Act (Germany,
  1952, 1972), 240
World Trade Organization (WTO)
  European Union and, 477
  France and, 168
World War I, Germany and, 182
World War II
  and Europe
    impact of, 453, 454
  France and, 123, 140–141
  Germany and, 180, 183–184,
    185–186
  Great Britain and, 104
  impact of, 8
  Italy and, 261

Marshall Plan, 454
  Germany and, 185–186
  Italy and, 279, 304, 311
  Netherlands and, 447
  Netherlands and, 408, 445–446,
    446f
WTO. See World Trade Organization

Yalta Conference, 183
Yaoundé Convention, 477
Yugoslavia, 3

Zimbabwe, 480
Zollverein, 181